Wine Myths and Reality

Also by Benjamin Lewin

What Price Bordeaux?

Wine Myths and Reality

Benjamin Lewin MW

Vendange Press
Dover
2010

Library of Congress Cataloging-in-Publication Data
Lewin, Benjamin
Wine Myths and Reality / by
Benjamin Lewin
Includes bibliographical references and index.

ISBN 978-1-934259-51-1

Library of Congress Control Number: 2010924591

Printed in China
1 2 3 4 5 6 7 8 9 10

For my anima figure

Contents

Preface

WINEMAKING IS NOT A MATTER OF CHANCE: the completely natural result of fermenting grapes would be vinegar. Every decision you make (or fail to make) in the vineyard or winery affects the style and quality of the wine that finally emerges in the bottle. Wine does not make itself. Never before has there been so much opportunity for the winemaker to direct viticulture and vinification to shape the wine. Wine has never been technically better, but these new possibilities create the dilemma of whether making better wine narrows differences between places, making wines more similar, so their character is lost. Heated arguments occur wherever there is a history of winemaking as to whether today's wine is better than yesterday's or has lost its soul. Increased opportunity to manipulate the process leads to the question of how far you can go before wine ceases to be natural and becomes an industrial product.

With all these conflicting forces, the question becomes: how and why did the wine in the bottle you buy today come to be like it is. "How" reflects what use the winemaker has made of his ability to influence the process; "why" reflects a mélange of historical, social, and economic forces. The reasons why Bordeaux tastes different from Burgundy, why Barolo is distinct from Rioja, why New World wines are more powerful than European wines, not to mention why wines everywhere have changed so greatly in recent decades, reflect an interplay of factors going far beyond the simple facts of what types of grapes are grown in each place. Never has there been so much experimentation with grape growing or wine making, and so much innovation in wine styles. Yet at the same time, the focus has been sharpening on a small number of varietals at the expense of diversity. Has this led to more or less choice for the consumer?

Many myths stand in the way of understanding why wine is like it is, myths about viticulture, myths about winemaking, myths about the historical verities of wine. I'm interested in the context of each wine, not just how it is made, but also why the winemaker decided to make it like that. "Why" extends beyond the individual winemaker into asking what issues determine the success (or otherwise) of each wine region? The basic question I want to ask in this book is what's really going on when they make wine?

This is not a muckraking book or an exposé, but I do want to debunk myths about wine and to set the record straight by throwing light on issues that have been murky or misunderstood. I believe in the value of transparency. And if the results are not always pleasing, the solution is to change production methods or to educate the consumer rather than to cover up.

When I mentioned the theme of this book to one of my MW colleagues, he was vaguely horrified. "Oh dear," he said, "you don't want to do that. It will destroy the romantic image." Perhaps it is its ancient origins that give wine its mythic aura. Or perhaps its central role in hospitality. Or the fact that every year is different. Or perhaps it's the halo effect of top wines that have become collectible items. Possibly it's no more than a great marketing success in making wine appear an artisanal product whatever its real origins. For whatever reason, the world of wine has an unusual gap between perception and reality.

When asked if they would like to try an organic wine, many consumers are puzzled. "Isn't all wine organic?" they often ask. Well, no, it isn't. Most of it is an industrial product. Most people think of wine as resulting directly from the fermentation of grapes. But wine production has never been entirely natural. In ancient times, herbs and spices were used for flavoring; in modern times adding sugar before fermentation was introduced to increase alcohol levels, and extraneous notes are introduced by exposure to oak or by other manipulations. In fact, manipulation during and after fermentation is extensive, and wine owes much of its flavor to decisions made by winemakers trying to satisfy the consumer market.

What goes into the bottle, what you actually drink when you open a bottle of wine, is determined not just by the vagaries of vintage and the hazards of winemaking, but also by market forces. Perhaps twenty or thirty years ago, the wine you were offered was what the producer wanted to make, or possibly what he was able to make. The transition to a consumer-driven market has caused a sweeping change, with wines tailored to demand. And of course the wine market is distorted by the iniquities of taxation like any other product, in fact, more than any other product, because alcoholic products are so attractive as targets for taxation. On top of this is the generally hostile attitude of the European Union to any form of alcohol consumption.

The wine you drink depends on the interplay of all these forces. Many of the wines of the Old World have long histories that still significantly impact the wines of today. Most of the wines of the New World are much more recent creations without the same historical constraints. Viticulture and vinification have evolved enormously in the past couple of decades, giving the winemaker far more control over the state of his grapes and what happens to them after harvest. Consumers, especially those who have come recently into wine, are driving a trend towards wines that are fruitier, and that can be drunk sooner than those of the past. Formidable export drives from new wine-producing countries have made new choices in wine widely available. Markets generally have become more open, with wine sold in supermarkets rather than specialist stores. Technological changes in grape growing and winemaking have combined with new sources for production and more open markets to change the face of wine, from plonk sold in 5 liter containers to rare bottles that can be had only on allocation by a happy few.

I begin where it all starts: with the grape. From there we go to how grape juice is turned into wine, to the nature of the international wine trade and its consequences for the consumer, and finally in detail to the wines themselves of the New and Old Worlds, where we look at the effects of contemporary forces in each country on its production of wine. This book makes no attempt to be comprehensive: it is not an encyclopedia but rather an account of trend setters, driving forces—the factors determining why wine is like it is. At the end of the day, we should see why plonk is different from fine wine, what determines the flavor profiles of different wines, how New World wines differ from Old World wines, what global warming is going to do to wine production, and how all these various forces will impact wine production in the future. Sometimes there are no answers, but the questions are thought-provoking.

This book is intended for anyone interested in why wine tastes as it does. If you don't care about the fine details, it can be read entirely without reference to the charts or notes. (If they look intimidating, just ignore them.) But assertions without support have little conviction, so charts contain supporting information for those who are interested in any particular aspect, and the notes give sources for those who would like to be sure I didn't just make it all up.

One of the pleasures of writing this book has been many fascinating interaction with winemakers and others in many regions, with far too many people to thank individually for interesting discussions, not to mention hospitality and tastings, but I must thank Kip Kumler, Jim Lapsley, Peter Sichel, Helio San Miguel, Liz Thach, and Vincenzo Zampi whose insightful comments on the book helped to improve it greatly. And as always, I was accompanied around the world of wine by my indefatigable traveling and tasting companion, without whom this would scarcely have been possible.

Benjamin Lewin MW

I   GROWING GRAPES

MAN HAS GROWN GRAPES since time immemorial. The production of wine can be traced back to 5400 B.C., and cultivation of the grapevine to 4000 B.C. Pictorial representations in frescos and detailed hieroglyphic information on the seals of amphorae show that viticulture and vinification in Egypt had become sophisticated by 2700 B.C. By the time of the Greeks and Romans, viticulture was an important economic activity, as shown by the publication of treatises on the subject. At the start of the Common Era, grapevines began to spread from the Mediterranean across Europe, and in the Middle Ages they were widely propagated under the aegis of the Church. The European wine industry began to take its present form in the eighteenth and nineteenth centuries, and then was drastically reorganized as a result of the phylloxera infestation at the end of the nineteenth century. Wine production started in the New World with colonization, but became a significant part of world production only in the last years of the twentieth century. Major differences in viticulture between Europe and the New World result from their different regulatory systems, the biggest effect being that whereas irrigation is mostly banned in Europe, it is used in most of the New World, resulting in different criteria for choosing vineyard locations.

Development of viticulture and the wine trade over 7500 years.

5400 B.C.	Pottery has traces of tartaric acid, presumed to come from wine.
4000 B.C.	Grapevine is cultivated as an agricultural crop in Mesopotamia.
2700 B.C.	Viticulture and vinification is extensive in Egypt.
300 B.C.	Theophrastus publishes book on Greek viticulture.
1000 B.C.	Phoenicians start extensive export trade in wine.
65 C.E.	Columella publishes manuals for winemaking in Rome.
600 C.E.	Ecclesiastical vineyards spread across Europe.
1880 C.E.	Vineyards reorganized as result of Phylloxera.
2000 C.E.	New World wines become important on world market.

1

The Spread of the Grapevine

IT'S A MYTH THAT VITIS VINIFERA, the grapevine variety from which all fine (and much other) wine is made, is a single species. Vitis vinifera belongs to the Vitis family, which has about 60 members. All form grapes, but only Vitis vinifera is suitable for making wine; the others all have aromas or flavors that become disagreeable in wine. The members of the Vitis family are traditionally referred to as species, and crosses between them are called "hybrids." But the fact that they can interbreed to form fertile offspring tells you at once that they are not different species. As all of these "species" of Vitis can interbreed, in reality they are distinct subspecies.[1] Although some of the hybrids produced by interbreeding vinifera with other Vitis (sub)species have been used to make wine, to all intents and purposes, all wines ranging from table wines to fine wines today are made from the many varieties of Vitis vinifera.[2] (Some of the hybrids or other members of the family have an important role in providing rootstocks onto which Vitis vinifera can be grafted.)

There are thousands of different varieties of Vitis vinifera from which wine can be made. Some of them have spread over the entire planet; varieties such as Cabernet Sauvignon or Chardonnay are now grown in virtually all wine-producing countries of the world. Some are still restricted to the places where they originated, and are used to produce wine only in one locale. Some have darkly colored skins and are used to make red wine; others have green or yellow skins and are used to make white wine. In a world where diversity is constantly narrowing, the grapevine, and the wine made from its fruit, stands out for its variety.

Where did Vitis vinifera originate? How did it spread worldwide to become the common grapevine used for wine production?

A Single Species from the East

At the end of the Tertiary period, more than 65 million years ago, give or take a few million, there was only a single type of grapevine. Vitis occurs naturally only in the northern hemisphere, and the primitive Vitis developed into different species suited to different environmental niches. Vitis vinifera originated in Eurasia. Almost all of the other species originated in North America.[3]

The original plant that gave rise to Vitis was a hermaphrodite, allowing self-fertilization. Primitive Vitis became dioecious; different plants had male or female flowers, so that both must grow close together for fruit to be formed.[4] (Only the female plants form berries.) Then the plant was domesticated. With domestication, it reverted to a hermaphrodite (possibly because rare naturally occurring hermaphrodites were selected for their ability to form fruit more reliably).[5]

During the Paleolithic era, more than 10,000 years ago, the first wine might have been made from wild grapes.[6] The most ancient traces of wine have been found on fragments of pottery from the Hajii Firuz Neolithic complex in the northern Zagros Mountains of Iran. The pottery dates from about 5400 B.C., and contains traces of tartaric acid, a compound that is produced in this area only by grapes.[7]

Wine probably became important in human culture when the grapevine was cultivated. The big question about domestication is whether it happened only once, so that all existing Vitis vinifera are derived from a single ancestral grape-vine. (This is sometimes called the Noah hypothesis.[8]) Alternatively, it could have happened on several different occasions, in which case subgroups of Vitis vinifera should have descended from different ancestral grapevines. One way to distinguish these possibilities is to compare the genetic profiles of Vitis vinifera found in different geographical locations with the profiles of wild grapevines.[9] Different groups of wild grapevines can be distinguished over regions from the Near East to the Western Mediterranean, and judging from their genetic contributions to cultivated grapevines, there may have been at least two different domestication events.[10]

One event most likely took place in Transcaucasia, possibly in the area around the Black Sea, where wild grapevines are still relatively abundant. From there the grapevine may have spread to the Near East, where it may have been cultivated from about 4000 B.C. (However, the main alcoholic beverages of the period were beer produced from barley and wine produced from dates, possibly because the major cities of Mesopotamia were close to the southern limits for producing wine from grapes.[11]) A second event may have occurred independently on the Iberian Peninsula.

The next important stage in development of winemaking was in Egypt, where hieroglyphs describe sophisticated approaches to viticulture and vinification.[12] The Egyptians grew vines in walled vineyards, developed methods for training the grapevine on an overhead trellis, and may have used irrigation. In making wine, they may have used the addition of chopped up fruit (containing yeast) to

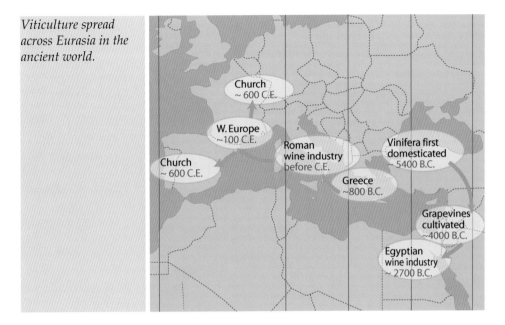

Viticulture spread across Eurasia in the ancient world.

initiate fermentation, and they developed methods for pressing the grapes. The entire wine production process, from viticulture to transport of the finished wine, was illustrated in tomb paintings.

By the time of the Greeks, viticulture was a regular part of farming and trade. Grapevines, together with wheat and olives, were basic agricultural crops. Around 320 B.C., the Greek philosopher Theophrastus (Aristotle's successor) published two series of books, *De causis plantarum* (The Causes of Plants) and *De historia plantarum* (The History of Plants). The Causes of Plants addresses many of the current issues in viticulture, including cultivation of the grapevine, pruning methods, and dealing with pests and diseases. It appears that vines were planted in tidy rows, like those of today, and there was attention to matching varieties to suitable soils.[13]

Cultivation of grapevines and the production of wine was a significant economic interest by Roman times. Around 160 B.C., Cato discussed vineyard management and vines in *de Agri Cultura,* giving a good deal of attention to issues such as pruning methods and the use of wine presses. Around 65 C.E. Lucius Columella published a 12-volume series on agriculture, *de Re Rustica,* including three books on viticulture. In one book he discussed the properties of different grape varieties. In the same century, Pliny also devoted a good part of his writing to descriptions of vines and wines, discussing in some detail the different grape varieties. Unfortunately, none of the names can be equated directly with modern varieties.

By the turn of the Millennium, viticulture was well established all round the Mediterranean. During the first century, the Romans spread the grapevine throughout the empire, extending north in Italy, up from the Mediterranean in France and through Iberia, and across Germany. (The extent of its growth into England at this time is more questionable,[14] although it seems likely that some of

The wine production scene from the tomb of Kha'emweset at Thebes, c. 1450 B.C. shows grapes being harvested, amphorae filled, and wine transported.[17]

the reputed vineyards really did exist.[15]) In 92 C.E., ostensibly to make more economic use of the land by growing more important crops, possibly in reality to protect viticulture closer to home, the emperor Domitian banned new plantings and ordered many of the plantings in the provinces to be uprooted.[16] It's dubious to what extent the edict was obeyed until it was repealed by the emperor Probus in 280 C.E.

With the fall of the Roman Empire, viticulture fell into decline everywhere. In Bordeaux, for example, there is little evidence for much commercial winemaking until the thirteenth century. The role that the Romans had played in spreading viticulture may have been taken over by the Church, which from roughly the fifth to tenth centuries propagated grapevines. "Fecit ecclesias et plantavit vineas,*" said a document of Charlemagne, concerning the foundation of a monastery in the eighth century.[18] Initially the purpose was to ensure the supply of sacramental wine, but production later became a successful commercial activity. The Church was certainly important in developing methods of cultivation, and individual sites, such as Clos Vougeot in Burgundy or Kloster Eberbach in Germany, attest to the success of the monks (especially the Cistercians).[19] Cer-

---

* Build the Church and plant vines.

tainly the Church had a role in spreading varieties and in matching them to local conditions, but it's not entirely clear how the overall economic contribution of the Church compared to that of individual landholders.[20]

By the year 1000, viticulture was well established across Europe, extending north and east of what had been the limits of the Roman Empire. The Loire and Champagne regions of northern France, and the Mosel and Rheingau of Germany were making wine by this time.[22] By 1086, the Domesday Book record-

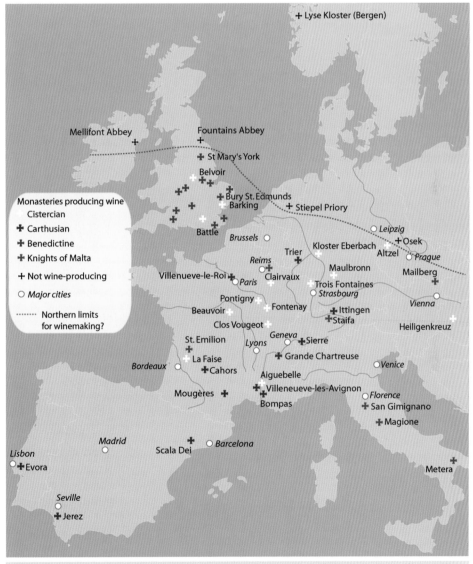

Monasteries of several orders spread across Europe in the middle ages, generally making wine wherever conditions permitted. The northern limits for winemaking must have been to the south of those monasteries that were forced to buy wine because they could not produce it themselves.[21]

ed 42 vineyards in the southern part of England.[23] The wine was not necessarily good, however; when King John tried the wine at Beaulieu Abbey in southern England in 1204, his reaction was to "send ships forthwith to fetch some good French wine for the Abbott."[24] Wine production continued in England until the sixteenth century.[25]

Viticulture extended surprisingly far north in the medieval period, up to Flanders in Belgium, Brandenburg in Germany, and northern Hungary.[26] As imports from the south became more accessible, the more northern vineyards were abandoned and given over to growing grain.[27] The largest areas for commercial wine production were in southwest France, the Rhône, and the Rhine (and some areas around the edges of the Mediterranean). The notable feature of vineyard locations was their concentration along navigable rivers, probably because the cost of water transport was vastly less than the cost of transport over land.[28]

The grape varieties that are predominant today can sometimes be traced back to mediaeval times, but it is hard to go back before that. As one example, Pinot Noir has certainly been grown in Burgundy for a very long time, but the first documented mention of the name occurs only in 1375. It's purely a matter of speculation whether the Romans brought it there or whether it originated later. But by the end of the mediaeval period, the grape varieties of today were being established in the most significant locales.

Vitis vinifera was unknown outside Europe until colonists transported it to the New World. Early colonists started wine production in South Africa in the seventeenth century, and in Australia in the eighteenth century. Cortés brought the first vines to Mexico, where they did so well that wine was exported back to Spain.[29] The vines were then taken down into South America. Vines were taken north to California during the eighteenth century. On the East Coast, after the failure of earlier attempts to produce wine from local grape varieties, Vitis vinifera was brought from Europe during the 17th century. But it did not do well because of the presence of a pest that devoured its roots: Phylloxera.

The Phylloxera Devastation

Phylloxera changed the face of viticulture for ever. This tiny insect, 1-3 mm long, is native to North America. Before human intervention, it extended from the East Coast to the Rockies. Now, of course, its domain is universal.

Its original name was Phylloxera vastatrix, which means phylloxera the destroyer.[30] It has an exceptionally complicated life cycle, with multiple forms, including male and female larvae, and various winged states. It can climb up the plant, it can fly from one plant to the next, and it can burrow down to the roots. It is adaptable: the winged forms are common in its native habitat in North America, but it manages perfectly well without wings in some other environments. Phylloxera is extremely fecund; with a generation time of less than one month, it can run through multiple generations in the course of a year in the vineyard.[31]

The burrowing form of Phylloxera feeds on grapevine roots.

Photograph kindly provided by Kevin Powell.

The burrowing form loves grapevines. It feeds on grapevine roots, using its long proboscis to suck sap out of the vine and to inject toxin. Once phylloxera starts feeding, it is only a matter of time until the vine dies. However, the lethal action is indirect. When damage reduces the pressure of sap below a critical level, phylloxera leave the vine and migrate to a fresh one. But the damaged sites provide entry points for other infections, such as fungal pathogens.[32] Finally the weakened vine dies.

Phylloxera was endemic in the Eastern United States, but the species of Vitis indigenous to North America are all resistant to it. These species are not native to Europe, and the trouble started when they were imported there. One reason was a craze for ornamental grapevines. Another was that some French winegrowers thought it would be interesting to experiment with American varieties. None of the American vines make wine that is particularly good, and some is quite un-drinkable, but growers in France thought it was possible that hybrids between these vines and the local Vitis vinifera might give more durable varieties that would make good wine. During the 1830s and 1840s, American vines were imported into France and became widely available.

Phylloxera came as an unwanted visitor with the American vines. Because Vitis vinifera had never been exposed to phylloxera, it had no resistance. Once phylloxera reached Europe, they rapidly migrated to the sensitive local vines. The first traces of phylloxera were found at Kew Gardens in England in 1863, but it was not long before it was omnipresent in Europe. The start of the infection in France has been traced to American vines planted in 1862 by a M. Borty at Roquemaure on the right bank of the Rhône, just north of Avignon (now part of the area where the wine of the Côtes du Rhône is produced). Already by the following year, local vines were infected and dying.[33]

Phylloxera spread amazingly fast through France. During 1870-1871, it traveled up the Rhône forming a triangle of infection with the peak at Tain l'Hermitage. At the same time, small, but isolated, centers of infection appeared around Bordeaux. By 1875, the Rhône triangle had broadened and there was a sizeable area of infection around Bordeaux. These areas widened further by 1880,

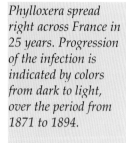

Phylloxera spread right across France in 25 years. Progression of the infection is indicated by colors from dark to light, over the period from 1871 to 1894.

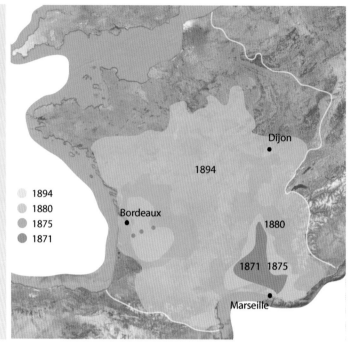

and by 1894 the entire map of winegrowing areas of France had been filled in.[34] The edges of infected areas reported by the Commission on Phylloxéra show a remarkable coincidence with the outlines of the administrative Départéments; it is unlikely that the insect respected the political boundaries, so one might suspect that reporting was less scrupulous in some Départéments than others, possibly understating the extent of the infestation.

Phylloxera was no more likely to respect national boundaries. It spread through Portugal around the same time as in France, wiping out wine production in the Douro by 1895. Its effects became apparent a little later in Italy and Spain, but both were heavily infected within a few years. It was much slower to reach Germany, where major effects did not become apparent until after 1945.[35]

The first reaction was incredulity. "Not in my house," as Lady Macbeth might have said. Denial usually took the form of insisting that well-tended vines would not be susceptible, even though Jules-Émile Planchon, Professor of Botany at Montpellier, quickly established that the cause was an infection with a previously-unknown insect. From the first identification of the insect in 1868, Planchon moved quickly to identify its origins, and in 1873 visited the United States to investigate phylloxera in its native habitat.

There was a scattershot search for solutions. Carbon bisulphide (a primitive neurotoxin) killed the insect, but vast quantities had to be pumped into the ground; the cost was beyond the means of most growers, and effects on the flavor of the wine were uncertain. Drowning the insects was partially effective, but required access to an inexhaustible supply of fresh water. Vineyards in sandy

The commission on phylloxera visiting the vineyards. The two figures at the back in top hats are J. E. Planchon and J. Lichtenstein, and the figure immediately in front of them is the American entomologist C. V. Riley.[38]

soil were relatively resistant, because phylloxera fails to propagate (possibly because it drowns when the soil becomes wet). The protagonists for carbon disulphide became known as *sulfuristes*, those for drowning as *submersionnistes*, but the march of phylloxera was inexorable.

The identification of the source carried the implication that native American vines were resistant to its ravages. By 1875, replanting the Midi (the area of the original infection) with American vines was extensive; more than 7 million cuttings of the Concord grapevine (a variety of Vitis labrusca[36]) were imported.[37] But the vines did not do well in their new environment. And tastings of wines made in France from imported American wines were judged to be fairly disastrous. The *americainistes* who wanted to replant on American vines were soon in a dwindling minority.

The idea of crossing Vitis vinifera with American Vitis was revived, in the hope of producing hybrid varieties that would both be resistant to phylloxera and make palatable wine. Many hybrids were produced, but most showed the "foxy" taste of American Vitis in the wine, although some of the hybrids continued to be planted until the end of the twentieth century. Out of all this, however, emerged the idea that the French Vitis vinifera vines could be protected by grafting onto roots of resistant American Vitis varieties.

Grafting was already well established as a technique for propagating fruit trees.[39] The technique is pretty simple in principle. One plant provides the root that extends below ground. It has a short stem extending just above ground level. A cut is made in the stem, and then a matching cut is made in the stem of the above-ground part of a different plant. The stem is inserted into the root-

Grafting involves fitting the scion into the stem of the rootstock. Two scions have been grafted on to one stem, and then secured with a tape that will be protected with a sealant.

Photograph kindly provided by Dai Crisp.

stock, the grafting site is bound up with tape and protected, and in a relatively short period the two parts seal together to generate a plant with a "rootstock" of one origin and a "scion" of a different origin. In a young plant, you can see a slight bulge in the trunk just above ground level where the graft was made.

In short order, American Vitis species were classified for their relative degrees of resistance to Phylloxera and their compatibility with different soil types. Vitis riparia became the rootstock of choice on clay soils, while Vitis rupestris tended to be used on calcareous soils. One of the main problems in adjusting American rootstocks to European conditions is the much higher content of limestone in Europe; if the rootstock cannot adjust to the low acidity of limestone, the plant develops the disease of chlorosis when the leaves turn yellow and fall off. (Chlorosis results from inability to take up enough iron.) An industry soon grew up in crossing American Vitis species to generate resistant rootstocks that were suited for particular soil conditions with regards to acidity, water retention, and so on. The problem of adaptation to limestone was solved by the discovery of Vitis berlandieri, an American Vitis species from Texas that thrives on chalk.[40] Grafted vines became the norm, and by 1895 more than a third of French vineyards had French vines growing on foreign rootstocks.

The fallout from the phylloxera infection was considerable. The planted area of French vineyards started the long march of decline, falling from 2.5 million hectares in 1875 to 1.5 million in 1914. (It is down to 1 million ha today.) Between 1875 and 1879, production of wine crashed by half; it did not recover until 1900. Some areas, especially those with marginal climates in the north, ceased production altogether. Others changed their grape varieties. The diversity of grape varieties was reduced; we shall probably never know how many simply succumbed to phylloxera and were never propagated on foreign rootstocks.

Phylloxera had a great effect on the way vineyards were planted. Previously, vines had been propagated en foule (literally: in a crowd) simply by sticking a

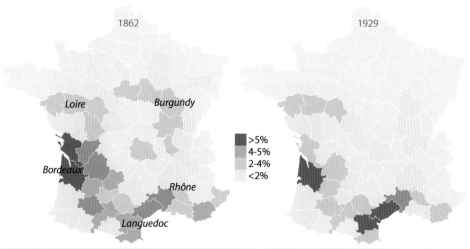

Vineyards retreated from the northern half of France after phylloxera.[41] Color indicates proportion of vineyards from >5% (darkest) to <2% (lightest) relative to total in France.

shoot in the earth. Usually a shoot from an existing vine was bent down into the earth nearby; once it took root, the connection to the mother plant would be cut, leaving a freestanding vine. A vineyard consisted of a haphazard array of vines, each supported by its own wooden stake. By contrast, grafted plants were usually planted in tidy rows (making it easier to work the vines with horse-drawn equipment), but also involving a reduction in the density of vines. This had been as high as 14,000 for vines planted en foule, but is rarely more than 8000 for vines planted on rootstocks. The density can have an effect on the quality of the grapes—at lower planting densities the vines don't have to struggle so hard, and quality is lower.

The major consequence for quality, however, comes from a more direct effect on the yield. Vines planted on rootstocks are usually more productive than those growing on their own roots. By 1914, when the majority of vines were grafted, production had reached the same level as in 1870, but from only 60% of the land area. Greater production is usually associated with lower quality (although tastings to compare the wines made from grafted and ungrafted vines in Burgundy during the period of replanting did not demonstrate any great difference).

Wine production was affected worldwide. During the worst period in France, wine was imported from Spain and Italy. Despairing of producing wine in their native country, some producers left Bordeaux for Spain. Some went to Rioja and revolutionized winemaking there. The boom lasted until phylloxera made it over the Pyrenees in the late 1890s. Then of course the blight followed them. There was no escape in Europe.

Phylloxera has spread worldwide, but it is not completely universal. It spread across the Rockies into California in 1876 and into Australia around the same time. But there are still some holdouts. Most of the grapevines of Oregon are planted on their own roots, Southern Australia is largely free of phylloxera, and Chile is free. A fascinating experiment is ongoing at the Reserva di Caliboro

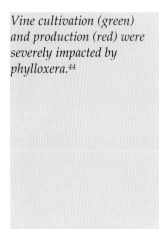

Vine cultivation (green) and production (red) were severely impacted by phylloxera.[44]

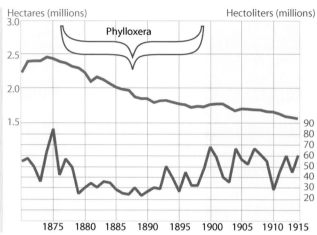

estate in Chile's Maule Valley (owned by Francesco Cinzano of Col d'Orcia in Montalcino, Tuscany), where Cabernet Sauvignon and Cabernet Franc have been planted side by side on their own roots and on rootstocks. The vines are managed, grapes are harvested, and wine is made, in exactly the same way for both grafted and ungrafted plantings. The first real harvest was only in 2008, but perhaps soon there will finally be a definitive answer as to the effect of rootstocks on quality of the wine.[42]

Even when you can, it's risky to plant vines on their own roots, because once phylloxera arrives it can spread extremely rapidly. In the late 1980s, California was hit with another phylloxera epidemic. A rootstock called AxR1 had been widely used as the result of advice from the viticulture department at the Davis campus of the University of California. AxR1 is a hybrid between Vitis rupestris and Vitis vinifera; like many hybrids with some vinifera parentage, it is not really very resistant to phylloxera. Like many other viticulture departments, Davis was more concerned with quantity of production (AxR1 is an abundant producer) than with quality or the long term.[43]

During the 1960s and 1970s, about 75% of plantings in Napa and Sonoma were on AxR1.[45] By the late 1980s, phylloxera was enthusiastically feeding on these rootstocks. Initially, there were claims that the epidemic was due to the emergence of a new "biotype" of phylloxera able to chew on rootstocks that had previously been resistant, but it's now clear this had little to do with the problem.[46] AxR1 is not employed at all in Europe because of its known susceptibility to phylloxera, so it was really only a matter of time before it succumbed in California. It was an expensive mistake: replanting on new rootstocks cost the California wine industry more than $1 billion.[47]

In Europe, there are isolated vineyards in several locations where vines have been able to survive on their own roots. The largest single area is the Mosel in Germany, where 55% of vines are still ungrafted. It's thought that phylloxera finds it difficult to propagate on the slate that dominates the region. (However, the German authorities recently banned planting of vines on their own roots. This is controversial. Some growers want to perpetuate ungrafted vines, but others feel it's time to move on; Annagret Reh-Gartner, of von Kesselstatt, told me, "It's irresponsible to plant ungrafted vines, since phylloxera is known to be there."[48])

More puzzling are small vineyards of surviving original vines where the surrounding vineyards have all had to be grafted. Bollinger has a small enclosed vineyard of vines on their own roots from which they produce the Vieilles Vignes Françaises Champagne; Lisini has a small vineyard of Sangiovese in Tuscany. You might wonder whether possibly the vines are rare resistant strains, but this is unlikely to be the case at Quinta do Noval in the Douro of Portugal, where the Nacional Port is made from a vineyard of vines of several varieties all growing on their own roots. As recently as the 1980s, there was still a small plot of ungrafted vines at Château Lafite Rothschild dating from around 1900.[49]

The number of exceptions where ungrafted vines can be found is dwindling. The heritage of phylloxera has made it the norm for vines to be grafted. Growers pay almost as much attention to their choice of rootstocks as to the choice of varieties from which the wine is actually made. Some years ago I was involved in a project to consider genetic engineering of grapevines to see whether it might be possible to introduce phylloxera-resistance into Vitis vinifera to allow it to be propagated on its own roots again.[50] More than one producer looked at me, puzzled, and asked, "Why would we want to do that? We have always grafted."

Old vines growing happily on their own roots in the Bernkasteler Doctor vineyard of the Mosel.

True, the combination of rootstock and scion gives more versatility in matching the grapevine to local conditions, but the basic parameter determining where each variety will grow best is the climate: within the overall zone for grape growing, each variety has a preferred range determined largely by temperature. Here the scion is all important.

Cultivars and Clones

There are more than 10,000 different varieties of Vitis vinifera, and thousands of them are used to make wine.[51] (About 2,000 varieties are characterized as table grapes.[52]) The most famous varieties are distributed around the world, but others are obscure, existing only in highly restricted places, known only to the locals and to the indefatigable cataloguers of the species. The largest diversity among varieties used to produce wine is found in the countries where wine production has been longest established; Italy, France, Greece, Portugal, and Spain have several hundred different varieties each. The term *cultivar*, meaning a *culti*vated *vari*ety of a plant, is often used to describe a distinct grapevine variety.

The differences between cultivars have arisen since Vitis vinifera was domesticated. Most of them have occurred naturally, but in the last century some new cultivars have also been created by crossing (the technical term is hybridizing) existing varieties. Because Vitis vinifera is self-fertilizing, the spontaneous generation of new varieties is an exceptional event, probably happening by cross-fertilization when two different varieties are growing close to each other. It's fair to say that none of the artificial crosses have produced anything as successful as nature itself.[53]

The differences between grapevine varieties are immense. Color is one of the most obvious. The progenitor Vitis was colored, and today's white varieties have lost the ability to produce skin pigmentation. Each cultivar has its own preferred conditions; the temperatures required for growth and ripening are the most critical for determining the zones where it grows best.

It is not always a trivial matter to tell the difference between cultivars. It may be hard to believe, but the traditional way of distinguishing varieties is by *ampelography*—assessing differences in the shapes of their leaves. (The name comes from *ampelos*, the Greek for vine.) Whole books have been written on the ampelography of the grapevine. Personally, I am inclined to view it more as art than science. Ampelography is susceptible to error by confusing varieties with similar appearance and growth characteristics. This has led to some famous mix-ups. Much of the Merlot in Chile was not really Merlot but was another variety that had come from Bordeaux, Carmenère; the two cultivars grow in similar locales and have a similar appearance.

Today we have a more precise method of defining cultivars and relating them to one another. The same technique of DNA fingerprinting used in criminal cases, or to determine human parentage, can be used to distinguish grapevine varieties. Each cultivar has a distinct DNA profile, and comparisons between cultivars can identify parentage. Using DNA fingerprinting has identified the origins of some varieties, such as showing that Zinfandel in California is really the same as the Crljenak grape of Croatia. (It passed through southern Italy, where it is called Primitivo before being brought by immigrants to California where it acquired yet another name.[54])

Each of the popular grapevine varieties has a number of subvarieties. These days, most varieties are propagated as clones. (A clone is a plant whose genetic makeup is exactly the same as a parent plant from which it was regenerated.) Many clones are available for most of the international varieties, and growers can pick those that are best suited to their particular vineyards with regards to the timing of the life cycle or productivity. The process of cloning is actually a bit more complicated than just taking a cutting; in principle, a clone should involve regeneration of the whole plant from a single cell of the parental plant. The advantage of cloning is that the new plant exactly reproduces the properties of its parent; and it can be guaranteed to be free of viruses, which are an ongoing problem in reducing the health of grapevines. (There's a procedure for eliminating viruses during cloning.)

New subvarieties are generated when a mutation occurs in a parent plant and is perpetuated in the cutting that makes the next generation. Some varieties are more prone to mutation than others. Pinot Noir is one of the most prone, and there may be several hundred subvarieties of Pinot Noir in Burgundy, including 200 defined clones. Not everyone uses the clones. Their importance varies with the grape varieties and the region. Usage of clones is much less of an issue in Bordeaux than in Burgundy: "In Bordeaux, you have in the same terroir, some good clones and some lesser ones. It's not a huge thing but it is another factor to consider, but after several others, like terroir. There is less variation between the clones of Cabernet Sauvignon or Merlot than in Burgundy, where clone is more important because there is a wider genetic variation between the clones of Pinot Noir," according to Paul Pontallier, winemaker at Château Margaux.[55]

Some growers believe in propagating the subvarieties that have given good results in their own vineyards. The belief is especially strong in Burgundy, where many feel that not only have the last few hundred years demonstrated the strength of the connection with Pinot Noir, but also that the vines have become adapted to growth in their particular vineyards. When they need to replant a vineyard, they take cuttings from existing vines that have performed especially well. This *selection massale* is the closest equivalent to the way things were before phylloxera. The difference is that now the cuttings have to be grafted on to new rootstocks instead of just sticking a free branch into the ground. The disadvantage is that any viruses or other diseases are likely to be perpetuated by selection massale. In Germany, where it's mandated that only certified clones can be used to replant vineyards, a grower can take his cutting to the institute at Geisenheim to have virus-free clones generated from it.

Selection massale is controversial because of its uncontrolled nature—it's hard to be really sure of the quality of the vines that have been selected. But it does ensure some variety when a vineyard is replanted. The greatest disadvantage of clones is simply that over-reliance on any one clone has a homogenizing effect on the nature of the fruit.

Zones for Grape Growing

The grapevine is amazingly hardy. It will grow anywhere it can get enough (but not too much) water and sunshine. As a practical matter, it grows well enough to make wine between the 50° and 30° latitudes. More precisely, the limits follow the 10 °C and 20 °C isotherms—lines of average annual temperature—which don't exactly coincide with the lines of latitude. In Europe, the grape-growing region extends from the northern limit of Champagne and the most northern wine-growing regions of Germany to the southernmost points of Spain and Italy. In North America, other climatic factors restrict production of fine wines to the West Coast of the United States, although there is also some production farther north in Canada. In the southern hemisphere, the production areas include southern Australia and New Zealand, the southern parts of South Africa, and central regions of Chile and Argentina.

Each variety has a characteristic annual cycle, from the time of flowering to the time of achieving ripeness. The response to temperature is usually characterized in terms of the average daily temperature during the growing season (the period from April to October[56]). Below a certain range, the variety will not ripen. Above the range, it ripens too fast, typically giving muddy or jammy flavors in the wine.

Most varieties have historically been grown in Europe at their northern limits, in regions towards the bottom of their preferred temperature range. The result is that traditionally there have rarely been more than three really good vintages each decade, when temperatures were high enough for full ripening. Poor vin-

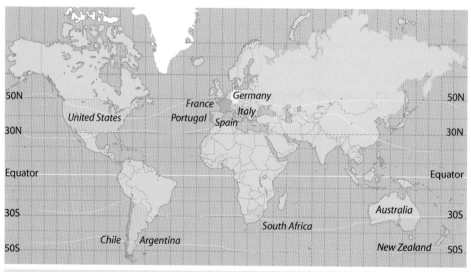

Major sites for grape growing are between the 10° and 20° isotherms in the northern and southern hemispheres. Isotherms are dotted white, the 30° and 50° latitudes are dotted red.

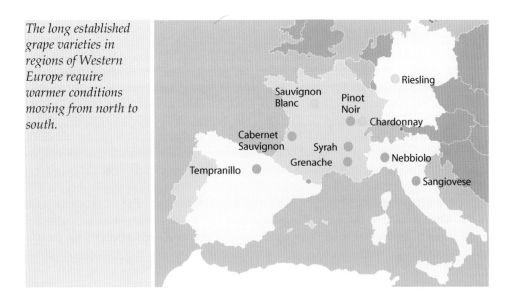

The long established grape varieties in regions of Western Europe require warmer conditions moving from north to south.

tages have resulted when the growing season temperatures were below the minimum for the variety. Of course, the recent warming trend is changing this situation. In the New World, where varieties were chosen more recently, temperatures in each region tend to be more at the upper end for the varieties grown there.

In the northern part of Western Europe, pushing up against the 50° latitude line, where temperatures are relatively cool, the varieties that are most successful are all white. Riesling is grown at the farthest north, in Germany and in Alsace; Sauvignon Blanc and Chenin Blanc are grown in the Loire, the northernmost regions in France for producing still wine. The Champagne region, a little north of the Loire, is an exception in growing Pinot Noir and Chardonnay, but this is due to the genius of making sparkling wine, where addition of a little sugar compensates for pushing ripening to its limits. Beyond the northern limits, England is another exception, where still wine is made mostly from special cold-resistant varieties, but remains marginal for production of fine wine.

Moving towards the south, Burgundy is famous for Pinot Noir, the most delicate of the red varieties, and Chardonnay. Just a couple of degrees warmer and farther south, Bordeaux is the paradigm for Cabernet Sauvignon and Merlot. Moving down to the Rhône, in the north comes Syrah, while the south grows Grenache and other hot climate varieties. The match between latitude and the temperature preference of each variety is not exact, since local temperatures are also affected by other factors, such as the elevation of the vineyards. The famous varieties of Tempranillo (in Rioja), Nebbiolo (in Barolo), and Sangiovese (in Chianti and Brunello) are all found in locales that are a bit cooler than might be suggested by their latitude. In general there's a good correlation between average regional temperatures and the preferred temperature range of the typical variety of the region.

Millennia of Innovation

Man has been improving the grapevine ever since it was first domesticated. New varieties have extended the range of places where it can grow. Specific clones have been selected for ability to ripen later, to produce smaller berries, or to withstand particular climatic conditions. The forced adaptation to grafting on to rootstocks has led to more refined control of productivity. Methods of training have improved the ability to withstand adverse climatic conditions, and management of the canopy has helped to produce riper grapes.

Once the grapevine was domesticated, its pattern of spread was partly due to economic factors, such as trading patterns and the rise and fall of empires, and partly due to more technical developments. It became possible to cultivate grapevines in Bordeaux and Burgundy around the first century C.E., for example, because new varieties developed that would grow and ripen in these cooler climates. These may have been the ancestors of Cabernet Sauvignon and Pinot Noir. In the period up to 1000 C.E., the Church was important in matching varieties to regions. By the late middle ages, the pattern was set in Europe.

There were probably relatively few changes in the way the grapevine was actually grown until the modern era. In ancient Egypt it was grown on a high trellis, a pattern that survives to the present day in the pergola system of Italy. In other places it was grown as a free-standing bush, with a dense array of grapevines perpetuated by rooting plants next to one another. Vineyards were worked exclusively by hand. All this changed with the twin events of the transition to grafting following phylloxera and the mechanization of vineyards, which led to the development of a variety of training systems for cultivating the grapevine, suited to specific climatic conditions. Management of the grapevine, together with developments in mechanization, is now the driving force in adjusting it to each region and climate.

Yet this vastly successful system now is subject to challenge as never before. Impending climate change threatens the established match of varieties to places. And there's a continuing narrowing of the range of varieties, with the same "international" varieties replacing indigenous varieties. Will continuing innovation help to maintain the variety of the grapevine or will it fall victim to homogeneity resulting from globalization?

2

Cultivating the Vineyard

GRAPEVINES ORIGINATED BY GROWING ON TREES in the wild. The shape and height of wild grapevines are constrained only by the limits of the tree providing support. They may be male or female, although both types must grow in the same vicinity if they are successfully to form berries. Today wild grapevines occur only in relatively small, isolated populations around the Mediterranean and towards the Caucasus.

The grapevine is extremely malleable and can be pruned into all sorts of different shapes. Various pruning systems are used to suit different locations. They affect how far the vine can spread out, what height its bunches of grapes hang above the ground, how much shade the grapes get from the canopy of leaves, and so on. The main factors affecting the choice of system are the climate and

Grapevines grow wild on trees. This female Vitis vinifera silvestris is part of a population of 132 vines at Ribera de Huelva river near Seville. Its leaves are brighter green than those of the tree.

Photograph kindly provided by Rafael Ocete.

Grapevines are pruned on to a training system consisting of a trellis with several horizontal wires.

Roses are often planted at the ends of rows to give early warning of pests and diseases.

whether harvesting will be manual or mechanical (mechanical harvesters like the rows of vines to be better separated and the canopy to be relatively high). Other factors can come into play: I remember visiting a vineyard in southern England that had an unusual canopy system, spread out and rather high. Eager to discover the basis behind this new adaptation to climate, I asked the proprietor about the rationale. "Oh," she said, "the previous proprietor had a bad back and trained the vines high so he wouldn't have to bend down."[1]

Vines can be free-standing, trained as a bush, which gives a relatively dense canopy that is suitable for warm dry climates; this is widely used around the Mediterranean. But a common feature in most modern systems is a trellis of horizontal wires, attached to a post at the end of the row of vines. As the vine grows during the season, its shoots are attached to the wires for support.

The type of training system determines the permanent structure of the vine. A "head-trained" system has only a vertical trunk; new shoots emerge from the head of the trunk each year, and are trained along the wires of whatever system is used. A "cordon-trained" system has permanent horizontal extensions along the trellis in one or both directions, and the new shoots grow out from the arms of the cordon.

Whatever system is used, effectively the vine starts out afresh each year. After the harvest, the last year's new growth is pruned off, except for some shoots that are used for the new growth in the next season. New growth is prodigious, and the shoots can easily extend for several feet.

The Grapevine Life Cycle

The grapevine is a sparse looking object at the beginning of the season, all stripped down to bare wood. The vertical trunk may be thin if the grapevine is young, or gnarled and thick if it is old, but will not show much sign of life. It may have a permanent branch extending horizontally in the most common types of pruning, or may stand alone with a barely perceptible bud at the top where a new branch will grow. Some time in March (when the temperature rises above 10 °C), bud break will happen. The first signs of growth are seen as the new shoots push out from the old wood. Shoots and leaves develop over the next couple of months, forming the canopy.

The first critical moment is when flowering occurs in May. Depending on the weather, this may happen relatively evenly or can be prolonged. The shorter the period for flowering, the better, because a more rapid flowering leads to a more uniform ripening of the berries at the end of the season. Typically the period between flowering and the completion of fertilization, called fruit set, is about two weeks. This requires the temperature to rise above 15 °C.

Problems with flowering have a major effect on the size of the crop. Coulure (sometimes called shatter in English) happens when flowers are not fertilized, so they do not develop into berries. Millerandage occurs a bit later, when flowers that were not properly fertilized (actually they were fertilized with dead pollen) fail to expand, giving small berries that ripen irregularly. And, of course, the vine is especially sensitive to a late frost between bud break and flowering, which can kill off the crop.

The size of the grapevine canopy increases over the next few weeks as more shoots and leaves develop, and the next significant moment occurs when the developing berries change color in July. This is called veraison. Until now, the berries have grown rapidly and chlorophyll has been the predominant pigment. At veraison, the skin of the berry becomes translucent for white varieties, and colored for black varieties. This occurs abruptly in any individual berry, but occurs over several days for the plant as a whole, and even for the berries within a bunch.

At the start of the growing season, everything has been pruned off the grapevine except for two of the last season's shoots, extending horizontally from the trunk, from which the new season's growth will come.

Growth slows after veraison, and photosynthesis is directed towards producing sugars for the berries and laying down carbohydrate reserves for the following year. The berries accumulate sugar and lose acidity. Harvest occurs when they are judged ripe. It used to be the case that harvest was generally set a regular 100 days after the flowering, but a trend to harvest riper berries means that the period is now often quite a bit longer.

After harvest, as temperatures drop, the leaves fall off, and then all of the past season's growth is removed by pruning, leaving only the permanent structure of the grapevine, ready to start again next year.

A grapevine does not demand much from the climate: simply more than 1500 hours of sunshine and more than 700 mm of water per year. Then photosynthesis will do the rest, using carbon dioxide from the air to build the structures of the growing plant. The requirement for sunshine translates into a need for the average yearly temperature to be around 14-15 °C. The grapevine is sensitive to cold: it stops growing below 10 °C and is killed by temperatures below –25 °C. It is also sensitive to too much heat: photosynthesis slows down over 30 °C and stops completely above 40 °C. And grapevines need a period of dormancy, a month or two below 10 °C to recover their strength for the next season. These parameters explain the vine's need for the climatic conditions found between the 30° and 50° latitudes.

The success of each particular vintage depends on conditions that year, especially how much sunshine and water (and when the water arrived). This influences the balance between vegetative growth (developing the structure of the plant) and the production of fruit. But it's not quite that simple, because the grapevine actually has a two year cycle. Grapevines start the season with dormant buds, which determine the crop potential for the coming season. These

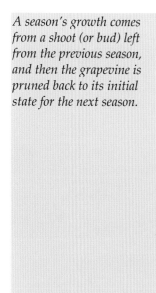

A season's growth comes from a shoot (or bud) left from the previous season, and then the grapevine is pruned back to its initial state for the next season.

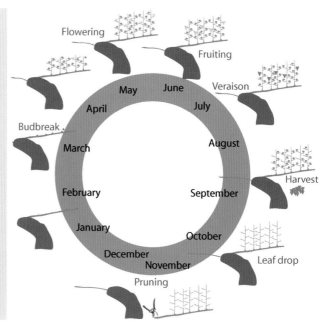

buds can develop into either foliage or fruit; the choice is influenced by exposure to sunlight, which drives development towards fruit. But the dormant buds were in fact formed during the previous year, and the level of budding depends on the amount of light they received that summer. The rationale is probably that the grapevine does not want to commit to producing fruit unless the shoot is in a place where the berries will be exposed to sun. Often the grapevine will compensate in one season for what happened the previous season: so a small crop one year will be followed by a large crop the next year.

From Deep Roots to Lofty Canopy

Well, actually, in a pruned grapevine, the canopy may not be so lofty, but the roots may well be very deep. The root system branches extensively, and it's the root tip that performs many of the most significant functions, including uptake of water and nutrients. If a plant gets the chance, it will follow the path of least resistance and spread its roots out near the surface. If it can't find enough nutrients at the surface, and especially if some stress is imposed by a surface ploughing to remove superficial roots, then it will send its roots down deeper, for several meters if necessary. Conventional wisdom is that grapevines produce the best results in poor soils, often in soils that would not be fertile enough to support any other crop, because this forces them to send their roots deeper.

Left to its own devices, the grapevine would grow as far up as the supporting structure allows. A cultivated grapevine, however, is pruned to form a relatively low canopy, a few feet up at most. (The canopy includes all parts of the grapevine above the root system.) The canopy has a great effect on exposure to sunlight and to wind, and on how much evaporation occurs from the leaves. "Canopy management" has been the focus of viticulture for several years and means that an active tuning of the plant, starting with the pruning system but extending to continual adjustment during the growing season, is used to try to equalize its production of fruit.

Different pruning systems are used in different climates, with cool climates emphasizing the need to expose berries to enough sunshine, and warm climates emphasizing the need to protect them from too much exposure. The canopy needs to be large enough to have a sufficient leaf area to support photosynthesis, but if it becomes too large, the shade can prevent sufficient sunshine from reaching the berries. The objective is to control the number of berries each plant produces and to try to ensure they ripen evenly. This starts with the number of buds that are allowed to develop. After the flowering, when it's possible to estimate the potential yield, further pruning may be used to reduce it. Vendange en vert (or "green pruning") is used to remove excess flowers or immature berries; it's somewhat controversial how much it improves quality, and is a bit undercut by the fact that the plant tends to expand the size of the remaining berries to make up for the forced reduction. Later in the season, leaf-pulling may be used to remove parts of the canopy where they are giving too much shade (actually the leaves can be removed with a machine that burns them off).

One of the critical features of the grapevine is that berries can ripen *only* on the vine. Some plants produce fruit that can be ripened after it has been harvested; it's common with tomatoes, for example, to collect them when still green, but then to ripen them by exposure to the plant hormone, ethylene. Strangely enough, with grapevines we are not really sure which plant hormones are needed for the ripening process, so it is crucial to get the berries to ripeness before the harvest.

The Limits of Yield

Yield is one of the most important (and misunderstood) concepts in viticulture. The amount of wine produced from a given area is usually measured in hectoliters of juice per hectare of land in Europe.[*] It's given in tons of berries per acre in the United States.[†] Yields can be anywhere from 35 to 80 hl/ha for quality wines. (An average production of 50 hl/ha would be equivalent to about 2700 bottles per acre. In a typical Bordeaux vineyard of 8,000 vines per hectare, this is roughly equivalent to producing 1 bottle of wine from every vine.) Yields can be much greater for producing bulk table wine, in the range of 100-150 hl/ha.

Immediately the comparison between quality wine and bulk wine makes the point that better wines are associated with lower yields. Why is this? When a vine produces more grapes, their juice is less concentrated—the vine puts roughly the same total level of energy into producing its fruit, so more fruit means less effort per berry. This is true only up to a point. It is perfectly clear that wine made from grapes at a yield of 50 hl/ha is more concentrated than wine made at 100 hl/ha. But there may come a point, perhaps around the 40 hl/ha level, where further reductions in yield do not have much effect upon perceived quality.

One of the reasons why old vines are highly prized is that the yield naturally goes down as the vine ages. There's no precise measure of when this happens, but French wines may carry the label "Vieilles Vignes" (old vines) as a marker implying higher quality from lower yield. There's no legal definition of the term, and it's left up to the individual producer to decide when the vigne has become vieille. Eventually, of course, production dwindles to uneconomic levels. Generally speaking, vines are replaced at around 25 years of age, as their yield becomes too low to be worthwhile for general production.

The ideal situation for quality is for every vine to have a low, but adequate yield, but it's a myth that measurement of yield in terms of production per unit area of land accurately reflects each vine's activity. A vineyard whose yield has

---

[*] A hectoliter is about 11 cases of wine; a hectare is 2.47 acres.

[†] Very roughly 1 ton/acre is about 16 hl/ha (although the ratio is somewhat different for red wine and white wine).

been reduced because some vines are diseased and are poor producers, while others are churning it out, will not make high quality wine. As a *reductio ad absurdum*, the average yield over the country as a whole is 30 hl/ha for Spain and 57 hl/ha for France;[2] but this is not because Spain routinely makes better and more concentrated wine than France, it is because the plains of Spain are full of diseased vines that reduce the yield without increasing the quality. If you have a significant number of dead or poorly producing vines in your vineyard, the yield per hectare may not correlate with quality at all.

It's the yield per individual plant that impacts quality, but this is something that's difficult to measure en masse. "M. Borie of Ducru Beaucaillou wanted to go from a maximum yield per hectare to a maximum yield per plant. But it's too complicated to survey, the INAO didn't have the means to maintain a file with the density of plantation for each individual grower," according to Jean-Michel Cazes of Château Lynch Bages in Bordeaux.[3] Cazes takes the view that extremely low yields in Bordeaux can be a sign of poor quality rather than the reverse: "It's not that you don't produce fine wines with 20-25 hl/ha, but it's not necessary, at least in Bordeaux... A low yield in a well-maintained vineyard with homogenous production of 40 or 45 hl/ha with old vines is perfect." Really low yields, he believes, mean either low density of planting, bad maintenance, or heterogeneity in the vineyard.[4]

Low yield is not a panacea for all ills. "Surely the predominant myth of the wine industry is that high yields result in low wine quality," says Australian viticulturalist Richard Smart.[5] He believes that low yields are a symptom, not a cause, and that they most commonly result from water stress. Limitations on the water supply, he argues, are the real basis for improving quality. So mimicking low yields, for example by green pruning to remove excess berries early in the season, will not necessarily have the same effect. "Method of yield control is more important than final yield in affecting sensory features," he concludes.

If all the vines are active, other things being equal, a vineyard planted at higher density will produce better quality berries than one planted at lower density. At least in the relatively poor soils of Europe, the extra competition between vines means that each vine produces a smaller number of berries. In Bordeaux, where there is a very wide range of wine qualities, it's noticeable that the best vineyards are planted densely at 8-10,000 vines per hectare, but those of generic Bordeaux are planted at around 4,000 vines per hectare. When yields are restricted, doubling the number of vines effectively halves the production per vine. At a yield of 50 hl/ha, a vineyard planted at 10,000 vines/ha produces 500 ml/vine, but a vineyard planted at 5,000 vines/ha produces 1000 ml/vine.

Vine densities traditionally have been less in the New World, originally because of the lack of tractors that could move along narrow rows, but more recently there's been a move in Napa Valley, for example, towards the narrow rows and high density of Europe. It's not entirely clear this has the same effects on quality in these richer soils as it does in Europe. As Paul Pontallier of Château Margaux says, "The soil is richer in the lesser class Châteaux, therefore the vines are more vigorous which calls for a lower density planting. Higher density works when the vines are very low in vigor."[6]

The Acid/Sugar Playoff

Sugar is at the core of wine production. Without sugar, there would be no alcohol. Fermentation converts sugar from the grape into alcohol in the wine. (Of course, any fruit or vegetable with enough sugar can be fermented to make wine. Unlikely as it may seem, even the cactus has enough sugar for fermentation to give an alcoholic product, which can then be distilled into tequila.) The amount of sugar in the grape is a key factor in determining how vinification occurs and what type of wine is produced.

When sugar levels are low, it may be necessary to help the grapes by adding some sugar before fermentation in order to get enough alcohol to balance the wine. At very high sugar levels, a wine may be brutally alcoholic, and there comes a point at which it is not possible to ferment all the sugar, so the wine is sweet rather than dry.

Grape ripeness is all about increasing sugar and decreasing acidity. In fact, the ratio between sugar and acidity is the most primitive measure of ripeness.[8] In the first few weeks of development, berries become loaded with acidity. Then there is a steady decline. Acidity is diluted as the berry expands, and some of the acids are converted to other compounds. Getting close to the harvest, acidity can drop rapidly. In warm climates, it may be necessary to harvest the grapes before the acidity falls so far that the wine becomes flabby. In cool climates, it may be necessary to wait longer to get rid of excess acidity.

The traditional measure of sugar level is the Brix—this is a number determined by using a refractometer to measure the optical density of the grape juice.[9] The result depends on the amount of dissolved solid matter, but 90% of this is sugar. The potential alcohol, the amount of alcohol that would be generated by converting all the sugar to alcohol, is given by multiplying the Brix by 0.55. Grapes are typically harvested between 21 and 26 Brix, corresponding to 11.5% to 14% alcohol.

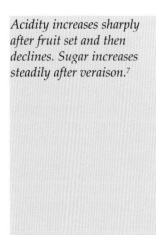

Acidity increases sharply after fruit set and then declines. Sugar increases steadily after veraison.[7]

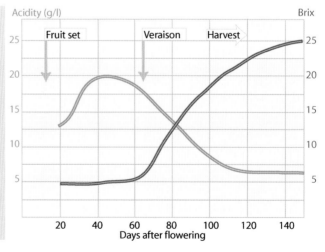

Sugar levels are assessed with a hand-held refractometer by putting a drop of juice onto the instrument and reading the result in the eyepiece (the inset shows a view through the eyepiece). More sophisticated refractometers with digital readouts are used in laboratories.

Sugars are synthesized steadily in the berry after veraison until a point about 130-140 days after flowering. Once Brix reaches 25-26, synthesis stops, but the sugar concentration continues to increase as the result of desiccation (as water evaporates through the skin of the grape).

There are two major types of acid in the berry: tartaric acid and malic acid. Their relative proportions have an important effect on taste.

Tartaric acid is synthesized by many plants, including the grapevine. In some geographical areas, the grapevine is the only natural source of tartaric acid, so its residue on ancient pottery leads to the inference that wine was present. It has no distinct taste, but is widely used as an acidifying agent in the food and drinks industry. The berry synthesizes tartaric acid from fruit set until after veraison, and then its level declines in the last few weeks of ripening.[10]

Malic acid is found in all living organisms. It is especially rich in green apples. Indeed, when you smell or taste green apples in a wine, it's due to high malic acid. Its level in grapes peaks around veraison, but then declines sharply. As berries ripen, the total acidity declines, but malic acid declines more sharply than tartaric acid. Loss of malic acid increases with temperature, which is why there is relatively less malic acid in grapes from warmer climates. There's also wide variation in malic acid levels with the grape variety; Chardonnay and Sauvignon Blanc are rich in malic acid, Riesling is intermediate, and Palomino (the grape from which Sherry is made) has almost none.

To make good wine, berries have to have enough sugar to give a decent level of alcohol, and must retain enough acidity to give freshness. There is a strong interplay between sweetness and acidity in the taste of wine: sweetness is much harder to detect as the acidity increases, or viewed the other way round, acidity is much harder to detect as sugar levels increase. At normal levels of acidity, say around 6 g/l (grams/liter), an average person can detect sugar at a level of about 4 g/l. But a wine with high acidity, say 8 g/l, may taste dry even with sugar levels of up to 9 g/l. (In fact, the various taste elements in wine all interact with one another; although alcohol itself tastes sweet, increased alcohol increases the perception of bitterness.[11])

The Taming of the Tannins

They knew some things in the past that have been forgotten today. In 1763, the Abbé Tainturier of Clos Vougeot explained the advantages of blending from their various terroirs: "We need [grapes that are] cooked, roasted, and green; even this last is necessary; it improves in the cuve by fermenting with the others; it is this that brings liveliness to the wine."[12] Has the need for flavor variety in creating complexity been forgotten today in the stampede to harvest grapes at riper and riper levels?

The moment of truth comes in deciding when to harvest. You have to get this right, because grapes ripen only on the vine. It used to be relatively simple: as soon as the berries reached a reasonable Brix, growers would pick at the first sign of impending bad weather so as not to take any risks. In cool climates, the need to see acidity levels drop would be balanced by concern that rain would dilute the harvest; in warm climates, the risk was more that acidity would decline rapidly, and sugar levels would increase too much. Growers were anxious not to let the level of potential alcohol get too high, because in the days before temperature control, fermentations would become hot, and run a risk of sticking. (Yeast is killed by excess heat, and it can be very difficult to get a stuck fermentation to start up again.) Typically this would lead to picking at a potential alcohol level around 11.5%.

But today sugar levels are only one criterion of ripeness. Berry maturity results from several pathways that may peak at different times. Maturity of grapes can be assessed in several ways depending on which criteria are applied. The size of the berry is important, especially for black grapes, where smaller berries give a higher ratio of skin to pulp. Polyphenols, which include the anthocyanins that give color and the tannins that give structure to a wine, are mostly found in the skin, so berry size influences both the color of the wine and the content of the tannins that are required for aging.

The current buzzword is "phenolic ripeness." As grapes mature, the tannin content increases, but the nature of the tannins also changes from harsher to better rounded. An early measure for phenolic ripeness was simply the appearance and taste of the grape: a ripe berry should come away cleanly when picked, and the color of the seeds should have changed from green to brown. This is not a new idea; around 65 C.E., Columella recommended the color of the pips as the best measure of ripeness.[13] More sophisticated measures now measure the level of tannins in the form of the IPT (Indice des Polyphénols Totaux). The scale for IPT is arbitrary,[14] but increased levels suggest that total phenols have increased from 5 g/l to 6 g/l since 1982, roughly a twenty per cent increase in twenty years.[15]

There's no good measure for the quality of tannins as opposed to quantity, but the concept that tannins mature from being "green" or "stalky" to becoming ripe goes back at least fifty years. Sometimes oenologists talk about "bad" tannins and "good" tannins.[16] At all events, "physiological ripeness" is associated with ripening to a later stage than formerly, and is influenced by color, stem maturity, tannin ripeness, berry shriveling, pulp texture, and seed ripeness. The basic change is that grapes are harvested at much higher sugar levels than previously in order to satisfy the demand for physiological ripeness. The most obvious effect is much higher alcohol in the wine, but prolonged ripening also has a big effect on the aroma and flavor spectrum of the wine, since volatile molecules as well as the phenols change significantly during the extra period on the vine.[17]

One reason why New World wines tend to be higher in alcohol than wines from Europe is that temperature and other climatic conditions lead to slower accumulation of sugar in Europe relative to phenols and other components. Because higher sugar levels are reached more rapidly in the New World, harvesting at the same sugar level as in Europe would mean the grapes had not reached phenolic ripeness.

Man versus Machine

Before phylloxera, when vines were planted on their own roots, they were densely packed. A new vine would be propagated simply by sticking a shoot from an existing vine into the ground close by. This "layering" resulted in a higgledy-piggledy arrangement of vines. Grafting on to rootstocks replaced this disorganization with a neat array of rows. The width of the row was typically set to allow a horse to pull a plough through without wandering to left or to right. Grapes would still be harvested manually by pickers who would work their way along the row, snipping off the ripe berries and placing them in baskets to be carried to the press.

The harvest at Moët et Chandon around 1900 at Le Mesnil-sur-Oger required pickers to collect the grapes by hand from tightly packed vines and place them in large baskets for transport to the press house.

Mechanization replaced the horse after the second world war when tractors were introduced, at first to pull along equipment for ploughing or spraying the vines, then with combined machines that could perform multiple functions. Special tractors were developed in France with a narrow gait that could move along rows with the traditional narrow spacing. Built high, they straddle the row. They were not available in the New World, where conventional farm equipment was used instead, requiring the rows to be more widely spaced. Now, of course, the same equipment is available worldwide, and vineyard work is generally accomplished by machines.

A move to using machines actually to harvest the grapes was driven largely by economics. Picking by hand is labor-intensive and requires a trained workforce to be available specifically for a few weeks per year. It's a relatively slow process, and can be difficult to arrange on short notice if the weather changes unexpectedly. A machine can be fired up at any time, picks the grapes more rapidly, and requires only one trained driver; the overall cost is about a fifth of picking manually. The ability to pick at night, when the grapes are cool, is a great advantage in hot climates. To use mechanical harvesting, the vines have to be organized on a trellis system that suits the harvester.

The big problem with mechanical harvesting is to distinguish between ripe and unripe fruit. The first machines simply beat the vine on the principle that ripe fruit would come off while unripe fruit would stay on. This was not terribly effective, and also resulted in the collection of a fair amount of material other than grapes (known as MOG in the trade). The machines improved when beating was replaced by a shaking mechanism; moving along the trellis, the harvester seizes the vine, moves it sharply in one direction, and then sharply back in the other direction. Mature grapes are released by this action, while immature or rotten grapes are not.

A mechanical harvester straddles the rows as it collects grapes.

Grapes are shaken loose as the machine passes over the vine; they are collected in a container within the machine.

The berries drop on to conveyer belts, and a sorting system removes leaves and other material before they fall into a container. Mechanical harvesters are becoming progressively more automated and sophisticated, for example, with controls to adjust the head for the difficulty of picking each particular variety. They are the norm for large scale producers and are widely used in both the New World and in Europe, accounting for almost all harvesting in Australia, for example, and about 75% of acreage in France.

The highest quality operations continue to use manual picking in the belief that a trained picker can still identify ripe fruit more selectively than a machine. And mechanical harvesters are limited by steep slopes (although they are getting better). Nor are they effective for late harvests when individual berries are selected in each bunch. But with such exceptions, they are now the norm worldwide in all but small-scale operations of the highest quality.

Going Green: Organic Viticulture

By the time you have fertilized with 50 kg/ha of nitrogen, 40 kg/ha of phosphorus, and 100 kg/ha of potassium, sprayed with herbicides to keep the weeds down, sprayed with pesticides to eliminate the insects, and treated with the latest steroids to prevent fungal infection, you may well have poisoned the soil in your vineyard. These are not healthy procedures; indeed they are supposed to stop several weeks before harvest so that the grapes are not contaminated. Remember that pesticides were actually developed from the nerve gases used in trench warfare in the first world war. Conventional viticulture is often encouraged by the authorities because it gives the most reliable results, with the highest yields. But it tends to homogenize the wine, eliminating differences between terroirs, reducing differences between vintages, and altogether turning out a bland product, in the same way that farmed fish never has the same flavor as wild. Of course, you don't have to go to extremes, and there is a growing trend towards "sustainable viticulture," in which use of fertilizers, herbicides, and pesticides is much reduced, although not eliminated. There's no knowing how widely it is practiced.

Organic viticulture goes the whole hog, and uses no chemical fertilizers, with only natural agents to control pests and diseases. Although adopted by many leading producers, it is still a miniscule part of world viticulture. Europe is the leader, but organic vineyards still account for only a measly 100,000 ha (about 2.5%); worldwide they are probably about 1.5%.[18, 19]

An organic vineyard uses natural means of fertilization and weed control. If fertilization is necessary (remember that grapevines give their best results in poor soils), manure is used. Cover crops are used to protect the soil. Instead of the pristine look of rows of vines separated by bare earth, now there is often a ragged cover crop around and between the vines. Sometimes it's a stripped down version of "Nature raw in tooth and claw," where the cover crops compete with the vines. Weeds are removed mechanically. Predatory insects or phero-

A conventional vineyard has bare earth between the vines (top), but an organic vineyard has cover crops (bottom).

mones are used to control pests. (Pheromones are the volatile compounds re-leased into the air that male and female insects use to find one another; saturating the air with pheromones protects the vineyard by causing "sexual confusion," when the insects don't know where to turn.) A vineyard is consid-ered organic only after three years of conforming to the protocol.

A century ago, vineyards could be worked only by horses. In fact, their layout was partially determined by the need to organize the rows so that horses could move through. Ploughing between the rows removed weeds, broke up the soil, and by removing the surface roots forced the vines to put down deeper roots. One of the problems with conventional viticulture is that the weight of the trac-tors compresses the surface soil, causing problems with drainage. Recently there has been a move towards bringing back horses.

Yields are lower in organic viticulture by about 20%, which contributes to higher quality. Costs are greater by about 20%. It's generally easier for small growers to go organic, because they are not giving up the economies of scale that a large grower gets from conventional viticulture. And they don't have the problem of needing to treat very large areas all at the same time when a problem such as mildew threatens. It's also easier when the vineyard has multiple grape varieties planted, each with different susceptibility to pests and diseases.[20] One problem is that it's hard to be organic if surrounding vineyards are not: pesti-cides or herbicides may waft across on to your vines. Some organic growers are forced to discard (or bottle separately) the production from the edges of their vineyards to ensure purity of the rest.

One of the biggest problems of organic viticulture is controlling mildew. Modern steroid inhibitors offer an effective control for both types of mildew (powdery and downy), for which there is no organic counterpart. Organic pro-ducers are restricted to using copper to treat downy mildew and sulfur to treat oïdium (powdery mildew), or stylet oils (which ironically are derived from petroleum distillate). In fact, concern about accumulation of high copper levels in

As part of the organic viticulture program at Château Pontet Canet, horses have been reintroduced to plough the rows between the vines. The equipment was designed especially and built by the château.

the soil is one of the major drawbacks of organic viticulture.[21] It's perhaps an open question whether it's the lesser evil compared to using steroid fungal inhibitors.

Lack of effective fungal treatments can be critical in humid climates, where mildew can spread rapidly. In Bordeaux, for example, high humidity caused outbreaks of mildew in 2007 that would probably have wiped out the vintage twenty years ago; but the new inhibitors rescued the crop, and the vintage is quite decent. There were some casualties among organic producers, however; at Château Pontet Canet, which had just gone organic, proprietor Alfred Tesseron decided he could not take the risk of losing the entire crop, and the mildew was controlled with modern inhibitors.[22] Pontet Canet is now starting back on the road to organic certification.

The details of what can be described as "organic" vary with the local certifying authority. One of the big issues is use of sulfur. To be labeled as organic wine, no sulfur preservatives can be added. This makes it difficult to safeguard the wine against contamination. Wine made by organic methods, but where sulfur preservatives are used, can be described as "made from organic grapes."

Organic growers tend to harvest sooner than conventional producers; they claim this is because chemical spraying delays ripening. It may also be because the grapevines are simply healthier.

Phases of the Moon

"Some call her sister of the moon
Some say illusions are her game"

These lyrics from Fleetwood Mac perfectly capture the controversy about biodynamics. Biodynamic viticulture sounds off the wall. Treatments are applied to the vineyards according to the phase of the moon. The current model for this is

Maria Thun's annual planting calendar (worked out in the 1970s), which relates ancient elements to organs of the plant (Earth to roots, Water to foliage, Air to flower, Fire to fruit and seeds), and assigns periods for actions according to the zodiac.[23] The biodynamic calendar has four types of days: fruit, flower, leaf, and root, which are defined in terms of four groups of star constellations. Each type of day defines a period when the moon is in one of the constellations. Suitable treatments for plants differ for flower days, fruit days, root days, etc.

Some of the more extreme measures are hard to understand. One of the best known (not to say mocked) procedures involves putting manure in a cow's horn and burying it in the center of the vineyard to make a preparation that is later spread over the vineyard. It is claimed that imitation horns do not have the same effects. Another use of the horn is when horn silica is prepared from finely ground silica buried over the summer in a cow's horn. The powdered preparation or solution is spread on the grapevines in the spring at 4 g/ha. Pests are treated by spreading the ashes of pests on the ground. This is definitely not going to do anything to discourage them. Solutions are made at very dilute levels and are supposed to transmit their effects through "activated water"; this nonsense has no scientific basis. Yet some of the top producers all over the world follow biodynamic practices, and there is absolutely no argument about the quality of their wines.[24] So what's going on?

Biodynamic methods were developed by Rudolph Steiner, a philosopher who created a theory of "spiritual science," which includes biodynamics. All artificial treatments, such as fertilizers or weed killers, are forbidden; compost is generated to replace fertilizers. Compost is based on waste from the vineyard (grape skins, seeds, cuttings from vines) and cow manure. But this is no ordinary compost, such as might be used in an organic vineyard. Steiner prescribed a set of six compost preparations made from plants (valerian, dandelion, oak, bark, nettles, yarrow, chamomile). They are known by numbers 502-507. Used to seed a conventional compost, they convert it into biodynamic compost. "The soil then becomes primed to receive energies streaming down from the cosmos and upward from within the earth itself," according to one modern writer.[25] This is simply beyond all reason.

The concept of the lunatic is a powerful testament to the long existence of beliefs in the effects of the moon. At what point does biodynamic treatment become superstition instead of good care of the land? "The good period for bottling is during the waning moon," says Guy Renvoisé in an otherwise completely serious book debunking nonsense about wine.[26] In fact, it is a common superstition, independent of biodynamics, that wine should not be bottled at the full moon (or, for that matter, during a thunderstorm). Can changes in atmospheric pressure really be significant enough to affect the condition of the wine?

A wide range of superstitions associated with the moon have found their way into wine lore. "Fermentation is quick when the moon is ascendant; if you ferment when the moon is descendant the process is much slower," says Serge Hochar of Lebanon's Château Musar.[27] It is quite widely believed that it is better to prune grapevines (and other plants) during a waning moon. The rationale is that less sap flows out of the cuts because the water table is diminishing.

To be certified as a biodynamic producer,[28] you don't have to follow the phases of moon, merely to apply all the preparations. The original concept for biodynamics envisaged each farm as self-contained, generating its own compost, but these days you can purchase certified preparations. (It's not always straightforward to obtain supplies: for example, cow manure, an essential ingredient for biodynamics, has to be obtained from a source where the cows are not treated with antibiotics.) Wine producers practicing biodynamics vary from those who are certified to those who are basically organic but use some of the biodynamic methods. Certified biodynamic viticulture is a vanishingly small proportion of total wine production.[29, 30]

Irrespective of skepticism about some of the biodynamic methods, the basic question is what effect they have on the soil. Claude Bourguignon is a scientist who has spent the last thirty years studying the soils in France. He is well known for his view that modern farming methods have destroyed the life of the soil. "In the last thirty years, around 90% of the soil life has disappeared... In France, I find soils that have less biological activity than the Sahara," he famously said.[31] He performed a highly quoted comparison showing that a biodynamic vineyard has more trace elements and microbial activity in deep soils than an organic vineyard.[32] Bourguignon believes that biodynamic treatments help support a population of mycorrhizal fungi in the soil that attach to the grapevine roots and transfer trace elements to the vine.

Other studies haven't shown any significant differences in the soil, but it's fair to say that the verdict is out on whether and what difference biodynamic treatments make.[34] It is certainly clear there's a substantial difference between the results of conventional and organic viticulture, but it's not so clear whether going biodynamic makes any further difference. So coming back to the central question: why do producers go to the extra effort and how do we explain the results? Could it be that increased quality is due more to the great care and attention given to the vines? They are not abused with fertilizers or herbicides, the vines are carefully tended, the canopies are adjusted for the conditions of the particular year, yields are kept low—it might be that absolutely identical treatment without the biodynamic additions would give virtually the same effects.

Maria Thun's calendar. The columns show date, constellation of the moon, solar and lunar events, which moon elements dominate the day, and which parts of plants are favored for treatment. A dashed line shows that all treatments should be avoided.[33]

June 2008

Date	Const. of Moon	Solar & lunar aspects	Trines	Moon Element	Parts of the plant enhanced by Moon or planets	Weather, etc.
1 Sun	♈	☉-♉		Warmth	Fruit	Tr
2 Mon	♉ 12^h			Warmth/Earth	Fruit to 11^h, Root 12^h – 19^h -----	
3 Tue	♉	☺19^h Pg 13^h		Earth	--------------------- Root from 23^h	
4 Wed	♊ 20^h	☊ 12^h		Earth/Light	Root to 19^h, Flower from 20^h	
5 Thu	♊			Light	Flower NPT from 0^h	St
6 Fri	♋ 17^h			Light/Water	Flower to 16^h, Leaf from 17^h	Vo St
7 Sat	♋			Water	Leaf to 11^h -----------	
8 Sun	♌ 5^h	☋9^h ♀☊♂●		Water/Warmth	----------------------	♄
9 Mon	♌			Warmth	------- Fruit from 7^h	
10 Tue	♍ 21^h	☽15^h		Warmth/Earth	Fruit to 20^h, Root from 21^h to 24^h	Tr
11 Wed	♍			Earth	--------------------- Root from 23^h	Tr ♄ St
12 Thu	♍			Earth	Root	St
13 Fri	♍		△	Earth	Root	♄
14 Sat	♎ 15^h		△	Earth/Light	Root to 23^h	

Northern Planting Tim

While it's entirely believable that biodynamic treatment of the soil improves grapes and therefore wine, it's much harder to believe that the calendar predicts when bottled wine will taste best. Biodynamic proponents claim that wine tastes best on flower and fruit days.[35] Are consumers likely to respect the biodynamic calendar when deciding whether they want to drink a glass of wine? Yet some major supermarkets in the U.K., not known for a romantic approach to their merchandise, only hold tastings for wine critics on days when the calendar predicts wines will taste best.[36] Jo Ahearne MW of Marks and Spencer tells me that some wines are affected more than others. "The more tannic, the more obvious; if they are very aromatic it's less obvious," she says,[37] and "we now only hold tastings on fruit, flower or (at worst) leaf days." What could be the basis for such an effect? Where is the line that divides unexplained, but plausible, effects from astrology?

Let me state my position explicitly. I am neither a believer nor a skeptic about biodynamic methods. Some of them are puzzling, but one is forced to recognize that there are some great wines made by winemakers who believe that biodynamic practices are an intrinsic part of the quality. However, I do demand that at the end of the day we can find a rational explanation for the effect, or at least that we can see how one may be possible even if we don't have a full explanation right now. So I am prepared to believe that organic methods make stronger grapevines that give better grapes and make better wines. I have a holding position on the various biodynamic treatments while we wait to find out whether they really affect factors such as microbial life in the soil.[38] I find it very difficult to believe that scattering the ashes of pests in the vineyards prevents those pests from returning. And it is completely impossible to believe that passing magnetic forces through water creates a "memory" affecting the way that water is used by the plants: this flies in the face of everything we know about the chemistry and physics of water. I reserve judgment as to whether pruning is better done at certain phases of the moon because it relates to the rate of sap flow while I wait for someone to actually measure that rate of flow; but I refuse to believe that the position of the moon in relation to other astrological bodies has any effect at all on anything other than superstitious behavior. And when I hear that "an important aspect of biodynamics is that we are not dealing with factors, we are dealing with forces, we are harmonizing the forces... [which] are impregnated through water, water has memory,"[39] I begin to wonder whether we are dealing with a rational position or trying to read the entrails as they might have done in ancient Rome.

Modern Trends

So vineyards of today run a gamut of styles, from fully fledged biodynamics where cow's horns filled with manure are planted by the light of the full moon, to industrial agriculture where everything is mechanized, and weed killing, pesticides, fertilizers, and irrigation are used to even out the crop as much as possible from year to year. Good wine is made at all levels: if biodynamic viticulture hits the heights of representing vintage variation in the individual vineyard, mechanized viticulture produces wine of a quality and consistency that was not previously available at this level on this scale.

Is the split widening between the small producer, who is turning more and more to organic viticulture, and the large producer, who takes more and more advantage of the modern techniques available in viticulture and vinification? To what extent (and at what levels of the market) is wine still a natural product?

It's true that we understand more today than ever before about the biology of the grapevine, how to make it productive or to limit its productivity, how to handle the problems of pests and diseases, but it's fair to say that we still do not understand in detail how the effects of different soils and environments (the *terroir*) are represented in the wine. And are the hard-won advances of recent years now threatened by a change in climate that may unsettle the balance between grape varieties and the regions in which they are grown?

3

The Mystique of Terroir

NOTHING IN THE WORLD OF WINE is more controversial than terroir. Opinions vary from belief that great wine comes only from great terroirs to denial that terroir has anything to do with quality. At its simplest, terroir can seem banal: it is not rocket science to suppose that a vine (or for that matter any other plant) grown in sunny, well-drained conditions at the top of a hill will produce different fruit from a vine grown in shady, water-logged conditions at the bottom of the hill. But terroir can be profound if you accept that wines made from even adjacent plots of land show consistent differences in their aroma and flavor profiles; while it is fanciful to suppose you can directly taste the properties of the terroir (Ugh, you might say, do I really want to smell and taste dirt anyway?), there has been a continuing debate as to exactly how its features might influence the fruit and the wine made from it.

Terroir is not in principle a difficult concept, but it occasions a great deal of argument in practice. *Terroir* implies that each vineyard has a unique combination of soil, aspect, and climatic features determining what type and quality of wine it is capable of producing. The basic concept is pretty simple: other conditions being equal, one plot of land will always produce different wine from another, even if it has the same grape varieties cultivated under the same conditions, because its terroir is different. In its purest sense, terroir refers strictly to natural features of the land.

The idea that differences in wine come directly from the land became honed into the concept of terroir in France. When the British philosopher John Locke visited the wine regions of Bordeaux in 1677, he described the basis for the difference between the top vineyards and the adjacent lesser vineyards: "The vine de Pontac [later to become known as Château Haut Brion, the famous first growth], so much esteemed in England, grows on a rising open to the west, in a white sand mixed with a little gravel, which one would think would bear nothing; but there is a such a particularity in the soil, that at Mr. Pontac's, near Bourdeaux the merchants assured me that the wine growing in the very next vineyards, where there was only a ditch between, and the soil, to appearance, perfectly the same, was by no means so good."[1]

Terroir is the pivot of winemaking in France, where the place of origin is found on the label of a quality wine, but the grape variety is not mentioned. Origin is all. The first traces of the modern concept of terroir appear in French literature of the eighteenth century, but the idea developed fully only during the nineteenth and twentieth centuries. In 1777, a French dictionary defined terroir. "On dit, que le vin sent du terroir, qu'il a un gout de terroir…" (it is said that wine smells of its terroir, that it has a taste of terroir… that is, it is has a certain aroma, a certain taste that comes from the quality of the terroir)." The entry distinguished between terroirs appropriate for different types of crops, helpfully adding, "Le terroir de Bourgogne (Burgundy) est bon pour les vins."[2] Actually, the concept that wines might acquire a "gout de terroir" may have preceded the development of the concept that the terroir influences quality of wine.[3] During the early nineteenth century, terroir was generally used in a disparaging sense, implying that the wine was rustic.

Terroir may first have made its way into the wine literature as a factor affecting quality when Dr. Denis Morélot wrote a book on the wines of Burgundy in 1831. Considering the basis for the differences between wines, he said, "I am far from denying this truth: that each of these wines has a particular quality, a taste absolutely different from the others… It is the soil that imprints its native properties on the wines and which creates the differences between them. I am completely convinced that the aspect, the dryness of the soil, the age of the vines, and their variety, powerfully influence the quality of the wine."[4] He went on to discuss in some detail the soils of each commune and their effects upon the wines produced there.

Some geologists are skeptical of the role of soil in the taste of wine. Geologist Jake Hancock commented, "Terroir is a concept which originated in France. It is difficult to think of another country where it could have started, since it has features so characteristic of second-class French thinkers: a combination of the obvious (the quality of a plant depends on where you grow it) and the mystical."[5] Other have been more accepting: James Wilson wrote an award-winning book called simply "Terroir," which attempted in great detail to correlate geology with properties of wine, largely in France.[6]

In the New World, terroir may be denied or disdained as no more than a marketing ploy. One sarcastic modern view sees terroir as a SCAM (Soil + Climate + Aspect = Mystique).[7] Refuting this position, wine critic Matt Kramer says, "A surprising number of winegrowers and wine drinkers— at least in the United States—flatly deny the existence of terroir, like weekend sailors who reject as preposterous that Polynesians could have crossed the Pacific navigating only by sun, stars, wind, smell and taste. Terroir is held to be little more than viticultural voodoo."[8] Kramer regards terroir as a "sense of somewhereness," which is not a bad definition.

One reason why terroir is emphasized far more in Europe is that the typical vineyard size is much smaller than in the New World.[9] Soil properties can change strongly over short distances, so variation in terroir is a feature of relatively small vineyards. But irrespective of whether vineyard size allows terroir to manifest itself in any particular wine, what's the reality here: is terroir a myth or does location of the grapevines determine the intrinsic characteristics of a wine?

And remember that the act of planting a vineyard must impact the terroir: at a minimum, the local ecology will be different when the land is planted with vines instead of whatever was there previously. Often enough, more extensive changes are made: land may be graded, terraces constructed for vineyards on slopes, drainage systems introduced, soil may be brought in—in short, the terroir is created by changes in the vineyard directly affecting the vines or by changes in the surrounding area indirectly affecting the vineyard. When these changes are old and hallowed by time, they are regarded as part of the natural terroir, to be protected from further change. When they are new, they may instead arouse protests about damage to the environment. So what's the balance of terroir: how does it arise and what effect does it have on the vines and wine?

Does the Answer Lie in the Soil?

If terroir exists, if the location where a vine is grown affects the characteristics of its grapes and then of its wine, the answer must lie in the soil.[10] Differences in the physical or chemical properties of the soil between one vineyard and the next must be transmitted to the grapes. This is evidently true at a gross level: differences in the structure of the soil determine how easily and how far down the vine's roots can penetrate, and differences in drainage determine how much water the roots receive. Together with the aspect of the land, which affects exposure to sunshine, it's easy to see how these factors may have an effect on quantity and quality of the berries.[11] Along the same lines, the general nutritive properties of soil, in particular its level of nitrogen and potassium, have a significant effect on growth; indeed, as a general rule, vines produce better wine in poor soil, and it is for this reason that rich soils are not associated with production of fine wine. It's harder to see how the properties of the soil might change the spectrum of aromas and flavors, making one wine "mineral" or another wine "earthy."

The idea that the quality of a wine depends on where it comes from is almost as old as wine production itself. In every civilization going back to the Romans, some wines have been more prized than others. Two millennia ago, the effects of the soil were considered by the Roman Vitruvius, who in a treatise on architecture commented, "These waters are given their different flavors by the properties of the soil, as is also seen in the case of fruits... We find wines of countless varieties and qualities produced in many... places. This could not be the case, were it not that the juice of the soil, introduced with its proper flavors into the roots, feeds the stem, and, mounting along it to the top, imparts a flavor to the fruit which is peculiar to its situation and kind."[12] Here is the very heart of the concept of terroir: the soil directly transmits characteristics to the grapes.

In a famous study of the Bordeaux vineyards, Gerard Seguin of the University of Bordeaux found no connection between wine quality and the chemical composition of soil. "It is impossible," he said, "to establish any correlation between quality of wine and the soil content of any nutritive element."[13] He went on to comment, perhaps a trifle sarcastically, that "if there were such a correlation it would be easy, with the appropriate chemical additives, to produce great wine anywhere." Indeed, Bordeaux alone demonstrates that great wines can be made on a wide variety of soils, acid and gravelly at Château Lafite, iron-rich clay with a limestone base at Châteaux Pétrus and Cheval Blanc, alkaline limestone at Château Ausone. But Seguin found a common feature to the terroirs of the great châteaux: bilan hydrique (hydric balance). The best have well drained soils with water tables just within reach of the vine roots; the consequence is that when the water table drops around veraison (the point at which the berries change color and begin to develop), the supply to the vines is restricted. This is precisely the condition needed to push the vine into giving priority to ripening its berries at the expense of vegetative growth.

Certainly the physical properties of soil may influence choice of grape varieties. The classic example is Bordeaux, where the gravel-based soils of the left bank favor Cabernet Sauvignon, whereas the clay-based soils of the right bank favor Merlot. The reason is that gravel is warmer than clay (stones retain heat from solar radiation, whereas more evaporation, with consequent heat loss, occurs from clay). The difference in temperature is sufficient to allow Cabernet Sauvignon to ripen on the left bank but not on the right bank, but Merlot (which ripens sooner) is successful on both sides of the river.

Rock is pretty solid stuff: vine roots cannot penetrate it directly, and it is important for its physical properties (such as drainage or heat retention) rather than for its chemical constitution. Rock of any sort at the surface has an important effect in reflecting heat back up to the vines. One famous example is the galets—a layer of pebbles at the surface in Châteauneuf-du-Pape—that absorb heat during the day and release it at night. A direct demonstration of the effect of stones comes from Tignanello, the famous super-Tuscan property in the Chianti

The white stones were brought to the surface when the vineyard at Tignanello was replanted.

region. The underlying soil had a high concentration of white stones, and when the vineyard was replanted, these were brought up to the surface. The resulting heat gain brought the harvest forward by one week.[14] And although no one has quantitated the effect, the heat-reflecting properties of slate—whether red, gray, or blue—has an important role in Germany in making it possible for grapes to ripen in marginal conditions.

Limestone is often regarded as favorable for vineyards—especially for white grapes—mostly because of its good drainage. It is also notable for its alkalinity, which is somewhat less advantageous.[15] The acidity of the soil has an important effect on growth of grapevines (and for that matter other plants), especially because it affects uptake of mineral nutrients. Vines prefer slightly acid or neutral soil (pH between 6 and 7); they will not grow in highly acid soils, and in alkaline soils their uptake of iron and other elements is reduced; at its extreme, lack of iron can cause the disease of chlorosis (when the leaves yellow and fall off). Remember also that the effects of the soil are filtered through the rootstock; one of the major issues when grafting was introduced to combat phylloxera was finding American rootstocks able to withstand the more calcareous soils in Europe.

It's a mantra that more alkaline soils give fruit with higher acidity. It's part of the rationale for planting white grapes on limestone, but the reason is not obvious. When I asked an oenologist in Bordeaux to support his assertion that alkaline soils give more acid grapes, he was dismissive: "I don't have any specific work in mind but I am sure you can find that in a good plant physiology book." Surprisingly there appear in fact to be no scientific studies to explain this. Is it another of those myths associated with supposing that terroir has direct effects

Kimmeridgian soil takes its name from Kimmeridge on the south coast of England.

on the grapes.[16] Certainly it's plausible that high calcium concentrations in the soil stress the plant, but we still need evidence that this creates higher acidity in the grapes.[17] With even less support, another stated reason for preferring white to black varieties on limestone is that soils derived from limestone contain less iron (which is true) and that black grapes require more iron[18] (which is a myth).[19]

Various grape varieties are associated with specific soil types, on which they are said to produce their best results. Riesling goes with slate, Chardonnay goes with limestone, and Syrah goes with granite. Does terroir plus cépage add up to that unique combination the French call typicité? To ascribe such specific influence to the terroir may be overstating the strength of the connection. Riesling, for example, is grown in cool climates under conditions that are marginal for ripening; so its best results are produced on the warmest soils, that is, those covered in reflective slate. Other varieties would no doubt also give their best results on the slate, but because Riesling is the top variety in the region, the best soils are reserved for it. So in Austria's Wachau, slate-covered vineyards are planted with Riesling, while the lesser loess-based soils are planted with the less well-regarded Grüner Veltliner; does this mean that Riesling and slate have a unique affinity, or is it simply that the less remunerative variety is not planted on the top soils?

The association of limestone with Chardonnay is often quoted as an example of a terroir-specific effect. In Burgundy's Côte d'Or, Chardonnay tends to be planted on limestone-rich patches, Pinot Noir elsewhere. The best example of specificity comes from a little farther north, in Chablis, where not only is the terroir based on limestone, but a distinction has traditionally been drawn between two types of limestone.

The famous Kimmeridgian soil is a soft mixture of clay and limestone, generally gray in color. It was laid down in the Jurassic period, when the sea retreated, leaving a bed of fossils that give the soil its calcareous nature. It is named for the village of Kimmeridge on the south coast of England, where the fossil beds are exceptionally rich. Kimmeridgian soil occupies about half of the Chablis region;

Chablis is divided into Kimmeridgian soil (outlined in white) and Portlandian soil (all other areas except for the alluvial land shown in green, mostly around the river). The grand crus and premier crus (indicated by names in red) are on Kimmeridgian soil.[20]

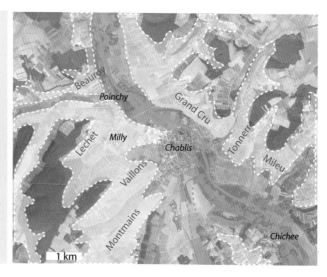

the rest consists of Portlandian limestone, harder in structure and browner in color (and taking its name from the village of Portland on the English south coast).

Chablis is divided into four quality levels: Petit Chablis, Chablis, Premier Cru, and Grand Cru. The original definition, in 1938 when the total vineyard area of 400 ha was less than 10% of today's 5,000 ha, confined all levels above Petit Chablis to terroirs of Kimmeridgian soil. This remained true as the area expanded: the AOC was described as comprising vineyards in a number of communes around Chablis but "with the exclusion of parcels not situated on Kimmeridgian soil."[21] It was felt that wines produced on the Portlandian limestone never achieved the same quality. But in 1978, when a further expansion occurred, the restriction was dropped.[22]

Was this the abandonment of a futile distinction or a cynical attempt to find a basis for increasing the area of production? Certainly there was a (justified) view that the expansion was associated with areas below the original quality. But was that quality due to the Kimmeridgian soil? The fact is that the Kimmeridgian soil is located on the south and east-facing slopes, where the good exposure helps to compensate for the cool climate, whereas the harder Portlandian soil occupies the plateaus at higher elevations (where the grapes are slower to ripen). So the original distinction was not ill-founded, but it had more to do with aspect and slope than with the underlying geology.[23]

Overt emphasis on terroir is less common in the New World than in Europe, but one of the most famous counter examples is the Terra Rossa soil of

The Terra Rossa soil of Coonawarra is evident in the exposed red bank of earth at the center. Underneath is the limestone ridge.

Coonawarra. This stretch of red loam with a limestone subsoil occupies about half the area of Coonawarra. Coupled with the coolest climate in South Australia, it supports the production of unusually elegant Cabernet Sauvignon (some Shiraz is also grown). The geological features are widely taken to be responsible for the unique quality of the wine, but have been generally misunderstood. It's usually been thought that the Terra Rossa soil, given its bright red color by a high concentration of ferric (iron) oxide, is the crucial feature, but in fact the key is the subsoil.[24] This is an unusually permeable limestone, which gives good drainage of excess water, but retains enough moisture to nourish the vines even in dry periods. Together with a water table that has seeped across from the mountains to the east, this provides a perfect water supply. The water table naturally would be around 1 m, but drains constructed in the region have lowered it to around 6 m, an example of (inadvertent) successful terroir modification.

There's often more than a nugget of truth in the conclusions resulting from generations of experience in matching grape varieties to terroirs, but the explanation may be somewhat different from conventional wisdom. It may owe more to indirect physical effects (such as heat retention or drainage) than to any direct interaction with the soil.

Licking the Slate

The concentration of blue slate covering the famous Bernkasteler Doctor vineyard in the Mosel gives its wines an intense mineral character, it is often said. In fact, from time to time you see people licking the slate to see whether they can detect the mineral taste of the wine. It's all very well to say that Chablis is flinty or that Riesling has a taste of gunflint, but just how would rocks of flint or shale leach flavors into the wine? Imagination plays its role: geologist Alex Maltman points out that the wines of Priorat are often described as tasting or smelling of

The Bernkasteler Doctor vineyard is covered with fragments of blue slate.

graphite (the unusual schist of Priorat is rich in graphite)—but graphite has no taste or smell![25]

Plants synthesize most of their components (almost 90%!) from air and water: the amazing act of photosynthesis enables them to obtain all the carbon, oxygen, and hydrogen they need from carbon dioxide and water. But inorganic components must be obtained from the soil, including macro-elements such as nitrogen, phosphorus, potassium, calcium, magnesium, sulfur, and a series of micro-elements required in lesser amounts.[26] Nutrient uptake is assisted by symbiotic microbes (mycorrhizal fungi) that live on the roots. Soils differ in their concentrations of these elements; deficiencies are manifested in poor growth. But it's a far cry from acknowledging that the soil's provision of nutritional elements influences growth, indeed is essential for it, to supposing that these elements change flavors.

Perhaps the biggest myth about terroir is that wines have a *gout de terroir*, that you can taste the components of the soil in the wine. This is not to say that the soil lacks influence on the chemical composition of wine. Efforts to distinguish the origins of wines by their contents of trace elements show there are differences. One study of 50 trace elements showed consistent differences between three areas of Margaret River in Western Australia.[27] But the levels of the elements are well below taste thresholds. Indeed, it is unlikely that any of the nutrients taken up from the soil reach levels you could taste in the grapes.[28] In fact, if they exceeded the threshold for taste, they would usually be regarded as problems requiring adjustment. The levels allowed by law for mineral salts (such as copper or iron) in wine are well below the threshold at which you could taste them.[29]

Nutrient concentrations may influence vine growth indirectly by their effects on symbiotic fungi that live on the roots, but there's no reason to suppose that any effects on flavor would directly reflect the properties of the mineral. Only some of the inorganic nutrients absorbed by roots find their way into the berries. And wine only partially reflects the constitution of the grapes; after all, wine does not taste like grape juice with some alcohol added, but has a different spectrum of aromas and flavors. Not only are the levels of the elements always well below taste thresholds, but they change significantly between the juice and the wine (many are removed by yeast during fermentation).[30] (And some fining procedures used during vinification, especially the use of bentonite clay, can make significant changes in the mineral composition.)

Flavors in wine are mostly due to complex organic molecules constructed in the grape or during fermentation; they are not ingested from the soil. Certainly wines can be found to have characteristic mineral or earthy flavors, but it is an act of imagination to suppose these come directly from the soil. It's fair to say that the jury is out on whether mineral contents of soil are reflected in any systematic way in berries or in the smell and taste of wine.

Grapevines can have deep roots, and it is generally agreed that the quality of berries increases as the roots go deeper. However, this is not due to differences in uptake of materials from the soil. It's due more to the fact that the vine gets a more even supply of water by using deep rather than superficial roots. It's commonly said that grapevines absorb minerals through more superficial roots, but take up only water from deep roots. Actually, mineral uptake may depend more on topsoil, but not for quite the reason stated. It's not so much that there is a difference in the behavior of deep roots versus shallower roots, but most absorption is done by the mass of the finest roots lying in the top half meter or so,[31] simply because this is where the greatest area of contact with soil occurs. But ascribing minerality to direct uptake from the subsoil is undoubtedly misguided.

Minerality is one of the most difficult qualities to define in wine. Described as flinty, sometimes as smoky, it represents a sort of precise, angular edge, usually associated with good acidity, often with crisp citrus flavors. Certainly it is associated with wines from certain areas, but does that necessarily mean it is a direct reflection of terroir as opposed to representing local winemaking practices or other extraneous influences? The only compound so far identified with minerality is benzene-methanethiol, which gives a smoky quality and has been found in Chardonnay, Sauvignon Blanc, and Sémillon.[32] Since this is a thiol (a sulfur-containing compound that is affected by exposure to oxygen), its involvement implies that smokiness will be enhanced by reductive winemaking (excluding oxygen) and minimized when wine making is more oxidative. Otherwise there's no scientific information on what might be responsible for minerality.

Some varietal characteristics owe as much to viticulture and vinification as to the intrinsic nature of the variety. Sauvignon Blanc has a unique combination of herbaceousness, citrus fruits, and tropical fruits, which display somewhat differently in the classic region of the Loire and the new region of Marlborough, New Zealand. Herbaceousness is due to a methoxypyrazine that forms early during the development of the grapes but declines sharply as they ripen. Tropical fruits result from volatile thiol compounds released during fermentation by the yeasts; their concentration is greatly influenced by choice of yeast and conditions of vinification. The difference between Sauvignon Blanc produced in the Loire and the same variety produced in Marlborough owes little to the difference in soils; it depends more on different regimes for obtaining ripeness, and differences in the styles of vinification which control the concentrations of these thiol compounds.

There is, incidentally, a fine distinction to be drawn between terroir and environmental effects. A classic example was the historical association of extremely earthy aromas and flavors with some red Burgundies. This was not in fact due to terroir, in fact it had nothing to do with the grapevines, but was the result of contamination with the yeast Brettanomyces. Opinion has evolved from regarding it as a corollary of quality to a possible flaw in the wine.[33] What other features of "terroir" might in the future turn out to be due to extraneous factors?

More recently, some Californian and Australian wines have shown a noticeable touch of eucalyptus. While this might be regarded as a feature of terroir, it is in fact due to oil blowing from eucalyptus leaves; sticking to the waxy skins of the berries, some finds its way into the wine.[34] Some might regard this as a feature of terroir, but personally I would regard it as adventitious since you could, after all, cut down the eucalyptus trees. More obviously, in south and west Australia a series of intense forest fires (starting in 2003) created the new phenomenon of "smoke taint" in some wines. Smoky aromas and flavors—which were perceived by tasters as flaws in the wine—were due to specific compounds absorbed by the grapes from the smoke, and the extent of the taint was determined by the timing and duration of exposure of the grapevines to the smoke.[35]

From Pompei to Clos Vougeot

In the century or so before the eruption of Mount Vesuvius in 79 C.E., one of the most renowned wines was Falernian, grown on the slopes of Mount Falernus near Naples. Falernian was a sweet white wine, made from partially dried grapes. Its quality was distinguished according to whether it came from the upper, middle or lower slopes. The middle slope was considered the best, and the wine was reputed to age for 10-20 or more years. The vintage of 121 B.C. was exceptionally fine, and became known as the Opimian wine after the name of the then Emperor. Falernian was in second place when Pliny compiled a list of 80 or so of the best regions for wine production around 70 C.E.[36] Pliny noted that new varieties of vines were becoming available, and commented on their suitability for particular climates, one of the first attempts to match cépages and terroir.[37]

Two millennia later, there was a measure of the value of position on the slope. "The wine, at the summit of the Clos Vougeot, one of the most celebrated vineyards of Burgundy, sells for 600 francs, that of the middle brings 900, and that of the base only 300," according to an Australian observer, James Busby, in 1825.[38] Anticipating concepts of terroir, Busby remarked on the importance of aspect and physical constitution of the ground: "The conclusion may even be drawn, that the intrinsic nature of the soil is of less importance, that it should be porous, free, and light... The soils of the best vineyards are those which contain little nutritious matter."[39]

Why does the middle of the slope give the best wine? The usual explanation is that drainage is most consistent in the middle of the slope. In a dry vintage, the bottom of the slope may do better than the top, in a wet vintage the relationship will be reversed, but from year to year the most consistent supply of water is in the middle.

Often enough, soil composition changes along the slope. A famous example is the rising slope containing the grand crus for white Burgundy, Bâtard Montrachet, Le Monrachet, and Chevalier Montrachet. Going up the slope, the soil changes from 20% clay and 80% pebbles at the bottom to 50% clay and 50% pebbles at the top.[40] Ahah! it is easy to say—the ideal soil composition for great white wine must be that of Le Montrachet (32-36% clay, 64-68% pebbles).

But some suspicion might be occasioned by the fact that mid-slope also gives the best results in many other locations where the underlying soil is different. So it may not be only a matter of drainage or soil composition, but rather due to exposure to the sun. On south-facing slopes (north-facing in the southern hemisphere), the middle of the slope gets the most sunshine. The effect depends on the angle of the sun, so is especially pronounced when the sun is low in the sky, that is, early in the morning and later in the evening.[41] This makes the slope particularly important for avoiding spring frosts and for ripening in the autumn.

Marketing the Terroir

Adam Smith, with his usual keen eye on the market, was the first to acknowledge the economic implications of terroir "The vine is more affected by the difference of soils than any other fruit tree. From some it derives a flavour which no culture or management can equal, it is supposed, upon any other. This flavour, real or imaginary, is sometimes peculiar to the produce of a few vineyards; sometimes it extends through the greater part of a small district, and sometimes through a considerable part of a large province."[42] With his customary skepticism, he went on to question cause and effect: "The whole quantity of such wines that is brought to market falls short of the effectual demand... [and]... therefore can be disposed of to those who are willing to pay more, which necessarily raises the price above that of common wine. The difference is greater or less, according as the fashionableness and scarcity of the wine render the competition of the buyers more or less eager... For though such vineyards are in general more carefully cultivated than most others, the high price of the wine seems to be, not so much the effect, as the cause of this careful cultivation."

The concept of terroir as a distinguishing feature in selling wines is relatively recent. When the appellation contrôlée system was originally conceived in France, it was by no means immediately obvious that it would be based on terroir. In fact, one of its principal protagonists, the politician Joseph Capus, no doubt influenced by the system of wine production in his native Bordeaux, argued in the Revue du Vin de France in 1935 that AOCs should be based on domains rather than terroirs.[43] (Bordeaux is the exception to the dominance of terroir as the defining characteristic of quality in wine; classification here is by the producer.[44]) By 1947, when Capus was President of INAO,* however, he was strongly defending the system of definition by terroir that had by then become entrenched.[45]

Burgundy was the battleground for establishing the importance of terroir. The 1920s and 1930s were a terrible time for Burgundy (as indeed for all of France), with demand for wine suppressed by economic conditions and production impacted by a series of poor vintages through the thirties. Battle was joined in Burgundy between the vins de marque (wines produced by negociants) and the vins de crus (producers' wines identified with particular locations). The producers argued that negociants subjected the wines to undue manipulation.[46] The argument as to whether the producer's label or the origin of the wine was a better guarantee of quality continued until a series of legal cases (collectively known as the Côte-de-Nuits trial) settled the issue in favor of labeling by terroir.[47] In 1935 the AOC system came into effect. The battle was won, but the war for authenticity continued for another fifty years.

The first topographic maps had divided Burgundy into small areas, each with its own name and reputation, falling into a hierarchy of qualities.[48] Following the nineteenth century delineation of vineyards, the AOC system divided Burgundy

---

* Institut National des Appellations d'Origine, the organization controlling the AOCs.

into village land, premier crus, and grand crus. The assignments have scarcely changed since then, and the hierarchy of pricing for each producer's wines faithfully follows the quality levels assigned to each terroir.

Before the AOC system was established, locations (lieu-dits) with different quality levels were defined by the history of the wines they produced: in Gevrey Chambertin, for example, the Chambertin vineyard was well known for producing better wines than the nearby Cazetiers vineyard. However, the boundaries do not reflect any exact definition of the underlying properties of the soil; they were based on the cadastral map, reflecting historical patterns of ownership. There was little thought to making the underlying geology the basis for the delineation of boundaries. A cynical view holds that when INAO began to classify vineyards, a rationalization was required because it was too much of a hot potato to classify the wines themselves.[49] The criteria for distinguishing AOCs are not necessarily well specified (perhaps a certain degree of ambiguity is essential), but some homogeneity of terroir is the unifying concept. This has since been adopted, albeit more in principle than in practice, by other classifications, such as the AVA system of the United States.[50]

Of course, focusing on origin provides a protection against imitation. You can make Cabernet Sauvignon anywhere in the world; but you can produce "Bordeaux" only in Bordeaux. Burgundy, where the concept is the most refined, perhaps has less need of it, because Pinot Noir is less malleable than Cabernet Sauvignon, and it remains difficult for other regions to match what remains (at least at the top end) uniquely elegant and refined. Yet Beaune producer Louis Latour comments, "When you try to analyze in detail the diverse elements of terroir, you find yourself with such uncertainties that it's better not to stick your nose in too far. That said, terroir is an excellent marketing tool, that's why everyone uses it."[51]

Is Terroir Immutable?

Terroir modification is very likely as old as vineyards themselves. Famous vineyards now considered to display the advantages of the terroir where they were planted may in reality owe as much to human reconstruction as to natural features. Among the more ancient of today's top vineyards are Côte Rôtie and Hermitage in the Northern Rhône, where immense efforts reworked the steep hillsides to make them accessible well before 1389, from which the first known descriptions date.[52] The Upper Douro, where Port is produced, is a series of man made terraces, carved out of the schist, after 1700.

Vines grow where not very much else will grow. This is one of the reasons why it so difficult to persuade vignerons to uproot plantings in unsuccessful European vineyards— wine production may be uneconomic, but there is no easy alternative. Sometimes vineyards have strange origins: the small (500 ha) Gimblett Gravels Winegrowing District in New Zealand's Hawke's Bay occupies land so unproductive that it became derelict, and a major part of it was intended for a gravel quarry before it became planted with vines.[53] Here the producers are unabashed about the need for human intervention: they say that "terroir manipulation" is part of the vigneron's art; the soil has no water-holding capacity, so without irrigation the vines would die.[54] They believe soil and climate are perfect, and that irrigation turns this into great terroir. Is that so different from building terraces to manage a slope where instead Nature is providing the rain?

Incidental changes in the local environment sometimes affect terroir. Forster Kirchenstück is the best vineyard in the Pfalz region of Germany. One reason why it stands out from the neighboring vineyards is that a grower constructed a sandstone wall around the 3.2 ha vineyard. Intended simply to emphasize his ownership, even though the wall is not terribly high (varying between 1 and 2 meters) it has two significant effects on the microclimate; it helps to keep wind circulating round the vineyard, so that it dries out well after rain; and some heat is reflected from the wall. Walls can also have the opposite effect; Helenkloster is a tiny vineyard at Mulheim in the Mosel, and a wall on the western edge retains frost, making it possible in most years to produce Eiswein, which requires keeping the grapes on the vine in frozen conditions into the winter.[56]

And in the Pechstein vineyard nearby, the "black basalt stones add a racy minerality to the sandy loam soil," according to famous producer Ernie Loosen, who took over the J. L. Wolf properties in the Pfalz in 1996.[57] In fact, Pechstein means "pitch stone," and the quality of the vineyard is attributed to its black basalt. This no doubt affects drainage and heat retention, but actually it's somewhat unlikely it does anything for minerality in the wine. However, the basalt in reality has two separate origins. A layer at about 3 meters depth resulted from ancient volcanic activity. But the surface layer of small stones, which gives the vineyard its characteristic appearance, comes from a quarry further over in the Pechstein valley. The stones were used in building streets, but those that were too small were thrown away. The closest open field for discarding the stones was the Pechstein vineyard, located at the entrance to the valley![58]

The hill of Hermitage looms over the town of Tain l'Hermitage on the Rhône river. Peak elevation is about 330 m. Vineyards are tenable only because of the construction of terraces and removal of boulders.[55]
Extending beyond Hermitage is the lesser appellation of Crozes-Hermitage.

300 m
250 m
200 m
150 m

1000 ft
200 m

The Kirchenstück vineyard is surrounded by a wall, which has a profound effect on the microclimate within the vineyard.

Photograph kindly provided by VDP Pfalz.

Draining the Marshes

If man cannot influence it, terroir should be immutable, but it's not as simple as that. Historical changes can be hallowed by time as part of the terroir. The Médoc, the area to the north of Bordeaux which produces many world-famous wines, including Châteaux Lafite Rothschild, Mouton Rothschild, Latour, and Margaux, was a hinterland of marshes in the middle ages. (Just a little north of the famous châteaux, the area was regarded as unfit for human habitation.) The classic phrase used to describe the region is "palus and marais," the palus being the waterlogged lands adjacent to the river, and the marais comprising marshy areas farther inland. Starting in 1599, Dutch engineers led by Conrad Gaussen drained the marshes under a mandate from King Henri IV. Basically this involved constructing a dike around each marais with a canal to drain out the water. It's often said that the terroir of the Médoc was created by the drainage of the marais, and that the famous areas for wine production would not otherwise exist. This is not entirely true. Certainly drainage greatly changed the terroir by creating large new areas of cultivable land, but few vineyards were established in the drained areas. Nonetheless, effects on the vineyards in the vicinity could be profound.[59] You rarely see reference to this change of the natural state when the Médoc is described as the perfect terroir for growing Cabernet Sauvignon.

The Médoc is superficially surprising as top terroir for wine because it is so flat and marshy. Most good wine-producing areas are relatively hilly, with slopes and angles that give good drainage. The highest point in the Médoc is only just above sea level (43 meters at Listrac-Médoc). Some areas are in fact below the level of the tide, with immediate consequences for the terrain. As a result of the successive drainage projects, what remain of the marshes in the Haut-Médoc today are mostly the palus extending out immediately from the river. But drainage remains a problem all over the region.

Accordingly, drainage systems are common in the vineyards to stop the accumulation of rainfall near the surface. Several of the top vineyards in the Médoc installed drainage systems following the recognition afforded by the famous 1855 classification. Château d'Yquem to the south of Bordeaux has 100 km of drains under its vineyards. So not only has the entire terrain been changed by major drainage projects, but individual vineyards are drained as necessary. Where does this leave the claim that the terroir of the Médoc should be protected from human intervention because it is uniquely suited to produce the greatest wines?

It has been known since before the eighteenth century that the best terroirs in the Médoc are based on gravel.[60] What are now recognized as the best vineyards were generally among the first to be planted on the famous "gravel mounds."[61] A gravel mound consists of topsoil on compact sand, sitting on top of a gravel bed that can range from a few centimeters to 2 or 3 meters in depth. Below that are alternating layers of compact sand and clay lens. Grapevines can establish deep roots on the gravelly soil, which has good drainage and a low water table. The gravel mounds are ideal terroir for Cabernet Sauvignon.

Because the gravel mounds are slightly elevated, they are not subject to flooding, although in some cases they were surrounded by marais. The second growth of Château Léoville Las Cases provides a famous example: its vineyards sit atop a gravel mound that was surrounded by marshes that flooded at high tide until the marais were drained. This illustrates one of the important effects of draining the marais: not only was the swamped land released for agricultural use, but the lowering of the water table on the adjacent gravel terraces improved their potential for quality wine production. By and large, the effects of the reclamation of the marais on the terroir of the vineyards were indirect rather than direct.

Gravel mounds provide the best terroir in the Médoc, forcing vines to develop deep roots.[62]

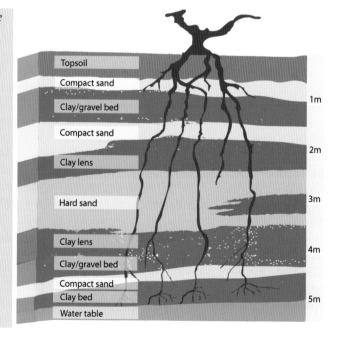

But the gravel mounds do not explain everything. Château Lafite Rothschild is immediately adjacent to three other châteaux. To its south is Château Mouton Rothschild. Both are first growths in Pauillac, but their styles are famously different, Lafite tending to elegance, Mouton more powerful. To the north of Lafite, separated from it only by the stream of the Chenal de Breuil, is Cos d'Estournel. But Lafite and Cos d'Estournel are at different elevations, and Cos d'Estournel has more of the underlying clay typifying St. Estèphe as compared to Pauillac. Although a most distinguished wine, Cos d'Estournel does not aspire to the same breed as Lafite. And to the west, no more than a stream separates Château Lafite from the adjacent fourth growth of Château Duhart Milon (which is actually owned by Lafite Rothschild, but never produces anywhere near the same quality). A little farther over, Château Latour achieves equivalent quality but differs in style from the others. Soils change significantly over short distances, so individual châteaux have variations within their terroirs, making the point that once you reach a size of tens of hectares, you are dealing with terroirs rather than terroir.

Terraforming the Mountains

No vineyard is natural, and the terroir is always influenced by man; just replanting the area with grapevines changes the local environment. But some changes are more extreme than others; indeed, the more extreme the terrain, the more violent is likely to be the effect of planting a vineyard. Mountain vineyards involve the greatest change of all, and nowhere is this clearer than in the plantings of the past two or three decades around Napa Valley.

Vineyards on slopes at elevated altitudes often offer advantageous terroirs. Drainage is good, the soil is not too fertile; often it is mineral or volcanic. There can be more diurnal variation in temperature (this is especially important in warm climates), and in the case of Napa Valley, the vineyards may be high enough to be above the fog line.

Napa Valley is surrounded by steep mountains on both sides, and many of its most famous cult wines come from vineyards on the mountain slopes. Yet constructing vineyards on mountains comes at a high price. It's rarely a matter simply of clearing the land and planting vines; often enough the process is more akin to terraforming, with massive clearance of forests and boulders, extensive reshaping of the terrain, even bringing in new earth by the container load. This can pose serious problems for the local environment, and the propensity to replace mountain tops with vineyards has become a major concern in Napa Valley. Several vineyards at elevated locations on mountains are controversial because of the methods used for their construction.

The Atlas Peak area, to the east of Napa Valley, is one of the most elevated locations for wine production. Only a couple of roads go into the area, and its dozen wineries are mostly at elevations above 1200 feet. When vineyards were first constructed there, no one was especially worried about environmental disruption. As Patrick Elliott-Smith recollected the construction of Elan Vine-

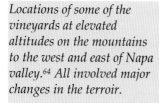

Locations of some of the vineyards at elevated altitudes on the mountains to the west and east of Napa valley.[64] All involved major changes in the terroir.

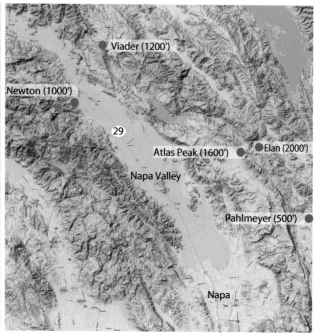

yards: "In 1979, I found my dream parcel of land at the top of Atlas Peak and began clearing the land with a 1953 International bulldozer. We removed boulders the size of cars to make way for the first vineyard."[63] This relatively small scale operation did not cause any particular trouble.

It was a different story when Atlas Peak Vineyards was constructed a few years later. Whitbread, the giant British brewers, purchased a plot of land that William Hill (of the eponymous Napa vineyard) had put together, and tore it apart to construct vineyards. As described by the project manager, Dick Peterson, "There are D10 Cats up there. This is a moonscape, but we're ripping it. We'll put terraces in there...We'll fill that canyon with rocks the size of Volkswagens, then cover it up with some muck from the caves we're digging."[65] This huge project did not pass unobserved. The neighbors sued Whitbread for failing to perform an environmental impact study, but they lost. [66]

Mounting concern about destruction of the environment led to fierce political fights, and ultimately to restrictions on vineyard construction. When Jayson Pahlmeyer constructed a vineyard in Wooden Valley, fifty acres were graded without an erosion control permit, and he was later forced to restore some of the land to its original condition.[67] The Sierra Club, an environmentalist organization, later sued Napa County for issuing permits to Pahlmeyer and others; they argued that erosion control systems on land brought under vineyard cultivation do not eliminate increased delivery of fine sediments to the stream system, which is detrimental to water quality and fish habitat. Construction of more than seventy vineyard projects was placed on hold as a result,[68] an indication of the magnitude of terroir creation in Napa Valley.

One of the most celebrated cases, and a trigger for subsequent regulations, was the construction of Viader Vineyards on Howell Mountain. A 90 acre plot was torn apart to construct vineyards. Boulders were blasted into smaller rocks that were then cleared out by bulldozers. The soil was "ripped" to a depth of 6 feet, by dragging steel rods through the earth. Just as the soil was completely bare, a major rainstorm came through. Sediment and mud ran off into the Bell Canyon Reservoir, a couple of hundred feet directly below the vineyard, polluting the water supply.[69] Subsequent problems with erosion and runoffs led to civil law suits and criminal charges.[70]

Perhaps at the end of the day (environmental issues aside) the question is not whether the terroir is natural or artificial, but whether it is good for wine production. Burgundy is the pre-eminent example of a natural terroir, perfectly suited to the Pinot Noir and Chardonnay cépages. There appears to have been little change in the terroir in several centuries; even the wall around Clos Vougeot, although responsible for maintaining the identity of this rather variable grand cru, has little practical effect. In the Médoc, the best terroirs were being used for wine production before the marshes were drained, but they were improved by drainage of the neighboring areas. In Napa, mountainside vineyards are often the results of wholesale reconstruction, but perhaps we are more conscious of man's efforts because they are so recent.

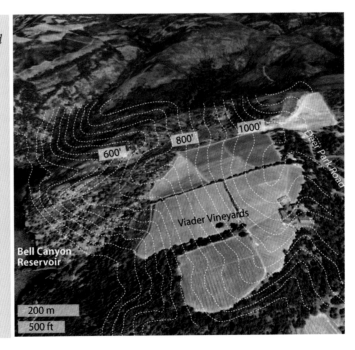

Viader Vineyards is located on land cleared at elevations of 800-1000 feet on Howell Mountain.[71]

Stress and the Single Grapevine

The grapevine is an extremely useful plant because it does best in poor soils that stress it to push its roots deep to find water and minerals, where other crops can scarcely be grown at all. When it is nutritionally challenged by growth in poor soil, water supply is the key to quality.

One reason why terroir is stressed much more in the Old World than the New is the ban on irrigation in Europe. If drainage is the most important feature distinguishing one terroir from another, as Australian viticulturalist Richard Smart points out, differences will be emphasized when water is provided erratically by rainfall, and reduced when irrigation is permitted, as it is everywhere in the New World.[72] According to California winemaker Randall Grahm, "The pernicious practice of drip irrigation, as routinely practiced here in California, essentially infantilizes plants, turning them into dumb, sterile consumers."[73]

Irrigation is a divisive issue. It is banned all over Europe, except in Spain where it was permitted from 1996, following the drought of the previous two

Vines gain water from rainfall or irrigation and lose it by transpiration from the leaves or evaporation from the soil.

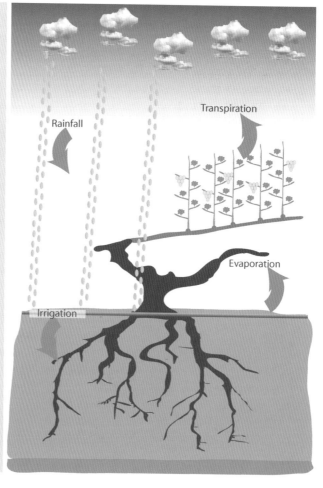

Rainfall

Transpiration

Evaporation

Irrigation

years. But much of Europe, especially France which has been a driving force on this issue, is relatively wet; the common problem is too much rainfall rather than too little. The concern is that permitting irrigation would vastly increase yields, and exacerbate the dimensions of the wine lake beyond even its present ridiculous proportions.

In the New World, vineyards are often planted in dry areas. Without irrigation, the vines would wither. Originally irrigation was quite crude, consisting of nothing more than a system of pipes connected to sprinklers that watered the vines from above. Later systems used pipes close to ground level, so the water falls closer to the roots, and the most recent developments use pipes buried underground that release water directly on to the roots. These, however, are expensive to install.

Stress is important for the grapevine because it influences how the plant uses its resources; under stress, it puts more effort into reproducing itself, which means producing fruit. Under good conditions, it just expands itself with vegetative production of more shoots and leaves. Water supply is the major determinant of stress. Water availability is controlled by the balance between provision by rainfall (and/or irrigation) and loss by transpiration from the leaves or evaporation from the soil.

The advantage of the latest irrigation systems is that water supply can be precisely controlled. Humidity meters in the soil make it possible to provide water only when the vine really needs it. Adjustments can be made during the season, so the vine gets more water at the beginning, when it needs to grow, but less towards harvest time, when water causes the berries to swell up. The latest technique is deficit irrigation, which limits the supply of water at critical points in order to stress the grapevine when deprivation is most effective in causing it to adjust its priorities between vegetative growth and fruit production.[74]

Do you make better wine by planting vines in a terroir where water is provided naturally by rainfall, but with erratic variations, and where the level in the soil depends on the balance between rainfall and drainage, or by planting in a dry climate that depends on irrigation, but where the supply can be precisely controlled at each stage of the growing season and adjusted to the soil level? Does modern New World winemaking obliterate terroir? By controlling the water supply through irrigation, and influencing exposure to sunlight through canopy management, are the differences between terroirs minimized so as to achieve more uniform homogeneity in ripe berries?

Garagistes and other Counter-Terroirists

Can you make great wine without great terroir? You can certainly make intense, powerful wines that occupy the commanding heights of the marketplace. But will they age like great wines: that is the question?

The recent phenomenon of garage wines captures the essence of the move to emphasize winemaking over terroir. Garage wines were so named because they are mostly produced under very modest conditions, some literally in basements or garages.[75] Produced mostly on the right bank of Bordeaux, these wines have very limited production (typically less than one thousand cases) from very small vineyards, typically less than 5 hectares. The wines are usually heavily dominated by Merlot (some are 100% Merlot), and generally associated with the new style of super concentration, reflecting very low yields, mature or over-mature grapes, increased extraction during vinification, and a strong emphasis on toasty new oak.

Most garage wines do not come from great terroir. Usually their terroir is quite ordinary. Extreme viticultural and vinification techniques have been used to compensate for the lack of terroir. Some proprietors of larger châteaux have been known to comment sourly that it is easy enough to produce high quality wine on a miniscule scale by using all the tricks of viticulture and vinification, but the real issue is to get quality wine when you have tens of hectares to cultivate.

So what does this tell us about terroir? The garage wines are rich and opulent, intense and powerful, delicious to drink when young, although for some tastes (including my own) really a bit overwhelming as an accompaniment for food. There is perhaps a certain sameness to them—the competition is to out-intensify one another rather than to reflect underlying properties of terroir. The jury is still out on whether they can acquire the complexity with age that used to typify Bordeaux, but personally I am doubtful. However, they remain a forceful demonstration of the effects of extreme winemaking and of the fact that you do not need terroir to make wines that are regarded as reaching the ultimate peak by some segments of the market.

The case against needing terroir for greatness is made better by Grange, the most striking example of a wine universally acknowledged to belong in the pantheon of great wines, but which is associated with no particular terroir.[76] Grange originated as the result of a visit in 1950 to Bordeaux by Max Schubert, the winemaker at Penfolds in South Australia. Impressed by the ageworthiness of Bordeaux, Schubert resolved to produce a wine of equivalent quality in Australia. He settled on Shiraz because it was readily available, whereas the only Bordeaux varietals grown in the region, Cabernet Sauvignon and Malbec, were in too short supply. Unable to blend varietals, he decided to blend Shiraz from two separate vineyards, one at the Penfolds estate in Magill close to Adelaide, and one farther south, which he thought would have complementary properties.[77]

The wine was made using methods comparable to those in Bordeaux, especially with regards to maturation in oak, but did not at first receive a good reception. "A concoction of wild fruits and sundry berries with crushed ants predominating," said one well known critic whom Schubert invited to a tasting of the first vintages (1951 to 1956). Others were less kind. It was the end of the decade before its early aggressive nature resolved to allow the wine to show its true quality. By 1962, it was winning gold medals at Australian wine shows. Since then, it has been internationally recognized as Australia's greatest wine.

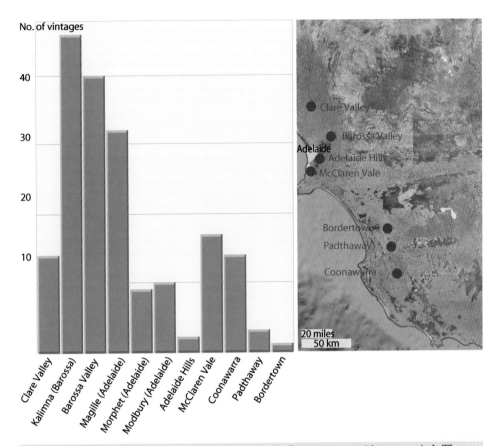

Many different sources were used for the grapes in Grange over a 46 year period. The histogram shows the number of years each source was used.[78] The map shows the varied locations of the vineyards.[79]

Grange started as a terroir wine, with the vineyard sources chosen to provide the same sort of complementary qualities that the Bordelais gain from blending different varietals. After the first couple of vintages, a little Cabernet Sauvignon was added to the Shiraz. However, vineyard sources changed. Grange comes today from a wide variety of vineyards, stretching from Clare Valley to Coonawarra, a distance of 100 miles (160 km), several times the distance across the left and right banks of Bordeaux, for example. Usually it includes wine from the Kalimna vineyard in Barossa, other vineyards in Barossa, and the Magill vineyard in Adelaide, but the other sources vary widely from year to year. On the other hand, in most years the blend is consistent, usually with 90-95% Shiraz and 5-10% Cabernet Sauvignon.[80] This is much less variable than the cépage variation in a typical Bordeaux vineyard over a comparable period. But Grange remains quintessentially itself, in spite of the diversity of sources and their variation from year to year, although you could no longer really call it a terroir wine; it is more a triumph of blending to achieve a consistent style.

The Far Reaches of Terroir

If we have to struggle to explain how the effects of terroir are manifested in grapes and then transmitted across the reaches of vinification to the wine, it becomes even more difficult to explain for wines with extra stages of vinification, such as Sauternes, Champagne, and fortified wines.

The dominant influence on dessert wines such as Sauternes is infection with botrytis, the noble rot. You might consider that terroir extends to the combination of humidity and sunshine that makes for conditions promoting infection, but this is stretching terroir well into the realm of climate.

As a wine relying extensively on blending, and with the flavor profile changed further by the second fermentation in the bottle, Champagne shows less association with terroir than any other fine wine. Yet the vineyards in the Champagne region are classified on the Echelle des Crus; vineyards classified on the bottom of the scale receive only 80% of the price for grapes of those classified at the top. The classification identifies a hierarchy, yet there are very few single vineyard Champagnes. Perhaps this reflects the fact that in a marginal region for wine production, the best sites are simply those that ripen more reliably; but in the context of a production system where the need is essentially for relatively neutral starting material, is it necessarily true that the best Champagnes would be produced from the top-rated vineyards?

There's a similar scale of vineyards in the Douro, top-rated as grade A, going down to the lowest grade of F. Quality of the base wine is more evidently related to the Port that will be produced by stopping fermentation half way; after all, the grapes are good enough to make vintage Port only in a minority of years. Classification is more puzzling in Jerez, where the best vineyards lie on the white chalk Albariza soils. But the grapes will be used to make a neutral white wine that is added to a solera containing wines commingled from the past several decades. What price terroir? The main difference perhaps is between those vineyards that usually give wines directed towards the light Fino style, compared with those that give wines directed towards the richer Oloroso style. Could this all go back to nutrient qualities in the soil?

If it's far from easy to see qualities of the soil reflected first in the grapes and then in the wine, how would we expect to see terroir manifested in spirits after distillation? Brandy's characteristic aromas and flavors are due to volatile compounds, synthesized in the berry or during fermentation, and effectively concentrated and selected during the process of distillation. This seems far distant from any property of the soil.

Yet soil is the basis for distinguishing different regions of Cognac. It all goes back to 1857, when geologist Henri Coquand distinguished six areas for growing grapes for Cognac: in declining order of quality, they form a sort of bull's eye radiating out from the town of Cognac: Grande Champagne, Petite Champagne, Borderies, Fins Bois, Bons Bois, and Bois Ordinaires. The Champagne regions have clayey, chalky thin soils on top of soft chalk from the Cretaceous; the limestone content is very high. "Grande Champagne... produces fine, light Cognacs

How can terroir survive distillation? Base wine is heated in the alambic still and then selected fractions are condensed to make Cognac.

Photo: © BNIC/ Gérard Martron

with a predominantly floral bouquet, requiring long ageing in casks to achieve full maturity," while Petite Champagne, although similar, has less finesse according to the local authority.[81] Borderies has clay and flint soils, producing "fine, round Cognacs, smooth and scented with an aroma of violets." The Fins Bois have more clay in the soil, which is known as "groies," and the cognacs age more rapidly. By the time we get to the Bons Bois, there is more sand in the soil, and the Bois Ordinaires is mostly sandy, although actually not much used for production. Sounds fine, except that it's obviously puzzling how the distinctive soil properties might survive the process of distillation.

But it may all be a mistake. Certainly it would be unusual for geological structures to form concentric circles, and in fact the stratum of chalk runs in a belt from northwest to southeast. Henri Coquand was President of the Geological Society of France; British geologists Jake Hancock and Richard Selley say he "was an experienced geologist and had been working in the Cognac area for several years. He must have known that he was talking nonsense."[82] How could this have happened?

The story goes that Coquand went around the Cognac region together with an expert taster. Coquand assessed the terroir and the taster assessed the brandy. They found that the level of chalk corresponded exactly with quality of cognac assessed by taste. "It's very much worth noting," Coquand wrote in his report, "that taster and geologist never once differed."[83] The very best cognac was produced from grapes grown on soft chalk, while the lowest quality came from soils of clay and sand. At the end of the visit, there was a grand dinner at which Coquand gave a talk describing his results. Selley thinks it was all a joke, based on the humorous suggestion that the quality of Cognac declines in ever increas-

*What is the correlation
between geology and the
Cognac AOCs?*[85]

*The band of chalk follows a
northwest-southeast axis,
but appellations are
organized as a bull's eye.*

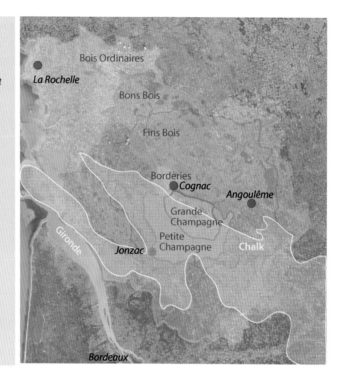

ing circles around the town, although if so, Coquand carried his sense of humor into the report he wrote for the Geological Society.[84]

There is some correlation between the extremes of terroir and the regions defined in the AOC: the best areas, Grande Champagne and Petite Champagne, are mostly on the belt of chalk; and at the other extreme, the Bois Ordinaires are the sandier soils nearer the coast. But there's no geological support for an organization of concentric circles, although the theory has been uncritically accepted ever since Coquand proposed it. Geologist James Wilson commented in his book on terroir, "Concentric bands of lessening quality encircle the bull's eye of Grands Champagne."[86] Yet at the same time he summarized the popular wisdom that "the worse the wine, the better the brandy." Indeed, the ideal wine for distillation should not have too much flavor but should provide a relatively neutral, slightly acidic, base for distillation. But in this case, shouldn't the chalky soils produce better wine that is less good for brandy production?

Does Terroir Matter?

A scientist who was interested in seeing whether terroir determines wine quality would need to have quantitative measures for both terroir and quality. Neither is easy to come by, but sometimes people have tried to devise numerical assessments to ask whether there is a relationship. But there is fatal flaw. To simplify, suppose we can divide wines into two broad groups. In one group, strong intervention in viticulture and vinification produces powerful, alcoholic wines, full of intense aromas and flavors in the "international" style. In the other corner, wine is made with less intervention, and shows less intensity, with more variation reflecting the vintage. It's not unfair to say that the second group is likely to be more representative of terroir than the first group. Now imagine that the critics favor the first group, and that prices follow the critics' acclaim. Any attempt to show an effect of terroir on quality or price will fall down on the fact that the "best" wines are those where grape growing and wine making have been tailored to reduce the effects of terroir; indeed, it may well appear that there is more correlation with some aspect of winemaking, for example, how much new oak is used. Just such a naive analysis indeed yielded the entirely predictable result (and regrettably newsworthy reports) that terroir does not matter.[87] I am afraid this is a demonstration of what computer people would call GIGO (garbage in, garbage out).

There's no doubt that, other things being equal, different plots of land will give different wines. But the differences depend more on physical factors, especially drainage, heat retention, and sun exposure, than on chemical differences. The main effect of these physical differences is on ripening; and the effect is magnified when vines are grown in a marginal climate. So on Burgundy's Côte d'Or, the grapes ripen best in the middle of the slope, creating the line of grand crus. It's hard to doubt that terroir has a significant effect on ripening and therefore in defining relative qualities. But the big question is whether terroir goes beyond changing quantity or quality of the grapes: can the soil change the nature of the wine? Do the grand crus of Chablis make wine that is different in its aroma and flavor spectrum from the premier crus because of their soil; or are all the differences simply the consequences of achieving a better level of ripeness?

Another age old question is whether you make the best wine by concentrating on a single vineyard plot that always gives fine results or by blending the products of plots with different properties. The effects of terroir are most obvious in areas where only a single variety is grown, and the vineyard plot is the only variable. The question is blunted in regions where wines are made by blending different varieties, which is perhaps why Bordeaux (typically made from several varieties) classifies wines, whereas Burgundy (the quintessential single variety wine) classifies terroirs. The debate has been most open, perhaps, in Barolo, where wines are made from a single varietal, Nebbiolo, but over the past two or three decades, production has shifted at most producers from "Barolo," consisting of a multi-vineyard blend, to an array of single vineyard bottlings. The traditional view was that the most complex wine was made by assemblage; the modern view is that the consumer demands the impression of precision given by individual bottlings. This is far from resolving the issue of terroir versus blending, but clearly enough resolves the issue of the dominant force in directing production: it's the market, stupid.

4

Vintage Variation and Global Warming

MOST FOODS HAVE A SELL-BY DATE, but wine has a vintage. As an agricultural product, grapes (and the wine produced from them) inevitably show variation from year to year. But the concept of the vintage is unique to wine. This reflects the fact that wine often is not consumed immediately, but is kept for a period of maturation.

In Roman times, the best wines were commonly kept for ten or twenty years before consumption. Distinctions were made between vintages; the Falernian (made from the slopes of Mount Falernus) was particularly fine in 121 B.C. Even then as now, the distinction was that the best wines were distinguished by vintage, but this was much less important for ordinary wines that were consumed immediately.

The Romans were able to age their wines by using amphorae, which were coated with resins to preserve the wine against oxidation, and sealed with corks. Resinated wines remained common until well into the Common Era. The Allobroges tribe, who occupied the area from Marseilles to Vienne in southern France in the first century C.E., and were admired by the Romans for their skill in wine production, made a wine called "pomatum" (meaning pitch).[1] It took its name from the use of resin to seal the containers, and may have been somewhat comparable to the Greek Retsina (in which pine resin is added to white wine). In fact, the quality of the pitch or resin was regarded as influencing the quality of the wine.[2] Flavoring wine with additional substances ranging from honey or spices to resin was common in both the Roman and Greek cultures. As can be seen from the flavor of Retsina (definitely an acquired taste), this has a profound effect on the nature of the wine.

The origins of the concept that wine is the unadulterated product of the grape are hard to trace, but by the time Europe emerged from the dark ages following the fall of the Roman Empire, wine was no longer being treated with resins or spices. One impetus may have been the belief that sacramental wine must be pure.

The Origins of Vintage

Vintage is a concept both old and new. It has always been important, but its meaning has quite reversed from time to time. The capacity to seal containers in an airtight way was lost after the Romans;[3] cloth or leather was used during the medieval period. This made it important to consume wine quickly, and the importance of vintage was that only the last year's wine was drinkable.

It was not until the late eighteenth century that it again became possible to preserve wine, so that vintage became associated with the ageworthiness of better years.[4] Up this time, wines were produced for immediate consumption. An old French proverb goes "the wine is drawn; it must be drunk," probably referring to the rapidity of spoilage.[5] Young wines were more valuable than older wines.[6] The exported wine was typically the "vin de l'année" of the last vintage. A "vin vieux" would be a wine of the previous vintage, considered less good, and sold off at less than half the price.

At the beginning of the eighteenth century, "New French Clarets" became the rage in the London wine market. These were wines from Bordeaux in a new style of higher quality, and advertisements often emphasized the fact that they were from the latest vintage. The key aspect of vintage in this period may have been the need to demonstrate that the wines were still fresh, effectively requiring that they came from the latest year.

Manufacture of bottles had begun in the early seventeenth century in England, but did not reach the Continent until towards the end of the century. At first, the bottles could be sealed only with ground glass stoppers (an expensive proposition that did not lend itself to mass manufacture). Cork had been rediscovered in the sixteenth century, but became available to seal glass bottles only around 1700.[7] By 1775 the production of bottles was standardized so they could lie flat, enabling the wine to stay in contact with the cork to prevent it from drying out.[8]

Towards the end of the century, distinctions begin to be made between wines on the basis of their potential longevity. Wine brokers in Bordeaux described wines as being "sèveux" (vigorous), meaning that they would age, as opposed to those described as "moins longue garde," which were appropriate for immediate consumption.[9] According to Thomas Jefferson, in his account of his visit to Bordeaux in 1787, at that time the 1783 vintage cost 2,000 livres per tonneau, compared to the 1,800 livres per tonneau of the 1785 and 1786.[10] This may be the first evidence for a premium paid for an older wine.[11]

Jefferson noted that the top wines of Bordeaux did not become ready to drink until after a few years of age. "Château Margau, La Tour de Segur, Hautbrion are not in perfection till four years old; those of De la Fite, being somewhat lighter, are good at three years, that is, the crop of 1786 is good in the spring of 1789."[12] He viewed them as remaining at their peak for a relatively short period. "All red wines decline after a certain age, losing color, flavor, and body. Those of Bordeaux begin to decline after seven years."[13]

By the end of the nineteenth century, a market in old wines had developed in England. Saintsbury, the celebrated author of "Notes on a Cellar-Book," purchased Lafite of the 1878 vintage when it was twenty years old (it had not been properly stored and he was not happy with it!), and mentions the fact that the 1870s were drinkable at 40 years of age.[14] During the twentieth century, the gap between young wines and old wines widened considerably, and by the middle of the century the concept was common that great vintages were marked by developing for many more years than lighter vintages. And the relationship between quality and ageability stretched into the view that great vintages required substantial time before it was appropriate to start drinking them.

Vintage Variation

When vintage was used only to distinguish the most recent year from older wines, variations between vintages were of academic interest, since anyway only one vintage was available. All the same, better vintages sold at higher prices.[15] But once it became possible to age wines for longer periods, and multiple vintages were available at the same time, older vintages became more valuable, better vintages attracted a higher premium, and there were more extreme price fluctuations from year to year.[16]

Vintage is more important in the Old World than the New. Temperature variations are greater from season to season in the traditional growing regions of Europe than in the more recently planted regions of the New World. In Bordeaux, for example, the average temperature over the growing season varies by around 2.5 °C during each decade. In Napa, the typical variation is only around 1.5 °C. On top of this, until 1982, temperatures in Bordeaux penetrated into the preferred range for ripening Cabernet Sauvignon only two or three times per decade. So successful vintages in Bordeaux alternated with poor vintages where the Cabernet could not really ripen. In Napa, by contrast, there was rarely any difficulty in ripening the Cabernet.

Temperature alone does not explain the quality of the vintage. In Bordeaux, rainfall is just as important, for both quantity and timing. Some warm vintages in Bordeaux have been poor, due either to lack of water or (more often) due to too much water, especially at the end of the season. But in the New World, by and large, the heat is reliable—and since water is often provided by irrigation on demand rather than falling from the sky, vintages are much less often spoiled by rain.

But even in Europe, the range of variation is less than it used to be. This is partly due to the warming trend, which has brought many regions up into a range where grapes ripen more regularly, and partly due to advances in viticulture and vinification that have saved vintages that previously might have been lost. In fact, the effects of technology are more significant for poor vintages than for good vintages. During the 2007 vintage in Bordeaux, problems with humidity provided ideal conditions for the spread of mildew; a generation ago, the crop

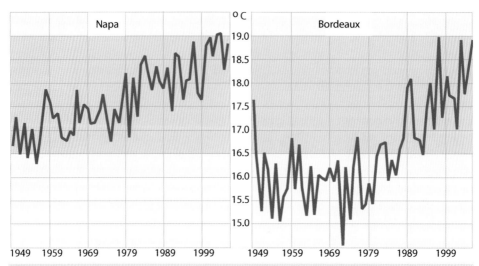

The range of average growing season temperatures is narrower in Napa than in Bordeaux. The shaded purple region shows the preferred temperature range for Cabernet Sauvignon (16.5-19.0 °C).[17]

might have been wiped out, but improvements in the ability to treat mildew rescued the vintage.

If the nature of the vintage depends largely on temperature and rainfall, can its quality be predicted from these factors? If you look at conditions during the year in Bordeaux, where there are records going back for most of the twentieth century, it's clear that the best vintages tend to be relatively hot and dry, and the worst vintages tend to be relatively cool and wet. Not very surprising, although it's certainly not an exact match, because there are vintages that were hot, but spoiled by rain at harvest; however, it's certainly true that it's impossible to get a really good vintage without adequate heat.

Princeton University economics Professor Orley Ashenfelter believes that the quality of a vintage can be predicted from the growing season temperature and the amount and timing of rainfall.[18] His formula for predicting vintage quality in Bordeaux gives about 85% of the importance to temperature, splitting the rest between points added for rain during October to March and points subtracted for rain during August and September.[19] The formula does not do a bad job of rating vintages, although it has some spectacular failures, mostly when the growing season was hot, but the vintage was spoiled for some other reason.[20] The details don't work perfectly, but support the general principle that temperature is good, rain outside of harvest season is good, and rain during harvest season is bad. The formula holds best when the main issue was lack of warmth in the growing season; it breaks down with the recent change in climate to regularly warmer vintages.

Vintage versus Blending

The importance of vintage is accepted without question in the world of fine wine, but it's not appropriate for all wines. The gap between wines intended for immediate consumption and those intended for aging has widened considerably since the late eighteenth century. While vintage is important for the best wines, which take some time to reach their peak, and vintage variation has interest for wines at higher quality levels, for others vintage serves more of its original purpose in ensuring that a wine has not become too old. Vintage dating would be inappropriate for the lowest tier of popular wines, and as a practical matter would make it difficult to move a poor vintage through the marketplace.

The market for short-term wines is dominated by large brands, for which consistency of flavor is all-important: the very antithesis of vintage, where variation is inevitable. In fact, many large brands do not have a vintage at all;[21] wines without vintage account altogether for roughly one third of sales of table wine in the United States.[22] Not only is vintage irrelevant, but a significant feature is the need to obliterate its effects when producing brands. Blending wines from different sources in order to maintain consistency is a much prized skill. The wine moves through the system fast enough that it is always fresh to drink, and like the wines from the early eighteenth century, once a new crop enters the system, the last one should all have been drunk.

The same skill is used at the top end of the market to produce Champagne. This is really making a virtue out of necessity. The Champagne region is marginal for wine production: in most vintages, grapes barely achieve ripeness. They can be turned into palatable wine only by making the transition from table to sparkling wine, and by adding a little sugar (the technical term is *dosage*) at final bottling. Even so, in many years the final product might be a little thin. So more than 90% of Champagne production goes into nonvintage wine, consisting of blends from different years. Only in the best years is a vintage Champagne produced. In fact, the critical measure of a champagne house is not so much the quality of its vintage wine, but its ability to maintain consistency of its nonvintage wine in spite of vintage variation.

A similar solution for handling vintage variation is found in Port. Most Port has no vintage. Vintage Ports are "declared" only in the best years; in a great year, all the shippers may well declare a vintage, in slightly less good years, only some shippers will declare one, depending on how well they feel their wine has turned out. Because vintage Port is produced only in some years, its share of the market fluctuates, but averages about 1%.[23]

Vintage is avoided altogether in Sherry, where wines are blended over a period of many years in the unique solera system. Age is important, but it's the length of time the average wine spends in the solera that determines its quality, not the vintage.

There's a handful of exceptional cases where great wines are blended across vintages. The great producer of Ribera del Duero in Spain, Vega Sicilia, produces a nonvintage Reserva Especiale that in fact sells for about the same price as a current release of its top vintage wine, Unico. But it's hard to break the mantra that great wine must have a vintage, although you might in fact get good results by blending vintages in the same way that blending is performed between wines coming from vineyards with different characters.

Vintage variation is part of the charm and interest of quality wines, but of course represents a range between the wonder of a great vintage and the risks and perils of a poor one.

The Temperature's Rising

Winemakers are in less doubt than anyone about the reality of global warming. A series of unusually warm vintages in Europe over the past couple of decades has increased the ripeness of the berries, leading to a richer, more alcoholic style of wine. So far, this has generally been associated with higher quality because there have been fewer vintages when the grapes failed to ripen properly. The effect in the New World has been less marked so far. There are dire predictions that if this goes much further, it will become impossible to grow the traditional grape varieties in many wine regions.[24]

Increased temperature is the best known effect of global warming, but not the only one that affects plant life; change in the water supply is important for grapevines, as is the increased rate of growth resulting from increased supply of carbon dioxide.[25] Higher temperatures cause the vine to awaken sooner from its winter dormancy, so that bud break occurs earlier; and increased growth shortens the growing season. The entire cycle of the vine is changing: harvest dates have been getting progressively earlier, with winemakers sometimes forced to scurry back from their summer vacations to get the grapes in.

To get a measure of the magnitude of the effect, consider those traditional rivals, Burgundy and Bordeaux. The average temperature difference between them during the growing season is 1.2 °C. The general temperature increase in European wine-producing regions since 1960 has been about the same magnitude. Every degree of warming has the same effect as moving the vineyards 200 km south.

Climate change has previously caused shifts in wine production. Until the sixteenth century, the Champagne region produced still red wines that were exported to Paris; however, the temperature plunge of the mini ice age was followed by sustained cooler temperatures, making it impossible to ripen the grapes fully. Burgundy then became the favored supplier. The change may have been only about 0.2 °C.

The effects of global warming may be most marked at the extremes for grapevine growing (nominally at the limits of the 50° and 30° latitudes). It might become impossible to make wine in southern Europe. Winters may become too warm in some areas, such as southern Spain, to allow vines to achieve dormancy.

By the same measure, regions that are presently marginal, such as England, might actually become attractive for winemaking.[26] The terroir in southern England is not unlike that of Champagne;[27] a small temperature shift could make this an attractive area for producing high quality sparkling wine. A team from leading champagne house Louis Roederer was spotted in England in 2007 hedging their bets by investigating the purchase of vineyards;[28] quite a reversal from the period when the English owned the vineyards of Bordeaux.

Matching the Climate

Average annual temperature has shown wild swings over the past thousand years, with warm or cold trends often lasting for a century. But beware: ten recent reconstructions for historical temperatures showed a serious lack of detailed agreement.[29] However, some general points are clear. It was relatively warm during the Roman period, and then cooled off during the Dark Ages. A warm medieval period started around 1000, but temperature reduced sharply during the Little Ice Age of the late Middle Ages. Vineyards in northern Europe were abandoned during the temperature drop of the mid fourteenth century. Then it stayed cooler from the sixteenth to nineteenth centuries until a generally warming trend culminated in the more exaggerated trend of recent decades.

In regions that have grown wine for centuries, the dominant varieties became established at various times between the Middle Ages and the modern period. These were the available varieties that performed best in the climate of that time. Of course, we can't always trace when varieties first became established in a region, but there are sufficient references to identify the rise to fame of several of the best known black varieties. The important point is that temperatures when these varieties were selected were generally significantly lower than they are today.

Despite large climatic differences between the coolest and warmest regions in Europe, the growing season has roughly the same duration, starting in April and ending between mid-September and mid-October. This is because early-ripening varieties, requiring less heat, have been planted in cooler regions, while late-ripening varieties, requiring more heat, have been chosen for warmer regions. This has an important effect on quality: quick ripening tends to reduce aromatic complexity, and a longer growing season gives the best results. "The best wines are produced with cultivars that just achieve ripeness under the local climatic conditions, as if quick ripening of the grapes burned the essences that make the finesse of great wines," commented Jean Ribéreau-Gayon and Emile Peynaud.[30]

The great expansion of vineyards in the New World over the past two or three decades means that their plantings are more recent. Also, in the absence of any regulations as to what may or may not be planted, there is a greater and more rapid response to market forces and fashion. The climate shows less annual variability, and varieties were chosen for their ability to ripen reliably to match the climate as it is today rather than the climate of past centuries, so the impor-

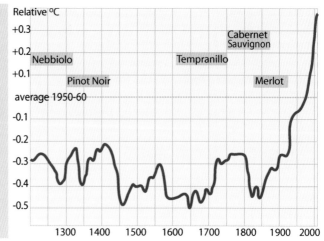

Average temperatures were lower when most of the great varieties were established in their characteristic regions. Nebbiolo and Pinot Noir were established in the Middle Ages; Cabernet Sauvignon, Tempranillo, and Merlot have more recent origins.

Average annual temperatures are relative to 1950-60.[33]

tance of vintage is decreased. The effect is most marked in Australia and New Zealand, where 50% of the vineyards have been planted in the past decade.[31, 32]

Climate is the most important factor in determining which grape varieties are appropriate for each region. The crucial factor is the temperature during the growing season. In the northern hemisphere, this is from April through October; in the southern hemisphere it is October through April.

One way to assess the potential of a wine-producing area by its temperature was invented by Albert Winkler at the University of California in the 1960s. The starting point for calculations is a base of 50 °F (10 °C), which is the temperature at which the vine comes out of dormancy and begins to grow. Each region is characterized by its number of *degree days*—the sum of the average daily temperatures in excess of the base temperature.[34] A day where the average temperature is 60 °F, for example, is worth 10 degree days (i.e., 60 − 50 = 10). To get the total, you add up the score for all days in the growing season.[35] Regions were divided into five zones from zone I (below 2,500 degree days), through zones II-IV at 500 degree day intervals, up to the top category (zone V, over 4,000 degree days).[36] Different grape varieties were recommended for each zone, from the cool climate of zone I to the warm climate of zone IV (zone V is not really suitable for quality wine).[37] Burgundy and Bordeaux fell into zone I at 2,300 and 2,390 degree days, respectively.[38]

The rationale for using degree days is that *only* temperatures above 10 °C contribute to growth, but pretty much the same result can be obtained in a simpler way by taking the average growing season temperature.[39] A change over the growing season of 1.3 °C corresponds to 500 Fahrenheit degree days (that is, one zone). Each variety does best in a characteristic temperature range; below the range it will fail to ripen properly, while above the range it is likely to give jammy wines. Comparing the two best known black varieties, Pinot Noir does best with an average growing season temperature around 16 °C, while Cabernet Sauvignon requires around 17.5 °C.[40] This explains why these varieties were planted in progressively warmer regions, Pinot Noir in Burgundy, Cabernet Sauvignon in Bordeaux.

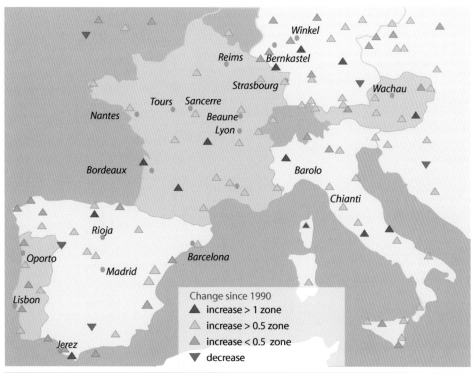

The growing seasons in the wine regions of western Europe have mostly been significantly warmer since 1990.[41] *(A zone is 500 Fahrenheit degree days.)*

The temperature range for best results is only about 2 °C for most varieties.[42] So the recent warming trend has a very significant effect on the match between grape varieties and regions. In most of the classic wine regions of Europe, growing season temperatures have increased by at least half a zone in the past two decades, and several have increased by more than a zone. According to the original concept of degree days, this would mean that different varieties should be planted. And there is every sign the trend will continue.

Average temperature is a relatively crude measurement, because diurnal variation—the difference between daytime and nighttime temperatures—is also an important issue for grapevines. Just like people need to sleep at night, grapevines need to rest. As the temperature goes down, the vine closes its stomata and stops respiration; this conserves water and retains acidity. In warm climates, it's especially important for there to be some respite from photosynthesis, as otherwise acidity is lost too rapidly. By pausing growth at night, the growing season is extended, which allows more time for other flavor components to develop before sugar levels become too high. A warming trend may have different effects depending on whether it increases peak daytime temperatures or reduces the cooling effect at night.

Changes in climate have the potential to alter significantly the effects of terroir. When vineyards are planted on a slope, for example, it is usually the middle of the slope that is the best terroir. Along the escarpment of Burgundy's Côte

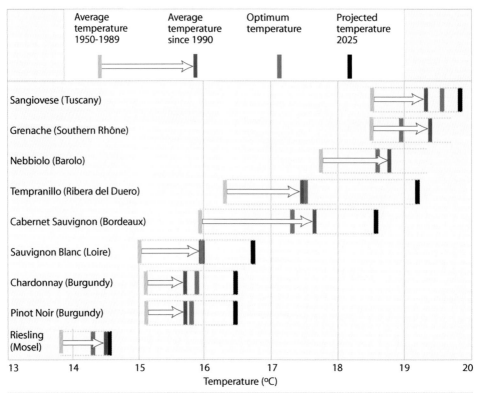

Average growing season temperatures have increased for classic wine regions since 1990.[43] The recent average temperature in most regions is now close to the optimum temperature for the best known varietal.[44] Projections show that by 2025 temperatures will be above the optimum in all regions.[45]

d'Or, the grand crus lie in the middle of the slope, because this is where the grapes reliably ripen best. This could be changed by global warming. And it's also true that terroirs higher up the slope do better in wet seasons, whereas terroirs at the bottom do better in dry seasons, because of drainage patterns, so a general change in rainfall could have a significant effect on relative qualities of terroirs. It would be dangerous to assume that the traditional hierarchy will be immune to change by global warming.

Varieties have traditionally been planted in Europe more at less at the northern limits for achieving full ripeness, with the result that usually there would only be a few really good vintages each decade. Between 1945 and 1990, average growing season temperatures in each classic region were between 0.5 and 1.0 °C lower than the optimum for the predominant variety. About three times every decade, a warmer year than average would bring really good ripening and create an excellent vintage. Global warming has increased the average in all regions since 1990, bringing it close to, or even over, the optimum. If the trend continues for the next decade or two, average temperatures will be well over the optimum, bringing into question whether these regions can continue to grow their traditional varieties.

Harvesting the Vine

Is it a myth that a thousand years of viticulture has enabled the Europeans to match each cépage to the perfect terroir? If you plot lines across Europe where the average temperatures in the growing season were optimal for ripening of the famous varieties, each of these lines (technically they are called isotherms) falls just to the south of the region that is best known for the variety. The Riesling band was to the south of the Mosel (Bernkastel) and Rheingau (Winkel), the Pinot Noir band just to the south of Burgundy (Beaune), and the Cabernet Sauvignon band just to the south of Bordeaux. Of course, temperature isn't the only factor in deciding what variety grows best, but the warming trend of the past twenty years has had a marked effect; the bands for optimum ripening have been pushed to the north, so the proportion of vintages with good ripening has increased significantly in all regions. The match between grape variety and climate is certainly now closer than it has ever been before.

The average increase of roughly 1 °C in growing season temperatures over the past two decades means that today's 16 degree isotherm is located more or less where the 15 degree isotherm was prior to 1990. This has moved each region to the temperature that used to characterize the region to its south. So Burgundy in the past decade has had an average growing season temperature of 15.9 °C, identical to that of Bordeaux in the 1960s.[47] That's a pretty big change given the distinction that is usually drawn between the suitability of Burgundy for Pinot Noir and of Bordeaux for Cabernet. Fortunately, all this has meant so far is better Burgundy and better Bordeaux, but if the trend continues, the temperatures may simply surpass the tolerance of the traditional varieties.

A real warning note was sounded in 2003, when the exceptionally hot conditions were fairly close to the projection for the average for 2050. The Burgundies of that year are too heavy to show the typical delicacy of Pinot Noir; many are more like the wines of the southern Rhône. And personally I don't buy the argument that Bordeaux came out with a great vintage; the wines of the right

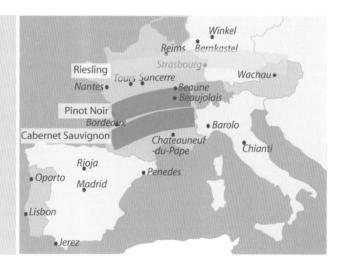

The band providing the ideal temperature for each variety prior to 1990 was just south of where the variety has traditionally been grown.[46]

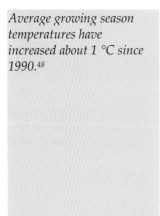

Average growing season temperatures have increased about 1 °C since 1990.[48]

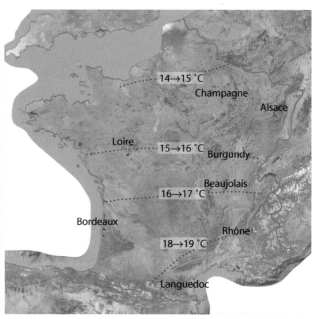

bank are often quite stewed, and those of the left bank seem clumsy by comparison with their traditional elegance. I will bet anyone who bought the propaganda and cellared the wines that they will fall apart in the next few years.

One of the most visible effects of global warming is that harvest dates have become progressively earlier all over Europe. There's a close correlation between higher temperatures and early harvest dates. The harvest in Châteauneuf-du-Pape now usually occurs at the beginning of September instead of the end, virtually a month's advance in half a century.[49] In Burgundy, the average for harvest dates in the past 50 years is earlier than at any time since 1370;[50] and the recent regression in harvest dates shows increasingly early spikes. In the exceptionally hot year of 2003, vignerons who had taken their traditional summer break in August—nothing much usually happens in the vineyard then—had to rush back to Burgundy and organize pickers for the earliest harvest on record (August 23). They started even earlier in the Beaujolais, on August 15.

Winegrowing regions of North America are not suffering as badly as Europe, but projections suggest that Napa Valley and other regions for quality wine production will become too hot for quality grape production in the next fifty years. It will become too hot altogether in the Central Valley to produce wine grapes, wiping out most of California's industry. Warming effects over the past half century have been more pronounced in the winegrowing regions of the northern hemisphere, but similar increases have occurred in the southern hemisphere. Growing season temperatures in Marlborough, New Zealand's best known wine-producing region, have increased about 1 °C since 1970, bringing it from just below the optimum for Sauvignon Blanc to just above it.[51] Climate change has been similar in South Australia.[52] The most striking effects in Australia, which may or may not be related to general climatic change, have been

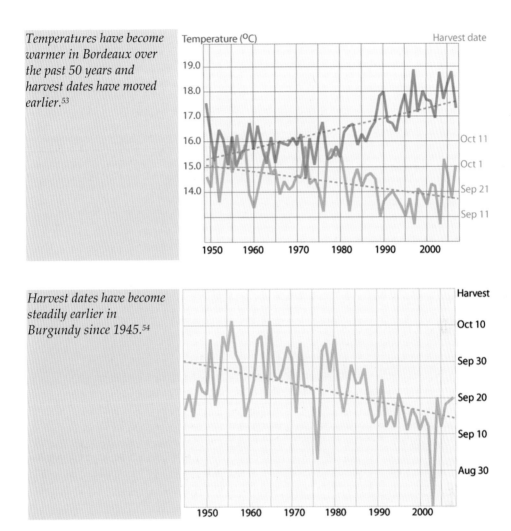

Temperatures have become warmer in Bordeaux over the past 50 years and harvest dates have moved earlier.[53]

Harvest dates have become steadily earlier in Burgundy since 1945.[54]

prolonged periods of drought, putting stress on the ability to provide sufficient water by irrigation, and rendering some wine-producing regions potentially infertile.

Is Global Warming the Enabler?

Global warming is by no means solely responsible for the steady increase in alcohol levels and decrease in acidity during recent years, but it has given a powerful push to the trend to harvest grapes at more advanced stages of ripeness. It used to be common for the harvest to occur 100 days after flowering, but now the period is often 110 or 120 days. Sugar rises and acidity falls continuously after veraison (when the grapes change color), and a significant change in the balance occurs with an extra week or two on the vine. Warmer climates enable

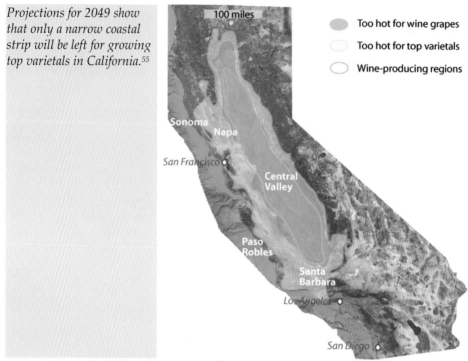

Projections for 2049 show that only a narrow coastal strip will be left for growing top varietals in California.[55]

Too hot for wine grapes

Too hot for top varietals

Wine-producing regions

grapes to reach ripeness more rapidly, and the combination of increased heat with later harvesting makes a powerful trend.

Alcohol levels in Bordeaux have increased about 20% since 1970, and acidity levels have fallen by about one third. Wines in Bordeaux used to be around 12.5% alcohol after chaptalization; now they are more often around 13.5%, in itself quite a difference in style. Higher to begin with, alcohol levels have also been increasing in the New World. Napa Valley has seen an increase in both red and white wines, just outrunning by a little the increase in growing season temperature. Grapes were usually picked at Brix levels of around 22 (potential alcohol about 12.5%) in Napa in the 1970s, but are now typically picked at Brix of 25 or greater (potential alcohol about 14%). While this is more a winemaker's choice than a direct consequence of global warming, it's certainly assisted by the generally warmer temperatures. Similarly, Australian wines increased steadily in alcohol level from 12.4% in 1984 to 14.2% in 2002,[56] although since then the trend has stabilized for reds and been reversed slightly for whites. The cause again is probably due more to seeking phenolic ripeness than to global warming per se.

Change is at its most marked at the limits for wine production. At the northern limits, a study of temperature increase at Geisenheim in Germany shows that already the climate has warmed past the average temperatures required to ripen Riesling and could now ripen Chardonnay; by 2050 it is predicted to be able to ripen Merlot![57] The effects are seen in an increase in the proportion of QmP wine produced each year. This is a direct measure of increased sugar level in the grapes, because for a wine to be classified as QmP it must reach specified sugar levels.[58]

The worldwide trend to harvest riper and riper grapes has pushed up alcohol levels generally. By concentrating on phenolic ripeness, grapes are harvested at much greater sugar levels than previously. But shouldn't the total alcohol level be considered an important criterion of when to harvest grapes? Isn't a wine with too much alcohol just as unbalanced in its way as a wine with insufficiently ripe phenols? Has the concept of phenolic ripeness gone too far and are producers missing the optimum in search of the maximum?

Far from attempting to counteract the trend towards higher alcohol and lower acidity that is promoted by global warming, winemakers seem more and more to be embracing the new "international" style of heavier, richer, fruitier, more deeply colored wines. This may well be rewarded in the marketplace: producers in Bordeaux whose wines today might be mistaken for those of Napa Valley have seen their prices jump over those producers faithful to the old style. How far can this go?

Potential alcohol has increased and acidity has decreased in Bordeaux since 1970.

Alcohol and acidity levels are for Cabernet Sauvignon at harvest.[59]

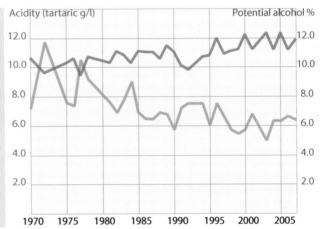

Alcohol levels have increased steadily in Napa Valley in parallel with average seasonal growing temperatures.[60]

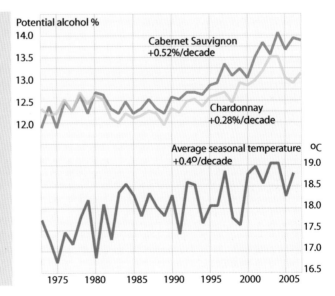

High alcohol is not confined solely to the New World or international-style wines. The wines of warm, southern regions in Europe have always been alcoholic. The winemakers can be quite trenchant about the need for high alcohol. "We don't want to give in to the craze for lower alcohol," says Victor de la Serna, who produces wine at Finca Sandoval in central Spain. "The wine would not be balanced, quality would suffer," if artificial methods were used to reduce alcohol. "People should just drink less or split the bottle between three instead of two people," he says.[61]

Convergence of Styles

The issue with early harvests is not just the inconvenience of interrupting summer vacations. The whole cycle of the vine is changed. The warming trend advances the entire cycle of grapevine maturation, from bud break (the start of the growing season), through flowering, veraison, to ripening and harvest. In fact, in France as a whole over the past 50 years, bud break has advanced by 5 days, and harvest has advanced by 17 days. This means that the overall growing season has become shorter. Longer growing seasons are associated with better ripeness (the technical term is the "hang time," meaning how long the grape hangs on the vine before it is harvested). Hang times have usually been longer in Europe than in the New World, and this has been felt to be an advantage in giving the wine more complexity.

Global warming therefore brings some convergence between Europe and the New World. The warming trend has been greater in Bordeaux than in California, so the gap in temperatures between Bordeaux and Napa Valley, one of the major New World competitors to Bordeaux, has narrowed considerably. In the past decade, Bordeaux has warmed up to reach almost the same average temperatures as those of Napa. This is part of the reason for the increased similarity in style between the regions, with Bordeaux now showing more of the riper, richer features associated with Napa valley.

The difference in the seasonal growing temperature has narrowed between Bordeaux and Napa since 1990.[62]

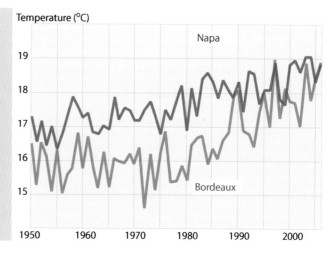

How reliable are the predictions that wine production (not to mention other agriculture) will be threatened by the future warming trend? I was not at all surprised at reports in 2009 that leading researchers had fudged their results in order to exaggerate the global warming trend.[63] Talks and papers on the subject tend to have an air of political commitment, with worst case extrapolations emphasized, although there is little factual basis for supposing we can simply assume the change of the last ten years will be exactly repeated every future ten years.[64] Nonetheless, the fact is that temperatures in wine-producing regions have increased significantly in the past two decades. Of course, this is a relatively short period in terms of environmental change, and there is little direct proof how much might be caused by natural cycles and how much by man-made activities; but the magnitude of the recent increase is greater than any occurring historically, and it would be a remarkable coincidence for this to be unconnected with human actions. The trend is at its most obvious in Europe where the change over the past twenty years has brought several wine regions close to the limits for producing quality wine from their traditional varietals. A blip like 2003 goes well beyond the limits and brings home the dangers if the present trend continues.

II MAKING WINE

THE TASTE OF WINE HAS BEEN CHANGING continuously since ancient times. The major problem with ancient wine was preservation. Because of the lack of inert containers, wine was often treated with wood resins as a preservative. This can have been no more than partially effective, so oxidation as well as the resins themselves must have had a significant effect on the taste. Soon after the start of the Common Era, wood barrels became used for storage; this made it necessary to consume the wine fairly rapidly, before it was spoiled by oxidation. There was a long interregnum before the next stage. During the eighteenth century, two developments made it possible for wine to be aged: the wine was protected by burning a sulfur candle before the barrel was filled (to generate sulfur dioxide as a preservative); and a truly inert container became available in the form of a bottle sealed with cork.

The basis for the process of fermentation that converts sugar in the grapes into alcohol in the wine was not discovered until the mid nineteenth century, and the ability to control malolactic fermentation (which reduces acidity and softens the wine) was not discovered until the second half of the twentieth century. The traditional bottle sealed by cork remained the only available container until the end of the twentieth century, but now is being slowly displaced by the screwcap (not to mention other types of containers such as bag-in-box).

Table II Development of winemaking over 6000 years.

4000 B.C.	Wine is stored in amphorae; resins are added to preserve it.
250 C.E.	Wood barrels used for transport and storage.
18th century	Sulfur is used to sterilize barrels. Corks become available and wine is bottled in glass.
1801	Chaptal introduces addition of sugar before fermentation to increase alcohol levels.
1863	Pasteur discovers that yeast catalyze fermentation of sugar into alcohol.
1939	Peynaud characterizes bacteria involved in malolactic fermentation.
1950s	New oak becomes widely used for red and some white wines.
2000	Screwcaps begin to replace corks, and bag-in-box used for cheaper wines.

5

Turning Grape Juice into Wine

WINE IS NOT A NATURAL PRODUCT, at least not in the form we know it. Wine is a transient stage in the transformation of grape juice to vinegar. Successful wine-making is about making the product as enjoyable as possible while it lasts, and (for fine wines) prolonging the period before the inevitable decay. If you had a completely natural wine, made spontaneously from grape juice without any human intervention, you probably would not like it very much, and it would be rather short lived.

The essential step for all wine production is the alcoholic fermentation, when yeasts attack the grape juice to convert its sugar into alcohol. The same yeasts are involved as those used in making bread, baker's yeast (Saccharomyces cerevisiae; Saccharomyces means "sugar fungus"). But yeast is far more than a mere catalyst for turning sugar into alcohol: it changes many of the compounds present in the grape juice, and creates many of the compounds in wine.

When alcoholic fermentation is over, the grape juice (or *must* as it is called in the trade) has been converted to wine.* But much lies ahead of it. For almost all red wines, as well as for some white wines, another fermentation occurs; cata-lyzed this time by bacteria, the malolactic fermentation converts malic acid into lactic acid, reducing acidity and generally softening the wine. Like alcoholic fermentation, malolactic fermentation (usually abbreviated MLF and known colloquially in France as "the malo") also has other significant effects on flavor.

We are not finished yet. Only the simplest wines are ready to go to market di-rectly after fermentation. Others go through a period of maturation, and the finest wines may spend months or years in oak barrels before they are ready. If the oak is new, the wine will pick up flavor components from it; even if it is old, the wine will change as the result of exposure to oxygen.

---

* If some sentences seem confusing because they refer to the *must*, remember that it is a noun describing the unfermented or fermenting grape juice, not a verb suggesting an imperative.

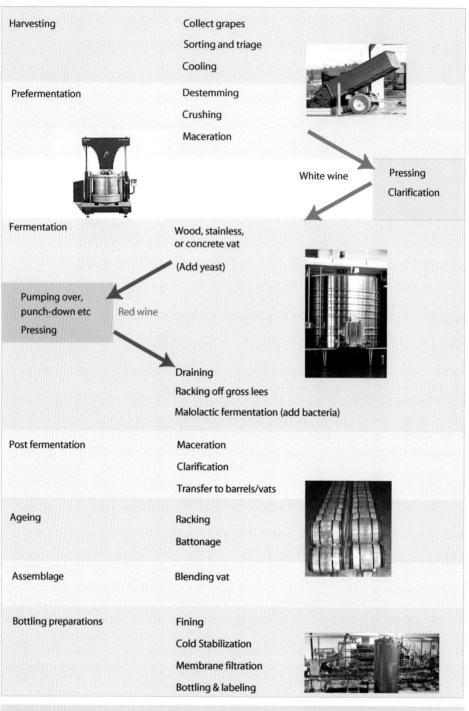

Winemaking involves the same stages for all types of wine, but they occur in a different order for white wines and red wines.

There's an important difference in winemaking between white wines and red wines, because color for red wine is obtained from the skins. Remember that almost all wine grapes have colorless pulp. (There are a few exceptional varieties, called teinturiers, but they are not generally very important in wine making.[1]) In fact, it's not only color that comes from the skins; other skin components, especially tannins, are important in making red wines different from white wines.

Common stages for all grapes are harvesting, sorting to remove extraneous material or damaged berries, destemming, crushing to release the juice, and (sometimes) maceration to allow the juice to extract compounds from the skins. Then for white wine the grapes are pressed; there are all sorts of presses, but the common principle is that the grapes are squeezed to separate the juice from the skins. The juice is then clarified by removing any large particles (broken bits of skin, and so on) to make it fairly clear and ready to be fermented.

For red wines, the grapes go directly from a destemmer/crusher into the fermentation vat, so the juice ferments in contact with the skins. Release of carbon dioxide pushes the skins to the surface where they form a cap. Various means are used to stop the cap from drying out; depending on the grape variety, the juice may be sprayed over the cap, or the cap may be punched down into the juice. When fermentation is over, the wine is run off into another vat; this is called the free-run wine.

So basically you can make red wine without any pressing at all. In fact, as long ago as the Middle Ages, this was the usual procedure, according to the recommendations of Olivier de Serres in the standard text book of the times (first published in 1600).[2] The grapes may later be pressed to extract whatever liquid has been retained in them; this vin de presse (or press wine) typically contains more extract and is less refined. In the Middle Ages the press wine was usually sold off separately at a lower price; today, a proportion is sometimes added back to the free-run juice to better balance the level of extraction.

At every stage along the way, the winemaker has an opportunity to influence the nature of the wine that will emerge at the end. No decision is without consequences, from the initial stages of deciding how long the juice can be in contact with the grape skins, to the final stage of deciding whether the wine is to be bottled in glass under a cork or screwcap, or is to be sold in some other type of container.

From Vineyard to Fermentation

The key transition from the vineyard to the winery is to keep the grapes in a pristine state. It is all too easy for them to become broken and oxidized en route. They need to be pressed (very gently for white wine) or destemmed/crushed (for red wine) before fermentation starts. Sometimes there will be a period of cold maceration first, when the juice is kept in contact with the skins at low temperature, before fermentation is allowed to start.

Grapes are emptied from containers on to the sorting table; the belt moves under the eagle eyes of the sorters, who remove unripe berries.

Photograph kindly provided by Bodegas Abadia Retuerta.

Whether harvesting is manual or mechanical, grapes are collected at the vineyard in small containers, so the weight of the grapes on top does not crush those in the lower layers. Mechanical harvesters may even have systems to keep the grapes under nitrogen to reduce the risk of oxidation.

One of the major advances of recent years has been increasingly refined sorting of grapes. One common device is a vibrating table, which causes small particles, such as fragments of leaves or insects, to fall through a grid. Other devices include flotation to separate unripe berries (they float on the surface, but ripe berries sink because of their greater specific gravity). Typically the last stage is examination by a keen human eye to pick out anything that is not a fully ripe grape, but the latest invention is an optical scanner that picks out undersized or discolored grapes and directs tweezers to remove them. With all this going on, there should be nothing in the press except nicely ripe berries. It makes you wonder, though, about what contribution the MOG (material other than grapes) made to the wine in the years before this level of sorting became common! Perhaps it contributed to greater variety of flavors.

Before all these developments, grapes were brought directly to the press and just shoveled in. The typical press was a vertical basket, basically a large cylinder that was forced onto the crushed mass of grapes. Control of the pressure on the grapes was fairly crude.

Grapes today are handled much more gently. Wineries are often built in multiple levels, so that the grapes enter at the top level, and then move gently down by gravity, first into the fermentation vats, and then into the maturation vats. Use of pumps to move the juice or wine around is minimized. Pressing is done at very controlled levels. The grapes for white wines are typically pressed in a pneumatic press, where they are squeezed gently against the walls of the container by a bladder that inflates slowly. The latest vertical presses have very delicate controls that allow much higher quality to be obtained when red grapes are pressed after fermentation.

At the start of the twentieth century, grapes were brought from the vineyard in large baskets and shoveled into the press. This view shows the press room at Moët & Chandon in Bouzy.

Once the grapes are in the vat, fermentation can begin. Fermentation converts complex substances to simpler ones. In the case of alcoholic fermentation, the sugars (glucose and fructose) are converted to alcohol. The energy that was stored in the sugars is released in the form of heat. Fermentation is extremely energetic, not to say vigorous. It releases clouds of carbon dioxide, and the must becomes turbulent and hot.

Heat used to be a major problem during fermentation. One of the great advances of recent decades is the introduction everywhere of temperature control.[3] This may take the form of stainless steel vats surrounded by water-cooled jackets, or coils that are inserted into wooden vats (the coils can also be warmed in cases where heat is needed to start fermentation). Before temperature control became common, fermentation could overheat if the weather stayed hot or the juice had a great deal of sugar. This could cause fermentation to become stuck or could result in infection with Acetobacter (bacteria that would convert some of the alcohol to acetic acid). (Fear of stuck fermentation was one of the motives that drove producers to harvest their grapes too soon.) In the old days, producers might even be forced *in extremis* to tip blocks of ice into an over-heated fermentation vat![4] Because it's a slow process to cool the must down, it's still important not to let the grapes get too hot when they are harvested.

Because of the need to extract color and tannins from the skins, red wines are usually fermented at higher temperatures (24-27 °C) than white wines (10-18 °C). High temperature makes the fermentation go faster, so a red wine fermentation is likely to last only a few days, whereas a white wine fermentation may take a

An old basket press (left) has a belt-driven cylinder that is lowered on to the mass of grapes. The latest version of the vertical press (right) employs computer-driven technology for gentle pressing.

couple of weeks. It's a delicate balance with red wines, because although you need extraction, volatile compounds, which are part of the aromatic spectrum, are lost at higher temperatures.

Fermentation temperature can have a significant effect on the aroma and flavor spectrum of a wine, especially in the production of esters. Esters are volatile, fruity substances formed when alcohols react with acids. They are responsible for the characteristic aromas of freshly fermented wines, such as banana, pineapple, or bubblegum, but the esters are rapidly broken down within a few months in bottle. That's why you may find these aromas especially concentrated in wines that are drunk very young. Reducing the fermentation temperature enhances production of esters, and some wines produced by very cool fermentation retain them even after some time in bottle.

Fermentation of red wine is extremely messy. White wine production is somewhat calmer, because the juice has been pressed. This creates another option: the wine can be fermented in barrel instead of in a large vat. (All those skins, seeds, and solid particles floating around would make this difficult with red wine.) Barrel fermentation is used for top-flight white wines that will subsequently be matured in oak, especially Chardonnay. It makes for a better integration between the intrinsic flavors of the wine and the flavors that come from the oak, because tannins inhibit the yeast and slow down fermentation, and the yeast modulates extraction of flavors from the oak.[5]

Bubble, bubble, toil, and trouble. Vigorous red wine fermentation pushes a cap of skin to the top of the vat; must is being pumped back over the cap from the bottom of the tank.[7]

Good Yeast and Bad Yeast

Before Louis Pasteur discovered the cause of fermentation, no one knew how alcohol was produced; it happened spontaneously after fruit was crushed, with varying results.[6] Basically it was known that sugar was converted into alcohol, but not why sometimes it was instead converted to acetic acid or lactic acid.

Pasteur showed that the differing outcomes resulted from infections with different microbes.[8] He demonstrated that infection with certain yeasts converts sugar to alcohol, and that during alcoholic fermentation they also produce many other organic compounds. The discovery that other yeasts (or bacteria) can spoil the wine led to a debate as to whether wine should be protected from further microbial action by pasteurization (heating to kill off any remaining yeast or bacteria).

Pasteur went on to show that fermentation does not require oxygen,[9] and suggested that exposure to oxygen is the cause of aging. His view that "it will be obvious to everyone that air has always been considered the enemy of wine,"[10] has resounded ever since, and indeed remains the subject of active controversy with regards to whether "breathing" occurs through the cork and has any effect on the aging of wine.

If you leave crushed grapes or must in a vat, fermentation will start spontaneously after a while. First the so-called grape yeasts or wild yeasts, which come from the skins of the grapes, will start fermentation. These yeasts are capable of fermenting until an alcohol level of 3-4% is reached, when they die off. Shortly after, the wine yeast *S. cerevisiae* takes over. It's unclear to what extent S. cerevisiae is present on the grapes themselves, but it is widely distributed in the winery, on buildings and equipment (as the result of earlier fermentations); it will continue fermentation until the sugar runs out or until an alcohol level is reached at around 15%.

There's an ongoing debate as to whether fermentation should be allowed to occur by the action of indigenous yeasts (those naturally occurring in the vineyard) or should instead be induced by adding a preparation of cultured yeasts. The process can be controlled by adding a low level of sulfur dioxide to kill the grape yeasts (which are more sensitive than S. cerevisiae) and then by adding a preparation of cultured S. cerevisiae to catalyze the alcoholic fermentation.[11] This gives a great deal of control, since cultured yeasts allow a winemaker to choose what characteristics to emphasize in the wine. Some yeasts bring out aromatic qualities, other suppress them; some help to reduce acidity by consuming more malic acid; specialized yeasts can allow fermentation to continue above the usual limit of 15% alcohol, or may be necessary to ferment juice with very high sugar content.

Traditionalists believe that the indigenous yeast population in the vineyard and winery constitute part of the characteristics of a natural wine; they are wont to refer to cultured yeasts as "industrial yeasts," which contribute to the general homogenization of flavors. This is one of the myths of winemaking. Well, to be more precise, there may be something to the criticism that use of the same yeast everywhere runs counter to diversity, but it is probably not true that indigenous yeasts are part of a vineyard or winery's character. "In a given vineyard, spontaneous fermentation is not systematically carried out by the same strains each year; strain specificity does not exist and therefore does not participate in vineyard characteristics. Ecological observations do not confirm the notion of a vineyard-specific yeast," according to eminent oenologist Pascal Ribéreau-Gayon.[12]

The fact is that a few yeasts become dominant in the course of fermentation; typically only one to three yeasts are present by the end of spontaneous fermentation. But winemakers who practice spontaneous fermentation argue that the variety of successive strains before the dominant strains establish themselves contributes to complexity. The same strain(s) are found for some consecutive years, but over time the dominant pattern changes.

There's a certain risk in relying on indigenous yeasts for fermentation. It's common for spoilage yeasts—yeasts that turn the wine sour or introduce other flaws—to be present among the grape yeasts; if they become established, they can ruin the fermentation.[13] There's also more risk the fermentation will become "stuck"—that it will just stop and be difficult to restart. It's safer to kill the indigenous yeasts with sulfur dioxide and add a culture of reliable yeasts. The cultured yeasts originated, of course, by isolating indigenous yeasts that had produced good results; and there's a fair variety of choice among them. The main criticism made by traditionalists is that the apparent variety is deceptive, because they all tend to have been chosen for vigor and reliability rather than for the quality of wine they produce. Using the same yeasts every year also diminishes vintage variation.

One interesting attempt to have the best of both worlds was tried at Sassicaia, the super-Tuscan winery in Bolgheri. The yeasts that had naturally fermented the wine were collected at the end of one season and cultured. Then they were used to inoculate the must to start the fermentation the next season. But the yeast population changed; the yeasts that were isolated at the end of the season were not the same as those that had been inoculated at the beginning.[14] So much for the consistency of vineyard-specific strains!

Spoilage yeasts can cause all sorts of flaws in wine. Most are simply to be avoided at all costs, but Brettanomyces is highly controversial. This yeast is not usually found on grapes at harvest time, but develops in the winery, often from contaminated wood barrels.[15] It generates a variety of compounds affecting flavor and aromas of wines, the most offensive being barnyard and mousiness.[16] The characteristic collection of aromas is usually known as Brett.[17] Some wine-makers believe that no level of Brett is acceptable, and that its presence is simply a flaw. Others hold that a (very low) level is a part of the complexity of wines fermented naturally. Château Beaucastel in Châteauneuf-du-Pape is famous for showing Brett in some vintages, and a survey of Syrah-based wines from the Rhône showed that many have Brettanomyces levels above the detection thresh-old.[18] Brettanomyces may have been responsible for the barnyard aromas once famously thought to be part of Burgundian terroir.[19] It's not always easy to determine whether a slightly earthy aroma is natural to the wine or results from Brettanomyces infection.

Chaptalization: Turning Sugar into Alcohol

Until the early nineteenth century, the alcohol level of a wine was determined solely by the effectiveness of native yeast in converting the sugar in the must into alcohol. Give or take a little, every 17 g/l of sugar in the grape juice gives 1% of alcohol in the wine.[20] But the yeast don't care where the sugar comes from. It's all the same to them whether it accumulated naturally in the grape or was extracted from beetroots and added to the must before the start of fermentation. It's all going to be turned into alcohol.

Jean-Antoine Chaptal was a chemist who rose to become Napoleon's Minister of the Interior in 1801. He had a strong interest in winemaking; in fact, you might very well call him the first oenologue. He believed that "alcohol is the essential characteristic of wine," and correspondingly that the problem with current wines was their low alcohol levels. His book on wine production went through several editions,[21] and introduced the concept that adding sugar before fermentation would increase the level of alcohol in the wine.[22] He recommended addition of sugar to a level of 5-10% of the weight of the must.[23]

Chaptalization, as it became known, slowly spread through winemaking from northern France to the south. It was not without controversy. Dr. Morélot, a well known contemporary critic on the wines of Burgundy, commented in 1831 that "one makes better wine, with a good taste; but this wine, I do not know if I am fooling myself, is no longer a true wine of Burgundy. Stronger, more alcoholic, and darker in color, it has lost its bouquet, and become more southern in style."[24] Nonetheless, by the 1850s chaptalization was widespread in France,[25] with Burgundy at the forefront.[26]

Dr. Morélot was undoubtedly right that chaptalization changes the character of the wine. The balance you get by adding sugar to increase the alcohol level is different from the results obtained when the same sugar level is reached naturally in the grape (because other compounds are produced by more extended ripening). The rationale for chaptalization in the nineteenth century was the need for the wine to reach a healthy level of alcohol[27] (a completely natural process typically produced wine at 9-10% alcohol). You might certainly argue that a better result was achieved by using chaptalization than by simply fortifying the wine by adding alcohol.[28]

But it's not at all clear that chaptalization is justified in the modern era. If a wine naturally would have an alcohol level of, let us say, 12%, wouldn't it be in better balance at this natural level than by bumping it up to 14% with chaptalization? The fact that chaptalization makes a heavier, some might say clumsier, wine is acknowledged in the AOC regulations in France, which limit chaptalization to a 2% increase in alcohol. That level, of course, was set many years ago, and if the process is to be allowed at all, it would certainly now be appropriate to significantly lower the permitted limit and to restrict more tightly when chaptalization can be used.[29]

A broader name for the procedure is "enrichment," which takes in other ways to provide the sugar, including preparations made from unfermented grape must. Enrichment, or *enrichissement* in French, is an interesting term, because what is enriched is more the grower than the wine. The economics of chaptalization are *very* advantageous. Producing wine from grapes might cost €9 per liter, but adding sugar costs only about €1.25 per liter of product.[30] And chaptalization increases the volume of the product, so you have more to sell.[31]

Producers who use chaptalization have to purchase the sugar through official channels and complete a form reporting the amount of sugar added to each volume of wine. But there are widespread suspicions that the rule has been honored as much in the breach as the observance. One producer in the Loire commented to me darkly that it was amazing how the supermarkets became full of large bags of sugar around harvest time. In the town of Beziers in the Languedoc (where goodness knows the weather is hot enough for addition of sugar to be unnecessary), the local supermarket used to announce "Le sucre est arrivé" by loudspeaker at harvest time.[32]

The sugar in grapes is a mixture of glucose and fructose, but the sugar in beets or maple syrup is largely sucrose. This doesn't make any difference to the outcome when it is fermented, but sugars from different sources have different characteristic levels of certain radioactive isotopes. Analysis of these isotopes in the wine by NMR (nuclear magnetic resonance) can be used to determine how much sugar was added from different sources, and is becoming a significant tool in combating fraud.

Periodically the authorities make an example: suspicion was aroused when large amounts of sugar were purchased from a supermarket near the Beaujolais wine region during the 2004 harvest season, and fines were later imposed on 53 producers and three branches of the Intermarché supermarket chain.[33] Very high fines (up to $27,000) aroused protest: "We want to make a good product, we didn't take the risk of ending up in court lightly, but we didn't have a choice—no one would have bought an 11% wine," said one of the winemakers, bowing to the God of high alcohol.

Even within the legal limits, the extent of chaptalization in France provides a significant proportion of the wine. Although the authorities have the detailed reports of sugar usage that must be completed by producers, they are strangely reluctant to release any information. (When I asked for details, Customs claimed that INAO—the organization responsible for administering the rules for AOC wines—have the information; INAO claimed that Customs have it.) But reports from the sugar producers proudly proclaim chaptalization to be one of the major uses of sugar in France,[34] and from their statistics, I calculate that chaptalization has applied to anywhere from 7% to 23% of the wine produced in France in recent years.[35] Is it comforting to know that at least three quarters of the wine is not chaptalized or disturbing to know that up to a quarter may be treated? If it wasn't for more than a century of tradition, it's entirely possible that chaptalization would be banned today as a swindle to turn sugar into alcohol.

The Mysteries of Malolactic Fermentation

"Malolactic fermentation happens in the wine in the spring by sympathy with the sap rising in the vines," used to be the vigneron's view. After alcoholic fermentation was complete in the autumn, the young wine was usually transferred to barrels to mature for a few months. It would remain quiescent typically until the spring, when another fermentation might (but did not always) occur. Called the malolactic fermentation (MLF), this reduces acidity and softens the wine by converting malic acid to lactic acid; not only is lactic acid weaker than malic acid, but it also offers a more creamy impression on the palate. No one knew why MLF happens, and it was often regarded as undesirable.

By the 1940s it was known that malolactic fermentation happens in the spring because at this point the cellars warm up enough to activate the bacteria that are responsible.[36] By the late 1950s, the great oenologist Emile Peynaud had isolated the bacteria and shown that inoculating wine with them could induce MLF.[37] Before Peynaud, producers tended to view MLF as a problem: after all, the wine had been quiescent for months, and now suddenly it started to bubble and release gas again![38] One of Peynaud's great contributions was to show that MLF could be controlled, and that in fact it usually improves the quality of the wine. Today MLF is regarded as essential for production of almost all red wines and for many white wines (especially non-aromatic, longer-lived wines such as Chardonnay). It is not usually performed with aromatic varieties, such as Riesling or Sauvignon Blanc, where it would interfere with the characteristic aroma spectrum.[39]

There is much more to MLF than simply the conversion of harsh malic acid (with its sharp taste of green apples) to soft lactic acid. It's malolactic fermentation that gives a wine those buttery aromas; this is due to formation of a compound called diacetyl, the same compound that gives buttered popcorn its characteristic smell. At low levels, diacetyl may be considered desirable, for example, in a buttery Chardonnay; but at higher levels it can become over-whelming. The level of diacetyl can be controlled by the duration of malolactic fermentation; it peaks before the end, so to maximize diacetyl, MLF is stopped (by adding sulfur dioxide), whereas to minimize it, wine is kept in contact with the malolactic bacteria as long as possible.

Where and when to perform the malolactic fermentation has become an issue in recent years. After the alcoholic fermentation (and any post-fermentation maceration) has finished, the wine is run off into new containers. In Burgundy, the tradition has been to go straight into barrels, whereas in Bordeaux, at least for the last century, the wine has been transferred to a larger vat.[40] Typically the wine would then rest until the spring before the malolactic fermentation began. More recently, and with much controversy, Bordeaux has been transferring the wine straight into barrel when fermentation is complete, and performing the malolactic conversion shortly after the transfer.[41] This makes the wine more attractive in the short term, especially at the point when the wines are first shown to critics just a few weeks later, but it's not clear that the exact timing or whether it's done in barrel makes any difference in the long term.

Heavier than Air

Carbon dioxide is heavier than air. Bubbling up through the must during fermentation, when one molecule of carbon dioxide is released for every sugar molecule converted to alcohol, it is responsible for the tumultuous appearance of a fermenting vat. After fermentation has been completed and the vat has been emptied out, carbon dioxide can sink into the vat to form a lethal layer devoid of oxygen. From time to time, people have been killed by carbon dioxide poisoning when trying to clean out vats after fermentation.

The release of carbon dioxide has both physical and chemical effects on fermentation. The act of bubbling through the liquid has a purging effect, and can carry volatile compounds along with the gas. This is another reason why it's important to control fermentation temperature; higher temperatures mean faster fermentation, which means a more rapid rate of release of CO2, and greater loss of aromatic compounds.

Under some circumstances, carbon dioxide forms a layer in the fermentation vat that changes the process of fermentation itself. This process, called carbonic maceration, originated naturally in the custom of putting whole clusters of grapes, uncrushed, into the fermenter. The grapes at the bottom are crushed by the weight of those above, releasing juice that is fermented by yeast in the usual way. The carbon dioxide released by this fermentation excludes oxygen around the intact grapes above them.[42] The lack of oxygen stops respiration, enzymes within the grapes are released, and they ferment the sugar within the grape. Yeast is not involved.

A lagar from the third century B.C. from Spain.

Carbonic maceration produces a wine that is purple, extremely fruity, and lacking tannins. It is suitable for short-term consumption. Malic acid is consumed during carbonic maceration, reducing overall acidity. Wines produced by carbonic maceration have lots of fermentation esters, resulting in aromas of banana, pineapple, bubblegum, and so on.

Beaujolais Nouveau is the classic example of a wine produced by carbonic maceration. These days the process is deliberately controlled. The vat is flushed with CO2 to remove oxygen and filled with whole bunches of grapes—the grapes must be unbroken in order to avoid an ordinary fermentation. The fermenter is kept under a blanket of carbon dioxide while fermentation proceeds. Carbonic maceration is usually just the first stage, and fermentation is not completed. Typically the juice is run off, the residue is pressed, and then the press-run juice and free-run juice are fermented together in the normal way.

Carbonic maceration has ancient origins. It's thought that wine was produced by semi-carbonic maceration in Roman times, when grapes were trodden in large lagares (troughs for holding wine with suitable holes for runoff), and the layer of carbon dioxide caused carbonic maceration in unbroken grapes. Lagares were also used for producing cider and olive oil, and have been excavated all over the wine-producing areas of Spain. Winemaking in Rioja in the nineteenth century used light treading in a lagar, which typically left the majority of grapes unbroken.[43] Similar methods are still used in Navarra, where they are called the método rural (rural method).[44]

Filtration: Stripping the Wine?

"Wine is a living thing." You see this said time and time again.[45] From this comes the concept that if you filter the wine, evisceration is inevitable. But no, wine is not alive: and if it provides a home for living organisms (bacteria or yeast) it will very likely be spoiled in short order. Certainly wine (or at least higher quality wine) is not static but evolves with time; and certainly we can ask what components are removed by filtration, and to what extent they might be necessary for this evolution. But let's base the discussion on a clear understanding that wine is a mixture of water and alcohol containing dissolved components, or perhaps more accurately that it is what chemists would call a colloidal suspension, in which some of its components aren't really dissolved into the liquid but rather are very fine particles suspended in it. If wine is a "thing," it is chemical not biological.

At the end of fermentation, the new wine is a cloudy solution with all sorts of gunk suspended in it. It is not attractive, and is far from the bright, clean appearance that the modern consumer demands. It may be clarified by a natural settling process (débourbage in French) or by the addition of various fining agents that cause suspended matter to precipitate out and fall to the bottom. Fining agents include proteins, siliceous earths, various synthetic polymers, and a clay called bentonite.[46] One current controversy is whether these agents, which don't remain in the wine, should be considered as additives for legal purposes. Also, they can affect whether the wine is considered suitable for specific purposes; for example, some agents would prevent a wine being kosher or being appropriate for vegans.

Before a wine is matured in barrel, the suspended matter (the *gross lees*) is allowed to settle for a day or so. This gives a cloudy solution, but without any large particles. The wine may stay in barrels for up to two years and more material will drop out of suspension to the bottom during this time. This is the *fine lees*, consisting of dead yeast cells and other materials. Fine wines may be kept in contact with the (fine) lees for several months to enable them to absorb compounds from the lees; this increases flavor complexity. The overall result of maturation on the lees is a creamy, richer texture.

The lees also have a protective effect on the wine. They provide a reducing environment, which antagonizes oxidation. Periodically the lees are stirred up (this is called battonage, because originally it used to be performed with a baton

The Oxoline system allows barrels to be stacked in rows and rotated on rollers.

Wine is being racked from the upper barrel to the lower barrel at a Bordeaux château.

The transfer tube is just above the level of the lees in the upper barrel, and transfer is stopped as soon as sediment appears in the tube.

or stick). Battonage prevents reductive flavors from developing in the vicinity of the lees. These days it can be performed more easily by keeping the barrels on a roller system that allows them to be rotated in place (some winemakers call them spinning barrels).

The alchemy of modern winemaking has developed preparations to substitute for aging on the lees. These include various compounds that enhance a round feeling in the wine, interact with tannins to soften red wine, and inhibit browning of white wine.

Maturation in barrel inevitably involves some exposure to oxygen, although it is probably not (as traditionally held) due to seepage of air between the staves of the barrel. Emile Peynaud calculated that oxygen penetration through the wood cask is insignificant.[47] Even though barrels are regularly topped up to compensate for evaporation, there's always some exposure to a headspace of air in the barrel. From time to time (typically every three months) the wine is racked off the lees into a new barrel. The traditional way of doing this is to burn a sulfur candle in the new barrel, and then to siphon the wine into it from a barrel at a higher level; these days there are gentler systems involving compressed gas to push the wine from barrel to barrel. Some oxidative exposure occurs under conventional racking, although it can be minimized by racking under a blanket of inert gas.

When the wine has completed its maturation, it is clarified to give a nice bright appearance. Traditionally for red wines this involves using egg whites, several per barrel. The albumin in the egg white catches suspended material and precipitates it to the bottom of the barrel. Because the albumin is positively charged, it interacts with negatively charged tannins, reducing the overall level and giving a necessary softening to the wine. Of course, it is now possible to use albumin or other preparations rather than egg whites themselves. This is a far cry from the old days: Maria Lopez de Heredia recalls that her bodega in Rioja had a farm with chickens in order to provide a supply of egg whites, and when times were really hard during the war, the chickens provided a source of revenue that kept the company going.[48]

Some treatments are unnecessary technically, but necessary (unfortunately) in order to pacify consumers. All wines contain tartaric acid, and in the form of potassium tartrate, it easily precipitates out in the bottle, forming colorless crystals. The crystals are completely harmless, but can be confused with shards of glass by less knowledgeable consumers. To avoid alarming people and having the bottles returned, producers use cold stabilization, which involves chilling the wine to –4 °C in a cooling tank. A thick layer of ice forms on the outside of the tank, while inside the cold precipitates the tartrate crystals. This prevents any crystallization from happening later.[49]

Cold stabilization largely fixes problems with precipitation for white wines, but red wines are naturally prone to throw sediments. Even after fining, wine is still a colloidal suspension, and tannins or other suspended material can fall out of solution to form a sediment. A whole host of filtration methods are available to treat the wine. This is one of the most controversial stages in wine production. The basic issue is simply how finely the wine is filtered. You will sometimes see a label on quality wines saying "unfiltered," to demonstrate that the wine has been bottled in its natural state.

Wine is a wonderfully receptive host for microorganisms, especially Aceto-bacter, bacteria that can turn it into vinegar. (The bacteria that like to live on wine are not at all dangerous to people, so there is little danger that a contaminated wine will be harmful, but it is not likely to be pleasant to drink.) The most stringent form of treatment to prevent contamination is a sterile filtration, passing the wine across a membrane with pores that are too small to let bacteria through.[50]

Filtration removes suspended particles from the wine. The question is how this changes the nature of the wine, and whether these particles are needed for the wine to mature. The answer is not straightforward, as different types of filters work in different ways. On the one hand, the holes in a sterile filter that are too small to let bacteria through are still more than a hundred times larger than flavor molecules. On the other hand, filters that work by absorption may not discriminate by size. Industrial production can use pretty brutal filtration methods that take everything out to leave a completely bright, clear wine.

The eminent oenologue Pascal Ribéreau-Gayon expresses the technical view: "Filtration... is intended to eliminate turbidity, foreign bodies, and impurities... It would be ridiculous to suggest that these substances make a positive contribution to flavor. Contrary to a widely held opinion, clear wine always tastes better than the same wine with even slight turbidity."[51] Ribéreau-Gayon believes that the complete absence of filtration is problematic for red wines and that some filtration is essential for white wines.[52]

The problem is probably not so much light filtration to clear the wine, but extensive use of the filters. The critic Robert Parker has been on a campaign against excessive filtration for years: "The effect of excessive manipulation of wine, particularly overly aggressive fining and filtration, is dramatic. It destroys a wine's bouquet as well as its ability to express its *terroir* and varietal character. It also mutes the vintage's character. Fining and filtration can be lightly done, causing only minor damage, but most wines produced in the New World (California, Australia, and South America in particular), and most bulk wines produced in Europe are sterile-filtered. This procedure requires numerous pre-filtrations to get the wines clean enough to pass through a micropore membrane filter. This system of wine stability and clarification strips, eviscerates, and denudes a wine of much of its character."[53]

You Can't Taste the Color

Red wine is all about extraction—extraction of color and tannins. Extraction used to be a relatively simple affair. When indigenous yeast were used, there was a lag period before fermentation started, so some exposure of juice to skins was inevitable. During fermentation the skins and other solid matter would rise to the top of the vat, and one technique or another would be used to immerse them periodically in the must. After fermentation, the wine would often be left for a few days before being run off. This would give a decent level of extraction of color and tannins; but anyone who remembers the wines of twenty or thirty years ago knows they were not so deeply colored as today, and measurements show a significant rise in tannin levels since then. The change is due partly to harvesting riper grapes and partly to better methods for extracting color and tannins.

Color and tannins are both in the general class of compounds known as polyphenols.[54] The "poly" in polyphenol indicates that the molecule consists of a chain of phenols linked together. Polyphenols come in a range of sizes, depending on the length of the chain, and one of their important properties is the ability to interact with one another to form longer chains. This softens their effect on the palate. And then as the chains extend (polymerize is the technical term), they reach a point at which they become too large to remain suspended in solution; they precipitate out to form the sediment at the bottom of the bottle. This reduces bitterness and color in the wine. This change in the tannins is an important aspect in the maturation of red wines, and explains why they may start out as bitter, but become softer and gentler with time.

The tannins give structure to a wine—that sense of texture extending beyond mere fruit flavors. More than half of the tannins are in the skin, but stalks and seeds also have a good amount. Tannins are bitter and the sense of a dry mouth you get after drinking a young Cabernet Sauvignon is due to the effect of the tannins in binding to the salivary proteins. In fact, one of the chemical methods for measuring the level of tannin is based upon its ability to interact with the protein serum albumin (found in saliva).

Tannins vary from relatively benign and ripe to astringent and stalky. Tannins in the stalks are somewhat harsher than those in the skin, which is why a noticeable softening occurred in Bordeaux wines when destemming (removing the stems before fermentation) was widely introduced from the 1970s.[55] The tannins in the seeds are the harshest of all, making it important to avoid pressing hard enough to extract tannins from them.[56] The quality of the tannins changes as the berries mature, going from green or stalky character to riper, better rounded

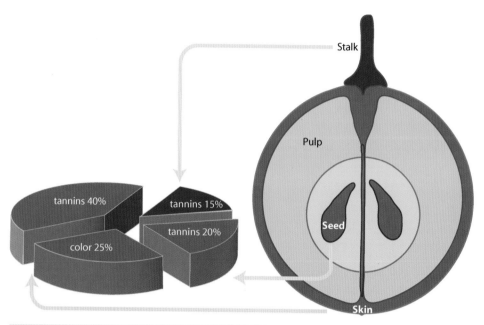

The skin of the berry is the major source of polyphenols, including all of the color and most of the tannins. Seeds and stalks contain harsher tannins than the skin. Per cents in the pie chart indicate the typical proportion of all polyphenols (total color = 25%, total tannins = 75%).

character. The amount of tannins depends on the grape variety, ranging from 1 g/l in a light-bodied red wine to 6 g/l in a heavily extracted full-bodied wine.

It's not straightforward to get a clear measure of the total quantity of tannins—different methods of measurement can give different answers.[57] There is even less agreement on how to assess the quality of tannins. As grapes develop, the total amount of tannins increases, and you can tell by taste that they become less bitter and astringent, but there's no chemical measure of how different tannins affect taste. The general concept that grapes should be harvested only when they reach "phenolic ripeness," is inevitably somewhat imprecise.

Tannins in wine come from the grapes, and are also extracted from the wood if the wine is matured in new oak barrels. Grape tannins are extracted into the juice by contact with the skin. Alcohol affects which tannins are extracted, so a cold maceration (when the juice is held in contact with the skin before fermentation) has different effects from maceration post fermentation (when alcohol is at its peak). During fermentation, extraction of color and tannins occurs as the cap of skins that forms on the top of the tank is pushed into the juice (*pigeage* or *punch-down*) or as juice is sprayed back over the cap (*pumping-over*). Pigeage is usually used for varieties where less overall extraction is wanted (such as Pinot Noir), whereas pumping-over achieves high extraction (and is usually used for Cabernet Sauvignon).[58] Today, enzymes that help to break down cell walls are sometimes added to help increase the level of extraction.[59]

The fact that color and tannins in wine both come from extraction of polyphenols often leads to the completely mistaken assumption that darker wines are better than light colored wines. But you can't taste the color! Subject to the caveat that some varieties are more pigmented than others, you might argue that a wine of some varietal that is darker than another of the same varietal is likely to have a greater level of overall extraction, because color is not extracted in isolation but in combination with other components. But it is not inevitably true that more extracted wines will be better than less extracted wines; and it is certainly not true that the density of coloring matter per se has any effect on the qualities of the wine.

Burgundy has always been a relatively light color, because Pinot Noir is not a heavily pigmented grape, and sometimes the light color is regarded as a disadvantage in the marketplace. Many of the more deeply colored Burgundies that can be found today owe their origins to the introduction of extended cold maceration in the 1980s by the oenologist Guy Accad. A much deeper color and level of extraction was achieved by keeping crushed grapes for up to 10 days before allowing fermentation to start.[60] Accad's techniques are deeply controversial: some believe they bring a modern approach to Burgundy, while to others the approach is an anathema that destroys typical wine qualities.[61]

By contrast with tannins, color can be more precisely measured in terms of both density and hue. Although it has no organoleptic effects, it is useful, as an indication of age and (sometimes) of the condition of a wine. Red wines lose intensity of color with age, and the hue changes from purple to orange. White wines show the reverse effect, and tend to darken with age.

Color is due to polyphenols, including both anthocyanins (purple or red pigments) and tannins (lighter red-brown colors), which are extracted from the skins during fermentation. The dark colors of varieties such as Cabernet Sauvignon and Syrah are due to the high content of anthocyanins. Varieties such as Pinot Noir, Sangiovese, and Nebbiolo give lighter colored wines, because they have less anthocyanins.[62] With age, anthocyanins polymerize (form longer chains) as

Fifty years of Lafite shows how the color changes from purple to red to orange and lightens as it ages.

The purple wine on the left is Château Lafite 2003; the garnet colored wine in the center is the 1978 vintage; the light colored wine on the right is Lafite 1945.

The 1945 was still vibrant and by far the best of the three in 2010.

Young dry white wine is pale, old white wine is darker.

The wine on the left is a Puligny Montrachet from 2005; on the right is the same wine from 1990.

The younger wine was fresh and steely; the older wine tasted somewhat oxidized.

Sweet wines also are deeper in color.

the result of oxidation and fall out of solution, causing both a change in hue (anthocyanins change from blue to red, and tannins change from red to brown) and a general lightening of color intensity.

But there is more to color than simply the concentration or types of anthocyanins. When black grapes are fermented, pigments are extracted from the skin, but this is not of itself enough to ensure good color. Anthocyanins are unstable and have to be "fixed" by conversion to a stable form.[63] The effect of other factors on the color pigments is called copigmentation;[64] it can account for up to half the color of young red wine, and also is responsible for shifting the color spectrum from red towards purple.[65] Low concentrations of cofactors add to the low color profile of varieties such as Pinot Noir.

Sometimes additional color concentration is obtained by cofermenting different varieties together, because one contains cofactors that act on the pigments of another. An especially striking demonstration of this effect is the ability of white grapes to increase color in red wines.[66] The effect depends on the relative proportions of black and white grapes included in the same fermentation vat; probably it peaks at around 10% white grapes, because up to that point, increasing cofactor concentration enhances color; above that point the white juice reduces color overall.[67] It used to be the case that black and white grapevines were intermingled in the vineyard, resulting in cofermentation of both types of grapes in the same vat, increasing color in the wine, whether the winemakers knew it or not.[68]

The basis for color in white wine is more mysterious. The pale yellow-green-straw color of most white wines is due to another class of phenolic compounds found in the skin, called flavonoids.[69] Oxidation of the flavonoids gives wine a golden color as it ages. Since skin contact is limited in white-wine production, the skin color of the grapes has little effect, although some color is gained if there is a cold maceration before fermentation. (Skin contact—called maceration pélliculaire—is used for some white varieties such as Muscat or Sauvignon Blanc, in order to extract aromatic compounds.) Some faint coloration of the pulps of some varieties contributes slightly to color, as in a faint pink in Gewürztraminer. Barrel fermenting or oak-aging produce darker yellow colors by extracting non-flavonoid phenols, principally lignins, from the oak. Deep color in a dry white wine is an indication of possible oxidation.

In the Pink

"Rosés are not wine," the sommelier at a Michelin-starred restaurant in London said to me in disgust when I mentioned that I would be visiting Provence and might try the local wines. True enough, many rosés are made for extraneous reasons—in many cases the main purpose is to improve a red wine rather than to make a good rosé—but rosé production has been increasing lately, with more serious attempts to make good rosé in its own right. So what are the real characteristics of rosé?[70]

How much pink is needed to be rosé and how much is too much? Rosé wines are not well defined, but are made from red grapes with low extraction of color. (Historically, before modern methods for extraction, red wines may have been not so much more deeply colored than the rosés of today.) Several different methods are used for making rosé, with varying results for quality. At its best, a rosé should be delicate, with the freshness of a light white wine, but with just that very faint touch of additional structure, a barely perceptible taint of austerity, coming from skin extraction.

The color intensity of a rosé wine depends on how much skin contact is allowed before the juice is separated. Using white winemaking methods with red grapes produces the lightest colored rosés; the grapes are pressed immediately, and the juice is kept in contact with the skins in the press for only a very short time, while the crushed grapes are being drained. Deeper colors are produced by allowing skin contact for a few hours, somewhat equivalent to maceration pélliculaire for white wines. As with white wines, this enhances softness and fruit, and reduces acidity.[71]

An alternative method is to use a saignée (literally a "bleeding") from vats used in conventional red winemaking. Most often, the main purpose of saignée is to improve the quality of the red wine, and the rosé is a byproduct. By drawing the first juice out of the vat, concentration is increased in the remaining red wine. This juice is rosé because it has not had much time to absorb compounds from the skins.

A major distinction between the two methods comes from their different purposes. When your main objective is a quality red wine, you are looking for fully ripe grapes. A saignée from the must gives different results from macerating grapes produced specifically for making rosé, where preservation of acidity and freshness is as important as ripeness. Jorge Muga, who produces a fine rosé at Bodegas Muga in Rioja, uses grapes from specific vineyards—"it is not a plan B used to improve the quality of the red wine," he told me, pointing out that the grapes are grown in shadier conditions to obtain the higher acidity and lower color appropriate for rosé.[72] Better results are obtained by using higher yields than you would for a red wine, so there is no green harvest, and by managing the vineyard so as to harvest the grapes a little less ripe than they would be for red wine production.

Of course you can make a rosé wine technically by blending in a little red to give color to a white wine. This is illegal in the European Union, except for Champagne where it's relatively common to put a little dry red wine in the mix to give a rosé its color. (Although some champagnes are made by extracting a little color from the red grapes during winemaking.) It is perfectly legal, and not uncommon, in the New World, however, to blend red and white to make pink wine.

But when E.U. Agriculture Commissioner Mariann Fischer Boel proposed early in 2009 to allow production of rosé-colored wines by mixing red and white wines, there was outrage. Presented as a reform that would allow better competition with the New World, the proposal was easily approved by the member states (including France). The fact that the proposal applied only to Vin de Table (meaning that quality wines would still have to be produced by traditional methods) was lost in the brouhaha. "The battle for rosé's nobility risks being lost with a wave of Europe's magic wand," says Xavier de Volontat, president of the French union of wine producers.[73] The blending option would lead to "economic and social destruction," he adds. First reactions at the E.U. were to dig in, but finally they were forced to retract the proposed rule change.[74]

So what is the difference? A "rosé" made by blending uses 3-4% of red wine to color a white wine, so it is essentially made from white grapes. A traditional rosé is made from a black grape variety; most often Grenache, Cinsault, Carignan, even Syrah, Mourvèdre, Cabernet Franc, and Pinot Noir, so the aromatic spectrum is different (although rosé shows the origin of the variety less clearly than either red or white wine). And carefully making a traditional rosé has a more subtle process of extraction. Also, it is more expensive than simply blending in a little red wine, which is why the change was such a threat to traditional producers. What would very likely have happened is that large quantities of unsellable white wine, stored as part of the wine lake, would have been turned into "rosé" to flood the market.[75] Would this be fraud or would this be fraud? The results of the controversy, however, do somewhat leave begging the question of why it is acceptable to blend in red wine to make rosé Champagne.

Rosés are usually dry in France, but are often off-dry in other winemaking regions. The "blush wines," in particular the white Zinfandels, of California are typical examples of pink wines made in an off-dry style.

Sulfur Dioxide: the Essential Preservative

Sulfur dioxide has been used in winemaking for several hundred years. When the Romans first started using wooden barrels, they discovered that burning a sulfur candle inside the empty barrel had a fumigant effect. Its specific effect in preserving wine was recognized when the use of burning sulfur was authorized for wine production in Prussia in 1487. The technique was introduced into modern winemaking by the Dutch in the eighteenth century.[76] Addition of sulfur dioxide as such (directly as a gas or by addition of potassium metabisulfite powder which releases sulfur dioxide when it dissolves) dates only from the twentieth century.[77]

Sulfur dioxide has two important roles: it is an antimicrobial agent that acts as a preservative by inhibiting growth of undesirable yeasts and bacteria; and it is an anti-oxidant that protects fruit and wine against damage from oxygen. Sulfur dioxide exists in two forms. The form that is most effective as an antimicrobial agent is the free gas (molecular $SO2$). When it dissolves in water, it generates sulfites, and this form is the most effective as an anti-oxidant.

Sulfur dioxide is used at all stages from harvesting to bottling. Grapes are often dusted with potassium metabisulfite (which releases $SO2$) when they are harvested, to protect them from oxidation before they make it into the vat. A low level of sulfur dioxide may be added at the start of fermentation to inhibit the wild yeasts. Sulfur dioxide is used as a protective agent while wine is maturing in barrels; and it is added at bottling as a sterilizing agent.

It's almost impossible to make wine without sulfur dioxide. Only "almost" because there are a few brave organic producers who do just that:[78] but it's an uphill battle to end up with wine rather than vinegar. And it's impossible to be sure of completely avoiding any sulfites in the wine because very low levels can be produced naturally during fermentation.[79] Any wine containing more than 10 ppm (parts per million) of sulfites has to carry the warning "contains sulfites" in both the E.U. and U.S.A: this means that all wines must be labeled irrespective of whether the level is actually likely to cause any health problems.

Used with a very wide range of foods, sulfur dioxide is probably the most common food preservative in existence. The reason for the warning is that some people are allergic to sulfites. But very few people are allergic to the levels in wine, although a small minority cannot tolerate any level.[80] Sulfur dioxide levels are actually much lower in wines than in foods in general; for example, preserved fruits may have more than 1000 ppm, whereas a wine typically will have somewhat less than 100 ppm.

Because the polyphenols in red wine have an anti-oxidative effect, red wine does not need as much $SO2$ as white wine. And because sweet wines have sugar that can provide an excellent medium for yeast to grow, they require much higher levels of $SO2$. The levels permitted in bottled wine are regulated everywhere wine is made, although of course the details vary with the country.[81] However, the regulations are a bit of a myth in the European Union, where they apply rigorously only for imported wines. Local producers can bypass them by taking advantage of the exceptions allowing higher limits for sweet wines.

There are simply no good alternatives to sulfur dioxide. Pasteurization by flash-heating the wine has been controversial ever since Pasteur proposed it as a means of sterilization.[82] Most producers feel it damages the organoleptic properties and inhibits the development of complexity. An exception is the Burgundian producer Louis Latour, which has used the technique virtually since it was invented, but some people feel the red wines fail to achieve their full potential as a result.[83] And in any case, pasteurization will not prevent oxidation.

It is, however, a myth that sulfur dioxide actually prevents oxidation from occurring. When wine is exposed to oxygen, alcohol (ethanol) is converted to acetaldehyde. This is a compound found in oxidized styles of wine, such as fino Sherry, where it contributes to the characteristic nutty aromas. What sulfur dioxide really does in wine is to combine with the acetaldehyde, forming an odorless compound that does not change the wine's aroma. (This is why sulfur dioxide is not used in the production of fino Sherry.)

Sulfur dioxide's action in removing acetaldehyde makes attempts to reduce it to absolutely minimal levels in order to reduce allergic reactions not exactly misguided, but possibly futile. Acetaldehyde is an allergen (something that provokes allergic reactions), and there comes a point at which reduction of sulfur dioxide is counterbalanced by the increase in acetaldehyde. Unfortunately, some level of allergens may be inevitable, irrespective of efforts made to reduce sulfur dioxide, histamines, or other components.[84]

The need for SO2 is significantly affected by the type of closure. The thinking about what levels of SO2 are necessary (and the regulations) go back to a time when all wine was bottled under cork. Because corks allow some exchange of air with the outside as they age, more sulfur dioxide is needed to protect the wine than in the case of a wine bottled under screwcap, which can come close to a hermetic seal. So producers are slowly rethinking their protocols for using SO2 as they move to other closures than corks in bottles.

Residual Sugar

Left alone, fermentation will continue until almost all the sugar in the must has been converted to alcohol. But the yeast have their limits. Most yeast cannot function at alcohol levels over 15%. So if the must has so much sugar that there is still some left when fermentation reaches 15% alcohol, the process will stop, leaving a sweet wine. Some of the great dessert wines are made in this way, by harvesting grapes very late, when sugar levels have become very high. Sauternes, the late harvest wines of the Loire and Alsace, the sweet wines of Italy, and the ice wines of Canada, all are made in this way.

In all of these wines, the high sugar levels get some help from natural processes. When grapes are left on the vine after the regular harvest date, a certain amount of dehydration occurs, called passerillage in France; by reducing water content in the grape, this increases the concentration of sugar, and the grapes are said to be passerillé. A more forceful concentration occurs when the fungus Botrytis cinerea infects the grapes. Forming a unpleasant looking mold on the surface of the skin, it extracts water and greatly concentrates sugar. But as well as being more concentrated, botrytized grapes have more intense flavors than berries that are merely passerillé, because the botrytis also adds notes of honey and increases volatile acidity (acetic acid), giving that delicious tang of honeyed piquancy.

Winemakers in warm climates have often developed methods for helping the natural process of dehydration after grapes are harvested. The old method of Vin de Paille (wine of straw) in the south of France consists of allowing the grapes to dry out on straw mats in the sun before they are pressed and fermented. Grapes are dried in warm attics to make the dessert wines Vin Santo and Recioto in Italy. Because the grapes are exposed to air during these processes, the wines usually have a slightly oxidized quality.

It's also possible to retain residual sugar in the wine by stopping fermentation before it is completed. One way to do this is to stop the yeast from working, most commonly by adding sulfur dioxide and/or lowering the temperature. This is how sweet German wines are made; and since fermentation is typically only a bit more than half complete when this happens, the resulting wine has relatively low alcohol, in the range of 8-10%. The result can be a beautifully balanced wine, sweet certainly, but with refreshing and lively acidity.

A more dramatic way of stopping fermentation is simply to add enough alcohol to bring the level over 15%, at which the yeast die, and the wine will be stable. This is the basis for all sweet wines based on fortification, such as Port. The sweetness of the wine is due to the sugar that had not been fermented by the time the brandy was added. Fortified wines have an advantage that they are stable against refermentation, whereas sweet wines with alcohol below 15% need to be protected against any reinfection with yeast, usually by keeping the level of sulfur dioxide high.

Natural Wine or Unnatural Practices?

So you are drinking a glass of wine. It is a clear, limpid red color, the nose shows the characteristics commonly associated with its variety, refreshing acidity supports the typical fruits on the palate, and it has a nice long finish. In short, it has precisely the characteristics you expect of that grape variety and place, and you would be able to identify it as such any day in a blind tasting. But is this typicity the natural and inevitable result of minimalist winemaking allowing the wine to establish its own intrinsic character; or is it the result of multiple small interventions and decisions by the winemaker, directing the wine's development down a path that satisfies the historical expectations and traditions of this variety and place?

Let's just follow the grape juice as it turns into wine. Grapes are crushed or pressed and fermented. Even for a minimalist producer, probably the fermentation will take place at a controlled temperature; the choice of this temperature will have a significant effect on how much color and tannin is extracted into a red wine, and whether a white wine emphasizes fruit or other qualities. And you have to choose whether to let the grapes macerate before and after fermentation; whatever you decide will also have an effect on the level of extraction. Malolactic fermentation can be used as opportunity for further control, although a minimalist producer may let it happen (or not) naturally. If the wine is matured in wood, you have to choose whether to use new oak or old oak, and if new oak is used, what toasting regime it has; this has a great effect on the transmission of flavors to the wine.

Sometimes people talk about winemaking in terms of intervention, the pre-sumption being that less intervention makes a more natural wine. Yet minimalist winemaking may not always be quite what it seems, or at least may not neces-sary involve the minimal extent of change to the wine after fermentation. Consider this tale of two wines produced by Nikolaus Moser at the Sepp Moser Weingut in Austria's Kremstal valley. Schnabel is a tiny vineyard just north of the Danube in the eastern part of Krems. Sepp Moser grow both Grüner Veltliner and Sauvignon Blanc here, and from the Grüner they make two entirely different wines from the same grapes.

Most of the wine is treated conventionally. It ferments (spontaneously) in stainless steel for about 2 weeks, and then the wine rests on the lees for 7 months and is bottled. It is pale in color, brilliantly clear, light and fresh, with faintly aromatic, spicy primary fruits, a very approachable example of a modern Grüner.

The smaller lot is called MINIMAL to reflect minimalist winemaking, with as little intervention as possible. The wine ferments in 300 liter barrels of old Aus-trian oak; fermentation takes 3 months to complete and the wine also goes (spontaneously) through malolactic fermentation. No sulfur is added, the wine is left on the lees for a year, then it is racked once with a little sulfur added, and bottled the following May. The wine is a medium golden color, not quite clear, and shows a complex, developed nose in a faintly oxidative style.[85] There's a creamy texture on the palate, and dense layers of flavor, somewhat in the style of gracefully aging old Burgundy.

The question is what's really the "minimal" treatment?[86] There was far less control by the winemaker for the MINIMAL wine, but actually much more hap-pened to it: oxidative exposure during prolonged alcoholic fermentation, malolactic fermentation, and a long exposure to the lees in the oak barrels. So you might quarrel with "minimal" as a description, but call this traditional at least. There's no doubt which wine most consumers would prefer: simple and fruity will fly off the supermarket shelf every time. But there's also no doubt which is by far the most interesting wine in terms of aroma and flavor variety, and for that matter, which will probably still be of interest several years from now. Minimalist or traditionalist, old versus new, it's all choices—and every choice changes the wine.

Even a minimalist can't but help make decisions that affect the nature of the wine. You could leave the wine to ferment with indigenous yeast and without temperature control (and periodically probably lose a vintage to spoilage or stuck fermentation), you can leave malolactic fermentation to chance, but you have to decide how long to leave the wine to macerate after fermentation before you run off the juice; and you have to decide what you are going to put the juice into, and how long it is going to stay there before you bottle it. And these days there is a good case to be made that the decision between cork and screwcap will influence the nature and development of the wine in the bottle.

No: wine does not make itself in the vineyard. The winemaker makes the wine.

6

The Alchemist's Delight

WINE IS BASICALLY A MIXTURE OF ALCOHOL AND WATER with various flavoring compounds dissolved or suspended in it. Its complexity derives from a very large number of compounds, each present in tiny quantities. The intricate relationship between aroma and flavor is explained by the presence of hundreds of small, volatile molecules; so far no one has been able to account for all of the components in any one wine, although we now have a pretty good idea of the principal aroma and flavor components that are characteristic of each major grape variety.

A purist might think that, in a natural wine, these components derive directly from the grapes that were harvested in the vineyard. But hold on a moment! With one or two exceptions, grape juice shows little varietal character; each variety develops its typical aromas and flavors during fermentation.

Yeast work furiously during alcoholic fermentation to modify or synthesize a wide range of compounds in the must. The resulting changes in the aroma and flavor spectrum are why wine smells and tastes different from grape juice. Then malolactic fermentation not only reduces the acidity, but also changes the flavor spectrum yet again. And, of course, when wines are matured in oak barrels, compounds leach into the wine from the oak to change it yet further.

All of these processes—alcoholic fermentation, malolactic fermentation, exposure to oak—can be used by the winemaker to emphasize or de-emphasize particular qualities in the wine. Winemakers like to say wine is made in the vineyard, and it's certainly true that getting healthy, ripe berries is a prerequisite: but it's one of the biggest myths of all that making the best wine requires only minimal intervention. Without intervention, wine is rapidly converted to vinegar.

Since some intervention is essential, and given that some means of intervention are hallowed by tradition, it's not always clear where to draw the line between artisanal winemaking and industrial process. Chaptalization, the addi-

The approach has become more scientific since Brueghel the Elder pictured the alchemist at work in 1558.

tion of sugar to the grape juice in order to increase the alcohol level during fermentation, is a couple of centuries old, and rarely arouses controversy. The use of modern techniques, such as reverse osmosis, evaporation under vacuum, or spinning cone, to remove water or alcohol is viewed with more suspicion. Dunking oak chips in the wine instead of putting the wine into oak barrels is on the edge; and what about the addition of oak flavoring compounds? Removal or addition of the typical volatile flavoring compounds of each grape variety is frowned upon; but addition of artificial coloring compounds, although not acknowledged, is practiced widely in the New World. Where does natural wine turn into an artificial beverage?

Is the winemaker of today the equivalent of the alchemist of the middle ages? The alchemist searched for a means of turning base metal into gold. The winemaker has a huge arsenal of devices for influencing alcohol level, acidity, sweetness, color, volatile aromas, and tannins. But the winemaker is a lot more successful in turning his grape juice into liquid gold than the alchemist ever was.

Alcohol: Finding the Sweet Spot

There wouldn't be much point to wine if it didn't have alcohol, and for one reason and another, the exact level is considered important. The first myth about alcohol levels is that the label accurately represents what is in the bottle. The European Union requires labels to identify alcohol levels within 0.5%; and the level must be stated in terms of an 0.5% interval. A wine labeled at 12.5% could have alcohol between 12% and 13%. The United States and Australia require accuracy only within 1.5%, so a wine labeled 12.5% could be anything between 11% and 14%.[1] Accuracy is further reduced by distortions resulting from the tax laws: tax on wine increases when the level goes over 14% alcohol in the United States, where it's strange how many wines are on the market with stated levels of 13.9%, just squeezing into the lower tax bracket.

When most wine was made from grapes grown under slightly adverse climatic conditions in Europe, more often than not it was a struggle to reach adequate alcohol levels. At least in more northern regions, it was only with the aid of chaptalization that a level approaching 12% or 12.5% was attained. But now far more wine comes from new wine-producing regions that are consistently warmer, and global warming has pushed up sugar levels in grapes from the old regions. It's ironic that alcohol levels in wine have been steadily increasing more or less in parallel with concerns about the effects of excess consumption that have led to more and more stringent regulations on what you can buy and how you can drink it. But whether the potential alcohol in the grapes is too low or too high, the winemaker now has a whole new range of ways to change it.

Chaptalization by tipping sugar into the must before fermentation remains the traditional way to increase alcohol. A modern alternative is to take some water out. Various machines, known generically as concentrators, can remove water. Some producers claim this gives a more natural result. This might be true when there's been rain just before harvest, and the grapes are nicely ripe except for this last minute dilution. But when the growing season has not been so good, and the grapes aren't perfectly ripe, removing water concentrates all components, not just the sugar, and so may intensify anything that's out of balance. And what does pushing it around do to the wine? It's an interesting contrast

This reverse osmosis machine is small and portable. To increase potential alcohol from 11% to 12.5% for 300 hl of must (equivalent to 40,000 bottles) would take about 10 hours.

Photograph kindly provided by Bucher Vaslin.

This evaporation sous vide machine is kept in a locked room at a Bordeaux château.

with the trend to building wineries where the wine moves only by gravity so that it is not disturbed by pumping.

The simplest and least expensive method to remove water is by reverse osmosis. This works on the same principle as osmosis, when water crosses a membrane to equalize the concentrations of substances dissolved in it. In typical osmosis, water crosses from the side of the membrane that has a low concentration of substances to the side that has a high concentration. In reverse osmosis, the direction of flow is reversed by applying pressure, so water can be extracted from must.

Some producers prefer the method of evaporation sous vide (evaporation under vacuum). This uses the principle that water boils at lower temperatures as the pressure is reduced. In a vacuum evaporation machine, the pressure is brought low enough for water to evaporate at 20 °C (68 °F). In Bordeaux, where in spite of global warming the climate still does not produce really ripe grapes every year, and where rain is common around harvest time, reverse osmosis machines and vacuum evaporation appear to be used about equally. They are usually hidden away from visitors.

Going in the other direction, the worldwide trend to harvest increasingly riper grapes has pushed up alcohol levels. For some producers, phenolic ripeness is all, and the wine is bottled with whatever alcohol level results. Others take advantage of new methods that allow alcohol levels to be reduced. The simplest method is actually the oldest: adding water to the must. This is illegal in Europe, where it is regarded as fraudulent. But it is sometimes practiced in California, although it was considered illegal until 2002, when there was a change in interpretation of the regulations (resulting from the need to add water to help stuck fermentations in musts of very high Brix). Nominally this is still the only reason why water can be added, but as a practical matter, water can now be added to dilute must or juice down to a level of 22° Brix to facilitate fermentation. (Watering back is limited to 7% dilution in California.) There are no statistics on how frequently it is employed, but its extension into general winemaking might be regarded as a swindle.

Saignée is the opposite of watering back. Some juice is run off at the start of fermentation of black grapes, increasing the ratio of skin to liquid in order to get a more concentrated red wine. The run-off juice is usually used to make a rosé. Saignée is most commonly used with varieties such as Pinot Noir that have less intense color. Like all techniques that change the balance of wine, this is contro-versial. Producers who use it believe it is a more natural alternative to other methods of concentration. "It is one of the most natural ways to enhance the flavor profile of a given wine without chemical manipulations," one winemaker told me.[2] "Any winemaker worth his salt will use this on occasion to get the best out of a particular style of wine or grape variety," says another.[3] Almost half the winemakers in California admit to using it routinely or occasionally.[4] The other half view it with disdain. "My rosés are made from pressed grapes because I believe wines should reflect the vintage and the place they were grown. If it was necessary, I would probably make a rosé out of the entire lot rather than manipu-late the red wine must!" says one winemaker.[5] "Usually this technique or sleight of hand does not produce wines of elegance (however wines of elegance are not in vogue)," another told me.[6]

The majority of winemakers see saignée as a remedial technique, and like other techniques for concentration, it may be appropriate when there has been dilution from rain at harvest. Some producers in California combine watering back with saignée; and there's a trend in California (legal but not publicized) of adding acid first to high Brix musts; some people call this "the acid whip." When you have a must that is simply too high in Brix, you add some water to bring the sugar level down to a level that will ferment, and then you bleed off some juice as fermentation begins, to mitigate the effects of dilution. Is this manipulation or is this manipulation?

Wine can certainly show a lack of richness at low alcohol levels, but can seem clumsy and out of balance at high levels. The "sweet spot" is a concept devel-oped by Clark Smith at Vinovation, in California's Sonoma Valley, which offers a service for adjusting alcohol levels. Vinovation advertises: "Since even small differences in alcohol content can have a large impact on aroma and texture, Vinovation offers the capability... to examine wine characteristics at 0.1% inter-vals to choose the wine of the best balance for the desired style. These "sweet spot" tastings remove the guesswork from discovering the best alcohol level for your wine."[7]

Clark Smith is passionate about wine and music. If you look at harmonics, he explained to me, you go suddenly from harmony to dissonance, and wine is the same: an 0.1% change in alcohol can completely reverse the feeling of integration. Sweet spots do not follow a continuous distribution, but occur at sharply deline-ated, separate levels. He makes his point by asking you to compare the astringency levels of three wines. It turns out that those at 13.7% and 14.2% alcohol taste well rounded (people differ in which they prefer), but a blend of the two that brings the alcohol to just under 14% tastes discernibly awkward (every-one agrees on this). So adjusting alcohol is not simply a matter of reducing (or increasing) it, but is a search to find the exact point at which it best integrates to give the most harmonious impression. Smith calls this "post-modern winemak-ing."

If you take your wine to Vinovation, they will use their reverse osmosis sys-tem to separate it into a permeate and retentate. The permeate is material that crosses the reverse osmosis membrane, containing water, alcohol, and other small substances. It is distilled to remove the alcohol. Then it is added back to the retentate, which contains all the other components of the wine. Typically about 25% of the total batch of wine is treated to denude it of alcohol; then it is recombined with the untreated material. In effect, this is the opposite of using reverse osmosis to remove water from must, because the trick of distillation has been introduced to treat the removed material before it is added back. Smith claims that the increase in alcohol in wines over recent years would be even more marked if it were not for Vinovation, which has taken an average of more than one percent alcohol from almost half of the wines produced in California.[8]

Reverse osmosis is a versatile technique that can be used to adjust components other than alcohol. The size of a molecule determines whether it is included in the permeate. Acetic acid is small enough to be included, and can be removed from the permeate by chemical means, which offers a way to treat wines that have volatile acidity (excess of acetic acid). But this is not legal in many jurisdictions.

The most sophisticated system for manipulating wine is the spinning cone, used to recover volatile aromas during production of tea or coffee, to obtain fruit and vegetable essences, and to remove alcohol from wine. The basic principle is that liquid is fed into the top of the spinning cone column (a vertical cylinder roughly 40" in diameter and 13' in height) and flows down over a series of alternating stationary and rotating metal cones. The liquid drips on to a rotating cone and is pulled by centrifugal force into a thin film on the surface, from where it drips on to the next cone. The thin film of liquid is exposed to a stream of nitrogen gas ascending from the bottom of the cone. By flowing across the surface of the liquid film, the nitrogen extracts volatile aroma and flavor compounds, and carries them up to the top of the column.

For treating wine, the process is split into two stages. The column is used first to extract volatile compounds, which are condensed and saved. The treated wine is collected from the bottom of the column. Then the wine is run through the column again at a slightly higher temperature to remove the alcohol. The compounds removed in the first stage can then be added to the dealcoholized wine.

The spinning cone is a industrial apparatus that can handle large volumes.

Photograph kindly provided by ConeTech.

Proponents of these treatments claim that in warm climates better wine is made by picking the grapes riper and removing the excess alcohol than by harvesting at the desired potential alcohol level. But how far should this be taken? If it's okay to adjust alcohol freely, why shouldn't the winemaker use similar techniques to adjust other aroma or flavor components? If it's okay to preserve volatile components by taking them out while the alcohol is removed, and then adding them back, would it be okay to adjust how much is added back?

Certainly the spinning cone can do a lot more than take out alcohol. By adjusting the conditions, individual volatile flavor compounds can be extracted. Pyrazines are volatile components that give Sauvignon Blanc much of its "grassy" character. Southcorp, the giant Australian producer, experimented at one point with removing pyrazines from a batch of unripe Sauvignon Blanc grapes and adding them to wine made from grapes that lost their pyrazines because they became too ripe.[9] "I regard that as natural," said Linley Schultz, the winemaker at the time. At the KWW in South Africa, winemakers went a step further and added pyrazines that had been purchased directly for use as flavoring compounds. The practice came to light after journalist Michael Fridjhon pointed to suspiciously high pyrazine levels in many South African Sauvignon Blancs.[10] It remains unclear how widespread the practice is.[11] No one would object if two wines were blended together to produce a better balanced product, but tinkering with individual flavor components is usually acknowledged to be another matter. At what point have we crossed the boundary between a natural product and an industrial fabrication?

Acidity: Essential But Not Too Much

The winemaker has quite a range of methods for increasing or decreasing acidity in wine, but by far the best result is obtained by picking berries with the right level of acidity. Acidity varies with the climate (higher in cool climates, lower in warm climates) and with the variety. The most important acids in grapes are tartaric and malic. Most of the acidity is tartaric acid, which has no flavor as such, but malic acid has a distinct flavor of green apples. Malic acid is generally more prominent in cool-climate varieties because it is metabolized during the later stages of development in warm temperatures. Red wines tend to have lower acidity than white wines, partly because they tend to be produced in warmer climates, partly because maceration with the skins extracts potassium (which reduces acidity).

Terms for describing acidity in wines range from "flabby" to "balanced" to "crisp."[*] Technically speaking, wine needs to have about 4-6 g/l of acidity to be in

---

[*] Acidity is usually measured as the amount of tartaric acid that would produce the same level of acidity as the mix of acids actually present in a wine. Acidity is expressed either in g/l (e.g., 4-6 g/l) or as a percentage (e.g. 0.4-0.6%). In France, acidity is given in equivalents of sulfuric acid, which must be multiplied by 1.5 to get the tartaric equivalent.

a "balanced" range.[12] Higher levels of acidity are needed to balance the sugar in sweet wines. The level of acidity drops with each fermentation; a little is lost during alcoholic fermentation, and then there is a much larger drop if there is a malolactic fermentation.[13]

All wines also have a small amount of volatile acidity, called VA in the trade. "Volatile" means that you can smell it, and for practical purposes in wine, this means acetic acid, the smell of vinegar. It is produced by oxidation of alcohol. At very low levels, it adds liveliness and piquancy, but if levels become high enough to notice directly on the nose, it's a problem. By contrast, you cannot smell the major acids in wine, tartaric and malic.

The most natural way to reduce acidity is by malolactic fermentation, usually considered appropriate for most reds and for many non-aromatic whites. By replacing malic acid with lactic acid, the wine loses the sharp taste of green apples, and gains more creamy textures.[14] In low acid vintages, by contrast, blocking the malo may be a way to retain more natural acidity. Some producers did this in the very hot 2003 vintage in Burgundy.

Wine can be deacidified chemically, which is legal in the cooler climates of Europe. Adding chalk (calcium carbonate) is an old method to remove tartaric acid, by precipitating out the calcium tartrate. More modern variations of this method use more complex chemicals.[15] (Reduction of acidity can also result from cold stabilization to remove potential tartrate crystals.)

Acidification is much easier—you just chuck tartaric acid into the must (or wine). This is legal only in the hottest parts of Europe but is common in much of the New World—many Australian wines are acidified, for example. When you taste a wine where the acidity seems out of whack with the rest of the palate, because you can taste it separately, it may mean that too much acid was thrown into the mix. You would probably get better results by blending in a high acid wine from a cooler climate, but then of course you may no longer be able to label the wine with the name of a single region.

An exception was made in Europe in the unusually hot conditions of 2003 to allow acidification in regions such as Bordeaux and Germany, where it is usually forbidden, but it's difficult to get the level right if you're not accustomed to doing it. Bordeaux producers who did not acidify felt that their wines came out better than those who did, although claims that the acidity levels miraculously corrected themselves during fermentation are hard to understand in terms of conventional chemistry.

The usual rule in Europe is that you can chaptalize in cool regions, and you can add acidity in warm regions. In some regions, both modifications are possible, but not at the same time. But even that limit is thwarted sometimes: the famous Hospices de Beaune in Burgundy bypassed the rule that a wine can be acidified *or* chaptalized by doing both on its wines from the 1997 vintage. Producer Jean Mongeard of Domaine Mongeard-Mugneret in Vosne Romanée argued that you could chaptalize the must and acidify the wine without breaking the rules.[16] How far can you go in manipulating the flavor profile before wine becomes just another processed product?

Dry Wine and the Sweet Tooth

Acidity and sugar are the yin and yang of wine. As acidity increases, sweetness becomes less evident; conversely, a little sugar can disguise excessive acidity. One of the most subtle playoffs is achieved in Champagne, where the cool climate is marginal for wine production, and a straight dry wine would be too acid to enjoy; but by making the wine sparkling, and by adding a little sugar when it is bottled (technically this is called the *dosage*), you get a perfectly delicious balance.

All wine has a little sugar. Even when a wine is fermented to completion, there will be a tiny residual amount that did not get converted to alcohol. Most people can taste sugar in wine at a level above 4 g/l (0.4%). Most dry red wines have less than 1 g/l of residual sugar, most whites are a little higher at 2-3 g/l. Of course, it's not only sugar that makes a wine seems sweet: alcohol gives a perception of sweetness, so a wine with a high alcohol level can appear misleadingly sweet. Glycerol also gives an impression of sweetness.

The legal definition of a dry wine is that it must have less than 4 g/l of residual sugar, but in recognition of the interplay with acidity, wines with sufficient acidity are allowed to have up to 9 g/l and still be described as dry. This is most often used for the Trocken classification in Germany. This can make "trocken" a somewhat misleading description. Fair enough: in some cases the high acidity will give the impression the wine is really dry, but in others, perhaps where the acidity is at the low limit, and the sugar is at the high limit for the category, you will be disappointed by a perceptible taste of sweetness.[17] The consumer would benefit if the European Union stuck rigorously to the notion that dry means less than 4 g/l of residual sugar; at least this is objective, since very few people can taste sugar below this level. Some other term could be used for wines that are expected to taste dry even though they have some sugar.

Residual sugar doesn't only make a wine sweet, it also makes it feel richer. It's a winemaker's trick to leave just a little residual sugar, right at the level of detection or maybe just a fraction above it, to give a bit of kick to the body and a superficial but misleading impression of richness. This panders to the well known fact that market surveys show consumers always claim to drink dry wines, but in blind tastings prefer wines with just a touch of residual sugar. Many of the leading brands, although billed as dry, have low levels of residual sugar. It would be extremely surprising if the sugar level was achieved by natural means. Indeed, Justin Knock, a winemaker at large Australian producer Fosters, says, "We do not practice arrested fermentation and I'd be amazed if anyone else did. It's far too difficult to control at the levels we are discussing (anywhere from 2–10 g/l)."[18] Adding sugar is just part of the final adjustments made before bottling. The extraordinarily successful Yellow Tail red wines have 5-7 g/l residual sugar, and several large American brands, such as Franzia "Chablis" have even more—at roughly 11 g/l, this would be classified as medium dry in Europe. Anything further from authentic Chablis would be hard to imagine. It would be illegal to represent it as a dry wine in Europe.

The most widespread technique for making sweet wine is simply to add sugar after fermentation has been completed. This is not legal as such in Europe, but can be done in the form of adding süssreserve or RCGM (concentrated and purified grape must).[19] This is merely a fig leaf: süssreserve is basically concentrated grape juice and RCGM is obtained from (unfermented) grape juice by a process of filtration and rectification, in which the solution is passed through decoloring resins and ion exchange columns. In reality, RCGM is a concentrated solution of glucose and fructose sugars. Its only difference from a solution made by dissolving purified sugars (more easily extracted from beets) in water is that it was made by partial dehydration of the must of cheap grapes.[20] These techniques are not used to make sweet dessert wine—the artificial nature of adding enough sugar would unbalance the wine—but are used for off-dry or medium dry wines. Known as back-blending, the technique was developed in Germany in the 1950s, but the results are rarely as satisfactory as causing some of the natural grape sugar to remain unfermented.[21]

In a bureaucratic fantasy, the authorities of the European Union have convinced themselves that using RCGM is natural in a way that raw sugar is not. This is one of the dirty little secrets of winemaking: it has no redeeming feature and should be stopped. It's also the case that chaptalization is used in producing sweet wines in other regions, for example in Sauternes, and it seems singularly pointless to add sugar before fermentation in order to leave some over when fermentation stops or is stopped. Shouldn't sweet wines be made from unsweetened must so that the sugar is entirely natural and in balance with everything else? If the must isn't sweet enough, maybe you shouldn't make a sweet wine.

Mega Color: Natural Additive or Snake Oil?

"Virtually everyone is using it. In just about every wine up to $20 a bottle anyway," says one winemaker in California.[22] "It" is Mega Purple, an additive made from grape juice concentrate, widely known to winemakers but kept as obscure as possible to the consumer. It's not even listed in the product catalogs of its producer.

Mega Purple is an extract made from grapes of Rubired, a hybrid variety developed in 1958 by Dr. Harold Olmo of the University of California, Davis, by crossing Alicante Ganzin and Tinta Cão. Tinta Cão is one of the quality black varietals used to make Port, but Alicante Ganzin is a French hybrid created by crossing Aramon Rupestris Ganzin #4 (a hybrid between the Aramon cultivar of Vitis vinifera and Vitis rupestris) [23] and Alicante Bouschet. Alicante Ganzin is a teinturier, meaning that its juice is colored red, and it's mostly used for breeding other teinturiers.

So Rubired is a hybrid with one eighth parentage from Vitis rupestris. It is not a very distinguished variety. "It produces a dark red blending wine, with little character or body, and is used to increase the color of generic or varietal table and dessert wines," says the University of California.[24] So why is it almost 5% of

8000 purple (right) gives a whole new meaning to a plain wrapper. The container has no identification except the name, but is claimed by its manufacturer, California Concentrate, to be the same as Mega Purple. It is dark, sticky stuff (left).

the total crush in California, making it one of the leading varieties, as important as Pinot Noir or Syrah?[25]

The Rubired extract is very deeply colored, very high in sugar, and because of its hybrid origin, has a slightly foxy aroma. It's most commonly used as an additive to give red wines a bit more color, but it also gives them a touch of residual sugar,[26] and a hint of that nasty foxy quality, known pejoratively to winemakers who use it as "Central Valley Red." It's used to overcome deficiencies in a wine, because it adds enough flavoring to hide vegetal notes or even a touch of the animal aromas introduced by Brettanomyces infection. It's been variously described as having "a sort of jammy taste, but with no fruit to it" or giving the wine "a tutti frutti aroma."[27]

Few winemakers admit to using it themselves, although they'll admit its use is widespread.[28] A little goes a long way; most winemakers who will talk about it say that more than 0.1% is noticeable in the wine. Rubired extracts have other purposes as well as treating wine (as food coloring or in fruit juices, for example), but their potency means that a small part of the entire production would be enough to treat all red wine produced in California.[29] Its homogenizing effect on wine flavor may partly explain the general similarities in style between many lower-priced red wines.

Mega Purple was produced by a subsidiary of the conglomerate Constellation Wines, who got into the business when they acquired Heublein in 1994. Heublein owned a grape juice concentrate factory at Madera, California. When the grape juice concentrate business later got into trouble due to over supply, Constellation closed other plants, but continued to produce specialist products at Madera. Mega Purple had been introduced in 1992 as a natural coloring agent, and in 2007 Anil Shrikhande, Vice President of Research and Development for Constellation Wines, said that twenty percent of the annual production of 200,000 liters is sold to the wine industry,[30] alone roughly enough to treat 10% of the red wine

MegaNatural is a series of products made from grapes (right). The Corporate logo of Polyphenolics is amusingly in purple.

MegaNatural™

produced in California. It is, of course, a vastly cheaper way to increase color than blending in a proportion of wine from a more deeply colored variety.

Today there is also a business in selling wine extract products to consumers. Polyphenolics is a wholly owned subsidiary of Constellation operating out of the plant at Madera with Anil Shrikhande as its President. It sells a series of products called MegaNatural, made from grapes, some of which are sold directly to consumers as dietary supplements, others to manufacturers (sold in 10 or 20 kg containers of powder for bulk use).

No one really knows exactly how widely grape concentrates are used, but by all accounts, they are commonly employed to bump up color and impression of extract in lower priced wines from California and Australia. Coming from hybrid grapes, these concentrates would be illegal in Europe, but of course the precedent for adding concentrate comes from the techniques developed in Germany for back-blending süssreserve. But whether used to add color or sweetness, grape concentrates should really have no place in modern wine making: any benefit from compensating for deficiencies in the wine is outweighed by that general homogenizing quality. There are simply enough opportunities now to make good wine without needing artificial coloring or sweetening. Elderberries (used to add color) were banned in wine by the nineteenth century: Mega purple is a modern equivalent that should be treated in the same way.

Wood *v.* Steel, Oxidation *v.* Reduction

Unless wine is matured in new oak, the containers it passes through on its way from fermentation to the bottle have little direct effect upon it. Fermentation vats can be made of wood, concrete, or stainless steel,[31] and although some producers believe that one or another gives better results, often enough you see all types at one place, just depending on the fashion at the time when they were bought. Some producers believe that one shape is better than another—conical vats rather than cylindrical, for example—mostly because of the way they dissipate heat through the fermenting must, but there's little objective evidence.[32] The general trend these days is towards stainless steel, with a handful of leading producers returning to oak because they feel it gives better aromatics, although one winemaker justifying the change admitted to me, "Science does not explain all the differences between oak and steel." So long as the containers are kept clean (certainly more difficult to accomplish with wood than with concrete or steel), they are not the most important factor at fermentation. One attempt to have the best of both worlds is to use vats with stainless steel construction at the top (where the cap is located) and at the bottom (where the vat is cleaned out), but with oak to contain the bulk of the must.

The major difference between containers, both at fermentation and during any subsequent maturation, is their impact on exposure to oxygen. How much oxygen a wine encounters en route from grape juice to the bottle has a major effect on its style. At one extreme, the new technique of micro-oxygenation increases exposure by bubbling oxygen through the must during or after fermentation. At the other extreme, reductive winemaking (reduction is the opposite of oxidation) uses closed stainless fermentation vats with a blanket of inert gas to completely exclude oxygen.

Oxidation and reduction are key determinants of wine styles. The properties of many components of wine depend on whether they are in oxidized or reduced states. The most dramatic effects are displayed by sulfur-containing compounds. When they are in a reduced state, they produce pungent smells of cabbage, garlic, burned rubber, or rotten eggs. They are known as thiols (more colloquially) or mercaptans (more formally). [33] Hydrogen sulfide, the smell of rotten eggs, is a pungent example of a sulfurous compound.[34] Excessive thiol concentrations resulting from flaws in winemaking can be removed by treatment with copper (an oxidizing agent); in fact, an old trick for dealing with a slight sulfur problem is to drop a copper penny into a glass of wine. The aromas clear almost instantly. While excess thiols are a problem in any wine, some varietals rely for their char-

Fermentation vats may be cylinders, cones, or cubes, made of stainless steel, wood, or cement.

Vats consisting of oak with steel tops and bases were specially constructed for Castello Banfi.

Photograph kindly provided by Castello Banfi.

acteristic aromas on the production of certain thiols at low levels, so the balance between oxidation and reduction is especially important in their winemaking.

Fermentation can occur in the absence of air, but usually gets off to a better start with a kick of oxygen. The most oxidative conditions for fermentation are provided by traditional open-topped wooden fermenters. This also leads to slightly less alcohol in the wine, as some is released into the atmosphere.[35] Modern stainless steel fermenters are closed, but have a valve to allow carbon dioxide to escape. A risk of performing fermentation anaerobically (in the absence of oxygen) is that reductive aromas (such as hydrogen sulfide) can form, and to counteract this, oxygen is sometimes injected.

Micro-oxygenation is the extreme form of oxidative exposure. It may be used during fermentation, it is usually avoided during malolactic fermentation, and its main use is during maturation. It was invented in Madiran in southwest France in 1991 to help reduce the violent tannins of the Tannat grape, and the technique is most suitable for producing wines for short to medium term consumption from tannic grape varieties. Oxygen is bubbled through the wine by using a sparger that distributes the gas in the form of tiny bubbles. By oxidizing the tannins, it advances the state of maturation, with a generally softening effect on the wine, and is most often used as a (cheaper) alternative to maturation in barrel.[36] It's effective because the oxygen is distributed evenly throughout the wine, instead of being restricted to the surface area of the barrel. There's no detailed theoretical understanding of how it works, and it needs to be used carefully to avoid spoiling the wine.

Reductive winemaking occurs in an oxygen-free environment, eliminating the reactions that occur when must or wine is exposed to oxygen in traditional winemaking. It produces wine with bright fruits, typically suited for earlier consumption. It has become especially well established for aromatic varieties such as Riesling and Sauvignon Blanc, where the aromatics are easily lost on exposure to oxygen. (Some of the characteristic features of Sauvignon Blanc are due to thiols, which react with oxygen but are preserved under reductive conditions.)

Reductive winemaking became popular in Australia and New Zealand under the influence of Brian Croser, a leading Australian winemaker,[37] and the reductive style is associated with the New World, although no longer exclusively practiced there. Fermentation occurs in stainless steel, oxygen may be excluded by using inert gas, and there is no exposure to wood. Dry ice (solid carbon dioxide) is used in the press to generate CO_2, which both avoids oxidizing the grapes and maintains the low temperature of the fruit. After pressing, the juice is transferred to stainless steel tanks where it is fermented at cool temperatures. The style of New Zealand Sauvignon Blanc, bright, steely, and full of sharp fruits, owes more to this treatment than to terroir.

The antithesis of reductive winemaking is a technique called hyperoxidation, which is sometimes used for white wines. Oxygen is bubbled through the must before fermentation, destroying anything that reacts with it. By removing compounds that are susceptible to oxygen (essentially tannins, which are undesirable in white wine because of their bitterness), this results in a wine that is more stable when it encounters oxygen later. In principle this can make a stable fruity wine, but the practical problem is stopping the process before the fruit is destroyed. It's useful only for neutral grape varieties, and cannot be used for those whose aromas depend on sulfur-containing compounds (which would be destroyed by the treatment).

Wood or steel, oxidation or reduction, are all perfectly legitimate ways to handle wine, but each treatment produces its characteristics in the wine. Nowhere is the hand of the winemaker more evident than in making choices among these alternatives. Stylistic preference here is clearly imposed rather than intrinsic to the grape variety or the terroir.

Oak: Barrels, Staves, Chips, and Dust

Oak barrels were originally used simply for storage and transport. Often enough wood was available from forests not too far from the vineyards, and the filled barrels could be rolled along, making transport easy. Barrels were replaced only when they became too decrepit to use any more. There was no thought at the time that oak would come to be a component of wine second in importance only to the grape.

Staves are being heated so they can be bent into a barrel, where they are secured by metal rings.

Photograph kindly provided by Taransaud Tonnellerie.

Use of oak not only ensures a certain degree of oxidative exposure, but when the oak is new, it directly transfers flavors to the wine. The big distinction between new oak and previously used oak, and the attention paid to the proportion of new oak, is a phenomenon of the last half century.[38] You see wine described as "matured in 100% new oak" or as using "50% new oak" (meaning that 50% of the barrels were new), because the transmission of flavors is by far the strongest with new oak; the effect is smaller after one year, and by three or four years, a barrel has become a relatively inert storage medium. However, exposure to oxygen is the same irrespective of the age of the barrel.

Barrels come in all shapes and sizes, but the most common is the 225 liter barrique of Bordeaux. For the best quality, planks of oak are seasoned outside for at least two years, and then cut into staves that are bent into barrels. The staves are heated for about 20 minutes to make them pliable. Once the staves have been secured with metal hoops, the barrel is "toasted." Traditionally this was done with an open flame, but today the process is often more precisely controlled by using a specified period of infrared radiation. Toasting is described as light, medium, or heavy, depending on the duration and temperature.[39]

Aromas and flavors derived from oak include coconut, vanillin, butterscotch, cloves, cinnamon, and smokiness.[40] In addition, tannins are extracted to add to those of the grape itself. (These are called ellagitannins, and they tend to be stronger than the grape tannins.) Extraction depends on the length of time the maturing wine spends in oak barrels. A more powerful wine with intense fruit extraction will benefit from longer time in oak than a less powerful wine, where the oak aromas and flavors could overwhelm the fruits. Extraction is also influenced by the level of toasting, which has quite an effect on transfer of flavors to the wine.[41] Toasting enhances some oak flavors and reduces others. Producers are fussy about specifying whether their barrels should have light, medium, or heavy toast.

The origin of the oak makes a big difference. French oak is usually considered the best, because of its tight grain.[42] American oak is a different species,[43] with larger sized pores, and, more to the point, conveys noticeably stronger flavors to the wine. You can detect its use in some New World wines by strong aromas of vanillin, and also in Rioja, where it has traditionally been used rather than French oak. Oak is expensive; barrels of top French oak run about $800 each (which comes to roughly $32 per case of wine). Back in the nineteenth century, Baltic oak was generally used in Bordeaux; recent economic pressure has renewed interest in oak from eastern Europe, although it tends to be sweeter and spicier than French oak (but not as pronounced as American oak).

A producer can play with a lot of parameters when choosing oak. Not only is French oak different from American, but oak from each French forest has its own characteristics. Even the barrels made by different coopers with oak from the same source with the same toasting can give different results; many producers in fact buy barrels from a variety of coopers, and the blend between the wines matured in the different types of barrels adds further complexity to the wine.

The effects of using expensive oak barrels can be mimicked by a range of cheaper options. It's an ongoing debate whether the results are really as good, but it's a rare producer who admits to using staves, chips, or dust, instead of barrels.

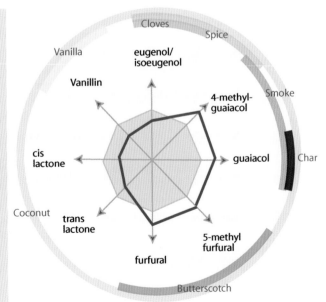

Aromas produced by oak are represented on a spider chart.

The gray octagon at the center shows equal representation of the aroma compounds; the red lines indicate the levels produced by heavy toasting, in which some components have been reduced and others increased.

The aromas associated with each compound are indicated on the circumference.[44]

A barrel room at Château Margaux contains millions of dollars' worth of new oak barriques.

Putting staves of new oak inside vats of stainless steel is the closest to using oak barrels. The planks can be of similar quality to those used in constructing barrels. They can be used to line the tank or simply placed in a matrix at the bottom. A cheaper technique is to suspend cubes of oak or chips (in some sort of bag) inside the fermenting tank. The smaller the format of the oak (chips are smaller than cubes, for example), the quicker the extraction into the wine. Inner staves might need a few months to mimic two years in oak barrels, cubes might need two months, and chips might be effective in only two weeks. Some exposure to air is also necessary to mimic the effects of maturation in barrels; this can be done by micro-oxygenation or other means. There is one possible advantage to the use of alternative oak formats: it's possible to expose red wine to oak during fermentation, thus providing an equivalent to fermenting white wine in barrels.

Just how well do these treatments mimic maturation in oak? The closer you stay to the original, the better you do. One manufacturer of oak beans (cubes) says that "beans, with their barrel-like gradation of color, provide a slow, controlled extraction... Chips offer immediate extraction. However, they usually leave wines with a monochromatic, disjointed flavor profile, along with a harsh and bitter mouth feel."[45] Without going so far, one study by a cooperage firm showed that tasters could detect differences in wines treated with different oak alternatives.[46]

The impetus for using oak alternatives is economic. Inner staves cost the equivalent of $150 per barrel, less than a quarter of the price of the real thing; cubes or chips cost an almost insignificant fraction of that; and of course a further incentive is that the wine can be taken to market much sooner. Going to extremes, you can use oak dust or granules, which are absorbed more or less instantly into the wine; and beyond even that, oak extract, basically a flavoring compound, is available on the market.[47] Indeed, as Michael Broadbent once asked sarcastically in his column in Decanter magazine, why not issue bags of

oak with every bottle so that each taster can adjust the wine to his own preference?

Certainly with staves, and perhaps with cubes, good results can be obtained.
It's a measure of how much consumers like the taste of oak, and the economics of
obtaining it, that the French authorities finally gave way and permitted oak to be
used in forms other than barrels. They had no alternative really, given the inroads that New World wines using oak alternatives have made into their
traditional markets.[48] But this is a sea change in abandoning traditional values.
One reaction was captured by the wine bar owner who said, "[This means] we
are going to make wines like we make food at McDonald's."[49]

Why are producers so secretive about use of oak? Wines that are barrel-
fermented will say so on the label often enough, back labels will often mention
the proportion of new oak or its origins, but producers who use staves, cubes, or
chips, will do no more than refer to oak flavors. If the procedure genuinely gives
results they consider just as good, if it is nothing to be ashamed of and there is no
attempt to trick the consumer, why not state it on the label? Regulations calling
for transparency in describing the sources of extraneous flavors would be no bad
thing. At least if oak is to be mentioned, the form of application should be stated.

Is it splitting hairs to regard the use of barrels, when some flavors transfer to
the wine, as a normal part of maturation, but to raise an eyebrow when oak
staves, cubes, chips, or dust are added solely for the purpose of flavoring the
wine? If addition of flavoring essences is clearly over the line, where exactly is
the line to be drawn?

Put a Cork In It

In most regards, cork is an ideal closure. It is inert, and it retains its elasticity for
decades. Granted you have to have a corkscrew to extract it, and it's not always
easy to reinsert it, but uncorking offers sommeliers a grand opportunity for
pomp and circumstance. The big problem with cork is a contaminant: TCA.

When you open a bottle of wine and you can't detect any fruits on the nose,
and then you get a rather musty or moldy, acrid odor of wet cardboard, the
reason is most likely that the cork was contaminated with TCA. The wine is
corked.[50] TCA is one of the most odiferous compounds known to man—most
people can smell it at levels of 3 parts per trillion, equivalent to a few drops in a
swimming pool—and TCA in the cork rapidly dissolves in the wine underneath
it.

Cork is a natural product. It comes from the bark of the cork tree (Quercus
suber). The best supplies are in Portugal, which has more than 30% of the world
total, and produces more than half of the world's cork. The cork industry is an
important economic factor in Portugal; the total value of cork exports is worth
more than the value of all Portuguese wine exports![51] The bark can be harvested
from a cork tree about once every decade. It comes off in large strips, which are
typically seasoned in the forest for about a year and then turned into planks.

They need a fairly extensive cleaning process, which is where some of the problems have occurred.

Natural cork consists of hollow cells containing air, is elastic, and has a non-slip surface that holds it in place in the bottle. Over half the volume of cork is air, which is why it is light and elastic. The cell walls contain suberin, a waxy substance that makes cork water-resistant. The cork is cut into cylinders, the corking machine compresses the cork to fit into the bottleneck, and then after insertion, the cork expands to fill the diameter of the bottleneck.[52] To improve the seal, the cork is coated with paraffin, which repels wine, and with silicone, which acts as a lubricant to ease insertion and extraction.

TCA (2, 4, 6-trichloroanisole) is produced by penicillin fungi that live naturally on cork trees. They act on a group of chlorine-containing compounds (the best known are the chlorophenols) to generate TCA and other compounds related to it.[53] Chlorophenols are used as pesticides and fire retardants, and they can come into contact with cork not only on the trees in the forest but during subsequent processing. One cause of TCA was the use of chlorine to bleach corks during preparation, but now that has been eliminated; even so, there is a certain ineradicable level of natural occurrence. Cork is far and away the most common source of TCA, but the problem can occur in other ways; whole wineries have been infected when penicillin molds have found chlorinated substances in wooden structures, for example. Cork taint typically spoils up to about 6% of bottles at random, but a winery infection can ruin the entire production.

Chlorine cleaning materials are now largely banned in wineries after a series of disasters. Realization of the extent of the problem goes back to the 1980s, when

Cork is harvested from the bark of the tree (left) and then stored as planks (right).

Photographs kindly provided by Amorim.

several French wine producers had large numbers of bottles spoiled by musty odors, too many to be due to individual cases of cork taint. Affected producers were all over the country, including Champagne Roederer, Châteaux Latour, Ducru-Beaucaillou, and Canon in Bordeaux, and producers in Sancerre to the north and Châteauneuf-du-Pape to the south.[54] Pascal Chatonnet, a research scientist at Bordeaux University, who became intrigued when a stainless steel vat at his family winery showed cork-like taint, chased the problem down to contamination of the wineries with chloroanisoles related to TCA.[55] TCA had been identified as the cause of cork taint by a German scientist, Hans Tanner, in 1982,[56] and Chatonnet's work showed that the winery problem was related, but not identical. The cause was usually a persistent contamination of wooden structures in the cellar.

The French producers were not exactly forthcoming about the problem. Critics sometimes pointed to a surprisingly high proportion of spoiled bottles found in tastings, but there was no public acknowledgement, although the châteaux were quietly rebuilding their wineries to eliminate the contaminated material. The full extent of the problem remains unknown, although as many as a quarter of the châteaux of St. Emilion may have had to rebuild their cellars.[57] This was no small undertaking: a contaminated cellar has to be completely destroyed before a new one can be built. It was not until 1998, well after the problem was resolved, that the lid came off in an exposé published jointly in the magazines L'Express and Que Choisir (a consumer review).[58] The authorities seemed to have had no regrets about concealing the problem: "Between a true case of cork taint, concerning 1-2% of bottles, and another taste, [also] described as "corked," more or less serious in individual cases, the consumer could become confused,"[59] says Jean-Louis Trocard, President of the CIVB.* The concern for the consumer is touching, but perhaps it would be better to be confused than to buy bad wine.

A decade later, similar problems surfaced at wineries in Napa Valley. Beaulieu Vineyards had levels of TCA just above the level of detection in its wine from the 1997-1999 vintages, Chalone Vineyards had problems around the same time, and Hanzell Vineyards stopped selling its 2000 Chardonnay because of noticeable TCA levels. The problem at Hanzell turned out to be due to contaminated hoses and drains.[60]

Winery contamination can be a disaster for the individual producer, but cork taint affects a random proportion of every producer's wines. No one knows what the proportion of corked wines was in, say, the first part of the twentieth century, but there is certainly an impression that the proportion has increased in recent decades, presumably due to more widespread use of chlorinated pesticides. Unfortunately, the likelihood of infection has nothing to do with the quality of the cork; the presence of TCA is completely adventitious irrespective of what grade of cork you buy.

---

*Conseil Interprofessionnel du Vin de Bordeaux, the organization representing the producers.

One of the worst aspects is the damage to the producer's reputation, especially when a low level of TCA contamination leaves uncertainty as to the cause
of the problem. When TCA is well above the threshold, it's obvious that a bottle
is flawed, and even someone who is not knowledgeable about the exact cause
will assume that the defect is a one-off. But at TCA levels around the detection
threshold, the fruits can be suppressed on the nose and palate without there
being overt signs of the characteristic musty odors. Faced with a bottle from an
unknown producer, you might easily conclude that this is his style, and he's no
good, whereas another bottle might in fact show real quality.

A early as 1982, in his research paper identifying TCA, Hans Tanner proposed
a solution: "Replacement of chlorine in the processing of cork should remedy the
cork taint problem."[61] You would think the cork producers would be grateful,
but not a bit of it. The chairman of Gültig Corks in Portugal reproached Dr.
Tanner for giving cork a bad image.[62] The cork industry remained in denial for
most of the next two decades. Only after they began to lose significant business
to screwcaps did they really try to remedy the problem at source. Progress was
partly impeded by the lack of vertical integration in the industry (no firms were
involved with all stages of production from forest to cork stopper), making
assignment of responsibility difficult, but that has been somewhat counteracted
by the growth of Amorim as a leading, vertically-integrated cork producer.
Abandoning the use of chlorine in cleaning corks brought the level of TCA
contamination down quite a bit, probably to around 2% or so. Some recent
techniques allow the corks to be treated to remove volatile compounds, including TCA.[63] Although relatively expensive, this is claimed to have brought the
level of contamination below 1%. I am a bit skeptical; it still seems common at
tastings to find almost one corked bottle in every other case or so.

In most industries, a rate of 1-2% loss due to poor condition when the goods
reach the consumer would be unacceptable, especially when care has been taken
to achieve high quality and the damage is due to something completely extraneous, far outside of the producer's control. (Think what would happen to
refrigerator manufacturers if 2% of fridges failed, spoiling the food.) The best a
wine producer can do with cork is to sample a supply to check that the proportion with TCA is below some limit (most producers use 1%), but there are always
some contaminated corks. There are also some losses due to oxidation when a
cork seals fails; this does depend on cork quality, and at the lowest levels, oxidation can be just of much of a problem as cork taint.

Cork has its (still) dominant position as the result of history. Imagine the
situation if screwcaps had always been used to seal bottles, and a salesman for
this new fangled product, cork, tried to sell it to a wine producer.[64] "Cork is a
natural product, made from the bark of the tree, by a complicated procedure
involving air-drying, washing, and preparation. Every sample is unique because
it is slightly different from all the others, and only a small proportion is spoiled
by contamination with a highly offensive compound to which people are extraordinarily sensitive. You need a special tool to remove the cork, and this
makes it difficult to reseal the bottle" Lots of luck!

Turning the Screw

The screwcap is older than you might think. There are now hundreds of patents for variations of the screwcap used to seal bottles with contents ranging from noxious liquids to water, but the original patent was granted to Dan Rylands in the United Kingdom on August 10, 1889. The first use of screwcaps for alcoholic beverages was for whisky; its introduction by White Horse Distillers in 1926 doubled sales in six months. (Until 1913, whisky bottles were sealed with corks that had to be removed with a corkscrew; the replaceable cork was invented in 1913 by Teacher's, described as 'The Self-Opening Bottle (Patented)," and sold under the slogan "Bury the Corkscrew.")

In the twentieth century, a screwcap was a sign of low quality wine, not necessarily rotgut, but certainly without the pretension of anything bottled under a cork. This changed in 2000, when a group of thirteen winemakers in Australia's Clare Valley, infuriated by damage to their wine, and suspicious (whether justified or not) that they were receiving corks inferior to those available in Europe, started bottling their wines under screwcap.[65] The trend snowballed; still strongest in the New World, where the majority of bottles are closed with screwcaps, it is now being seen more frequently in Europe.

Known in the trade as Stelvins (after the name of the dominant manufacturer), screwcaps got a bad name in the wine industry when early attempts to use them in the 1970s met consumer resistance.[66] Technical trials in Australia, however, produced satisfactory results, so the stage was set for their reintroduction when exasperation with cork taint and oxidation problems passed all bounds. Until the early 2000s, screwcaps remained technically the same as in the 1970s: an outer metal closure that fits on to a thread on the bottle, with an inside liner that fits tight against the top of the bottle to seal the contents.

This matchbox advertising Teacher's whisky shows an early attempt to get rid of the corkscrew.

At first, the wine makers were just relieved to have got away from the problems with cork, and, no doubt, somewhat nervous about consumer acceptance.
No one thought much about whether changing the seal on the bottle would have
an effect on the wine inside. But it soon became apparent that there can be significant differences between wines bottled under cork or sealed under screwcap.

The main player in investigating the effects of screwcaps has been the AWRI
(Australian Wine Research Institute), which started an interesting series of trials
when the same wine was bottled in 1997 with different closures. Sample bottles
were opened each year to see what differences had developed in taste or chemical composition. It rapidly became clear that the types of closure provide very
different levels of seal. Screwcaps are the tightest: less sulfur dioxide gets out of
the bottle and less oxygen gets in. They are also very consistent: all screwcaps of
the same type give the same result. As you might expect from the old idea that
wine "breathes" through the cork, natural corks show more exchange; and
individual corks also show somewhat wider variability.[67] As anyone who has
bought a case of old wine can attest, that is not a surprise: out of 12 bottles originally all in the same condition, after 10-20 years there will be significant variation
in the level of the wine in each bottle. And synthetic corks, made of plastic,
showed much the fastest rate of exchange; in fact, by four years after the start of
the trial, levels of sulfur dioxide in bottles with synthetic corks were down to the
levels at which oxidation becomes overt.

One of the implications of screwcaps' reduced rate of exchange is that you can
use less sulfur dioxide at bottling. In fact, it may be essential to do so. A stir was
created at the International Wine Challenge in 2006, a competition where more
than 9,000 wines were tasted, when many screwcap wines showed rubbery,
reductive aromas. (Reductive aromas arise when there is too little oxygen, allowing compounds such as hydrogen sulfide, the smell of rotten eggs, to form.) In
fact, 2.2% of the screwcapped wines were spoiled, compared to 4.4% of wine

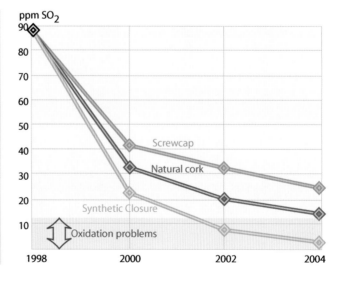

*Each type of bottle seal
causes the wine to
mature at a different
rate.[68]*

*All bottles started with
90 ppm (parts per
million) of total sulfur
dioxide in December
1997. The level at which
oxidation problems start
to appear is typically
about 12 ppm.*

bottled under cork that been tainted or oxidized.[69] However, there's a solution to the problem with screwcaps, which is to use less sulfur dioxide at bottling or to arrange for some subsequent exposure to oxygen.

Tasting comparisons between corks and screwcaps make it perfectly clear that if a wine is going to be consumed within a few months, screwcaps offer a much better chance of drinking it in the original condition that the winemaker intended when he bottled it. There's much less certainty about using screwcaps for wines that are intended for long aging. Part of the concern is that some exposure to oxygen may be necessary for aging—and the recent problems with screwcaps suggest that at a minimum, some oxygen may be needed to avoid reductive problems.

The hot issue of the moment is the OTR—the oxygen transmission rate. This describes the rate at which oxygen gets into the bottle. The variability of natural corks makes this difficult to control. Screwcaps show a level similar to the very tightest corks. The OTR of a screwcap is determined by its liner, the flat cylinder that the metal top compresses against the top of the glass. Research is now taking place to develop new liners that have precisely controlled levels of OTR. The original screwcaps have a layer of metal inside the liner, which makes it basically impermeable. New types of liners are using plastics with defined permeability to oxygen. In the near future, a producer who decides that his Sauvignon Blanc should be kept fresh for rapid consumption will be able to choose a screwcap with a minimal OTR, whereas a producer who is selling a Cabernet Sauvignon intended for long aging would be able to choose a screwcap with an OTR that he thinks is appropriate for development of this wine.

And what of synthetic corks, those molded plastic closures that can be so difficult to get out with an ordinary corkscrew? They certainly did not come out well from the AWRI study. And excessive passage of oxygen is not the only problem. They have a tendency to "scalp" wine, to extract volatile compounds from it that are part of its usual character. Riesling, for example, often shows petrol-like aromas that are due to the presence of a compound called TDN.[70] When TDN levels were measured in bottles two years after the same wine was put under different closures, screwcapped bottles kept all their TDN, corks retained about half—but synthetic corks had less then 5% left.[71] But they are improving all the time, and efforts are being made to develop synthetic corks with controlled OTR, and to make them more neutral to avoid scalping. However, right now they remain suitable only for wine that will be rapidly consumed.

All of which brings us to the question of ageing, and whether oxygen is really necessary. The idea that oxidation is an intrinsic part of ageing goes back to Pasteur, and was widely accepted until the mid-twentieth century. Since then there has been a split. Surveys of winemakers show they continue to believe oxidation is needed for ageing. But most expert technical opinion argues that ageing takes place in reductive conditions. "Reactions in bottled wine do not require oxygen," said Pascal Ribéreau-Gayon.[72] "It is the opposite of oxidation, a process of reduction or asphyxia, by which wine develops in the bottle," according to Emile Peynaud.[73]

Yet there is surprisingly little scientific evidence. The myth here is not that oxygen is, or is not, involved in ageing: the myth it is that we really know what is involved. The AWRI's comparisons between corks and screwcaps opened up the whole issue by demonstrating that the closure is not necessarily inert, and that wine ages differently depending on how much oxygen is available to it. The real question is what's the optimum amount of oxygen for a wine to age to reach its maximum potential? No one has done a definitive experiment. If it were up to me, I would bottle wine under natural cork and under screwcap, and I would keep one set of bottles under normal conditions, and the other set under nitrogen. This would show definitively whether oxygen was needed and whether there is any difference between cork and screwcap aside from oxygen permeability. All of the recent demonstrations of reductive problems in screwcapped wines suggest that a rather small amount of oxygen exposure may be needed for great wines to develop their potential.

Sparkling wine is a completely different case. Bottled under several atmospheres of pressure, with a metal cage to ensure the cork cannot come out, there is no prospect of oxygen seeping into the bottle. (Great Champagne can age in the bottle, but the processes do not depend on oxidation.) Cork isn't completely sacrosanct, because some New World sparkling wines have been bottled under crown caps (the same sort of closure used for beer bottles), but Champagne and all European sparkling wine have stayed resolutely under cork. But now a new alternative threatens this last sanctuary of the cork. Alcan, a major force in screwcaps with their dominant Stelvin closure, spent a million euros developing a new closure for sparkling wine. A lever ejects a plastic cork from the bottle, specially engineered to maintain the satisfactory popping sound of a traditional cork.[74] The lever closure is being tried on Duval-Leroy Champagne on an experimental basis; it remains to be seen whether the original cork will be threatened.

Screwcaps are widely accepted in Australia and New Zealand, but European consumers don't like screwcaps, or at least, when asked about preferences they

In this new Champagne closure, the traditional foil cover extends over the lever at the right, which opens the bottle.

tend to choose natural cork, going back to the old view that screwcaps are associated with lower quality. Resistance remains strongest in Continental Europe,
but in the U.K. has slowly given way to the predominance of screwcaps in New
World wines, although there is still resistance to using screwcaps for red wines
intended for aging. And these days it's not always so easy to tell the difference:
screwcap packaging is getting better and better, and the latest version from
Stelvin uses a soft insert around the threads under the foil capsule, so at a casual
glance there is a little difference from a bottle under cork. Indeed, no one has
ever done the critical survey of consumer tastes, which is to ask whether people
knew whether a bottle was sealed by screwcap or cork when they bought it.

"God Made the Wine"

Some vignerons would lead you to believe that they are merely the agent of the
Almighty in converting grape juice to wine. But wine is a human invention.
"God made only water, but man made wine," said Victor Hugo.[75]
    True enough, if there were no interference, the level of sugar in the grapes
would determine the level of alcohol in the wine. But how many wines actually
have "natural" alcohol levels between the Scylla of chaptalization and the
Charybdis of watering back (or other adjustments)? Except for wines made from
exceptionally ripe, late harvest grapes, all wine naturally would be dry; how
many sweet wines owe their sweetness entirely to nature? Winemaking more
naturally is oxidative than reductive; special precautions are needed to exclude
oxygen, but how much oxidation is experienced depends very much on the way
the wine is handled. The aromas, flavors, and structural components that wines
obtain from oak may meld seamlessly with the product of the grape itself, but
you have to recognize that their origin is extrinsic to the grape. Even how you
bottle (or otherwise package) the wine will affect how it smells and tastes just a
couple of months later. Winemaking is intrinsically an interventionist activity.

7

A Thousand Cultivars Bloom

THERE IS A HUGE DISCREPANCY between the large diversity of Vitis vinifera varieties and the increasing focus in winemaking on a small number of internationally recognized varieties.

Roughly 10,000 distinct varieties of Vitis vinifera are known. About half are found in France or Spain, with most of the rest in Italy, Greece, and Eastern Europe, reflecting their long wine-growing histories and emphasis on domesticating or developing grape varieties. Most of these are varieties that have arisen naturally since Vitis was domesticated. Varieties that have originated in the Americas are more recent, as are many of the varieties in Germany (which have been bred for adaptation to cool-climate conditions).

Several hundred varieties are used to make significant amounts of wine, but fewer than a hundred or so varieties account for half of all plantings. Among these leading varieties, fewer than twenty account for a quarter of the world's vineyards. The concentration of plantings into the leading international varieties has intensified over the past two decades, but this does not necessarily represent a significant loss of diversity in wine since the varieties that have declined are by no means high quality. The top positions on the world planting list are now split between quality varieties and the remnants of the old bulk plantings.

Cabernet Sauvignon now is the most widely planted black varietal in the world, followed closely by Merlot and Grenache (although this latter is far from being uniformly treated as a quality variety). The most striking change in the past twenty years is an almost three-fold increase in Syrah, which was not anywhere near the top ten list in 1990. The area of Carignan, which rarely gives wine of any quality, has halved.

The world's most planted white wine grape remains Airén, a completely nondescript source of white wine in Spain.[1] But its plantings have dropped dramatically since 1990, when it was far and away the most widely planted grape in the world. Chardonnay was not even in the top ten in 1990, but is now

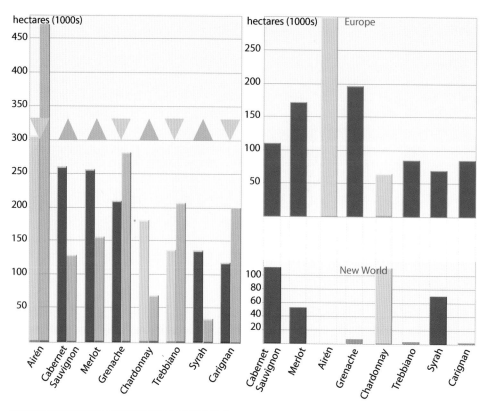

Plantings of the leading varieties changed greatly between 1990 and 2004 (left). Red and yellow show hectares in 2004 and gray shows hectares in 1990. Pink triangles indicate a decrease; green triangles indicate an increase.[2] The top varieties are different in Europe and the New World (right).[3]

the world's leading quality white grape. There is still plenty of Trebbiano (Ugni Blanc), although quite a bit of it is used to make wine for distillation into brandy rather than for drinking.

There's a great difference in distribution of these varieties between the Old World and New World.[4] In spite of attempts at what the French call "cépage amelioration" (improving the types of planted varieties), Europe is still stuck with large quantities of the old bulk production varieties, led by Airén and Trebbiano (Ugni Blanc) in the whites, and Carignan in the blacks. In the New World, where most plantings date from the last two decades, the motto has been "plant the usual suspects." Cabernet Sauvignon production is now split more or less equally between New World and Europe, and there is actually more Chardonnay in the New World than in Europe. The detritus of Airén, Trebbiano, and Carignan is completely missing from the New World. Is this part of the reason why the Old World producers are struggling so hard for market share in the global economy?

Noble Varieties and Commoners

The range of grape varieties is immense, from household names to obscurities known to only a few remaining growers. Going back to the glory days when France *was* wine, its best grapes were called the noble varieties: Cabernet Sauvignon, Merlot, Pinot Noir, basically representing Bordeaux and Burgundy for the reds; and Chardonnay, Riesling, and Sauvignon Blanc for the whites, with more diverse origins.

The criteria for a noble variety are that it should have an international reputation, and that the quality of its top wines can be demonstrated by their aging potential. By this measure, there is no doubt about the position of the first five. Depending on whether your allegiance is to Bordeaux or Burgundy, you might

Grape varieties form a quality tree, with a small group of noble varieties broadening into groups making classic wines, groups that can be interesting (more could be added to this list), a very large number of indifferent varieties (not shown), and the old bulk production varieties right at the bottom.

Noble Varieties	
Cabernet Sauvignon	Chardonnay
Merlot	Riesling
Pinot Noir	Sauvignon Blanc

Classic Varieties	
Cabernet Franc	Chenin Blanc
Nebbiolo	Gewürztraminer
Sangiovese	Sémillon
Syrah	Viognier
Tempranillo	
Touriga Naçional	

Interesting Varieties	
Barbera	Albariño
Carmenère	Aligoté
Dolcetto	Cortese
Gamay	Garganega
Grenache	Grüner Veltliner
Malbec	Marsanne
Montepulciano	Muscadet
Mourvèdre	Pinot Blanc
Pedro Ximénez	Pinot Gris
Petit Verdot	Roussanne
Tannat	Muscat Blanc à Petit Grains
Touriga Franca	Friulano
Zinfandel	Torrontés
	Verdejo

No Name Varieties	
Alicante Bouschet	Airén
Aramon	Bourboulenc
Bobal	Chasselas
Carignan	Clairette
Cinsault	Crouchen
Lambrusco	Folle Blanche
	Malvasia
	Trebbiano

regard Cabernet Sauvignon-Merlot blends or Pinot Noir as the epitome of red wine; and although Chardonnay today is far and away the best known quality white grape, a century ago Riesling was held in higher esteem, as judged by auction prices in London. All of these varieties produce very high quality wines in multiple locations. But I would question whether Sauvignon Blanc really belongs in this group. Vinified as a monovarietal, it's a rare Sauvignon Blanc that ages well; blended with Sémillon, it makes some great white wines in Bordeaux, but the number with high aging potential is miniscule—I can count them on my fingers.

Those who feel that this traditional list shows an outdated bias towards France have a point. The most obvious omission from the list of noble black grapes is Syrah, which actually has long made wines of the highest quality in the northern Rhône, but really is if anything more prominent now under its Australian name of Shiraz. Wines from Syrah (or Shiraz) or blends based on it can show as much complexity as the noble black varieties and can age as well. I would certainly include Syrah in the very top group.

Other varieties that can reach equivalent quality, but in a more geographically restricted way, include Cabernet Franc (back to Bordeaux again), Nebbiolo (who can quarrel with the assertion that Barolo can be as great a red wine as any?), Sangiovese (where Brunello di Montalcino has reached its peak in recent years), Tempranillo (the basis for the great Riojas), and Touriga Nacional (perhaps a special case since its greatest role is achieved in Port, which after all is fortified). Among the whites, claims could made for Chenin Blanc, Gewürztraminer, Viognier, although none is quite so convincing.

The existence of some great wines made from these varieties has given them an international reputation. However, all attempts have failed at reproducing the qualities of Nebbiolo, Sangiovese, or Tempranillo outside of their native habitats, preventing them from joining the list of true "international varieties." Some people say the same about Pinot Noir, but that would be to provoke an argument.

There's a sizeable group of interesting varieties, which from time to time make really good wine, although most of the production is at a much lower level, and there's a huge number of fairly indifferent varieties. The joker in the pack is a large number of indigenous grapes that can make interesting wines in their local conditions, although for one reason or another they have failed to penetrate the outside world. A sizeable bunch of no-name varieties make large amounts of wine, but you don't often see these varietal names on the label; it's rare indeed that there's anything of interest.

A handful of varieties make great wines in very special circumstances, but only in those circumstances. Palomino Fino makes great Sherry, but is pretty indifferent as a dry white wine. To quote Jancis Robinson, Palomino makes a potentially great style of wine, but is not inherently a great grape. Malvasia under its synonym of Malmsey has been known to make great Madeira, but otherwise is of little interest. Sémillon achieves greatness principally for its role in the blend of sweet wines such as Sauternes. And I admire the effort, but have been unconvinced by attempts to produce quality wine from old Carignan vines.

Ancient Origins and Newbies

Originally all grapes were black. Color is due to production of the anthocyanin pigments in the skin. Grapevines producing white grapes arose by mutations inactivating the production of anthocyanins. Most major white cultivars have the same mutation, which suggests that the distinction between black and white grapevines must have occurred early in the evolution of the grapevine.[5] Of course, white varieties continue to arise, sometimes by new mutations inactivating the anthocyanin genes.

Today's grapevines can be grouped into sixteen clusters that fall into four general groups. Each group has a geographical bias but there is overlap between the groups, indicating that grapevines were often transported from their sites of origin to new locations. Three of the clusters of the French group contain wild grapevines, suggesting that the traditional French cultivars are closest to the ancestral grapevine (Vitis vinifera silvestris).[7] Two groups contain principally eastern Mediterranean or central European varieties. The group of table grapes is genetically distant from the wine grapes and wild grapes; they probably originated from intense selection during ancient agriculture. Virtually all of the modern grapes with international reputations belong to one of the clusters in the French group.

Grapes have been grown in most of their present locations in Europe for between one and two thousand years. But the names and descriptions of the

Genetic relationships between cultivars identify four groups: three groups of wine grapes and one group of table grapes.[6]

Branch points show how far back in evolution each cluster diverged.

The 16 individual clusters in the groups vary in size from 4 to 33 cultivars and/or wild grapevines; one representative member of each cluster is named.

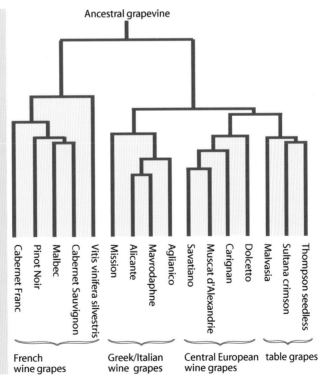

varieties grown one or two millennia ago cannot be equated with modern varieties. Indeed, some of the modern varieties, such as Cabernet Sauvignon, Merlot, or Chardonnay are relatively recent arrivals on the scene; they were generated by spontaneous crosses between existing varieties at points in the last five or six hundred years. The oldest of the modern varieties can be traced back to the medieval period. The two most anciently established of the important varieties grown today are Nebbiolo and Pinot Noir. Nebbiolo wins for the oldest known description by a short head (a mere century or so).

It's generally thought that Nebbiolo originated in Piedmont and that its name refers to the nebbia, the local fog forming in the Piedmont hills in the autumn. Several references from the thirteenth century probably identify this variety growing in Piedmont. The Rivoli estate (located in what is now a suburb of Turin) described production of 300 sextaries of wine made from "nibiol" vineyards in 1268.[8] "Neblori" and "nebiolo" are mentioned in documents from 1292 in Alba and 1295 in Asti.[9] There is a continuous stream of subsequent references to the importance of the grape, and it is viewed as the highest quality grape of the region in a famous treatise of 1606.[10]

Pinot Noir is thought to be one of the most ancient varieties, and it is believed that it may have been cultivated in Burgundy from the fourteenth century, although real evidence for its origins is pretty scanty. A grape called Pinot, presumably Pinot Noir, possibly previously known as Noiren, was first mentioned in Burgundy in 1375.[11] In the closely related group of Pinot varieties, Pinot Noir is the ancestral parent, and several different Pinot Blanc clones arose as independent mutants.[12] Indeed, most recently one occurred in the vineyards of Henri Gouges in Nuits St. Georges where it is used to produce a white wine.[13]

Riesling is another old variety, possibly dating back to 1348, to a reference to "Russelinge" in a map in Alsace, but almost certainly known by 1435 when "Riesslingen" grapes were purchased near Hochheim in the Rheingau.[14]

Romantic fancies have wonderfully embroidered the real origins of Syrah. The resemblance between the identity of its alternative name, Shiraz, with the city of the same name in Iran has provoked theories that the grape may have originated in Persia, and was brought to France by the Romans. An early nineteenth century catalog of French grape varieties repeated the local tradition that "Seyras" was originally brought from Shiraz by a hermit who resided in Hermitage.[15] However, DNA fingerprinting shows that it originated in a cross between Dureza (found in the Ardèche region on the west bank of the Rhône) and Mondeuse (a grape of Savoie, well to the east).[16] This places its origins in France, well away from the romance of the East.[17]

Sangiovese is another grape attracting some amusing theories. Translation of the name as "blood of Jove" spawned proposals that it dates from the days of Rome. Soderini mentioned a grape called Sangiogheto in Tuscany in 1590, but there is no proof this was Sangiovese.[18] By the eighteenth century, there are references to Sangiovese as being one of the most planted grapes in Tuscany (together with Malvasia and Trebbiano).[19] DNA mapping identifies the parents of Sangiovese as Ciliegiolo, a Tuscan grape, and Calabrese Montenuovo, a grape from the south.[20] When and where this cross occurred is unknown.

Cépage Plus Terroir Equals Typicité

Or does it? The case for typicity is that each cépage grows best in a specific terroir; the combination brings out unique characteristics of the wine that the French call *typicité*. At its ultimate, the argument supposes that a cépage may be capable of giving its best results in only one place. The case against is that the association of particular qualities with specific combinations of cultivar and place is no more than a historical accident, that the same cultivars can be grown elsewhere; the fact that the wine may be different from historical impressions merely reflects the fact that it produces different results in different conditions.

Certainly some varieties are difficult to grow successfully away from their traditional locales: Pinot Noir is closely associated with Burgundy, Tempranillo with Spain, Nebbiolo and Sangiovese with Piedmont and Tuscany.

Growing Pinot Noir elsewhere to give wines like those of Burgundy has been a holy grail of winemakers; and the quest has yet to be fulfilled. Yet excellent wines are made from Pinot Noir in New Zealand, in Oregon, and more recently in Germany. Do we say they fail to show the typicité of Pinot Noir because they are not easily confused with the wines of Burgundy; or do we say that if history had been different, and Pinot Noir had been grown first in New Zealand, we would regard Burgundian Pinot Noir as failing to achieve New World richness?

There is to date a pretty good case that Nebbiolo gives good results only in Piedmont, at its peak in the regions of Barolo and Barbaresco, and that Sangiovese gives top results only in Tuscany, at its best in Brunello di Montalcino. Efforts to reproduce these wines by growing the varieties elsewhere have so far failed, making a case for saying these cépages have indeed found a unique match with their terroir.

Tempranillo is an ambiguous example. This great grape of Rioja has not been grown successfully outside of Spain, but it has certainly been widely propagated in Spanish regions other than Rioja in the past couple of decades. Is this a case where it has been possible to produce wines with the same typicité in new regions, or one where we have accepted changes in the style of the varietal wine as its boundaries have expanded?

Some varieties are more easily transportable. Cabernet Sauvignon originated in Bordeaux, Syrah originated in the northern Rhône, Chardonnay may have originated in Burgundy. But all now have reputations based on wines made all over the world. New World versions tend to be richer, fuller-bodied, more powerful, more alcoholic than those of Europe, but it is an exceptional taster indeed who can guarantee consistently to distinguish Old and New World wines of these varieties in a blind tasting.

Steven Spurrier's famous "Judgment of Paris" tasting in 1976 makes the case forcefully. This was a blind wine tasting held in Paris when French judges compared Napa Valley Chardonnays and Cabernet Sauvignons with white Burgundy and red Bordeaux. The judges, a distinguished group of top tasters, were confident they could tell the difference, that the contest was not at all serious, and that they had identified the French wines as superior. There was an outcry when the results were tallied and Napa wines came top in both categories; some judges tried to take back their results.[21] The French press ignored or denigrated the results, but journalist George Taber reported the results in Time magazine; not surprisingly, quite a fuss resulted in the United States. The tasting is regarded as a pivotal moment in international acceptance of California wines, but the point is not so much which wines "won" the tasting, but the fact that the judges were completely confused as to which wines originated in France and which in California. What price typicité?

Yet there is a difference. The slightly herbaceous aroma and flavor spectrum of a traditional Bordeaux is distinct from, say, the intense blackcurrant fruits and aromaticity of a Barossa Cabernet Sauvignon. But wait: note that I said a "traditional" Bordeaux. It is not so easy to distinguish today's wines from the left Bank of Bordeaux from those made in California's Napa valley or in South Australia. Warmer climatic conditions and a trend to later harvesting have led to Cabernet Sauvignon in Bordeaux that often more resembles a New World Cabernet Sauvignon than a wine from Bordeaux of fifty years ago. So what's the typicité of Cabernet Sauvignon and has our view of it changed from herbaceous to fruity?

White pepper used to be regarded as part of the typicity of Hermitage, but this is actually a characteristic of Syrah before it reaches full ripeness; today's Hermitage is more often closer to the spectrum of aromatic black fruits found in Shiraz from Barossa Valley. Chardonnay, that most malleable of varieties, takes its character as much from winemaking style as from origin of the grapes; I defy anyone to define typicité for Chardonnay, since even within its traditional Burgundian home there is a great difference between a steely, mineral, unoaked Chablis, and a fat, nutty, buttery Meursault full of new oak from the Côte d'Or.

The aromas and flavor spectrum of each varietal are influenced greatly by ripeness. Perhaps there is a slightly less than ripe typicité for Cabernet Sauvignon (such as traditional Bordeaux) and a fully ripe typicité (as found in the New World). Is the difference between Cabernet Sauvignon and Pinot Noir that we have accepted a change in typicité for the former but are reluctant to do so for the latter?

The Bitterness of the Super-taster

Smell is vastly more complicated than taste. You can distinguish probably around a thousand odors, using hundreds of different types of receptors for odors in the human nose, but there are only five different types of receptors for taste on the tongue.[22] It used to be thought that receptors for different tastes are located in different areas of the tongue, but we now know that a single taste bud contains up to a hundred taste cells and has receptors for all five taste types (sour, salt, bitter, sweet, unami [savory]). Basically the taste of any one of these groups can be distinguished from another, but two tastes in the same group (such as two bitter compounds) cannot be distinguished. More of the complexity of wine is due to its smell than to its taste, although this may not be obvious as the two senses mingle when a wine is tasted. People's abilities to smell and taste vary widely. How far does this bring into question the whole idea of describing wines in a way that is universally meaningful?

We have known for almost a century that individuals' sense of smell differ widely (the first report concerned differences in ability to detect the aroma of verbena).[23] Recent scientific discoveries show that odors are detected by a vast set of receptors with overlapping sensitivities, so a particular odor may be recognized by several different receptors with different sensitivities to it, whereas taste receptors are nonoverlapping (with the sole exception of a partially shared receptor for sweet and unami). Odor receptor genes in the human population vary more widely than taste receptor genes.[24]

Individual capacity to detect specific odorants can vary greatly.[25] Sometimes the same aroma is perceived differently, such as androstenone which some people find unpleasant (urine-like), but others detect as sweet and floral. It's noticeable when people describe wines that their terminology for taste (for example, for sweetness or alcohol levels) is more consistent than their descriptions of aromas, where different people may well use different terms to describe the same odors, often reflecting the fact that the odorant is found in many different sources in nature. When you add these differences in description to differences in detection, it becomes complicated to provide an objective description. But scientific analysis comes to the rescue: many of the characteristic aromas of specific varietals can be identified with particular chemical components, whose concentrations can be measured.

Judging from the number of genes devoted to each type of taste, bitterness may be the most important. There are 25 different genes coding for receptors for bitter compounds, compared with 3 genes responsible for both sweet and unami tastes.[26] (The receptors for salty and sour tastes have not been unequivocally identified.) There is significant variation in ability to taste unami, and generally less variation in sensitivity to sweet, salty, and sour.[27] The widest range comes in sensitivity to bitterness, which is important because bitterness is often associated with toxic compounds.[28]

One of the first insights into taste differences came in the early 1930s when Dupont chemist Arthur Fox accidentally released some PTC (phenylthiourea) in his laboratory. A colleague reacted to the bitter taste, but Fox himself could not detect it.[29] In fact, about 70% of people taste bitterness in the compound. It turns out that this difference is due to a single gene; you can taste PTC as long as you have one active copy of the gene.[30] Although a quarter of the population can't taste PTC, the sensation of bitterness for those who can taste is affected by various factors other than the gene itself, so when tasters are tested, there is a more or less continuous range of sensitivities.

The PTC gene codes for a receptor that binds a set of related chemical compounds, all of which trigger the bitter sensation. Among them is a chemical called PROP,[31] which is now routinely used to test for ability to sense bitterness. Testing with PROP shows that some people are extremely sensitive to it. This sensitivity correlates with a need to add sweetening to counteract the perception of bitterness; in fact, it defines a category of people who have significantly enhanced sensitivity to bitterness. These so-called super-tasters make up about 20%

of the population.[32] The story in the wine world goes that super-tasters can be recognized by taking sugar and cream in their coffee, finding red wine too bitter to enjoy, preferring slightly sweet white or rosé (white Zinfandel is their favorite tipple), finding that artificial sweeteners have a bitter metallic taste, and (where information is available) the occurrence of morning sickness in their mothers.[33]

The larger puzzle for wine drinkers, however, is why enhanced sensitivity to PTC or PROP should imply a difficulty with handling tannins in red wine (or caffeine in coffee), since PTC and PROP are chemically different from tannins or caffeine.[34] No one has systematically tested what range of bitter compounds respond to the PTC receptor, but certainly the super-taster phenomenon seems to have a big influence on tastes in wine.[35]

It's clear that super-tasters have an exaggerated response to bitter compounds, but it's not entirely clear why. They have a higher density than usual of the cells containing taste receptors on the tongue.[38] The usual test for a super-taster is to apply a little blue food coloring to the tongue; the taste buds stand out as bumps in the middle of the blue stain, and you simply count how many there are per square centimeter; roughly speaking, a tolerant taster (not sensitive to bitter taste) has about 50, an average taster has about 100, and a super-taster has about 150. You can apply the test to yourself simply by placing a paper cut-out on the tongue and applying the blue dye to the circle in the center.

But this has never completely made sense, because an increased number of receptors would predict increased sensitivity to all tastes, not just to bitterness. Indeed, it turns out that super-tasters are more sensitive to a range of bitter compounds (not just those recognized by any one bitter receptor) and also to salty, sweet, and sour tastes.[39] In fact, if you define super-tasters as people with

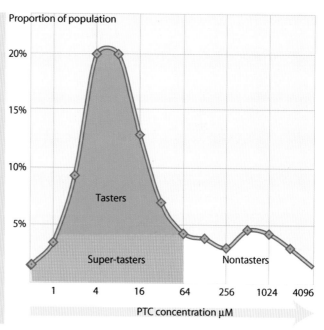

Measuring the threshold level at which people can taste PTC classifies those requiring >64 µM as nontasters.[36]

Super-tasters are defined by their psychological response rather than by the threshold, and comprise about a third of all tasters.[37]

 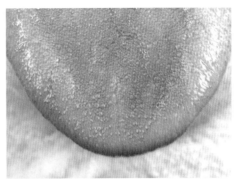

Super-tasters (left) have a much greater density of taste buds, shown by the blue stain, than normal tasters (right). Photographs kindly provided by Tim Hanni MW.

heightened sensitivity to all tastes, PROP isn't the only or best stimulus that reveals them. Super-tasters have been specifically diagnosed from the population of PTC/PROP tasters, but the basis for super-tasting remains undefined. It's possible that the effect depends on the way taste stimuli are interpreted by the brain rather than on the sensitivity of detection. There is in fact no scientific definition of super-tasters: they are basically people who self-diagnose extreme reactions to bitter compounds.[40]

By contrast, differences in detecting sweetness are only about 10-fold (compared with 10,000-fold for bitter), but a major part seems to be due to variation in the amount of a sweet receptor. People who have less of this receptor are less sensitive to sugar.[41]

Most attention is focused on the fact that super-tasters report disagreeable sensations when they drink red wine, but the real implication for wine tasting is that everyone's reaction will be different, depending on exactly where they are along the curves for detecting bitterness and sweetness. Super-tasters are simply the extreme end of the distribution.

Just to add to the puzzle, tannins are usually detected more by astringency than by taste. Astringency is a feeling (not a taste) due to a tactile sensation, created (for example) by tannins when they bind to salivary proteins in the mouth. Super-tasters don't seem to have any increased sensitivity to astringency.[42]

What does all this mean for objectivity in describing the aromas or the bitterness or sweetness of a wine?[43] Should there be a standard for calibrating critics?

Aromas of Grapes and Wine

If you try to classify grape varieties into groups, the criteria owe as much or more to smell as to taste. Certainly acidity and fruit flavors come into it, but the first measure for identifying an unknown wine tends to be its aroma.

Red wines are most often grouped according to whether they convey an impression of red fruit or black fruit. Among the red fruit group, Sangiovese and Nebbiolo usually convey a savory rather than overtly fruity impression, and this can be true also of Pinot Noir and Tempranillo. Among the black fruit group, there's a gradation from herbaceous, to fruity, to overtly aromatic. Some grapes might move from one group to another, depending on their degree of ripeness: Cabernet Sauvignon, for example, tends to be herbaceous when under-ripe but can be jammy when over-ripe.

White wines divide into neutral and aromatic by flavor profile. Some neutral whites have a real affinity for oak, and can be greatly enhanced by time spent in wood, when the oak flavors may come to be as important a part of the profile as the grape flavors themselves. It is less common for aromatic varieties to be exposed to wood. At one extreme, Sauvignon Blanc can be "grassy" or herbaceous; at the other, Muscat (or its relative Torrontés) are rare varieties that actually show grapey aromas.

More than a thousand volatile compounds contributing to aromas have been found in wine.[44] (This compares with a mere fifty volatile aromas in coffee.[45]) The characteristic aroma and flavor spectrum of any wine is due to complex interactions between these components, but as we learn more about smell and taste, often the dominant characteristics of a grape variety can be identified with a few components. The herbaceous qualities of Cabernet Sauvignon or Sauvignon Blanc, those petrol notes of Riesling, the pepper of Syrah, the lychees of

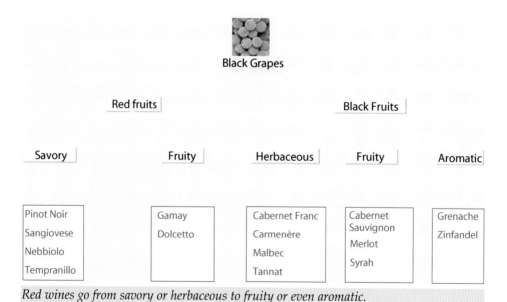

Red wines go from savory or herbaceous to fruity or even aromatic.

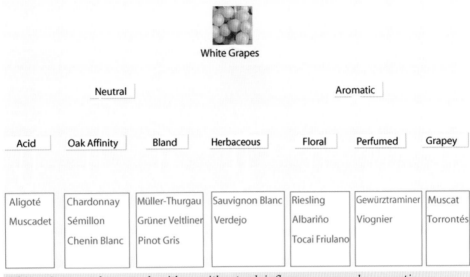

White Grapes

Neutral				Aromatic		
Acid	Oak Affinity	Bland	Herbaceous	Floral	Perfumed	Grapey
Aligoté Muscadet	Chardonnay Sémillon Chenin Blanc	Müller-Thurgau Grüner Veltliner Pinot Gris	Sauvignon Blanc Verdejo	Riesling Albariño Tocai Friulano	Gewürztraminer Viognier	Muscat Torrontés

White wines may be neutral, with or without oak influence, or may be aromatic.

Gewürztraminer, for example, each resides in particular molecules. Knowing the conditions that favor or disfavor the formation of these components opens up a whole new range of possibilities for influencing wine flavor.

This knowledge reinforces the usefulness of describing wines by their aromas. To the outsider, it may seem fanciful, even pretentious, to say that Cabernet Sauvignon offers an impression of bell peppers, that Sauvignon Blanc shows traces of asparagus and passion fruit, that Pinot Noir is characterized by overtones of earthy strawberries, or to find suggestions of chocolate or coffee in a wine—but finding that the wines have traces of the same chemical components contributing to the characteristics of the fruits or vegetables validates the approach.

The compounds that contribute to flavor and aroma are a dizzying array of chemical types, including thiols (sulfur-containing compounds), esters (formed by reaction between alcohols and acids), and terpenes (hydrocarbons formed by a wide variety of plants, which take their generic name from turpentine). Sometimes the compounds responsible for the characteristic aromas of a grape variety are found in the grape itself (Muscat is a classic example), but more often they are generated during fermentation and maturation, sometimes by directly converting an inactive precursor in the grape into an active odorant, sometimes as the result of a more complex pathway catalyzed by yeast. Some aromas and flavors develop only with bottle aging. And of course some have an extraneous source, the oak of the barrels in which the wine is matured.

Many grape varieties have characteristic aromas of fruits or vegetables that are due to specific identified compounds.

Grape Variety	Aroma		Compounds	Type
Pinot Noir	strawberry		Ethyl acetate, ethyl butyrate, ethyl formate, ethyl hexanoate, furaneol, methyl cinnamate	esters
Cabernet Sauvignon	bell pepper		3-isobutyl-2-methoxy-pyrazine	pyrazine
Syrah	pepper		Rotundone	
	blueberry			
Sauvignon Blanc	gooseberry		4-MMP (4-mercapto-4-methyl-pentan-2-one) (effect depends on concentration)	thiol
	passion fruit, cat's pee			
Riesling	petrol		TDN (1,6 trimethyl-1,2-dihydronaphthalene)	
Gewürztraminer	lychees		*cis*-rose oxide	ester
Muscat	grapes		Geraniol	terpene
Sémillon	figs		ethyl propionate, isobutyl acetate	esters
Carbonic maceration, e.g. Gamay	bananas		isoamyl acetate	esters
Botrytized wines	honey		Sotolon	lactone

It depends a lot on the varietal how much difference yeast make at fermentation. For aromatic varieties such as Sauvignon Blanc, where they play a key role in releasing aromas, the effect is much greater than for neutral varieties. Don't be fooled into thinking yeasts are only machines for converting sugar to alcohol.

Winemaking conditions can therefore have a strong influence on varietal character. For example, thiol compounds are reducing agents, so it follows that their properties are emphasized by winemaking under reductive conditions and minimized under oxidative conditions. This particular aspect of winemaking becomes of prime importance for varieties such as Sauvignon Blanc where a large part of the aroma is provided by thiols.

Aroma and flavors in wine may be generated at any stage of vinification.

	Source	Influenced by	Example
	Grapes	Berry ripeness	Herbaceousness (bell peppers) in Cabernet Sauvignon
	Released from grape precursors during fermentation	Strain of yeast	Gooseberry/passion fruit aromas in Sauvignon Blanc
	Created by yeast during fermentation	Strain of yeast	Esters (isoamyl acetate) in carbonic maceration, such as in Beaujolais nouveau.
	Created by bacteria during malolactic fermentation	Strain of bacteria	Diacetyl (buttery)
	Botrytis cinerea fungus	Extent of botrytis infection	Honey and piquancy in dessert wines
	Oak	Type of oak, barrel toasting	Vanillin
	Bottle development	Age	Petrol aromas in Riesling

The Bell Peppers of Cabernet

Cabernet Sauvignon may be the most famous black variety in the world, and certainly it is now the most widely planted of the quality black varietals, but its fame originated in the Bordeaux blend rather than as a one hundred percent varietal. On Bordeaux's left bank, it would be thought unsophisticated to make a wine solely from Cabernet Sauvignon; usually it is blended with Merlot, and sometimes Cabernet Franc and Petit Verdot are also added. Cabernet Sauvignon brings structure and austerity to the blend, Merlot contributes fruitiness and fleshiness, Cabernet Franc has leafy notes of tobacco, and Petit Verdot brings a touch of spice. Malbec and Carmenère are varieties that used to be common in Bordeaux, but that today have become rare. On the right bank, Merlot dominates the scene, usually with Cabernet Franc as the subservient variety. Wines labeled

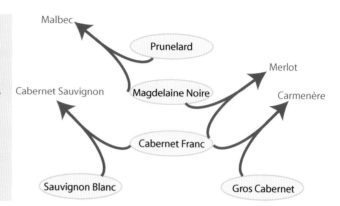

Bordeaux black varietals have incestuous relationships.

Parents are shown in pink ovals; progeny varieties are in red.

as Cabernet Sauvignon are common in the New World, although often they contain a small amount of Merlot (legally limited to 15% if the wine is to carry the varietal label).

The black Bordeaux varieties are relative newcomers to the viticultural scene. They show a tight relationship stemming from several common ancestors. Ironically at the center of the history, since if not exactly marginalized, it has certainly decreased in importance recently, is Cabernet Franc. This turns out to be the common ancestral grape of Bordeaux. A chance cross between Cabernet Franc and Sauvignon Blanc created Cabernet Sauvignon, probably a few hundred years ago.[46] Another cross involving Cabernet Franc, this time with a lost cultivar (examples of which were found in an abandoned vineyard in the Charente region to the north of Bordeaux) created Merlot.[47] The second parent of Merlot, named Magdelaine Noire des Charentes after its rediscovery, was one of the parents of Malbec.[48] Cabernet Franc is also one of the parents of the old Bordeaux variety, Carmenère (now scarcely grown at all).

Cabernet Sauvignon is thought to have been introduced to Bordeaux by Baron Hector de Brane (the proprietor prior to 1830 of Brane Mouton, which was later to become Mouton Rothschild). Armand d'Armailhacq also grew the grape at his château and advocated its use in his book (published in various editions from 1855).[50] It does best on well-drained, gravel soils.

Merlot is a relative newcomer to the list of top varieties. It was a secondary cultivar in Bordeaux in the nineteenth century, increasing in popularity in the

France has one quarter of the world's Cabernet Sauvignon; most of the rest is in the New World.[49]

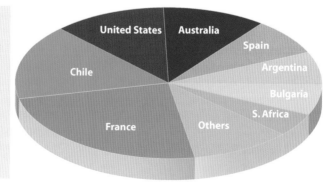

The small, darkly colored berries of Cabernet Sauvignon bring structure to a blend.

second part of the century because of its relatively low susceptibility to powdery mildew, which was becoming a problem. It became significant when it replaced Malbec during the replanting resulting from the phylloxera epidemic.[51] Today it is the major variety in Bordeaux,[52] the most widely planted black variety in France, and close behind Cabernet Sauvignon in worldwide popularity. One of the most famous (and most expensive) wines of the right bank of Bordeaux, Château Pétrus is made almost exclusively (95%) from Merlot, and many of the successful small-production, cult wines are monovarietal Merlots.

Cabernet Sauvignon has spread around the world from its origins in Bordeaux. France remains the country with the most plantings, more than half in Bordeaux, but overall there is now more Cabernet Sauvignon in the New World than the Old. Most of it is grown in climates that are warmer than Bordeaux, and this has had a major effect on our perception of the nature of the variety.

The traditional aroma of Cabernet Sauvignon, as seen in the wines of the left bank of Bordeaux, has a herbaceous note usually described as bell peppers. The fruit aromas and flavors are black, and sometimes young wines, especially from

As Cabernet Sauvignon ripens, its aroma and flavor spectrum changes from bell peppers to blackcurrant to cassis to jam.

Cabernet Sauvignon is usually planted in the gravel soils, as here in the Médoc.

warm vintages, show clear notes of blackcurrants. Wines from the warmer climates of the New World often show blackcurrant aromas, and these can intensify into the more aromatic notes of cassis. In really hot climates, this turns to an impression of jam (as it does with all black varieties). This variation reflects a progression of aromas as the grapes become increasingly riper. Indeed, as Bordeaux has been overtaken by warmer vintages, the traditional herbaceous notes have become unfashionable, and château proprietors may bristle visibly if you describe a wine as showing herbaceousness.

We may now be at the last point in history when one can talk about the bell peppers of Cabernet. The trend is moving so firmly away from the traditional herbaceous flavor spectrum towards the blackcurrant flavors of modern fruit-forward wines that in another twenty years there may be no one left who remembers that Cabernet Sauvignon used to be herbaceous or who does not regard this as a flaw. Yet the blend of very faintly herbaceous Cabernet Sauvignon (on the left bank) or Cabernet Franc (on the right bank) with the fruity Merlot made for some wonderfully complex wines in top vintages. Personally, I believe that something has been lost, and that wines are less complex, when all the fruits are uniformly ripe; it's that very faint (but only very faint) touch of herbaceousness that gives Bordeaux its classic elegance and complexity.

The herbaceous quality of Cabernet Sauvignon is due to its production of a single compound, a pyrazine (3-isobutyl-2-methoxypyrazine, known as IBMP). Not surprisingly, since Sauvignon Blanc is one of the parents of Cabernet Sauvignon, the same compound is also responsible for the characteristic herbaceous notes of Sauvignon Blanc, although in this variety it usually manifests itself more as grassiness or asparagus. Methoxypyrazine synthesis is related to vegetative growth, occurring in the berries between fruit set and the period just prior to veraison. Sunlight triggers its destruction, and its level drops sharply between veraison and harvest. Warmer climatic conditions, coupled with the trend to harvest grapes at greater levels of ripeness, may mean that the level has dropped below detection by the time Cabernet Sauvignon is harvested.

So the aromas and taste of Cabernet Sauvignon from different regions are much influenced by the typical level of ripeness. The transition from herbaceous to blackcurrant reflects how much heat and light the berries have had, and how late they were harvested. Blackcurrants have become more evident than bell peppers as vintages have become warmer in Bordeaux. California Cabernet Sauvignon varies from relatively soft and amorphous black fruits at the generic level to intense blackcurrants from Napa, somewhat leaner from Sonoma. Cabernet Sauvignon from Australia tends to exuberance, with intense aromatics accompanying the blackcurrants from Barossa Valley, less aromaticity from McLaren Vale, and more precise, elegant fruits from Coonawarra. Chile and Argentina produce Cabernet Sauvignon in the style of California, but the fruits tend to be less well focused and less intense.

Syrah or Shiraz?

Syrah, Sirah, Syra, Sirac, Seyras, Schiras, Shiraz are all names by which Syrah has been known in the Rhône. It is the sole red grape of the Northern Rhône, where it is vinified as a monovarietal (the old habit of including some white grapes for softening now being quite rare). The oldest established appellation is Hermitage.

Although wine was being produced in Hermitage in Roman times, there is no knowing what grape varieties were cultivated then, and the modern history of Hermitage starts with a royal visit in 1642, when Louis XIII was offered the wine.[53] Syrah has been grown in the Northern Rhône at least since the seventeenth century, when it became known as Sérine at Côte-Rôtie and as Petite Syrah at Hermitage.[54] Petite Syrah refers specifically to cultivars with small berries,[55] as opposed to those with larger berries, known as Grosse Syrah. The old cultivars now represent less than 10% of modern plantings, however, as they have been replaced by modern clones of varying quality.[56] Current plantings mostly date from clones of Grosse Syrah developed in the 1970s and 1980s, which unfortunately follow the model for higher production at the expense of quality.[57]

Australian Shiraz dates from cuttings taken from Hermitage in 1831 during James Busby's tour of France. Busby (who played a formative role in the early Australian wine industry) referred to it as Ciras or Seyras, and the vines were

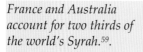

France and Australia account for two thirds of the world's Syrah.[59]

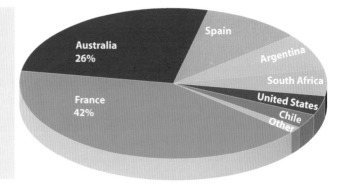

made freely available; by 1860 they had been widely planted in Hunter Valley.[58] The earliest references to the grape in Australia often use "Scyras" as a description, but by the 1860s the wine was generally known as Shiraz or Hermitage. Hermitage ceased to be used in the 1980s to avoid conflict with the wine from France. Australia's most famous example of a Syrah-based wine, Grange Hermitage, changed its name to Grange in 1989.

Syrah is dry, dense, rich, alcoholic, and tannic. It is deeply colored with black hues; perhaps it is not as densely colored as Cabernet Sauvignon. The nose tends towards a mineral blueberry, often with spiciness or peppery overtones, sometimes showing a tarry or burned rubber aroma. Classic notes of white pepper tend to come out in wines made from grapes harvested at lower ripeness levels.

Syrah has spread around the warm climates of the world, with wine styles somewhat indicated by whether it is called Syrah or Shiraz. The wines of the Rhône tend to be relatively backward, often with gamey notes (but these may be due to infection with the yeast Brettanomyces rather than to the variety or terroir). Eventually Hermitage ages toward a similar flavor spectrum as old Bordeaux. The wines of the Languedoc, the other major locus for production in France, tend to be fruitier and richer, but less refined. In hot vintages, Rhône wines can show fruits of black plums, closing the gap quite a bit with the New World style, but they are rarely as full-throated as the Shiraz of Australia or South America. New World Shiraz can be aromatic (more so than Cabernet Sauvignon). Australian Shiraz is often made in an exuberant style, bursting with forward fruits, dominated by notes of aromatic plums, tannins obscured by the fruits, tending to high alcohol of 14% or more. It is at its most forward from Barossa Valley.

Some successes with Syrah are now found in South Africa, where the wines tend to follow the Australian model but with less intensity, more of a halfway house between Australia and the Rhône. Syrah in Chile, often named Shiraz to indicate relationship with the Australian style, can be aromatic, with damsons and black plums showing on nose and palate, with the same high alcohol as Australia, but less weight and lower acidity, sometimes with slightly herbaceous notes reminiscent of the Rhône. Argentina makes Shiraz with soft upfront fruits, usually black plums, in the Australian style but less exuberant, concentrated, and alcoholic.

The Ancient Pinot Family

Burgundy continues to define the essence of Pinot Noir. No other region can reliably aspire to its capture of the delicacy of Pinot, although individual wines from other regions may sometimes be mistaken for Burgundy. France dominates worldwide production of Pinot Noir. However, about 40% of France's Pinot Noir is used for Champagne; in terms of production for red wine, its lead is much smaller. Burgundy's 10,000 ha are roughly twice the area found in any other single region.[60] Germany's position as a significant producer is relatively recent, a result of the trend towards red wine drinking combined with the opportunities opened by warmer climatic conditions. The United States, especially in Oregon and California's Sonoma Valley, and New Zealand are the main New World challengers in Pinot production, although the styles are usually somewhat distinct from Burgundy.

Pinot Noir is definitely a grape for cool climates. All the classic locations for Pinot production in France are in the northern part of the country: Burgundy, Sancerre, Alsace, and Champagne. The regions of Germany are farther to the north yet, Baden just to the north of Alsace, and the tiny region of the Ahr, the most northern region for wine production in Germany, able to ripen Pinot Noir only because of its special properties as a micro climate. In the United States, Oregon might be compared climatically to Burgundy (Sonoma Valley is somewhat warmer), while in New Zealand the move towards Central Otago takes Pinot Noir production into the coolest climate in the country.

There is still generally a distinction between Pinot Noir from the Old World, epitomized by Burgundy, where the wine tends toward a lighter more savory style, and the New World, where it is richer, with more powerful fruits and a fuller body. In France, Burgundy is at its weightiest in the Côte de Nuits, with fruits tending to black cherries, lighter in the Côte de Beaune with fruits tending to earthy strawberries, lighter yet in the surrounding satellite regions. Sancerre in the Loire produces light-colored Pinot Noirs with good acidity and (in a warm year) something approaching the earthy strawberry fruits of the satellite regions around Beaune. Pinot Noir in Alsace can be pale to the point of confusion with rosé, but more intense examples can now be found (although their "typicity" has been questioned), with good acidity and notes of earthy strawberries.

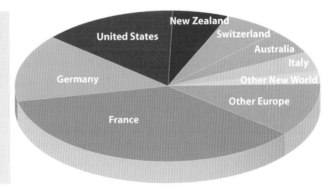

France has almost 30% of the world's Pinot Noir. The rest is distributed between Europe and the New World.[61]

Sweetness of fruits is a marker for all regions from New Zealand. Marlborough shows the bright, forward fruits that typify New Zealand wines, with red and black cherries on the palate, and precise fruit flavors supported by good acidity. The wines often show prominent aromatics. Martinborough (just to the north) is similar to Marlborough, but slightly denser and fuller in style, with more intimations of black fruit, especially cherries. To the south, the cooler climate of Central Otago, a more recent convert to Pinot Noir production, shows earthier aromas and flavors, with more upfront, softer fruit flavors tending to the classic strawberries. Fruits can be lifted by the higher acidity. Winemakers often compare it to Oregon.

South Africa Pinot Noir can be similar in style to New Zealand, but with less bright fruits and less noticeable aromatics. Chile is similar, with a mix of cherries and strawberries, but less fruit intensity and less aromatic than New Zealand, and sometimes a tell tale touch of menthol, often a faintly herbaceous note. Yarra Valley in Australia shows rather soft, earthy flavors, with strawberries predominating, and acidity on the lower side, sometimes marked by a very faint medicinal edge. The wines are lighter than those of New Zealand, the fruits are less lifted. Willamette Valley in Oregon varies more significantly with climate, from wines that can be relatively thin and acid, to those that have palates dominated by earthy strawberries.

Carneros was one of the first regions in California to emphasize Pinot Noir. Its wines have fruits of black cherries, sometimes notes of eucalyptus, and can be lean and spicy. Russian River Valley in Sonoma shows quite weighty fruits in the same spectrum but with more precise delineation of flavors, fuller bodied, and often a little spiciness. Santa Barbara produces Pinots in a softer style, but often too alcoholic. Napa Valley Pinot Noirs tend to be over-ripe, with rather jammy, and sometimes too heavy, fruits.

If there's a single word to describe Pinot Noir, it should be "elegant." Pinot Noir is very easily destroyed by over-extraction, which can be a problem with New World Pinots. Personally, I am somewhat inclined to the view that it becomes difficult for Pinot Noir to retain typicity once the alcohol level goes over 13%. Of course there are exceptions, but the elegance of the aroma and flavor spectrum tends to be lost at high alcohol.

Pinot is an ancient grape family, often thought to have originated fairly closely from wild grapevines. Of course, no one really knows. Speculation about ancient origins is encouraged by Columella's description of a variety resembling Pinot Noir in the first century C.E., although the first clear references to Pinot Noir are not until much later, in the fourteenth century. Pinot is particularly prone to mutation and throws off new variants at a greater rate than most other varieties; there are several hundred clones under cultivation.[62]

Clonal variation affects a wide range of properties, from the size of the berries and overall yield to the time of ripening. All this plays out in the aroma and flavor of the wine. It can be really important to plant the right clone. When they started growing Pinot Noir and Chardonnay in Oregon, producers had a lot of trouble because they planted clones recommended by the University of California at Davis that ripened relatively late. The clones had been chosen for

California in order to get a more extended growing season. The problem was that this required harvesting around the time of the autumn rains in Oregon, with generally disastrous results. In the early 1990s, the so-called Dijon clones were imported to Oregon, giving much better results because they came to ripeness about two weeks earlier. In fact, Dijon clones of Pinot Noir have generally now replaced Oregon's traditional clones (Pommard and Wädensvil). The Dijon clones have acquired an almost mystical significance to the extent that they are sometimes now mentioned on labels, but actually they have nothing much to do with Dijon; the name appears to have arisen simply because the clones are described by D numbers and were imported from Burgundy.

The Pinot family consists of closely related variants: Pinot Noir, Pinot Gris, Pinot Meunier, and Pinot Blanc. The first three are black grapes, the last is white. Their genetic maps are almost indistinguishable, implying they all originate from the same ancestor.[63]

The differences between them are subtle. Pinot Blanc's lack of color is due to the same mutation that prevents anthocyanin production in other white grapes. Pinot Gris has rather variable color, possibly the result of a mutation specifically affecting only the cell layer that produces the skin. Pinot Meunier differs from Pinot Noir in having leaves that are densely covered with fine hairs, whereas the leaves of Pinot Noir are smooth. This gives the underside of the leaves a slightly white appearance, somewhat like dusting with flour, hence the description Meunier (French for miller). The difference between Pinot Noir and Pinot Meunier is due solely to a genetic change affecting only the outer layer of cells. It turns out that this results from a single genetic difference in the pathway for producing giberellic acid, a plant hormone that controls growth.[64] (In fact the mutation is identical to one that has been used to increase production in wheat.)

The relationship between the Pinots is made possible because grapevines are propagated vegetatively, by making cuttings, instead of being grown from seeds.

The Pinot family varies from black/purple (Pinot Noir), red/pink (Pinot Gris) to white (Pinot Blanc). The grapes of Pinot Meunier have the same appearance as Pinot Noir. Photographs kindly provided by the Institut für Rebenzchtung Geilweilerhof, Germany.

When a plant is grown from a seed, all its cells have the same genetic constitution. But when it is propagated by cuttings, each cell layer can inherit the properties of the cell layer of the parental plant. So all Pinot Meuniers are descended from a single plant in which a somatic mutation changed the properties of just the outer cell layer. In fact, if new plants are generated from the cells of this layer (the "true" Pinot Meunier?), they form dwarf grapevines of much reduced size but with increased fruit capacity. If new plants are generated from other cell layers of Pinot Meunier, they are identical to Pinot Noir! So Pinot Meunier is a chimera, with all its cells exactly the same as Pinot Noir, except for the outer layer which is the same as the cells of the dwarf plants. In fact, all the Pinot varieties are chimeras, in which the genetic constitution of the layer of skin cells is different from the constitution of the cells of the inner layer.[65]

Anything but Chardonnay

Anything but Chardonnay, dissenters used to say at the peak of the craze for Chardonnay. A surprising attitude given the enormous variability of Chardonnay. Chardonnay is the most widely propagated white grape in the world; almost every wine-producing country has some. The bulk of production is split between France, the United States, and Australia. The stylistic split between Europe and New World is not always straightforward to define for Chardonnay, because the use of oak can be at least as important as terroir or climate. At one extreme, Chardonnay may be vinified in stainless steel; at the other it may be fermented in new oak barrels and then kept in new oak for months.

Unoaked styles range from the mineral Chablis of northern France to the piercing citrus of New World Chardonnay. Oaked styles range from subtle Burgundies to rich, fat, buttery wines dominated by the aromas of malolactic fermentation from Napa or South Australia. South America and South Africa produce some positively exotic wines with tropical fruits. Perhaps there's an element of caricature in these descriptions, but even if each is an extreme manifestation of match between cépage and locale, certainly the range illustrates the malleability of the variety. Chardonnay is an extraordinary vehicle for displaying the wiles of the winemaker, although it is generally felt that it produces its best results on soils with high chalk content.

Almost three quarters of the world's Chardonnay is in France, the United States, and Australia, but the rest is widely distributed.[66]

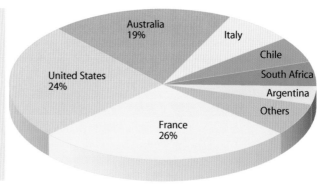

Chardonnay is planted on chalk in Chablis, as can be seen from the white soil on the hill.

Burgundy is the heartland for Chardonnay, producing several classic styles. In the northern outpost of Chablis, reaching full ripeness can be a problem, and the style depends on whether the wine is unoaked (at its best displaying a steely minerality) or oaked (adding hints of smoke and liquorice to the minerality, but not vanillin since the oak is rarely new). Even at grand cru level, Chablis is rarely as full bodied as wines from the Côte d'Or to its south, where use of new oak increases in proportion to the quality of the wine. The style in the Côte d'Or is at its steeliest in Puligny Montrachet, creamier in Chassagne Montrachet, and softer in Meursault, sometimes with a nutty edge. Corton Charlemagne can be fat and opulent. Strength of oak depends on producer style but is not usually obtrusive and tends to be smoky rather than buttery. When you get to the grand crus, with Le Montrachet at the peak, there can be more overt oakiness when the wine is young.

California Chardonnays tend to noticeable oak, with overtones of vanillin and butter even when French oak is used. The style is at its fullest in Napa, similar but a little less rich in Carneros, somewhat leaner in Sonoma, with Russian River Valley providing a more elegant style. Like everything else, Chardonnay from Australia tends simply to be bigger and bolder than the same grape from elsewhere. In the oaked style, Australian Chardonnays are big, oaky, buttery, and alcoholic; in the unoaked style they tend to lime and other citrus flavors. The unoaked style is distinguished from the Old World by the intensity of its bright, forward lemon fruits, absence of minerality, and higher alcohol. A move away from excessive oak in the oaked style leaves citrus flavors noticeable on nose and

Chardonnay clones vary greatly in berry and bunch size. Clone 4 is the most widely planted clone in California, and gives consistently high yields. Clone 15 comes from Washington State and gives smaller berries and much smaller bunches.

Photographs kindly provided by Chalk Hill Estate.

Clone 4 (Martini 5V21; Olmo #66)   Clone 15 (Prosser LR2V6)

palate, with sweet oak aromas and flavors following on the finish. Tropical notes can be a mark of New World Chardonnays from Australia, New Zealand, or Chile, but not usually California. (Sometimes this is due to fermentation at low temperatures.) Chile and South Africa tend to follow the Australian style, but with less intensity. Northern Italy (Piedmont, Tuscany, and Umbria) produces some heavily oaked Chardonnays, distinguished from the French by a touch of vanillin from the oak, sometimes coming close to a New World style.

Clonal variation of Chardonnay is usually stated to have relatively little effect on flavor.[67] The emphasis on Chardonnay clones is usually placed more on features such as time of ripening, but in fact there are quite noticeable effects on flavor profile when you look for them. The range of difference was shown by an interesting experiment when seventeen different clones were planted at Chalk Hill winery in Sonoma.[68] The clones varied widely in the sizes of the berries, the sizes of the bunches, the overall yield, and the Brix at harvest.[69] Each clone was vinified separately under identical conditions, and when I tasted wine made from six of the clones, the differences were striking. Clone 16 from Rutherglen, Australia was clearly heavier than any of the others, powerful rather than elegant; clone 76, one of the so-called Dijon clones from Burgundy, was more elegant and Burgundian with a better balance of acid to fruit; clone 17, a selection from Robert Young in California, was more mineral than most; clone 22 from Coneglio, Italy, and clone 352 from Espiguette, France were distinctly lighter and fresher than the others, and clone 4 (originating from Stony Hill Vineyard in St. Helena), had distinctly sweeter fruit.[70] You shouldn't expect different clones of any varietal to taste the same any more than you would expect Red Delicious, Granny Smith, Fuji, Gala, or Macoun apples to taste the same.

You can in fact produce Chardonnay in almost any style from any place. The distinctions between Burgundy, Napa, Australia, and so on, owe more to winemaking choices in these locales than to intrinsic qualities of the terroir.

Herbaceous Sauvignon Blanc

Some wines have no character to speak of (the world is full of amorphous white wines with little flavor beyond the basic solution of alcohol in water), some have character thrust upon them by exposure to oak or other means, but some have such powerful intrinsic aromas that, love or loathe them, there is certainly no mistaking their character. The most distinctive white wines have powerful aromas provided by volatile compounds. All wines have volatile compounds, of course, but their presence is an especially strong feature of varieties such as Sauvignon Blanc, Riesling, Gewürztraminer, and the Muscats.

Sauvignon Blanc stands at an intriguing interface between the herbaceous and the fruity. The traditional grape of the eastern part of the Loire, where it is vinified as a single varietal, it is now associated with Marlborough in New Zealand, whose forceful style has come to typify the variety for many people. France remains the largest producer of Sauvignon Blanc, with almost a third of the world's vineyards, but New Zealand is close behind. Other New World countries make up most of the rest, mostly following the bright stainless style of New Zealand.

Sauvignon Blanc from the Loire is classically aromatic with a smell of green unripe fruit. The wines are fresh and soon ready to drink, but typically do not last long. Sancerre and Pouilly Fumé are the best known appellations. Vinified in a neutral manner (old oak or stainless steel), the result is a crisp wine, with high acidity resulting from the cool climate, and mineral overtones. Often failing to achieve full ripeness, the wines can be characterized by the herbaceous aroma known pejoratively as cat's pee.

Sauvignon Blanc's importance extends farther south in France to Bordeaux, where it is one of the two major white varieties. Blended with Sémillon, it is the major component in the dry white wines, but a minor component in the great dessert wines. Typical proportions for the blend are 80:20 for the dry wines and 20:80 for the sweet wines, although some of the most famous dry white wines use 50:50. Most production uses old oak or stainless steel, but the top white wines are matured in new oak, which makes for complexity and age worthiness. The fatter qualities of Sémillon ameliorate the leanness of the Sauvignon Blanc.

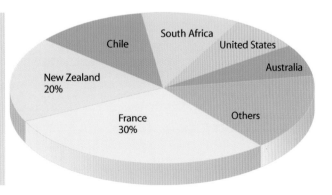

France and New Zealand together account for half of the world's production of Sauvignon Blanc.[71]

(Sémillon is also important in the sweet wines for its high susceptibility to botrytis.) Today there is a tendency to make pure varietal Sauvignon Blanc using stainless steel like the New World.

The herbaceous qualities of cool climates turn to more perfumed notes in warmer climates. The revolution in Sauvignon Blanc came from New Zealand. Introduced into New Zealand in the 1970s, Sauvignon Blanc became commercially established in the 1980s, and became the paradigm for the modern stainless steel style of production by the 1990s. Made famous by wines from the cool climate of Marlborough, the New Zealand style is achieved by rapidly crushing the grapes, followed by low temperature fermentation (10-14°C) in stainless steel. This gives strong citrus fruit flavors (often showing as grapefruit) and tropical aromas and flavors (typically showing as passion fruit). Accounting for two thirds of Sauvignon Blanc production in New Zealand, the Marlborough region typifies the unoaked New World style of Sauvignon Blanc. Other New World countries follow the style of strong, forward, often piercing fruit, but usually the fruits are not so bright as from New Zealand. In South Africa, acidity tends to be relatively low for the variety, and aromatics of exotic fruits, especially passion fruit, are more noticeable than herbaceous or grassy notes.

Yet another aspect of Sauvignon Blanc is revealed by the Fumé Blanc style pioneered by Robert Mondavi in Napa Valley. The story goes that Mondavi was offered Sauvignon Blanc grapes at a time when the variety was little known in the United States. Reasoning that people were familiar with the Pouilly Fumé wine from the Loire even though they did not know it was made from Sauvignon Blanc, and after experimenting with various styles of production, Mondavi gave the wine the name Fumé Blanc (which also served to distinguish it from those Sauvignon Blancs that were being produced in a sweet style). Half is fermented in oak barrels, to get softness and complexity, and half in stainless steel, to retain freshness; then the wine matures briefly in oak barriques, the result being to introduce creamy and smoky aromas cutting the usual herba-

IBMP level falls after veraison.[72]

Harvesting at 13% potential alcohol would give an IBMP level just at the detection threshold in this example.

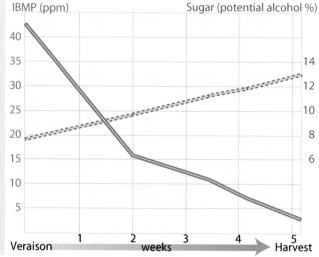

Different aroma profiles result from fermentation with two yeast strains.

The red strain of yeast releases more volatile thiols than the blue strain, resulting in increased concentration of the aromas associated with 4-MMP and the other thiols.[73]

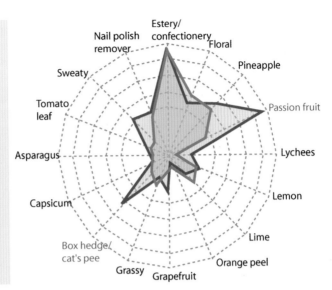

ceousness of Sauvignon Blanc. Imitating Bordeaux, it also has a little Sémillon. First marketed with the 1966 vintage, it remains one of Mondavi's staple wines, and the style has been imitated by other producers in Napa valley and elsewhere. Today most of the grapes come from Mondavi's own vineyards in Napa.

Two types of compounds are responsible for the characteristic aroma and flavor spectrum of Sauvignon Blanc, and their different natures explain the effects of viticulture and vinification on the typicity of the variety.

"Green" characters, variously taking the form of grassy or asparagus-like aromas, result from methoxypyrazines. Synthesized by the plant, they are found in the berry, and the most important is the same IBMP (3-isobutyl-2-methoxypyrazine) found in Cabernet Sauvignon. Humans are very sensitive to methoxypyrazines, and almost all Sauvignon Blancs have a level above detection.[74] (One reason we are so sensitive to methoxypyrazines is that they are an indication of unripeness in fruit.) Exposure to sunlight causes levels to decline, and there is a rapid drop as grapes approach maturity, with losses of 10-fold or more in the last 6 weeks of ripening. The timing of harvest is a key determinant of the level in the grape. Methoxypyrazines are easily extracted from the grapes, so the level in the mature berry essentially determines the level in the wine.

The "tropical" characters in Sauvignon Blanc come from volatile thiols, which are formed during fermentation. The most important is 4-MMP.[75] This is very potent; levels in wine are usually well above the threshold for perception.[76] Its effect is greatly influenced by its concentration; at low concentrations it gives an impression of broom or box, turning to gooseberries, passion fruit and tropical fruits at higher concentrations, and ultimately showing as cat's pee when in large excess.[77] 4-MMP exists in the grape as an odorless precursor. During fermentation, yeast enzymes release it from the precursor form.[78] Different yeasts vary by up to ten fold in their ability to release the volatile thiols, so the strain of yeast used in fermentation makes a significant difference to the aroma of the wine.[79]

The combined effects of IBMP and 4-MMP and their related compounds give Sauvignon Blanc that unique combination of herbaceousness and exotic fruits. How the two types of compounds respond to viticulture and vinification explains the differences between the classical style of the wines from the Loire and the new style of the wines from New Zealand and elsewhere in the New World. High levels of methoxypyrazines are associated with less ripe grapes, so the wines of the cool-climate Loire tend to herbaceousness. Volatile thiols are destroyed by oxidation, so winemaking in traditional conditions, typically using barrels of old oak where exposure to oxygen is high, reduces their levels. The New Zealand style of winemaking in stainless steel, often in deliberately reductive conditions (when a layer of nitrogen is used to exclude oxygen) preserves the thiols, which is why you tend to find notes of passion fruit in Marlborough Sauvignon Blanc.

The Petrol of Riesling

Does a whiff of petrol identify the essential character of Riesling or is it a flaw? It's created in Riesling by TDN (trimethyl-dihydronaphthalene). which is rarely found in grapes but develops in the bottle by slow chemical actions.[80] TDN levels are increased by low yields, warm weather, and high levels of acidity in either fruit or the wines.[81] Petrol develops slowly over some years in French or German Rieslings, but typical growth conditions favor more rapid development of TDN in Australian Riesling, where critic Tom Stevenson comments that, "TDN is typically so precocious that judges are expected to mark down wines showing too much petrol too quickly."[82] When rather young, Riesling can be deceptively simple; the characteristic steely, mineral citrus fruits develop slowly in the bottle. When TDN develops in the same time frame, the result is a dry, perfumed finish perfectly complementing the fruit spectrum; but when it develops first, the impression can be a little raw.

Riesling is the most racy and elegant of grapes, marked by good acidity, with light almost perfumed fruit, showing a range of flavors from green apples to minerals. The focus on sugar made sweetness the major determinant of style in Germany, and indeed, some believe that, because of its very high acidity, the full delicacy of Riesling is only revealed in the presence of at least some residual sugar. Once again the New World has brought a new intensity to bear, with fruit-driven Rieslings from South Australia always showing a completely dry style. Now Germany is following the lead of the New World, with its new emphasis on the trocken (dry) style.

The traditional quality grades of German Riesling are nominally distinguished by the concentration of sugar in the grapes at harvest, but in practice they are also associated with increasing residual sugar in the wines going up the scale through Kabinett, Spätlese, Auslese, and the higher grades of dessert wines. All show soft aromatics, with the fruit spectrum starting with citrus and then showing increasing notes of apricot going through to the highest levels. Even in the trocken style, German Riesling is distinguished from Alsace or the New

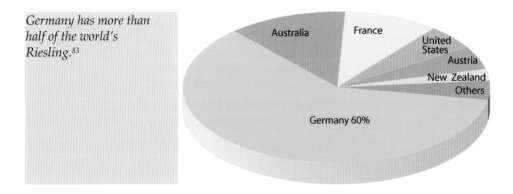

Germany has more than half of the world's Riesling.[83]

World by a certain softness and perfume on the nose, although differences between regions are harder to see in the dry wines. Petrol developing with age increases the sense of minerality.

Riesling shows the playoff between sugar and acidity. When the high acidity has been ameliorated by a little residual sugar, it's an education to taste a series of half-dry Rieslings and try to guess sugar and acidity levels: the interplay is so subtle that it's extremely difficult simply to place the wines in order of ascending residual sugar. The move towards dry wines, better suited to accompany modern food, has seen increasing focus on dry or half-dry styles in German production; indeed, the objective of the new style called Classic in Germany is that the wine should taste dry, even though it may have a little sugar.

Elsewhere in Europe, Riesling is usually dry. Austrian Rieslings tend to have more mineral tones and sometimes higher overt acidity than German (trocken) Rieslings. Alsatian Rieslings have a steely mineral character, lean and austere, with the palate often showing citrus fruits. (But the recent warming trend in Alsace has led to more production of wines with residual sugar.) They are often chaptalized and have higher alcohol than the trocken Rieslings of Germany.

Australian Rieslings usually have those bright, piercing citrus fruits characteristic of the New World. Clare Valley produces high concentration, often with predominant notes of lime as well as lemon. Watervale is the best part of Clare Valley for Riesling. Eden Valley tends to be more floral. Both can have strong notes of petrol or kerosene even when young.

New Zealand Rieslings follow the same style as Australia, but usually have a little residual sugar to soften and balance the acidity. This gives something of a Germanic quality, but without the delicacy or perfume. The generality about New Zealand Riesling is that it has more aromatic complexity but simpler, purer fruits, whereas Australia has more marked fruit complexity.

Beware the Welschriesling! Also known as Riesling Italico, this is widely planted in central Europe, and when labeled as Riesling can fool the unwary buyer. This is a bulk-production grape, giving wine that has little connection with the real Riesling.

Riesling is considered to be a "terroir grape," one that reflects the conditions of viticulture more than most. You see this most clearly in Germany, where wines from the Mosel are the most elegant, with precisely delineated fruits; from the Rheingau there is a little more weight with a delicious sweet/sour balance in the traditional style; and then going farther south the wines become somewhat heavier, with less minerality. The best soils are slate. It is said that the calcareous soils of Alsace give Riesling with more weight and body than the slate soils of Germany; perhaps there is an effect from acidity of the soil, but the difference is more likely to reflect the effects of climate on ripeness, and length of the growing season, than to be due to mineral in the soil. After all, the much larger differences between the styles of German and Australian Rieslings are attributed not to terroir but to winemaking (aided by the climate).

Riesling's characteristic fruit spectrum depends on terpenes, a group of organic compounds that also dominate Gewürztraminer, Muscat, and Albariño.[84] They are also found in Muscadelle, and Sauvignon Blanc, but at levels below the threshold for detection. An overlapping set of terpenes is found in all these aromatic varieties, but relative and overall quantities give each a different aroma spectrum. Muscat is dominated by geraniol (smell of roses), Gewürztraminer by cis-rose oxide (smell of lychees), Albariño has high hotrienol (notes of lime), and Riesling has a complex set of aromas in which no single influence dominates.

Terpenes have their characteristic odors only when they are free volatile molecules. The grape contains a mixture of free terpenes and precursors that are odorless because they are bound to sugars. In most of these varieties, the majority of terpenes are in the inactive bound form.[85] Breaking the chemical bond linking the terpene to the sugar, called a glycoside, releases the odiferous form. This happens to a small degree naturally in the grape itself, and during fermentation, but if you want to increase the concentration, the most effective way is to use cultured yeasts with increased enzyme activities or even directly to treat the must with an enzyme that breaks glycoside bonds.[86] Once again, varietal character is not entirely intrinsic but can be controlled by choices during winemaking. No one has done a systematic tasting test to see whether the results of using

Riesling grows on slate in the Mosel.

Terpenes are major components of the aroma spectrum of Riesling, Gewürztraminer, and Muscat.

Terpene	Riesling	Gewürz-traminer	Muscat	Odor	Other sources
Linalool	✓		✓	Rose	Lavender, bergamot, jasmine, cinnamon, clove, nutmeg, coriander, cardamom, ginger.
Alpha-terpineol	✓	✓		Lily of the Valley	Lilac, pine, bitter orange (Citrus aurantium).
Citronellol	✓			Citronella	Rose, geranium, ginger, black pepper, basil, peppermint, cardamom, lemon eucalyptus
Nerol	✓	✓	✓	Rose, lime	Orange blossom, ginger, basil, cardamom, mint mandarin.
Geraniol	✓	✓	✓✓	Rose	Geranium, lemon, citronella, nutmeg, ginger, grapefruit.
Hotrienol	✓	✓		Hyacinth, linden	Japanese Ho Tree (Cinnamomum camphora), grapefruit peel.
cis-Rose oxide	✓	✓✓		Rose, lychee	Lychee

enzymes produces wines as subtle as those produced by nature, or whether the wines are unbalanced by excessive release of terpenes.

Germany remains the world leader in overall production of Riesling, but Australia has an importance beyond its position in second place for pioneering the New World style of bright, piercing fruits—in the case of Riesling, the fruits can be quite aggressive. Production of Riesling in the traditional sweet styles has been declining steadily in Germany, with trocken or halbtrocken wines now reduced to half of production. Germany remains the leader for producing very sweet dessert wines in the botrytized Beerenauslese and TBA styles, and also for its ice-wine. Botrytized sweet Rieslings are also produced in Alsace and in Austria. The high acidity of Riesling gives it a fantastic ability to age, and the best examples can match any dessert wine in the world for complexity and ageworthiness.

Is Riesling the world's most undervalued grape? At one time, it was the most highly valued white grape in the world; at the end of the nineteenth century, prices for Riesling were higher than for any other white grape at Christie's auctions in London. Today Riesling rarely commands prices comparable to top Burgundies. Yet its versatility is extraordinary, from completely dry wines with the precise delicacy of the Mosel to sweet TBA. The development of complex aromas and flavors over time places it high in the group of wines that become increasingly interesting with age, and it is a perfect match for a surprisingly wide range of foods, with none of the buttery or oaky notes of Chardonnay that can sometimes clash with a meal. What stands between Riesling and wider success?

The Grapes of Muscat

Muscats are thought to be one of the oldest grape varieties, sharing the distinctive feature that the aroma and flavor of the grape comes out directly in the wine. There is no mistaking the perfumed, "grapey" quality of Muscat grapes or wine. The strong aroma makes the grapes especially attractive to bees, leading to suggestions that Muscat was the variety identified by Pliny as Uva apiana (grape of the bees).[87] As might be expected of an ancient grape, there is a huge range of Muscat varieties, from the most refined, Muscat Blanc à Petit Grains to the ordinary Muscat d'Alexandrie (used for both wine and table grape production).

About twenty distinct varieties of Muscat have been identified; most are white, but some are red or pink. Muscat Blanc à Petits Grains is also known as Muscat de Frontignac, and may have been cultivated in southern France by the Romans; it was the dominant grape of Roussillon from the fourteenth until the nineteenth centuries. Muscat d'Alexandrie is widely disseminated around the Mediterranean, its name being sometimes being taken to suggest it may have originated in Egypt.[89] Two varieties that are really only half-Muscats are also widely grown. Muscat Hamburg is principally a table grape, and is the only Muscat that can be classified as a black grape; it may have originated in a cross between Muscat d'Alexandrie and the Black Morocco grape. Muscat Ottonel is the lightest in both color and aroma; the variety is most often used for table

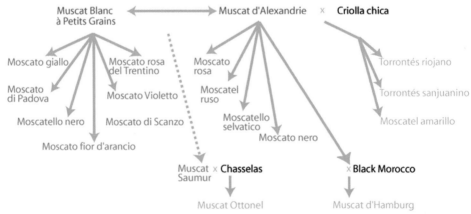

The large Muscat family falls into two main groups, based on Muscat Blanc à Petits Grains and Muscat d'Alexandrie (shown in red). Related members of each group are in gray. Varieties where Muscat is one parent are shown in pink. Non-Muscat parents are in black.[88]

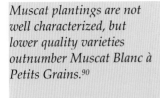

Muscat plantings are not well characterized, but lower quality varieties outnumber Muscat Blanc à Petits Grains.[90]

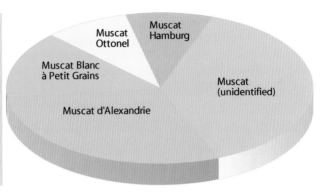

grape production, but is not always considered to be a full fledged Muscat since it originated in a cross between Muscat of Saumur and Chasselas.

The genetics of the group show that Muscat Blanc à Petit Grains and Muscat d'Alexandrie are related to one another, and each appears to be the progenitor of a large group of subvarieties. Also related to Muscat are the Torrontés varieties of Argentina, which originated in crosses between Muscat d'Alexandrie and the local Criolla chica (a variant of the Mission grape of California). Torrontés have inherited the characteristic grapey aromas of their Muscat parent, although it's not strong as in the original. And the aroma of Muscat d'Alexandrie is less intense than that of Muscat Blanc à Petit Grains.

Muscat Blanc à Petits Grains is of vastly higher quality than the other Muscats, but it is only a small part of worldwide plantings; Muscat d'Alexandrie is about twice as common. Muscat is mostly planted in the warmer areas of Europe; it has not really been taken up in an important way in the New World, with perhaps the exception of the Brown Muscats of Australia (used for sweet, "sticky" wines). The most important plantings of Muscat Blanc à Petits Grains are in southern France, where it is the sole variety permitted in the fortified sweet dessert wine, Beaumes de Venise (from the southern Rhône), and in several appellations for Vin doux Naturel (sweet fortified wines) in the Languedoc, including Frontignac. Being somewhat obscured by the sweetness, varietal character does not usually come through as strongly in dessert wines as in dry wines, but Muscat is an exception, where the strongly perfumed grapes blend beautifully with the sweetness.

The most notable wines made from Muscat d'Alexandrie are at Rivesaltes (in the Languedoc) and at Setúbal in Portugal. Most of the Muscat in Spain is Muscat d'Alexandrie. Red (well, really pink) varieties of Muscat Blanc à Petits Grains are used to make rosé wines in Italy (the variety is called Moscato Rosa or Rosenmuskateller locally) in both sweet and dry styles. The most extreme versions of Muscat are made in Rutherglen, in Victoria, Australia, from a pink variant, Muscat Rouge à Petits Grains, where the must is fortified to block fermentation after only a day, giving a very sweet wine with primary fruit character.

Muscats owe their characteristic aromatics to the same monoterpenes found at lower levels in Riesling and Gewürztraminer. The major terpenes in Muscat are geraniol, linalool and nerol. Geraniol is the most important, with an odor generally described as rose-like, but in high concentrations, as its name suggests, it can give a strong aroma of geraniums, which can become unpleasant in wine. This is one of the reasons why Asti Spumante, made from Muscat Blanc à Petit Grains as a somewhat perfumed sparkling wine, needs to be drunk young; as it ages, it can acquire too strong an aroma of geraniums.

Deus ex Machina

Descriptions of the specific aromas associated with aromatic grape varieties, and their identification with known compounds, make it seem as though it should be possible to identify wines from at least some varietals by their aromas. So if there are objective criteria for assessing wines, could a machine replace the MW (Master of Wine)?

The aroma wheel gives a sense of the complexity of the aromas in wine. It suggests descriptors grouped under topics such as green fruit, tropical fruit, floral, spicy, and so on, with around a hundred individual types of descriptions for either white or red wine. Probably we know the chemical basis (or at least a major part of the chemical basis) for something approaching half of these aromas. They could be measured in a mass spectrometer, which is pretty good at discriminating volatile compounds. In fact, this is what an electronic nose does.

"Electronic nose" is basically a fancy term to describe any piece of scientific equipment that detects volatile aromas. Mostly this is useful for rapidly detecting dangerous compounds, a sort of replacement for the canaries that miners used to take down mines to detect carbon monoxide. Electronic noses have been used by NASA to detect release of ammonia on the space shuttle, there are devices to detect chlorine, nitric acid, or sulfur dioxide when they reach dangerous levels, and there's even one to determine whether meat is safe by detecting volatile compounds released by contaminating bacteria.

An electronic nose has been made to distinguish between espresso coffees on the basis of their aromas.[91] This is somewhat less complex than wine, since 32 volatile compounds represent more than 95% of the total. The machine can distinguish eight different types of coffee (made from beans from different sources)—but it can't tell whether an individual taster will prefer one to another.

A machine could certainly measure visual criteria: it could assess color in terms of density and hue (as measured by the wavelengths). It could objectively analyze some important taste criteria: alcohol level, acidity, residual sugar, all are crucial to any assessment of wine. It might be able to use the ratio of acid to sugar to assess perceptible sweetness. It could measure tannins, but is it possible to give any universal impression of bitterness? It could test for the aroma characteristics of specific varietals: TDN would be an unequivocal marker for Riesling, for example. By assessing relative levels of various volatile components, it could probably do a pretty good job of identifying several aromatic varietals. It would be more difficult to find criteria to identify neutral varieties.

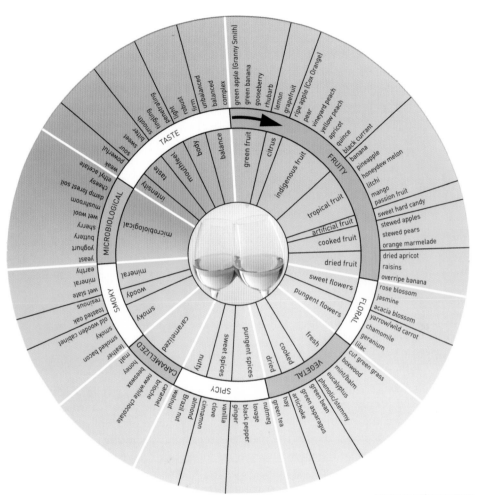

A version of the aroma wheel prepared specially for German white wines has all of the aromas found in Riesling except petrol, which is evidently a sensitive subject. Photograph kindly provided by the German Wine Institute (www.germanwineusa.com).[92]

But could it identify quality? That's a much more nebulous concept, based on assessing the complexity (how many different aromas and flavors contribute to the spectrum), balance (do all the components meld together or does any one stick out), ageworthiness (is there a sense of structure, how will the present aromas and flavors develop over the future). This is essentially a human concept: the best a machine could do would be to try to calibrate the various parameters it can measure against an expert's assessment of quality to see if a pattern could be detected. There are so many different paths to quality—and one of the marks of the highest quality wines is the sheer difficulty of deconstructing their makeup—that success here seems dubious.

Perhaps the measured physical and chemical qualities of wine, from acidity or sweetness to quantities of every volatile compound, could be matched to the

taster's descriptions for acid, sweet, floral, perfumed, and so on. At a pinch we
might be able to put into software-ese descriptions of tannins ranging from silky
and ripe to green and harsh. But how would we describe in terms that a computer could understand qualities such as balance, harmonious, texture, grip—all
readily understood but hard to define quantitatively. Personally, I am relieved
that I do not have to resolve the conflict behind my scientific training and the
value of MWs; I think human tasters are safe from being replaced by an electronic nose.

Engineering the Grapevine

The first genetically engineered crop (a tomato with increased resistance to
bruising) went on the market in 1994. Since then, many types of plants have been
altered by genetic engineering, and for some crops, genetically engineered plants
are now the majority (72% of soybeans worldwide in 2008 were genetically
modified).[93] Yet although more than 60 genetically engineered foods have been
approved in the United States, not a single case involving vines and wine production has come to fruition.

Suppose you take a cultivar of Vitis vinifera—let's say Chardonnay—and
cross it with some other variety. The progeny will have half its genes from Chardonnay and half from its partner. Now let's take those progeny and cross them
back to Chardonnay again; the next generation will be 75% Chardonnay and
only 25% from the partner. If we keep doing this, with each subsequent cross
back to Chardonnay we reduce the proportion of genes from the other variety by
50%. By the time we've done ten generations, only 1 in 1000 genes come from the
partner. By 15 generations, virtually all the 30,000 genes should come from
Chardonnay.[94] If at each generation we select the plants for some property that
comes from the partner cultivar—perhaps this might be resistance to some
pathogen—we'll end up in principle with a plant that is basically Chardonnay
plus the resistance gene and a handful of others from the partner. No one would
object to this process, and in a sense it's what happens naturally as new cultivars
develop, but of course it would take several decades to accomplish. In principle,
genetic engineering lets us short circuit the process by inserting the foreign gene
directly into Chardonnay. So what's the problem?

Scientists are in fact trying the direct approach with powdery mildew, a serious fungal disease that affects Vitis vinifera cultivars. The related grapevine
species, Muscadinia rotundifolia, has a single gene that makes it resistant to
powdery mildew.[95] Vitis vinifera becomes resistant if the gene is crossed into it
by conventional breeding.[96] The Muscadinia gene is now being cloned with the
objective of introducing it directly into Vitis vinifera cultivars. People who object
to genetic engineering on principle should answer this question: would it better
to use grapevines carrying this gene or to continue treating powdery mildew
with sulfur or with steroid inhibitors, neither particularly good for human consumption?

Of course, it's relatively rare that a single gene from another grapevine species will be sufficient to confer a specific trait. More often multiple genes will be required. While this could make it even more complicated to construct a resistant strain by conventional breeding, it wouldn't pose any problem in principle for genetic engineering. But there's only a limited number of cases in which the requisite genes will be found in other grapevines; more often it will be necessary to go to other plant species or even to other sources altogether. The same issues apply here that apply to genetic engineering of any crop: will the process lead to reduction of diversity because of increasing reliance on a small number of cultivars that have been engineered? Could it have adverse side effects (such as allowing genes for pesticide resistance to spread to other plants)?

The grapevine is prone to a large number of pests and diseases, and in many cases there are no conventional cures. Nematodes are a perennial problem (in fact, in some areas, rootstocks are chosen just as much for nematode resistance as for resistance to phylloxera). As well as attacking the roots directly, nematodes are vectors carrying diseases such as fanleaf virus. INAO[97] has been testing rootstocks genetically modified to resist the nematode that carries fanleaf virus, against which there is currently no protection, in an experimental plot at Colmar in Alsace. The experiment has been continuing in spite of protests from the Terre et Vin group of producers, who believe that genetic modification will reduce diversity and risk loss of typicity in the wines.[98]

Loss of diversity in rootstocks is not really so much of an issue, but it's a fair point that, since clones have to be modified one by one, the introduction of some desirable gene into a specific clone of some cultivar could lead to its use at the expense of diversity. But is this more than enhancing the trend that is already reducing diversity? The authorities are always pushing clones that are reliable and productive rather than known for their quality.[99] The wine industry is no exception to the trend that commercial production of strains is associated with loss of flavor quality.

The grapevine is a bit different from other plants because of its dependence on grafting. On the one hand, genetic engineering of a scion will be needed to affect resistance to any pests that function above ground or to modify the properties of the cultivar with regards to production of berries. Since the scion cannot survive by itself, it is unlikely any of its traits could be transferred to other plants. On the other hand, it is the rootstock that needs to be modified to affect soil pests such as nematodes; but whatever is done to the rootstock is unlikely to be transmitted to the berries (and therefore to the wine that people consume).

There's a further practical difficulty in genetic engineering scions. Like other plants, grapevines have different cell layers whose lineages separate early in plant development. When a plant is propagated by cuttings, as has been the case for grapevines for thousands of years, these layers are inherited by the progeny. In fact, many grapevines are chimeric—there are genetic differences between their two layers. But genetic engineering is performed with single cells: so the engineered plant can represent the genetic constitution of only one of the layers of the original plant. Any significant differences between the layers of the original (chimeric) plant will be lost.

Personally I am inclined to the view that it's better to perform simple engineering of the grapevine to make it resistant to viruses, bacteria, fungi, and other diseases, than to treat the crop with potentially dangerous inhibitors or pesticides. Although applications are supposed to stop several weeks before harvest, residues can be hard to remove from the grapes; surveys of table grapes sold in European supermarkets have shown significant residues.[100] A grapevine with additional genes coding for natural resistance to pests or diseases would not offer any comparable hazard to human health. However, engineering to "improve" fruit quality is likely to be counter-productive in the same way as other more conventional approaches at breeding; have you ever had a farmed fish with anything resembling the flavor of a wild fish? But in spite of much research, no genetically engineered grapevine has yet been used to produce wine.[101]

Genetic engineering of yeast is a lot simpler than with the grapevine, and it has just as much potential to affect the flavor of wine. Potential targets for modification of yeast are at fermentation (to change features such as how much alcohol is generated), to make the process more resistant to spoilage (by introducing antimicrobial agents), or to affect specific wine properties (such as release or synthesis of aromatic compounds that affect varietal typicity or to increase production of agents such as resveratrol). In contrast with the failure to utilize genetically modified grapevines, there has been more interest in customizing yeasts.[102]

One of the most dramatic developments in genetic engineering has been to produce strains of yeast that can perform both the alcoholic fermentation and the malolactic fermentation. This was done by transferring the genes needed for the process from a bacterium into yeast.[103] Then malolactic fermentation occurs simultaneously with alcoholic fermentation instead of separately.[104] This has major implications for big commercial producers, who can cut time required for production. But it is almost certainly going to result in changes in the aroma and flavor spectrum of the wine in ways that are hard to predict. The ML01 strain is already in commercial use, but its creators are extremely coy about how much and where it is used.[105]

The End of Evolution?

Has evolution of the grapevine come to an end? Well, no, but over the past century it has largely taken a different form from previously. When many different grape varieties grew in close proximity, there were greater opportunities for sexual mating between them to produce new types. Some of the most important modern varieties originated in this way: Cabernet Sauvignon from an adventitious cross between Cabernet Franc and Sauvignon Blanc, Merlot from a cross between Cabernet Franc and a (now lost) variety retrospectively called Magdelaine Noire des Charentes, Chardonnay from a cross between an ancestral Pinot and Gouais Blanc. Some of the parents of the most successful varieties were themselves of no great account—Gouais Blanc produces indifferent white wine. In fact, it was so poorly regarded that several attempts were made to ban its planting in the middle ages;[106] if they had succeeded, we might not have Chardonnay today! Like people, you can never tell how the progeny will turn out.[107]

Opportunities for sexual recombination have been much reduced by the decline in the diversity of planted grapevines and by the modern method of planting each variety in its own separate vineyard block. And if a new variety were to occur, it's unlikely it would noticed or exploited, given the increasing pressure to focus on the tried and tested. There are some minor exceptions: Pinot Gouges (the white strain of Pinot Noir found in Henri Gouges's vineyards in Nuits St. Georges) is used to make white wine, for example. But for the last couple of centuries, new strains of the grapevine have come from breeding programs rather than occurring naturally.

Breeding programs have not done nearly such a good job as Nature. No great varietal has emerged. The most prominent of the man-made crosses is Müller-Thurgau, produced in Germany in 1882 by a cross between Riesling and the table grape Madeleine Royale.[108] The most widely planted grape in Germany, it has the important attributes of growing more easily and offering greater resistance to frost than Riesling. But it's basically good for producing bulk Liebfraumilch rather than quality wine. In fact, breeding programs have generally had their greatest successes in producing new varieties that do well in marginal climates, often because they have greater resistance to cold weather. While useful in allowing the range of viticulture to be extended where natural varieties might not succeed, almost by definition this does not produce great wine.

Selection of clones from existing varieties has had more impact.[109] Whether for good or bad depends on the criteria applied in the selection. There has been too much of a trend for breeding institutes to concentrate on reliability and productivity rather than quality. Often enough this has led to homogeneity and blandness in the wine. But when clones are selected for quality of fruit, or for criteria such as ripening at the most appropriate time for a specific climate, they can improve the wine. There remains, of course, the concern that lack of diversity will offset the advantages gained by having healthy grapevines, and clones cannot do more than allow the best subvarieties to be selected from a cultivar; they will not offer the range of new possibilities created by a sexual cross. If evolution has not ended, then, certainly it is more restricted today.

III THE WORLD MARKET

REGULATION AND TAXATION are as old as wine itself. In ancient Egypt, wine had to be cleared by the authorities as fit for sale, and it was taxed according to its quality level. In Greece, speculation was prevented by refusing to allow wine to be sold before it was bottled and by banning sales on credit. Wine production became a sufficiently important economic factor in the Roman Empire for planting of vines to be regulated. For the next couple of thousand years, regulation was local and sporadic. The modern era started in the first part of the twentieth century with the introduction of legislation in France, culminating in the system of Appellation Contrôlée, to ensure the authenticity of the stated origin of a wine. This evolved into the system that now rules the classification of all wine in the European Union into three categories: table wine, wine with geographical indication, and quality wine. Place names as descriptors for wine remained a free for all outside Europe until recent treaties granting protection to the European place names. In the New World, production of wine is much less regulated, and description focuses on varietals, with less concentration on place of origin, but the marketing of wine is tightly controlled, reaching a ludicrous epitome in the three-tier distribution system of the United States.

Development of regulations.

2500 B.C.	"Inspector of the Wine Test" approves wine for sale in Egypt. Tax determined by quality.
400 B.C.	Laws in Greece prevent watering down wine and require airtight amphorae. Wine cannot be sold as futures.
92 C.E.	Roman Emperor Domitian requires vines to be uprooted in many regions.
~800	Emperor Charlemagne bans treading grapes and introduces other regulations.
1487	Sulfur dioxide authorized as preservative by decree of Prussian Royal Court.
1935	Appellation contrôlée introduced in France.
1962	European Union extends regulations to define quality wines in member countries.
2000	Agreements to protect European place names on wines in New World.

8

Global Wine Trends

INTEREST IN WINE HAS NEVER BEEN SO GREAT AS TODAY. Going back to the ancient world, wine was a focus for the leisured classes. The best wines were treasured, and, much as today, connoisseurs would boast about old wines they had drunk. The Satyricon, a sharp satire of the first century C.E., describes a dinner party at which a rich parvenu, Trimalchio, serves a wine described as real Opimian—the fabled Falernian wine from the year 121 B.C. when Opimius was consul. The wine was supposedly labeled as "one hundred years old," a pointed give-away as to lack of authenticity, but the description emphasizes the social importance of being able to brag about the vintage.[1] Not so much has changed at the top end in the past two millennia.

But in the past half century, the wine market has broadened enormously and quality has improved out of all recognition. "We've converted from being a cottage industry into a competitive consumer luxury-goods industry," says Michael Mondavi, formerly of Robert Mondavi winery in Napa valley.[1] The contrasting directions of two countries at opposite ends of the wine spectrum illustrate worldwide trends. France is the world's largest consumer, with an average annual consumption of roughly 75 bottles per person. In the United States, individual consumption is relatively low, at roughly 11 bottles per person.

"French drinking habits are well known. Essentially they consist of fairly continuous consumption over the course of each day."[1] It took an Anglo-Saxon to make this disapproving comment; it was probably not true even when it was written in 1990, and it is certainly no longer true today. Any French wine producer will tell you that there has been a dramatic fall in consumption over recent decades. Total consumption has almost halved since 1965.[2] But the proportion of wine at the highest quality level (AOC) has increased three-fold over the period. They say, "Les Français boivent moins mais boivent mieux." (The French drink less, but drink better).

By contrast, the United States has slowly been becoming a wine-drinking country, with consumption per person having increased three-fold since 1965.[3] And over that period, there has been a transition from low quality, sweet, fortified wines made from no-name grape varieties to dry wines made largely from quality varietals. With high population compensating for low individual consumption, the United States is set to become the world's largest wine-consuming nation. The decline in France shows the abandonment of wine as an ordinary beverage (much of it was rotgut consumed by workmen on their way to work); while the increase in the United States shows how wine is being embraced as a lifestyle choice.

From Plonk to Cult Wines

Should we measure a country's success on the wine stage in terms of its total volume of production, the value of its sales, or the reputation of its top wines? In most cases, the top wines attract attention, sometimes they create a halo effect helping the others, but if volumes are small their overall sales may make little direct contribution to the health and wealth of the wine region. The volume of lower-priced wines may be more important.[4] There is one major exception to this rule: Bordeaux, where the top wines are the major economic sector.[5]

France still dominates the production of high-end wines. The number of French wines whose price puts them into the category of luxury goods is far higher than for any other country. The United States runs second. Within France, Burgundy outstrips Bordeaux about 2:1 in terms of individual high-end wines—but many of the Bordeaux wines are relatively widely available, while almost all the Burgundian wines are available in only very small amounts. In fact, it is only from Bordeaux that wines at a price level over $100 per bottle make a large contribution to the economics of the region.[7] As you might expect, the Rhône is in third place for high-priced wines from France.

The top regions in the United States are Napa followed closely by Sonoma; in Australia Barossa is followed by McLaren Vale. In Italy the honors are shared between Piedmont and Tuscany; Spain is represented mostly by Rioja.[8] Cham-

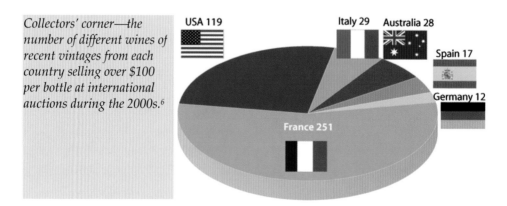

Collectors' corner—the number of different wines of recent vintages from each country selling over $100 per bottle at international auctions during the 2000s.[6]

USA 119

Italy 29   Australia 28

Spain 17

Germany 12

France 251

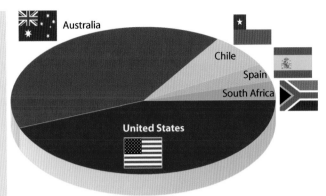

The United States and Australia together account for three quarters of the market share of the most powerful brands.[9]

pagne, Alsace, Madeira, and Port also produce collectible wines. The penetration by the New World is recent; in the 1990s, Australia scarcely figured; in the 1980s Napa was not significant. In fact, it was the legalization of wine auctions in New York in 1995 that really led to the rise of Napa as a prominent region for wine collectibles.

It's a very different picture looking at the distribution of top brands. The United States and Australia dominate by far, each with several brands in the top twenty worldwide. No other country has more than a single brand, and France does not appear at all in the list. Of course, there are wide differences in brand penetration in different countries. In the Anglo-Saxon world, brands dominate the market. In France and Italy, they have a much smaller market share.

Innovations in winemaking technology have had a major effect on the nature of the brands. The introduction of anaerobic methods, in which oxygen is excluded and the wines become brighter with more aggressive, forward fruits, has pretty much led to a new style of wine, as epitomized by New Zealand Sauvignon Blanc. At the other end of the spectrum, the ability to stabilize wine with sterile filtration allows wines with small amounts of residual sugar to avoid spoilage problems, allowing many major brands to make "dry" wines that in reality have low levels of residual sugar. The ability to use oak in cheaper forms than barrels has been responsible for allowing oak-flavored wines to penetrate lower levels of the market.

A Faithful Follower of Fashion

Wine styles are enormously influenced by fashion and limited by the available technology. The deeply colored, intensely extracted, powerful wines of today are made possible by modern methods of viticulture and vinification.

Both red and white wines were made in ancient times. The Egyptians must have made red wines, because most pictures show black grapes and juice. The Greeks prized their sweet wines, made from grapes that had been dried in the sun. The most famous wine of the Romans, Falernian, was white and sweet. In the middle ages in Bordeaux, most wine was white (known as vin clair), but a small amount of red wine was also made. With very short fermentation periods (around two days), the red cannot have been much more colored than a light rosé of today, and presumably the wine was low in alcohol.[10] By the nineteenth century, color and alcohol were prized in many markets; so wines such as those of Bordeaux, which were still relatively light with low alcohol, were habitually strengthened with wines from farther south to give them more color, body, and alcohol.

Auction prices give some idea of the fashion of the moment. Wine was included in the very first Christie's auction in London in 1766, and continued to be sold until the first world war. There were a few sales between the wars, but wine sales then stopped until the department was reopened in 1965. Two centuries of changes in wine fashions can be tracked through the catalogs.

Through the early nineteenth century most sales were of generic wines. Wine was wine. Lots offered in the early 1820s included "Port" and "Sherry" (occasionally the name of a shipper was mentioned), "Madeira" (the best was qualified as East India Madeira), "Champagne" (occasionally named as Sillery), "Hock" (from the Rheingau) was distinguished from "Moselle," and "Claret." Occasionally the name of the bottler was mentioned, but the only producer distinguished by name was "La Fitte." Burgundy was extremely rare. The price range was narrow for all quality wines, roughly £2-5 per dozen bottles.[11] Vintages were mentioned only sporadically.

Things changed little by the middle of the century. The classification of the great châteaux of the Médoc in 1855 had little direct effect on the consumer in London. Not much of a premium was paid even for the first growths; at one auction in 1860, "Claret" sold for £6 6s. per three dozen, whereas "La Fitte Claret" sold for £7 2s. (neither being given the benefit of vintage). The châteaux mostly remained unidentified.[12] Claret continued to sell a bit below Port, Madeira, and Sherry.[13]

By the end of the nineteenth century, the pattern was very different. Wine auctions focused on Champagne, Claret, and to a lesser degree, Port and Sherry. Champagne was by far the most expensive item: at the top, Pommery 1874 was selling for up to £12 per case at Christie's in the 1890s. The most expensive hock was Steinberg Cabinet, usually £5-6 per case. Sales of Burgundy were not common, but Romanée-Conti sold for £6.50 per case and Le Montrachet for £4 per case on the rare occasions they were offered. Lafite Rothschild was generally the most expensive claret, at under £5 per case for the 1870 vintage. Sauternes were even cheaper, with Château d'Yquem at £4-5 per dozen.[14]

Over the past century, a major rearrangement has taken place. Burgundy and Bordeaux hold positions as producers of the most expensive wines; white wines are less in demand than red; and Champagne only rarely rises to the extreme heights. Some wines from new regions make it into the lists of high-priced rarities, including the Rhône and the New World, especially Napa Valley. Hock and fortified wines have dropped off the list.

Today the gap between the top and bottom of the market is far higher in wine than any other beverage. Even aside from scarce cult items, wines at release vary from around $2 per bottle to more than $2000 per bottle.[15] There's nothing like a thousand-fold range of prices for beer or spirits—or soft drinks.

Sweet versus dry, white versus red, fashions come and go. It's a common pattern for wine regions to start by producing sweet wines, and then to move towards production of more sophisticated dry wines. All over the New World, production started with no-name varieties, often fortified to achieve a sweet style, and then made a transition to a dry style with higher quality varietals. The only significant difference in this pattern between the United States, Australia, South America, and South Africa, is the time at which they made the transition. But this is not to sneer at the New World; until the eighteenth century the white wines of Bordeaux were all made as sweet as the vintage allowed.[16]

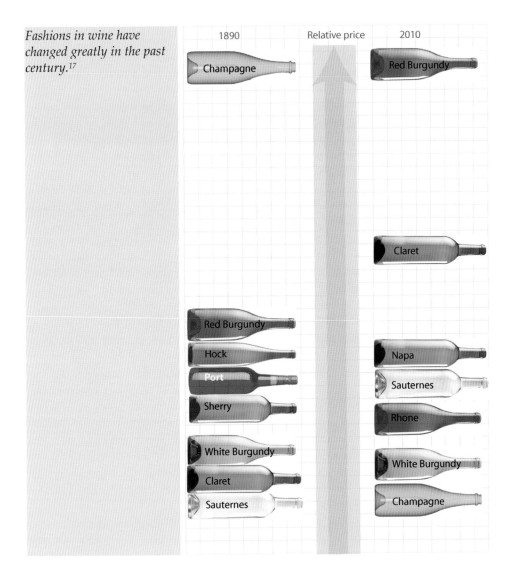

Fashions in wine have changed greatly in the past century.[17]

The Eggheads of Oenology

At the start of the twentieth century, wine production was mostly on a small scale, but by the end of the century most wine was mass produced. As industrial techniques replaced artisanal production, reliability and consistency became more important, creating increased need for technical support. The industry puts relatively little direct effort into research—much less than the food industry, for example—but as wine production has become an economic force in a region, centers for technical support develop at local institutions. Among the best known institutes of oenology today are those at Montpellier in southern France, Geisenheim in the Rheingau of Germany, the Davis campus of the University of California, and the AWRI (Australian Wine Research Institute) in Adelaide.

Oenology departments tend, of course, to specialize in the issues that are important in the vineyards surrounding them. They can be pretty good at solving local problems. The University of Bordeaux was instrumental in rescuing white Bordeaux from the dumps by discovering how to preserve character and freshness. The AWRI has been at the forefront of research into the differences between screwcaps and corks. But while research at the universities can bring helpful insights into viticulture and vinification, there is also more than an element of dead hand coming from the impetus to play it safe rather than to innovate. Oenology departments everywhere tend to favor quantity over quality and to prefer technical sophistication and reliability rather than artisanal variation. One of their most important roles today is to turn out trained oenologists who become winemakers with high levels of technical expertise. The crucial issue here is that the technical expertise should be a means for producing wine of interest rather than an end for homogenization.

University departments tend to place more emphasis on bringing up the general standard from the bottom than diffusing the highest quality down from the top. The institute at Dijon bears some responsibility for the spread of Pinot Droit in Burgundy in the 1960s; this cultivar of Pinot Noir (named for its upright stance) is a reliable producer, but gives quantity rather than quality. Its large berries with thick skins gave a wine that looked better than it tasted. Many of those characterless Burgundies of the period reflect the lack of focus and concentration in Pinot Droit.

Rootstocks might seem to be somewhat less interesting than varietals, but can have a huge effect on viticulture. Witness the debacle of AxR1. This cross between Vitis vinifera and Vitis rupestris is not used as a rootstock in Europe because of its sensitivity to phylloxera, but was recommended by the University of California at Davis for local use because of its reliability in various soils and climates and its high productivity. So widely accepted was the advice, that when AxR1 was duly eaten by an onslaught of phylloxera, almost all of the vineyards in California had to be replanted between 1989 and 1996, an economic devastation for the region.[18]

It's fair to say that the Department of Viticulture and Enology at Davis is no exception to the inclination to favor quantity over quality. Their role has not changed since their reaction in 1964 to the proposal of Fred and Eleanor McCrae to plant a Chardonnay vineyard at Stony Hill. "The professors disapproved of amateurs pretending they were in Burgundy, where Chardonnay was grown, when they were in northern California, where white wine was made out of French Colombard, Chenin Blanc, and other white grapes better able to withstand frost," says historian James Conaway.[19] Stony Hill Chardonnay duly became one of the most famous wines of Napa Valley.

Of course, it's easy to take potshots at academics who rely on the status quo. Many of the most interesting wines of today come from entrepreneurs who took a risk in planting a variety in a location which all conventional wisdom said was designed for failure, from Mas de Daumas Gassac's planting of Cabernet at Aniane in the Languedoc to Cloudy Bay's planting of Sauvignon Blanc in Marlborough, New Zealand. No university department would countenance such risky ventures. To get the best out of the departments, you have to understand where they are coming from, which is reliably raising the general standard. The mistake is to let their influence become so dominant that an entire region follows a single practice.

Flying Winemakers and Globalization

Oenology is almost as old as winemaking. Around 200 B.C., Cato (the Elder) in his book *de Agri Cultura* advised on a whole gamut of activities, from cultivating vineyards to detailing procedures for making wine. Some of his concerns were unique to the period: advice for looking after slaves, for example, including giving them the equivalent of a bottle of wine per day. But many issues have scarcely changed: how to train the vines, what grape varieties might best be cultivated, when to harvest, and how to run the presses.[20] The average vineyard was not so different in size then from a large vineyard today, in the region of 20-40 hectares.[21] Much of the attention given to grape growing and wine production no doubt reflects their economic importance; Cato regarded the business as profitable, although later writers on the subject, such as Columella during the first century C.E., were less convinced.[22] At all events, the tradition of commentary and advice on vineyards and wine production continued for the next millennium or so.

It was only in the second half of the twentieth century that oenology became a hands-on experience in the sense that visiting oenologists would advise wine producers on the spot. This simultaneously brought significant technical improvements to winemaking and generated assertions that all wines were beginning to taste the same.

The first of the great oenologists, who did more than anyone to bring vinification into the modern era based on rational analysis, was Emile Peynaud. He revolutionized winemaking in Bordeaux in the 1950s by introducing methods based on understanding the processes of vinification. Before Peynaud, malolactic fermentation was a mysterious event that might (or might not) happen in the spring. Peynaud demonstrated that malolactic fermentation is caused by bacteria that are sensitive to temperature; they become active as the cellars warm up in the spring.[23]

Peynaud convinced winemakers to replace old barrels, often infected with spoilage bacteria, with clean, new barrels—leading to criticism that he had introduced the taste of oak into wine. The changes that he championed, from using the best grapes to maintaining cellar hygiene, made wine easier to drink sooner. To those accustomed to the view that young wine was tart, tannic, unpleasant, and even undrinkable, this was heresy. Traditionalists distrusted him and claimed that his wines had been homogenized, "Peynaudized," as they put it. "I am not sure of the appellation, I do not recognize the vintage, but I can tell this wine was made by Emile Peynaud," was one famous comment. (Similar comments have been made since, with perhaps more pertinence, about the oenologues of today.) Peynaud's retort was that, "The wines of yesterday were more stereotyped than today's. They were all similar because they shared the same defect. They were oxidized."[24]

Similar accusations reverberate, but with more force, in the present era. Many Bordeaux châteaux are advised by oenologues, of whom Michel Rolland, Stéphan Derenoncourt, Denis Dubourdieu, and Jacques Boissenot are the best known. Each advises a considerable number of château—Michel Rolland more than 50, Stéphan Derenoncourt around 40, Denis Dubourdieu and Jacques Boissenot some 20-30 each. Altogether some 200 of the leading wines of Bordeaux depend on advice from these four oenologues.[25] (And of course they also advise wineries in other regions and countries.)

Michel Rolland in particular is known for producing wines with intense fruit and new oak, very much the modern style of Bordeaux, in some ways more resembling wines of the New World than those of Bordeaux in the past. He is the proprietor of Château Bon Pasteur in Pomerol, and among the châteaux he advises on the right bank are the producers of many of the garage (intense small-production) wines. He is often felt to be the arch apostle of the international style, and was portrayed as a somewhat Mephisophelean figure in the film Mondovino, which took aim at the globalization of wine.

The "international style" wines depend on changes in both viticulture and vinification. Not only are grapes harvested at increased levels of ripeness, with greater sugar levels (giving higher alcohol levels) and more (and riper) tannins, but the wine is exposed to new oak at an earlier stage. The new style wines tend to be powerful rather than elegant, bursting with fruit, sometimes with jammy rather than savory aromas and flavors. These wines tend to show well at comparative tastings because their intense flavors make it difficult to appreciate wines with more subtle constitutions; even experienced tasters can be fooled. Personally I would question whether these wines are really suitable to accompany food. However, they are much favored by some influential wine critics, including Robert Parker; reflecting the extent of his influence, in France, they sometimes say that a wine made to this prescription has been *parkerisé*.

The Most Powerful Critic in the World

Wine criticism is a relatively new phenomenon. It used to be that critics were essentially the same people who sold you the wine; writing was a subsidiary activity. In the absence of any genuine independence, their corruption was legendary. "Have you received your case of Lafite from the château this year?" one would ask another. Stories used to abound about critics who visited famous châteaux and left the trunks of their cars open, ready for a few complimentary cases of wine.

The absence of genuine critical comment was part of the impetus that led Robert Parker to start *The Wine Advocate* in 1978. Since then The Wine Advocate has become by far the most important newsletter on wine, and Robert Parker so dominates wine criticism that many feel no other critic has any comparable significance. But Parker's importance may perhaps lie not so much in his dominance as in the fact that he really developed the whole idea of independent criticism. Now there are many others earning their living by wine criticism (although it has to be said that many regrettably lack his independence.) Since the 1970s, the transition from a producer-driven to a consumer-driven industry has seen enormous growth of consumer magazines and newsletters focused on assessing and recommending individual wines.[26]

The Wine Advocate established the paradigm for assessing wines with a quantitative score out of 100, much simplifying the process of selection for the consumer. Right from the start, Bordeaux was a major focal point, spurred by the fact virtually no critics had exposed the poor quality of some first growths during the preceding decade. The Wine Advocate was different, starting off by slamming the quality of the 1973 vintage. Château Margaux was described as "a terrible wine… very thin and acidic."

The Wine Advocate reports its ratings in plain text, but Decanter and the Wine Spectator are glossy consumer magazines.

It was with the (then) atypical 1982 vintage in Bordeaux that Parker made his reputation. Relatively warm, prolonged vintage conditions led to a harvest of unusually ripe grapes, giving wines with lower acidity, much riper tannins, and higher alcohol than had previously been common. The low acidity caused many critics to write off the year, at least in terms of a classic long-lived vintage. Among these was Robert Finigan, author of the Private Guide to Wines, then the leading wine newsletter in the United States. This mistake, together with some financial problems, led to the decline and ultimate failure of the Private Guide,[27] opening the way for the Wine Advocate to dominate the market in fine wine assessment.

Robert Parker was one of the first to recognize the quality of the vintage, and his argument that 1982 would be a long-lived great vintage elevated him to become the high priest of wine criticism. From its initial issue of a few hundred copies in the local Washington-Baltimore area, the Wine Advocate has grown to tens of thousands of copies distributed worldwide. In April each year, the Wine Advocate now offers a detailed assessment of the preceding Bordeaux vintage complete with scores out of 100 for most wines.

Its dominance, initially of the market in the United States, later in Europe and Asia, has led to the description of Parker as the world's most influential critic. Indefatigable in his tasting, now supported by a team of writers with responsibilities for particular wine regions, he has built the Wine Advocate into a voice that cannot be ignored by wine producers. Nowhere is this more apparent than in Bordeaux, for which he still takes personal responsibility.

A score of 90 from the Wine Advocate is the tipping point. The saying goes that a wine with a score above 90 cannot be kept on the shelf; but at a score below 90 it cannot be got off the shelf. The Bordelais both rely upon and deplore Parker's influence. One château owner recently said to me, without any perceptible sense of irony, "Nobody pays any attention to the Wine Spectator—it all depends on God's rating." (It goes without saying that God is Parker.) The proprietor said sadly that now the negociants just quote Parker, essentially replacing what used to be their own comments with his ratings.[28] Indeed, Parker scores are commonly appended to wine bottles in wine shops around the world.

The Wine Advocate shows a preference for wines that are dark colored, full bodied, with obvious fruits, and often high in alcohol. This is the modern style pioneered by the New World, and of which the 1982 vintage was a forerunner for Bordeaux. Given this perception, it is ironic that early issues of the Wine Advocate (in common with other commentators of the period) took the view that California wines had alcohol levels that were too high, had too much oak, and were altogether too massive. An early issue commented, "The better Bordeaux are elegant, delicate wines that possess incredible subtlety and complexity, whereas the best California Cabernets are massive, powerful, assertive wines often bordering on coarseness." Parker went on to comment that the California Cabernets did not age well beyond a few years, compared with the much greater longevity of Bordeaux. It is not easy to relate these early views to the wine reviews of the past decade.

Everyone agrees that Parker's scores have a major effect on the price of Bordeaux. There is no doubt that his views affect the general reception of a vintage. The 2008 vintage in Bordeaux is a case in point. This is a decent enough, but not top, vintage, and when the wines first went on the market in April 2009, in rather difficult general financial conditions, prices dropped some 30% from the previous year. Halfway through the campaign, Parker reported that the vintage was much better than had been generally appreciated; prices for those wines that had not come out previously went up sharply. (Many believe this is a fool's paradise.)

The critics' ratings for individual châteaux can swing widely from year to year, but prices show good stability from one year to the next (relative to the overall scale for the vintage). There are certainly exceptions where an extraordinary result by a château may cause a dramatic (but usually transient) spike in its price (corrections in the other direction are much less common), but there is considerable inertia with regards to changing the relative prices of châteaux. Parker's view of a château certainly affects the price of the wine, but he reacts much faster than the market, and it can take some years for a château to change its general position in the rankings. In fact, none of the critics' ratings show close relationships with one another or with release prices of the wines.[29]

Parker's opinions are so important in the world of wine that there is a whole company devoted simply to adjusting wines in order to get better Parker points. Based in California's Sonoma Valley, Enologix was started in 1993 by Leo McCloskey. He's a somewhat controversial figure because his methods are secret, consisting of software that he claims can predict the critical score of a wine from chemical analysis. His database of tens of thousands of wines is used to advise his clients what they need to do in order to bump their score over the magic 90 point level. Few winemakers will acknowledge using his services, but McCloskey claims that tens of wines advised by Enologix score over 90 points in the Wine Advocate.[30]

Whether you agree with Parker's ratings or not, whether it is healthy for any one opinion to be so dominant, there is one thing that can be said with certainty: Parker's ratings reflect his palate. The Wine Advocate takes no advertising and exists solely on its subscription income. That is more than can be said for the vast majority of wine magazines and critics. The leading magazines, the Wine Spectator in the United States, Decanter in Britain, and La Revue du Vin de France, all depend heavily on advertising from wine producers and distributors.

With a circulation of 350,000, the Wine Spectator is by far the largest wine magazine. It's influential in the United States to the extent that retailers rush to stock wines it recommends; it is regarded more or less with indifference elsewhere. Its market position has been captured by Michael Steinberger: "Its content appears tailored to attract two groups of wine drinkers: trophy hunters and people fairly new to oenophilia. For the uninitiated, the Spectator is a superb gateway product: informative, topical, easy on the eyes, mercifully light on the jargon... To appeal to the poseurs, the magazine runs lots of unctuous stories about insta-billionaires and their custom-designed cellars, invariably stocked with a millennium's supply of swank wines. It is partly for this reason that the Spectator is considered a joke by many wine sophisticates; some call it the

"Speculator" after the aforementioned trophy hunters. The magazine is also knocked for its ratings, which are seen as inconsistent and inflated relative to other critics, and for its coverage, which often tends toward the sensational... It's never been proved that advertisers influence scores, but suspicions run deep, especially in wine chat rooms."[31] All too often, the Wine Spectator loses its focus and publishes issues with little to say about wine, but with a lot about lifestyles of the rich and famous.

With articles written mostly by its own staff, the Wine Spectator offers a certain unanimity of opinion in liking bold, fruity, forward wines. This can lead it into error. Barolo had a unprecedented run of wonderful vintages from 1996 to 2001 due to the good weather in Piedmont. But there was general hilarity when the Wine Spectator rated the 2000 vintage. "Italy's jewel box of a wine region produced its greatest vintage ever in 2000—a year I rate a perfect 100 points," James Suckling, their man in Europe, said with characteristic pomposity.[32] True, it was a good, perhaps even a great vintage, but by 2004 when the wines began to appear, cognoscenti were waiting for the wines from 2001, a truly classic vintage. The producers could not believe their luck in having the preceding vintage rated as the best ever, and laughed all the way to the bank as the wines sold out in the United States. The 2001 vintage epitomized the ethereal style of Barolo, but 2000 was just a little too warm to display classic character. The wines showed more obvious fruit than usual, drinking well in their youth; lovely wines, but not classic long-lived Barolo. The Wine Advocate showed much better judgment in rating vintage 2000 at the same 95 points as 1999, and rating 2001 at 96 points.

Among the Wine Spectator's most notable features are its annual publication of the Top 100 wines of the year, released just in time for the Christmas buying season, and the Restaurant Awards issue in August. Both have been tarnished by awards for nonexistent wines or restaurants, and for inexplicable choices. The Top 100 list is a particularly big deal, especially for wines at the very top, which rapidly escalate in price and become scarce, even though the mandate for inclusion on the list is that wines are produced in good quantities and sold at reasonable prices.

In 1999, the top-rated wine on the list was the 1996 Cinq Cépages, a Bordeaux blend made by Chateau St. Jean in Sonoma Country.[33] The magazine commented: "The rise of the 1996 Chateau St. Jean Cabernet Sauvignon Sonoma County Cinq Cépages to our Wine of the Year won't surprise those who've tasted this remarkably rich and polished wine as it has evolved. With its uncommon depth, ripe, juicy flavors and plush, velvety texture, Cépages won votes and admiration from our editors for its quality (a 95-point rating on the Wine Spectator 100-point scale), its $28 price and its availability."

The problem is that the 1996 vintage was only released on to the market in a very small tranche during 1999. It was not generally released until the following year (and at double the price).[34] At the least, it's questionable how supplies could have been adequate to allow people to follow the wine as it evolved. Just to add to the confusion, in replying to criticism, Thomas Matthews of The Wine Spectator referred to the award-winning wine as the 1999 vintage (which certainly could not have been available).[35]

Equally incredible was the Wine Spectator's choice of Guigal's 1999 Châteauneuf-du-Pape as its wine of the year in 2002. There is no doubt that Guigal is a master winemaker: his single-vineyard Côte-Rôties are widely acknowledged to be among the finest wines on the planet. But his wines from the southern Rhône, including Châteauneuf-du-Pape are simply not in the same league. The Châteauneuf is well enough crafted, but it's a middle of the road wine without any particular distinction, and there are any number of other, more interesting wines of the appellation. In response to criticism, the magazine did not provide any further enlightenment about the choice. "This 1999 Châteauneuf-du-Pape is an outstanding effort by an extraordinary winemaker in a difficult vintage," said Thomas Matthews of the Wine Spectator.[36] Fair enough: but does a good result from a "difficult" vintage justify a wine of the year, when other regions may have performed better? There was nothing wrong with this wine, indeed it was commendable, but its choice as wine of the year simply casts doubt on the value of the whole exercise.

But worse was yet to come. Every August, the magazine rates restaurants for their wine lists, placing some 4,000 restaurants in three ascending categories: Award of Excellence (3,249 winners at last count), Best of Award of Excellence (797 winners), and Grand Award (72 winners). The restaurant gets a certificate for the appropriate level of award, which it can display.

An exposé in the New York Times reported that for the basic level of Award of Excellence, all that is required is for the restaurant to send its wine list to the Wine Spectator with a check.[37] The current fee is $250, so the thousands of restaurants on the present list have paid more than a million dollars to the Wine Spectator between them for the year's listing. (You have to reapply every year.) The Wine Spectator makes no claim that it visits restaurants except for those given the Grand Award, but certainly it was not widely appreciated outside of the trade that basically the Award of Excellence is cheap advertising for the restaurant.

Just how easy it is to gain an Award became clear as the result of a spoof application made by writer Robin Goldstein as part of his research. He submitted the wine list from a mythical restaurant, called Osteria l'Intrepido in Milan, created a web site for the restaurant, and obtained a Milan phone number and fax.[38] The rub comes in the wines on the list: they were terrible. The "reserve" list contained three vintages of the great Tuscan wine Sassicaia; but also contained twelve wines that the Wine Spectator had rated poorly, from 58 to 81 points, with comments such as "tasted metallic and odd," "unacceptable, smells like bug spray," "turpentine, hard acidic character."

Certainly Goldstein took some trouble to make the fake restaurant appear real. If it had actually submitted a consistently good wine list, there would be little with which to reproach the magazine, which, as Executive Editor Thomas Matthews pointed out, does not claim to visit the restaurants à la Michelin. "This is a program that recognizes the efforts restaurants put into their wine lists," he said.[39] But when the list includes wines that the Wine Spectator itself has trashed, isn't the wary diner entitled to wonder whether that Award of Excellence certificate on the wall isn't simply a cheap substitute for buying in some good wines? What faith does the Wine Spectator have in its own ratings?

All this is perhaps an illustration of the naïveté with which consumers regard supposedly authoritative magazines. Yet naïveté is not restricted to consumers. An academic study tried to determine whether wine had improved in quality and price by examining the Spectator's Top 100 list.[40] The thesis was that if average scores have increased, wines must have got better; if average prices have decreased, values must have improved. There was no significant variation in average scores over the period, but average price declined 44%. A large part of the price reduction was due to the replacement of French wines by less expensive wines from the New World. The authors concluded that American consumers are getting equally good wine for less money. The study may well be a testament to the power of the Wine Spectator in the market; it suggests that producers have made increasingly successful efforts to provide inexpensive wines made in a style that the Wine Spectator scores well. But unless you believe that Wine Spectator scores represent some objective measure of quality, this sadly proves nothing about value.

Published from London, Decanter magazine modestly bills itself as "quite simply, the world's best wine magazine." It started as a relatively serious, consumer-oriented magazine, with articles from good contributors. Most articles are written by outside contributors, so there is some variety of opinion, and it still retains some heavyweight and knowledgeable writers, but now selling 40,000 copies under the aegis of IPC (International Publishing Corporation, a mass market magazine publisher), it has distinctly more of an LCD tone, personality-driven articles, "promotional supplements" that make it easy to confuse advertising and editorial content, and a host of extra-mural activities including wine tastings, dinners, wine awards, and so on. Its major influence is in Britain, but its impact is not at all comparable to The Wine Advocate or Wine Spectator in the United States.

The Revue du Vin de France really was the world's best wine magazine (granted you had to read it in French), albeit strongly focused on France. Published since 1927, its circulation of more than 40,000 gave it a commanding position. Articles were knowledgeable and wide-ranging, and contributors included two of France's most renowned tasters, Michel Bettane and Thierry Desseauve. But concerned about future policy, Bettane and Desseauve quit the magazine after it was taken over by Marie-Claire (part of the Lagardère publishing group), which had previously purchased a rival magazine in the 1990s, Cuisine et Vins de France, and taken it down market. Unfortunately, their fears were only too well founded.

The increasing diversity of sources for wine, coupled with increasing numbers of new consumers, creates more and more need for informed criticism at all levels from retail to restaurant wine lists. The time when wine was a pursuit of a few, who knew where to obtain reliable advice, is long since past. The problem is the gap between the newsletters, such as the Wine Advocate, whose main readership consists of enthusiasts at some level, and the magazines, now increasingly consumer-oriented, and like all magazines of their type, prone to confuse editorial and advertising content. More of a ladder is needed to enable consumers to climb from dependence on ratings of variable quality to reliance on their own palates.

International Brands: Sourcing Wine

Terroir is irrelevant. The origins and sources of the wine are of relatively little importance. For the majority of today's consumers, the name of the wine brand is the crucial factor. Wines are bought on the same basis as other products: on the reputation of the manufacturer, and on the price.

A wine brand used to be relatively simple. It would typically consist of a single wine, such as Blue Nun Liebfraumilch or Mateus Rosé, the leading brands in Britain during the 1960s and 1970s. Each had its own style and following, and there was none of what today would be called "crossover" to other products of the same company. If you wanted a red wine, rather than a white or a rosé, you wouldn't look to Blue Nun or Mateus to provide it.

Today a brand attempts to provide a complete line offering the consumer a range of options (typically around the same price point). Take Blue Nun, which has been revitalized to provide a range of 20 wines, including red, white, rosé, and sparkling. Most people were probably aware that Blue Nun Liebfraumilch came from Germany (although very few consumers in Britain are aware that Mateus comes from Portugal).[41] But today the only category the brand represents is itself. In the Blue Nun range, the closest to the original Blue Nun is now a Qualitätswein (nominally a step up in grade) that comes from Germany's Rheinhessen region, but the range also includes a Shiraz from Australia, a Cabernet from France, a Zinfandel from the United States, and wines from many other sources. The two important features are the name, Blue Nun, and the varietal.

Some brands add geography as part of their character. The extraordinary success of Yellow Tail started with a single wine in 2001. It became the largest

Blue Nun includes wines from several countries.

imported brand in the United States in 2003, and now is on the list of top ten brands worldwide. Today Yellow Tail includes 13 varietal-labeled wines and also a reserve line (at higher price). But all share the same logo that was associated with the original success: a jumping wallaby, pointing to the origin in Australia, which remains a major selling point. You might view Yellow Tail as a sub-brand of "Brand Australia."

There can be strong reactions when a brand with national origins goes multinational. Lindemans, a well-known brand from major Australian producer Fosters, was accused of "using [a] highly-rated and well-recognized Australian brand with a reputation for quality and integrity and raping it," when they introduced lines from Chile and South Africa.[42] Fosters defended themselves by saying that consumer research indicated that most purchasers recognized Lindemans as a brand but had no idea it originated in Australia.

With their increasingly broad remit,[43] brands are taking over more and more of the market. At the start of the millennium, the top ten global wine brands had 5% of the world market.[44] By the end of the first decade, the list was strengthened by some powerful growing brands from the New World, Jacob's Creek, Lindemans, Blossom Hill, and Yellow Tail.[45] The top brands of still wine have more than achieved parity with sparkling wines, where brands have always dominated the market. Granted that leading brands remain a much smaller share of the wine market than their counterparts in the spirits or beer market, still they are progressing in both market share and increasingly global distribution.

Packaging the Product

As long ago as the 1950s, the giant American producer Gallo used screwcaps, based on the belief that corks were unreliable; unfortunately, however, all this did was to reinforce the general impression that screwcaps were associated with low quality production.[46] It took a while before consumers accepted that a screwcap did not necessarily imply lower quality, but since 2000 there has been a sea change, although there are still big differences between individual countries. Screwcaps are strongest where they started, in Australia (where more than half of the wines use screwcaps) and New Zealand (where virtually all of them do so). Slowly the effect has spread through Europe, led by large supermarkets in Britain that insisted on their suppliers using screwcaps. Germany has been somewhat of a holdout for the traditional view that screwcaps indicate lower quality, but on a recent visit, several producers told me they were now bottling wines for export under screwcap, because corks were not acceptable to their importers in the New World, a complete reversal from how things used to be. Screwcap usage in France is sporadic, but there are examples of important producers in every major region using screwcaps, although the overall proportion remains small.

What would be the ideal container for wine? It would be completely inert, incapable of reacting with water, alcohol, or any of the dissolved components. Glass fits that description better than anything else available. But the ideal con-

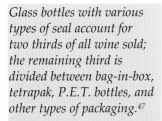

Glass bottles with various types of seal account for two thirds of all wine sold; the remaining third is divided between bag-in-box, tetrapak, P.E.T. bottles, and other types of packaging.[47]

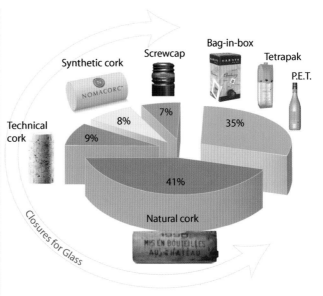

tainer would also be light and easy to transport. Glass is heavy and also (rela-tively) fragile. The seal for the container would be inert, and preferably reusable: cork has been much improved in the past decade, but there is still an unaccept-able level of contamination with TCA, and cork is not easy to reuse. Screwcaps may turn out to be the answer when the issue of oxygen permeability can be resolved.

Another issue is that some wines are aged for long periods, up to several dec-ades, so the container needs to be stable. Glass lasts for ever (although corks sometimes have to be replaced after 25 years or so). Nothing else with the same durability has been found, but there are several alternative packaging media for wines that will be consumed in the short term. Bottles made of aluminum or P.E.T. (a plastic like that used for bottled water) are light, and the tetrapak (adapted from the cardboard cartons for juice or milk) is easily transportable. And the ingenious bag-in-box is well suited for large quantities: it contains a collapsible plastic bag inside a cardboard carton, with a tap. As wine is drawn out, the bag collapses to exclude oxygen, so the wine stays fresh. Bag-in-box is the most rapidly growing segment of the market among the alternatives for cheaper, short-lived wines.

All these new possibilities have significantly changed the way wine is deliv-ered. Glass now accounts for only two thirds of the market, although admittedly it's the more expensive two thirds. Natural cork, which sealed virtually all glass wine bottles two decades ago, is now used in about two thirds of bottles. Techni-cal corks (consisting of agglomerated particles of natural cork) and synthetic corks (made of molded plastic, sometimes colored like real cork, sometimes brightly colored like children's toys) come next in importance. Screwcap is the most rapidly growing segment, increasing roughly five-fold in the five years since 2003. It's probably going to be second after natural cork in the not too distant future.

Winemaking is a natural enough activity, but is it "green?" Obviously enough, organic viticulture makes fewer demands on the environment than conventional agriculture, but the difference hasn't been quantitated. Running a winery is an expensive proposition in terms of energy consumption, but if you calculate how much energy goes into a bottle of wine, the result is a bit surprising. The energy cost of producing bulk wine is just a bit less than half the energy cost of producing bottled wine: the difference is due not only to the materials involved, but also because of the high costs involved in transporting the bottled product.[48] Bottles may be colored green, but they have a high carbon footprint, affected somewhat by the type of closure.

The cork producers have been feeling themselves under attack lately, with problems of cork taint leading more and more producers to switch to screwcaps, and they have gone to some pains to try to show that cork is environmentally the most friendly closure.[49] If a bottle has a carbon footprint of 180 tons of CO_2/million units, a natural cork adds another 10, a synthetic cork another 16, a technical cork another 21-25, and a screwcap another 35-50 depending on exactly how it's made. There's been quite a bit of fuss as to whether corks or screwcaps are better for the environment, but it's obvious that if you really want to make an impact, eliminating or improving the glass is the way to go.

Taxation: Extortion or Distortion?

Alcohol has been a favorite target for taxation even well before it became attractive as a sin tax. In early agricultural economies, wine (and beer) were simply targets among many for possible taxation. In situations where wine became a significant part of the economy, its importance for taxation increased. The Romans received considerable revenues from taxes on wine imports (recorded by stamp marks on the amphorae).[50] Colbert, the great finance minister of France in 1670, commented that the state needed to know how much wine people would buy each year in order to assess the level of revenue.[51] At the peak of production before the phylloxera epidemic, in 1875, taxes on wine and spirits were the largest single item of state revenue in France.[52] But from ancient times until the last century, wine (and other alcoholic beverages) were assessed on the basis of the ease of tax collection and the extent to which taxes could feasibly be raised.

Taxation of wine was used in the same way as other fiscal measures, as part of general policy. During the seventeenth century, for example, English policy was to tax wine imports at rates intended to encourage trade with territories owned by the Crown and to discourage trade with countries with which England was at war.[53] Certainly wine was regarded as a luxury rather than necessity, and therefore appropriate for increases in indirect taxation, but it attracted no particular hostility. One of the first signs of the transition to use taxation of wine to influence social policy was the attempt to reduce alcohol consumption in Britain during the first world war by increasing taxes on alcohol. Yet this was pragmatic, based on concern to increase industrial productivity, rather than representing a moral stance.

The temperance movement of the nineteenth century agitated against consumption of alcohol, but its extreme position, that any form of alcoholic drink was dangerous, caused its efforts to be directed towards prohibition rather than increased taxation. The collapse of Prohibition in the United States dealt a blow to the movement; but the concept that alcohol consumption is a problem for society that should be addressed by fiscal and social policies developed as part and parcel of the politically correct movement in recent decades.[54]

Tax rates on wine vary widely in Europe, but the general rule is that the farther away you are from the producing countries, the less value you will get in a bottle of wine. The countries of the north, ranging from Scandinavia to Britain have very high excise duties, basically a flat tax per bottle. This means that the value of the wine in an inexpensive bottle can become vanishingly small—when you buy a cheap bottle of wine, you are paying tax and getting remarkably little product. In the producing countries of the warm south, excise taxes are much lower, so the overall tax bite depends on local sales tax and is more proportionate to the value of the bottle. Maybe that's why you can get a delicious bottle of wine more cheaply when on holiday.

Whatever the reasons for the variation in tax rates, attempts to use them for social policy are rarely successful. Countries with punishingly high tax rates (Sweden, Britain, and Ireland) have widely varying consumptions. Countries with high consumption (Portugal, Spain, France, Austria, Germany, Ireland) have a huge range of tax rates. Ireland, with the highest tax rate, has one of the

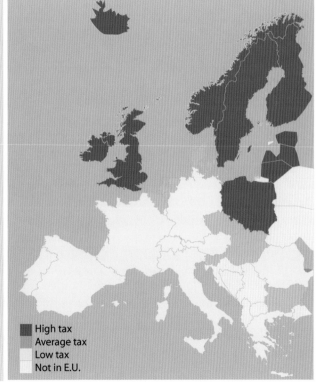

Although Europe is supposed to be a Community, tax rates on alcohol vary enormously. Low tax rate countries are typically less than €1.5, high tax rates are more than €3 for an average bottle.[55]

High tax
Average tax
Low tax
Not in E.U.

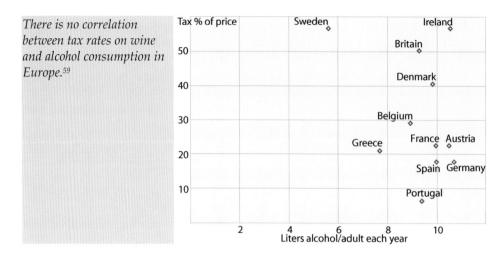

There is no correlation between tax rates on wine and alcohol consumption in Europe.[59]

highest consumptions. Statistics show that people do generally drink less when the cost of alcohol is raised, but it's really a futile endeavor to use taxation to try to stop people drinking.[56] Probably the major consequence for wine drinkers is that people who buy cheap wine get increasingly poor value for money, partly because of the tax bite, partly because quality is compromised by the intense pressure on price. And binge drinking among adults is greatest in countries with high tax rates (Britain and Finland are at the top of the list) and lowest in countries with low tax rates (Spain and Italy are at the bottom).[57]

The consumer who buys an average bottle of wine is ripped off everywhere in the Anglo-Saxon world, although it varies a bit as to who is ripping him off. In Britain, the combination of a standard excise tax with a swingeing rate of VAT means that less than a third of the cost of a £3.99 bottle actually reflects its content. The situation is even worse for someone who buys a bottle at the next price point down, say at £2.99—the wine will be worth only about 50p. In the United States, the stranglehold of the three tier system means that the distributor takes a major share before the wine even gets into the retail chain; the average profit to the winery on the bottle is only about 60¢, so the producer is actually getting the smallest share of the pie of anyone in the chain.[58]

There's not much doubt about extortion with regards to taxation on wine—things haven't changed much since the English were forced to pay Danegelt to head off Viking invaders in the middle ages. And market distortion almost inevitably results from the tax authorities' perpetual attempts to find clever ways to maximize revenues. It's common for different rates to apply, for example, depending on the alcoholic strength. After this was introduced in Britain in the 1860s, merchants began importing wines at different strengths and then blending them to avoid paying the higher tax on the whole lot. You might say that the more intricate the forms of taxation, the more intricate the tricks that are practiced to bypass them.

The distortion of the market affects producers more than consumers. In Britain, for example, the supermarkets try at all costs to keep their wines to crisp price points, £3.99 and £4.99 being the most common. When the tax is increased,

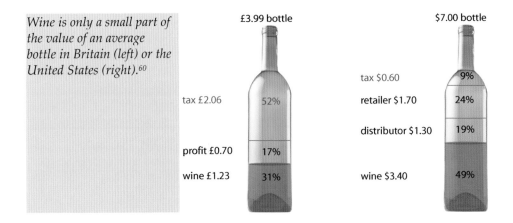

Wine is only a small part of the value of an average bottle in Britain (left) or the United States (right).[60]

£3.99 bottle

tax £2.06   52%

profit £0.70   17%

wine £1.23   31%

$7.00 bottle

tax $0.60   9%

retailer $1.70   24%

distributor $1.30 19%

wine $3.40   49%

their efforts to keep below the price point require the producers to cut prices—but even though the tax increase may only be a few pennies relative to the total cost of the bottle, this can be a major proportion of the producers' profits. The pressure this puts on the system distorts the whole market.

The Fanatics of Prohibition

Where on earth could a newspaper be prosecuted and fined for an article reviewing recent releases from Champagne? Some part of the world where religious beliefs have been enshrined into laws banning alcohol? A dictatorship where free speech has been abolished? Incredible though it may seem, the answer is France. In December 2005, the weekly magazine Le Parisien published an article, "The Triumph of Champagne," a normal enough event in the run-up to Christmas, you might think. But a fanatical anti-alcohol society (AMPAA)[61] sued the newspaper on the grounds that the article was not editorial but constituted advertising—which would be illegal under French law. Le Parisien was fined €5,000.[62]

Perhaps only Kafka could understand the extreme irrationality of the law in France, which after all is one of the great wine (and spirits) producers of the world. "There are three countries in the world which ban the discussion of alcohol: Iran, Afghanistan and France," says Frédéric Delesque, marketing director of Camus Cognac.[63] The French Ministry of Health has published guidelines saying, "The consumption of alcohol, and especially wine, is discouraged." One wonders about the rationality of "especially wine."[64] In another report, alcohol was placed in the same category as heroin and cocaine (very dangerous).[65]

It started with the Loi Evin, a law passed in France in 1991 to control advertising of alcohol and tobacco. The law completely bans all advertising on television, or sponsorship of cultural or sports events; and advertising in the press allows only a very limited description of the product. (It was this restriction that was supposedly breached by Le Parisien.) It's illegal to show people drinking in advertisements. In a context where consumption was falling anyway, the law has had a dramatic effect in further exacerbating the ills of the industry, and it's no exaggeration to say that wine producers feel they are being demonized.

But worse was yet to come. The fanatics of AMPAA sued Heineken for maintaining a web site about its beer in France. In February 2008 the court duly ruled that it was illegal to provide information to users in France; Heineken was given three weeks to close down.[66] Access from computers in France is now blocked not only to local sites, but also (for example) to Orlando wines in South Australia because they are owned by the French company, Pernod-Ricard. Outside of France, you may think it's pretty stupid when you click on the web site of a wine producer and get a message asking you to certify you are over the legal drinking age when the site does not sell wine but provides information; but the inconvenience is as nothing compared with the very real possibility that wine producers will be banned entirely from maintaining web sites in France. The effect on free speech is chilling; there's about as much Liberté, Egalité, Fraternité on the internet in France as in Tiananmen Square in China.

The famous French statesman Talleyrand said sarcastically of the Bourbon kings of France, "They have learned nothing, and forgotten nothing." The same could be said of the fanatics who make laws about wine in Europe, and even (perhaps especially!) in France. Their arrogance surpasses even that of the ignoramuses responsible for the disaster of Prohibition in the United States. The rationale for Prohibition was based on a mistaken moralistic view of the evils of alcohol; such naïveté is understandable in the context of the early twentieth century, but one would hope to see a more sophisticated understanding in the present era.

Today the pressure comes mostly from Europe, but also from some international bodies. WHO has the objective of classifying the danger of consuming alcohol on the same level as tobacco. Back to the same McCarthy-like objective of tarring all with the same brush; it worked at Prohibition, when wine was lumped with spirits, so why shouldn't it work now by lumping wine with tobacco? But there is a difference. Tobacco is harmful not only to the smoker, but also to those subjected to passive inhalation; there is no safe dose. Alcohol is harmful to an individual only in excess; and only to others as a result of inebriated behavior. Truly the lunatics are running the asylum in the European Union.

Indeed, free speech goes out of the window everywhere that alcohol is regulated. If I go into the tasting room of a winery in California, ask for a glass of red wine, and comment that I've heard this has health benefits, the winery can lose its license to produce and sell wine if it responds positively. What happened to the First Amendment?

Certainly there is no question but that alcohol abuse can have serious consequences not only for the individual but others. But that does not make the quiet enjoyment of a drink a criminal offense, although sometimes we seem to be getting close to such a position. And it's curious how binge drinking is a problem in countries where it's illegal or strongly discouraged for the young to have any exposure to alcohol (especially Britain),[67] whereas it's far less of a problem in countries where children are encouraged from an early age to treat wine as part of a normal meal (such as Italy).

Save your Heart or Sacrifice your Liver?

There is no doubt about the damage caused by excess alcohol consumption. Death rates from cirrhosis of the liver correlate with overall consumption of alcohol for countries worldwide.[68] And the decline in alcohol consumption in France since the 1960s has been followed by a decline in liver cirrhosis.[69] The big question is always to what extent you can extrapolate an extreme situation like this to normal levels of consumption.[70] Also, wine consumption has beneficial as well as harmful effects, and it's not clear that there is any simple answer as to the balance at moderate levels of consumption. Unfortunately, commentary, if not the literature itself, is so politically motivated as to make it anything but reliable.

Before clean drinking water became available, wine was undoubtedly a beneficial alternative. In fact, diluting the contaminated water with wine had a significant effect in reducing bacterial infection. And even as recently as the eighteenth century, wine was prescribed as a cure for illness. When the great philosopher David Hume became ill in 1730 with what sounds like a nervous breakdown, his physician diagnosed "the Disease of the Learned;" the prescription for recovery included claret.[71] It would be a bold doctor who would make such a recommendation today.

Health benefits have long been claimed for wine drinking. In 1926, Raymond Pearl, a researcher at Johns Hopkins University, published *Alcohol and Longevity*, a book in which he reported that moderate drinkers had increased life expectancy.[72] He studied death rates in a population of 5,000 people; since the study extended into Prohibition, the sources of alcohol must have been somewhat rough and ready! Heavy drinkers had clearly reduced longevity, but moderate drinkers had a small advantage over abstainers.[73] Subsequent studies confirmed the effect but were largely ignored: rationality had little place in this discussion.

The direct benefits of drinking wine first came to public attention with the report of the French Paradox. The CBS news program "60 Minutes" in the United States reported in 1991 that rates of heart disease in France are lower than those in the United States although the diet in France has relatively more fat. A protective effect was attributed to the high consumption of red wine, and started a move towards drinking red rather than white wine. Actually, the association goes back a long way, starting with a paper in the medical journal Lancet in 1979 showing a strong negative association when wine consumption was plotted against coronary disease. Subsequent studies confirmed that there is a U- or J-shaped curve with a 10-40% reduction in heart disease at levels of moderate consumption. The bottom of the curve is reached at 2-3 drinks per day for males, 1-2 drinks per day for females. The effects are specific to wine: consumption of spirits shows no effects, and beer is less effective than wine.

This type of information is notoriously difficult to interpret because of confounding factors, ranging from smoking to socio-economic status. But allowing for these complications as best as possible, it seems that low levels of wine consumption have a protective effect against diseases with an oxidative component. Red wine is more effective than white because of its content of polyphenols such

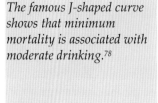

The famous J-shaped curve shows that minimum mortality is associated with moderate drinking.[78]

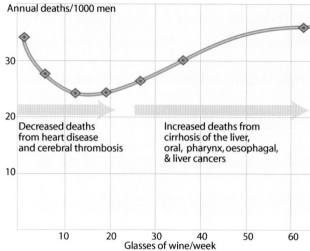

as tannins, which are anti-oxidants. Among the polyphenols is resveratrol, which has been implicated as an anti-aging agent. You would have to drink so much red wine to get a benefit from resveratrol, however, that you would probably develop cirrhosis of the liver first.[74]

Cancer risks associated with alcohol appear to be determined by cumulative exposure, with both level and duration of consumption playing a role in development of cancers in tissues exposed to alcohol.[75] It's probably true that the balance of benefit to harm is more dubious for women than for men, partly because the curve turns upward sooner,[76] partly because there is probably a connection between alcohol consumption and breast cancer.[77]

Whether pregnant women should drink is another, and more difficult, matter. Fetal alcohol syndrome affects babies whose mothers have consumed alcohol during pregnancy: the syndrome takes the form of some or all of the symptoms of short stature, facial disorder, and neurocognitive defects.[79] There's no cure for this lifelong affliction. FAS was diagnosed as a consequence of chronic alcohol consumption, originally found in specific high risk populations such as the native Americans. Now, but without any further evidence being presented, there has been an elision to concluding that there is no safe level of consumption.[80, 81] This is more the behavior of a witch doctor than a scientist or physician.[82]

There is no evidence for supposing that the risk is directly proportional to total consumption, as opposed to arising over a threshold. If the risk factor is the peak alcohol blood level, a pregnant woman who goes in for binge drinking a bottle of wine at one sitting may be at risk, even if it is the only alcohol she drinks during a week, whereas a women who drinks that same bottle one glass at a time with dinner over a week probably has little risk.[83] Given that alcohol may be a teratogen (an agent that causes birth defects), it is certainly appropriate for pregnant women to be cautious about alcohol consumption; whether abstinence is required is something reasonable people might discuss, rather than be subject to government edicts based on ill-founded extrapolations.

None of the factual information about the balance of risks and benefits appears to have had much effect on expert opinion. After the Royal College of Physicians in London published its recommendations in 1987 that weekly intake of wine should be limited to around 3 bottles per week for men and 2 bottles for women, a member of the working party described the process: "Those limits were really plucked out of the air. They were not based on any firm evidence at all."[84] Yet these unsubstantiated recommendations became the basis for government policy. "More than 10 million people, 31% of men and 20% of women, are now regularly drinking above the guidelines set by Government, and many of these are likely to suffer ill-health or injury as a result," stated a parliamentary report in 2009.[85] Surely if as many as a third of the population are ignoring your recommendations, you might at least question the connection of those recommendations to reality?

Unfortunately, extreme positions have taken over the argument about alcohol consumption, and the "experts" who have extrapolated from their data to the real world have done no favors to the cause of logic.[86] The authorities, who after all tend to be politicians lacking scientific expertise, find it all too easy to take the demagogic course of targeting anyone who enjoys a glass of wine. We all pay the price, literally in higher taxation, and metaphorically by loss of liberty.

9

The International Wine Trade

EXCEPT WHERE BANNED BY RELIGIOUS BELIEFS, alcoholic beverages provide the most common form of relaxation in cultures worldwide. The most popular form of beverage depends on the culture. Wine may be common or may be restricted to the rich or upper classes. In ancient Egypt, for example, wine was a privilege of the rich, and beer was the drink of the poor; whereas in Greece, advances in viticulture made wine available as the preferred drink at all levels of society (although the wine given to slaves was certainly inferior to that drunk by their owners).[1]

The international wine trade has been vigorous for several thousand years. In ancient times, Egypt produced only some of its own wine and imported a considerable proportion. The Phoenicians were notable traders in wine. By the time of the Roman Empire, trade in wine was a significant economic factor. Much of this ceased during the collapse of the dark ages. As the Church extended its tentacles through mediaeval Europe, one of the mandates for priests was to produce locally the wine that was needed for sacramental purposes. This led to the planting of grapevines in most unsuitable places, apparently as far north as Scandinavia, but also provided one of the spurs for developing viticulture.

As commerce picked up, vineyards tended to be planted in locations that made it possible to transport the product, typically along rivers. Improvements in transport, such as the construction of canals, changed the economics, so that vineyards succeeded where the best wine could be made, rather than where locations offered the easiest transport options. Within France, vineyards were all over the country until the eighteenth century, when the railways put the kibosh on outlying areas, and vineyards retreated to areas where wine could be more reliably produced.[2] As wine became more available on the international market, ability to transport well became more of an issue; the relatively light wines of France were at a disadvantage compared to the more alcoholic wines of Spain and the Mediterranean, which traveled better.[3]

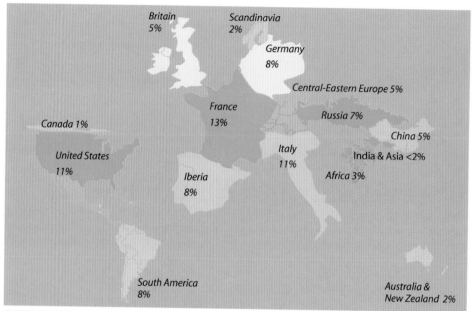

Britain
5%

Scandinavia
2%

Germany
8%

Central-Eastern Europe 5%

France
13%

Russia 7%

Canada 1%

China 5%

United States
11%

Italy
11%

India & Asia <2%

Iberia
8%

Africa 3%

South America
8%

Australia &
New Zealand 2%

The world distorted according to wine consumption emphasizes the importance of the European and American continents, and diminishes India, Asia, and Australia.[4]

The modern era is caught between history and innovation. Many of the vineyards of Europe are planted according to historical imperatives; they are not necessarily where you would choose to plant vineyards today if you had quality wine production in mind. In the New World, modern technology has made it possible to plant vineyards in places where historically the vines would not have succeeded, especially where irrigation is necessary to avoid desert conditions. Today, transport is just another cost factor rather than determining where wine is produced.

There are huge geographical disparities in production and consumption. The countries of western Europe remain both the largest producers and consumers. France and Italy together account for a quarter of the world's production and consumption. The United States is rising to prominence as the largest single market, following the European model of being both producer and consumer. It is already the largest market by value, and is projected to become the largest by volume by 2012.[5] The small populations of Australia and New Zealand mean that although they are now important producers, they have little importance as consumers. Central Europe, Russia, and China are significant consumers; but Asia and India disappear to insignificance on the map in terms of consumption.

Choose your Tipple

In the context of the craving for alcohol, wine is only a small part of worldwide consumption. Beer has the lion's share of volume (80%), with wine representing

11%, and spirits making up the other 9%.[6] Economically beer remains the most important sector in the alcohol business, providing about half the value of the total market; wine is in second place with just over a quarter. Western Europe dominates the wine market, the most important countries within it being Italy, France, Germany, and Britain in terms of value.

The 32 billion bottles (or equivalents) of wine sold each year have a production value around $100 billion. So the average price is only just over $3 each. More than 75% of all wine sold is at a level of under $5 per bottle. The total value of the world wine market fluctuates widely according to whether it is assessed in terms of receipts by producers, retail sales, or all sales including restaurants, with estimates ranging up to about $250 million depending on the basis.[7]

Europe leads the world in alcohol consumption. France, Spain, Germany, and Britain all have around an overall consumption of 11-12 liters of pure alcohol per adult per year;[9] Italy is somewhat lower.[10] Consumption of alcohol has been declining steadily in Continental Europe, but increasing in Britain (and also in the United States). But the drink culture varies greatly between countries. Britain and France may never break out of their love-hate relationship so long as the French mainly drink wine while the British mainly drink beer. The difference may reflect the fact that in each case the predominant alcoholic drink is largely produced within the country. France imports relatively little wine, and most of the 400 million cases it drinks each year are produced in France. Britain imports all of the 200 million cases of wine it drinks each year, but produces virtually all of the 500 million cases of beer it consumes.[11]

But the culture gap is narrowing between traditional wine-producing countries, where wine consumption is falling, and the Anglophone world, where it is increasing at the expense of other forms of alcohol. In France, there has been a small decline in consumption of beer and spirits in the past fifty years, but a dramatic decrease in wine consumption (the present level is about a third of that in 1965). Similar but less severe declines have occurred in Italy and Spain. The

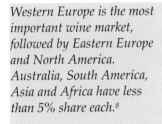

Western Europe is the most important wine market, followed by Eastern Europe and North America. Australia, South America, Asia and Africa have less than 5% share each.[8]

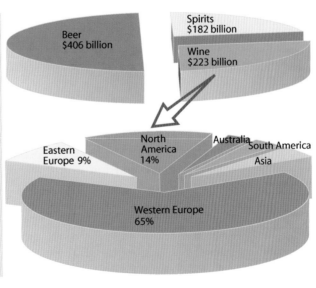

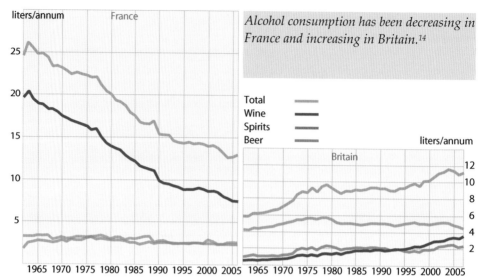

Alcohol consumption has been decreasing in France and increasing in Britain.[14]

decline in wine drinking is largely responsible for the overall fall in alcohol consumption. In Britain, beer has gone up and down again, spirits have increased somewhat, but wine consumption has increased about ten fold (albeit from a very small base in 1965). Wine consumption per person in Britain has now reached about half of the French level.[12] The increase in wine drinking is responsible for most of the overall increase in consumption.

There are some new markets, although their importance is hard to assess. China and India are the most rapidly growing markets, with the small proportion of drinkers compensated by large populations. China is growing as a producer as well as a consumer: some estimates place it as the world's sixth largest producer.[13] Its movement towards becoming an important worldwide player in wine is encouraged by the government, which believes that a switch to wine from rice spirits will reduce alcoholism. If production in China continues to grow at the present estimated rate of 30%, it could become the world's largest bulk exporter of wine within a decade.

Inequality of Supply And Demand

Looking at the variety of brands available in your local store, and their constantly changing nature, you would never think the wine industry was in crisis or decline. Yet worldwide consumption has shown little increase for years, there is a surplus of supply compared to demand, competition between new producers and old has created turmoil, and much of the change represents a desperate attempt to hold on to existing markets. The ramifications go all the way down to the diversity and pricing of the bottles available in each market.

There has been a worldwide glut of wine for more than three decades. Consumption declined steadily through the 1980s and 1990s before stabilizing, and although production has been reduced, it still remains typically about 15% in excess of consumption. If all of that surplus was bottled for sale, it would amount

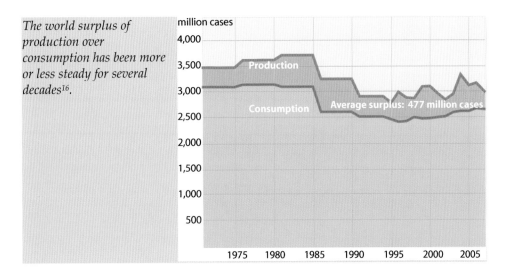

The world surplus of production over consumption has been more or less steady for several decades[16].

to about 500 million cases each year. However, a significant part of it is diverted to other uses, often by distillation to produce spirits or industrial alcohol.[15] But the glut places a pall over the whole industry, putting downward pressure on prices, especially at the highly competitive lower end of the market. The ill-advised policies of the European Union in subsidizing production suggest that this situation will not be easy to change.

Until relatively recently, most wine was consumed in the countries that produced it. There was a clear division between producing countries and consuming countries. The major producers, France, Italy, and Spain, imported little wine and consumed a major part of their own production. Most of the wine consumed in the United States was produced in California. Countries that did not produce wine, such as Britain, provided the major markets for those wines that were not consumed in the countries of origin. The major exception was Germany, which is an established producer, but which does not produce enough for its own consumption, and is therefore also a significant importer.

Today all that has changed. Overall, the proportion of wine that is exported has increased from 15% to almost 30% in twenty years. Almost 50% of the trade is accounted for by the three major importers: Britain, Germany, and the United States. The new producers, most notably Australia and New Zealand, consume little of their own wine; most is exported. In South America, there is a split between production from indigenous varieties for home consumption, and production from international varieties for export. The United States is the only New World producer to be a major importer; consumption of imported wine has reached more than 30%.

Some of the international exports are finished product, sent in bottles from the exporting country. Some is sent in bulk and bottled in the country where it is to be sold—England, not exactly renowned as a wine producer, can bottle the equivalent of 450 million bottles per year (about a quarter of the 1.7 billion imported each year).[17] Packaging close to the market is especially advantageous for wine that is sold in formats other than bottles, such as bag-in-box, which is

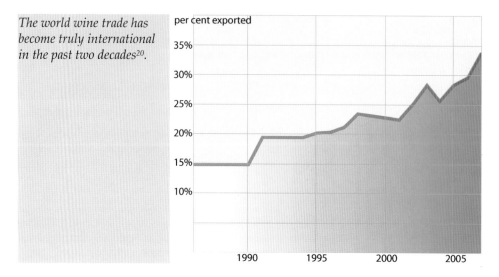

The world wine trade has become truly international in the past two decades[20].

difficult to transport and is intended for rapid consumption. Sometimes it's simply a financial calculation, based on the cost of bottling at source versus the cost of bottling at point of sale that determines what route is followed. On occasion, wine follows a circuitous route that isn't intuitively obvious; a major brand in Britain, Blossom Hill, is produced in California, shipped to Diageo's plant at Santa Vittoria d'Alba in Italy where it is bottled, and then exported to Britain.[18,] This accounts for a quarter of all Italy's wine exports to Britain, and a third of all its imports.[19]

Crisis in Europe: the Rise of the New World

Wine production was relatively stable in the nineteenth century. Just before phylloxera devastated the industry, France was the clear market leader with almost 40% of world production; Italy and Spain accounted for another 25% and 20% respectively. Even today these three remain the market leaders, but their combined proportion of world production has shrunk to about half. Production in France is about 50% greater than before phylloxera; Italy and Spain have roughly doubled. The largest decline in production may have been in Hungary, a major producer in 1880 but a struggling one today.[21]

Since the phylloxera epidemic, wine production has increased universally, but the pattern of production today is very different from a century ago. At the start of the twentieth century, wine production in Europe was the only game in town. At the start of the twenty-first century, having more or less doubled over a hundred years, Europe accounts for only about two thirds of world production.

The greatest change is the rise of the New World. Virtually insignificant in terms of quantity in 1900, and even less significant in terms of quality, the New World now accounts for almost 30% of world production, with a range from plonk to the very finest. The United States is its largest producer, with 90% coming from California; Australia and Argentina vie for second place.

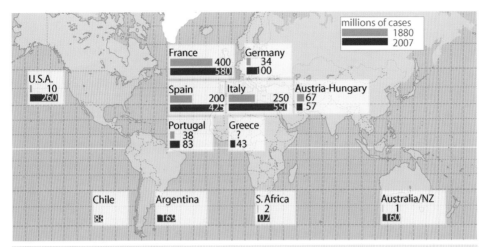

France 400 / 580
Germany 34 / 100
U.S.A. 10 / 260
Spain 200 / 425
Italy 250 / 550
Austria-Hungary 67 / 57
Portugal 38 / 83
Greece ? / 43
Chile 8 / 88
Argentina 16 / 169
S. Africa 2 / 102
Australia/NZ 1 / 160

millions of cases
1880
2007

Europe has increased production since 1880, but the New World now accounts for almost a third of all production.[22]

The change has aroused outrage in Europe. "Until recent years, wine was with us," stated a report commissioned by the French Ministry of Agriculture in 2001. "We were the center, the unavoidable reference point. Today, the barbarians are at our gates: Australia, New Zealand, the United States, Chile, Argentina, South Africa."[23]

Production in Europe rose steadily during the twentieth century until peaking in the 1970s-1980s; after falling back about a quarter, it has been more or less stable for the past couple of decades. By contrast, production in the New World has continued its inexorable climb, from about 275 million cases in 1950 to 725 million cases today. This leaves the situation now with the big three of France, Italy, and Spain still dominating European and world production, but with the United States and Australia making important inroads from the New World. (Argentina is a larger producer than Australia overall, but not such an important exporter).

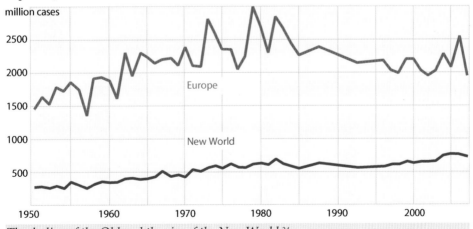

The decline of the Old and the rise of the New World.[24]

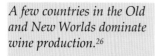

A few countries in the Old and New Worlds dominate wine production.[26]

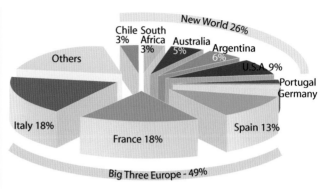

One of the major changes in the wine industry has been the yield—the amount of wine produced from a vineyard area.[25] Advances in viticulture have led to yields increasing everywhere over the past century. Today, low yields are associated with higher quality. But for the first half of the twentieth century, low yields were generally due to the poor state of the vines and their inability to withstand pests and diseases. Increasing yield in the second part of the century resulted from the improved state of the vines and more productive viticulture.

Yields are not regulated in the New World, where they are limited simply by the intentions of the producer. With irrigation and fertilization, it's perfectly possibly to achieve 120 hl/ha—although the wine is unlikely to be very good. The figures for California and Australia include a mix of high yield production for bulk wine with production of quality wines at lower yields. The same is true in Europe, but yields are restrained in the AOC (or equivalents in other countries) by the regulations. In France for example, about half of production is within the Appellation Contrôlée system, where yields are usually restricted to 55 hl/ha or below.

But the trend to higher yields is pretty much parallel worldwide, and has evened off only in the past decade. So although the total area of vineyards worldwide declined from about 8.8 million hectares prior to 1990 to just under 8

Yields have increased steadily for the past century.[27]

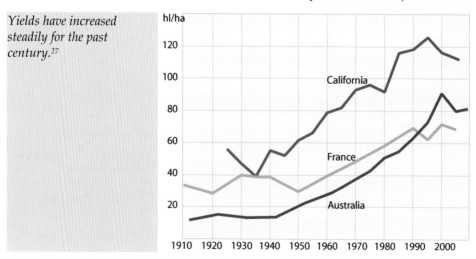

million hectares by 1995,[28] production has declined less, staying more or less around 2.5 billion cases annually. Control of yields has only had a real effect for the smaller part of the market represented by fine wines.

The New World became significant in exporting wine only in the past quarter century. Figures for the overall increase in production underestimate its importance. Certainly production has greatly increased, but a key factor has been a general trend to replace low quality varieties with high quality international varieties.[29] The change in quality was just as important as the change in quantity in becoming competitive in export markets.[30] Quality varietal plantings, producing wines suitable for export, have increased four fold in the New World since 1990.[31]

Rapidly falling consumption in Europe made it impossible to cut production enough to close the gap. And rapidly increasing production from the New World made it impossible for Europe to increase exports. The result has been a steady surplus of about half a million cases of wine produced every year by France, Italy, and Spain. This is actually not far from the total annual production of the New World. Increasing production in the New World has widened its surplus over consumption, but this became a major problem only recently with the worldwide financial crisis of 2009.

There's been a similar move to quality in Europe as in the New World. The trend is to replace poor varieties with better ones, especially in areas previously known for bulk production of wine, such as the south of France or Castille La Mancha to the south of Madrid. And as the total number of vineyards has contracted, it has been producers in the poorer locations who have gone to the wall. The surplus production is much larger with table wine than with quality wine. There is a clear trend to less production of table wine and more production of quality wine (as defined by the European Union).

Taken at face value, consumption of quality wine and table wine are at almost equivalent levels in Europe. However, the official figures have to be viewed with a certain amount of skepticism, because in some cases the change is simply that

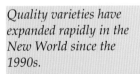

Quality varieties have expanded rapidly in the New World since the 1990s.

The graph for each country shows the total of international varieties.[32]

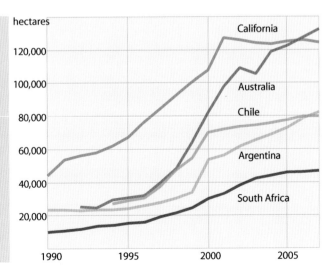

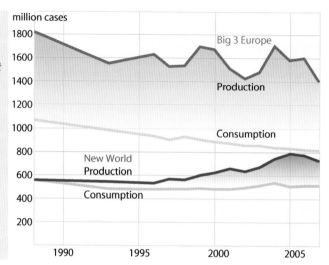

Production and consumption have fallen in France, Italy, and Spain, with a more or less constant surplus (red); production has increased in the New World, exacerbating the surplus (purple).[34]

reclassification has promoted vineyards from table wine to the level of quality wine. For example, appellation controlée vineyards are 99.8% of Bordeaux today, but were only 53% of the area in 1950;[33] but it's pretty much the same vineyards that are making the wine (albeit under the tighter conditions of the AOC).

What does Europe do with all its excess wine? Well, the European Union had a plan to handle the surplus. It consisted of two seemingly contradictory policies. (Fortunately contradiction never worried the bureaucrats.) First, subsidies were offered to grub up vineyards. Actually this was not completely unsuccessful: more than 500,000 hectares of vineyards were removed between 1988 and 1996, a reduction of more than 10%, albeit not enough to eliminate the wine lake.[36] The other half of the policy was to buy up the surplus wine and distill it to generate

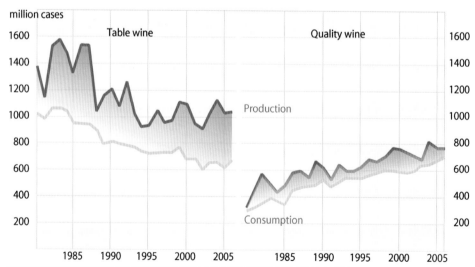

Table wine production has decreased steadily, while quality wine production has increased in Europe.[35]

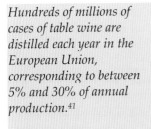

Hundreds of millions of cases of table wine are distilled each year in the European Union, corresponding to between 5% and 30% of annual production.[41]

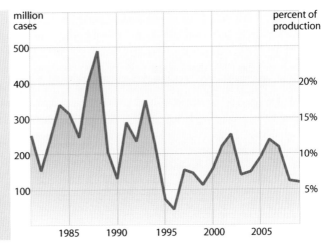

alcohol for industrial or other uses.[37] Whether this was successful depends on your criteria. On the one hand, the wine was removed from the marketplace. But since there was little diminution in the quantity of wine being distilled over the years, the policy had little permanent effect on the glut. Indeed, it created a dependency culture in which wine was produced solely for the purpose of being sold into the subsidy program. (History should have shown the futility of such interventions. A prime d'arrachage [payment for pulling out vines] was introduced in France in 1936, and payments were introduced for distilling excess wines,[38, 39] so the recipe seems to be to try more of the same old failed policies.) In a belated recognition of reality, the system is due to be reformed over the next few years, including phasing out the distillation subsidies.[40]

Boom and Bust in the Vineyards

Boom and bust cycles have been accompanied by attempts to regulate vineyard plantings since time immemorial. One basic problem is the time lag between deciding to plant vines and harvesting a crop, typically at least three years. High demand causes everyone to rush out and plant vines, no one know how many other vines are being planted, of course, until three or four years later they all produce wine. Suddenly shortage turns to glut. One of the earliest documented examples was the rush of planting in response to the eruption of Vesuvius in 79 C.E., which destroyed the local vineyards that were the main supply for wine for Rome. The result was a glut by the next decade.[42]

With some rare exceptions, attempts to direct plantings have not been very successful. Sometimes, of course, the regulations had ulterior motives. When the Roman Emperor Domitian banned new plantings and ordered half of the existing vineyards to be uprooted in the provinces in 92 C.E., his motives were probably mostly to protect producers in the home region near Rome.[43] In any case, it appears that no one paid much attention to the edict. Two hundred years later, Emperor Probus encouraged planting vines in Gaul, with more success.

The seventeenth century saw attempts to discourage plantings in unsuitable areas (the forerunner of the complex system controlling all vineyards in Europe today). Colbert, Minister of Finance under Louis XIV in 1682, noted the problem caused by "the excessive multiplication of vines in terrains that are not appropriate."[44] In Bordeaux, a "fureur de planter" (rush of planting) was triggered by the winter freeze of 1709 that killed many of the vines in the region, together with the end of the war with England that had suppressed trade. Planting became so excessive that it may have impacted production of other crops, and it sparked proposals to pull up many of the vines.[45] Expressing a characteristic free market view, Adam Smith commented that the real motive was "the anxiety of the proprietors of the old vineyards to prevent the planting of any new ones," rather than any genuine concern to promote production of corn rather than wine.[46]

Fast forward to Europe at the present, where the creation of vineyards is controlled by the arcane regulation of "planting rights." If you own a vineyard in the European Union, essentially you have the rights to that many hectares of vines. You cannot plant any more vines unless you can acquire additional planting rights. If you pull up the existing vineyard, you can replant it in the same place or plant the same number of hectares elsewhere. You can also pull up the vineyard and sell the planting rights to someone else. One producer in Tuscany told me that in order to plant a new vineyard, he had purchased planting rights from a producer who was relinquishing a vineyard in Sicily!

There is not much to be said in favor of this system. In an ideal world, it would work by encouraging producers in uneconomic areas to sell their planting rights to producers in areas better suited for viticulture. But like so many distortions of the free market, the law of unintended consequences triumphs. The negative effects of preventing good producers from expanding when they have identified good locations for new vineyards much outweigh any effects in limiting the wine glut. And it adds to the expense of innovation; at roughly €30,000 per hectare, planting rights in some areas almost double the cost of land for a new vineyard. The E.U. has announced plans to abolish the system in 2016 as part of an attempt to "phase out wasteful and expensive market intervention measures"[47]—but one wonders, if the deficiencies of the system are so obvious, why wait until then?

The Price of Everything

The price of land was never much of an issue before wine became a luxury item. Historically grapevines tended to be planted on land that could not grow other crops successfully, so land values were relatively low. But today the prices for top vineyard land have followed the prices of the wines into the stratosphere. Even the rise of garage wines in Bordeaux or cult wines in Napa Valley, often owing more to extreme measures for viticulture and vinification than to unique terroir, has not dented the inexorable rise of land prices.

Burgundy probably has the most expensive vineyard land in the world. The piecemeal nature of vineyard holdings means it is relatively rare for anything other than a tiny plot to change hands on the Côte d'Or, but the rate can put local housing prices quite to shame. Grand Cru Burgundy can sell at a rate of €4-6 million per hectare. Top châteaux in Bordeaux run at about half of that rate, although much larger sums of money are involved when a château with tens of hectares is sold.

Outside of France, the most expensive vineyards are in Barolo, where small parcels of the Cannubi vineyard (the local equivalent to a first growth) are reputed to change hands for around €1 million per hectare. The most expensive land in the New World is probably in the top-rated Rutherford region of Napa Valley, somewhere under $1 million per hectare.

The price of land becomes an expensive part of the cost of wine. Carrying costs on purchasing land alone could be the equivalent of $25 or more per bottle,

The surreal price of Le Montrachet floats in the stratosphere, even above other grand cru Burgundy. Pomerol is the most expensive area in Bordeaux, but the communes of the Médoc can come close. Although there is wide variation in each region depending on the reputation of the individual vineyard, land prices correlate approximately with the price of wine.[48]

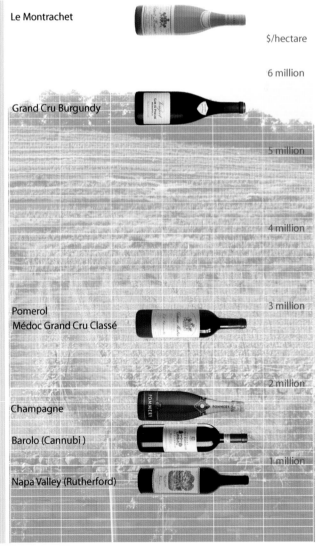

Le Montrachet

$/hectare

6 million

Grand Cru Burgundy

5 million

4 million

3 million

Pomerol
Médoc Grand Cru Classé

2 million

Champagne

Barolo (Cannubi)

1 million

Napa Valley (Rutherford)

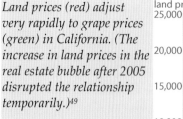

Land prices (red) adjust very rapidly to grape prices (green) in California. (The increase in land prices in the real estate bubble after 2005 disrupted the relationship temporarily.)[49]

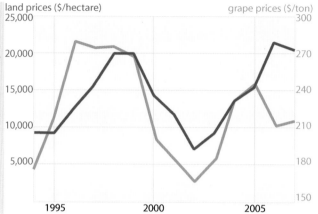

so the wine has to sell at a very high price to justify such a purchase. Of course, the relationship is driven the other way, with high prices for wine encouraging purchasers to pay correspondingly higher prices for the land.

As a rough working rule, the price of land tends to be about 100 times the price of grapes per ton, which in turn is about 100 times the price of a bottle of wine. So if wine sells for $100 per bottle, you can expect the vineyard to be worth about $1 million a hectare.

The Supermarket Crunch

Supermarkets are the 600 pound gorilla in wine sales. Their penetration into wine is most evident at the consumer level in high-economy countries, where the majority of wines are now purchased in supermarkets,[50] whereas twenty years ago, specialist shops reigned supreme. But the effects go far beyond the visible stacks of bottles or piles of bag-in-boxes and are felt all the way down to the wine producer. Supermarkets naturally require to be supplied in larger bulk than small outlets, and this goes hand in hand with the consolidation among distributors and producers, since each requires a partner of appropriate (i.e., large) size.

The rise in supermarkets is largely responsible for the increased concentration in the retail market. In much of Europe, 50-60% of the retail market is in the hands of the five largest wine retailers. Monopoly situations, such as in Scandinavia, increase this to more than 80%; regulatory restrictions in the United States have the opposite effect, and restrain it to about 20% nationwide.[51]

Supermarkets are hated and feared by small specialist shops, and the usual reaction is epitomized by the owner of Young's Liquors on Long Island in New York State, where the fight to allow supermarkets to sell alcohol was intense in 2009.[52] "I've heard that if this bill passes a thousand licensed liquor stores will go under," said Edward Wassmer, adding that wine makes up 75 percent of his sales.[53] This parallels the popular impression of what has actually happened since supermarkets started to sell wine in Britain in the late 1970s; supermarkets have gone from a minor player to about 70% of the market.

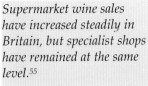

Supermarket wine sales have increased steadily in Britain, but specialist shops have remained at the same level.[55]

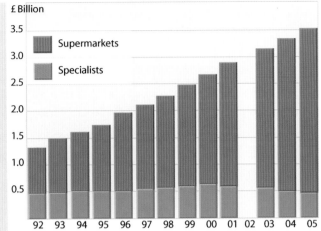

£ Billion

Supermarkets

Specialists

92 93 94 95 96 97 98 99 00 01 02 03 04 05

Has this been at the expense of other retailers? Well, yes and no. Supermarkets sell roughly three times as much wine today as they did at the start of the 1990s. But this is due more to the increase in the size of the market than to encroachment on the customers of other retailers. In fact, the total sales by small specialist shops have stayed more or less steady—not a great result against the background of inflation, but scarcely decimated as popular impression would have it. There's a good argument for saying that it is in fact the supermarkets that have expanded the market by making it possible for people to purchase wine in circumstances when they would not otherwise have done so.[54]

A common complaint against supermarkets is that the apparent choice offered to the consumer is deceptive— superficially there may be great variety, but actually all the wines fit the same, rather simple mold. There's more than a grain of truth in this. British supermarkets concentrate on wines in the fruit-forward New World style at the lower end of the price range, so that although a typical supermarket may have tens or even hundreds of different wines for sale, the focus on price makes it difficult to find distinctive wines.

More to the point may be the concern within the wine trade that the extreme price sensitivity of the supermarkets not only trains the consumer to regard wine as a cheap item, but also puts downward pressure on producers with regards to quality. Wines are commonly discounted. According to Jean-Manuel Spriet, the CEO of Pernod-Ricard in Britain, "[other wine suppliers] make the wines designed for sale at £3.99, introduce them at a higher price, and then bring the price down... they start at £7.99 and are discounted down to half price, which is crazy."[56] Indeed, according to Jon Moramarco, Constellation's former European chief executive, more than half of their wines are sold at discounts of 50% from the nominal price.[57] The attempt to create the impression of bargains just destroys any possibility of giving the consumer any sense of real value. (The favorite type of promotion is known as a "bogof"—buy one get one free.)

The contortions needed to sell wine at the "magic price point" of £3.99 in Britain[58] put huge pressure on producers. There are endless stories about supermarkets squeezing producers in order to sell wine at this price point;

Increased choice for the consumer in the serried ranks of bottles at the supermarket, or simply more of the same?

believing that a foot in the door will lead to better prices in the future, the producer may cut his price to an uneconomic level, but if so, he is operating under a sad illusion. Only the largest producers can afford to play the game, further emphasizing lack of diversity. For the supermarket, profit margin is everything, as captured by a story from Tim Atkin MW: "[A Tesco buying manager] was given a new wine to taste in Australia last year and was asked for his reaction. He swirled the contents of his glass, sniffed it, tasted it and replied: 'Not enough margin'."[59]

The Great Wine Agglomeration

There is continual moaning all across the world of wine about the effects of increasing concentration at all levels of the industry. The giants of the industry such as Constellation or Diageo are gobbling up wine producers worldwide. In the United States, the amalgamation of distributors makes it difficult for small wine producers to get to market. In France and Britain, supermarkets have an increasing share of the retail market. Yet wine remains the least concentrated of any part of the wider drinks industry. Constellation, the world's largest wine company, has sales of under $4 billion[60] out of the world's $220 billion spent on wine.[61] Yet large as Constellation seems to people in wine, it is dwarfed by companies in soft drinks, beer, and spirits.[62]

What a difference a decade makes! At the turn of the millennium, the top ten drinks companies in the world had a combined cash flow of $10 billion. At the end of the first decade of the new century, mergers and acquisitions brought the total cash flow of the top ten companies involved in alcoholic drinks close to $70 billion. About $16 billion came from sales of wine; not chump change, surely, but definitely taking second place in many cases to the other interests of the companies. During the decade, three of the top companies were swallowed by others in a continuing frenzy. Diageo acquired Seagrams, Fosters took over Southcorp, and Constellation bought Mondavi.

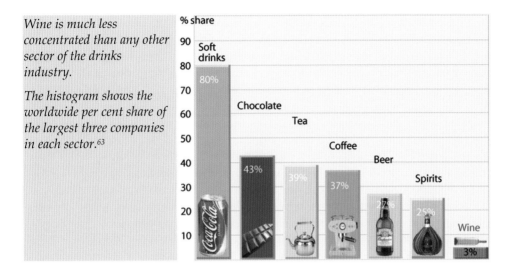

Wine is much less concentrated than any other sector of the drinks industry.

The histogram shows the worldwide per cent share of the largest three companies in each sector.[63]

The history of the world's largest drinks company, Diageo, started in the eighteenth century with whisky (J & B) and Guinness. It grew steadily by acquisition of spirits brands, including whisky, gin, vodka, and rum. Guinness, as it was known then, merged with another drinks company, Grand Met, in 1997 to form United Distillers & Vintners, which then became known as Diageo. Its holdings of beer and spirits remain far more important in revenue terms than wine, which accounts for only about 6% of total.

The world's top wine companies in 2008.

Company	Origins	Nature	Revenues ($billion)[64]	Wine ($billion)	Wine %	Principal Activities
Constellation	USA	public	$5,213	$3,842	74%	wine
Gallo	USA	private	$3,800	$3,200	84%	wine
Pernod-Ricard	France	public	$9,689	$2,240	23%	spirits, wine
LVMH	France	public	$24,098	$2,200	9%	luxury goods
Fosters	Australia	public	$3,642	$1,600	44%	beer, wine
Castel	France	private	$2,820	$1,297	46%	wine, beer, water
Diageo	Britain	public	$16,120	$967	6%	spirits, wine
Brown Foreman	USA	public	$3,282	$755	23%	spirits, wine
The Wine Group	USA	private	$735	$735	100%	wine
Freixenet	Spain	private	$730	$730	100%	sparkling wine

Pernod-Ricard was formed in 1975 by the merger of the two leading competitive producers of spirits in France—they had started with Absinthe, when it was legal. Wine was of little importance until 1989, when Pernod-Ricard purchased the Australian Company Orlando Wyndham, bringing them one of the world's largest brands, Jacob's Creek. When Seagrams was sold in 2001, Pernod-Ricard split the spoils with Diageo. Then in 2005 they split Allied Domecq (the British conglomerate) with Fortune Brands. This brought them Montana, making them the largest winemaker in New Zealand.[65] In little more than a decade, Pernod-Ricard went from insignificance to one of the top half dozen producers of wine.

No company may have achieved worldwide dominance, but several countries are dominated by their largest single producer. Gallo was for long the largest wine company in the world; still privately owned by the Gallo family, it is the dominant player in the United States market. Fosters has grown by gobbling up all of its former competitors in Australia, and now includes Southcorp, Rosemont, Mildara Blass, Beringer Blass, and Penfolds, giving it by far the most powerful position in Australian wine production.

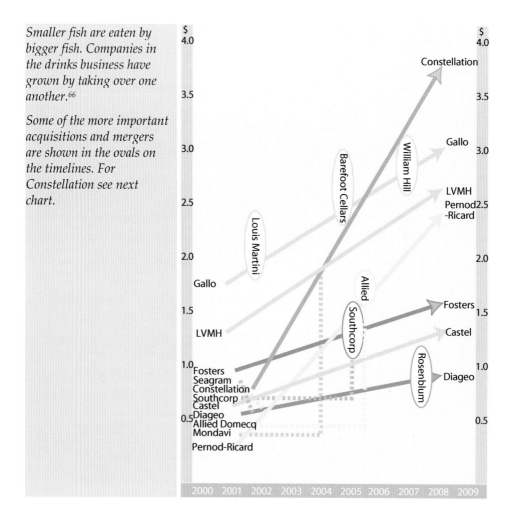

Smaller fish are eaten by bigger fish. Companies in the drinks business have grown by taking over one another.[66]

Some of the more important acquisitions and mergers are shown in the ovals on the timelines. For Constellation see next chart.

Often enough, these giant players trade divisions, somewhat like dealing out playing cards—or perhaps in the present climate of world recession, rearranging the deckchairs on the Titanic. Look at how the old Inglenook winery, once one of the top names in Napa Valley, has been run down. The brand was sold to United Vinters in 1964, became part of Heublein in 1969, Heublein sold it to Constellation in 1994, Constellation sold it to The Wine Group in 2008, and now The Wine Group has converted it from bottled wine to bag-in-box. None of this is apparent to the consumer, of course, indeed, you never see most of the über-company names on a label, but the Franzia brand is owned by The Wine Group, Mondavi by Constellation, Korbel by Brown-Foreman, Jacob's Creek by Pernod-Ricard, and Blossom Hill by Diageo.

Constellation is not the largest company involved in producing wine, but it is the largest company whose principal purpose is the production of wine. It has grown steadily by a series of acquisitions. It started out as the Canandaigua Wine Company in upstate New York in 1945, taking its name from the local town. Founded by Marvin Sands in 1945, its first year sales amounted to $150,000. Its initial products were not illustrious, consisting of wine made from indigenous varieties in the eastern United States, including the infamous Scuppernong.[68] Canandaigua moved into California wines only in the early 1990s, including its acquisition of Almaden and Inglenook when they were spun off after their disastrous period as part of Heublein. The move into more serious wines intensified with the acquisition of Franciscan (in Napa Valley) at the end of the nineties. In 2002 the name was changed to Constellation, and then a series of major purchases followed in Australia (BRL Hardy), California (Mondavi) and Canada (Vincor), the latter two each over the billion dollar level. With sales of $3.8 billion

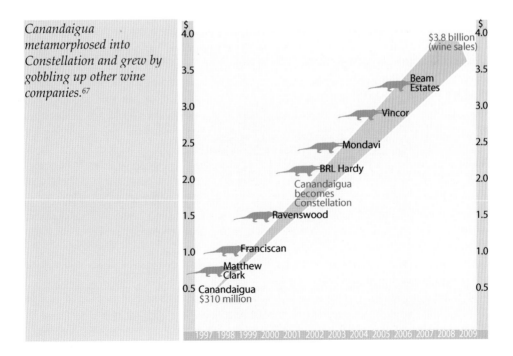

Canandaigua metamorphosed into Constellation and grew by gobbling up other wine companies.[67]

today in wine alone, the company is still run by the Sands family. True to its roots, it still produces Manischewitz kosher wine at its winery in Naples, New York. Made from Concord grapes in an old fashioned sweet style, Manischewitz remains consistent but—well, let's say idiosyncratic in order to avoid a snobbish value judgment.[69]

Certainly it seems easier to grow by buying someone else than by building your own business. But how much have all these acquisitions and mergers contributed to increased concentration in the industry? The wine revenues of the top ten companies have almost doubled in a decade during which wine revenues overall increased by perhaps 30% worldwide.[70] Like other industries, the big players are becoming more important.

If You Can't Beat 'Em, Join 'Em

There's a very long tradition of people or companies from outside wine-producing regions investing in wine. Perhaps the English takeover of Aquitaine was one of the first foreign investments, although from the perspective of the Bordelais maybe it was more of an invasion. Certainly the English—or the British as they had by then become—built the trade in Sherry and Port. The prestige of the Grand Cru Classés in Bordeaux has always made them particularly attractive to foreign investors, and at any given time there have usually been several foreign owners.[71] American investors have become important in France, starting at the top with banker Clarence Dillon's acquisition of Château Haut Brion in Bordeaux in 1935, followed in recent times by investments elsewhere, such as the takeover of the Burgundian producer Jadot in 1985 by their American distributor, Kobrand Corporation. Of course, some potential investments have been rebuffed, such as Robert Mondavi's attempt to establish wine production in the Languedoc, but for the most part foreign investment has been a welcome fillip to wine production in Europe, especially in France.

Wine production tends to be much more concentrated in the New World than the Old World, where it is especially fragmented. The major players have a large share of the market in New World countries, but a much smaller share in Europe, where there are far more producers, and individual vineyard holdings are far smaller. In Europe, no single company has more than 7% of total production in its home country, but in the New World, single companies can dominate production, as with Distell in South Africa, Concha y Toro in Chile, and Gallo in the United States. Of course, the actual level of production also varies widely, so the largest companies in France and Italy, although small in the context of their country's total production, each produce more than the total amount of New Zealand.[72] On the other hand, as in the case of Distell in South Africa, domestic dominance is nice for the company, but does not necessarily make it a major player on the world stage.

Concentration tends to go along with publicly owned conglomerates, and some of the same names appear in multiple places. Constellation is dominant in the United States and important in Australia, Fosters is dominant in Australia and owns Beringer in California, and Pernod-Ricard is French by origin but now more a global player. There are exceptions, most notably Gallo in the United States, Garcia Carrión in Spain, and Castel in France, all of which remain privately owned. Some of the most important companies, such as Constellation or Diageo, now have such widespread holdings that they can scarcely be identified any longer with their country of origin. Certainly there is a long-established trend for companies originating outside the major European wine-producing countries to buy up producers, most notably in France.

The largest wine producer's share of production in each country varies widely.[73]

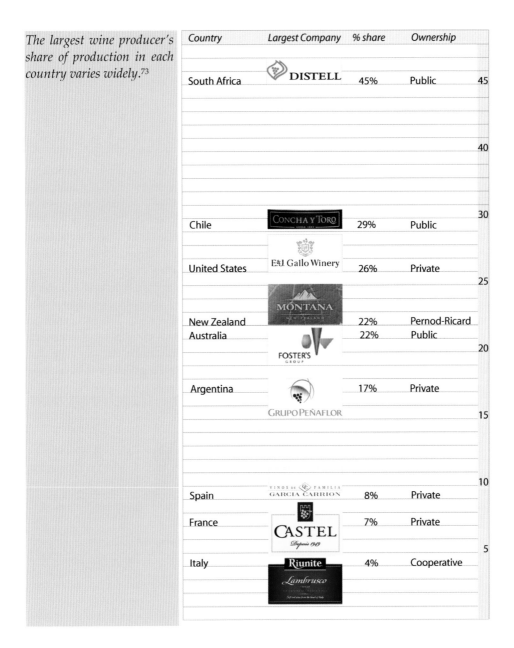

Country	Largest Company	% share	Ownership	
South Africa	DISTELL	45%	Public	45
				40
Chile	CONCHA Y TORO	29%	Public	30
United States	E&J Gallo Winery	26%	Private	25
New Zealand	MONTANA	22%	Pernod-Ricard	
Australia	FOSTER'S	22%	Public	20
Argentina	GRUPO PEÑAFLOR	17%	Private	15
				10
Spain	GARCIA CARRION	8%	Private	
France	CASTEL	7%	Private	5
Italy	Riunite Lambrusco	4%	Cooperative	

Concentration of wine production in major producing countries.[74]

Country	Average vineyard	Number of producers	Top-3 share	Top-5 share
New Zealand	50 ha	463	75%	80%
United States	100 ha	3,606	64%	80%
South Africa	25 ha	560	55%	
Australia	75 ha	2,320	48%	70%
Chile	1 ha	300	34%	51%
Argentina	5 ha	1,275	25%	41%
Spain	3.5 ha	6,355	12%	30%
Germany	1 ha	30,470	13%	
France	2 ha	36,440	13%	40%
Italy	1 ha	43,000	7%	10%

It's a more recent phenomenon for European wine producers to acquire subsidiaries in the New World. Sometimes the connection with the original producer is evident, more often it is obscure. The pioneers were the rich Champagne houses, whose subsidiaries are usually clearly identified. Among the first to realize the potential were Roederer, who established Roederer Estate in Anderson Valley in Sonoma in 1983, and Moët et Chandon, who set up their subsidiary Domaine Chandon in Napa Valley in 1986. The subsidiaries make sparkling wine—they are scrupulous about avoiding use of the term "Champagne." Champagne houses have also have set up subsidiaries in Australia or New Zealand. It's fair to say that, with rare exceptions, the warmer climates of the New World make a less refined product than Champagne itself, which is really a triumph in turning adversity of wine making in marginal climates into a luxury product. It's a bit too easy in the New World, the fruits are a little too ripe, the acidity is a little too low, but all the same, the wines can be good, even if lacking

Moët & Chandon have expanded out of Champagne to establish subsidiaries in Napa Valley and Australia. They use their own name in Napa, but use Greenpoint for exports from Australia, although the wine is available in the country as Domaine Chandon.

the finesse of Champagne. And now the trend has extended to other wines. Bordeaux châteaux have set up operations in California or South America. Major Spanish producer Torres first expanded around Spain and now is a major producer in Chile. Less obvious, because they don't necessarily operate under their own names, foreign companies own about 20% of Napa Valley vineyards. Globalization has definitely become a two way process.

The Bootleggers' Heritage

Most people who are interested in wine have some sense of which producers they like, whether it's a simple choice among leading brands or a sophisticated selection of artisan winemakers. They also are able to choose where they buy their wine, whether at supermarkets or specialist shops. But the pipeline from the producer to the shop is a black hole: there is little awareness of the extent to which the distributor in the middle affects the available choice and price.

Freedom of choice varies greatly, depending on where you live. In most of Europe, wine is a free market: in principle you can buy any wine you like, although of course choices are influenced by local conditions, such as preference for the local product over imports. Sweden is an exception, where monopoly rules: Systembolaget's 400 stores in Sweden have a monopoly on retail sales. You can buy anything you want, so long as Systembolaget decides to import it. Choice is inevitably more restricted than it would be in a free market, although not as much as in Canada, where the regional wine boards have a monopoly ensuring that 40% of sales are Canadian wine.

The contrast between the organization of the wine industry in Europe and the United States is ironic. In Europe, centuries of tradition now mean that producers (especially for quality wine) function under a wide range of legal constraints regulating what type of wine they can produce. Promotion is becoming impossible, but they can actually sell their wine to anyone, anywhere who wants it. But in the United States, where the experiment of Prohibition failed so ignobly, producers can make wine pretty much as they like, and there are relatively few restrictions on promoting it. Yet consumer choice is restricted by the mess in distribution resulting from ill-thought out features of the repeal process.

Distributors gained a stranglehold on the market during Prohibition. The illegality of distribution made it not only criminal but also highly lucrative. Inevitably the mob moved in. By the time Prohibition ended, they were well entrenched. Repeal forced the industry into the so-called three-tier system, designed to prevent concentration in the hands of the mob or anyone else. Producers are kept separate from distributors who are kept separate from retailers. Together with the ability of each State to impose its own regulations, the system is truly Balkanized.

We need producers: without them there would be no wine. We need retailers: without them it would be difficult to buy wine. But do we need distributors: are they the parasites of the system? You might argue that large producers are perfectly capable of undertaking their own distribution, but that for small producers, distributors provide the essential connection to market. Ironically, how-ever, it is larger producers in whom distributors are interested; small producers often fall through the net.[75]

Whatever essential role distributors may have filled in the past in enabling producers to market their wines in spite of the confusing welter of state regula-tions, today they are the bottleneck in the system. Distribution tends to be the most concentrated part of the wine industry, and nowhere is this better illus-trated than the United States. There are 2,800 wineries in California;[76] the national number of retailers is unknown, but even the largest (Costco) has less than 5% of the market—but there are only a few hundred distributors.

The number of distributors is declining while the number of wineries and brands is increasing. There were more than 10,000 wholesalers in the 1960s, but fewer than 300 at the turn of the century.[77] Mergers and acquisitions, increasing the market share of the giants at the top, have driven the decline. The top five distributors now have 43% of the market; the top 10 have 60%. Consolidation of distributors is driven mostly by consolidation in the distribution of spirits (affect-ing wine because the same distributors handle both wine and spirits). The higher profit margins in spirits place companies that handle only wine at a disadvan-tage, pushing the trend toward mergers. The better returns on spirits encourage investments there rather than in wine. The biggest distributor (Southern Wines and Spirits) has an annual cash flow of $7.0 billion, whereas the biggest retailer (Costco) weighs in at $0.8 billion. [78]

Southern started in a small enough way in 1968, with a $200,000 loan from Miami National Bank to a New York liquor executive, Walter Jahn. The bank was later reported to be a conduit for mob money. Its chairman, Samuel Cohen, was convicted of money-laundering charges, but became a business partner of Jay Weiss, who became a top executive of Southern. These connections were the basis for rumors that Southern was connected with the mob.[79]

Southern remains privately held, and handles its business secretively. By 1999, it was operating in 8 states, with an annual cash flow of $2.8 billion, repre-senting close to 12% of all domestic wine and liquor consumption.[80] Growing by gobbling up smaller distributors, its most recent acquisition of another large distributor, Glazer, brought it to operating in 38 states. It has close to a quarter of the national market.

Together with other wholesalers, it is not afraid to exercise political influence. Southern contributed equally to Democrats and Republicans in recent elections, and the WSWA (Wine and Spirits Wholesalers Association) was one of the top donors to politicians.[81] A major objective is to uphold the restrictions of the three-tier system, which protects distributors' profits by restricting sales within a state to distributors licensed by that state. Preventing shipment across state lines is one of the main causes for inflating the cost of wine and depriving the consumer of choice.

When Prohibition was repealed by the 21st Amendment to the Constitution, states were given the authority to regulate sales of alcohol, in particular to regu-late imports into the state. This was interpreted by many states as giving them the right to prevent producers from shipping wine directly to a consumer; instead the producer is supposed to sell only to a licensed distributor. Put simply, this conflicts with the provision of the Constitution that states shall not have the power to interfere with inter-state commerce.

The clash was finally tested in a case that reached the Supreme Court on the rights of wineries to sell directly to consumers in states with restrictive laws. The immediate commercial interest is relatively small, since direct sales are only about 2% of the whole market, but the implications are almost unlimited, since opening up direct shipping from wineries would almost inevitably release the other restrictions enabling the distributor to strangle the consumer. The Supreme Court decided in 2005 that restrictions on direct shipping were unconstitutional.[82]

The point was hammered home by another case, in which Costco fought the Washington State Liquor Control Board on the grounds that its limitations on the distribution of wine and beer violated federal antitrust law. Basically Washington State had in place a whole set of restrictions, ranging from minimum markups to bans on volume discounts and central warehousing—all designed to protect the distributors who no doubt had been hand in glove with the state legislators. Costco, which comes close to a national retailer of wines, won its case in April 2006.

Together the two cases opened up the market, and it became possible for consumers in many states to purchase wine directly from wineries or from retailers in other states. There has been a vigorous rearguard action from distributors desperate to protect their monopoly. Southern's attitude is best summarized by a note that was produced in a court case in 1995; scrawled on an advertising flier from a California wine retailer, offering to ship wines directly, was a note from Mel Dick, a senior Vice President of Southern, to the president, Wayne Chaplin: "Is there any way to stop this?"[83] Southern used its influence to make it a criminal offense for a consumer in its home state of Florida to ship wine from a winery in California; the penalty was the same as for burglary—five years in prison![84] This gives you some sense of the forces behind the scenes and the pressure to prevent choice for the consumer.

As a private company, Southern does not have to publish its accounts, so no one knows how much it spends on "lobbying," but it is thought to be the single largest source of funds for opposing liberalization of the wine laws. So every time an American consumer buys a bottle of wine distributed by Southern, part of the costs goes to efforts to deny freedom of choice. You might have thought that the growing power of Southern, which is now by far the largest wine distributor in the United States, would attract the attention of the anti-monopolies unit of Justice Department; one can only marvel at its immunity, especially since one of the stated purposes of the repeal of Prohibition was to prevent monopolies in wine and spirits distribution.

What public interest could be served by preventing consumers from having the same freedom of choice in purchasing wine as for other commodities? The excuses presented to preserve the remnants of the old system grow steadily feebler. "Social responsibility plays an integral role at Southern Wine & Spirits of America," said Lee Schrager, a Vice President of Southern.[85] But Southern and the other distributors are no doubt maneuvering even as you read this to prevent you from having free access to the market. State by state, legislators who put the interests of the distributors ahead of those of their constituents have been struggling to put the genie back in the bottle; let's hope they don't succeed.

The Unequal Equation of Supply and Demand

It's enough to make an economist despair. Not only is wine an inefficient market, but the imbalance of supply and demand has been perpetuated for decades; the worldwide surplus has really hardly shifted since 1970. Production has declined in parallel with the decline in demand, but never enough to close the gap. On top of this, wine remains an agricultural product, so there is unpredictable fluctuation in supply from year to year.

The basic problem in demand is the transition in Europe away from wine being a daily beverage, consumed in large quantities at cheap price. This has vastly reduced the total market. Growing consumption in new markets, such as the United States and Asia, has not been enough to compensate for the loss; and anyway, the new consumption is at a different level. There is little prospect that demand will be restored to the overall level of twenty years ago.

Europe will never solve the problem of its wine surplus so long as it subsidizes production that has become uneconomic. With a shifting world economy, other industries have moved out of Europe; why should wine be different? But having peaked in the 1970s-1980s, wine has merely gone back to where it was in the 1960s. It's not an easy problem to resolve, because there is no often no obvious alternative usage of the land; the fact that you can't even make decent wine often means that no other crop will be successful. Whether Europe will really allow another few hundred thousand hectares to be ploughed under remains to be seen, but nothing much else will restore balance.

While the surplus in the big three—Spain, Italy, and France—remains the major problem, there has been a shift of who gets stuck with the parcel when the music stops. Europe's problems in disposing of its surplus were exacerbated by the growth of production in the New World, which at first had little problem in selling its wines. But the rapidity of growth in supply, especially from Australia, has finally outgrown demand, leading to a classic boom and bust cycle in which wine cannot be sold, prices are dropping, grapes are unpicked, and finally some vineyards are being pulled out.[86] There are similar problems in South America, albeit lesser in magnitude.

The wine market is almost never in balance. Supply fluctuates with the vintage; and it's rarely practical to stockpile large vintages to even out the supply in small vintages. The transition from a cheap beverage to a drink which, if not a luxury item, is at least dispensable, makes wine more susceptible to general fluctuations in the economy.[87] The combination of the general worldwide surplus, annual fluctuations in supply, and unpredictable fluctuation in demand depending on the economy, makes for a roller coaster.

10

Fraud and Scandal

FRAUD IS THE INEVITABLE COMPANION OF REGULATION AND TAXATION. And regulation and taxation are as old as wine itself. By 2500 B.C., the "Inspector of the Wine Test" was required to approve wine for sale in Egypt.[1] By 400 B.C., laws in Greece prevented watering down wine and required it to be sold in airtight amphorae. Fines were imposed for selling wine on futures.[2] The major problem has always been adulteration in one form or another; Pliny the Elder complained in 77 C.E. that "genuine, unadulterated wine is not to be had now, not even by the nobility."[3] The most famous wine of the time, Falernian, made on the slopes of Mount Falernus near Naples, was apparently so ubiquitous as to arouse suspicions of authenticity.[4] Just before the lava came down over Pompeii, Falernian was available in bars for the unbelievable price of only four times that of the house wine.[5] Galen, the famous Roman physician of the second century, who had some experience of the real thing and thought it was at its best after 15 years or so, commented that "other wines like it are prepared by those who are skilled in such knavery."[6]

Adulteration varies from harmless dilution with water to addition of lethal concoctions. Mediaeval laws commonly forbade the watering of wine. An English law of 1327 required innkeepers to draw wine from casks in the view of their customers. The law provided not only that new and old wine could not be blended, but they could not even be kept in the same cellar. Wines from different sources could not be sold by the same merchant.[7] Punishments were public. In 1364, John Penrose, a vintner in the city of London, was found guilty of selling bad wine, and condemned to drink a draught of his own wine, before having the rest poured over his head, and being banned from selling wine.

Passing off inferior wine as better wine is a more subtle form of adulteration than watering down. This is particularly difficult to prevent in a context in which wines are being blended anyway. Although the history of wine is replete with regulations to prevent dilution, adulteration, or inappropriate blending, until the present century, concern was more about making sure the wine was sellable than protecting its authenticity of origin. In Carthage, around the sixth century B.C., Mago described how to produce high quality wine and what additives should be used to disguise wines of lower quality.[8]

During the nineteenth century in Bordeaux, wines were commonly blended with imports that were a bit stronger, brought in from Spain or from the Rhône valley in France. "Hermitager" became a verb describing use of the wines of Hermitage (in the northern Rhône) to strengthen those of Bordeaux or Burgundy. In fact, a major part of the skill set of the negociants who shipped the wine from Bordeaux was to adjust it to suit the tastes of their customers.[9] This blending was so important that arguments continued from the seventeenth through the nineteenth century about who should have the right to perform it. During the nineteenth century, Bordeaux shippers purchased vineyards in Hermitage in order to assure their supply, and as much as 80% of the production was shipped to Bordeaux.[10]

Blending with foreign wine was regarded as normal practice in Bordeaux, even for the top wines. It was regarded with skepticism only by outsiders. Cyrus Redding, an English commentator on wine, remarked in 1833 that, "Bordeaux wine in England and in Bordeaux scarcely resemble each other. The merchants are obliged to 'work' the wines before they are shipped, or, in other words, to mingle stronger wines with them, such as Hermitage, or Cahors, which is destructive almost wholly of the bouquet, color, and aroma of the original wine."[11] Thomas Jefferson was highly skeptical of the negociants' activities: "The vigneron never adulterates his wine, but on the contrary gives it the most perfect

Vignerons protested in Montpellier in 1907. The slogan on the barrel says "war on fraud, keep wine natural."

and pure care possible. But when once a wine has been into a merchant's hands, it never comes out unmixed. This being the basis of their trade, no degree of honesty, of personal friendship or of kindred prevents it."[12]

It was not until the twentieth century that authenticity of origin became an important issue. When the phylloxera epidemic devastated wine production, first in France and then in the rest of Europe, the market was opened to competition by cheap imports (from Algeria) or with synthetic products (basically made from sugar). Vignerons rioted in the Languedoc in 1907, setting a tradition for protest that continues to the present day. In Bordeaux, the negociants struggled to protect their vested interest in blending wines, and succeeded in delaying the implementation of laws protecting origin until 1912.[13] Finally, it became true that a bottle stating "Bordeaux" actually contained nothing but wine from the region.

Authenticity became of increasing importance and was the basis for the system of Appellation Contrôlée that was formally introduced in 1935. Initially this covered a relatively small proportion of vineyards, restricted to the top areas, representing about 10% of wine production. Since then it has spread to include more than half of the vineyards of France. It was the forerunner for the European Union system of QWPSR (Quality Wine Produced in a Specific Region); every country in Europe has its own system, but wines in the top category always have a label saying where they come from. Similar systems, although somewhat less well defined and less effective, are now spreading through the New World.

Authenticity of origin is a major characteristic for defining a quality wine. Usually it goes hand in hand with procedures to ensure that a certain standard is maintained, at a minimum that the wine has not been adulterated with non vinous components. The famous frauds alternate between passing off inferior wine as coming from a better location and actually adulterating the wine in order to "improve" it.

Plumbing the Depths

A variety of motives are responsible for adulterating wine, mostly to make it look better (typically more darkly colored) or taste better (most often to compensate for the results of a poor vintage). All involve an amount of deception in making the wine appear as something it is not. But the most lethal form of adulteration started more as a means of protecting the wine.

Needing preservatives to conserve their wine, the Romans often added a preparation called *sapa*. Columella, author of a famous series of books on agriculture in the first century, detailed how much sapa should be added to preserve the wine until the next vintage without letting the flavor become noticeable enough to discourage purchasers.[14] Sapa was a sweet syrup, prepared by boiling acidic wine in lead-lined vessels, and its active component was lead acetate. From Columella's recipe, it's possible to calculate that the lead content of the wines would have been about 20 mg/l, so consumption of a liter would give more than 40 times the level of 0.5 mg/day that produces chronic lead poisoning.[15] Indeed, there is a school of thought that lead poisoning may have

City officials escorting a wagon of confiscated wine casks for dumping in the river at Nuremberg, probably about 1630.[18]

contributed to the fall of the Roman Empire.[16] Since Columella's books continued to be available through the mediaeval period, lead poisoning did not stop with the Roman Empire.

The Romans had no idea that sapa contained a lethal dose of lead, but a millennium later, lead was added intentionally because it had been discovered that it improved wine flavor. In particular, it corrected the problem with sour wines by making them taste sweet. Once it was realized that the addition of lead was toxic, attempts were made to ban it. One of the very first edicts concerning adulteration is attributed to Charlemagne in 802, banning the use of leaded wines.[17] In Ulm, the center of the German wine trade, an edict of 1487 required all innkeepers to testify to the purity of their wine; and a list of banned ingredients included lead oxide. Fifteenth century edicts in both France and Spain banned the use of sapa to sweeten wine. A seventeenth century etching from Nuremberg shows a wagon of confiscated wine being taken to the river for dumping.

But the attraction for the wine merchant of correcting unsellable wine overcame any concern for the consumer. In the late seventeenth century, a recipe similar to Columella's was used in southern Germany, involving addition of litharge (a powder of lead oxide) to wine vats. Increased use probably resulted from a series of poor vintages that produced sour wines. In 1695, Eberhard Gockel, a physician in Ulm, pinned down outbreaks of chronic colic to lead poisoning caused by the use of litharge.[19] By 1696, the Duke of Württemberg issued another decree on adulteration of wine, banning the addition of litharge.

By the mid eighteenth century, such laws were common, and penalties included death.[20]

This was by no means the end of epidemics of lead poisoning. Subsequent outbreaks occurred in England at the end of the eighteenth century (due to contaminated cider, rather than wine), and a British physician complained in 1820 that the use of lead "adds the crime of murder to that of fraud."[21] There's a theory that the ill-health (and bad temper) of the composer Handel was due to lead poisoning.[22]

Lead in wine has continued to be a sensitive issue. Lead can get into wine from the environment, although the sources have effectively been eliminated in recent decades. In the early part of the century, vineyards were sprayed with lead arsenate, and lead paints were common in wineries.[23] Capsules on bottles used to be made of tin, and this seems to have been a source of lead in wine; apparently wine became contaminated during pouring, from lead residues deposited on the bottle.[24] Lead capsules were banned in 1996 in the United States, and capsules are now made of plastic.

The most recent excitement was the discovery that lead could leach from crystal decanters into wine.[25] Port kept in a decanter for several months achieved dangerously high levels (whether aside from that it was still drinkable after such a period is another question), but later studies showed that under normal conditions of consumer use, any level of lead in the wine was far below dangerous levels.

Red, Red Wine

You can make wine from elderberries. In fact, it's popular with home winemakers. But what does that have to do with the product of the grape? Well, there's a very long history of elderberries being used to improve the color of wine.

Elderberries grow on bushes that can become large, up to 4 meters high. They are relatively small, deeply colored berries. The color is due to a high concentration of anthocyanins, and they also contain tannins at levels comparable to the less pigmented red grape varieties. Sugar levels are much lower than grapes, typically about 75 g/l (a Brix of about 8, equivalent to 5% potential alcohol). Citric acid is the most abundant acid, and a lot of sugar is used to counteract the acidity when making elderberry wine. It's important to use ripe berries, and to avoid contamination, because the unripe fruit, leaves, shoots and bark are all harmful if not entirely poisonous.

So elderberry wine is no threat to the established order, but winemakers have been known to look enviously at the high anthocyanin concentrations in the dark blue skins of the small berries.

Elderberries have been employed from Champagne to Port. During the nineteenth century, the town of Fismes (in the Marne) was famous for providing elderberries for tinting rosé Champagne.[26] The Teinte de Fismes was made by "digesting 250 to 500 parts of elderberries, and 30 to 60 parts of alum [aluminium

Elderberries have a long but not very distinguished history in wine production. They are small and very deeply colored, and have been used widely for increasing color in wine.

potassium sulfate] with 800 to 600 of water, and then submitting the mixture to pressure."[27]

Its use was even more pronounced in Port. "It is my belief that the peculiar color of nearly all Port wines hitherto drunk in England... can only be produced by artificial means and is effected by an infusion of elderberry juice," commented the British representative in Lisbon in 1867.[28] The situation was so bad that in 1756 the Portuguese government had required that all elderberry trees in the region should be destroyed,[29] but the edict evidently had little effect.

Why Is Antifreeze Delicious?

Many noxious substances smell or taste bad, a clear warning to avoid them. But ethylene glycol, a syrupy derivative of alcohol, which lowers the freezing point and is widely used as engine antifreeze, actually tastes sweet and pleasant. A fair number of people are hurt by accidentally consuming it each year; and there've even been murder cases where it's been fed to victims by spiking their drinks.[30] The so-called antifreeze scandal in Austria in 1985 was actually somewhat mis-named; winemakers had been adding diethylene glycol to make their wine appear richer, but this is not the same as ethylene glycol. It is, of course, related, and it does have a slight antifreeze effect, but it's not as toxic. The sweet taste means it's relatively easy to ingest large amounts and reach a toxic level, how-ever, so it is banned for use in foods and drugs.

Diethylene glycol owes its infamy in wine to the chemist Otto Nadrasky. He had been working on a means to produce "wine" simply from chemicals, with-out the inconvenience of needing to ferment grapes. During his research, he discovered that diethylene glycol masks the presence of additional sugar, with the result that sugar could be added to wine without being detected during analysis.[31] In the context of regulations rating wines according to grape sugar levels, this was a profitable discovery. One story has the fraud discovered in December 1984 when a wine producer tried to reclaim the VAT that he had paid on purchases of diethylene glycol.[32] Another places the discovery later, in March 1985 when a tax inspector queried purchases of large quantities of diethylene glycol by an obscure wine merchant in a village on the Hungarian border.[33]

The affair was covered up, but came to light in Germany (where much of the treated wine had been sold) in July; and by August all Austrian wine for sale in Britain was withdrawn. The scandal affected everyone, even impeccable producers, who had unknowingly purchased treated wine from others. More than a thousand different wines were found to have been treated, amounting to several millions of bottles. This could have accounted for as much as 10% of the wines produced in Austria over the period.[34]

With their usual irrelevance, the authorities finally announced that the regulations would be tightened, but current law was in fact adequate: addition of glycol was completely illegal, taking place against a background of general disregard for regulations. A warning sign had been sounded previously when the annual sales of the red Hirondelle brand (popular in Britain in the 1970s), which was labeled as Austrian red wine, were reported to exceed the entire production of red wine in the country.[36]

The events of 1985 are still referred to in Austria as "the scandal"—the word antifreeze is never mentioned. It was a drastic wake-up call. By the year following the scandal, exports of Austrian wine, which previously had accounted for a half to a third of production, collapsed to almost nothing. It took more than a decade before recovery even began.

In spite of press hysteria, there was no hazard to human health from the tainted wines. By far the worst case affecting health was the 1986 wine scandal in northern Italy when four large producers added methanol to their wines.[37] Twenty-six people died and many more were hospitalized. It emerged from the investigation that this was the extreme manifestation of a general disregard for regulations regarding blending of wine from different sources.

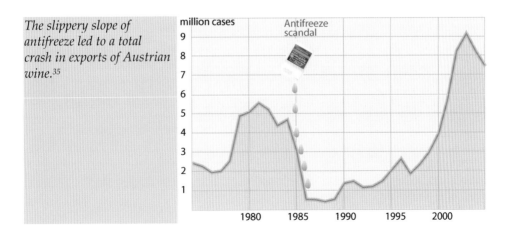

The slippery slope of antifreeze led to a total crash in exports of Austrian wine.[35]

A Spoonful of Sugar

You can't make wine without sugar, in fact you can't make any alcoholic beverage without it since alcohol comes from fermentation of sugar, but that very fact makes it extremely simple to abuse the process. Not only can the alcohol level be bumped up by adding sugar before fermentation occurs, but by using dried raisins and sugar, or even just by making a solution of sugar in water, fermentation followed by addition of some flavoring compounds will produce "wine." A recipe was published in a scientific encyclopedia in the 1760s: "Take 250 pounds of sugar; put in a cuve of 2 muids; fill within 16 pints of the top; put in a warm place; add 3 or 4 pounds of yeast from fresh beer... Color with sunflower extract to make red wine and add a little oil for aroma."[38]

At the peak of the crisis caused by the loss of production resulting from the phylloxera devastation (1885-1890), there were substantial sales of "sugar wines" consisting of industrial fabrications from alcohol, tartaric acid, flavoring compounds, and so on. During this period as much as 10-20% of total wine production in France[39] may have come from fermenting dried raisins that had been mixed with water and a little sugar (a large part was produced in industrial establishments in the Parisian region; if you weren't going to grow grapes, why not eliminate the costs of transport to the consumers).[40]

Today, addition of sugar is legal in the cooler parts of Europe; probably up to 20% of French wines have their alcohol level increased by this chaptalization.[41]

Wine scandals involving sugar are endemic. The stakes are highest in Germany and Austria, where the classification system grades wine according to the level of sugar in the grape must. By adding sugar to the must, the wine achieves a higher, and more valuable, grade. A similar, if less pronounced, effect is created whenever a wine is classified by alcohol level, for example, Beaujolais requires more than 9% alcohol, but Beaujolais Superieure must be above 10%.

It's really a scandal that sugar can be added legally in Germany so long as it is in the form of RCGM (rectified concentrated grape must, which is a sugar preparation made from grapes), although it's restricted to wines below the quality grade of QmP. It's not legal to add sugar from other sources, but it emerged in 1980 that addition of liquid sugar (a solution of fructose and glucose known as invert sugar) was common. Two hundred sugar merchants had illegally supplied 1,800 wine producers, who had artificially sweetened 300 million bottles of wine between 1977 and 1979.[42] Sugar had been added to wines in regions extending from the Mosel to the Nahe and the Pfalz; overall up to a ton of sugar was added per thousand hectoliters of wine.[43] (Proportionately, the most sugar was added in the most northernmost region, the Mosel.) A scandal involving people in high places erupted in the Mosel, where the President of the German Winegrowers' Association turned out to have illegally sweetened several million bottles of wine.[44] One wonders how much German wine was authentic before the authorities clamped down.

For whatever reason, Beaujolais seems to attract more scandal than most. As recently as the 1950s, when Beaujolais was producing less than 60 million bottles per year, it was estimated that the Paris region alone consumed more than 250 million bottles annually.[45] More recently, large purchases of sugar from supermarkets during the 2004 season led to the discovery that alcohol levels had been increased more than the legal limit of 2%.[46] The motive wasn't so much the classification of the wine as simply to reach a high enough alcohol level to be competitive in the modern world.

With sugar scandals continuing right up to the present day, perhaps the only solution to guarantee authenticity would be to ban chaptalization in any form and to make it illegal to have sugar in a winery. This would prevent accidents such as Christopher Fielden was encouraged to precipitate in the Médoc: "I was asked to stumble when I passed a certain problem vat and, just by chance, empty the open sack of sugar, that I happened to be carrying, into it."[47]

You Pays Your Money and You Takes Your Choice

Nominally a quality wine in Europe should be at least 85% of what is stated on the label, since in theory it's permitted to include up to 15% of wine from another vintage. Similarly, in cases where a grape variety is stated, 15% of another varietal can be included. But the place name has been sacrosanct since the enforcement of appellation rules throughout the European Community.

Nowhere was the impact of the regulations felt more keenly than in Britain, where for years appellation names had been used as folkloric descriptions of wines rather than referring to actual origins. Christopher Fielden quotes the complaint of the manager at the bottling plant of the giant Societé de Vins de France in England: "You English are such individualists. Each one wants a different blend for a different wine... As a result I have to keep halting my bottling line, pumping wines from tank to tank... just to satisfy old-fashioned quirks."[48] The plant, which became known as Château Ipswich, was stocking eight base wines, three white, three rosé, and two red, which were blended as necessary to make a series of different wines for sale. The two red base wines had alcohol levels of 12% and 11.5%, respectively. "Châteauneuf-du-Pape" was produced from the twelve percent; "Nuits St. Georges" was made by mixing in a little eleven-five; the mix was lightened a little more for "Beaujolais" by increasing the eleven-five a bit further; while the eleven-five alone was used when "Médoc" was required.[49] The operation was a great success until exposed by journalist Nicholas Tomalin in the Sunday Times in November 1966.

While this may have been an extreme case, the traditional practices of wine merchants in Britain were certainly threatened when the country joined the European Union. Nuits St. Georges, for example, was used as a generic name for Burgundy with a good body. Often enough the same wine would be labeled as Volnay, Nuits St. Georges, or Gevrey Chambertin, depending on the client.[50] There was enough wine in the pipeline that Britain needed to be given a three year derogation from joining in 1973 to requiring full compliance in 1976.

And certainly it is not unknown for Burgundies to be mislabeled at source. (I once inadvertently caused great offense in the cellars of a Burgundian producer, when looking at cage after cage of bottles whose contents were identified only by half-legible marks on chalkboards, I innocently asked if mistakes were ever made at labeling.) The Grivelet scandal in 1979 was stated by its protagonist, in the time hallowed way, to be nothing extraordinary because everyone was doing it. Faced with rapidly increasing demand for fine Burgundy in the United States, Bernard-Noël Grivelet took out full page advertisements offering individually numbered bottles of Burgundy from such prestigious appellations as Chambertin, Bonnes Mares, and various vineyards in Chambolle Musigny and Morey St. Denis. Five thousand cases were shipped (and consumed!) before it was discovered that M. Grivelet had in fact filled the bottles with non appellation wine.[51] Despite his claims that the practice "was widespread throughout the district," bankruptcy followed.

Sometimes the fraudsters are caught up by simple discrepancies in the numbers. Export figures showed that between 2005 and 2008, the Aude region of the Languedoc sold 1.3 million cases of Pinot Noir to the United States each year. The problem is that the whole Languedoc produces only 500,000 cases of Pinot each year! Winemakers and cooperatives sold the wine to the negociant firm Ducasse in Carcassone, which sold it to the huge producer Sieur d'Arques.[52] Sieur d'Arques then sold the wine to Gallo, for their Red Bicyclette brand. In the best French tradition, it remains unknown exactly who perpetuated the scam, but the profits must have been huge, since Pinot Noir sells for about twice the price of other black grapes. Everyone along the chain was prosecuted;[53] the defendants were found guilty in February 2010 and given suspended jail sentences and fines ranging from €,500 to €180,000, [54] rather piddling compared to the millions made in the fraud. [55] The defense was the same as usual: "There is no prejudice. Not a single American consumer complained," said the lawyer for Sieur d'Arques. Others defended themselves by arguing that they delivered a wine that had "Pinot Noir characteristics." Indeed, this doesn't say much for the ability of those farther along the chain to distinguish Pinot Noir from generic red wine! What's the point in paying a premium for a varietal if even the producer can't tell the difference?

The Scandal of the Century

Bordeaux had about ten vintages of the century between 1900 and 2000. But there was surely only one scandal of the century. Winegate had everything: a protagonist larger than life, Pierre Bert, who when he lost the case turned to the tax inspectors and said, "You've won, let me buy you a glass of champagne;" a judge at the Court in Bordeaux who palpably knew absolutely nothing about wine; the dogged tax inspector Destrau who pursued Bert for months while he untangled the threads of an extraordinarily ingenious fraud; inspectors whose bungled attempts to raid the headquarters of a suspect negociant made Inspector Clouseau look supremely competent; and the old-line major negociant, Cruse, who made no distinction between Vin de Table and top quality Bordeaux or Burgundy, and who went bust a year later.

The authorities thought they had an infallible system for control. "Our system of control has been perfected so that [fraud] is impossible. All these stories of coupages [blending], of wines from the Midi that are sold as Beaujolais or Bordeaux, are nothing but a tissue of ridiculous lies," said Pierre Perromat, the President of INAO[56] in 1973.[57] But there was a fatal flaw in the system.

Bert's system was so cunning that even after the tax inspectors knew there was a fraud, it took months for them to figure it out. But it would never have been successful but for the Cruses' cupidity and willingness to cooperate. They should have known better since Pierre Bert was a broker with a history of wine frauds.

The fraud occurred in the context of an overheated, speculative market. Prices rocketed in 1972 to 1973 and then collapsed in 1974. Early in 1973, Bert set up a small negociant business that he called Balan et cie (after the name of his driver, Serge Balan). Like many others, he was under financial pressure because in 1972 he had sold wine that he did not actually possess, expecting prices to fall before he needed to deliver. Confounded by a continued rise in the market, he was faced with a ruinous situation in the form of a deficit of 300,000 francs.

The "infallible" system for controlling wine in France provided a certificate of origin with every lot of wine. AOC wines had an acquit vert (green certificate), while table wines had a white certificate. The certificate was issued by the producer's local tax office, where the original remained. A copy of the certificate with detachable coupons traveled with every lot of wine. When the wine was moved from one location to another, for example from a grower to a negociant, an approved shipper could stamp a coupon, detach it, and return the copies to his local tax office and to INAO.

Balan et cie obtained a franking machine from the local tax office. (Machines were routinely available to reliable negociants.) The secret of their success was that they simultaneously purchased red table wine and white AOC Bordeaux. The red wine came with an acquit blanc, and the white wine came with an acquit vert. By swapping the acquits, that is by stamping the acquit vert when the red wine was sold and by using the acquit blanc for the white wine, Bert could sell the red wine as AOC Bordeaux and the white wine as table wine. The system fooled the authorities because the AOC of the wine is noted on the coupons, but the color of the wine was stated only on the original that remained in the originating tax office.

The price differential between white AOC Bordeaux and white table wine was small, about 10%, and Bert took a corresponding loss on that transaction. But the differential on the red wines was much larger, with AOC Bordeaux selling for about 3 times the table wine. So Bert trebled his money on that side of the transaction. A single tanker trundling from warehouse to warehouse where the switches were made was sufficient to move the equivalent of 4 million bottles and make several million francs of profits in a period of four months.

The stakes increased when Bert recruited Cruse as a client. They set up a trade in which Cruse purchased the fake red AOC wine at a price some 15% below market, while simultaneously selling the same amount of vin de table (of which they had an excess) to Bert. "We will deal with you," the Cruses said to

Bert bought white Bordeaux AOC, which he sold for a loss as table wine. But he made a profit by buying red table wine that was sold as Bordeaux AOC.

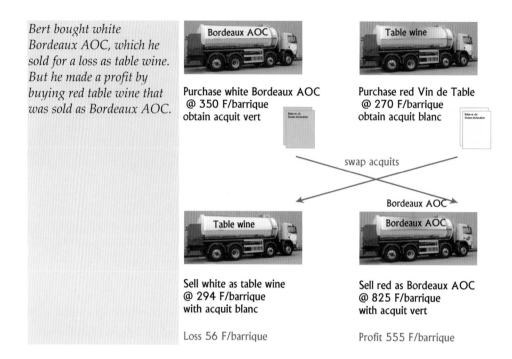

Purchase white Bordeaux AOC
@ 350 F/barrique
obtain acquit vert

Purchase red Vin de Table
@ 270 F/barrique
obtain acquit blanc

swap acquits

Bordeaux AOC

Sell white as table wine
@ 294 F/barrique
with acquit blanc

Sell red as Bordeaux AOC
@ 825 F/barrique
with acquit vert

Loss 56 F/barrique

Profit 555 F/barrique

Bert, "on condition that we can exchange wines for current consumption [table wines] for the appellation wines that you deliver to us."[58] In due course, the system was simplified to the extent in which no wine actually changed hands, although for the sake of appearances a single tanker load of wine made the rounds from Balan to Cruse and back again. Essentially, Cruse received an acquit vert from Bert in exchange for an acquit blanc, but the wine stayed in the tanker. This enabled Cruse directly to sell their excess of vin de table as AOC Bordeaux.

The situation descended into farce when the tax inspectors appeared at Cruse headquarters on June 28 and demanded to take an inventory. There had for years been a gentleman's agreement between the negociants and the tax authorities that due notice would be given of inspections, and on these grounds, Cruse refused to allow the inspectors entry to the cellars. It took another two months before the inspectors were able to check the records, starting on August 28, when it soon became apparent that the fraud practiced by Bert was only a small part of the problem, and that Cruse had habitually sold the wine of one appellation as coming from another, labeled the same wine as coming from different appellations, sold the same wine under different château names, or had changed vintages, as well as promoting vin de table to AOC.[59] Only one wine, and from the Midi at that, apparently was used to compensate for ullage of the casks of the various AOC wines.[60] There were also accusations of chemical adulteration. Descriptions of vats were give-aways, such as "could be Beaujolais for the American market."

The trial started in October 1974, with Bert and the Cruses as the principal targets. Bert was accused of adulterating wine as well as changing its appellation. He defended himself vigorously on the grounds that, whether his actions were legal or not, they were no more than accustomed practice in improving the wine—"baptizing" was the term he used. He took the classic defense that he had never received any complaints from any of his customers. In one exchange that became famous, Bert conceded that he had mixed white wines with red, because "a little white wine does not harm the quality when there is too much tannin in the red." "Yes, but it's not legal," said the judge. "No, but it's good," Bert answered. He claimed that much of the wine labeled as AOC Bordeaux was in fact so poor in quality that it could be sold only after improvement.[61] When the verdict came in December, only Bert received a jail sentence jail; the Cruses were given suspended sentences.

The postscript was a mixture of farce and tragedy. Pierre Bert emerged after a short period in jail to write a humorous book about his experiences and became a minor celebrity. Unable to stand the disgrace, Herman Cruse committed suicide by jumping off a bridge into the Gironde. The house of Cruse went bust the following year, although more as a result of misjudgments in the market than because of the scandal.

Thomas Jefferson Was Here

It's not that Thomas Jefferson was omnipresent in wine regions when he was United States Minister to France from 1785 to 1789, but he left such a detailed record of his travels, and such perspicacious notes on wines and producers, that you feel he was a major authority of the late eighteenth century. He was an avid wine collector, known to have purchased the first growths of the Médoc and Graves as well as Château d'Yquem, not to mention later being involved in efforts (inevitably unsuccessful because of phylloxera) to grow Vitis vinifera at his home, Monticello, in Virginia. So it was a major event to find preserved bottles of Château Lafite, labeled 1787 and engraved with the initials Th. J. It was a pity that the engraving was later found to have been done with twentieth century power tools.

When Michael Broadbent brought the hammer down on lot 337, the first item in the afternoon session at Christie's wine auction in London on December 5, 1985, it was the most expensive bottle of wine in the world. Sold for a bid of £105,000 to the son of billionaire Malcolm Forbes, it was hand-blown in dark green glass; there was no label, but etched into the glass was "1787, Lafitte, Th. J.". This was one of a cache of bottles supposedly discovered in a bricked-up cellar in Paris that had been bottled for Thomas Jefferson.

Several of these bottles were later purchased by Bill Koch, an American tycoon. Koch became suspicious about their authenticity when the Thomas Jefferson Foundation cast doubt on the provenance of the bottles. Investigations of the wine itself, using techniques such as carbon dating, were inconclusive in most cases (although they did suggest that at least some of the bottles contained wine one or two centuries younger than claimed), but an examination of the bottles suggested that they had been engraved using twentieth century power tools.[62]

The seller of these, and many other old wines, was Hardy Rodenstock, a German living in Munich, who was originally a manager of pop music groups. Interested in wine as an amateur, he was a regular contributor to one of Germany's wine magazines (Alles über Wein) and a regular buyer at the London wine auctions. He acquired an almost mystical reputation for his ability to sniff out caves of old bottles. The Jefferson collection, supposed to have been revealed when a hidden cellar was exposed during the destruction of an eighteenth century house in Paris, was only one of these. Others included a supply of Pétrus in large format bottles, reported to be from an English cellar, a cache of old Bordeaux in Venezuela, and a cellar in Russia of first growth Bordeaux that was claimed to have belonged to the Tsar. By the 1980s, Rodenstock had become a professional wine trader, and hosted a series of high-end tastings at which a seemingly endless supply of extraordinary old bottles appeared. One of these tastings went through 125 vintages of Château d'Yquem.

The Jefferson cellar supposedly contained about a hundred bottles, including many of the first growths, and a couple of dozen bottles engraved with the initials "Th. J." Rodenstock has never revealed the source of the bottles, in spite of considerable pressure after the problems emerged. Believing that the bottles were fakes, Koch started an extensive investigation, not only to analyze the bottles, but also to search into Rodenstock's background. The investigation discovered that Rodenstock had changed his name, revealed various legal problems in Rodenstock's past, and culminated in a lawsuit in New York. There was of course an argument as to whether this was the appropriate jurisdiction, and to date the lawsuit has not brought any final resolution to the question of authenticity.

Several collectors have been burned by buying very expensive old bottles that could be traced back to Rodenstock and which now have dubious value. Bottles from Rodenstock were sold by Farr Wine Merchants in London, The Wine Li-

A bottle supposedly of Château Lafite from 1787 that was engraved for Thomas Jefferson. (Artist's impression.)

The affair remains so sensitive that Christie's refused permission to reproduce an original photograph of the bottle, as did its owner, Bill Koch.

brary in California, and various auction houses in London and New York. Finally this has led to sensitivity on the question of fraud, and the auction houses are refusing to accept suspect bottles. Is the apparent increase in the number of fakes due to fraud becoming more profitable with the rise in prices or has it been going on all along and only now is anyone paying attention?

With the very old wines, more is at stake than the authenticity of the particular bottles. Over the years, Rodenstock's supply of rare bottles included a significant number from the eighteenth and nineteenth centuries. Indeed, one writer pointed out that much of our knowledge about the supposed taste of these rare old wines depends on bottles provided by Rodenstock.[63] It now seems that, at the very least, the basis for all this knowledge is highly questionable. Is it a myth that we really know anything about the taste of nineteenth century wines?

IV THE NEW WORLD

WINE PRODUCTION IN THE NEW WORLD has deeper roots than is sometimes realized, but a universal feature is that originally most wines were produced for local consumption, often in a sweet style, and usually from low quality varieties. The move to fine wine production is relatively recent everywhere.

Although there was in fact some quality wine production in the United States early in the twentieth century, it was brought to a grinding halt by Prohibition. The industry did not really begin to produce quality wines again in any significant proportion until the 1960s, and it was not until 1967 that production of dry wine surpassed sweet wine, with quality varieties coming to the fore in the 1970s.

In Australia and New Zealand, wine has been produced since the nineteenth century, but production was dominated by cheap fortified wines. The transition to table wines began in the 1950s, but surpassed fortified wine production only in the 1970s; quality wines became predominant only in the 1980s. Much production in South America still is from local varieties, and the move towards quality wine production dates only from the 1990s. South Africa has grown vines since the seventeenth century, but the industry is only now recovering from years of abusive monopoly.

Distribution patterns are very different in each region, with the United States consuming the majority of its domestic production, Australia and New Zealand exporting the vast majority of their production, and South America and South Africa consuming their own low quality production but trying to export the higher quality wines.

The recent reconstruction of the industry in the New World has concentrated on a few "international varieties." In many cases, the wines compete with classic wine regions of Europe. So Napa Valley's best known wines are Cabernet Sauvignon (competing with Bordeaux) and Chardonnay (competing with Burgundy). Barossa Valley is famous for its Shiraz, the Australian name for the Syrah of the Northern Rhône. New Zealand has brought a new meaning to Sauvignon Blanc, previously the preserve of the Loire Valley. In South America, both Argentina and Chile are trying to compete on the international stage of Cabernet Sauvignon, although each makes a point of a rediscovered variety, Malbec in Argentina, and Carmenère in Chile. South Africa has not yet quite found its focus.

Top regions and varieties in the New World.		
Country	Region	Variety
United States	Napa Valley	Cabernet Sauvignon
Australia	Barossa Valley	Shiraz
New Zealand	Marlborough	Sauvignon Blanc
Argentina	Mendoza	Cabernet Sauvignon
Chile	Casablanca Valley	Cabernet Sauvignon

11

North America: The Varietal Engine

WHEN YOU THINK OF NEW WORLD WINES, you think of varietals. Most wines from the New World carry the name of their predominant grape variety. When you think of the comparable wines from Europe, however, most carry place names, with a bewildering range from the familiar to the barely pronounceable; almost none identify the grape varieties. Varietal labeling is now seen as a brilliant move that gave New World wines a major boost compared to the complicated place names of Europe, but it met with enormous hostility when it was first suggested. Frank Schoonmaker, a major figure in the New York wine world, was the driving force behind the idea. The author of a general book on wine in 1935 (which lacked enthusiasm for California wines),[1] he imported European wines to the East Coast. With the interruption of supplies by World War II imminent, in 1939 he added a handful of wines from California to his portfolio.[2] He demanded that the wines should be identified by varietal names. Well ahead of its time, his catalog stated, "The labels give specific information concerning their origin—where they were made, by whom, when and from what grape."[3]

Most California wines of the period were labeled with generic names imitating places in Europe.[4] This custom had started in the late nineteenth century as a means of competing with imports from France; "Claret" was used as a description to compete with cheap reds from Bordeaux.[5] Ironically, because varietal labeling went hand in hand with discouraging the use of European place names on American wines, Schoonmaker was seen as the enemy incarnate by the winemakers. Varietal labeling was viewed as nothing more than an attempt by the importers to protect European place names by implying that varietal-labeled wines were inferior. An editorial in the Wine Review thundered against importers who "wish to preserve their profits by keeping alive the myth that the wines of this country are inferior to those of Europe."[6] The vehemence of the argument did not diminish for several years.[7] Yet today it is varietal labeling that gives the New World an advantage in the modern marketplace.

Varietal labeling had in fact started in California in the nineteenth century. Maynard Amerine, of the University of California, commented, "The idea that varietal labeling was invented by Frank Schoonmaker is mainly malarkey... it had been very actively used in California in the 1890s," although he went on to concede that it was Schoonmaker who really developed the idea in the market.[8, 9] In more modern times, from the 1930s, it was Louis Martini (in Napa Valley north of San Francisco) who first produced vintage-labeled varietal premium wines in significant quantities (together with Inglenook).[10, 11] But it was Schoonmaker's initiative, together with Frederick Wildman, another New York importer, that really forced the association between varietal labeling and quality. The lower quality California wines continued to be labeled as "Burgundy" for heavier reds, "Claret" for lighter reds, "Sauternes" or "Moselle" for white wines.[12]

There was no connection between the European place name used on the label and the type of grape variety used to produce the wine in Europe. Jacob Schram (founder of Schramsberg winery) observed in 1861 that Zinfandel (a variety unknown in France) looked like the best grape for clarets![13] A century later, Gallo's Hearty Burgundy was based on Petite Sirah (Durif) and Zinfandel, while Gallo's "Chablis" was made from Colombard and Chenin Blanc grapes,[14] neither grown anywhere near Chablis in France.

A view of quality wine production in California, probably in the 1940s, emphasized estate bottling from wineries in the regions north and south of San Francisco.

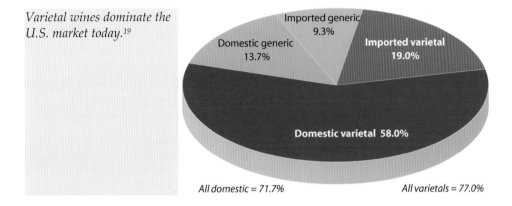

Varietal wines dominate the U.S. market today.[19]

Imported generic 9.3%

Domestic generic 13.7%

Imported varietal 19.0%

Domestic varietal 58.0%

All domestic = 71.7%   *All varietals = 77.0%*

Things have certainly changed since 1934, when Frank Schoonmaker wrote: "Fully nine-tenths of the wine from California… will necessarily be of second rate quality because it will necessarily come from vines that can produce only second rate wine grapes."[15] But today quality varietals dominate California, and wines carry varietal labels at almost all price levels.[16] There used to be a price barrier, reserving the lower price levels for generic labels, but now varietal wines have penetrated even the low end of the market. Only the cheapest California wines still carry generic names derived from Europe.[17] Generics are a majority only under $5/bottle; by $15/bottle, 90% of wines are varietal-labeled.[18] Proprietary names come back at the highest price levels (more than $50/bottle) due to wines that are made from blends of different high quality varieties (often based on a Bordeaux-like mixture of Cabernet Sauvignon and Merlot).

From Scuppernong to Varietals

Wine production in the United States started with the failure to grow imported European vines on the East Coast. No one knew at the time that the reason was the ubiquitous presence of phylloxera, which simply ate the roots of the grapevines. The problem with making wine from the native grape varieties (such as Vitis labrusca) was their idiosyncratic taste, a smell and flavor often described as "foxy," which is due to the presence of the compound methylanthranilate in the grapes.

Nonetheless, the Concord grape, a cultivar of Vitis labrusca developed in 1853, is the most widely cultivated grape in the United States outside of California.[20] It is used to make juice, grape jelly, wine, and also as a table grape. Plantings have been declining, but Concord still occupies almost two thirds of the vineyards in New York State.[21] (Vitis vinifera is just over 10%.) In the south, a cultivar of Vitis rotundifolia[22] called Scuppernong was used to produce the most popular wine in the country before Prohibition.[23] The early introduction of Vitis vinifera from Europe was not entirely in vain, because some chance hybrids (formed between vinifera and the native species) made wine that was at least reasonably palatable. One such hybrid was Catawba (produced by a cross between vinifera and labrusca), which was widely used during the nineteenth century to produce wine on the East coast.[24]

I admit to the prejudice that wine is made from Vitis vinifera, and this book scarcely touches on wine made from other sources. The story of the native grapes is mentioned for two reasons. First, a considerable amount of table wine was produced from sources other than Vitis vinifera in the United States;[25] no distinction is made in the official records, so it is necessary to be aware that statistics on the growth of the domestic wine industry are colored by the inclusion of these wines. Second, given the considerable economic importance of these wines in the early period, many of the regulations concerning wine production allow for their peculiarities.

The grapes of native vines do not accumulate high enough sugar levels to give good wine, and they have far too much acidity. As a result, it is legal to adjust the juice by adding both sugar (to increase production of alcohol during fermentation or to sweeten the wine afterwards) and water (to reduce the acidity). In fact, dilution of 35% is permitted for wine made from non-vinifera species. This is euphemistically (not to say misleadingly) described as "amelioration."[26] Furthermore, making the wines sweet and fortifying them with brandy is a good way to hide their characteristic aroma. They were also often blended with more neutral wine from California to hide their offensive qualities. (The State made it illegal in 1887 to add sugar to wine in California, but addition of water is still possible, although the limit is 7%.)

The first Vitis vinifera vines were brought into California from the south. Previously imported into South America by Spanish missionaries, Vitis vinifera reached California with Franciscan monks in the eighteenth century. The vines were a single variety, named for its origins as "Mission." Although no doubt better than the wine made from native or hybrid varieties, quality was poor, since the Mission grape is a rather characterless black variety. It is still grown in South America, where it is known as País in Chile and Criolla Chica in Argentina.[27]

Wine production from imported European vines started in California in the 1860s. A Hungarian entrepreneur of slightly uncertain origins, Agoston Haraszthy, who owned the Buena Vista vineyard in Sonoma, is officially designated as the "Father of California Viticulture." With a commission from the state of California, he visited European vineyards in 1860, and the following year reported on the prospects for improving viticulture. With practical effect, he

Development of wine production in the United States	
1700s	European vines fail to grow in on the East Coast
1860	Wine production from European vines starts in California
1920-1933	Prohibition suspends wine production
1960s	Napa Valley becomes known for quality wine production

imported a wide range of grapevine varieties and offered them for sale; his catalog claimed 492 varieties.[28] It is not clear how much impact Haraszthy actually had on plantings. Arpad Haraszthy claimed that his father had introduced Zinfandel (which would certainly have been his longest-lived legacy), but it is doubtful whether this is true.[29]

At all events, by the end of the century two significant changes had occurred. Zinfandel had largely replaced Mission. And phylloxera had arrived, making it impossible to grow Vitis vinifera in California on anything other than rootstocks of native varieties.[30] The industry continued to develop for the first two decades of the twentieth century until it was stopped in its tracks by Prohibition.

The Long Shadow of Prohibition

Far from being a "noble experiment," Prohibition was an entirely ignoble expression of intolerance that increased societal problems by pushing alcohol consumption into illegality. Its effects were devastating. It distorted the industry by eliminating quality wine production; it took almost half a century to recover. Wine appreciation in the United States was retarded for the same period. Prohibition's effects are still with us in a panoply of regulations whose only purpose is to enrich entrenched interests at the expense of the consumer; the main beneficiaries are the distributors, the inheritors of the mantle of the bootleggers.

When the idiocy of Prohibition was introduced in 1920, California had 40,000 hectares of vineyards and was producing the equivalent of about 20 million cases of wine annually.[31] The most common plantings were Zinfandel, Carignan, Mourvèdre, Grenache, and Durif (Petite Syrah).[32] Production of dry table wine was a bit greater than production of fortified (sweet) wine.[33] A breakdown of production soon after the turn of the century shows "Claret" as representing by far the greatest named type of wine (more than half); Zinfandel accounts for another third.[34] White wine, in the form of "Riesling" was less than 10%.

Prohibition significantly affected the patterns of production and consumption, but both increased rather than declined. It remained legal to produce wine for sacramental and medical purposes; and in fact wineries were allowed to continue to produce wine (although they could not sell it unless it satisfied one of the exemptions) because the vines continued to produce crops.[35] For the most part, however, the industry turned to producing grapes rather than making wine.[36] The grapes could be sold by virtue of an exemption in the law that allowed home production of grape juice (it was not supposed to be fermented). Each household could produce 200 gallons (roughly 1000 bottles) annually for personal consumption. This had two consequences.

People enthusiastically set about making wine from grapes shipped from California, but fine wine grapes did not transport well. This created a demand for growing thick-skinned grapes (especially Alicante, which also gave good color) that resisted damage en route.[37] Carloads of grapes were sent east by train, mostly to major distribution centers in Chicago. Grapes were also turned into

A police raid in New York at the start of Prohibition in 1920.

dried bricks of grape juice concentrate (sometimes known as "bricks of Bacchus"), which were sold with a boldface warning label "Caution: Do Not Add
Yeast or Will Ferment and Turn into Wine" detailing precisely what abuse was
necessary to cause this terrible outcome.[38]

And people became used to the somewhat rougher quality of the wine (not to
mention the fact that a proportion made by bootleggers was toxic, because the
government had poisoned industrial alcohol with methanol in a futile attempt to
prevent it being diverted for consumption).[39] When Prohibition ended, there was
far more demand for sweet wine. California adjusted to the new market, in
which fortified wines outsold dry wines by three to one.[40] It was to take 40 years
to reverse the trend.[41] (The industry persuaded the government to use "dessert
wine" as a description instead of "fortified wine," to avoid the implication that
something abnormal had been added.[42]) A huge proportion of this wine was sold
as an alternative to spirits at the very low end, and became known as the "Skid
Row Trade."[43]

In a striking demonstration of the counter productive nature of legislating to
control private social behavior, changing patterns of consumption saw wine
increase significantly at the expense of beer during Prohibition.[44] Wine production followed suit.[45] During the first five years of Prohibition, annual home wine
production totaled twice the amount of commercial production before Prohibition![46] The habit continued for several years: by the late 1930s, 30% of national

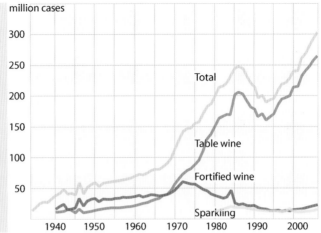

Table wine consumption has increased in the U.S.A. since the 1930s, but fortified wine consumption has decreased.[52]

consumption was still produced at home.[47] In California, there was a planting boom during the first few years of Prohibition, when the area of vineyards doubled, although they were increasingly given over to inferior varieties.[48] But by the end of Prohibition in 1933, the boom had bust, and many vineyards were in a sorry state.

Wine consumption continued to increase steadily after the repeal of Prohibition. Wine was shipped from California to bottlers all over the United States.[49] A boom resulted from the lack of availability of European wine during the second world war, when transport difficulties forced a transition to bottling at source.[50] But it was not until 1967 that sales of (dry) table wine passed those of fortified wines.[51] From the 1970s, the market became more mature, dominated by dry red and white wine.

AVAs: Variable Appellations

The Repeal of Prohibition gave individual states the rights to control production and distribution of alcohol. This created a Byzantine mess of regulation that has plagued wine production and consumption in the United States to this day. One odd legacy was the assignment of alcohol regulation to the BATF (Bureau of Alcohol, Tobacco, and Firearms). Perhaps that explains why it is easier to purchase a gun than wine in much of the United States. In 2003, these functions were separated, and regulation of wine became part of the TTB (Alcohol and Tobacco Tax and Trade Bureau).[53]

When the first regulations were introduced following Repeal, varietal labeling had not yet become important. All the same, any commonsense view would assume that a wine carrying the name of a variety should consist basically of that variety. But when federal regulations were established in 1936, a wine required only 51% of a variety in order to be labeled with its name. This was increased (against some opposition) to 75% in 1983,[54] still a lax regulation; you would certainly be surprised if you bought orange juice and discovered that 25% of it was grapefruit juice. Little attention was paid to geographical origins at the time, but the rules allowed names (such as those of counties or towns) to be used, subject to the same 51% rule.[55]

Geographical descriptions for American wine were introduced as the result of an overhaul of regulations initiated by the BATF in 1976, reflecting increased American interest in wine.[56] An AVA (American Viticultural Area) is supposed to describe a region with historically recognized boundaries and distinctive geographical features. But the process is far from objective. The BATF did not set out to divide up winegrowing regions into some logical framework. Establishing an AVA requires an initiative from the growers or other local interests. The BATF (and now the TTB) considers petitions requesting the definition of specific AVAs. The petitions can be contested, and sometimes the process becomes contentious. The AVA describes only the geographical area; it does not specify varietals, yields, or any other details of viticulture or vinification as is common in Europe. In fact, the regulations do not require that wine actually is produced there for a region to be described as an AVA. The AVA is America's closest equivalent to the Appellation Contrôlée of France, but while it is certainly an appellation, it is not very contrôlée! It is basically a marketing device.

Almost 200 AVAs have been created since the first one in 1980.[57] And no, the first wasn't Napa Valley (which became the second AVA in 1981) but Augusta, in Missouri. This makes the point that AVAs are nationwide, although more than 100 are in California, and another 25 in Oregon and Washington. The AVA system has the same sort of organization of Russian dolls found in European appellations. Wine labeled "California" can come from grapes grown anywhere in the state. "North Coast" includes Napa, Sonoma, Mendocino, Lake, Marin, and Solano. Napa County is not an AVA but can be used to describe wine from anywhere within the political unit. And within the famous AVA of Napa Valley are several smaller appellations.

AVAs vary enormously in size. Some are so large as to be completely meaningless. Virtually all the wine produced in Washington State is entitled to the Columbia Valley AVA, which brings the concept to the point of absurdity. Sonoma Coast covers a region of 205,000 hectares (although there are only about 2,800 ha of planted vineyards).[58] Napa Valley is large with 18,000 planted hectares (about 9% of the total area of the valley).[59] The Oakville or Rutherford AVAs within Napa are only 2,700 ha each. But many AVAs are the results of compromises to satisfy vested interests, and only a few have any real homogeneity of terroir. There's a huge range of variation between the north and south ends of Napa Valley, for example, but the AVA does not distinguish between them. Basically the boundaries were drawn to include all vineyards regarding themselves as producing Napa Valley grapes.[60]

For a wine to carry the name of an AVA, 85% of the grapes must come from within it. That's still not really good enough: if you are paying a premium for Napa Valley Cabernet, you do not expect 15% of the grapes to come from the bulk wine production region of the Central Valley. For a political unit, such as Napa County, only 75% of the grapes must have the named origin.

And as for vintage, the rules have finally been tightened to specify that wine from an AVA must have 95% of its grapes from the stated vintage, although the rules were adjusted in 2006 to reduce the proportion to 85% for wines from state or county designations. (Napa Valley therefore requires 95% but Napa County requires only 85%.) So take a worst case scenario of a bottle labeled as Napa County Cabernet Sauvignon. If it contains 75% of Cabernet Sauvignon, 75% of grapes from Napa County, and 85% of grapes from the stated vintage, actually only just under half (48%) of the wine will be exactly what the label states.

Perhaps because the system is so inconsistent and poorly designed, the AVA descriptions have scarcely penetrated the consciousness of the American consumer; one or two AVAs, such as Napa Valley, are well known, but the rest fade into obscurity. It's even been claimed that that many consumers think Mondavi (the well known producer in Napa) is an AVA.[61]

But there have been even worse onslaughts on the integrity of the system. Wines without a trace of grapes from Napa Valley have been sold under labels where "Napa" is the most prominent identification. The rules don't allow the name of an AVA to be used on a label unless the grapes come from that AVA (subject to the 85% rule). But there's a grandfather exemption allowing the use of names that existed before the AVA was created. This loophole was exploited by Bronco Wine Company to the point at which you could drive a trailer load of jeroboams through it. (Trading on the name of Napa is not a new problem: there were attempts in the early twentieth century, long before the introduction of the AVA system, to prevent Napa producers from including grapes from the Central Valley in their wines. Oddly enough, they were cheerfully including grapes from Yolo County, to the north, without generating the same level of controversy.[62]) By 1988, probably 50-60% of the wine bottled in Napa was made from grapes imported from outside the valley.[63]

Bronco Wine Company is owned by Fred Franzia and other members of an old California wine dynasty. (The original Franzia brand was sold by the family in 1973 and now has no connection with them.) In 1994, a year after the Rutherford AVA in Napa Valley was established, Bronco purchased two existing trade names, Rutherford Vineyards and Rutherford Vintners. Although those brands had previously produced their wines from Napa grapes, the new owners were able to use grapes from other sources under the grandfather rule. And then in 2000, Bronco spent $42 million to purchase the Napa Ridge brand from Beringer.[64]

Beringer had been producing large quantities of Napa Ridge wine from grapes purchased outside the valley.[65] People weren't happy about this, but following the purchase of Napa Ridge, Fred Franzia announced plans to build a huge bottling plant in southern Napa County, with a capacity of 18 million cases per year. The scale of the enterprise is indicated by the fact that the entire production of Napa Valley is roughly 9 million cases per year. Under existing regulations, Napa Ridge wine bottled at the plant could be labeled "bottled in Napa Valley," irrespective of the origin of the grapes. In fact, most of the grapes came from that Mecca for bulk production, the Central Valley.

*The prominence of Napa
Ridge on the label belies the
fact that the wine actually
comes from the North Coast
of California, not from
Napa.*

Prompted by concern that the reputation of Napa would be tarnished by this vast expansion of wine labeled with its name, California passed a law in 2000 stating that wines with Napa on the label must be made from at least 75% of grapes produced in Napa county. Fred Franzia sued to prevent implementation of the law.[66] Decisions went to and fro over several years, but in 2005 the California Supreme Court ruled in favor of the law.[67] By 2006 it was all over, and if you see Napa on the label, then at least a decent proportion of the wine comes from there. Is this a triumph for the consumer? Well, only partially: 75% is a pretty lax standard. You would be horrified today to be sold a Burgundy in which 25% of the grapes came from the south of France.[68]

What should be done about AVAs? Granted that the AVA is intended to describe only geographical origin, surely for it to mean anything, it should be an imprimatur indicating an area of some consistent quality. I suggest this means that the larger AVAs should be abolished. There's nothing wrong with putting Napa County or Sonoma County, or some similar term on a label to indicate the origins of a (relatively) generic wine, but it should not be an AVA. The term should be reserved for relatively small areas where there is some coherence of terroir and wine style, and it should be strictly limited to wines made *exclusively* from grapes of that area. Vintage should also be 100%. The label should mean exactly what it says: so let's stop trying to fool the consumer.

1000 Miles of Vines

Wine is produced all along the western seaboard of the United States, a stretch of roughly one thousand miles from north to south. This is about the same distance as the most extended range in any European country, from the northern wine-producing regions of Italy to its southernmost regions. But the range of styles is more consistent in the western United States. Much of the quality production focuses on the classic grape varieties of Bordeaux and Burgundy, although they are not organized on a north-south axis comparable to European viticulture. Temperature is influenced more by proximity to the cooling effects of the Humboldt current in the Pacific Ocean than by the latitude. Any attempt to relate the varieties grown along the north-south axis parallel with the Pacific with those

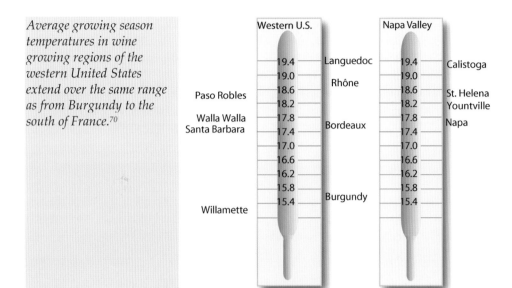

Average growing season temperatures in wine growing regions of the western United States extend over the same range as from Burgundy to the south of France.[70]

grown on a north-south axis in France or Italy is confounded by microclimates: the results have to be judged on their own merits.

A line of latitude running from Bordeaux, where Cabernet Sauvignon triumphs, would pass through Oregon, where the focus is on Pinot Noir, the great grape of Burgundy (which is on a latitude a couple of hundred miles to the north of Bordeaux). Willamette Valley, the best known locale in Oregon, has an average growing season temperature slightly below Burgundy. Yet Oregon is sandwiched between Washington State to its north, and California to its south, both of whose quality red wine production focuses on Cabernet Sauvignon. Parts of Washington's Columbia Valley, such as Walla Walla, have temperatures similar to Bordeaux. Napa Valley, the best known locale for Cabernet production, ranges in temperature from just above Bordeaux to much warmer. So Cabernet Sauvignon dominates over a range of several hundred miles from Washington State to northern California. No comparable geographical separation is found in Europe without significant changes in the cultivated varieties.

Four states account for almost all production of wine from Vitis vinifera in the United States.[69]

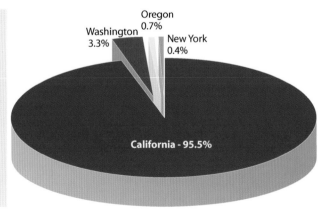

Only in the southern part of California does quality wine turn to the varieties associated with the south in Europe, most notably in the Rhône-like blends of Paso Robles. Farther south in Santa Barbara, cooler temperatures place us back in a microclimate that attempts to produce Pinot Noir. All the way up the west coast, Chardonnay is the variety of choice for quality white wine, although a focus on Riesling has developed in Washington State. The one unique American variety, Zinfandel, is grown all over California, although under the name of Primitivo it is grown in the far south of Italy.

The major wine-producing regions extend over 1000 miles of Washington, Oregon, and California.

Major AVAs are outlined in orange. The most common varietals for each state are shown in the boxes.

Washington
Riesling
Chardonnay

Oregon
Pinot Noir
Pinot Gris

California
Zinfandel
Cabernet Sauvignon
Merlot
Chardonnay

100 km

100 miles

California is usually said to account for 90% of wine production in the United States. In reality, this understates its importance, since the official national figures include production from all types of grapevines.[71] If only Vitis vinifera is considered, wine production is pretty much a West Coast phenomenon (with a nod of apology to a handful of producers in New York state).[72] California's production makes it the fourth largest producer of wine in the world, behind the major European countries (France, Italy, Spain).

The Move to Varietals

Prohibition eliminated most fine grape varieties in the United States.[73] At its end, Zinfandel, Alicante, and Carignan were two thirds of plantings in California.[74] White varieties had all but disappeared. The trend towards mass production varieties continued for the next half century. In fact, things were even worse than suggested by the list of varieties, because roughly half of the wine was produced from grapes not even listed as wine grapes.[75, 76] Of course, much of this "wine" was fortified. "Any grape may be utilized for wine or brandy," according to the Growers' Grape Products Association in 1941.[77, 78]

The move to quality started in the 1970s: since then the old blending grapes have to a large degree been replaced by quality varietals. The transition to varietal labeling went hand in hand with the progression from a market dominated by sweet fortified wines to a market of dry table wines.

At the start of the 1970s, bulk production varieties altogether accounted for more than 80% of all production. Cabernet Sauvignon was only 5%. The transition to quality occurred in the last two decades of the century. By the twenty-first century, Cabernet Sauvignon was almost a quarter of production, with almost equal quantities of Merlot and Zinfandel (although much of the Zinfandel is used to produce white Zinfandel, basically a rosé of low quality). Pinot Noir has stayed steady around the 5% level, but Syrah shows a striking increase since the mid 1990s. Today, named varieties account altogether for 70% of production.

The concentration in white varieties is even more striking. In the 1970s, Colombard (not a variety usually associated with quality) was the major variety with 40% of plantings, but by 2002 there was more Chardonnay than any other white variety.

Total production has increased about three fold since the 1970s; about a third of this is due to increase in yields, and about two thirds to increased plantings. And the price gap between different regions in California has steadily widened. In the 1960s, grapes from Napa began to be worth more than those from the Central Valley;[79] today the difference is more than ten-fold.[80]

Production in all three wine-producing western states has increased dramatically in the past two decades, although production in Washington and Oregon is tiny compared to California. Production in California goes back more than a century, but production of Vitis vinifera in Washington and Oregon dates only from the 1970s.

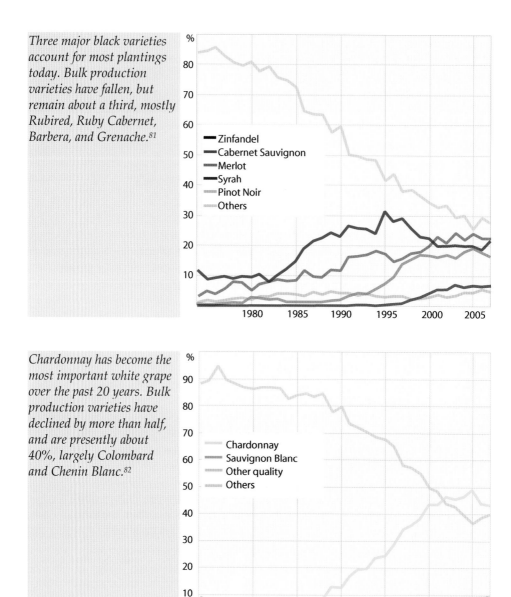

Three major black varieties account for most plantings today. Bulk production varieties have fallen, but remain about a third, mostly Rubired, Ruby Cabernet, Barbera, and Grenache.[81]

Chardonnay has become the most important white grape over the past 20 years. Bulk production varieties have declined by more than half, and are presently about 40%, largely Colombard and Chenin Blanc.[82]

Wine production in Washington was held back by the attitude of the authorities. After Repeal, wine produced in the state had a protected market.[83] Until this was abolished in 1969, Concord grapes (and worse) dominated the state industry.[84] A merger between two producers of fruit wines formed the American Wine Growers in 1954, which was the predecessor to Chateau St. Michelle, the oldest winery in the state, but serious production of wines from Vitis vinifera did not start until a decade later.[85] By 1970, all but three of the existing wineries closed; and plantings of Vitis vinifera began. Today production focuses on quality

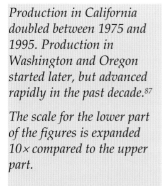

Production in California doubled between 1975 and 1995. Production in Washington and Oregon started later, but advanced rapidly in the past decade.[87]

The scale for the lower part of the figures is expanded 10× compared to the upper part.

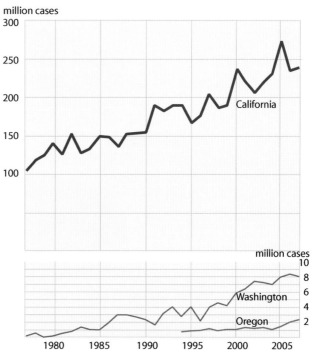

varietals. Concord is still grown, but not for wine production. Although the number of wineries has increased dramatically, from 80 in 1996 to more than 500 today, the industry is actually very concentrated, with more than half of all production coming from wineries owned by the Stimson Lane company (the owners of Chateau St. Michelle).[86]

Oregon's production also started with fruit wines, but it was not competitive, and was largely defunct by the 1960s. The first vinifera vines were planted in 1961, and by the end of the decade wineries were becoming established in Willamette Valley.[88] By 1980 there were 34 bonded wineries in the state, and steady increase has brought this to more than 250 today.[89]

California: the Land of Plenty

California wines are two thirds of all wines sold today in the United States.[90] This represents a drop from the peak of 90%.[91] However, the decline has been partly compensated by a continuing move towards premium wine production. The increased diversity of sources and the up-market trend reflect the increasing interest in wine, which is making the United States the world's largest market.

The wine trade draws a distinction, not entirely well defined, between inexpensive jug wine and "premium" wine. At one time, the distinction was semi-facetiously defined as "premium wine comes in a bottle with a cork." That no longer stands up, of course, due to the increased quality of wines bottled under screwcap, and for that matter in other formats. When California producers who

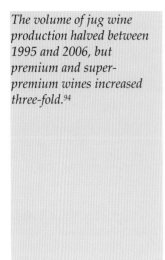

The volume of jug wine production halved between 1995 and 2006, but premium and super-premium wines increased three-fold.[94]

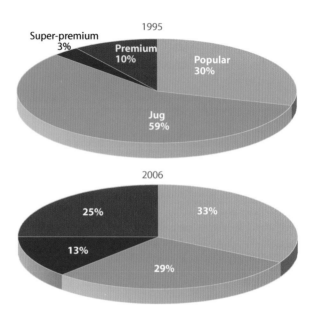

considered themselves to be making quality wine got together in 1955 to form an association called the Premium Wine Producers of California, they had a hard time agreeing on a definition, but finally came up with price as the criterion: premium wine was sold at more than $1 per bottle.[92] Only 2-5% of California wine was thought to qualify.[93]

The cut-off point between "popular" wine and "premium wine" is particularly hard to define. There's the same tendency in the wine industry to grade inflation that's found in the schools; it's fair enough to divide wine into the ascending qualities of jug, popular, premium, and super-premium, but perhaps less reasonable to rename the second class as "popular premium" starting at $3 per bottle. A reasonable division would have jug wines at under $3 (the name reflecting the fact that usually they are sold in larger containers), popular wines at under $7, and premium from there up to $14. Above that everything is lumped into super-premium; some people add a class of "cult wines" for anything over $50 or so.

No matter what the names, the main point is that California wine production has made a transition from being driven by the bottom end of the market to focusing on more expensive wines. Part of the reason for the change is the increasing difficulty in competing on price at the lower cost end of the market with imports, especially from Australia and South America. The volume of production of jug wines in California fell by about half in the decade following 1996. In economic terms, premium and super-premium wines now account for roughly two third of revenues compared with one third a decade ago.[95]

California has a wide range of climates and terroirs. Wine is made in the coastal portion of the state from Mendocino county in the north down to San Diego County on the border with Mexico. In the center of the state lies the Central Valley, a rich agricultural area. This area between the coastal foothills and the Sierra Nevada mountains really comprises two river valleys: the Sacramento valley to the north and the San Joaquin valley to the south. Grapevines are widely grown all over San Joaquin valley because the fertile soils produce large yields, giving grapes that are used for cheap wines. This accounts for more than half of all California's production. To the north of San Francisco, Napa and Sonoma valleys are the best known quality wine regions, emphasizing reds of Bordeaux varietals and whites of Chardonnay. Quality wine production in the south is more recent, with Paso Robles now producing Rhône-like blends, and the Santa Ynez and Santa Maria Valleys of Santa Barbara split between Burgundian varieties in the cooler western part and Rhône varietals in the warmer eastern half.

Geography has a large role in the division between wine classes. The bulk of lower end wine comes from San Joaquin Valley. Running north to south for 200 miles, wine is made from just south of Sacramento all the way down to Bakersfield (just northeast of Los Angeles). The main difference between the San Joaquin Valley and premium regions, such as Napa, is more in yields than in the varieties planted. Chardonnay is more than two thirds of plantings in both the San Joaquin valley and the Napa Valley; although in black varietals, Zinfandel is the major variety (43%) of the San Joaquin valley, whereas Cabernet Sauvignon is the major variety of Napa (52%).[96] The difference in the yields is large: San Joaquin gets almost three times the yield obtained in Napa.[97]

The average yield for California varies with vintage, of course, but has risen steadily from around 50 hl/ha in the 1930s after the end of Prohibition to a current value around 110 hl/ha.[99] The increase has been mostly in the lower quality areas; while Napa, for example, has had yields around 60 hl/ha since 1990, San Joaquin has doubled over the same period from 80 hl/ha to an average 160 hl/ha.[100]

The traditional criticism of California wine has been to consider it somewhat clumsy: "Every critic of California wines before the 1880s hit upon their earthiness, heaviness, harshness, their heavy alcohol content, and their low acidity."[101] The basic reason was that winemakers were following the European model for cooler climates, where grapes were harvested as late as possible to obtain decent

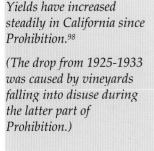

Yields have increased steadily in California since Prohibition.[98]

(The drop from 1925-1933 was caused by vineyards falling into disuse during the latter part of Prohibition.)

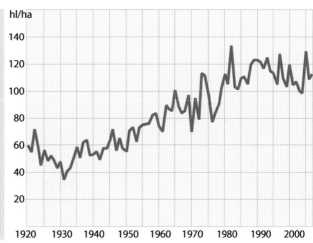

Wine is produced all along the western half of California to the north of Los Angeles. The San Joaquin Valley produces only bulk wine. Quality areas are found in the north (Napa and Sonoma) and in the south (Paso Robles and Santa Barbara).[102]

alcohol levels. In California, this produced high alcohol and low acidity. This continued for at least a century. Part of the reason for Napa Valley's early prominence was that its wines showed less susceptibility to these perceived failings. Yet as recently as the 1970s, Robert Parker complained in the Wine Advocate that the best California Cabernets were "massive, powerful, assertive wines often bordering on coarseness." Parker went on to comment that the California Cabernets did not age well beyond a few years, compared with the much greater longevity of Bordeaux.

The current style of Napa is relatively recent. When Napa grape grower Andy Beckstoffer says that phylloxera was the point at which everything changed in Napa, you do a double take and think that surely he's not going back to 1880 as the turning point. But of course he means the more recent problem, when most of the vineyards had to be replanted between 1989 and 1996 because the predominant AxR1 rootstock succumbed to phylloxera. Beckstoffer dates the switch to harvesting grapes at increased ripeness and making wine in Napa's current lush style from this period. The replanting gave an opportunity to experiment with rootstocks and varieties; planting clones that developed physiological ripeness later, combined with the late harvesting trend, saw levels of alcohol and extraction increase significantly.

"Wine making changes every 5-10 years. If you asked winemakers in 1995 whether they would still like to make the same wine they made in 1985, the answer would be no. The last big issue was ripeness and alcohol, but that is now solved. 15 is the new 13," says Scott MacLeod, winemaker at Napa's Rubicon

Estate. By moving to later harvesting, "I'm capturing more of what the vintage is," he told me.[103] California wines today are probably somewhere in the mid-range of New World wines with regards to alcohol and acidity levels—lower alcohol and higher acidity than their Australian rivals, perhaps, but more powerful than those of South America. Although alcohol levels in European wines have increased steadily, they have stayed behind those of California, but the distinction between Europe and California has much diminished in the past twenty years.

Napa: the Cabernet Locomotive

Napa Valley is by far America's best known wine-producing region. About 30 miles long and generally less than a mile wide, nestled between the Mayacamas mountains to the west and the Vaca mountains to the east, it has less than 10% of California's vineyards and accounts for under 5% of all production,[104] but it has set the standard for quality wine production for more than a century. Yet although its name is a clear imprimatur on a bottle, the valley is actually far from homogeneous in terroir and climate. Its growing temperatures increase by more than one day degree zone from south to north.

The collision between the three tectonic plates that created the valley some 150 million years ago left detritus of a great variety of soil types. Climate is subject to a variety of local effects, so the Valley escapes the European rule that things get steadily warmer going south; the northern end is decidedly warmer than the southern end. The reason is that the more open southern end gets cooling breezes from San Pablo bay, whereas the northern end is effectively closed. Napa itself, at the very southern end, is close in temperature to Bordeaux; but Calistoga at the far north is more like the south of France. Moving from south to

The narrowness of Napa Valley means that the mountains are evident even from vineyards on the valley floor. This view looks northwest.

north, the soil changes from sediments deposited by past oceans to more volcanic terrain. A major factor, of course, is the consistent difference between the warmer, and more fertile, valley floor, and the cooler terroir of the slopes to the west and the east. The east is drier than the west, because rainfall gets blocked by the Mayacamas Mountains separating Napa Valley from Sonoma. Because a high pressure system usually settles over the California coast each summer, the growing season is usually warm and dry. Fog is not usually a welcome component of the climate for grape growing, but it's different in Napa. Fog rolls in from the Pacific regularly each morning and clears later in the day; this is an important factor in moderating the daily temperature. There is also an important difference for those vineyards located high enough on the slopes to be above the fog line.

Recognizing politics more than terroir, the Napa Valley AVA was defined on an inclusive basis, extending to most of the vineyards in Napa County. Wild Horse Valley, Atlas Peak, and Chiles Valley are distinct from the valley itself. Within the valley, the heart of the AVA is at Rutherford and Oakville, which have the terroir known as the Rutherford Bench, although its boundaries are not well defined. (The Rutherford Bench is a gravelly terroir deposited on an alluvial fan by the Napa river.[106] References to "Rutherford dust" refer to a supposed dusty note in the wines reflecting the terroir, and the local association of producers calls itself Rutherford Dust.[107])

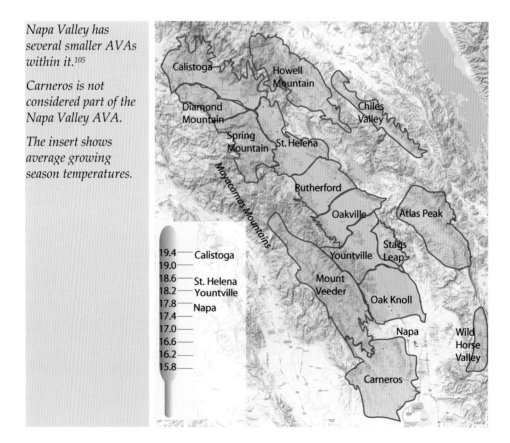

Napa Valley has several smaller AVAs within it.[105]

Carneros is not considered part of the Napa Valley AVA.

The insert shows average growing season temperatures.

The terrain is fairly different on the mountains, notably Mount Veeder on the western side and Howell Mountain on the eastern side; and, of course, temperatures decline with elevation. The large number of sub-appellations led to concern that Napa's image might be diluted, and in 1990, at the urging of the Napa Valley vintners, California passed a law stating that all wines attributed to any AVA within Napa should in addition mention Napa Valley.[108]

Napa was not the first of the fine wine regions to be planted in California. Vitis vinifera vines probably reached northern California in 1817, and in 1823 the Sonoma Mission was established, where there was a working vineyard within a year.[109] The Mission system gave way to secularization, and around 1838 George Yount established what was to become the first vineyard in the area now occupied by the town of Yountville in Napa Valley.[110] At this point, California was still Mexican; the town of Napa was founded in 1848 after California became part of the United States. At the end of the 1850s, Napa was still only a minor wine-producing area, with roughly a third of the vineyard area of Sonoma; plantations in the vicinity of Los Angeles to the south were far more important.[111]

The first of many planting booms started in 1880; vineyards increased from under 1500 ha to almost 5,000 ha by 1882.[112] By 1891, Napa was close to parity with Sonoma. Then phylloxera wrought the same devastation as in France; combined with an economic depression, it reduced vineyard areas to a low of around 800 ha in 1897.[113] In the last part of the nineteenth century, Napa was making progress toward quality, with Zinfandel as the major variety (roughly a third of plantings), and assorted Bordeaux varieties making another 5%. Prohibition caused the same havoc here as elsewhere; after Repeal, Petite Sirah and Alicante were two thirds of plantings.[114] Quality production was confined to a

The Sonoma Mission was established in 1823. This view shows it about 1900, before it collapsed and was restored. The surrounding vineyard had about a thousand vines.

handful of exceptional producers.[115] At the end of the 1930s, quality varietals still accounted for less than a third of total production.[116] However, Napa largely produced dry table wines, selling at higher than average prices, making it something of a quality leader relative to a national market dominated by fortified sweet wines.[117]

Shortages of European imports during the second world war led to increased national interest in quality wines from California, with particular emphasis on Napa. This was the beginning of the move to varietal labeling. By the late 1940s, Inglenook was the leader, with its entire production labeled by varietal; no other producer came close, but Louis Martini had a substantial proportion, and Beaulieu and Beringer had small amounts.[118] The increase in varietal labeling was slow but steady, and by 1971 varietal-labeled wines were probably about 30% of premium production.[119] Today, quality varieties account for almost the whole crop in Napa Valley.[120]

The move to quality is even more striking than in California as a whole. The focus has wavered as to red versus white wine; in 1961, Napa Valley was two-thirds red, then an emphasis on white wine led to a brief period in the early 1980s when whites were in the majority,[123] but now Napa is firmly red territory again, with three quarters black grapes. The context for these changes was a dramatic planting boom between 1968 and 1974 (in 1973, half of the planted vines were so young that they were not yet producing wine[124]), followed by quiescence for the rest of the decade, before things took off again in the 1980s.

In 1961, almost the only quality grapes in Napa were small parcels of Caber-

Napa Valley become almost exclusively devoted to high quality varieties during the 1980s.[121, 122]

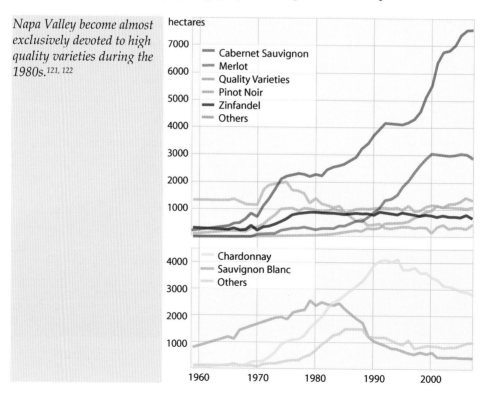

The striking architecture of the Mondavi winery set the standard for developments in Napa Valley. Photograph kindly provided by Robert Mondavi.

net Sauvignon, a meager 150 ha in all. There was also a little Zinfandel, although Zinfandel has never been really important in Napa. There was virtually nothing in the way of quality white production. Cabernet Sauvignon became the most planted black variety during the planting boom of 1968-1974, and Chardonnay became important in the whites. The increase in Cabernet Sauvignon still seems exponential; but Chardonnay seemed the same way until it leveled off.

Some date the modern era in Napa from 1966, when Robert Mondavi opened his winery, the first new winery to be built in Napa since Prohibition.[125] Today, Bordeaux varieties account for 80% of black plantings, and Chardonnay accounts for almost 70% of white plantings. Quality varieties account for most of the remaining 20% of black plantings (sometimes planted experimentally in small amounts); and Sauvignon Blanc is the second most important white variety.

The Grapes of Wrath

Conflict is endemic in wine-producing regions. There may be profound differences of view as to whether the future of a region lies in quality or quantity. Growers and producers may have very different interests, and large producers may react differently from small producers. The needs of wine production may conflict with those of neighboring towns. The arguments in Napa have been especially stormy, with particularly extreme results.

It's been a battle to keep Napa Valley as an area devoted to wine production. Like any area within commuting distance of a major city, land value prices are higher for subdividing the area into cookie-cutter plots for housing than to maintain it for agricultural use. This has led to fierce fights about the future of the valley, including limitations on planting new vineyards, and culminating in restrictions on subdivision for housing purposes.[126] The agricultural preserve, created in 1967, prevented subdivision into lots smaller than 20 acres, essentially preventing vineyards from being sold off for housing developments. Of course, there is an example in the immediate vicinity of the loss of a prime wine-growing area. South of San Francisco, extending from San Jose, Santa Clara Valley was one of the first areas of California to be planted for wine production; relatively

Aerial views of vineyards of Napa Valley (left) show little change since 1940, but views of Santa Clara (right) show that vineyards have been entirely replaced by houses. Photographs kindly provided by Napa Valley Vintners Association.

important in the nineteenth century, it moved towards premium wine production after the repeal of Prohibition, but by the late 1950s, wineries were abandoning production. Today it has been turned into Silicon Valley.[127]

Wineries by no means necessarily own their own vineyards. Ownership in Napa is divided between wineries and growers. The wineries claim to own roughly two thirds of the vineyards,[128] but the true number is probably nearer one half.[129] At all events, it is clear that growers represent a substantial interest. However, wineries often lease vineyards or have other long-term relationships to ensure a consistent supply of grapes. It is not uncommon for wineries to both own land and purchase grapes. But a significant part of the harvest goes into a free market for grapes.

The conflict between growers and producers has been exacerbated by the move towards later harvests to obtain riper grapes. When growers are paid for the weight of the berries, longer hang times generally mean less weight, because the berries become dehydrated. "What do you get for the last twenty days on the vine? The growers say they've lost 20% of the weight, the wineries say they are getting better grapes; the growers say, so you win and I lose," comments Scott MacLeod, winemaker at Rubicon Estate.[130] Andy Beckstoffer, the largest individual grower in Napa Valley, has an answer: he links the price of his grapes to the price of the wine made from them. "The switch to pricing by quality instead of as a commodity puts growers and producers on the same page, as opposed to the tradition that growers want to over-produce and vintners want to underpay," he told me.[131] The model is not widely followed, however, and there still tends to be a "them and us" attitude between growers and producers.

As a premier wine-producing region, Napa has the usual fatal attraction for large corporations. Much of the history has been unhappy, with venerable old wineries ruined by corporate greed after a takeover. The move started when four of the major American distillers bought wine producers during the second world war; they actually controlled about 25% of production in California before they withdrew in the 1950s.[132] There was another flurry of activity from large American companies in the 1970s, and in the 1980s international interest was spearheaded by sparkling wine producers from France and Spain who established wineries in Napa and Sonoma, led by Moët and Chandon.[133]

The history of the old Inglenook winery in the Rutherford region reflects in microcosm many of the twists and turns of winemaking in Napa Valley. Some people regard it as the birthplace of fine wine, or at least of fine wine based on Cabernet Sauvignon, in Napa. Finnish sea captain Gustave Niebaum, who made a fortune trading furs in Alaska, decided after a visit to France that the gravelly loam soils of Rutherford resembled Bordeaux and might reward attempts to produce the same blend of wine. He planted Cabernet Sauvignon, together with Cabernet Franc and Merlot.[134] About twenty years later, Georges de Latour came to the same conclusion and planted Beaulieu's first vineyard, later to be used for the famous Private Reserve wine, on an adjacent plot.

Niebaum was well ahead of his time, planting vines at a density of 10,000 per hectare, sorting grapes when they arrived at the winery, using gravity flow to ensure minimal disturbance of the wine, and generally running his vineyard

The Inglenook winery is a gothic structure in appearance, but was constructed by techniques well ahead of its time, using concrete poured on to steel cables to give the flexibility to withstand earthquakes. Today it is the headquarters of Rubicon Estate, owned by Francis Ford Coppola, and although the exterior has not changed at all, the interior does somewhat now resemble the Hollywood view of a winery.

along the lines of top vineyards today. A splendid Gothic mansion was constructed to house winemaking and to be the headquarters of the business.

The Inglenook winery was as much a passion as a business, making a profit for only one year in its existence,[135] and subsequently fell on hard times. It survived Prohibition without making any wine. In the post Prohibition years, Inglenook made some splendid Cabernet Sauvignons; rare bottles are still eagerly sought by collectors. But the winery was sold to United Vintners in 1964, and then became part of Heublein when United Vintners was itself sold in 1969. Quality went out of the window. In 1975, film director Francis Ford Coppola purchased Niebaum's former home together with 49 hectares of surrounding vineyards, and then in 1995 Heublein tired of the business and sold him the Inglenook winery and the rest of the vineyards.[136] The original holdings are now reunited under the name Rubicon Estate. The Inglenook name was sold to Constellation, who sold it to The Wine Group in 2008; now, sadly, it is used for jug wine.

Today, ten international conglomerates own roughly a quarter of the vineyards. Another 13 individuals or corporations each own more than 200 hectares (500 acres) of vineyards. Altogether then, fewer than 25 individuals or corporations own half the vineyards.[137] The other half is distributed among several hundred owners. The average size of a vineyard holding is hard to determine, but is fairly sizeable, probably on the order of 35 ha with a production around 150,000 bottles per year (a bit less than the average size of a classified growth in

Roughly a quarter of Napa's vineyards are held by large corporations, mostly international conglomerates.

The figure shows the original country of origin. Single owners include both individuals and corporations.[139]

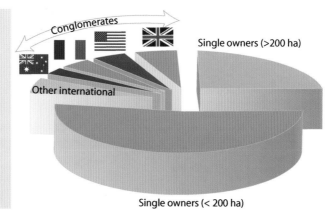

Conglomerates

Single owners (>200 ha)

Other international

Single owners (< 200 ha)

Bordeaux[138]). This average disguises a wide range from very large corporate owners to small family wineries.

Where does the future of Napa Valley lie—with large scale production of value wines or with boutique production of cult wines? "Making the distinction between artisanal wine and commodity is the challenge; as technique drives the process towards a more standardized product, individuality is lost. The focus on everyone producing the same stuff is the mutual assured destruction of terroir," says Rob Sinskey of Robert Sinskey Vineyards.[140] For some time, there have been problems at the lower end of production, where the same range of varieties is produced at lower prices by Australia or South America. And then the financial crisis of 2009 extended the problem to higher priced wines, especially those at the very top. As it became difficult to sell wines above the $100 per bottle level, there were some dramatic price cuts. Among the smaller properties are a fair number of "lifestyle wineries," where rich investors have enjoyed the prestige of owning a Napa Valley winery; with the financial crisis, prestige began to be replaced by the pain of needing to work much harder to sell the wines, and the general disparaging view among other owners is that a shakeout would not entirely be a bad thing.

Nowhere in the United States—indeed, perhaps nowhere in the world—is there the same concentration of cult wines. Cult wines are produced in small quantities, often less than a thousand cases annually, and sold at prices bearing little relationship to the cost of production. Many are not available in general distribution, but sell out to members of a wine club or mailing list. Sometimes it takes several years just to get on the mailing list. The general mark of the cult wines is extreme extraction to give intense flavors. When I met Paige Pahlmeyer at Cult Wine Central to taste the Pahlmeyer wines, she captured the whole phenomenon in a phrase when she explained, "My husband Jayson believes that if a thing is worth doing, it is worth doing to excess."[141] Some feel the trend to increased ripeness and intensity has run its course, and that fashion is turning back to more moderate wines. But I am not so sure that the trend has really reversed. It's still rare to find wines from Napa below 14% alcohol, and if there's any move to moderation, it's certainly not evident yet at the consumer level. "It's popular to bash Napa now on the basis that the wines are too big and brawny,"

Many small producers share a tasting room at the Napa Wine Company in Oakville, indicated by the sign to Cult Wine Central.

says Rob Sinskey, who makes wines in a distinctly more moderate style in the Stag's Leap district of Napa. "We are so caught up in the big Cab that we are missing the potential of the region," he told me. [142]

The nature of the top wines has changed in Napa over recent decades. Twenty, or perhaps thirty, years ago, the tendency was for a producer's top wine to be a "Reserve" bottling—a selection of the very best cuvées. Today there is much more emphasis on single vineyards, with some producers offering multiple bottlings to showcase each vineyard. Could it be that the Californians are coming around to the French view of terroir?

Sonoma: Running Second

"Napa is all about Cabernet Sauvignon and Bordeaux varieties, Sonoma is a jigsaw of varieties and is about diversity," says Mark Lingenfelder of Chalk Hill Winery.[143] Indeed, the Chalk Hill estate shows in microcosm the diversity of terroir in Sonoma, going from warm, south-facing areas that resemble Bordeaux to cool north-facing areas that resemble Alsace on the other side of the same hill. It's much harder to pin down any unifying factor for Sonoma than for Napa, with no single variety or style dominating.

Sonoma County is a relatively large area, extending from the coast to the Mayacamas Mountains separating it from Napa County. Labeled Sonoma County, a wine can come from anywhere in the area. Only a minor step up, Sonoma Coast is a vast coastal area without particularly distinguished terroir, although within although within it are some individual vineyards with good reputations. Coming to the regions of highest quality, it might be more appropriate to talk about Sonoma Valleys in the plural, since in addition to the eponymous Sonoma Valley itself, there are several other valleys, each with its own characteristics. The AVA of Sonoma Valley is to the north of the town of Sonoma, centered on the Sonoma river. The other areas of interest are the valleys formed by rivers that drain into the Sonoma river (a contrast with Napa Valley, where the areas of interest are the mountain slopes on either side of the valley bottom). The best known valleys in Sonoma are the Russian River Valley (for Pinot Noir), Alexander Valley (for Cabernet Sauvignon), and Dry Creek Valley (for Zinfandel).

Closer to the breezes and fogs from the Pacific, Sonoma has cooler climates than Napa, and the average grapes have about 0.25% less alcohol at harvest.[144] Fog is the main climatic element, and may persist well into the day. Black grapes are about two thirds of plantings (less than Napa's three quarters).[145] Total production in Sonoma is about 10 million cases annually, compared with 7 million in Napa.[146] Average grape prices are the second-highest in California, with the inland valleys achieving prices just below those of Napa Valley.

They tell you that Napa Valley is a more commercial environment than Sonoma, and that the whole scale is more artisanal in Sonoma. There are elements of truth to this, but it's a bit misleading. Driving up Napa Valley, at first sight it seems if anything less developed than Sonoma. The major road through the valley is Route 29, a divided highway that narrows to a single lane in each direction half way up the valley at Yountville. On the eastern side of the valley is the Silverado Trail, no longer a trail, but scarcely a thruway. As you drive up to Sonoma from San Francisco, a much broader valley separates the Coastal Range along the Pacific from the Mayacamas Mountains to the west; you feel far less confined than in Napa Valley. The freeway of route 101 drives right through Sonoma Valley, a fast track with the usual depressing industrial developments on either side once you enter the valley above Petaluma. However, when you get off the beaten track, there are numerous small winding roads running through hillside slopes patterned with vineyards in the various component valleys. Several of the valleys come together at Healdsburg, a gentrified town just off the freeway, with a yuppified air of up-market artisan activities.

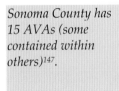

Sonoma County has 15 AVAs (some contained within others)[147].

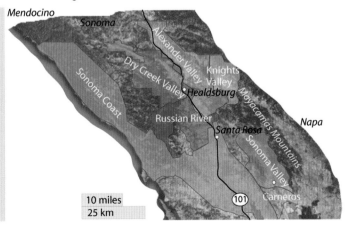

Russian River Valley, running to the south of Healdsburg, is Pinot Noir Central. The style is richer than Burgundy. "We don't make Burgundy and don't try to. We make Russian River Pinot Noir, " says Bob Cabral, winemaker of Williams-Selyem, whose single-vineyard Pinots sell exclusively to a mailing list that isn't easy to join. "Russian River Pinots are deeply textured wines with dark fruits," he says, adding that "we make really ripe wines but we try not to get too ripe."[148] There is also, of course, a good amount of Chardonnay produced in Russian River.

Dry Creek and Alexander Valleys run parallel to the north of Healdsburg. Closer to the coast, Dry Creek is a broad valley, cool at the southern end and warm at the northern end, growing a wide range of varietals from Pinot Noir at the south, to Cabernet in the middle, and Zinfandel in the north. It's by far best known for its Zinfandels, and indeed perhaps this is the one region in California where Zinfandel can be taken seriously as a grape that reflects terroir and produces ageworthy wines.

With that perverse reversal of the usual north-south, cool to warm, relationship, Alexander Valley, the most northern AVA of Sonoma, is where Cabernet Sauvignon does best. The Cabernets lack that extreme lushness found in Napa Valley and can offer a more restrained impression, as indeed also can the Zinfandels, especially those from around Geyserville, which rival those of Dry Creek Valley.

The Gallo Wine Empire

Central Valley is a huge area dominating the central portion of California. From north to south, this flat valley stretches for 500 miles. Ideal for agriculture, it accounts for more than two thirds of crop production in California. The dry southern part, San Joaquin Valley, depends on irrigation, and is a Mecca for agriculture. It is not known for fine wine, but grapes are an important crop, although historically Thompson seedless (used both as a table grape and for wine production) has been the most important grape crop. The recent trend towards premium wine production, however, means that even in San Joaquin Valley, Chardonnay has become the most important white grape (although yields are vastly higher than in other regions to the point of caricature).[149] Zinfandel is most important black grape, but this is deceptive since most of it is used to produce white Zinfandel.[150]

If you drew a map of the American wine industry based on the importance of the producers, Modesto, California would be right at the center. Pretty much at the mid point of the Central Valley, this fertile, hot area is completely undistinguished for fine wine production. Yet from modest beginnings after the repeal of Prohibition, the Gallo winery located here has grown to dominate the American wine industry in a way rarely equaled elsewhere.

Gallo started as a small operation shipping grapes during Prohibition. Joe Gallo (father of Ernest and Julio) bought a vineyard in Modesto, then a railway town, and in 1925 set up a shipping business near the freight yards.[151] Grapes

Modesto, where Gallo has its headquarters, is in the heart of the Central Valley[153].

from their own vineyards plus those of other local growers were shipped to the great yards at Chicago, the major center for grape sales during Prohibition. The move into wine production was almost inadvertent; when the market for grapes crashed in 1929, Gallo constructed underground tanks to store the unsold production as wine.[152]

After their parents' death in 1933, Ernest and Julio Gallo took over the vineyard and (illicit) winery. With about 500 acres (200 ha) of vineyards, they obtained a permit to produce wine and run a winery.[154] By 1935, E & J Gallo Winery was producing the equivalent of 145,000 cases of wine annually.[155] They expanded rapidly, purchasing more land and constructing a new winery, effectively built on assembly-line principles,[156] possibly the first of its type. The winery also had a distillery and produced brandy, sold as such, and also used in the production of fortified wines.

The second world war was a profitable period, with the winery operating under contract to the government. During this period, the Gallos extended their vineyards, including the purchase of a 1000-acre ranch planted with Thompson seedless (used to make raisins), and began the move to vertical integration by purchasing the railroad cars used in shipping.[157]

The basis for their huge expansion after the war was the foresight in signing contracts with other growers for taking their crops at prices slightly higher than the existing market. By the time wartime price controls on wine were lifted, they had rights to 75% of the crop from Napa and Sonoma counties as well as the surrounding areas of the Central Valley.[158] With this level of control, they were able to sell the grapes that were surplus to their requirements very profitably.

A shrewd understanding of the markets, coupled with technical innovations designed to fit wine to the consumer's taste, contributed to their success. Ahead of their time, they emphasized light, fruity qualities in table wines, which were sealed with screwcaps. By the 1950s, Gallo was the largest winery in the United States, although behind Guild (a major cooperative) and Italian Swiss Colony in sales.[159] What pushed them to the top was a retrogressive move to a sweet, fortified, flavored wine in 1957:[160] Thunderbird (named after the American

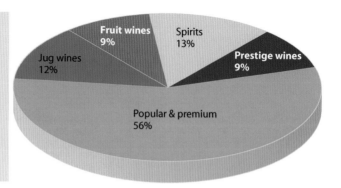

Gallo has widely diversified interests in the American wine and spirits industry.[165]

Figures are relative to Gallo's total production.

muscle car) was based on a mixture of lemon flavoring and white Port, with an alcohol level of 21%. Largely sold into the black community, it rapidly became the best selling "wine" in the nation. But it took Gallo years to live down the criticism that profits came at the expense of the "misery market" of skid-row drinkers.[161] (Thunderbird is still available on the market, although no longer overtly identified with Gallo, and labeled as "An American Classic"![162]) Gallo's reputation remained associated with these "pop wines;" in 1971, Gallo was reported to produce 90% of all pop wines[163] (which were about 20% of all wine sales). Today they manufacture flavored wine coolers under the Bartles & Jaymes brand name.[164]

Gallo is privately owned (with about 15 members of the family in the business), and perennially secretive. Its wineries include the original site in Modesto, another in Livingston (a few miles to the south), and one built more recently in Healdsburg, Sonoma in the late 1990s. All are surrounded by high fences and guarded gates.[166] Finances are even more closely guarded, but Gallo is thought now to produce 76 million cases of wine each year,[167] roughly a quarter of the total consumption in the United States.[168] It probably owns about 13,000 acres (5,000 ha) of vineyards in California[169], but this provides only a small part of its needs, and it is a major purchaser of grapes from many growers. It's the largest wine company by sales in the United States, the largest privately-owned wine company in the world, and the second largest producer in the world.[170] I estimate that it probably has annual revenues of about $3.7 billion; the profit margin is generally thought to be around 5%.[171]

Gallo has dominated jug wine production for half a century, but more recently has moved into premium wines. It's a microcosm—or perhaps given Gallo's size a macrocosm—of what has happened in California over the last half century. Today more than half of Gallo's income comes from sales of popular and premium wines, with an increasing contribution from prestige wines from Napa and Sonoma, but there is still also significant income from jug wines, fruit wines, and spirits.

It's a measure of the enormous change in California wine that the introduction of Hearty Burgundy in 1964 was regarded as a move towards quality—a well made, full bodied, fruity red wine rather than the flavored fortified wines that were the success of the 1950s. The timing was propitious, just preceding (and perhaps contributing to) the transition to the preference for dry table wine

*The Gallo Winery in Modesto is a sprawling plant covering about 65 acres (25 ha).
Photograph kindly provided by Seaman Corporation, FiberTite Division.*

over sweet wines. By 1972, Robert Balzer, the wine critic of the Los Angeles Times, commented, "Gallo Hearty Burgundy is the best wine value in the country today."[172] It was then priced at $1.25 a bottle. But today, Hearty Burgundy is one of Gallo's few remaining generic wines, selling as the only non-varietal in the Twin Valley brand. In their lines of table wines, Gallo now produces more than 130 different varietal-labeled wines, and a mere handful of generics.

After the second world war, Gallo began to purchase grapes from the North Coast, which it blended with supplies from the Central Valley in order to improve quality. By 1954, Gallo was buying 40% of the Napa Valley crush.[173] But the real transition to quality started in 1967, when Gallo offered incentives to its growers to plant better varieties. Within two years, Gallo controlled the majority of the 170,000 acres (70,000 ha) of varietal vineyards in California;[174] by 1972 they stopped using the infamous Thompson seedless table grape for wine production. A further move towards quality was accomplished by acquiring other producers; the purchase of Frei Brothers in 1977 brought 2,000 acres for planting varietals in Sonoma's Dry Creek Valley. More recent prominent acquisitions have been the Louis Martini Estate (with holdings in Sonoma and Napa) and the William Hill Winery in Napa.[175]

Their overall holdings reflect the state of California wine as a whole. The least distinguished Gallo wines—although still almost all varietals—carry only "California" as the origin. Selling in a price range from $3 to $10, most of this wine is sourced from San Joaquin Valley.[176] A notch up come wines from the somewhat meaningless Central Coast AVA (a long region running halfway down the coast

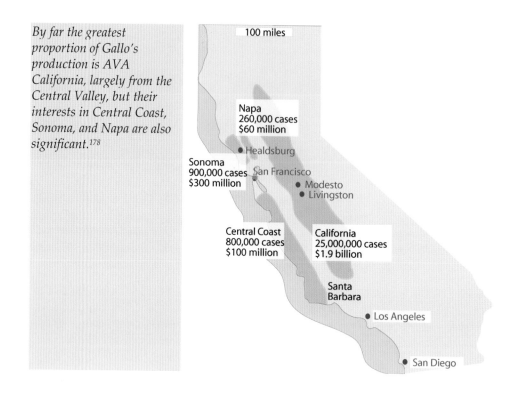

By far the greatest proportion of Gallo's production is AVA California, largely from the Central Valley, but their interests in Central Coast, Sonoma, and Napa are also significant.[178]

100 miles

Napa
260,000 cases
$60 million

● Healdsburg

Sonoma
900,000 cases San Francisco
$300 million ●
● Modesto
● Livingston

Central Coast
800,000 cases
$100 million

California
25,000,000 cases
$1.9 billion

Santa
Barbara

● Los Angeles

● San Diego

of California from Monterey to Santa Barbara), selling at $10-$16. The wines from Sonoma, some labeled under Gallo's own name, achieve super-premium prices of $10-$28 (the lowest being the "Reserve" line from the Turning Leaf brand), and the wines of Louis Martini and William Hill of course stand out over the $35 level.[177]

The Northwest: Rain and Dessert

You would hardly know that Washington and Oregon are in the same country as California to judge from their viticulture and winemaking. Both states are divided by the mountains of the Cascade Ridge, which separate the wet western side (continuously soaked by rains from the Pacific) from the dry eastern side (where agriculture is possible only when supported by irrigation). The climate in the west is cooled by the Pacific. The climate in the east is Continental, with extreme heat in the summer, and winter freezes that sometimes kill the vines. Wineries in Washington are often relatively small, but (unlike California) tend to be part of larger agricultural enterprises in which other crops are more important.[179] Polyculture rules. Most agriculture is in the east, relying on irrigation. Oregon is more given to treating viticulture as an isolated activity, but the enterprises tend to be relatively small. Oregon's vineyards are concentrated in the western part of the state, with Willamette Valley as the best known area.

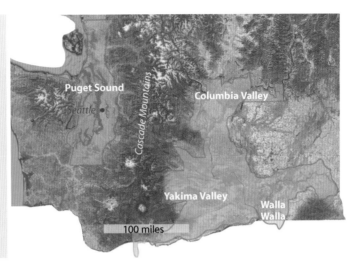

Washington is divided into two AVAs. Columbia Valley AVA includes the bulk of winemaking, with all areas to the east, and includes several smaller AVAs, including Yakima Valley and Walla Walla. Puget Sound mops up the east.[180]

The map of Washington State shows AVAs on both sides of the Cascades, but this is misleading. There are only a handful of wineries in Puget Sound. Columbia Valley includes virtually all the wineries, although all the AVA means on the label is that the winery is not among the one percent located in Puget Sound. The real indication of quality here comes from the sub-appellations, all located within Columbia Valley, of which Yakima and Walla Walla, the first to be given AVAs, remain the best known. Basically this is a desert plateau, where viticulture is completely dependent on irrigation.

Washington's production is split between red and white, with slightly more red. Chardonnay has been the main staple of the whites, but in the past few years Riesling has increased, and now is fractionally in the lead. Most of the blacks are Bordeaux varieties (85%), the remainder largely being Syrah (grown in the warmer spots).[182]

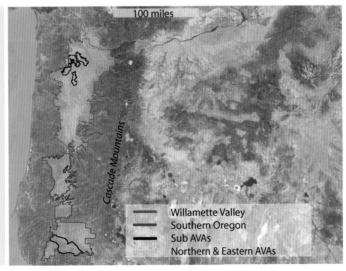

Willamette Valley and Southern Oregon are the two major AVAs of Oregon. Willamette has some smaller AVAs within it; Southern Oregon is effectively divided into three major AVAs, with smaller ones within them. There are also some AVAs to the north and east.[181]

Oregon's plantings are three quarters in black varieties, with Pinot Noir accounting for about three quarters of that. Pinot Gris accounts for about half of the white varieties; Chardonnay is the runner up.[183] North Willamette Valley, a relatively fertile environment, is by far the most important region, with roughly two thirds of the vineyards and most of the wineries.[184] Some smaller AVAs are located within it. The small scale of production is indicated by the calculation that an average winery produces only 12,000 cases per year.

Canada: Retarded Development

The wine situation in Canada was until very recently a tribute to the stupidity of the belief that it is appropriate for government to regulate choice in alcohol consumption. The whole engine of progress was firmly in reverse. Control of wine production and consumption has been in the hands of the provinces since the mid nineteenth century, and Prohibition became widespread during the twentieth century. The Provinces generally repealed Prohibition during the 1920s.

After Repeal in Ontario in 1927, the atmosphere remained hostile: Ontario did not grant any new licenses to produce and sell wine until 1974! (This was to Iniskillin, now famous all over the world for its ice wines.) During the interim, wine was produced more or less exclusively from native varieties, such as Concord, and the focus was on producing sweet, fortified wines to hide the taste. The local market was highly protected by strong tariffs on imported wines. On top of this, each province established a liquor board, which had monopolistic rights to sell wine. Only under such conditions could the local industry have prevailed to the point at which Canadian wine could occupy a major proportion of the market. Pity the poor Canadian consumer.

Protectionism ceased in 1988 when there was a free trade agreement with the United States.[185] You might expect that domestic production would have been seriously impacted, especially by California wines, but curiously, the Canadian consumer appears to have acquired a taste for the local product, and domestic sales even today have 40% of the market.[186] However, this is undercut by the deceptive "Cellared in Canada" scheme, which allows this label to be used for wine that is up to 70% foreign in origin. So much of the wine that the poor consumers think is local product is in fact bulk wine, bought at rock-bottom rates on the international market, and blended with a minor component of Canadian wine.[187] The worst offenders are the largest companies, Vincor (a subsidiary of the American giant Constellation) and Andrew Peller; you have to read the small print on the back label to determine that the wine in fact consists of foreign imports.[188] Some of the wines' production origins are identified only by post office box numbers: "If they have a winery there, they have certainly hidden it well," says David Bond, of the Association of B.C. Wine Growers.[189]

The two leading wine grape regions in Canada are the Niagara Peninsula in Ontario and the Okanagan Valley in British Columbia.[190] The number of wineries in Ontario, the major wine-producing state, increased from thirty in 1990 to more than a hundred by the end of the decade. Both Ontario and British Columbia introduced appellation of origin schemes in the form of the VQA (Vintners Quality Alliance) label, with 85% rules for vintage year and place of origin.

Extreme cool climate conditions limit the possibilities for wine production, but Vitis vinifera has begun to replace the native and hybrid varieties. Grape-vines are grown in microclimates where they can escape the harsh winter, but even so, Vitis vinifera is vulnerable to the impact of cold weather. In Ontario, Vitis vinifera has now increased to two thirds of production, but cool climate hybrids are 20%, while Concord is still 13%.[191] The most widely planted grape is the hybrid Vidal,[192] but it is followed by Chardonnay. There's actually a substantial proportion of black Bordeaux varieties.[193]

One of the most remarkable features is the production of ice wine, where grapes are kept on the vine well into winter, and wine is made by pressing the frozen grapes, giving a very concentrated and sweet wine. The best are made from Riesling, but there is also substantial production from hybrids that withstand the cold winter weather well. Following Iniskillin's initiative at Niagara-on-the-Lake in Ontario, ice wine is now also made at wineries in British Columbia, and even as far north as Quebec and Novia Scotia.[194]

North America Growth

Regulation of wine production and consumption in the United States offers a complete opposite to Europe. Contrasted with the panoply of regulations concerning every aspect of viticulture and vinification in Europe, in the United States there is very little regulation of production. A producer can plant his grapes where he wants, cultivate them in whatever manner he wishes, and use most of the available technology for winemaking. But he can sell the wine only under an intricate set of conditions that vary with each individual State and which severely limit his ability to make contact with the consumers who actually drink the wine. In Europe, although production is highly regulated, there is in general nothing to stop a producer making whatever arrangements he wishes to sell the wine, directly to the consumer, via distributors and wholesalers, or through retail stores. However, advertising involving alcohol is much more controlled in Europe, especially in France where fanatics have got hold of the bureaucracy.

North America is a locomotive. The United States is predicted to become the world's largest consumer of wine in the immediate future (in fact, if you take value rather than volume, it has been the most important market for several years). Domestic production accounts for two thirds of this consumption and continues to grow along with consumption. California's importance vastly outweighs all else, although Washington is developing a niche in Riesling, and Oregon in Pinot Noir. Production has recovered from the impact of Prohibition, and the wine made in the country is better technically than ever before; it is ironic that choice still remains restricted for the consumer by the legacy of Prohibition in the form of a market still distorted by an artificially controlled distribution system. Corresponding to its small population and northern climate, Canada is both a minor consumer and producer on the world stage, about the same in size as Oregon, but it does excel in the niche of producing ice wines. It took much longer to recover from Prohibition, and indeed still offers poorer consumer choice than it should.

It's a mark of the increasing importance of the United States as a wine producer and consumer that Napa Valley has become one of the New World's trend-setting wine regions. In the 1970s, Napa was struggling to make wines more like those of Bordeaux, and Steven Spurrier's "Judgment of Paris" tasting in Paris in 1976 shocked the world of wine when wines from Napa Valley took first place over Chardonnays from Burgundy and Cabernets from Bordeaux.[195] This was the first sign that Napa could make world-class wines. Today the tables are turned, and over the past decade the wines of Bordeaux have been made increasingly in richer styles resembling those of Napa. Imitation is, after all, the sincerest form of flattery.

12

Australia & New Zealand: Pushing The Envelope

"THE VISION IS THAT BY THE YEAR 2025 the Australian wine industry will achieve $4.5 billion in annual sales by being the world's most influential and profitable supplier of branded wines, pioneering wine as a universal first choice lifestyle beverage." This was the stated aim in Strategy 2025, a strategic plan developed by the Australian wine industry in 1996.

The plan got off to a fantastic start. The target was surpassed by the end of the first decade, twenty years early![1] By year 2000 Australia had displaced France from its domination of the British market, and was making major inroads into the United States. The campaign to sell "sunshine in a bottle" was an unbelievable success. But then success was overtaken by a classic boom and bust cycle.

The achievement of the plan is striking when you compare the growth of production in Australia with that in Bordeaux, the Old World wine region that is perhaps most threatened by Australia. In 1970, the entire production of Australia was not much more than half that of Bordeaux. By year 2000, Australia was producing twice as much wine as Bordeaux. Australian production increased five times over, while Bordeaux did little more than stay steady. And production in Australia increased steadily (until a recent downturn), while Bordeaux shows an uneven pattern, with sharp declines in production in bad years.

The plan called for vineyard plantings to increase from 63,000 ha at the start in 1996 to 100,000 ha by 2025 (to reach a size roughly comparable to that of Bordeaux). But by 1999 there were already more than 120,000 ha; today there are about 165,000 ha.[2] Exports simply could not keep up with the pace of increased production.[3] Indeed, exports started to decline in 2008; and global financial problems pushed the situation into crisis by 2009, with a glut causing growers to leave grapes unpicked or to sell at distressed prices.

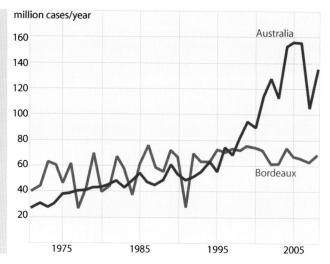

Wine production in Australia has increased 500% since 1970, while production in Bordeaux has been flat.[4]

Australia's dilemma is that its success has been achieved by providing a consistent quality of premium wine at lower price levels than either Europe or the United States. "Cheap and cheerful" would be derogatory, but certainly the wines offer explosive, forward fruit flavors at a reasonable price. But focusing on price builds little consumer loyalty; the wines almost all come from "international" varieties, and there are few unique distinctions of origin to stop other countries from competing. Some believe that the way out is to move to higher quality levels, but it's far from clear that this could absorb the volume of production. So has Australia reached the natural peak of its cycle; is it now set for an inevitable decline, or is there a way out?[5]

Sunshine in a Bottle

Australian wine used to be easy to distinguish. As Jancis Robinson comments, "Gamboge [resin]... in the eighties was a give-away for an Australian white."[6] Not a favorable impression, certainly, but things have changed vastly in the past decade.

Wine has been produced in Australia for more than two centuries, but it is really only in the past decade that it been devoted to full bodied dry red or white

Development of wine production in Australia.

1788 First vines planted in Australia

1971 Table wine production surpasses fortified wine production

1996 Australia announces Strategy 2025, a plan to become the world's most important wine producer by year 2025

2000 Australia passes France as most important exporter of wines to Britain.

2009 Production glut causes prices to collapse.

Penfolds advertised their brandy in the Adelaide Advertiser in 1948, emphasizing the medical connection.

Look for the Maison Marnay Label!

MAISON MARNAY

A Penfolds Hospital

BRANDY

wines, in the case of reds most famously from Shiraz (its own name for Syrah) or Cabernet Sauvignon, in the case of whites most successfully from Chardonnay. The first vines were planted at the end of the eighteenth century, but production focused on cheap fortified wines, largely made from the Sultana grape (the Australian name for Thompson seedless). It was only in the 1970s that the industry came into the modern era, when production of dry table wine overtook the production of fortified wine.

The progression is perfectly illustrated by the history of Penfolds, started by Dr. Christopher Penfold in 1844. The first winery at Magill, just south of Adelaide, still exists. The good doctor produced "Sherry" and "Port," which he believed had medicinal value for his patients. Even in the 1940s, Penfolds was advertising its brandy with an implied medical value. There was little emphasis on wine, and so little belief in the value of quality wine, that when winemaker Max Schubert set out to make a high quality wine, Penfold's management forbade him to do it.

The wine was called Grange, and it was to become Australia's icon wine. The first vintage, 1951, was experimental, but the 1952 vintage was sold commercially.[7] The wine was not initially a great success, and in 1957 Penfolds management banned Schubert from producing any more.[8] But Schubert contin-

Australian wine of the 1892 vintage was sold at Christie's in London on May 12, 1899. The lot of three dozen bottles fetched £3. 6s.

Photo: © Christie's.

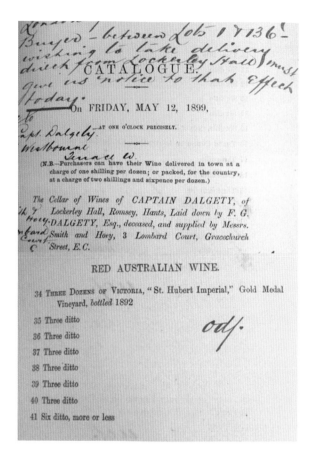

ued to produce the wine in secret, scrounging oak barrels in which to mature it. In 1960, as the quality of Grange began to be recognized, Schubert was officially allowed to resume production. But notwithstanding this success, even by the 1970s, Penfolds was still better known for its fortified wines than for dry table wine.[9]

Australian wine production lives and dies by its capacity to export. Exports started in 1854, and by the end of the century roughly 20% of production was being exported to Britain.[10] Most of the wine was fortified and cheap, but some quality wines emerged, including some St. Hubert's 1892, which reached an auction at Christie's in 1899.[11] Total exports stayed around a quarter of production until the 1990s,[12] when exports became the driving force to fulfill Strategy 2025. The relatively small population of Australia could not possibly support the scale of expansion, making this the first example of a wine-producing country whose industry depended on export rather than domestic consumption.[13]

With no entrenched traditions, or at least with a willingness to change, wine production in Australia has gone through several transformations to respond to the market. When the industry emerged from the agonies of fortification, most production was of white wine. There was a mini boom in red wine in the 1970s, but production still reached only about a third of white wine levels.[14] But as the

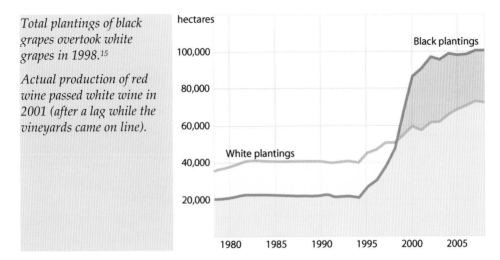

Total plantings of black grapes overtook white grapes in 1998.[15]

Actual production of red wine passed white wine in 2001 (after a lag while the vineyards came on line).

worldwide preference for red wines became apparent, new plantings focused on quality red varieties. By 1998 the area of black grapes surpassed that of white. The gap widened steadily until leveling off soon after the millennium.

With the transition came an improvement in the quality of both black and white grape varieties. Plantings were led by Shiraz (Syrah) and Cabernet Sauvignon, followed by Chardonnay. At the start of the 1980s, less than a third of plantings were quality varieties;[16] by the turn of the century, the proportions had more than reversed, with only 20% left of nonpremium varieties.[17] A striking demonstration of the transition is the contrast between the decline of Sultana (a remnant from the days of fortification) with the dramatic rise in Chardonnay, from zero plantings in 1978, to more than 30,000 ha (almost half of all white grapevines) today.

Red wine production overall leads white wine production, but not by a huge margin. Shiraz is the most widely planted grape, with Cabernet Sauvignon as the runner up. Merlot is the other important black variety. The boom in Chardonnay

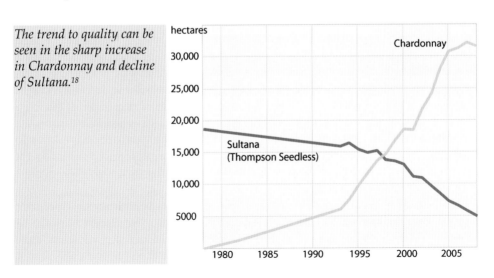

The trend to quality can be seen in the sharp increase in Chardonnay and decline of Sultana.[18]

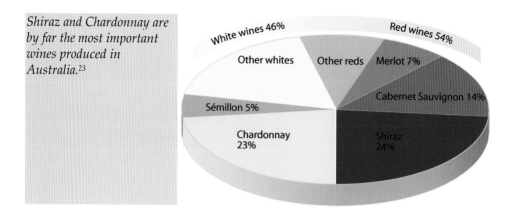

Shiraz and Chardonnay are by far the most important wines produced in Australia.[23]

has brought its production almost up to that of Shiraz. Together Shiraz and Chardonnay account for almost half of all wine production. The whites fall off rapidly from Chardonnay, with much less production of Sémillon, Sauvignon Blanc, and Riesling. Although Australian Riesling has made an impact on the world stage, it's only 2% of all production.[19]

Australian winemakers are fairly forthright, not to say trenchant, in their view that Australia provides better conditions for winemaking than Europe. "Our geology and soils are old, generally much older than those of Europe and California, our sunshine hours are greater and more intense and our air is cleaner and drier. And don't let the apologists claim those differences as disadvantages in the quest for the world's finest; they are an essential part of our uniqueness," says Brian Croser, one of Australia's most distinguished winemakers.[20] The reliability of the climate means there is less vintage variation, consistent water supply is provided by irrigation, and there's rarely any difficulty in getting grapes to full ripeness (especially since the varieties have mostly been chosen in the past twenty years with the present climatic conditions in mind).

Irrigation is a key factor in Australian viticulture. Almost all vineyards are irrigated,[21] and this is a both a benefit and a limitation. The benefit is that supply can be more exactly controlled than is ever possible with rainfall, but the limitation is that the supply can itself become restricted, especially in the aggravated conditions of drought in recent years, and where there is competition from neighboring towns. There might well be more vineyards in the vicinity of Adelaide but for the fact that the needs of the population for water outrank those of the vines. With the exception of Hunter Valley, where summer rains can be a problem, few viticultural regions obtain enough water from rainfall during the growing season for grapevines to survive.[22] Many of the vineyards have lakes to catch the winter rainfall so it can be used for irrigation in the dry summers. In drier regions, pressure from the drought makes it uncertain whether there will be enough water in future years.

Viticulture in Australia produces full bodied wines with intense, ripe, fruit flavors, usually with higher alcohol levels than those of European wines. The intensity can blow you away at tastings, but the alcohol can put you under the table. Is there a certain—how shall we put this?—lack of subtlety to the wines, and a failure to reflect interesting differences due to place of origin? But reverse the argument: if wine historically had been Australian, and France had started its production only in the past twenty years, would we criticize French wines for their lack of intensity and for excessive variability depending on the vintage and place of origin?

Well it depends what sort of wine you are drinking. With large brands, where vintage is really not very relevant, and consumers want consistency, it's difficult for small-scale European wine production to compete with the reliability of larger scale production from Australia, or for that matter, other New World countries. At the high end, where people are interested in vintage variation and look for nuances between wines coming from different places, it's more of an open question. So how do we get beyond "sunshine in a bottle"?

Regional and National Origins

Given a land area larger than all the wine-producing countries of Europe combined, it's surprising that Australia should have created such a single image of "Brand Australia." This was pushed by the combination of large-scale winemaking, blending wines from different regions to make brands, and sometimes an overt view that skillful winemaking renders nuances of terroir irrelevant. Of course, some areas have always commanded a premium, with Barossa Valley as the best known. The one area that has usually been regarded as having unique terroir is Coonawarra, with its red Terra Rossa soil. But it's fair to say that although individual producers in Barossa or Coonawarra may be recognized for the unique nature of their wines, there is little emphasis on terroir differences within each region.

There was no official distinction between wine-producing regions in Australia until 1994 when Geographical Indications were introduced to protect the names of individual areas. The hierarchical system defines 29 zones, 64 regions, and 10 subregions. The sole restriction on use of the name is the usual 85% rule for the origins of the grapes. "Geographical Indication" seems a somewhat obscure choice as the new name for regional designations in a country usually given to more forthright expressions. Can the Australians be coming round to the view that terroir matters after all?

It's fair to say that most of the place names have little significance for the consumer. The names you see on labels tend to be those whose reputations were established well before the system came into place. Among big bold reds, Barossa, Coonawarra, and McLaren Vale in South Australia are the best known. For cooler climate wines, Yarra Valley, well to the south in Victoria, is noted for Pinot Noir; and Margaret River, way over in Western Australia, is known for Bordeaux-like reds and for Chardonnay. The best locales for other white wine production are Eden and Clare Valleys in South Australia. Hunter Valley, the old stamping ground for bulk wine production in New South Wales, is still known for its Sémillon-based wines. The outlier for cool climate wines is Tasmania, off the coast to the south.

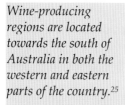

Wine-producing regions are located towards the south of Australia in both the western and eastern parts of the country.[25]

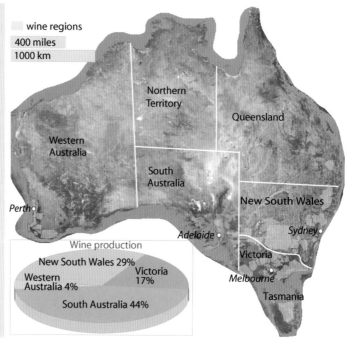

But the whole is greater than the sum of the parts. From the most famous wines to the generic brands, "Australia" is still a common identifier on the label. Penfold's Grange, by far the best known top wine, usually says just "Wine Made in Australia."[24] Of the two leading brands, Jacob's Creek may identify itself with South Australia, and Yellow Tail sometimes is so specific as to identify the wine with South Eastern Australia.

It is typical for Australian brands to be blended from different regions. The large scale of production would make it difficult for any one region to supply sufficient product; and blending from different sources allows consistency to be maintained across vintages. The source wines for Yellow Tail, for example, come from 33 different wine regions in Australia, and are blended at Casella Wine's huge plant in the Riverina region of New South Wales.

Brands sourced from a variety of regions probably make up more than half of Australia's production, minimizing the opportunity to develop recognition of regions.[26] These brands were called "Brand Champions" in a revision of Strategy 2025, called Directions to 2025, undertaken in 2007. The conclusion was that Brand Champions have run their course, and future expansion for Australia requires a move up market, with more recognition for regional variation. The report called for development of Regional Brands, "wines which reflect the remarkable number of successful combinations of classic grape varieties with Australian wine regions."[27] The emphasis is still on brands, because nothing else can absorb the volume requirements, but the proposed combination of regional typicity with large scale production seems just a bit unlikely.

Whether or not Regional Brands will succeed, the question at the higher end is just how much regional variation there is anyway. There's not a lot to be

Australia's most famous wine has little indication of geographical origin.

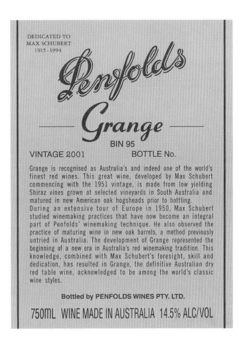

discerned in the bulk wine regions of New South Wales and Victoria to the east, with perhaps a nod of exception to Hunter Valley Sémillon. Most wines produced from specified areas come from South Australia; what typicity do Barossa, McLaren Vale, or Coonawarra bring to their powerful red wines, and are the Rieslings of Clare Valley and Eden Valley more distinguished by regional origin or by winemaking characteristics? How distinctive are the cool climate regions of Margaret River and Yarra Valley?

The Barossa Mother Lode

South Australia is the engine of Australian wine making. Accounting for almost half of all production,[28] it has been the most important wine-producing region in Australia since the start of the twentieth century.[29] It's also the major focus for quality and for trend setting in both reds and whites.

The wine-producing regions are located in the eastern and southern part of the state. To the north of Adelaide are Barossa Valley (famous for red wines) and Clare and Eden Valleys (famous for Rieslings). More wine-growing regions surround Adelaide and extend to its south, including McLaren Vale just beyond the city's suburbs. Some hours away to the south and east, near the border with Victoria, is a group of regions including Coonawarra.

Barossa nominally accounts for just over 10% of production in South Australia, but its reputation and importance spread far beyond that. Some of Australia's most famous wines originate in Barossa, but "originate" is the right word since many have now expanded far beyond its boundaries. About an hour's drive to

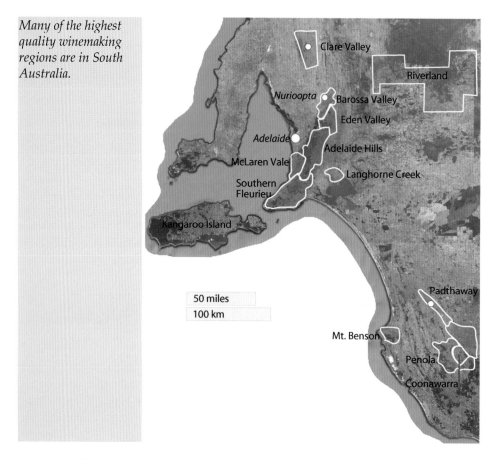

Many of the highest quality winemaking regions are in South Australia.

the north of Adelaide, Barossa has vineyards extending all around the main road running from Lyndoch (to the south) through Tanunda to Nuriootpa. Mountains to the east separate Barossa Valley from Eden Valley; to the west the terrain opens out to fields of other crops. Barossa Valley is relatively flat, generally below 400 m elevation. Eden Valley is at slightly higher elevations, typically 400–600 m, and the climate is correspondingly a little cooler. Rainfall increases going from west to east, but its importance is reduced by the common use of irrigation.

Barossa Valley was settled by German immigrants in the mid nineteenth century. Some of today's vineyards originated with the first settlers of 1842; by the 1850s at least fifty vineyards had been established. By the end of the century there were about 2000 ha of vineyards, producing almost half of South Australia's wine. Some of the famous names of today originated during this period. Johann Gramp planted vines at Jacob's Creek in 1847, and then founded the Orlando company in what was then the village of Rowland Flat; in due course this transmogrified into Australia's largest wine brand (now owned by Pernod-Ricard). On a much smaller scale, Henschke was founded in Eden Valley, and today still produces its Hill of Grace, one of Australia's most famous quality wines.

Barossa is no longer an exclusive focus for artisan wines. Huge wine processing plants are evident on the satellite map of the valley. The Jacob's Creek plant covers about 10 hectares—larger than most vineyards in Europe. Production far exceeds that of Barossa Valley itself, with grapes coming from all over South Australia or even farther afield. The plants of Jacob's Creek, Penfolds, and Wolf Blass alone could account for a significant fraction of all Australia's wine production.

Barossa Valley lies on a north-south axis and is separated by the Barossa range from Eden Valley to the east. It opens out to the west, where other crops as well as vines are planted.[30]

The plant where Jacob's Creek is produced is at Rowlands Flat in the middle of vineyards in Barossa Valley, but the grapes come from all over the region.

An Extravaganza of Shiraz

So what is the character of Barossa itself? It is one of a trio of locations producing the most powerful red wines in Australia: Barossa Valley, McLaren Vale, and Coonawarra. The gradient of varieties goes from Shiraz at Barossa to the north, to Cabernet Sauvignon at McLaren Vale, and to Coonawarra to its south.

Brought back from France by James Busby in 1831, cuttings of "Ciras" were first cultivated in Hunter Valley. By the second half of the nineteenth century it had spread through all winemaking areas and was one of the most important varieties. The Australian style of full-flavored fruits finds its epitome in Barossa, a relatively warm climate where the vines reach high levels of ripeness giving wines with alcohol levels approaching 15%.

The most widely grown grape in Australia, Shiraz has come a long way from the days when it was used as a workhorse grape or to make fortified wine. The wines are at their most dense and concentrated from Barossa, where Shiraz shows distinct aromatic notes of black plums and cherries; they are perhaps a little more refined from the cooler climate of Coonawarra, and one might say perhaps a bit rustic from other regions. Sometimes the wines from Victoria show slightly spicy or peppery notes resembling those of Syrah from the southern Rhône.

Actually, in terms of resemblances the tables have been quite reversed. It used to be the case that Syrah of the northern Rhône, the best known being Hermitage, was often peppery, even a touch herbaceous, but this is a feature of grapes that aren't completely ripe. These days, the Syrahs of the Rhône, and even more so those of Languedoc farther south, are prone to imitate those of Australia, showing very ripe, almost jammy fruits, with strong aromatic notes, if not usually as high in alcohol. Perhaps it is fair to say that Australian Shiraz has become the dominant global model for fruit-driven wines produced from this varietal.

Shiraz has always been an important grape in Australia, but until the recent revolution was used more in blends labeled by generic names than as a varietal. In what is now its best known home, Barossa Valley, it was the only quality grape variety forty years ago, when it was about 15% of all plantings, but much of it was blended with other varieties to make "Claret" or "Burgundy."[31] The plantings of Shiraz in Barossa today are comparable to the total area planted in the valley in 1970, and almost all the wine carries a varietal label.

Whereas Barossa Valley is a popular tourist destination only an hour from Adelaide, Coonawarra is isolated midway between Adelaide and Melbourne in what appears to be a flat wasteland. Aficionados claim it's not really the flattest place in Australia, and it's true that the best terroir, the famous Terra Rossa red soil on top of the limestone ridge, is just high enough to be clear of the water table.[32] The climate is about 0.75 °C cooler than Barossa over the growing season, just enough to tip the balance from Shiraz to Cabernet Sauvignon. Unfortunately, Coonawarra is not synonymous with Terra Rossa. The area legally entitled to describe itself as Coonawarra includes sandy soils to the east and heavy black soils to the west, as well as the authentic Terra Rossa (some of which isn't even included in Coonawarra). Once again politics have triumphed over winemaking.

Almost half the production in Barossa is Shiraz, with Cabernet Sauvignon following as the second most important variety.[33] In Coonawarra the proportions are reversed, with Cabernet Sauvignon representing over half the crop and Shiraz as the runner up. Vines were planted in Coonawarra in 1890, but Shiraz was virtually the only variety grown until 1950, when Wynns Coonawarra Estate successfully introduced Cabernet.

Coonawarra is now generally recognized to produce Australia's best Cabernet Sauvignons, but once again they do not have much common ground with the wines made famous by the Médoc of Bordeaux. They are richer, fuller, and riper in the typical Australian style, often produced as single varietals. There is certainly no trace of the herbaceousness that used to characterize Cabernet Sauvignon from Bordeaux (and which still appears occasionally, although many vintages now resemble the wines of the New World). I suppose you might argue that whereas the austerity of Cabernet Sauvignon in Bordeaux demands blending with Merlot to give a softer note, the full ripeness achieved in Australia makes this unnecessary.

One intriguing aspect of red winemaking in Australia, and certainly something not seen in Europe, is the production of blends from Shiraz and Cabernet Sauvignon. Here are the two most powerful black grape varieties, each of which can stand alone in the Australian context, being melded together. What does each bring to the blend? The traditional justification is that Syrah rounds out the austerity that sometimes appears on the middle palate of Cabernet Sauvignon, although you might think that Merlot would be more obvious for this purpose, and anyway, it's not obvious that austerity is really much of an issue in Australia.

The blend probably started in the late nineteenth century for the production of generic "claret." But there were no wines of note until the 1950s, when some of the earliest vintages of Grange included a little Cabernet Sauvignon with the Shiraz. The best known wine in this category today is probably Penfolds Bin 60A, which since 1962 has consisted of a blend of roughly equal proportions of powerful Shiraz from Barossa with cooler Cabernet Sauvignon from Coonawarra. Cabernet-Shiraz blends are not exactly a curiosity, certainly they are in no danger of extinction, but they are overshadowed by varietal Shiraz or Cabernet Sauvignon to the extent that a competition called "The Great Australian Red" has been started to promote the blend. It attracts about 150 entries annually.

The Steely Rieslings of Eden

Just the other side of the Barossa range is Eden Valley. Wine production in both valleys dates from the same year—1847— when Johan Gramp planted vines at Rowland Flat in Barossa Valley, and Joseph Gilbert planted vines at Pewsey Vale in Eden Valley. By 1854, Pewsey Vale was producing Riesling as well as Shiraz and Cabernet, so the origins of Riesling are just as old as the black varieties.[34] The elevation of the vineyards in Eden Valley, and their exposure to prevailing winds, makes for a significantly cooler climate than in Barossa Valley. Somewhat farther south, Clare Valley was settled around the same period, and shares with Eden Valley a focus on white wines, especially Riesling (although Clare has a warmer climate and correspondingly also has a greater proportion of black varieties).

Production of Riesling in Australia has been left way behind by the growth in Chardonnay. In fact, total Riesling plantings have been declining, but this has mostly been due to grubbing up in inferior regions, so that production is now concentrated on where it does best, in Eden Valley and Clare Valley. Together, Eden Valley and Clare Valley have sparked a revolution in the recognition of Riesling. Until their dry Rieslings penetrated the export market, Riesling was more prized for its sweet styles than for dry wines to accompany food. Germany was (and still is) by far the largest producer of Riesling, but most of its production was in off-dry or sweet styles. France was in second place with Rieslings from Alsace made in a variety of styles from dry to sweet.

Today Australia is the second largest producer of Riesling (just ahead of Alsace), with about a quarter of its production coming from Eden Valley and Clare Valley.[35] Only about a million cases of Riesling are exported each year,[36] but the novelty and intensity of the style has had a disproportionate effect on the international market. The effect hasn't just been on the style of Riesling: the screwcap revolution started when a group of winemakers from Clare Valley abandoned corks and collectively turned to screwcaps.[37] It just happens that Riesling was the perfect wine for such an experiment.

Australian Rieslings show piercing fruit intensity marked by strong citrus flavors, bright and even aggressive in the New World style. The style of Clare Valley is the most austere and acidic. One of the best regions within it, Watervale, tends to show pronounced lime and other citrus flavors. Polish River, the other famous subregion, has great intensity. Eden Valley tends to be a little lighter and more floral. The aromas and flavors of these Rieslings are a great contrast with the view of Riesling largely dictated by exports of German wines in a variety of sweet styles. Now, of course, Germany is coming somewhat more into line with the New World with its trocken (dry) styles, but it is still true (at least in Britain and the United States) that if you want to drink a dry Riesling, your best chance of finding one lies in the Australian section of the wine store. The distinctively steely style is an interesting contrast with Australian Chardonnay, which at least in its full-blown form can have difficulty in distinguishing itself from other New World Chardonnays.

The Cool Reserve of Margaret River and Yarra Valley

Two of the best known cool climates in Australia lie almost at opposite ends of the continent: Margaret River in the far west, and Yarra Valley just to the east of Melbourne. Both coming into the limelight in the past couple of decades, they have taken different paths to fame.

Australia's best chance of making wines that compete with Europe on its own terms (as opposed to the more common exuberant style) may come from the (relatively) cool climate region of Margaret River, on the western edge of the country. Margaret River is best known for its clean, elegant Cabernet Sauvignons and Chardonnays. Australian wine writer James Halliday says that the distinctive quality of the red wines, immediately apparent when they first became available on export markets in the 1970s, was due to the absence of malolactic fermentation as a result of the sterile conditions of the new wineries.[38]

Western Australia had been making wine for more than a century before it gained any repute, when the wines from Margaret River hit the international scene. Margaret River is still pretty much the only region in Western Australia with a reputation for quality. Its rise was triggered by a report by John Gladstones, at the time working on lupins, but since then the author of a respected book on viticulture,[39] that its climate resembled Bordeaux.[40] The climate is generally maritime, and about a quarter of the rainfall occurs during the growing season (an unusually high proportion for an Australian wine-growing region). Soils tend to be gravelly. There are now about 120 wineries, typically located within two or three miles of the ocean, whose cooling breezes play a large part in maintaining a relatively cool climate. It's generally a little warmer than Bordeaux, but varies from the warmer parts north of the river to the cooler parts to its south.

The suggestion that Margaret River was suitable for making wine was originally received with skepticism. The Western Australian Department of Agriculture greeted Gladstone's paper with a press release entitled "Southwest Wine Growing 'Not Practical'."[41] But today Cabernet Sauvignons from Margaret river run second to Coonawarra on Langton's classification of the top wines from Australia;[42] its Chardonnays share the honors with some (relatively) cool climate wines from Victoria. Leeuwin's Art Series from Margaret River, with the label for each vintage provided by a different artist, is perhaps Australia's best regarded Chardonnay. It's a sign of how far things have come that the original vineyard at Leeuwin was planted by casual labor who put in the vines upside down, with their roots sticking up in the air, so many had to be replanted.[43] You would never know it from today's immaculate estate.

Yarra Valley is in fact Victoria's oldest established wine-growing region, starting in 1837, but production ceased by 1921, killed by the move away from table wines to fortified wines. Replanting began at the end of the 1960s. Yarra Valley is now most notable for its production of Pinot Noir, which accounts for a quarter of all plantings —although not all of it is used for dry red wine, since Yarra Valley's second claim to fame is as a choice site for producing sparkling wine (Moët & Chandon have established their Australian operation here). A good deal of Chardonnay is also produced, in fact a little more than the Pinot Noir. Average temperatures are somewhere between those of Burgundy and Bordeaux, so the Pinot Noirs tend to be fuller and softer than those of Burgundy; there are also some Bordeaux blends made in a style that can be lighter than elsewhere in Australia.

Old Australia

Two very different regions typify the origins of wine production in Australia. Hunter Valley in New South Wales was where wine production first got its start, and is now an area more or less for bulk production. And the old tradition of sweet fortified wines is perpetuated in the "stickies" from Rutherglen in Victoria, although today's wines show a level of refinement far indeed from the old fortified wines.

Hunter Valley has an unsuitable climate for wine production. Actually the area is divided into Upper Hunter Valley and Lower Hunter Valley, with most wine production in Lower Hunter Valley, although both parts have more coal mines than wineries. Rainfall is the big problem here: there's enough rainfall to support grapevine growth—but most of it falls around harvest time. Most of the soil is unsuitable for grapevines.

Red wines from Hunter Valley are inevitably uninteresting, and its one claim to fame is its Sémillon. This is often ungiving in youth, to the point that one wineshop chain in Britain that had been a leading advocate told me they had given up, because consumers simply would not drink the green, hard wines. Aficionados claim that if you hold the wines long enough—we are talking at least a decade here—they soften and become complex and interesting in a style that can be confused with old white Burgundy.

Rutherglen's wines are sui generis. Well inland, at the northern boundary of Victoria, the climate is Continental and hot, suitable for the production of fortified red wines. The region did well in the days when fortified wine was Australia's main export, and large amounts continued to be sent in barrel to Britain until the 1950s.

The two famous styles are the Muscat and Tokay, the former made from a brown clone of Muscat à Petit Grains, giving rise to the name "Brown Muscat," the second made from the unrelated Muscadelle (a very minor component of some Sauternes). Grapes are kept on the vine for a very late harvest, until they have shriveled and become more concentrated by desiccation. They are crushed, but fermentation is scarcely allowed to proceed before they are fortified (typically after one day) to bring the alcohol up to 17-18%. So most of the sugar remains in the wine.

The method of production means they show more in the way of primary fruit influence than aromas and flavors developing from fermentation. But then the wines are matured in small barrels of old oak for protracted periods—up to ten or twenty years. The wine becomes more concentrated as the result of evaporation and the color turns dark brown. Viscous and very sweet, the wine is in some ways more like a liqueur. Casks are topped up from younger vintages, akin to a solera system, so there is usually no vintage. The Muscats are classified into the ascending levels of Rutherglen Muscat, Classic, Grand, and Rare (without any formal definition of any of the levels).

The Yellow Tail Explosion

A major part of the Australian export success has been due to one label, but is this the country's Achilles heel? The Yellow Tail phenomenon started in 2001, when Casella Wines introduced the brand to fill a gap in the United States market at the $6-7 level, between cheap jug wines and the lowest priced premium wines. Casella offered Deutsch & Sons, one of the largest U.S. wine importers, a 50/50 partnership for North American distribution, giving Yellow Tail immediate access to distribution networks in 44 states. From 200,000 cases in 2001, the brand exploded, becoming the number one imported wine in the United States in 2004, with worldwide sales passing 12 million cases. Yellow Tail now amounts to 9% of Australia's production and 15% of its exports. The original brand consisted of one white wine and one red; now there is a series of varietals and also a Reserve range.

"They are soft, enjoyable and easy to drink," says John Casella.[44] Is the hidden message here that the wines tend not to be completely dry—in fact they have sometimes been criticized for having residual sugar. The brand was initially designed specifically for the American market. "We brought back hundreds of these wines from the U.S. Then we looked at how we could best interpret these styles from what we produced here, and what would fit in a price category of under $US10," says John Soutter, the Export Manager of Casella Wines.[45] On the principle that 20 million lemmings can't be wrong, Casella can afford to laugh at the critics.

Australian exports to the United States more than doubled in the first five years of the century—but most of the increase was due to Yellow Tail. By 2006, Yellow Tail was selling 8 million cases a year in the United States alone, which amounted to a third of all Australian wine imports. The following year, Austra-

Australian wine exports to the USA have shown little growth, but Yellow Tail has increased explosively.[46]

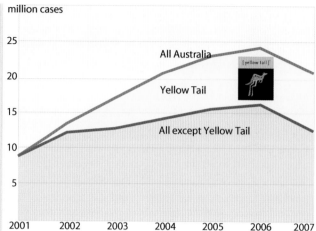

lian imports declined but Yellow Tail stayed steady, becoming 40% of all Australian imports. Part of the success has been attributed to the distinctive name and label (its use of a wallaby started the whole rush to "critter" brands). But the problem is that it stamps "Brand Australia" as representing the low end of the market (not to mention a slightly frivolous expectation created by the "critter" image). Together with the success of other mass-market brands, such as Jacob's Creek, this makes it more difficult for other producers to defy the image and to break out of the box by moving to production of higher quality, more expensive wines.

Brand Australia

No country has more collective awareness of its wine identity than Australia. "Brand Australia" has become a watchword for a certain style and quality—forward, fruit-driven, reliable. But does Australia's success carry with it the seeds of its own destruction? Three quarters of its exports go to two markets: Britain and the United States. In Britain it has displaced the traditional European providers; in the United States it has made it impossible for California to compete at the lower end of the market.

Outside of wine circles in Australia, there is little awareness of the extent to which the industry is dominated by the leading brands, because they are largely exported. Take the extreme of Yellow Tail, which is almost exclusively an export phenomenon— it became available in Australia in 2003, but domestic sales are insignificant. This situation is common to several Australian brands, but when a wine is not well rooted in its domestic market there is nothing to fall back on if exports falter. "One of the interesting features of the Australian wine industry is that the most successful Australian export branded wines are often unknown to Australians, because these wines are entirely developed and produced with the export market in mind," one marketing study commented.[47] Lack of a home base has not been a problem for Yellow Tail, however, which dominates Australian

Leading brands account for a quarter of all production in Australia.[52]

Brand	Production	Export	Owner
Yellow Tail	12 million cases	97%	Casella Wines
Jacob's Creek	8 million cases	50%	Pernod-Ricard
Lindemans	4 million cases	67%	Fosters
Wolf Blass	4 million cases	67%	Fosters
Banrock Station	3 million cases	65%	Constellation
Penfolds	3 million cases	67%	Fosters

exports to the United States to the point at which for many consumers it defines the image of Brand Australia.

Brand Australia has been based on pleasing the consumer. Nowhere is the contrast clearer between Europe's focus on tradition and the Australian focus on the future. Comparing French and Australian attitudes, Australian winemaker Brian Croser commented on a report commissioned in France on how to improve French wine exports.[48] "M. Berthomeau... poses the question, 'Do we need to get rid of our restricting rules and produce wines 'a la carte' in order to please the new consumers? Do we need to strongly enter the ruthless universe of world-wide brands and manage our winegrowing industry so it produces standard raw materials for wineries?' Reading this I thought they finally understand. However by the end of the report he has answered firmly no to both of these questions."[49] Banging home a similar point, Phil Laffer, winemaker of the successful brand Jacob's Creek, says directly, "A large part of Australia's wine success is that we'll make the wines you would like, rather than tell you what wines you should drink."[50] The French for their part express incredulity at the laxness of regulation. "You do not have a system of geographical indications for wine. You have a system of indications for sources for your grapes," said Madame Bienaymé of the OIV.[51]

Croser points out that Australian wine production can be divided into two types: roughly 60% comes from large scale, irrigated vineyards, tending to be in the warmer inland regions, and used for producing branded wine; the other 40% comes from more temperate regions and includes all the regionally differentiated wine. He does not believe that regional identification is useful for branded wine. "The regional identification of branded commodity wine, at least beyond country, is irrelevant; destructive where it interferes with the production process as it does in France and where the region is also a recognized producer of premium differentiated wine."[53] In fact, he believes that Australia's problems come entirely from the large producers, at the expense of the small producers. "The biggest problem for the fine wine community is the negative and deteriorating image problem created by the behavior of the branded commodity wine industry," he says.[54] So the big question becomes whether the dominance of the branded wines prevents Australia from solving its dilemma by moving up market. Does "Brand Australia" obliterate recognition of the regional differences that may be necessary for success at higher price points?

Oil refinery or winery? The tank farm at Casella Wines, where Yellow Tail is produced, stretches as far as the eye can see.

Production is mostly on a huge scale, with a divide between grape growing and winemaking, so that producers purchase many of their grapes from outside growers. As production scales back in response to the crisis, more and more vineyards will become surplus to requirements. Painful though it may be, the only solution is likely to require reduction of the over-supply. The bodies representing the industry collectively reported in 2009 that over-supply was between 20 and 40 million cases (relative to annual production of about 140 million cases), and that around 20% of the vineyards simply could not produce wine at an economic cost.[55] Programs are being developed to prevent further expansion and to help growers pull out uneconomic vineyards. Certainly this is a more active program than has been seen anywhere in the Old World to address the European wine lake.

The crisis in branded wine is evident in the struggles of Fosters, formerly a brewer, which now owns the wine-producing properties of the old Southcorp operation. Even though many brands have been abandoned, they simply cannot scale back fast enough to maintain profitability. There are also problems at the high end, where opinion seems to be turning against the styles of the past. Those jammy, fruit filled, alcoholic extravaganzas often do well at tastings and win accolades from publications such as the Wine Advocate and Wine Spectator. But are consumers tiring of them and looking for more variety? Does the image carrying over from the brands impede them from finding it? Perhaps a bit defensively, Robert Parker remarked in The Wine Advocate that, "One of the perennial criticisms of these South Australian wines is that they are no more than one-dimensional fruit bombs that will fall apart with age... Another myth about Australian wines is that they all taste alike... the top-notch wines are dramatically different, even within the same general viticultural regions... [Some of the best values] are undeniably industrial wines, but they are the finest industrial quality wines being made in the world today."[56]

One measure of success at the high end is increasing value on the auction market. Taking a leaf from the famous 1855 classification of Bordeaux, Langton's, the leading auction house for wine in Australia, has classified Australian wines based on auction results. The basic criterion for inclusion is the price. The first classification, in 1991, had 34 wines; revised every five years or so, the latest classification has 101 wines, divided into the categories Exceptional, Outstanding, Excellent, and Distinguished.[57] Almost half the wines are Shiraz, and another quarter are Cabernet Sauvignon. But the dominance of single varietals is slipping, with quite a few blends based on Shiraz or Cabernet Sauvignon, and including some Shiraz-Cabernet blends. The honors go by far to South Australia, with just over half of the wines, led by Barossa closely followed by Clare Valley and Coonawarra. It's interesting that at this level almost all the wines have distinct geographical origins, with fewer than 10% relying on broad regional descriptions. So maybe there is some belief in the importance of origin?

New Zealand: A Tight Commercial Focus

In some ways New Zealand is similar to Australia; in others it is a complete antithesis. Like Australia, the growth in wine production has been recent—even more recent in fact—and is very largely based on export. Like Australia with Shiraz, much of its success is identified with a single varietal—in this case Sauvignon Blanc—where it has given a new twist to a classic French grape. Ownership of its industry is even more concentrated than Australia's. The big difference is that its focus is clearly on premium wines.[58] At 20 million or so cases a year, total production is tiny, only about fifty percent more than Burgundy. But the effect on the world stage has been pronounced.

Wine production dates from colonial times, but was largely devoted to fortified wines. Because of difficulties in growing Vitis vinifera, hybrid vines were widely planted, mostly Baco 22A (which is forbidden in Europe). Until 1960, Albany Surprise, a clone of the Isabella variety of the American grapevine Vitis labrusca, was the most widely planted variety. With a heavy foxy taste, the wines cannot have been pleasant. Even worse, a government commission in 1946 admitted: "A considerable quantity of the wine made in New Zealand would be classified as unfit for human consumption in other wine-producing countries."[59] Much of this was because of excessive chaptalization, followed by diluting the must with water, a practice that was not really abandoned until modern times. When it was finally made illegal in 1983, there was a sharp drop in the total volume of wine produced.[60]

A revival started in the 1960s, but the focus was on cheap sparkling wine, white wine (often made from the infamous Müller-Thurgau), and fortified wine. Slowly the emphasis shifted to dry table wine, increasing from 12% in 1962 to 91% by 1985.[61] Although by the mid 1980s Vitis vinifera had taken over most

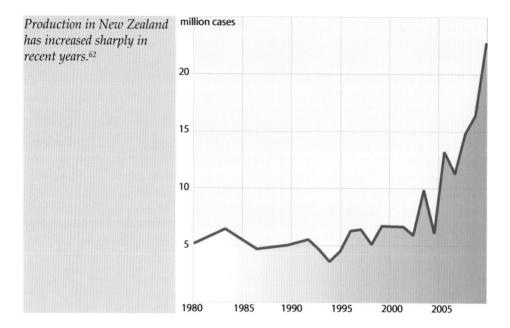

Production in New Zealand has increased sharply in recent years.[62]

plantings, the most widely planted variety was still Müller-Thurgau, used to make slightly sweet, characterless wines.

Vastly increased vineyard plantings in the mid 1980s led to the usual bust following the boom. As the dust settled, the industry was reorganized, and a grubbing up scheme pulled out almost a quarter of the vineyards. By 1990, vineyard areas were increasing again, but the difference was that much of the Müller-Thurgau had been eliminated, and new plantings concentrated on quality varietals. The increase in production that followed two or three years later has continued to the present. You will not see "Old Vines" on a bottle of wine from New Zealand because the entire industry is less than thirty years old.

New Zealand has the coolest climate for wine production in the New World, but there is a very wide range from the warmest areas in the north (Northland and Auckland, which some people consider not really suitable for wine production) to Central Otago in the south (the world's closest wine-producing region to the South Pole). Climate varies significantly with vintage, and there is sufficient variation between regions that a good vintage in the south does not necessarily mean a good one in the north.

Soils tend to be relatively fertile, so excess vigor in the vine can be a problem. Can the fertility really be ascribed simply to the relative geological youth of the land mass (50 million years compared with, for example, Chablis' limestone of 180 million years)? A more down to earth explanation is the relatively high water table and high moisture retention.

Marlborough is by far the best known wine-producing area of New Zealand, accounting for more than half of New Zealand's total wine production. Marlborough owes its success to an accident. In 1973, Montana, New Zealand's largest wine producer, was looking to expand; because land in Hawke's Bay was too expensive, they purchased some farms in Marlborough, and planted vineyards.[63]

These were the first vines to be planted in Marlborough! Most of the planting was Müller-Thurgau, but they included 24 ha of Sauvignon Blanc as an experiment.[64] The decision to plant in Marlborough was controversial; many people thought it was mad, and the board of Seagrams, who had just bought Montana, at first refused to approve the decision, before reversing themselves.[65] The rest is history, as they say.

Marlborough offers cool climate production, because although the summers can be warm (with a typical maximum temperature around 24 °C), there is strong diurnal variation, and it can be cool at night. Average temperatures are just a little cooler than Burgundy, and have seen the usual 1 °C increase in global warming over the past twenty years.[67] Although there is nominally enough rainfall for the vines, strong cooling breezes cause an unusually high rate of transpiration, so irrigation is common. Most of Marlborough's wine comes from the Wairau Valley, where there is a wide variety of soil types, ranging from gravelly to more alluvial.

The other important areas in terms of volume are in warmer climates on the north island, Hawke's Bay and Gisbourne, which are somewhat more devoted to

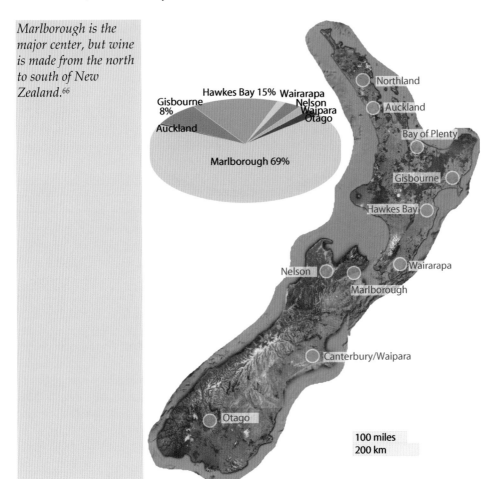

Marlborough is the major center, but wine is made from the north to south of New Zealand.[66]

bulk wine production. In fact, until the 1970s there were more vineyards on the north island, although today the south island has about three quarters of all plantings. The general trend over the past decade has been for grape production to move from the wetter, warmer north towards the cooler, drier, south. But although grapes are now grown all over New Zealand, much of the wine is actually bottled in Auckland, where the three largest producers have their plants. Grapes are brought from all over to the central facilities.[68]

The most recently developed region is Central Otago. Vineyards are typically at elevations of 200 – 400 m, so that although the summers are hot, the vines cool down due to high diurnal variation at night. It's the most extended wine region in New Zealand, so there is a lot of variety in vineyard conditions. (Originally it was thought to be too cold; the Department of Agriculture said in 1958 that the "economics of grape growing" were "not very favorable."[69])

A rapid increase in the number of wineries, now totaling more than 500, belies the highly concentrated ownership of the industry. Takeovers since year 2000 have brought most of the industry under foreign ownership. Montana, which was New Zealand's largest producer, passed from Seagrams to Pernod-Ricard. Nobilo, another large producer, was purchased by Australian BRL Hardy, which in turn was swallowed up by American Constellation Brands, which also owns Kim Crawford and Monkey Bay. Cloudy Bay (of which more shortly) is owned by French luxury house LVMH. Matua Valley, formerly one of the largest independent producers, is now owned by Australian Fosters. The two largest companies remaining independent are Delegat and Villa Maria.

The Sharp Edge of Sauvignon Blanc

Sauvignon Blanc from New Zealand burst on to the world stage with the success of Cloudy Bay's 1985 vintage. The style was and is archetypal: piercing citrus fruits with a touch of gooseberries, exotic notes of passion fruit, a distinctly herbaceous edge—altogether lively and zesty.

Cloudy Bay was established as a subsidiary of Cape Mentelle, the well regarded winery in Western Australia.[70] The story goes that Cape Mentelle had been failing to produce Sauvignon Blanc that satisfied them, tried by chance a bottle brought by some visiting New Zealand winemakers, and decided that this terroir would give them what they were looking for. The first vintage was a winemaking triumph: neither winery nor vineyards existed, and the grapes were bought from Corbans and vinified at their winery in Gisbourne (under the direction of Cloudy Bay's first winemaker, Kevin Judd). Then land was purchased and vineyards planted. The winery was constructed the following year at Matthews Lane (between Renwick and Blenheim in Wairau Valley), but even today its own grapes supply only about half the winery's needs, and the rest comes from grapes purchased from outside growers on long term contracts. In 1990 Veuve Clicquot purchased Cape Mentelle, so Cloudy Bay became part of LVMH. The winery is actually nothing much to look at—a workmanlike collection of

Sauvignon Blanc represents the majority of wine production in New Zealand.[74]

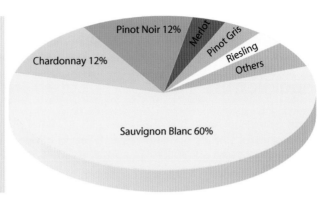

industrial buildings—but the effect of its success on New Zealand's reputation for Sauvignon Blanc has been global.

Sauvignon Blanc is by far New Zealand's most important grape variety, accounting for more than half of all wine production. Marlborough is the paradigm for New Zealand, and accounts for three quarters of the production of the variety in the country.[71] Sauvignon Blanc from Marlborough has the sharpest style, with citrus fruits usually the dominant influence, showing intense grassy aromatics; going farther north, notes of passion fruit become more noticeable. Bright fruits result from winemaking in stainless steel, although some winemakers—including notably Cloudy Bay—do use some oak to soften the edges. Originally, all the Sauvignon Blanc in New Zealand came from a single clone, but now others have been imported.[72]

They are rightly proud of their Sauvignon Blanc in New Zealand. Its innovative style has displaced Sauvignon Blanc from the Loire in many markets. Winemaker Brett Bermingham at Nautilus says, "It's not the technology or the clone, and it's not even our skill and hard work that is rattling the French. It's the Marlborough climate that makes our wines distinctive, and the French can't copy that."[73] It's funny to see the tables turned with New Zealand claiming unique climate: back to terroir? Climate has something to do with it, but I think winemaking style also plays a significant part.

Chardonnay was actually the predominant grape variety in New Zealand in 1985, but was pushed into second place as plantings of Sauvignon Blanc expanded rapidly in view of its success. Then Chardonnay was (just) pushed into third place as the phenomenon was repeated with Pinot Noir. Chardonnay can represent the same New Zealand style as the Sauvignon Blanc with bright, forward fruits and little exposure to oak, although there are also wines made with buttery flavors from malolactic fermentation and heavy use of oak. There's also a tendency to use very low temperature fermentation to bring out tropical fruit flavors; personally I'm with French oenologist Emile Peynaud who famously said, "If I want to drink fruit juice, I'll drink orange juice," but some people like the style.

The other significant white varieties are Pinot Gris and Riesling, but neither achieves great distinction. Pinot Gris has expanded steadily in the past few years to take third place, but a tendency to leave a little residual sugar in the wine somewhat muddies its flavors. New Zealand Riesling has never managed to achieve a reputation to compete with Australia.

Pinot Power

Pinot Noir is the latest buzz in New Zealand. Total plantings have doubled in the last five years, and its percentage of all production has increased sharply to bring it into second place behind Sauvignon Blanc. It's mostly planted in the Wairarapa area, especially Martinborough, but is also successful in Marlborough. The most recent development is its extension to Central Otago, well down in the south island.

Pinot Noir from Martinborough or Marlborough shows an aroma and flavor spectrum focused on aromatic black cherries, whereas Otago tends more towards red fruits of strawberries. [75] The difference is perhaps a little akin to that between the Côte de Nuits and Côte de Beaune in Burgundy, but one would not mistake these wines for European: they show forceful fruits, aromatic intensity, and rather high alcohol. They are interesting wines in their own right, but definitely a New World expression of Pinot Noir. I would not accuse them of subtlety. Their nearest competitors in terms of style are the wines of the United States; you might compare Martinborough or Marlborough to (say) Russian River in California, and Otago to Oregon.

It's fair to say that other red varieties have not had the same success. The warmer climates of the North Island offer the best chance of success for Cabernet Sauvignon or Bordeaux blends, with Hawkes Bay considered to be the promising region, but the problem—reminiscent of Bordeaux—is getting full ripeness.

While the emphasis on Sauvignon Blanc perhaps reflects a risk of overdependence on one variety and style, so far New Zealand has encountered no major block to continued growth. Production declined slightly in 2009, but a 4% drop is pretty minimal compared to the devastation in Australia. [76] Although there have been declines in exports to Europe and the United States with the world financial crisis, New Zealand has compensated by making inroads into the Australian market. [77] Sauvignon Blanc overtook Chardonnay as the largest selling white wine variety in Australia by value in March 2009. [78] New Zealand supplies most of that Sauvignon Blanc (it accounts for 40% of total wine exports). [79] It's known locally as the savalanche. New Zealand wine writer Michael Cooper says, "Kiwis drink heaps of Australian wine so why shouldn't Australians drink heaps of Kiwi wine? I mean, trade works both ways." [80]

New Zealand's success is increasing the present problems of Australian producers, but possibly in the long run may create problems at home, because the increase in volume is associated with drop in price, risking New Zealand's reputation for premium quality. At all events, climate dictates that New Zealand must continue to focus on white wine; whether Sauvignon Blanc alone can carry the burden remains to be seen as fashions come and go.

13

Up And Coming

in the Southern Hemisphere?

THE COMMON PROBLEM FOR SOUTH AMERICA and South Africa is the struggle to make the transition from producing wines from poor quality or over-cropped varieties for local consumption to competition on the international market. Chile was dominated by the black País grape, the same as the Mission variety that initiated wine growing in California. Almost half of Argentina's vineyards are cultivated with local varieties generically called Criollas, which are thought to have originated in Argentina as descendants of imported Mission vines, but now are distinct from traditional European varieties. South Africa has a long established industry, but a monopolistic system focused on quantity at the expense of quality, with vast amounts of characterless white wine produced from over-cropped Steen (the local name for Chenin Blanc). A significant amount of production was used for sweet white wines.

With a move towards international varieties, these emerging countries have some natural advantages. Climate is reliable, and costs are lower than those of the more established New World countries. By producing wines such as Chardonnay or Cabernet Sauvignon in an international style, they can nibble away from below at the markets established by California and Australia. On the other hand, they have no cult wines to cast a halo on those below, nor for the most part do they have a natural lead into the international market. Are they condemned to be providers of wines in the bottom tier?

Each country does have one variety to provide a more or less unique focus. Argentina and Chile have both brought back lost varietals of Bordeaux. Argentina makes varietal Malbec, and Chile makes varietal Carmenère. Both were important in Bordeaux in the nineteenth century, but disappeared during the replanting after phylloxera. South Africa makes Pinotage, the strange result of a cross between Pinot Noir and Cinsault. But none of these really compete with the current international varieties. In these generally warm climates, reds tend to be more interesting than whites, but Argentina has its unique Torrontés (a mixed bag given its half Muscat parentage, which can make it overly aromatic).

Argentina and Chile produce wines in the New World style, although they are rarely so intense as Australia or so refined as California. South Africa is often considered to be a half way house between the New and Old Worlds. Argentina is the most important in terms of total volume, reaching fifth place in world production, just ahead of Australia. Chile and South Africa come next on the list.

Argentina: Value and Malbec

Argentina's history of wine production goes back to the settlers of the sixteenth century. The industry developed in the direction of quantity rather than quality, however, with most wine made from low quality Criolla grapes. By 1973, annual production was more than 300 million cases; and vineyards continued to expand during the 1970s to more than 330,000 hectares as the result of inexpensive water being made available for irrigation. The boom led to an inevitable bust, and by 1993, vineyards were down to 200,000 hectares, and production was below half of the peak of the 1970s.

Total production has been fairly stable since then, but there has been a steady increase in the proportion of wine made from quality varietals, currently just under 40%. Today Argentina is both the largest wine-producing and consuming country in South America, but its importance on the world stage is overstated by its position as the fifth largest producer. Its production of quality wine is only

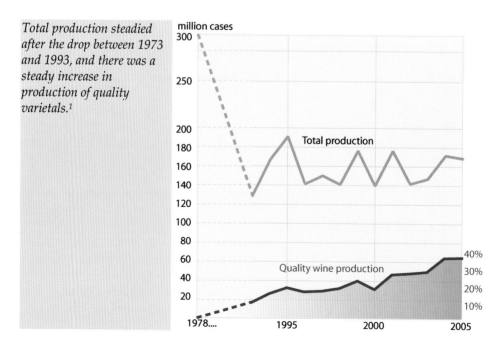

Total production steadied after the drop between 1973 and 1993, and there was a steady increase in production of quality varietals.[1]

Black quality varieties focus on Malbec, Cabernet Sauvignon, and Syrah, white on Torrontés and Chardonnay. The varieties shown in the chart account for about 40% of all production.[4]

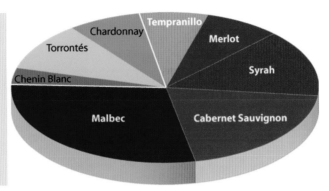

about half that of Australia, and it is well behind in terms of exports. Exports were minimal through the 1990s, and although they have increased sharply since 2004, Argentina today exports only about half the amount of Chile (which is nominally a much smaller producer), and is more comparable in importance to South Africa. A strategic plan follows the precedent of Australia in aiming to increase exports strongly over the next decade.

Among the growing proportion of quality varietals, whites make up about a quarter.[2] Torrontés is the most important of any named white variety. A similar grape of the same name is found in Spain in Galicia and in Córdoba, but it may not be the same as Torrontés in Argentina, which exists in several varieties. Torrontés Riojano has the highest quality, while Torrontés Sanjuanino and Torrontés Mendocino are considered to be of lower quality. Torrontés Riojano and Torrontés Sanjuanino are the progeny of crosses between Muscat of Alexandria and Criolla Chica (a black variety).[3] Torrontés Mendocino is probably also descended from Muscat of Alexandria, although the other parent has not been identified. The Torrontés parentage is often noticeable in the wine in the form of grapey aromas, although not usually as intense as in Muscat itself.

Bonarda was the most widely planted black grape in Argentina, but no one knows whether it is the same as Bonarda from Piedmont. At all events, it is more often used to make table wine than a quality varietal. And now it has been overtaken by Malbec, Argentina's own version of an international varietal. Malbec was an important variety in Bordeaux in the nineteenth century, but was not replaced after phylloxera hit. However, it continues to be grown in the southwest of France, most notably in Cahors, where the grape is called Auxerrois and the wine was known as the "Black wine of Cahors." It is usually blended; Cahors must contain at least 70% Malbec. It is also grown in the Loire, where it is called Cot.

Malbec was probably imported into Argentina from Bordeaux in the mid nineteenth century. By the present era, it had adapted to its new home, but unfortunately many of the old vines were pulled out during the decline of the 1970s. But now there is more in Argentina than anywhere else. At one time it was mostly included in blends, but the recent trend is for it to be vinified as a monovarietal in a modern style. This tends to be less deeply colored and tannic than the traditional Malbec from Cahors, with better ripening giving soft, plum fruits.

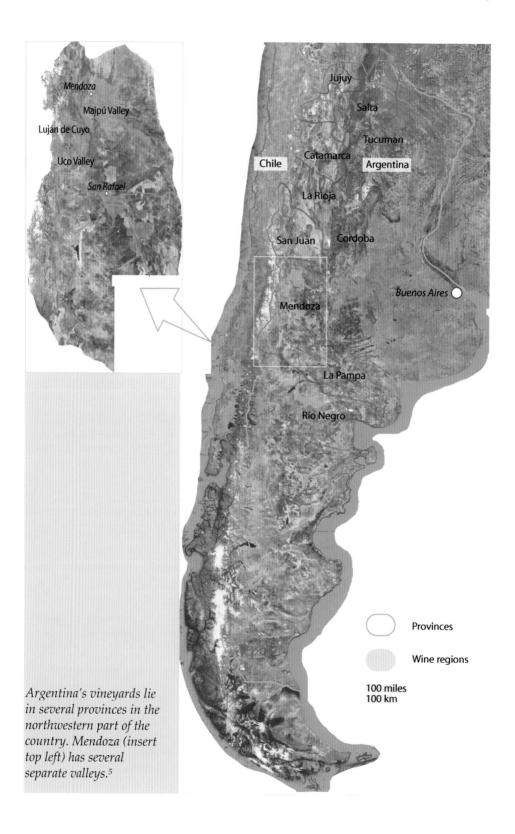

Argentina's vineyards lie in several provinces in the northwestern part of the country. Mendoza (insert top left) has several separate valleys.[5]

It does not have the complexity of Cabernet Sauvignon or the aromatic appeal of Syrah, but it has become Argentina's own.

The usual international suspects are also grown in Argentina, with Chardonnay in second place in the whites, and Cabernet Sauvignon important in the reds. The style of the wines is distinctly New World, but there is a tendency—how shall we put this?—towards rusticity. It's fair to say at least that the style of the wines follows the precedents of California and Australia, although achieving less intensity.

Argentina shares the southern half of South America with Chile. In fact, their vineyards face one another, as it were, across the Andes. Argentina's vineyards are located in the northern half of the country. Mendoza is by far the most important region, with 70% of the vineyards and 80% of all production. From its latitude you would think it was a warm climate, but vineyards are planted at high elevations, reducing temperatures and making for greater diurnal variation. Originally the area was a desert with a sandy soil, but irrigation has transformed it for viticulture. There is no phylloxera, so most vines are not grafted. (It is not clear why phylloxera has failed to penetrate South America—Chile is also free of it. There is no obvious explanation in terms of the terrain.) Within Mendoza, Luján de Cuyo concentrates on Malbec, while Maipú focuses on Cabernet Sauvi-

Malbec growing in Mendoza is just below the Andes.
Photograph kindly provided by Archaval-Ferrer, copyright Manuel Ferrer.

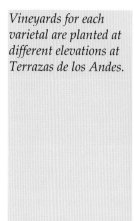

Vineyards for each varietal are planted at different elevations at Terrazas de los Andes.

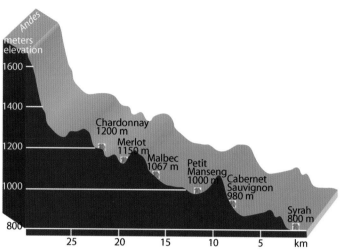

gnon. The high elevation (900-1250 m) of the Valle de Uco gives a cool climate suited to aromatic whites and Chardonnay. East Mendoza has the biggest volume-producing areas.

Altitude is an important determinant of style and quality in Argentina, where the vineyards range from about 450 m above sea level in Río Negro to over 2,000 m in Salta. Within the Mendoza region, elevations vary from 500 m to 1,450 m. Part of the effect this has on the wine is due to the temperature; with an average temperature drop of 0.6 °C per 100 m, the difference between the lowest and highest vineyards (within 100 km of one another as the crow flies) is comparable to going from the south of Italy to the north of France. There's much more diurnal variation at the higher elevations and also an increase in solar radiation.[6] So the climate ranges from hot to cool all within this geographically restricted region. The harvest occurs about a month later at the highest altitudes compared with the lowest.

One interesting illustration of the effect of elevation is shown by the vineyards of Terrazas de los Andes, a winery established by Moët & Chandon in Luján de Cuyo, just south of the town of Mendoza. Going west from Mendoza towards the Andes, the land rises up from 800 meters to 1200 meters within some 20 km. Syrah is planted in the warmest vineyards, near Mendoza, and then as the land rises, varietals are chosen for successively cooler temperatures, culminating in Chardonnay at 1200 m elevation.

Malbec produced in the Mendoza region has more acidity as vineyard elevation increases, resulting from the combination of lower temperatures and greater diurnal variation.[7] The color becomes more intense and violet, and the quantity of tannins increases, up to a limit at about 1000 m, most likely due to the effect of solar radiation on anthocyanin synthesis. (Production of anthocyanins is partly a defense mechanism to protect the grape from ultraviolet radiation, so increased solar exposure causes increased anthocyanin production in black varieties.) General balance and complexity of the wines is better above the lowest elevations. The basic message is that style and quality are determined more by altitude than any other geographical factor; in fact, increasing elevation achieves somewhat similar improvements to reduction in yields. With global warming a factor of increasing importance worldwide, the ability to choose your vineyard's elevation may give Argentina a significant advantage in the future.

San Juan to the north of Mendoza is the second largest wine-producing region, and with its warmer climate is best known for producing large volumes of low quality wine from lesser varieties of grapes. It can produce decent reds for everyday drinking. La Rioja in the north is known for the plantings of Torrontés, giving wines with high sugar concentration and low acidity. The vineyards are flanked by two low mountain chains, Famatina on the west and Velazco on the east.

Farther north, at the southern tip of Salta, Cafayate is considered the most important name in the province, accounting for more than 70 per cent of its production. Vineyards are found at an elevation of 1,600 m, with a somewhat extreme climate (very hot during the day, cool at night). Water for irrigation is supplied by the rivers that formed the valleys of Calchaquí and Santa María, and is complemented by water pumped from wells. Torrontés produces delicate, perfumed wines here, but there has been a gradual shift to reds, including Cabernet Sauvignon, Tannat, and Malbec.

Climate is generally reliable, to the point at which vintage was once regarded as unnecessary information. "The quality does not differ fundamentally from one crop to another as happens in some European countries. Because of this it is not usual to mention the vintage on the label," according to the Director of the Instituto Nacional de Vitivinícultura in 1977.[8] Today, of course, with the international market in mind, Argentine wines carry a vintage whether it matters or not.

Chile: Finding its Voice

Wine production started in the sixteenth century in Chile, brought by settlers in much the same way as in Argentina, but the industry has followed a somewhat different course. One driving force is that Chile has a much smaller domestic market, with consumption at levels only around a third of those in Argentina, so producers need alternatives. Deprived of an easy home market for table wines, they turned sooner to producing international varieties for export. Vines were imported from France as early as 1850, and a strong French influence developed, especially after phylloxera drove many winemakers out of France towards the end of the century.[9] Production was split between the local variety (País) and the imported French varieties. The industry was suppressed by an anti-alcohol movement from the 1930s until the mid 1970s, when winemaking might have revived but for the political environment.[10] (First the Allende regime threatened to nationalize all wineries, then the country became a pariah under Pinochet.) It was only after the fall of the Pinochet regime in 1989 that wine production was able to take off. Famous Bordeaux oenologist Michel Rolland said that when he started consulting in Chile in the 1990s, "Winemaking was not about making good wine, just about stopping it being bad."[11]

Production in Chile is driven by exports.[13]

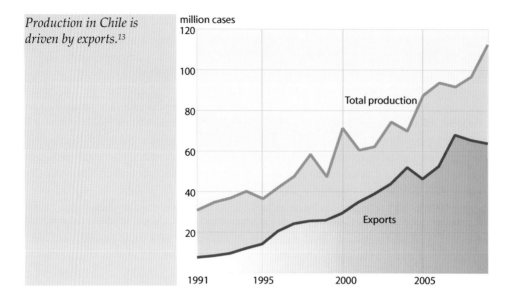

Chile's most important producer, Concha y Toro, was founded in 1883, and its story is a microcosm of wine production in the country. By the end of the 1960s it was producing 25 million bottles a year, but virtually all was sold on the domestic market. Indeed, the wine would scarcely have been attractive in any international context; like most Chilean wines, the main flavor component was oxidation. In the 1980s, Concha y Toro began to modernize its production facilities, and by the 1990s it became an important exporter, especially to the United States. At one point, Chile was in third place for wines imported to the U.S., and Concha y Toro accounted for half of those imports. Today the company owns 15 properties located all over Chile and produces 135 million bottles per year; it has almost a quarter of the domestic market and exports half its production.

Since 1989, production in Chile has increased more than three-fold, and exports almost ten-fold, a feat worthy of Australia; at around 60%, the export proportion is actually the highest of any wine-producing country. But the total export figure is a bit misleading; only 60% is actually bottled wine, and the rest is exported in bulk (at about 15% of the price), a large part of it to China, where it tends to be mixed with local production and sold as domestic product.[12] Allowing for this, Chile, Argentina, and South Africa all have roughly equal importance as exporters of bottled wine on the world market.

Chile has a strong focus on international varieties. The total area of vineyards has doubled since 1994, but the increase has been almost exclusively in international varieties, which now comprise about 70% of the total 117,000 ha.[14] The emphasis is clearly on black varieties. Cabernet Sauvignon alone is more than a third of all plantings, with Merlot in second place among quality varietals. Chardonnay and Sauvignon Blanc are about equally important among the whites.

Carmenère deserves a word. One of the lost varieties of Bordeaux, in the mid nineteenth century it was widely planted, but by the end of the century it had already declined. Because it did not graft well, it disappeared from Bordeaux after phylloxera, and now there is very little left in Europe. Chile's involvement with Carmenère was an accident, when it was discovered that many vines that had been described as Merlot were really Carmenère. Actually a distinction had been drawn previously, with Merlot known as "Merlot Merlot" and Carmenère called "Merlot Chileno." But there was no escape from reality after an investigation by a visiting French ampelographer, Jean-Michel Boursiquot, in 1994. The two varieties are not obvious to distinguish visually, and older vineyards have them intermingled. This causes problems with harvesting, because Carmenère ripens three weeks after Merlot. New plantings separate the two varieties, but no one really knows how much of the remaining "Merlot" is really Carmenère—it could be more than half.[15]

Carmenère tends to savory green pepper flavors (which are exaggerated when the grapes are unripe). It has low acidity and when really ripe can give lush fruits. However, it reaches high sugar levels before phenolic maturity, and more often gives somewhat one dimensional flavors as a result. It is similar to Merlot with black fruits, but has slightly lower acidity than Merlot, and less tannic structure. It is usually vinified as a monovarietal, but I am inclined to wonder whether it might be more interesting to use it to revive the old Bordeaux blend. It might be facile to say that Merlot doesn't give as good results as Carmenère in Chile given the questionable antecedents of so much of the "Merlot," but it does generally seem to be a little undistinguished.

Confusion about varietals is something of a tradition in Chile. A significant part of the Sauvignon Blanc isn't really Sauvignon Blanc at all but is a grape called Sauvignon Vert or Sauvignonasse locally, probably the same as Tocai Friulano of northeastern Italy. Sauvignon Vert is a much softer, and less characterful, variety than Sauvignon Blanc. As vineyards are replanted, it's no doubt being replaced, but in the meantime this explains the lack of varietal typicity of much Chilean Sauvignon Blanc. No one knows how much Sauvignon Blanc isn't really Sauvignon Blanc, but it could be a majority of the plantings.[17]

Quality wines are named according to a system of Regions, Subregions, Zones, and Areas, and 85% of production meets the standard for this Denominación de Origen. Most of the rest is described as varietal wine without

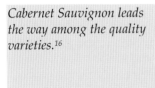

Cabernet Sauvignon leads the way among the quality varieties.[16]

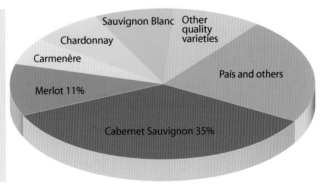

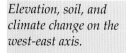

Elevation, soil, and climate change on the west-east axis.

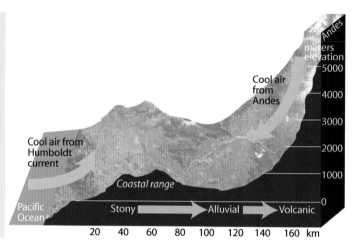

description of origin,[18] and only a tiny proportion of less than 3% is labeled as table wine (Vinos de Mesa).[19]

Chile is longer and skinnier than Italy, so there is plenty of choice for climate variations in which to make wine. With only a hundred miles between the ocean and the mountains, the climate depends more on position on the west-east axis, and on elevation, than on latitude. The low mountains of the Coastal range separate the Pacific from the broad valley leading to the Andes. Most wine regions extend from the Coastal range to within sight of the Andes. The soil changes from stony to more alluvial going from the Coastal range into the valley, and then into volcanic ash at the Andes. Rainfall is inadequate, so irrigation is usually required, provided by run-offs from mountain streams. In some areas, however, obtaining irrigation rights is a limiting factor. The entire country is free of phylloxera, so many vines are planted on their own roots (although rootstocks are becoming more common as a precautionary measure).

The major influences are the Pacific Ocean to the west and the Andes to the east. The cold Humboldt Current flows north up the coast, generating cool, humid air that blows from the Pacific across to the east. On the other side, cold air descends from the Andes into the valley. Between the ocean and the Coastal range, the weather is subject to high humidity and strong breezes. The eastern side of the Coastal range is more protected. It can be warm in the valley between the Coastal range and the Andes, but cools off approaching the mountains.

The important wine regions lie in relatively constricted latitudes. Wine-producing regions are usually divided into three broad areas: the Aconcagua region to the north of Santiago (comprising Aconcagua and Casablanca Valleys); the central valley region to the south of Santiago (where the bulk of wine production occurs); and the southern region consisting of the Itata and Bio Bio valleys.

In a reversal of the usual relationship between quality and latitude (for the southern hemisphere), the higher quality regions are in the north. The southern region still mostly makes wine from País. Aconcagua Valley is the home of Errázuriz, one of Chile's leading quality producers, which was established in 1890, and now has more than 250 ha of vineyards there, as well as other vine-

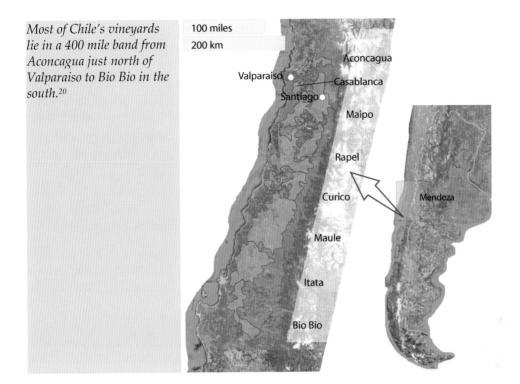

Most of Chile's vineyards lie in a 400 mile band from Aconcagua just north of Valparaiso to Bio Bio in the south.[20]

yards elsewhere. Vineyards run right up to the base of the mountains. The wine region follows the Aconcagua river, from close to the Pacific, across the Coastal range, and up to the foothills of the Andes. The focus is on black varietals following Bordeaux. Casablanca Valley is a more of a newcomer, planted in 1982 as an experiment by Concha y Toro, and now a focus for production of Chardonnay and Sauvignon Blanc. It's not really a valley, but lies between the Pacific and the Coastal range. There are no major rivers, rainfall is low, and it is difficult to obtain water rights to support irrigation for new plantings.

Most of the important producers are located in the Central Valley region. French varietals were first planted in Maipo Valley, and a major proportion of Chile's Cabernet Sauvignon comes from here. Most of the major wineries were established in the nineteenth century, close to Santiago. The region extends from the Coastal range to the Andes. It remains important because of its history, but it's not at the cutting edge. Fine wine is also produced in Rapel Valley and Colchagua Valley, which is relatively warm and focuses on black varieties. Colchagua is one of the most rapidly growing areas in Chile, especially with its newly recognized subregions, including Apalta, which is being developed by Viña Montes. By the time you get down to Maule Valley (which altogether has about half of Chile's vineyards), the emphasis is more on País.

At one extreme, Chile is exporting about 30% of its production in bulk at prices equivalent to around $1 a bottle; at the other extreme, there are also prestige wines running close to a hundred times that. Most are Cabernet Sauvignon or blends based on it. The first was Concha y Toro's Don Melchor, first produced

Vineyards in Aconcagua Valley extend to the base of the Andes.
Photograph kindly provided by Viña Errázuriz © Eugenio Hughes.

in 1987, from Cabernet Sauvignon planted in the Puente Alto Vineyard in the highest, coldest region of the Maipo Valley. Other prestigious labels produced by leading local producers are Montes Alpha M, from Via Montes, and Clos Apalta from Casa Lapostolle, both in Colchagua Valley.

Foreign producers are also taking stakes in Chile, and one resulting high-end wine is Almaviva (produced in Maipo Valley by a collaboration between Mouton Rothschild and Concha y Toro). Not to be outdone by their cousins, Lafite Roths-child have an investment in Viña Los Vacos in Colchagua. The influence of Bordeaux is also seen in the presence of flying winemakers, most notably Michel Rolland, who advises Casa Lapostolle. Perhaps the most important foreign investor is Miguel Torres of Spain, whose arrival in 1979 far preceded other foreign investors. His winery in Curicó Valley, in the Maule region, introduced temperature-controlled fermentation in stainless steel, pneumatic presses, and other features of modern technology, and had a significant impact in bringing Chilean wine into the modern era.

South Africa: Industry in Renovation

Wine production in South Africa was in crisis for more than a century, or to be more precise, it suffered from a cure that was as bad as the disease. Dutch settlers planted vineyards in the seventeenth century, but it was only in the early nineteenth century that production took off as the result of increased trade with Britain following its occupation of the Cape. The market collapsed when Britain turned to French wine following a trade treaty in 1861. Half a century later, in 1918, the KWV (Koöperatieve Wijnbouwers Vereniging[21]) was formed with government backing. Virtually all the farmers joined the new cooperative, and it was able to use its power to improve prices, but was undercut by huge harvests. The government then gave it power to set the minimum price each year for excess wine to be purchased for distillation; and when this was not enough, extended its power in 1940 to control prices of all wine, and indeed to control all production. The intention was to alleviate the situation by eliminating surpluses, but, hand in hand with large wholesalers, the KWV favored bulk production. The dead weight of the KWV squashed quality wine production until the industry was deregulated in 1997, when finally quality producers could get out from under. At this point, the KWV was split into two parts, a cooperative representing growers, and a private company that became the largest wine producer. (It was overtaken in 2000, when SFW and Distillers, two other large wine producers, merged to form Distell.)

The change in two decades has been remarkable. Plantings of quality varietals were minimal under the old regime: only 6% in 1980. There was a slow increase over the next decade, but things really took off after deregulation. Today about half the vineyards are planted with international varieties. If Chenin Blanc is included, the total goes up significantly, but in the context of South Africa, Steen (the local name for Chenin Blanc) is often a workhorse grape rather than used to make premium wine. Judging from its decline during the period when quality varietals increased sharply, the South African producers do not esteem it highly. Indeed, much of it has been used for production of brandy rather than wine.

Chenin Blanc remains the most widely planted grape in South Africa. Sauvignon Blanc and Chardonnay have displaced almost all other white varieties; there is still a little Hanepoot (the local name for Muscat), Sémillon, Riesling, and

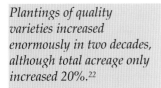

Plantings of quality varieties increased enormously in two decades, although total acreage only increased 20%.[22]

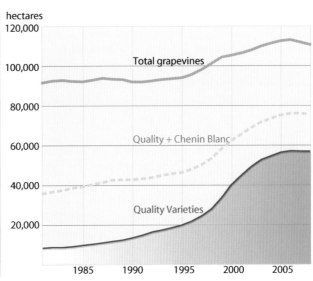

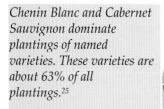

Chenin Blanc and Cabernet Sauvignon dominate plantings of named varieties. These varieties are about 63% of all plantings.[25]

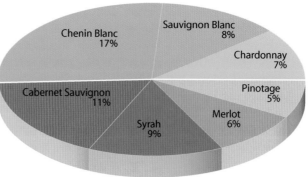

the infamous Cape Riesling (which is really Crouchen Blanc). Cabernet Sauvignon takes the lead as the most planted black grape variety, followed by Syrah (known here as Shiraz to reflect its New World style) and Merlot, with a little Cinsault (best forgotten), Cabernet Franc, and Pinot Noir.

Pinotage is South Africa's own variety.[23] Not much cultivated anywhere else in the world,[24] it is regarded in South Africa as a quality varietal. I would say this is open to question. The name reflects its origins as a cross between Pinot Noir and Hermitage (the local name for Cinsault), created in 1925 by Abraham Perold, the first Professor of Viticulture at the University of Cape Town. Perold created four seedlings, which were subsequently propagated by his successor at the University, C. J. Theron. The first Pinotage wine was made on an experimental basis in 1941, followed by commercial planting in 1943. Four vineyards planted Pinotage in the 1950s, and the first varietal-labeled wines were produced in the 1959 vintage. The variety was propelled to fame when Bellevue Estates Pinotage won a prize at the National Wine Show.

The variety was appealing because it ripened early and achieved high sugar levels. But initially the wines often showed notes of acetone (nail polish remover); this was partly responsible for its poor reputation. The cause has been ascribed to both viticulture (when the vines are cultivated under high temperature and water stress) and vinification (using too high temperatures for fermentation), but it is fair to say that although it discouraged many early consumers, it is not now usually a problem. Pinotage can be made in fresh and fruity styles for early drinking, or given exposure to oak to become a more serious wine, but perhaps the most significant fact is that nowhere do you find any claim for its typicity. There's no core style for Pinotage akin to that for its Pinot Noir parent.

Pinotage remains controversial in South Africa, with some producers advocating it, but others embarrassed by it. "Astringency and bitterness are two of the inherent risks in making Pinotage," says Seymour Pritchard, a Pinotage enthusiast who owns Clos Malverne.[26] It's most often vinified as a single varietal, and although there are some interesting wines, they are in a small minority. My own view of Pinotage is somewhat akin to Dr. Johnson's view of the dog walking on hind legs: "It is not done well; but you are surprised to find it done at all." When I encounter a good example of Pinotage, after an initial reaction of relief, I am left

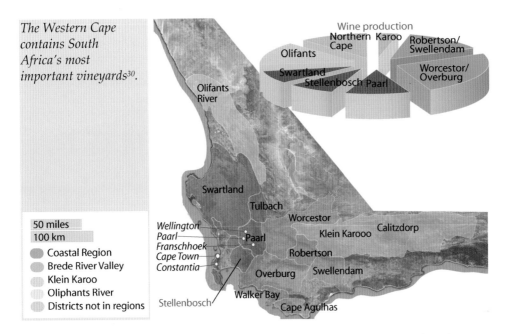

The Western Cape contains South Africa's most important vineyards[30].

with a suspicion that probably a better wine could have been made by planting the vineyard with another variety.

Pinotage is sometimes used as the basis for the "Cape Blend," which is as controversial as the varietal itself. Attempts to define a varietal composition for the blend proposed that it should be based on Pinotage, with a minimum of 30% and a maximum of 70%. But it was impossible to reach agreement, and the only defining characteristic of Cape Blend is that it is a red wine coming from the Cape Region.[27] As a practical matter, however, most Cape Blends do contain some Pinotage.

One ongoing controversy is whether and why South African wines have a "peculiar, savage, burnt rubber and dirt odor," according to British journalist Jane MacQuitty[28] Not everyone finds the same offensive quality; other critics refer to smoky, earthy, or sometimes tarry aromas. WOSA (the industry body Wines of South Africa) took the criticism seriously enough to establish a commission to investigate; it reported that a small number of wines do have an aroma that can be recognized as burned rubber, but there is no other common feature to these wines. Probably the odor simply results from poor winemaking allowing accumulation of sulfur compounds.[29]

Dry table wine is about 90% of the total production of 75 million cases, with half exported.[31] There is still some production of fortified wine, but almost all of it is sold domestically. Sparkling wine is made by both tank fermentation and by fermentation in the bottle, although the latter is described as Method Cap Classique; the more appropriate description of Méthode Champenoise is not used because of objections from the French Champagne mafia.

Most wine production occurs in the Western Cape, which has the coolest areas at the very southern tip of Africa. There's also some wine made farther north, in the Northern Cape. South Africa has a hierarchical system for describing wine

Vineyards of Stellenbosch protected by the Helderberg mountain.
Copyright Erica Moodie/Wines of South Africa.

regions, with several broad Regions, each divided into Districts, which may in turn be divided into Wards. By far the most important in terms of international reputation is Stellenbosch, a district in the coastal region about thirty miles from Cape Town. Paarl, especially the Franschhoek ward, and the Walker Bay district are also well known. These are the coolest regions. Constantia was important historically for its famous sweet dessert wines.

Stellenbosch is the wine capital of South Africa, with its climate dominated by a ring of neighboring mountains. Three quarters of its plantings are high quality varieties, with Sauvignon Blanc well in the lead.[32] The only other district with a comparable emphasis on quality is Paarl. The tiny ward of Constantia is devoted almost entirely to classic grape varieties, producing dry wine, although the Klein Constantia and Groot Constantia companies have reintroduced the Constantia dessert wine that was famous in the eighteenth century. This is an unfortied, late harvest wine made from Muscat Blanc à Petits Grains.

What's the overall impression of South African wine? The difficulty is that it's not clear it really has a coherent identity. The traditional varieties of Chenin Blanc and Pinotage don't really cut it on the international market. A handful of Chenin Blancs are competitive, but most are nondescript. Pinotage remains a niche at best. There are certainly some good cool climate results with Sauvignon Blanc and with Pinot Noir; but of course the areas where these can be made are relatively restricted. The verdict is still out on whether Bordeaux blends or Shiraz will develop into distinctive enough wines, or at least offer a price advantage over other New World alternatives. It does not seem likely that South Africa can become a competitive source for bulk production of inexpensive wine, so that will not be the way out.

V THE OLD WORLD

WINE PRODUCTION IN EUROPE represents 2000 years of experiments in matching grape varieties to regions, with a range from cool climates where wine growing is marginal to hot climates that are barely tenable in the era of global warming. A notable feature of the classic wine regions that represent the best of each country is the lack of overlap among their grape varieties. In France, Burgundy has several hundred years of experience with Pinot Noir; by comparison, Cabernet Sauvignon is a relative newcomer to Bordeaux. Italy has the widest range of climates, with the top wines coming from cooler northern half of the country; Piedmont's Nebbiolo is the oldest established variety. Based on Tempranillo, the great wines of Rioja go back at least to the fifteenth century, but owe their present success to developments resulting from an influx of French winemakers at the time of phylloxera. For dry white wines there is little to match Chardonnay from Burgundy; for sweet white wines there is a panoply of choices with Bordeaux and Germany at the top. Champagne owes its success to the happy accident of discovering sparkling wine when the mini ice age of the sixteenth century made it impossible to mature black grapes. There is no rival for dry fortified wines to Sherry or for sweet fortified wines to vintage Port.

The top wine regions of the Old World.

Region	Wine style	Top Varieties
Bordeaux	Dry red	Cabernet Sauvignon and Merlot
Burgundy	Dry red & dry white	Pinot Noir and Chardonnay
Hermitage & Côte Rôtie	Dry red	Syrah
Barolo	Dry red	Nebbiolo
Brunello di Montalcino	Dry red	Sangiovese
Rioja	Dry red	Tempranillo
Rheingau & Mosel	Dry and sweet white	Riesling
Champagne	Sparkling	Pinot Noir, Chardonnay
Port	Fortified sweet	Blended
Jerez	Fortified dry	Palomino, Pedro Ximénez

14

Bordeaux and Burgundy: Classic Rivals

IS IT A CARICATURE TO SAY that Bordeaux epitomizes the commercial approach to winemaking while Burgundy represents the artisanal? The die was cast in 1855, when the great châteaux of Bordeaux were classified by the prices of their wines, whereas in Burgundy the focus was on mapping the vineyards where the grapes were grown. The 1855 classification of Bordeaux was almost incidental, yet the consequences have reverberated throughout the region ever since.[1] In the same year, a detailed map of the vineyards of the Côte d'Or appeared;[2] and a century later this effectively became the basis for a description of quality, assigning each vineyard to a position in a hierarchy from village wine to grand cru. Branding the wines versus mapping the terroir: how have these different approaches served each region?

Bordeaux has the diversity that comes from blending different grape varieties. Indeed, the dominant variety is different in different parts of Bordeaux. Total production has been steady around 70 million cases annually for the past decade (subject, of course, to vintage fluctuation), 90% of it red. Burgundy is much smaller, currently producing about 15 million cases annually, roughly double the amount of production in 1980; only a third of production is red. Burgundy is devoted to Pinot Noir for its red wines and to Chardonnay for its whites; the concentration on single varietals emphasizes the differences that come from individual plots of land.

The difference between Bordeaux and Burgundy is typified by the way they describe themselves. Almost all of the several thousand producers in Bordeaux are called "Châteaux."[3, 4] The name can be misleading with regards to their size and importance, since châteaux vary from the grand estates of the Médoc, typi-

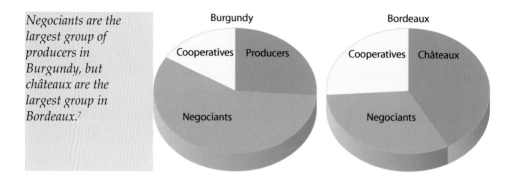

Negociants are the largest group of producers in Burgundy, but châteaux are the largest group in Bordeaux.[7]

cally with 40-50 hectares of vineyards, to much smaller family producers with only a couple of hectares. Bordeaux's 100,000 ha are divided among roughly 8,000 "châteaux," so the average vineyard holding is only about 13 ha, corresponding to about 7,000 cases of wine annually. The name of the château is by far the most important determinant of reputation. Most châteaux produce only a single wine, but the more important often also have a second wine.

Burgundy producers usually bottle their wines under the name of the family—in fact, the multiplicity of overlapping hyphenated names resulting from the break up of family holdings under French estate law can be confusing. Production is on a much smaller scale in Burgundy. Its 28,000 ha are divided among 3,800 growers, so the average holding is only 7 ha. And those 7 ha are rarely a contiguous plot. With almost 500 different vineyard appellations in Burgundy, most growers' total holdings are divided into many, much smaller holdings that are bottled individually (although sometimes holdings are so small that it's not economic to produce an individual wine). The name of the producer and the appellation are both important.

Both Bordeaux and Burgundy show a split between wine bottled by its producer and wine bottled by a negociant who amalgamates lots purchased from many growers or producers. In Bordeaux, château bottling accounts for the greatest part of the market, and negociants' wines are usually sold under brand names, distinct from the château-bottled wines. In Burgundy, many negociants' wines are sold under the same appellation names as the producers' wines, although some at lower levels are sold as brands. The distinction between a small producer and a large negociant is not necessarily obvious from the label. Although growers are bottling an increasing proportion of their own wine, negociants still bottle the major proportion of Burgundy.

The fame of Bordeaux and Burgundy is international, yet both are firmly rooted with the majority of sales in France;[5] and the majority of exports is to other E.U. countries.[6] Bordeaux's overall economic importance is about three times that of Burgundy. Always skillful at finding new markets when old ones falter, the Bordelais have greatly increased sales in Asia recently, to a point at which China has displaced the United States as the largest importer of Bordeaux outside the E.U. For Burgundy, the most important two markets outside of France are the United Kingdom and United States. Exports are relatively more valuable than domestic sales, especially when there is a great vintage on line.

All Bordeaux is Divided into Three Parts

Bordeaux is divided into two parts, the left bank and the right bank, separated by the Garonne river, which joins the Dordogne river just north of the city of Bordeaux to form the Gironde estuary (which gives its name to the local political and administrative unit, the Département de Gironde). (The region between the Garonne and the Dordogne is called Entre-deux-Mers, which literally means "between two seas.") But in terms of the dominant grape varieties, Bordeaux really falls into three areas. The left bank is divided into the Médoc, the peninsula to the north of the city, and the Graves, which extends south from the suburbs of the city. The right bank stands alone, well separated from the city.

Virtually all wine in Bordeaux falls under the Appellation Contrôlée system. Generic Bordeaux AOC can be produced anywhere within the region, but each district also has its own, more restricted AOC. With a total of 57 different appellations under the general rubric of Bordeaux, the system might seem to offer a usefully detailed classification, but this is deceptive. The right bank contains most of the areas that produce wine at the lowest level of AOC Bordeaux, and broad district appellations, consisting of the Côtes and Entre-deux-Mers.[9] All of these areas produce both red and white wines. The most important appellations on the right bank are the Libournais, a small cluster of appellations taking their name from the town of Libourne on the Dordogne river. The best appellations in the Libournais are St. Emilion and Pomerol, surrounded by a group of satellite appellations. They produce only red wine.

The Garonne divides Bordeaux into the left bank and right bank.[8]

The Médoc and Libournais produce only red wine, other regions produce red and dry white, and a cluster of appellations around Sauternes produce sweet white wine.

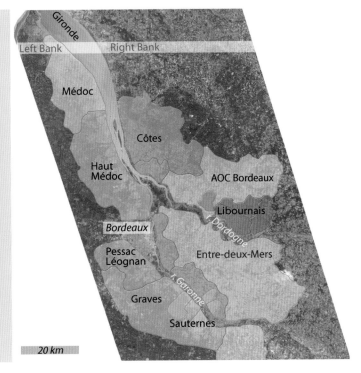

On the left bank, the most important areas are the Haut-Médoc, which forms the southern half of the Médoc, and Pessac-Léognan at the northern tip of the Graves. The Médoc produces only red wine. The Graves produces both red and white wines, and the best white wines of Bordeaux come from Pessac-Léognan. The sweet wine regions around Sauternes lie towards the southern tip of the Graves (opposite some regions for sweet white wine production on the other side of the river).

The majority of producers are on the right bank; more than half make wines only of the lowest level appellations, AOC Bordeaux and the Côtes. The left bank altogether has roughly a quarter of the producers. There is a huge price gap between generic Bordeaux at the bottom and the Haut-Médoc, Pessac-Léognan, and Libournais at the top, so the latter regions are far more important in terms of revenues.

Virtually all Bordeaux, whether red or white, is a blended wine. Six types of black grapes and six types of white grapes are allowed in Bordeaux,[11] but most black plantings are Cabernet Sauvignon, Merlot, or Cabernet Franc, and almost all whites are Sauvignon Blanc or Sémillon. Any of these grape varieties can be grown anywhere in the region, but some appellations apply only to red wine (if you make a white wine in a red wine appellation, it must be labeled as Bordeaux AOC).

There is no single prescription for Bordeaux wine. There can be wide variation in the proportions of the different grape varieties. The appellation rules nominally allow the same grape varieties to be grown anywhere in Bordeaux, but in fact there is a major difference between left bank and right bank. Cabernet Sauvignon and Merlot dominate the left bank, whereas Merlot and Cabernet Franc dominate the right bank. This is a response to their different soils, gravel-based on the left bank creating a slighter warmer environment than the cold clay-based soils of the right bank. The result is that Cabernet Sauvignon ripens reliably only on the left bank.

The difference between the red wines of the left bank and right bank is due to the different grape varieties as much as to the terroir itself. For white wines, it's not so much the geography as the type of wine you want to make that determines the blend. Bordeaux white wines are produced from Sauvignon Blanc and Sémillon, with the former comprising the majority of the blend for dry wines, and the proportions reversed for sweet wines.

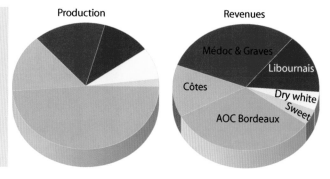

Generic Bordeaux and the Côtes account for two thirds of production, but less than half of revenues.[10]

Production

Revenues

Médoc & Graves

Libournais

Côtes

Dry white

Sweet

AOC Bordeaux

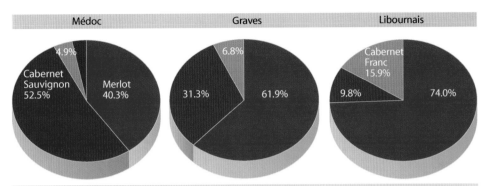

Cabernet Sauvignon dominates the Médoc, but Merlot dominates the Graves and Libournais.[12] There is a small (but increasing) amount of Petit Verdot in the Médoc, shown by the black sector.

The Haut-Médoc is the only part of Bordeaux with any degree of hierarchical organization. Wine from the Haut-Médoc may be Haut-Médoc AOC, but within the Haut-Médoc are six communal appellations at the top of the hierarchy. Their wines are labeled with the names of the communes, including the famous appellations of Margaux, St. Julien, Pauillac, and St. Estèphe.

Although Bordeaux's great reputation was built on wines based on Cabernet Sauvignon (and references to the "Bordeaux blend" almost always mean wines dominated by Cabernet Sauvignon), this is really true only of the Médoc; actually by far the dominant grape variety in Bordeaux as a whole is Merlot. Merlot is approaching two thirds of all plantings, and Cabernet Sauvignon in fact is only a quarter, but the distribution is different in the Médoc, Graves, and Libournais.

Cabernet Sauvignon is (just) the majority grape in the Médoc, where it is concentrated in the best appellations.[13] In fact, it is only in the four top communes that Cabernet Sauvignon is really in a clear majority. Most of the other plantings are Merlot. There is a little Cabernet Franc and a small proportion of Petit Verdot, a variety that is difficult to ripen, but is considered to add spice to the blend, and that has increased a bit with the recent warming trend. The top châteaux have the highest proportions of Cabernet Sauvignon.[14]

The right bank is three quarters Merlot, with very little Cabernet Sauvignon—where Cabernet is grown it is more often Cabernet Franc. Although Graves is usually considered to be part of the left bank—well, of course, it is part of it geographically—in terms of cépages it is almost exactly half way between the Médoc and the Libournais, roughly one third Cabernet Sauvignon to two thirds Merlot.

In spite of its reputation for sticking to tradition, Bordeaux has actually seen significant change. Its renown over the past two centuries has been based on its red wines, but in terms of overall production, its devotion principally to black varieties is relatively recent. Until the 1960s, plantings of white grape varieties were in the majority. As recently as 1968 they were still 50%, but fell dramatically to a small minority by 1988. Today, Bordeaux produces 90% red wine.[15] And the nature of the red wine is changing.

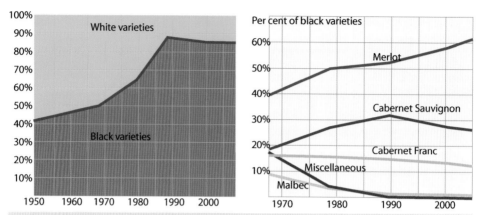

Bordeaux has changed from white to red wine production and has continuously increased the proportion of Merlot in red wine.[16]

There has been a steady movement towards Merlot over the past half-century. On the left bank, this is seen in a decline in Cabernet Sauvignon and an increase in Merlot;[18] on the right bank it involves a further emphasis on Merlot, which is heading towards monovarietal territory. Cabernet Franc is decreasing. The miscellaneous varieties have all but disappeared (there is still some Petit Verdot in the Médoc, and tiny amounts of Malbec in various vineyards). The increasing proportion of Merlot is a significant factor, changing the style of Bordeaux so that it is fruitier and can be drunk when younger.

The trend towards Merlot is seemingly irresistible, but even so, the nature of Bordeaux is that the blend can vary greatly from year to year, depending upon which varieties are successful in each vintage. At Château Pichon Lalande in Pauillac, for example, the vineyard has a majority (58%) of the two Cabernets, but the actual level of Cabernets in the wine over a decade has varied from as little as 50% to as much as 85%. So different vintages in Bordeaux differ not only in how the basic quality of the year affects the nature of the wine, but also in what blend was used that year.

Cabernet Sauvignon together with Cabernet Franc forms a majority in Pichon Lalande, but actual proportions vary depending on vintage conditions.[17]

The dashed white line shows the level of Cabernets planted in the vineyard.

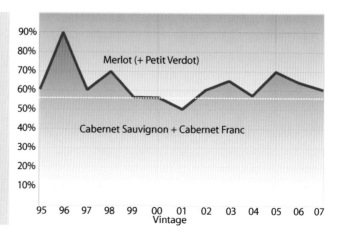

Châteaux, Negociants, and You

Bordeaux originated as a wine exporter rather than producer. When the Romans arrived in 56 B.C., Bordeaux was recognized as a center for commerce, and the city was already an active port. (The Bordelais were probably actually drinking wine produced in Gascony, to the southeast.) Bordeaux became a major wine exporter during the three centuries of English control of Aquitaine (1152-1453). The 40 or so English vineyards recorded in the Domesday book in 1086 went nowhere near supplying England's pressing need for wine,[19] and over the first century of English rule, Bordeaux displaced the port of La Rochelle to its north as England's major supplier. By the start of the fourteenth century, half of Bordeaux's exports went to England,[20] but only about 15% of the wine came from the vicinity of Bordeaux itself.[21]

Even by the fifteenth century, wine production was of relatively small economic importance in the Médoc.[22] Certainly it was never more than a secondary culture. Steady growth turned viticulture into a major economic contributor by the end of the seventeenth century. During the second half of the eighteenth century, viticulture became important on the left bank, where vineyards already occupied the areas that are cultivated today; by the end of the century, Bordeaux had become an important producer as well as exporter. Production was mostly from the left bank; although wine was being made in a wide area of the right bank, viticulture was far less important than on the left bank.

Whether the wine was produced in the immediate vicinity or brought in from the right bank or the southwest, the city of Bordeaux established itself at the center of the developing wine trade. Its role as the export center for both local and foreign wines led to the development of its unique system for distribution, which controls the way you buy Bordeaux to this very day. All wines passed through the hands of the merchants, who developed into the powerful class of negociants, maturing the wines to suit the palates of their customers. The pro-

Bordeaux first became known for its importance as a port, as illustrated by the prominent ships in this map by Munster from 1598.

ducer was unimportant (at least to the consumer), and the negociant would purchase wines, and blend them (often from a variety of sources) into a marketable product.

Until the eighteenth century, wines were produced for immediate consumption,[23] and young wines were more valuable than older wines.[24] Negociants would buy from the châteaux as soon as the grape juice had been converted into wine. They would transport it to their cellars in Bordeaux, ready for shipping once they had performed their various magic tricks on it. The wine would be shipped as soon as possible, while it was still fresh, young, and valuable. Later in the century, when it became possible to age wine, the position of the negociants was reinforced as they became responsible for maturing the wine in their large *caves* until it was exported. And when exports shifted from barrels to bottled wine, for the most part it was the negociants who undertook the bottling.[25]

Establishing their companies on the Quai des Chartrons, close to the port, and outside the old city walls, the negociants became known as the Chartronnais. Their central position evolved into an arcane system for distribution called the *Place de Bordeaux*. The roles and relative importance of the players have changed over the years, but the basic system has remained unchanged, created by the need to connect the negociants located in Bordeaux with producers distributed all over the left bank and right bank. Until the railway was extended through the Médoc and the Libournais in the late nineteenth and early twentieth centuries, travel to the far reaches of the wine country was by no means easy. The connection was made by courtiers, whose role is much like that of a real estate agent in bringing together the buyer and seller. Courtiers would have detailed knowledge of the producers, and so would find whatever wine was needed to make up a

A view of the Quai des Chartrons around 1907 shows a busy scene. Only a few courtiers and negociants still have their headquarters on the Quai.

particular blend for a negociant. Even today, negociants purchase wine from châteaux only via the mediation of courtiers, although the process is now little more than a formality.

The dominance of the Place de Bordeaux is intimately connected with that unique system for selling the new vintage: *en primeur*. This means that wine is sold in the spring following the harvest, even though it will not be bottled for another one to two years. The system has its origins in the role of the negociants in buying the wine from the châteaux immediately after the harvest.

A diminution in the role of negociants was sparked in the early 1920s when Baron Philip Rothschild persuaded the first growths to join him in bottling their own wine. The wine was still sold via the negociants, but the difference was that although the negociants continued to purchase it soon after the vintage, they did not take receipt until the château bottled it two years later. The wine was kept at the château, but at the negociants' risk.[26]

The change imposed by château bottling basically affected the location of the wine between fermentation and bottling. The arrangements for nominal transfer of ownership became formalized in the en primeur system, when contracts were exchanged in the spring after the vintage. The negociants maintained their grip on distribution, and remained the power in the land because they controlled access to the market. Sales en primeur for wine that would be bottled at the château slowly became the norm over the century.

The arrangement stayed largely within the trade until 1967, when château bottling was made mandatory for the Grand Cru Classés of the Médoc. This forced negociants to trade only in contracts for subsequent delivery of bottled wine from the leading châteaux; possibly to assist with their cash flow, it was around this time that the wine began to be offered at that stage to retailers and hence to consumers.[27] This was a significant part of the move to a consumer-driven wine market.[28] The system was reinforced when château bottling was made generally compulsory in 1990. From relatively small beginnings with a few châteaux offered by a handful of merchants to cognoscenti, the en primeur offerings have now become a major annual event of full-scale consumerism.

Roughly 700 châteaux offer their wines en primeur today (including most although not all of the top châteaux) and the majority of them become immediately available to the consumer. The negociants have been reduced to mere distributors, who have done no more than pay the château, while simultaneously selling the wine on to retailers. Consumers have to purchase en primeur on the basis of reputation, or market hype, rather than on tasting. In a good vintage, the wine will sell all the way through to the ultimate purchaser, the consumer, who pays up front, although he will not receive the wine for another two years. In a poor vintage, commitments to buy the wine may stick with negociants and distributors.

Like a drug addict, Bordeaux is now completely dependent on selling en primeur. Of course, once you have started to sell en primeur, you are locked into the system, because to make a transition to selling after bottling would eliminate your cash flow for two years. En primeur wines are first shown to the world during the last week of March, when Bordeaux becomes a circus with the en primeur wines as the entertainment. By the end of the week, faxes and emails are flying around the world with reports of the vintage. Soon after, the first wines are actually offered for sale via the Place de Bordeaux, and slowly more are released, culminating with the first growths.

The Place de Bordeaux famously insulates the châteaux from the ultimate purchaser: the consumer. This can mislead châteaux into setting prices for a vintage that may bear little relation to consumers' interest. Even as recently as the 1970s, negociants, who after all have to sell the wine, had a key role in setting prices. The change to château bottling, coupled with the transition to a consumer-driven market, was a powerful force for pushing the seesaw from the negociants to the château proprietors. Even in 1982, only a third of wine produced in the Gironde was bottled at the château; today most is château bottled. The change in the balance of power was also given a major impetus by a market crisis in 1974, caused by the peak of a boom and bust cycle, when many negociants went to the wall.

The disconnect in pricing exacerbates a long tradition of conflict between the châteaux and the negociants. In a good vintage, the châteaux may find that they have under priced the wine when they see it increase rapidly in price as it leaves the negociants. Determined to see the profits stay with those who have actually made the wine, they may then increase prices substantially in the next vintage, irrespective of its quality. The negociants wail that they cannot the sell the wine at this price, but are forced to take it under threat of being cut out from the next good vintage. It's really a game of pass the parcel, with whoever is left holding the wine running the risk.

In a great vintage where demand outstrips supply, there is no risk; the negociants can take the money, and run to the bank as they sell the wine directly on to the consumer. In a poor vintage, they may be stuck with it. The much overpriced 2006 and 2007 vintages are a case in point. After the great 2005 vintage, prices backed off only a little for the much less good 2006 vintage; then when the world financial crisis forced prices lower for the 2007 vintage, the dilemma was that 2007 seemed such better value than 2006, that anyone along the chain left holding 2006 was stuck with it. The balance of terror is perpetuated along the whole chain, with the vendor at each stage saying to the purchaser that buying the wine this year is prerequisite to maintain the allocation for next year. When you are trying to purchase a Bordeaux en primeur from a hot vintage, it's the relationship your local distributor has with the negociant in Bordeaux that will determine whether you can get it.

Discontent over profits being taken further along the chain has led over the past twenty years to the development of the system in which the first growths no longer simply release their wines en primeur, but divide them into tranches. In a good year, the first tranche (also known as the prix de sortie) may be quite small to test the waters; usually the price is relatively attractive, but quantities are restricted. Second and then third tranches are released later at steadily increasing prices if the campaign is going well. At the consumer level, you see tranches at all levels of classified growths, not just the first growths. Usually this is due to shortage of supplies on the after market. Below the first growths, the châteaux usually have a single release price. However, negociants who sell out their initial allocation from the château (at what amounts to a first tranche price) may then go back into the market to re-purchase from the Place (the château having now sold out), and the higher cost means that they sell the wine on at a higher price, effectively amounting to a subsequent tranche.[29] Châteaux may try to hold back some of the crop in good years to sell later.

Boom and bust cycles are no doubt an integral part of selling any product that fluctuates so widely in quality every year, but they are certainly much enhanced by the combination of selling wine before you really know its quality together with maintaining protective layers between the producer and the consumer. Consumers have no chance to taste the wines, and have to decide whether to buy on the basis of balancing hype from producers with recommendations from critics. It's fair to say that it's not an easy job to assess wines at such a young stage. Indeed, the increasing number of people engaged in tasting en primeur (and their lack of traditional expertise) is partly responsible for a recent trend to make changes in vinification ensuring that the wines seem flattering at this stage, a source of much controversy. One negociant says, "At best [the blend] is an approximation of what the wine will ultimately be."

The perception that Bordeaux became terribly expensive with the incredible increase in prices in the 2005 vintage is well founded, but this is true really only of the few hundred leading châteaux. The thousands of producers of generic Bordeaux—petit châteaux, they are sometimes called— have gone in the other direction. With essentially no increase in price over a decade, the price they can gain for their wine is below the cost of production; and the value of their land is no higher than the *prime d'arrachage* (a payment from the government for pulling up the vines).[30]

The importance of the Place has diminished, but 70% of the wine produced in Bordeaux today is still sold via the Place.[31] Today there are about 400 negociants, of whom about forty account for 85% of the market. Their combined turnover is about €2.1 billion, so this is pretty big business. Some are still located in Bordeaux, although those still engaged in production have often moved to new facilities outside the city.[32]

Some large negociants still behave in the old style, buying wine to produce blends. The largest are the negociant arm of Château Mouton Rothschild, which produces Mouton Cadet, and CVBG, who own a series of châteaux and vineyards and produce the well-known Dourthe #1 brand. But brands are handled in a completely different way from châteaux. Negociants do not hold substantial vineyard areas in order to produce brands; in fact, they directly own less than 5% of the vineyards.[33] Most of the wine for the brands comes from independent vignerons, often under long-term contract.

A Panoply of Classifications

The first thing you ask about most French wines is where the wine comes from: what is its appellation? But Bordeaux is different. The first thing you look at is the name of the château. The place of origin and the quality of the producer are all tied up in this one name. How did this happen?

Until the sixteenth century, little attention was paid to the exact origins of a wine. During the seventeenth century, the main distinction was between the plateaus a little inland and the alluvial palus (wetlands) closer to the river. By the eighteenth century, individual regions were being distinguished. By the middle of the century, there was a steady relationship between the prices of the appellations; within the Médoc, individual communes had much the same relationship as today.[34] Prices for the right bank were not thought worth recording; in fact, the prices for left bank wines remained well above those of the right bank throughout the first half of the twentieth century.

Individual producers began to fall into a hierarchy during the eighteenth century,[35] and what were to become the first growths separated from the rest.[36] The Bordeaux broker Abraham Lawton maintained a classification of the Crus (best producers) of the Médoc; a list of his prices between 1741 and 1774 shows many names that are recognizable today among the leading properties.[37] Because the brokers dominated the trade in Bordeaux, their pricing for the various châteaux determined reputation. Over a century, châteaux moved slowly from one category to another, although the four first growths always stayed at the top. The classification was largely an internal matter, a tool used among the brokers, although classifications found their way into some books on the subject. It was really just due to an accident that the classification of the time became fixed for perpetuity in 1855, when the Emperor Napoleon III organized a Universal Exposition in Paris to provide a showcase for French products.

The Bordeaux Chamber of Commerce was invited to display the wines of the Département of the Gironde as well as other regional products at the Exposition. The wines were to be submitted to a jury that would consider them for medals on the basis of tasting. To accompany the display, and to give some significance to the individual wines, the Chamber of Commerce commissioned a wine map of the Gironde. They asked the brokers who usually handled the wines in Bordeaux to provide a list of the leading châteaux, identified by class and commune, to accompany it.[38]

Over the following two weeks, a committee of brokers drew up a list of red wines (all from the Médoc except for Haut Brion) and a list of Sauternes. The intention was not to classify the wines of the Médoc as such, but the quality of wine produced on the right bank was generally considered lower, and its producers were less well known to the brokers, who naturally enough concentrated on where their business came from: the left bank. The main criterion for the classification lay strictly with the commercial basis of pricing in prior years, as reflected in the brokers' records.

The classification divided the most important châteaux into a series of five narrowly separated price bands, from Premier Grand Cru Classé (first growths) to Cinquième Grand Cru Classé (fifth growths).[39] The first growths at the top of the hierarchy sold for roughly twice the prices of the fifth growths at the bottom.[40] The 1855 classification covers 61 châteaux, 60 in the Médoc, with the addition of Château Haut Brion in Pessac-Léognan.[41] The classification also

The Grand Exposition of 1855 at the Palais de l'Industrie in Paris displayed products from all over France. Napoleon III and Empress Eugénie were pictured visiting the exposition. The arrangements made to include the wines of the Gironde had a permanent effect upon the classification of wines in Bordeaux.

divided the sweet wine producers of Sauternes into three tiers, with Château d'Yquem at their head as Premier Cru Supérieur, and the others as Premier Cru Classés and Deuxième Cru Classés.

There was nothing official about the classification; it was (and is) no more than a snapshot of the brokers' commercial opinions at this particular point in time, but the system has stuck. So unlike other regions in France, Bordeaux classifies producers rather than land. Indeed, the classification has been so successful in improving the reputations of the châteaux—the prices of all the classified châteaux increased after the classification, and the first growths became more widely separated from the rest—that it was imitated in all subsequent classifications in Bordeaux.

The next step down in the Médoc is the Cru Bourgeois classification, which applies to châteaux in the Médoc that missed out in 1855. It classifies 247 châteaux into the ascending levels of Cru Bourgeois, Cru Bourgeois Supérieur, and Cru Bourgeois Exceptionnel.[42]

The 1855 classification preceded the establishment of the AOC system by the best part of a century. When the AOC was initially described for Bordeaux, in 1936, six communes in the Médoc were given their own AOCs. Châteaux in Pauillac, for example, state "Appellation Pauillac Contrôlée" on the label.[43] But the classification system is separate from the Appellation Contrôlée, and is far more important. Being a first or second growth has far more impact than which commune you come from.

One of the problems of Bordeaux is that while the Médoc is classified with the care and attention of angels dancing on the head of a pin, classification elsewhere is sporadic. Every classification system is different. Classification systems now exist in Pessac-Léognan and St. Emilion, although Pomerol (whose wines are close to those of St. Emilion) famously remains unclassified. But beware: the same term on the bottle may have a somewhat different meaning in the Médoc or in St. Emilion.

It was a full century after the 1855 classification before any other appellations were classified. Classifications could have followed the systems that had by then been established for the rest of France on the basis of terroir. However, the producers were the driving force, and perhaps unsurprisingly, the common feature of all these classifications is that the châteaux are classified.[44] So the model of the Médoc has been more or less followed as other areas have introduced classifications. However, because INAO was responsible for these classifications, they became part of the AOC system.

The Graves was classified for red wine production in 1953, but in fact, all the classified châteaux are in the subregion that was later split off as Pessac-Léognan. The classification system simply picked out the better châteaux to be described as Cru Classés.[45]

Classification of St. Emilion is slightly different. First published in 1955, the classification divided the châteaux into two groups. The first group is called "Premier Grand Cru Classé," the same term used for first growths in the Médoc, but is subdivided into two further groups. The two châteaux subclassified as group A, Ausone and Cheval Blanc, are equivalent to the first growths of the Médoc; the several châteaux in group B (13 at present count) are roughly equivalent to second growths of the Médoc. Then there are about 50 châteaux simply described as Grand Cru Classé. In addition, all the producers of St. Emilion (roughly 600 châteaux) can describe themselves as St. Emilion Grand Cru (a term which has little significance except to undermine completely the concept of "Grand Cru"). There is a world of difference between a Grand Cru Classé, which is classified, and a Grand Cru, which has no classification at all.

Following the initial release in 1955, the St. Emilion classification has been revised four times.[46] The criteria for classification are a mélange of terroir, quality of wine, and commercial considerations. The system is not exactly objective, especially with regard to the commercial considerations, which are influenced by the fact that the jury is weighted with brokers, who are biased against proprietors who sell their own wine instead of using Bordeaux's distribution system.

As part of the regular legal system, reclassifications have been subjected to challenges in the courts. In fact, the classification systems for the Cru Bourgeois of the Médoc and for St. Emilion were overthrown by court orders in March 2007 (the challenges were based on accusations of unfair practices when the classifications were drawn up).[47] The objections may be well founded in procedural principles, but in practice there is little sympathy for them. Nicolas Thienpont (whose Château Pavie-Macquin was promoted in the 2006 reclassification), says that "the case was brought by four properties who produce rubbish. Whatever the tribunal decides they will still produce rubbish."[48] Both systems are in the process of being reinstated, but it may be a while until the situation is fully resolved.

Terroir and Classification in the Médoc

The main issue in understanding the relationship of terroir to classification in Bordeaux is that there is no relationship. Châteaux have been classified in their role as producers, as judged by the price fetched by their wine on the Place de Bordeaux. Furthermore, the scale of production on the left bank would make it very difficult to assign a single classification for the terroir of any individual château. The holdings of individual châteaux are rarely in single, contiguous blocks; often they are interspersed with the holdings of other châteaux. And there is significant heterogeneity in the details of the underlying terrain in the Médoc, which can change rapidly over short distances. So usually there is appreciable variation within the terroir of a single château.

The best vineyards in the Médoc are the most elevated, associated with thick gravel mounds (geological structures that give good drainage). To a casual eye, the terrain looks quite flat, and you would never suspect there was a significant difference, but even a small elevation is enough to lift the land significantly higher above the water table. The importance of drainage is emphasized by the old Médocain saying, "The best vines can see the river," meaning that the vine-

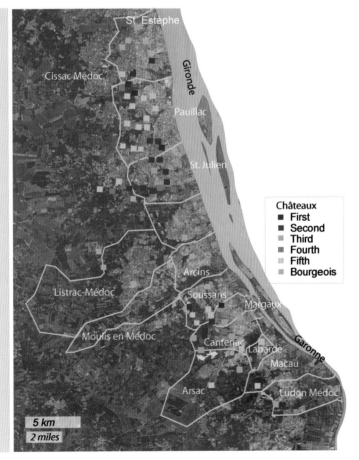

On the left bank to the north of Bordeaux, wine is grown in a broad band parallel with the Gironde.

The Haut-Médoc extends from the outskirts of Bordeaux to St. Estèphe. The Bas-Médoc is farther north.

Within the Haut-Médoc are the individual communes where the best châteaux are located.

The appellations are single communes, except for AOC Margaux, which includes Margaux, Arsac, Labarde, Soussans and Cantenac.

yards are located on slopes draining into the Gironde (or sometimes into one of the streams running into it).

The gravel mounds are large structures extending for several kilometers.[49] They form a line of outcrops more or less parallel with the river, all the way from Graves (south of the city of Bordeaux) to St. Estèphe (well to the north). Château Haut Brion is located in Graves on one of the largest of the gravel mounds; then there is a break in the line until Margaux is reached. The largest of the gravel mounds in the Médoc runs through the famous communes of St. Julien, Pauillac, and St Estèphe and includes several first growths as well as other important châteaux.

The first growths really do have an advantage in terroir, with their key vineyards located on gravel mounds up to 9 meters deep with a relatively low water table.[50] The other leading châteaux, including those classified in 1855, also mostly lie along the band of the gravel mounds, but terroir varies significantly among them, even between adjacent châteaux. With the exception of the first growths, there is not really any geological evidence to support a hierarchy among them, or necessarily to distinguish them from other châteaux close by, given the extent and diversity of their vineyards.[51] This is not to decry the importance of terroir, or of making the best matches between grape varieties and individual vineyard parcels, but other factors, including restriction of yield and the assignment of lots to the grand vin and second wine, are equally important in establishing the brand of each château.

There's nothing wrong with a classification system based on price, but it should be clear that what this represents is the relative success or failure of each château during the period of assessment. Success may depend on the intrinsic quality of the terroir, but it also reflects the quality of viticulture and vinification. And of course the terroir itself may change as a château sells or buys land. Present reputation is simply an assessment of how successful a château has been in exploiting its terroir of the moment.

The explicit connection between price and classification has had long-term effects upon the whole attitude to pricing in Bordeaux. With price the exclusive marker of quality, proprietors have felt ever since 1855 that there is far more at stake than mere profits in setting the price: there is the reputation that will be inherited by future generations. Allowing your price to slip below your neighbor's has the possible implication that your wine should really be at a lower classification. There are endless stories of châteaux waiting for their close rivals to set prices in order to ensure they will not be beaten.

The vineyards of a château today are not necessarily the same as those it held in 1855. Châteaux can (and often do) change their terroir by trading land, and this does not affect their classification. The château is in effect a brand name, and the proprietor can change its terroir without affecting its classification. There are no regulations specific to the Grand Cru Classés; their status was conferred once and for all by inclusion on the brokers' list of 1855. This is unique to the left bank of Bordeaux.

Sales and purchases of land by the classed growth châteaux is an extremely delicate issue in Bordeaux. Indeed, all but one of the Grand Cru Classés refused to tell me how their vineyards differ today from those when the château was classified in 1855. However, it's clear that very few of them have the same terroir they had at the time of classification. The total vineyard area of the Grand Cru Classés has gone down and up again; today it is close to twice its minimum in the middle of the twentieth century.[52] Total production is about five times greater than in 1855.

These bare statistics disguise much greater changes, since land has often changed hands between châteaux, sometimes associated with changes in owner-ship, sometimes under the impetus of rationalizing piecemeal holdings. Some classified growths all but became derelict during difficult periods, with most or all of their vineyards sold off: but Lazarus-like, they have come back from the dead, reconstituted with new vineyards (not usually related to their holdings when they were classified originally).[53]

A common feature between 1855 and today is the economic concentration of a small number of leading châteaux. The Grand Cru Classés are the smallest group of châteaux in the Médoc, but have by far the most economic importance. They are relatively large estates, with an average vineyard of 55 ha (135 acres) and an annual production of 300,000 bottles. Although the classed growths have about 20% of the planted vineyards and production in the Haut-Médoc, they account for at least twice that proportion of revenue.

Second Wines versus Brands

Thirty years ago, most châteaux in Bordeaux produced a single wine. Quality would go up and down with the vintage, there would be some variation in the blend depending on the success or otherwise of each variety, but basically you would be getting the same wine each year, made from the same vineyards, subject to individual vintage variation. And supposedly the châteaux with the best terroirs made the best wines. Today, many châteaux also produce a second wine, sold at a price well below the eponymous grand vin; and a few have gone in the other direction by creaming off the best of the crop to make a super-cuvée.

The story is that a second wine is made from lots that, for whatever reason, do not meet the objectives of the grand vin. Initially, second wines were impor-tant for protecting the name of the château in poor vintages by finding a use for lots that did not make the grade. But from these humble beginnings, second wines have become a phenomenon in their own right. Their growth has been explosive since 1982. Except for some châteaux that are too small, or whose proprietors object in principle to the concept, most leading châteaux now pro-duce a second wine.

What does this do to the economics of production? The châteaux would have you believe that the second wine gives the consumer an opportunity to experi-ence the style and expertise of the château in a wine that is readier to drink sooner at a much lower price But is the second wine simply a brand extension that sells at a price inflated by the reputation of the château?

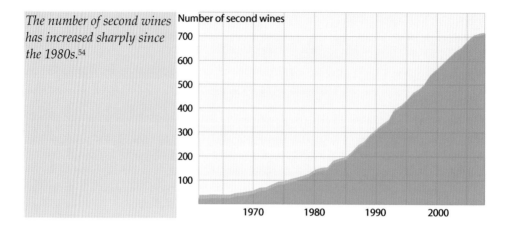

The number of second wines has increased sharply since the 1980s.[54]

The origins of second wines are less obvious than they appear. The general perception is that a second wine is produced by declassifying those lots that are deemed not good enough for the grand vin. In reality, they encompass a range of sources: inferior plots of land, production from young vines (which are generally felt to produce wine of lower quality), cépages that were less successful in a given vintage, use of vin de presse (what's made by pressing the grapes at the end of fermentation, which is of lower quality than the wine made from the juice released earlier). At one extreme, they may come completely from lots that are declassified from the grand vin; at the other, they may come from vineyard plots that never contribute to the grand vin. If the best lots going into the second wine might be regarded as a sacrifice of wine that could have gone into the grand vin (at higher price), the worst lots probably make a much better price in the second wine than would have been obtained had they been sold off in bulk.

Declassified lots most often come from young vines.[55] Overall about 75% of second wines are related to the grand vin, while 25% come mostly from separate terroir. 10% of second wines come exclusively from specific parcels (irrespective of vintage), and therefore are really an independent marque of the same producer, rather than a second wine related to the grand vin. Larger châteaux have almost inevitably accumulated some plots of lesser terroir over the years, so they need to find a use for the inferior lots of wine. Indeed, second wines offer châteaux an opportunity to hide the mistakes of previous proprietors, but using separate parcels rather undercuts the concept of the second wine, at least insofar as it might be used to improve the quality of the first wine.

The most famous second wines largely coming from distinct plots are Les Forts de Latour (of Château Latour) and the Clos du Marquis (of Léoville Las Cases). The main source of grapes for Les Forts de Latour (probably the best second wine in Bordeaux) is a separate vineyard to the west of the "Grand Enclos" around the château. But the second wine also includes production from vines that are under 12 years old within the Grand Enclos, and (depending on the year) some individual lots that are not good enough for the grand vin. Clos du Marquis is a separate plot of land within the estate of Léoville Las Cases, and

Second wines have various origins[56].

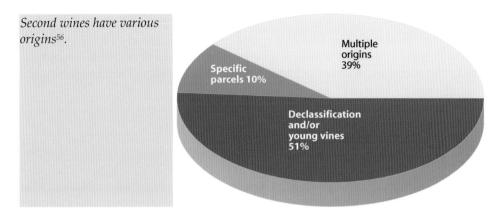

Specific parcels 10%

Multiple origins 39%

Declassification and/or young vines 51%

was used to make a separate wine at the start of the 20th century; now it is the basis of the second wine.

Relative proportions of production of second wines to grand vin vary widely. The vast majority of châteaux put most of their production into the grand vin. However, the increasing trend towards second wines means that some châteaux routinely use less than half of production for the grand vin, therefore making their "second wine" the major product! Of course, proportions vary significantly each year, with the second wine increasing sharply in poor vintages.[57]

Market forces have propelled the growth of second wines. Second wines typically spend less time in oak, and use much less new oak, than grand vins.[58] Second wines are therefore ready to bottle (and to release on the market) quite a bit sooner. Second wines also usually have more Merlot than grand vins. This gives the second wines a fruitier, more forward and approachable style, making them ready to drink somewhat sooner.[59] Partly a response to criticism that consumers no longer want to have to cellar wines for many years until they are ready to drink, this difference casts some doubt on how far the second wines really represent the style of the grand vins.

Are second wines second best? How does the taste of second wines compare with that of other wines at the same price level? At the end of the day, irrespective of the origins of the grapes in the second wine, the question becomes whether the wine genuinely offers the consumer a chance to experience the style of the grand vin at a cheaper price and earlier time, or whether the second wine is effectively trading on the reputation of the grand vin, possibly selling at an inflated price without offering any special value.[60] Second wines tend to sell at a price level one or two notches below the grand vin; for example, the second wines of the first growths are usually available at price levels corresponding to the second growths, the second wines of the Deuxième Crus sell with the third or fourth growths, and so on.

At tastings I held specifically to compare second wines with other wines of the same price from the same commune, both professional and amateur tasters concluded that most often they preferred the other wine. There was a slight, but not very significant difference, in second wines being regarded as just a little readier to drink than alternatives. The moral is pretty clear: if you want a wine at a certain price from a given appellation, you will usually do better to avoid a second wine, whose price is elevated by the glory of the grand vin.

The growth of second wines as a new category has effectively bypassed the tight rules that govern the appellations. (True they must conform to the rules of the appellations in which they are located, but their relationship with the grand vin is entirely unregulated). The authorities are trying to prevent confusion with grand vins by insisting that terms such as "château" are reserved for an "exploitation viticole," which is interpreted to exclude second wines.[61] Most second wines now have a description such as Moulin, Petit, Pavillon, Fleur, Chapelle, Cadet, Benjamin, Dauphin, accompanied by some play on the château's name.

But the consumer would certainly benefit from a clearer distinction between second wines and other products. Certainly there is no way to distinguish a second wine made by declassifying lots from the grand vin from one that is really an independent marque. Indeed, there is no simple way to distinguish between second wines, third wines, or commercial marques. Personally, I would go further and limit a château to using its name on only its grand vin and second wine, excluding its use on wines that come from lesser appellations (such as an Haut-Médoc produced by a château in one of the communes).

More than 12,000 names appear on Bordeaux labels, although the number of actual properties is somewhat less. Châteaux are no longer supposed to sell the same wine under different names (often enough a separate name will be used to supply a supermarket to make it appear that the wine is unique), but the rule is honored as much in the breach as in the observance.[62] Although it's thought there are about 9,000 independent producers or growers, the fact is that no one knows exactly how many châteaux there really are. Mythical châteaux have been damaging the reputation of Bordeaux for more than a century, and it's really time to clean up the mess.

During the 1990s, château-labeled wines represented about 50% of all AOC Bordeaux. They began to decline as sales increased in supermarkets at the expense of specialist stores. Things are now different at the level of generic Bordeaux, where only about 25% is sold under the name of a château, with the rest divided roughly 2:1 between brands developed by negociants and house brands produced specifically for supermarket chains.[63] At least with the brands it is pretty clear what you are getting, but it remains true that you can by no means be certain that a generic Bordeaux labeled Château Quelquechose really represents the sole product of an individual château.

Garage Sales

Garage wines are the antithesis of bargains. Few in number and tiny in production, they are Bordeaux's version of the cult wine. Because most of these operations started in rather modest accommodations, some literally in basements or garages, the French writer Nicolas Baby came up with the name vins de garage and called the vintners *garagistes*.[64] Few garage wines produce more than 1000 cases per year. Most come from the right bank, where the estates have always been small, but garage wines take the principle of small is beautiful to the limit. Perhaps it would be more to the point to describe the movement as small is expensive. The wines are usually dominated by Merlot, and the common feature is a super-concentrated style achieved by extreme methods of viticulture and vinification.

The craze for garage wines really took off in St. Emilion at the beginning of the 1990s, with Jean-Luc Thunevin's Château de Valandraud leading the way. Thunevin came to France from Algeria, worked as a bank teller, opened a wine bar, and eventually bought a tiny parcel of less than an hectare. Together with his wife Murielle he started producing wine, and created Valandraud (named by combining *val* for valley with Murielle's surname, *Andraud*). Their first harvest in 1991 produced only 1280 bottles, made from a relatively sandy plot of land. Since then Valandraud has been produced from better terroir—but the wine is basically the same.

There were only about five garage wines when they made their first widespread impact on the market in 1991. Since then, numbers have increased fairly steadily until reaching a plateau in the past five years at the present level of 30-40.[65] The majority of garage wines still come from St. Emilion, but a handful of garage wines on the left bank follow the same general principles, although here more often dominated by Cabernet Sauvignon.

Most garage wines come from rather ordinary terroir. Their market success has led to various imitations. Garagistes have gone into terroir, purchasing small but special plots of land from which very concentrated wines can be made. Some established châteaux began to produce super-cuvées along the same principle, either using grapes from a small, superior terroir within the estate, or simply selecting the very best barrels, to produce a more concentrated wine than that of the château itself. This is the reverse of the phenomenon of second wines, where the grapes from inferior terroir that are not considered good enough for the grand vin are relegated to a second wine. Of course, whereas the production of a second wine may improve the Grand Vin, taking the best lots for a super-cuvée is likely to have the opposite effect.

Garage wines have had an effect out of all proportion to their number and size. There are probably less than 200 ha of vineyards devoted to producing garage wines, generating fewer than 40,000 cases each year in total. This is roughly equivalent to the size and annual production of a single Grand Cru Classé of the Médoc. But they have moved the whole market.

Garage wines remain intensely controversial, and are especially subject to derision on the left bank. There is some doubt about the staying power of the wines themselves, but not much question about the extent of their influence, which has been widespread. It was the garagistes who introduced viticultural techniques for reducing yields that have become common all over Bordeaux and led the trend towards harvesting riper grapes. From the epicenter in St. Emilion, the trend towards richer wines spread across the right bank and then to the left bank. "St. Emilion in the nineties was the engine for change for fine winemaking," says Jonathan Maltus of Château Teyssier.[66] Whether you love or loath the garage wines, there is no denying the vibrancy they have brought to the wine scene first in St. Emilion and then elsewhere in Bordeaux. Have they pushed the style of production past a tipping point into a new Bordeaux? Between traditional producers, producers making wines in a more modern style, second wines, and garage wines, it can be hard to discern the true typicity of Bordeaux.

Burgundy: the Reign of Terroir

Burgundy is a substantially older wine producer than Bordeaux. Viticulture in France started on the Mediterranean coast, probably somewhere around Marseilles. During the first century it was carried steadily north by the Allobroges tribe, whose capital was Vienne in the northern Rhône. According to that acute observer, Pliny, the expertise of the Allobroges in viticulture surpassed that of the Romans.[67] Their principal grape was a black variety known as Allobrogica, which resisted cold weather. People like to think this may have been an ancestor of Pinot Noir, but of course there is no evidence.

By the second century, negociants were dealing in wine from Lyon, but viticulture had not yet pushed farther north.[68] The Côte d'Or of Burgundy may have first been planted during the third century.[69] Certainly vines had been planted in Burgundy by 312, when Emperor Constantin visited Autun, and there was discussion of the economic conditions of wine production in the region.[70] Little is known about wine production in Burgundy during the centuries following the fall of the Roman Empire. But by the 13th century, the wines of Beaune and Bourgogne were known in Paris (Beaune referring to the region around today's Côte d'Or, Bourgogne to the region farther north around Auxerre).[71] The vineyards around Beaune were regarded as one of the most important economic assets of the Duchy of Burgundy; and the wines were widely exported. There was a set back in the sixteenth century when Burgundy was absorbed into France, but by the seventeenth century, the wines of Burgundy were well placed in the French hierarchy.[72]

The name "Pinot" appears for the first time in 1375, when the Duke of Burgundy, Philip the Bold, ordered a shipment of "vin de pinot vermeil" (red Pinot wine).[73] A strong advocate for quality in wine production, twenty years later he issued a famous edict requiring "bad and disloyal" Gamay grapes to be uprooted from Burgundy, and to be replaced by Pinot. The basic objection to Gamay was that it was too productive (giving at least twice the yield of Pinot Noir), and the Duke also banned several common agricultural practices, including fertilization.

Like many other such attempts at regulation, his edict was counterproductive; it resulted in a general decline in Burgundy's importance as a wine-producing region.[74] In fact, until the twentieth century, Pinot Noir and Chardonnay were concentrated in the narrow strip of vineyards running from Chagny through Beaune to Dijon (the Côte d'Or), with other, inferior varieties planted in the surrounding areas.[75] But since then, Pinot Noir has taken over and now is regarded as the premier (and for the most part the sole) black grape variety of Burgundy.

The only exception is generic Bourgogne Rouge, which can include Gamay (in a blend with Pinot Noir called Passe-Tout-Grains, which loosely translated means "chuck in all the berries"). White wine is virtually all Chardonnay at higher levels, although a fair amount of Aligoté is found at the level of generic Bourgogne. Aligoté is an old grape of the region that was displaced by Chardonnay when phylloxera forced replanting. It can give wine that is somewhat sharp and acid, but producer Laurent Ponsot believes it represents the original authenticity of white Burgundy, and makes a very good Morey St. Denis premier cru (Clos des Monts Luisants) from it to prove his point.

Burgundy is now a mature wine region, and you might think it must have long since reached the limits of its expansion, but in fact production has more or less doubled since 1980. The increase has come almost entirely in white wine and the sparkling Crémant. White wine production is about twice that of red at the present. Quality has gone up and down over the past half century. A good deal of damage was done in the 1960s by planting an overly productive clone, Pinot Droit. And then the excessive fertilization of the 1970s all but poisoned the soils with excess potassium, giving flabby wines of low acidity. It wasn't really until the 1990s that quality fully recovered.

The region of Burgundy is geographically diverse. At its extremes, Beaujolais in the south has soils ranging from clay and limestone to granite, while Chablis in the north is famous for its Kimmeridgian limestone. Beaujolais remains distinct in producing red wine from the Gamay grape, and although it's part of the general region, it's not considered to be "Burgundy" as such. The total production of Beaujolais is roughly the same as the production of red wine in Burgundy proper. The relationship between Beaujolais and Burgundy has become rather sensitive. Growers in Burgundy are concerned about signs that the labels Bourgogne Rouge and Bourgogne Blanc, presently restricted to Burgundy proper, might be extended to Beaujolais, allowing Bourgogne Rouge to be Gamay, and allowing the Beaujolais growers to use 200 hectares of recently planted Chardonnay to compete with the existing Bourgogne Blanc. "The BIVB [Bureau Interprofessionnel des Vins de Bourgogne] liner is heading straight for the iceberg of

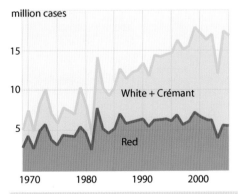 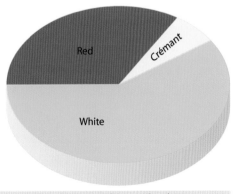

Production has doubled since 1980, but the increase has been in white and crémant (left). Today red is about one third and white is about 60% of all production.[76]

The region of Burgundy stretches from Chablis in the north to Beaujolais in the south.

Chablis produces only white wine, the Côtes de Nuits, Beaune, and Chalonnaise have both white and red, the Mâconnais is mostly white, and the Beaujolais is almost all red from the Gamay grape.[77]

Excluding Beaujolais, Burgundy has 46% Chardonnay and 36% Pinot Noir. There is also 6% of the white grape Aligoté and 11% of Gamay, both used in generic Bourgogne.

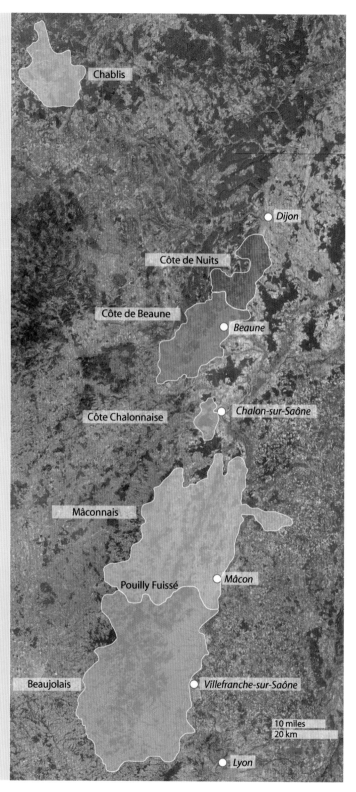

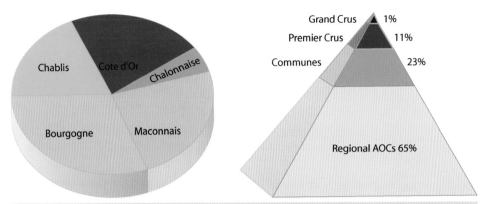

Generic Bourgogne and Mâconnais are the largest parts of production (left); grand crus and premier crus (in the Côte d'Or and Chablis) are only a small part of production (right).[79]

Beaujolais, risking drowning those who paid for the voyage," said a statement issued by the Syndicat des Bourgogne.[78]

Just north of the Beaujolais is the southernmost region of Burgundy proper, the Mâconnais, whose best known appellation is Pouilly Fuissé, producing almost exclusively white wine from Chardonnay. Going north, we then come to the heart of Burgundy. The small region of the Côte Chalonnaise lies just to the south of the Côte d'Or.

Côte d'Or might perfectly well mean "hillside of gold" judging from the prices that the wines of Burgundy fetch today, but actually it derives from Côte d'Orient, meaning a slope facing to the east. It is a narrow escarpment running roughly south to north, from the white wine appellations in the south, through the city of Beaune, almost to Dijon in the north. All the great names of Burgundy are here, with a group of appellations devoted to red wine in the northern half, the Côte de Nuits, and both red and white wine produced in the southern half, the Côte de Beaune. White grapevines tend to be planted where there is more limestone in the soil. Exquisitely detailed mapping places every site somewhere in a hierarchy from generic Bourgogne, through the broad appellations of the Côtes de Nuits and Côtes de Beaune, to the famous communes and their premier and grand crus in the Côte d'Or. Position on the slope is the main determinant of place in the hierarchy, with the upper middle of the slope considered to produce the best wine.

The crème de la crème are the premier and grand crus of the Côte d'Or and Chablis. The name of a premier cru is stated on the label, together with the name of the commune and the statement Premier Cru AOC. But grand crus of the Côte d'Or are so grand that they state only the name of the grand cru, as in Grand Cru Chambertin AOC. The hierarchy is similar in Chablis, where only white wine is produced, but Chablis is always stated on the label in addition to any premier or grand cru name.

There is a long tradition of lieu-dits (individually named vineyards) in Burgundy, and they are freely used on the label, together with a communal AOC

The Côte d'Or
consists of the Côte de
Nuits (from Nuits St.
Georges to the north)
and the Côte de
Beaune (from Aloxe
Corton to the south).

Gevrey Chambertin,
Morey St. Denis,
Chambolle Musigny,
Vougeot, Vosne
Romanée, and Nuits
St. Georges are the
great communes in
the Côte de Nuits, all
devoted to red wine.

In the Côte de Beaune,
Aloxe Corton and
Beaune produce more
red than white,
Pommard and Volnay
are exclusively red,
while Meursault,
Puligny Montrachet,
and Chassagne
Montrachet are white.

The AOCs of the Haut
Côtes and Côtes de
Nuits and Beaune lie
on either side of the
line of communes.

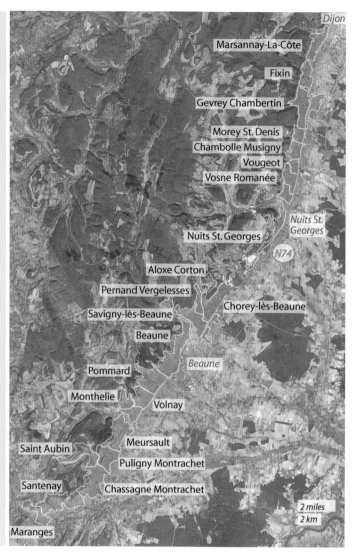

The best terroir lies in
the middle of the slope
along the Côte d'Or.

The grand crus have
an elevation of 250-
300 m.

Illustration from Ecole
des Vins de Bourgogne /
L. Groffier.

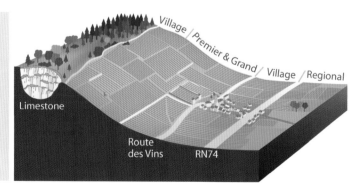

description. Some of them are well respected and considered to be significantly better than a communal AOC as such. But beware: casual brand descriptions for bottlings are also used, and since no distinction is made between them and the authentic lieu-dits, when you see an additional name on the label under the communal AOC, you have no means of knowing whether it really represents wine from a special vineyard. It is probably too much to expect this practice to be stopped, as of course it should be.

Beaune is the center of the wine trade. Most of the old negociants have their headquarters here. Although it's the names of the growers who bottle their own wines that grab attention, the fact is that most Burgundy continues to be bottled by negociants. Most of the negociant names are recognizable from fifty years ago, unlike Bordeaux where there has been extensive turnover.

In the center of the old town of Beaune is the Hospice de Dieu, established as a hospital in the middle ages, and funded by wine produced from its own vineyards.[80] One of the highlights of the year in Beaune is an auction at which the latest vintage from the Hospice is sold to local negociants, who then take possession of the barrels and mature it in their own particular styles. At one time these wines were well regarded for their quality.

A charity auction of wines made from vineyards owned by the Hospice de Beaune has been held in the courtyard of the Hôtel Dieu in Beaune annually since 1859. It is part of a series of events called Les Trois Glorieuses at the end of November, and helps set the price for Burgundy for that year. This photograph shows the scene early in the twentieth century.

The château at Clos Vougeot stands in the middle of the clos. Part dates from the middle ages, but it is no longer used to make wine. It is now the headquarters of the Confrérie des Chevaliers du Tastevin, which in spite of its medieval robes was formed in 1934 to promote Burgundy.

Up in the northern part of the Côte d'Or is another relic from the past. Clos Vougeot, which indeed has a wall around the entire vineyard as its name suggests, is one of the most famous vineyards in Burgundy. It was here that the Cistercians started making wine, and very possibly may have initiated the cultivation of Pinot Noir. After the Burgundian vineyards were seized in the French Revolution, the Clos was broken up into many individual holdings. Today more than one hundred growers own part of the Clos. It's a living illustration of how history can adversely influence the present, because the entire Clos Vougeot was classified as a grand cru under the illusion it was still a single vineyard; in fact, it extends from the top to the bottom of the famous slope, and just like everywhere else along the slope, while the center may be of grand cru standard, the top and bottom are not better than communal. Clos Vougeot is the center of nostalgia, having now become the headquarters of the Confrérie des Chevaliers du Tastevin, an organization established to promote Burgundy during the terrible period of the 1930s. This was part of a successful "folkloric" movement to market Burgundy through fairs, tastings, and various pseudo-historic spectacles.[81]

The different regions of Burgundy were already priced separately by negociants in the eighteenth century, but until the Appellation Contrôlée rules came into effect, the names were used as much to indicate style as to authenticate origin. "A wine with the characteristics of Pommard or Volnay would be named as Pommard or Volnay," says one historian of Burgundy.[82] Differences may also have been somewhat muddied by the common practice of blending with stronger wines brought in from the Rhône. Until the mid twentieth century, virtually all Burgundy was sold under the name of a negociant:[83] growers' names were virtually unknown to the public.[84]

Conflicts between the negociants and the growers developed between the first and second world wars. In 1919 the negociants proposed the principle of equivalence, in which the names of wines would be regarded as interchangeable within levels classified as tête, première, seconde, or troisième.[85] Quality and style were considered more important than origin.[86] Growers fought back by bringing court actions to restrict the use of appellation names. The conflict was emphasized by a public battle between Colette, the author, who was involved in promoting the wines of the negociant Chauvenet, and Gaston Roupnel, a leader of the growers, who went so far in the heat of battle as to say, "The majority of wines sold behind respectable labels are more often the product of the chemist's laboratory rather than the vintner's cellar."[87] The growers finally won when the Appellation Contrôlée came into effect in 1936.

Emphasizing the importance of origins strengthened the position of the growers. Domain bottling began in the 1920s when growers such as the Marquis d'Angerville, who led the growers' syndicate, began bypassing the negociants as the result of the dispute. Still a relatively small proportion until after the second world war, domain bottling began to increase in the 1960s and 1970s, becoming most common with the wines of most valuable origins: the premier and grand crus. Roughly 25% of premier and grand cru production was estimated to be domain bottled in 1969, increasing to 45% by 1976.[88] Actually this was a mixed bag in terms of results: a fair amount of domain bottling was performed by mobile bottling plants, carried on the back of a truck, and quality was variable, to say the least.[89] By the 1970s, growers were installing equipment and gaining expertise. From the premier and grand crus, domain bottling has spread to become the norm for the communes today.

As this movement gathered force, some of the old negociants protected their positions by buying vineyards. Today the major houses mostly produce wines from their own vineyards as well as from grapes bought from outside growers. The largest houses (Bouchard, Patriarche, Louis Latour, Louis Jadot, Faiveley, and Joseph Drouhin) collectively own more than 400 hectares on the Côte d'Or.[90] More to the point, perhaps, they own around 15% of the premier and grand crus.

The Artisanal Scale

The detailed mapping of the land into several hundred different classifications imposes a much smaller scale of production on Burgundy. Every individual plot of land has a level in the hierarchy. The base levels are the regional and district AOCs (such as Bourgogne or Côtes de Nuits). The first of the real quality levels, and the heart of the system, are individual communes, named for villages that have become famous, such as AOC Vosne Romanée. And then within each commune, the best vineyards are classified as premier cru or, at the very top, grand cru, and the label says "AOC," followed by the name of the Cru.

Going up the hierarchy, the average sizes of the appellations decrease. Communes are not large, but the premier crus contained within them can be small, and the grand crus may be tiny, sometimes just individual vineyards. The 11,000 hectares (27,000 acres) of the Côte d'Or are divided into 27 communes, varying mostly from 100 to 300 ha. They include 375 premier crus and 32 grand crus, mostly less than 10 ha each. The descriptions of land in the Côte d'Or are organized into a relatively steep pyramid, steadily narrowing from the base of two thirds of regional AOCs (such as Bourgogne) to 11% of premier crus and 1.4% of grand crus at the peak.[91]

Most premier and grand crus are split among several owners. Take Clos Vougeot, very large for a grand cru in Burgundy, whose 50 hectares are roughly equivalent to the average of a Grand Cru Classé in the Médoc. It is divided among 60 growers; the largest has only 5.5 ha, and the smallest has only a few rows of vines.[93] Take Chambertin, where the largest proprietors have a couple of hectares, producing less than 10,000 bottles per year, and the holdings of smallest proprietors are measured in Ares (a hundredth of a hectare or 100 square meters), producing at most a few hundred bottles. Of course, each proprietor has a variety of holdings, perhaps extending from generic Bourgogne in the vicinity of the village, some village AOC, and perhaps some parcels of separate premier or grand crus. But each wine has to be vinified and matured separately, a very different scale of production from a Bordeaux châteaux producing one or two

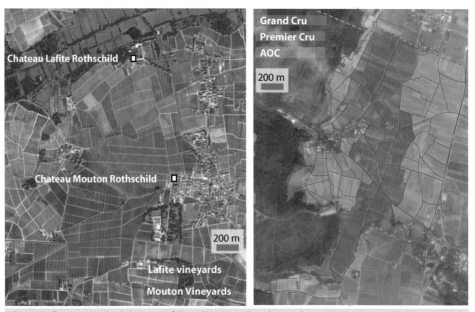

The two first growth châteaux of Pauillac together have about the same total vineyard area (180 ha) as the entire appellation of Chambolle Musigny, which has 23 individual premier crus, and 2 grand crus.[92]

wines from its entire holdings. (Burgundy's closest parallel to Bordeaux would be the exceptional situation where a premier or grand cru has only a single owner; this is called a monopole.)

This seemingly uneconomic situation has two basic causes. The first, of course, is the highly detailed definition of terroir. The second is the ludicrous state of French inheritance laws imposed by the Napoleonic code. Completely the opposite of the emphasis of primogeniture that holds estates together in the Anglo-Saxon world, this requires that everything in an estate is divided equally among all the children. So a perfectly viable holding of a hectare in Burgundy may be subdivided into several uneconomic holdings of a few rows of vines each if the owner was unwise enough to have too many children.

The emphasis on family holdings in Burgundy means that each successive generation breaks up its already small holdings into multiple parts. Of course, sometimes holdings are united as the result of marriage, and the history is evident in the series of overlapping compound names for the producers in each village. Only the largest producers in Burgundy, who own vineyards across several villages, have adopted the model of the Bordeaux châteaux in turning their operations into corporations whose shares, rather than individual holdings, are distributed with an estate. High inheritance taxes add to the difficulty of maintaining an estate, and contribute to the trend for estates in Burgundy or châteaux in Bordeaux to fall into the hands of larger organizations.

Bordeaux is more reliable than Burgundy with regards to vintage variation. Bordeaux's larger scale, and the ability to vary assemblage depending on which cépages are more successful in each vintage, gives better capacity to iron out vintage fluctuations. Within Burgundy, each bottling represents only one variety from a small vineyard area, so inevitably this means there is more variation from one year to the next.

While it is true that the scale of production is different at the highest levels between Burgundy and Bordeaux, this is not nearly so evident at the generic level. Certainly the largest brands in Bordeaux are much larger than the largest brands in Burgundy. Bordeaux's most successful brand, the misleadingly named Mouton Cadet,[94] sells about 13 million bottles per year (somewhat down from its peak, a mere pittance compared to successful New World brands, but large in the context of France). The total amount of all branded Bourgogne is probably only around 30 million bottles. But although the morcelated appellation system makes it difficult to produce a substantial amount of any individual wine, negociants remain powerful in Burgundy, still accounting for more than half of all production.[95]

The Old, the New, and the Brutal

After the retrenchment imposed by phylloxera, the area of Bordeaux stabilized around 135,000 hectares at the start of the twentieth century. After the second world war, it declined fairly steadily to a minimum just below 100,000 hectares, and then recovered through the 1980s. It now stands around 120,000 hectares.

The steady increase in yields since then means that Bordeaux has 20% less vine-yards than a century ago, but 50% more production.[96] With vintage variation reduced somewhat by modern viticulture, production has been steady for some years at around 800 million bottles. By comparison, Australia, which was producing only about 300 million bottles in the late 1970s, has increased steadily, passing Bordeaux in 1996, and now producing about twice as much wine.[97] And that is only part of the problem.

Bordeaux is a paradox between success at the top level and failure at the bottom. The Grand Cru Classés and other leading châteaux have been selling their wines at unprecedented prices in top vintages. But at the same time, producers of generic Bordeaux cannot compete with the flood of New World wines that are fruitier, more reliable, and cheaper. A top Bordeaux can be worth $1000 two years before it is even bottled, while a generic Bordeaux cannot be sold even at $5 per bottle. The result is that in spite of its success at the top, Bordeaux is a signifi-cant part (about 10%) of the European wine lake; about a fifth of its crop simply cannot be sold.[98]

Superficially Bordeaux has not done too badly in the past couple of decades. With 3 billion euros worth of sales each year, it is the most important wine-producing region in France after Champagne. Allowing for the ups and downs of normal vintage fluctuation, since 1990 production has increased about 1% per year, but the total value of sales has increased by 4.5% per year. This is nicely ahead of inflation.

But the overall growth hides some serious underlying structural problems. Generic red Bordeaux, selling on average for under €3 per bottle, accounts for half of the market. The various Côtes appellations, accounting for another 15%, have seen no increase in average price since 1999. Dry white Bordeaux is in the doldrums, with production declining 40% in the past decade,[99] and an average price only just over €1 per bottle.[100] There is growth only at higher levels in the

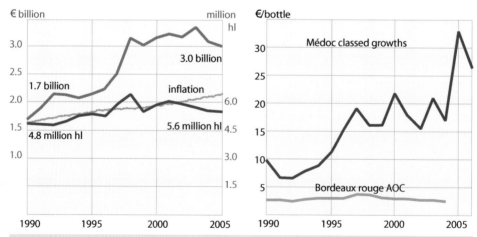

Production in Bordeaux has been steady (left, red) but total revenues have almost doubled (left, green). However, prices of top châteaux, such as the Médoc classed growths, have increased sharply, while Bordeaux AOC has not increased (right).

more quality-driven regions. The CIVB (the organization of producers) believes that 20% of the vineyards in Bordeaux need to be pulled up in order to bring supply back into proportion with demand. But offering compensation to growers to abandon their vineyards has been almost completely ineffective.[101, 102]

Mathieu Chardronier, managing director of major negociant CVBG Dourthe, says that Bordeaux needs to make a transition to larger scale production. "We have a system of production and distribution which is effective for the Grands Crus but it is a real weakness for the rest of Bordeaux... Our biggest handicap is the fragmentation of our wine industry. I don't think a region of this size can have 10,000 producers."[103] That's certainly part of the problem, but is it the whole story? Could the underlying problem be that the terroir and climate simply aren't good enough to make the types of wines consumers now want at entry-level prices?

The latest proposal to fix the crisis is amazingly counterproductive. Perhaps on the principle that you simply can't confuse consumers too much, INAO has been asked to approve a new category of wine, called Bordeaux Premier Cru, which would be added on top of Bordeaux Supérieur and AOC Bordeaux. Already the 57 different appellations in Bordeaux confuse the consumer to the point of distraction, and here is another one that sounds awfully like the top classifications of premier grand cru classé, but in fact would be distinguished from the lowest categories only by having higher alcohol.[104] "The consumer will see through it," says Simon Staples of Berry Bros & Rudd in London, who sell a good deal of Bordeaux.[105] Yes indeed: what can they be thinking in Bordeaux?

Much depends on your cost structure and the amount you are producing. While €3 per bottle is a sort of tipping point, it elicits very different reactions in Bordeaux and the Languedoc. "Selling our wine below €1000 per tonneau [equivalent to €3 per bottle] is suicidal for our producers," says Alain Vironneau, President of the Syndicat of Bordeaux & Bordeaux Superieur.[106] But the Syndicat des Vignerons Coteaux du Languedoc has different expectations: "Coteaux du Languedoc wines sold in hypermarkets are at good price levels, with 35% of sales at over €3 a bottle."[107]

At the level of generic Bordeaux, the cause may be lost. But in the better appellations, Bordeaux has been changing. Over the past twenty years or so, Bordeaux wines have become deeper in color, richer in tannins, and higher in alcohol. Does this suggest a convergence with the New World, perhaps with Napa Valley in California? In the 1970s, stung by criticisms that their wines were too heavy, winemakers in Napa were desperately trying to emulate Bordeaux. In the new millennium, Bordeaux winemakers are increasingly trying to emulate the success of the New World in providing wines with more obvious fruit-forward aromas and flavors and—heaven forefend—not a trace of herbaceousness.

The new Bordeaux started in 1982. The vintage was warm, harvest conditions were ideal, and unusually ripe grapes gave wines loaded with sweet fruits emphasized by lower acidity. In fact, the low acidity led some critics to question whether the wines would age well; reputations were made and broken by the debate. Certainly the wines were ready to drink amazingly early, and in the

The Gironde froze in the unprecedented cold of February 1956, but since then it has become steadily warmer in Bordeaux.

nineties there did seem to be a period when they were fading; but the best began to revert to type after 2000, some even showing those classical faintly herbaceous notes. The judgment of history so far remains that this is a great vintage.

Since 1982, grapes in Bordeaux (and elsewhere) have been harvested at increasing levels of ripeness, with higher alcohol, softer tannins, and lower acidity. The trend is due partly to improvements in viticulture allowing grapes to be harvested at a later point in the ripening cycle, and partly due to new techniques in vinification that allow better control of extraction. It has also been reinforced by a series of vintages that have been significantly warmer than those of previous years. The question is hotly debated as to how far this trend can go before wines in the new style of Bordeaux lose their character and their traditional age worthiness. (Cooler vintages that do not conform to the trend are now sometimes called "classic" to contrast with the new style.)

No one wants to make wine from under-ripe grapes any more. Vegetative flavors from vintages when the grapes failed to ripen are really something of the past. But has the reaction gone too far the other way, towards super-ripe grapes? More recent vintages pose the same question as 1982 but even more forcefully: can wines that are enjoyable so young be expected to mature and develop for fifty years like the greatest vintages of the past?

Acidity has decreased as alcohol has increased. Acidity has been declining at roughly 10% per decade, so that it is now only about two thirds of the level in the 1970s. The average alcohol level in Bordeaux wines has increased steadily from a range of 12-12.5% thirty years ago to a range of 13-13.5% today. The trend to higher alcohol is a significant factor in a transition to the more powerful new international style at some châteaux, and has been especially marked in the past decade. Personally, I believe this represents a decline in elegance—if you go back to older Bordeaux at lower alcohol levels, you can see what we have lost. One oenologue of the old school said to me recently, "In a vrai [true] Bordeaux you have no alcohol perception—if you feel alcohol it is not a true Bordeaux."[108]

Rendement de Base: a Farce in Three Parts

It's hard to quarrel with the idea that yields should be limited in order to ensure quality, unless perhaps you are a vigneron desperate to sell more wine. The role of the authorities is supposed to be to maintain standards by setting appropriate yields for each AOC. They have the right to conduct inspections and to fine producers or prevent them from selling wine under the AOC label if yield limits are breached. But the connivance of the authorities in relaxing the limits is as much of a problem as producers flouting the regulations. The situation is better than it was, but still fails to ensure quality all around.

Originally the limits applied to labeling rather than production.[111] So if you were producing wine in a grand cru with a limit of 35 hl/ha but actually you produced 60 hl/ha, you could label wine as the grand cru until you reached the 35 hl/ha limit. The rest of the production could still be sold, but had to be labeled according to the limits for the lower parts of the appellation hierarchy. You might label the next 5 hl/ha as village wine, to bring you to a village limit of 40 hl/ha, the last 10 hl/ha as Bourgogne to bring you to the limit of 50 hl/ha for the region, and then the rest would have to be sold outside the AOC. So there could be a whole range of bottles, labeled from Vin de Table to Grand Cru Burgundy, but all containing exactly the same wine.

The authorities came to their senses in 1974 and changed the rules so that the limits actually applied to production: in a grand cru with a limit of 35 hl/ha, you could only produce that much. But in case that was too onerous, they increased

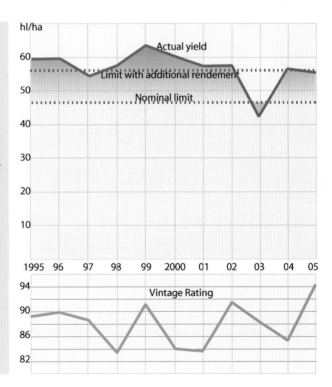

The peaks of rendement.

Over a decade, yields in Burgundy were usually substantially in excess of the nominal legal limit (lower dashed red line).[109] The upper red dashed line shows the limit with a maximum PLC (20% above the rendement de base).

There is no correlation between the yield and the quality of the vintage.[110]

the limits. The normal yield limit, which is quoted as indicating the quality of the particular AOC, is called the rendement de base (base yield). But the limit can be increased in any particular year by (nominally) up to 20%. This is the PLC (plafond limite de classification). In theory, this is intended to allow a response to the particular conditions of the year, for example, allowing an increase in good years that produced high yields. However, this is a rule that is honored more in the breach than the observance. INAO sets the PLC at 20% (and occasionally even higher) irrespective of vintage conditions. In effect, grand crus are habitually allowed to produce at levels that would be appropriate for premier crus, premier crus are allowed to produce at limits that would be appropriate for village wine, village wines have limits more appropriate for the region, and as for the region—well here we are beginning to approach Vin de Table territory.

Only once in an entire decade was the actual yield in Burgundy remotely close to the rendement de base. That was 2003, when the excessively hot vintage conditions caused the vines effectively to shut down. In most years, production was slightly above even the maximum 120% level. From 1998-2000, the excess was closer to 30%. And there can be no excuse that the high yields relate to vintage conditions; there is absolutely no correlation between the permitted increase and the quality of the vintage.

The system changed again in 2004 by introducing the notion of allowing variation around an average based on a decade for the Côte d'Or. The RMD is the rendement moyen décennal (ten year average) and has replaced the rendement de base. Yields can be varied up or down by 3 hl/ha each year, provided that the rolling ten year average is within the limit. The RMD levels are around 35-37 hl/ha for the grand crus, 40-45 hl/ha for premier crus and village wines, and 55 hl/ha for regional wine, so the system is starting off on the high side.[112] Whether it will stem the seemingly inexorable rise in yields remains to be seen.

Yields remain an extremely sensitive issue. When the rendements were published for the 2005 vintage in Burgundy, some were below the levels that had been requested by the vignerons. To express their displeasure, a group of vignerons vandalized the local INAO center in Macon.[113] INAO put out a press release defending itself for lowering limits to maintain quality in view of the world surplus of wine.[114]

Yields in Bordeaux don't seem to be such a sensitive issue, perhaps because the appellation is not so directly tied up with quality. The range of yield limits is less, nominally from 55 hl/ha for generic Bordeaux AOC to 45 hl/ha for the communes of the Médoc. But in fact it's a nonsense. For 2008, the Haut-Médoc was increased to 55 hl/ha, the same as Bordeaux, and *higher* than Bordeaux Supérieur which was 53 hl/ha. The communes were even higher yet at 57 hl/ha! "Numbers mean what I say they mean," as Humpty Dumpty might have said.

Quality in Bordeaux is associated with a classification that reflects success after the fact; it may well be that the more successful châteaux have restricted yields more than others, but none of the classification systems in Bordeaux sets any level on yield limits. There is nothing to say that a Premier Grand Cru Classé should be made at a lower yield than a Cru Bourgeois. Indeed, given the fact the most châteaux now produce a grand vin and a second wine, and that their production is supposedly intermingled, it might be difficult to set yield limits simply for the grand vin.

1855 And All That

The wine was scarcely darker than a pale rosé, quite acidic but not very tannic, with an alcohol level around only 10%. Was this a modern Beaujolais nouveau in a poor year? No, it was claret of the 1855 vintage, as originally produced in Bordeaux, at the time of the classification of the wines of the Médoc. Bordeaux wine is very different today. Of course, it is no surprise that Bordeaux has been changing continuously, indeed all wine production has changed, but the critical question is whether the producers making the best wines in 1855, very different in type from the wines of today, would necessarily be expected to be the producers making the best wines in the twenty-first century under rather different conditions? Yet after a century and a half, the classification of the top wines of the Médoc has never changed.

If there is any rhyme or reason to classification in Bordeaux, it is not obvious to the casual observer. Although all classifications are based on price, every region has its own system. Of the top appellations, only Pomerol has no classification at all, although some of its wines are the highest priced in Bordeaux. The variety of classification systems really begs the issue of the relative positions of wines in different appellations, especially between the left and right banks. It's obvious anecdotally that the right bank has been rising, since its wines were priced well below those of the left bank until 1945, whereas right bank wines surpass left bank prices today, but just how far has this trend gone? The top wines of the left bank clearly outpaced their counterparts on the right bank until the early 1970s. But since then the top wines of the right bank—Pétrus, Ausone, Cheval Blanc—have been regarded as essentially equivalent to the first growths of the Médoc, followed by a strong range of wines at the next level.

Using records from the Place de Bordeaux, I have produced the first joint classification of left and right banks based on the same principle as existing classifications: price. This classification of the top 100 wines shows that today the honors are split more or less equally between the left and right banks. The rise of the right bank is the shown by the way its wines dominate the top fifty. A few

Red Bordeaux has become more intense over 150 years.[115]

Year	Color		Alcohol	Tannins
1850	rosé		10%	1 g/l
1900	red		10.5%	1 g/l
1950	dark red		12%	5 g/l
2000	purple		13.5%	6 g/l

The top 100 wines of Bordeaux classified by price include:

43 Right Bank

42 Left Bank

8 Sauternes

7 White Bordeaux

Wines are listed in descending order of average price for the period 1996-2005.[116]

Pétrus
Ausone
Cheval Blanc
d'Yquem
La Mondotte
Haut Brion Blanc
Latour
Valandraud
Margaux
Mouton Rothschild
Lafite Rothschild **11-20**
Bellevue Mondotte
Haut Brion
l'Evangile
Pavie
Eglise Clinet
Magrez Fombrauge
Pape Clément Blanc
Clos l'Eglise
Mission Haut Brion
Léoville Lascases
Palmer
Laville Haut Brion
Péby Faugères
Angélus
Fleur de Gay
La Conseillante
Vieux Chateau Certan
Pavie Decesse
Cos d'Estournel
Clinet **31-40**
Pichon Lalande
Ducru Beaucaillou
Figeac
Pavillon Blanc de Margaux
Climens
Domaine de Chevalier Blanc
Bon Pasteur
Monbousquet
Montrose
Pape Clément
Canon La Gaffelière
Pichon Baron
Canon
Nenin
Troplong Mondot
Petit Village
Lynch Bages
Chapelle d'Ausone
l'Arrosée

Rol Valentin
Petit Cheval
La Dominique
La Gaffelière
Rauzan-Ségla
Beauséjour Bécot
Léoville Barton
Rieussec
Fieuzal Blanc
Quinault l'Enclos
Gruaud Larose **61-70**
Suduiraut
La Tour Haut Brion
Forts de Latour
Pavie Macquin
Clos Fourtet
Guiraud
Grand Mayne
Beauregard
Smith Haut Lafitte
Léoville Poyferré
Haut Bailly
Grand Puy Lacoste
Pontet Canet
Lascombes
Pavillon Rouge de Margaux
Gazin
Fieuzel
Domaine de Chevalier
Langoa Barton
Clos du Marquis **81-90**
Brane Cantenac
Beauséjour Duffau
Calon Ségur
Carruades de Lafite
Carmes Haut Brion
Talbot
Rayne Vigneau
Beychevelle
Haut Marbuzet
Saint Pierre
Lagrange
Sociando Mallet
Clos de l'Oratoire
d'Arche
Branaire Ducru
Filhot
Clerc Milon
Prieuré Lichine
Barde Haut

white Bordeaux, all but one from Pessac-Léognan, make into the top 100, together with a similar number of top Sauternes.

If you look at prices for wines from Bordeaux châteaux over the past two or three decades, change today is far more rapid than it was during the more leisurely period leading up to the 1855 classification. One of the reasons why the classification of 1855 was not controversial was that it represented 50 years of received wisdom. But today you get different results depending on whether the period is the past 20, 10, or 5 years. A 20 year period may not allow sufficiently for recent changes, but over 5 years a transient fad may over-influence results. A decade seems the right balance to strike between stability and change, as adopted by INAO for the classification of Saint Emilion.

My reclassification of the wines of the Left Bank has been done on exactly the same basis as the original classification, from prices on the Place de Bordeaux, except that the period has been shortened to a decade.[117] There are dramatic differences from the 1855 classification. Only about one third of the classed growths would be in the same group today as they were in 1855. The best relationship with the classification of 1855 is right at the top, where the first growths (now including Mouton Rothschild, which was promoted in 1973 in the only change ever made to the classification) remain unchallenged. In fact, the first growths have greatly expanded their lead over all other châteaux, from a mere 15% price advantage in 1855 to around 100% today.[118]

The large group of the original second growths, together with some newcomers, now falls into three subgroups. At the top, La Mission Haut Brion, Léoville Las Cases, and Palmer occupy somewhat the position that Mouton Rothschild occupied in 1855: significantly below the first growths, but above the next few wines, which consist of six châteaux headed by Cos d'Estournel. This group of nine châteaux identifies one of the most significant changes, the development in just the past 25 years of the whole new class of "super-seconds." The super-seconds consist of a few of the old second growths that have risen above the rest of the seconds plus Palmer and Lynch-Bages. There is a large price gap between the super-seconds and the first growths. There is also a significant gap to what remains of the old second growths. Usually the super-seconds are just described in terms of the Médoc, but La Mission Haut Brion, the sister property of Château Haut Brion in Pessac-Léognan, would price at the head of this group if the Graves were included (and Pape-Clément would also be included).

Defined by the single criterion of price, the super-seconds are quite distinct between the first growths and the following group, which has a diverse set of châteaux—some second growths and others from the old classification, additions from Graves, and second wines. After this, there is a more or less continuous range of prices, making it difficult to divide the wines into clear groups. The dividing line between the last two groups is more or less arbitrary. A couple of the old seconds have fallen right down the list into the fifth group. To allow for inclusion of Graves, I have slightly expanded the total number of châteaux to 71.

A novel feature of this classification is the appearance in the list of some second wines. The second wines of three of the first growths (Latour, Lafite Rothschild, and Margaux) make it into the group below the super-seconds.[119] The close ranking of Léoville Las Cases to the first growths is indicated by the appearance of its second wine (Clos du Marquis) just below the second wines of the first growths. The second wines of two further super-seconds (Pichon Lalande and Palmer) appear at the head of the fifth group. Given the unregulated, not to say slightly irregular, nature of second wines, this would no doubt be a problem for any official reclassification.

A new classification shows the top wines of the Médoc and Graves ordered by average price for the period from 1996-2005.[120]

Colors indicate positions in the 1855 classification.

Purple = first growths

Red = second growths

Brown = third growths

Blue = fourth growths

Green = fifth growths

Black = cru bourgeois or unclassified

Pink = Pessac-Léognan

Gray = second wine.

Latour
Margaux
Mouton Rothschild
Lafite Rothschild
Haut Brion

Mission Haut Brion
Léoville Lascases
Palmer
Cos d'Estournel
Pichon Lalande
Ducru Beaucaillou
Montrose
Pape Clément
Pichon Baron
Lynch Bages

Rauzan-Ségla
Léoville Barton
Gruaud Larose
La Tour Haut Brion
Forts de Latour
Smith Haut Lafitte
Léoville Poyferré
Haut Bailly
Grand Puy Lacoste
Pontet-Canet
Lascombes
Pavillon Rouge de Margaux
Domaine de Chevalier
Langoa Barton
Carruades de Lafite
Brane-Cantenac
Calon Ségur
Clos du Marquis
Carmes Haut Brion
Talbot

Beychevelle
Haut Marbuzet
Saint Pierre
Lagrange
Sociando Mallet
Branaire Ducru
Clerc Milon
Prieuré Lichine
Giscours
Malescot St Exupéry
Kirwan
Duhart Milon Rothschild
La Lagune
d'Issan

Tourrelles Longueville
Rauzan Gassies
Alter Ego de Palmer
Cantenac Brown
Bahans Haut Brion
Ferrière
Haut Batailley
Dauzac
Phelan Segur
Durfort Vivens
Lafon Rochet
Gloria
Pibran
Cos Labory
Armailhac (Mouton Baronne)
Haut Bages Libéral
Marquis de Terme
du Tertre
Siran
Larrivet Haut Brion
Labégorce
Ormes de Pez

Below New Classification

Carbonnieux
Haut Bages Averous
Poujeaux
Grand Puy Ducasse
Haut Bergey
Chasse Spleen
Lynch Moussas
Olivier
Pagodes de Cos
Labégorce Zédé
Cantemerle
Boyd Cantenac
La Tour Carnet
Pédesclaux
Croizet-Bages
Camensac
Potensac
Latour Martillac
Belgrave
Desmirail
Marquis-d'Alesme-Becker
Meyney
Dame de Montrose
Sarget de Gruaud Larose
Fiefs de Lagrange
Coufran
Croix de Beaucaillou
Batailley
Pouget

The impossibility of being included in the 1855 classification means there may be more to be lost than to be gained for unclassified châteaux in participating in any other classifications. Sociando-Mallet was classified as a Cru Bourgeois in the original classification of 1932, but now by any standard would be well up the list of Grand Cru Classés if there were any reclassification. However, the château decided not to be included in the 2003 classification because in effect that would stamp the wine at the Cru Bourgeois level: "There are the Grand Cru Classés, there are the Cru Bourgeois, and then there is Sociando-Mallet."[121]

The châteaux that would be dropped from the classification are mostly the perennial under-performers from the old group of fifth growths, but a fourth and some thirds are found as well. Some of these wines in fact fail to make the top list by a fairly wide margin. Several Cru Bourgeois would be ahead of them if the classification were extended, as it probably should be, to include another 10 or 20 wines.

I suppose the question is whether classification matters at all. If the market can reassess the values of the châteaux so that prices no longer correlate with position in the classification, is the old classification anything more than an irrelevance? But it has a surprisingly effective hold on reputation, with an especially strong effect seen at both the top and bottom. The very existence of the class of first growths sets a glass ceiling that other châteaux, even the super-seconds, cannot penetrate. The one exception, indicated by the promotion of Mouton Rothschild, is a tribute to Baron Philippe's political influence, a factor that is unlikely to be emulated by anyone else.[122] And it is probably true that the very best of the unclassified châteaux, such as Haut-Marbuzet or Sociando-Mallet, are kept from achieving yet higher prices by the fact they are excluded from the classification, By the same measure, the classified growths that would not make the cut today probably have their prices inflated by those magic words "Grand Cru Classé du Médoc en 1855."

Altogether 500 châteaux are classified in Bordeaux, a very thin layer of icing on the cake. Some proprietors feel that classification conveys a clear advantage. "[Classified châteaux] rake in money while the rest, no matter how good, struggle, says Daniel Cathiard of Château Smith Haut Lafitte in Pessac-Léognan.[123] But far from dominating the ranks of the top-priced wines, classified châteaux actually account for only half of the most highly priced wines.[124] The rest are from Pomerol, garage wines from St. Emilion, second wines of top châteaux, and some châteaux who have refused to be classified in the twenty first century because they were ignored in the nineteenth. Half of the unclassified wines consist of châteaux (or second wines) that did not even exist 25 years ago. So classification in Bordeaux is a mixed bag; where it exists, it may help producers who are included, but the market is quite capable of functioning without it. Of course, you have to ask whether there is any point classifying solely by price: if the classification corresponds exactly with current prices, it gives no extra information over and above the price itself. Yet if the classification differs from current price, you have to ask which is right: the classification or the market? Which brings us to another means of classification: the intrinsic quality of the terroir.

Terroir is for Ever

All classification is based ultimately on price. It's an objective measure of market assessment, although how far it correlates with quality is another matter (what is quality anyway?) The big difference is whether the wines are classified directly or whether the land where the grapes are grown is classified. It might seem simpler and more direct to classify the wines—after all, that's what you drink—but this is fraught with difficulties because the wines change in every vintage. Only in Bordeaux are wines classified, in the form of the producing châteaux. Everywhere else in France, it is the land that is classified, with Burgundy providing the epitome of detailed classification; every plot in Burgundy is assigned to a level in a hierarchy which effectively predicts its potential for wine quality. But what was the basis for this classification: detailed geological surveys, other means for assessing terroir, tasting the wine (remember that a single vineyard may have multiple owners in Burgundy, each producing a different wine)? No, it was basically the average price that wine from that vineyard reached in the negociant market of the nineteenth century. Better wines fetch higher prices, but that brings us back, of course, to the question of what is quality? Wine today is somewhat different from wine of a century ago; fashions change, and the view of what is desirable and therefore makes quality can change significantly.

Definition of terroirs in Burgundy has become more complex, but if pricing is a measure of underlying quality, the hierarchy has remained in principle the same over the past two centuries and is holding up well today. Prices from 1810 onwards show a hierarchy similar to that of today, with a price range between

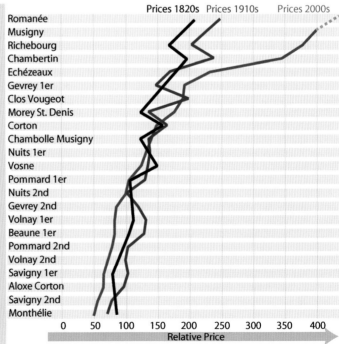

The Burgundian hierarchy has been stable for two centuries.[125]

Appellations are given by the names used in 1910; uncertainty in identifying exactly which modern appellations correspond to some of the old categories may be responsible for some of the variation.

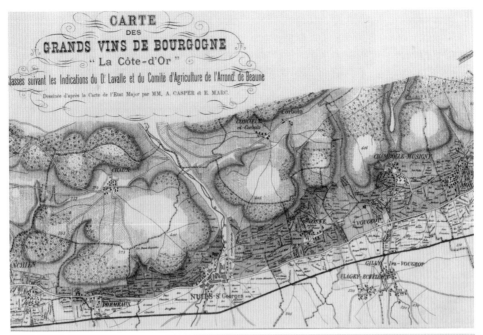

An extract from the map of the Burgundian hierarchy prepared in 1860 could be used as a guide to the present appellations.

the top and the bottom of about 2.5 fold. Wines were sold by negociants with little attention to individual producers, and prices were based on areas more broadly defined than those of today. Just as the negociants in Bordeaux found it useful to maintain a stable relationship between the prices of different châteaux, so the Burgundian negociants had a fairly stable price hierarchy for the regions.[126] A century later, finer distinctions were being drawn, with Nuits, Gevrey, Volnay, Pommard, even Savigny, all split into 1er and 2nd classes. The price range widened to 3.5 fold between the top and bottom. By the second half of the twentieth century, the premier and grand crus were distinguished from the village wines, and the producer's name had as much effect on price as the appellation. The range between the averages for the top and bottom widened enormously to more than ten-fold.

The order of the various appellations today closely follows that of a century ago. In the nineteenth century, Romanée and Chambertin were level pegging at the top, with Richebourg close behind.[127] At the top a century ago was Romanée, just ahead of Musigny, Chambertin, and Richebourg: the same four occupy the top positions today, although Romanée-Conti is farther out in front, and Richebourg and Musigny have moved in front of Chambertin. The biggest change is that the very top wines seem to have expanded their lead (much in the same way that the first growths of Bordeaux have expanded their lead over neighboring châteaux). The move towards quality at any price might perhaps more cynically be regarded as a move towards fashion at any price in an era when wine has become a luxury item with bragging rights.

In a parallel with the famous 1855 classification of Bordeaux, the appellations in Burgundy today closely follow those of the map of 1860 that was prepared in order to show the wines at an exposition in Paris in 1862. Remarkably little has changed since then, but the difference of course is that the Burgundy classification was based on terroirs, and remains valid, whereas the Bordeaux classification of producers retains only partial connection to reality. The Burgundy appellations were finalized in the 1930s, but closely follow the assignment in earlier assessments, in fact the 1860 map of the Côte d'Or was actually the basis for the AOC assignments in 1936.[128]

Just as in Bordeaux, the nature of the wine has changed over the past centuries from lighter and less extracted to darker and more intense. Take Romanée-Conti as an example. In the eighteenth century, it contained 20% Pinot Blanc and Pinot Gris, was made by 12-36 hours fermentation, and emerged relatively light in color. By the nineteenth century, white grapes were reduced to 6%, fermentation was 4-5 days long, and the wine was getting darker. Today the only grape is Pinot Noir, fermentation lasts 2-3 weeks, and the wine is dark and far more tannic.[129] Yet it remains constant as the most highly prized wine of Burgundy.

So is the hierarchy of terrors immutable? The context is that grape varieties were often planted at their northern limits for ripening, so achieving ripeness became a major criterion when terroir was defined. Those plots ripening reliably, that is, even in the poorer vintages, were valued more highly. In the Côte d'Or, that really gives the prize to the vineyards in the middle of the slope. But will this still be true in the era of global warming or will some of those plots ripen too quickly to give the highest quality wine? Certainly it was not clear in 2003, an exceptionally warm year close to the average predicted for 2050, that the traditional order prevailed.

How does the definition of terroir in terms of village, premier cru, grand cru, relate to the market's more practical eye? Classification has a great effect on the price of land. Village vineyards sell for around ten times the price of regional vineyards, premier cru vineyards are two or three times more expensive than village vineyards, and grand crus are three or four times more expensive than premier crus.[130] Vineyards are equally valuable whether used to produce red or white wine. In 1939, when his vineyard Les Blanchots Dessus in Chassagne Montrachet was classified as premier cru, vigneron Jules Morey said, "Why bother? It's only white wine," when it was suggested that he should appeal for promotion to grand cru status.[131] But today a small parcel of Le Montrachet that sold recently may have set the all-time record for vineyard prices.[132]

When I analyzed Burgundy along the same lines as Bordeaux, and ordered the appellations by average prices, I discovered better consistency for the wines of Burgundy. Grand crus come out ahead of premier crus, which come out ahead of villages. There isn't complete consistency: some premier crus would be promoted to grand crus if assessed solely on price, especially Les Amoureuses in Chambolle Musigny and Clos St. Jacques in Gevrey Chambertin. Some grand crus would be demoted (possibly Clos Vougeot and probably most of the lieu-dits of Corton, which are rather variable). There are certainly large differences among the premier crus, with those of the Côte de Nuits generally fetching high-

Romanée-Conti
La Tâche
Musigny
Richebourg
Romanée St. Vivant
Chambertin
Chambertin Clos de Bèze
Griottes Chambertin
Grands Echézeaux
Les Amoureuses, Chambolle Musigny
Bonnes Mares   **11-20**
Mazis Chambertin
Clos St. Denis
Chapelle Chambertin
Latricières Chambertin
Ruchottes Chambertin
Clos de la Roche
Charmes Chambertin
Echézeaux
Clos St. Jacques, Gevrey Chambertin
Clos Vougeot
Les Hauts Doix, Chambolle Musigny
Aux Reignots, Vosne Romanée
Les Petits Monts, Vosne Romanée
Les Malconsorts, Vosne Romanée
Les Gruenchers, Chambolle Musigny
Les Suchots, Vosne Romanée
Corton Bressandes
Les Fuées, Chambolle Musigny
Les Sentiers, Chambolle Musigny
Corton Rognets   **31-40**
Clos des Epenots, Pommard
Les St. Georges, Nuits St. Georges
Les Brûlées, Vosne Romanée
Les Orveaux, Vosne Romanée
Corton Combes
Les Cras, Vougeot
Les Beaux Monts, Vosne Romanée
Corton Clos du Roi
Grèves Vigne De L'Enfant Jésus, Beaune
Corton Pougets
Le Corton
Les Hautes Maizières, Vosne Romanée
Corton Grèves
Clos de la Perrière, Vougeot
Clos des 60 Ouvrées, Volnay
Les Procès, Nuits St. Georges
Estournelles St. Jacques, Gevrey Chambertin
Les Vaucrains, Nuits St. Georges
Clos des Ducs, Volnay

Les Cras, Chambolle Musigny
Corton Renardes
Les Cailles, Nuits St. Georges
Clos de Réas, Vosne Romanée
Les Combettes, Gevrey Chambertin
La Petite Chapelle, Gevrey Chambertin
Les Corbeaux, Gevrey Chambertin
Les Baudes, Chambolle Musigny
Corton Maréchaudes
Les Cazetiers, Gevrey Chambertin
Les Feusselottes, Chambolle Musigny **61-70**
Clos de la Bousse d'Or, Volnay
Les Boudots, Nuits St. Georges
Aux Murgers, Nuits St. Georges
Les Charmes, Chambolle Musigny
Les Chaumes, Vosne Romanée
Lavaux St. Jacques, Gevrey Chambertin
Clos Fonteney, Gevrey Chambertin
Les Roncières, Nuits St. Georges
Corton Perrières
La Perrière, Gevrey Chambertin
Les Meurgers, Nuits St. Georges
Corton Clos de la Vigne au Saint
Les Chatelots, Chambolle Musigny
Combe aux Moines, Gevrey Chambertin
Les Millandes, Morey St. Denis
Le Poissenot, Gevrey Chambertin
Les Pruliers, Nuits St. Georges
Combe d'Orveaux, Chambolle Musigny
Petits Vougeot, Vougeot
Les Damodes, Nuits St. Georges   **81-90**
Clos des Mouches, Beaune
Les Rugiens, Pommard
Les Caillerets, Volnay
Les Jarollières, Pommard
Les Champonnets, Gevrey Chambertin
Bel Air, Gevrey Chambertin
Les Chaboeufs, Nuits St. Georges
Les Perrières, Nuits St. Georges
Les Champeaux, Gevrey Chambertin
Clos des Chênes, Volnay
Les Chaffots, Morey St. Denis
Les Crots, Nuits St. Georges
Les Chaignots, Nuits St. Georges
Clos de Corvées Pagets, Nuits St. Georges
Clos Sorbè, Morey St. Denis
Clos des Porrets, Nuits St. Georges
Les Taillepieds, Volnay
Aux Beaux Bruns, Chambolle Musigny
Les Grands Epenots, Pommard

The top 100 appellations of the Côte d'Or for red wine are led by grand crus (purple) followed by premier crus (red).[133]

er prices than those of the Côte de Beaune, and dominating the top 100. The top village appellations of the Côte de Nuits—Vosne Romanée and Chambolle Musigny—get higher prices than the lowest premier crus of Beaune, which probably should be demoted. But overall, if Burgundy appellations were reclassified today on the basis of price, the results wouldn't come out very differently from the existing order. Certainly there has been much less change than in Bordeaux.

Of course, it's a different matter if you look directly at producers. The reputations of existing producers are largely recent, since the second world war. Although some of the names remain the same, the constant reorganization with each generation as vineyards are divided and combined reduces consistency over decades. A small group of producers stands out above all the others.[134] Domaine Leroy has now displaced DRC (Domaine de la Romanée-Conti) as relatively the most expensive producer (although of course only DRC produce Romanée-Conti itself and La Tache). Leroy and DRC achieve at least twice the price of any other producer, making them the clear equivalent of the first growths.[135] The importance of the producer is emphasized by a huge price range for wines from any single appellation. No negociant comes into the top fifty, emphasizing the importance of making your own wines from your own vineyards.

So in the end, whether it's Bordeaux or Burgundy, it's the name of the producer you look for first. The appellation or other classification is ancillary information that may be helpful in indicating style— left bank versus right bank in Bordeaux, Côte de Nuits versus Côte de Beaune in Burgundy. But it's the man who makes the wine who really matters. The advantage of terroir-based classification is that price differences between different producers' wines for the same appellation tell you what the market thinks of each producer, and price differences between ascending levels of the appellation hierarchy usually do relate to increase in quality.

Beaujolais: Nouveau Tarnished

Should it really be labeled "fermented grape juice"? Beaujolais Nouveau is certainly different from any other wine. And it dominates the image of Beaujolais. Fresh, tart, and (sometimes) fruity, it needs to be drunk within a few weeks.[136]

Between the city of Lyon and the south of Burgundy proper, the gently rolling hills of the Beaujolais represent the final devotion of France to Gamay, a black grape that was common all over Burgundy until Philip the Bold ordered it to be uprooted in 1395. Beaujolais' present position as a favored supplier of wines to the Parisian region dates from the opening of the Canal de Briare in 1642.[137] By the start of the eighteenth century, Beaujolais was dispatching 80% of its production to Paris, with the rest being consumed locally or in Lyon.[138]

Most Beaujolais has always been made for early drinking, but Beaujolais Nouveau, which amounts to a third of all production, is the extreme case. Barely has fermentation finished when the wine is bottled. Still redolent with fermentation esters, it is released to the public on the third Thursday in November. Since 1951, the general regulation has been that AOC wines cannot be sold until December 15 following the harvest, but an exception was made for "nouveau" wines sold "en primeur." There was already a tradition of making the wine available in the bistros of nearby Lyon, but the release date became formalized, and the rule today is that the wine can be shipped from the second Thursday in November in order to be available worldwide for sale a week later.[139]

Beaujolais Nouveau was about 15% of all production when it first became known as such in the 1950s.[140] Production of Beaujolais doubled by the 1980s, and Nouveau increased to more than a quarter. At the peak it reached as much as 50%, but today it is in decline.[141] In its time, Beaujolais Nouveau was a lifesaver. Sales of Beaujolais were depressed through the 1950s, and the novelty, or perhaps one might say the gimmick, of Beaujolais Nouveau gave a much-needed lift. The slogan "Le Beaujolais Nouveau est Arrivé" became so effective that it was a rare wine shop that did not have it on a placard in the window on November 15.[142] Races to get the first Beaujolais Nouveau to Paris or to London by unusual means attracted publicity.

Some part of the phenomenon must be attributed to Georges Duboeuf, who established a negociant business in the Beaujolais in 1964. Known for his remarkable palate and eye for quality, he produces a range of Beaujolais from Nouveau to individual vineyard bottlings. By far the largest producer of Beaujolais Nouveau, his firm alone is responsible for 15% of all Beaujolais production, buying grapes from more than 400 growers.[143]

LES VENDANGES – Un Cuvage en Beaujolais
Départ du vin nouveau

The dispatch of the new vintage of Beaujolais was a sedate affair early in the twentieth century, contrasted with the hoopla of balloons, parachutes, motorcycles, racing cars, or even Concord at the end of the century.

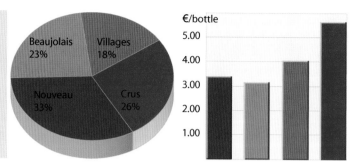

Beaujolais Nouveau is the single largest category of Beaujolais. Price increases only slightly from Beaujolais to the Villages level; it is about 20% higher for the average Crus.[147]

Demand for Beaujolais Nouveau is certainly on the decline. Sales are falling worldwide, except for Japan, where the rhythm of the annual ritual remains appealing. Japan takes about a million cases of Beaujolais Nouveau, roughly 20% of all Nouveau, and more than a third of exports.[144] Elsewhere it's kept partially afloat by the annual marketing, but it's hard to see Nouveau wine as offering any sort of value relative to competition at the same price from "real" wine.

Not only may the phenomenon have run its course, but it shows all the typical signs of a short-term gain at long-term expense. During the 1970s and 1980s, when the phenomenon peaked, Beaujolais Nouveau really pulled the region out of trouble. But its reputation among more serious wine drinkers is terrible. "The nouveau has destroyed our image. All of Beaujolais is confused with nouveau," says Jean-Pierre Large, director of Domaine Cheysson in Chiroubles,[145] pointing to the problem that putting "Beaujolais" on the label is tantamount to telling the consumer that quality (and price) must be limited. Indeed, a local magazine, *Lyon Mag*, published an interview with oenologist François Mauss in 2002 under the title "Le Beaujolais, c'est de la merde." The producers did the worst possible thing: they sued for libel.[146] They won an award (what happened to free speech?) in a decidedly pyrrhic victory; the resulting publicity did nothing to help Beaujolais. (The award was subsequently overturned on appeal.)

The major part of production in Beaujolais is simple Beaujolais or Beaujolais Villages (from the same origins but with higher alcohol). Its price is barely distinguishable from that of Nouveau. The wines of distinction in the region come from the ten Crus,[148] of which Moulin à Vent, Fleurie, and Morgon, all at the northern end of the Beaujolais, are the best known (and best). Some of these wines can be very good, even demonstrating ability to age. They are allowed to put only the name of the Cru on the bottle, and often do so in the hope that people will not realize they are associated with Beaujolais. While this may be necessary for the Crus, of course it denies the rest of the Beaujolais any uplift from the halo of its best wines.

The future of the region is unclear. The practical difficulty is whether there is any alternative for the vineyards used to produce Beaujolais Nouveau at the present. Needless to say, these are not the best vineyards. Perhaps it's better that they produce Beaujolais Nouveau rather than join the lake of wine to be distilled,[149] but the price is a lowered reputation for the rest of Beaujolais.

15

Three Parts of Gaul:
North, Rhône, and Languedoc

THE FRENCH WINE INDUSTRY is in a perpetual state of hypochondria. Books and articles appear continually with "La Crise Viticole" in the title. In spite of its success in defining the major grape varieties and establishing paradigms for their styles, wine production in France is now under threat as never before. The best wines of Bordeaux and Burgundy remain the classic definitions for Cabernet Sauvignon and Pinot Noir, but there is competition everywhere for the role of trendsetter. French dominance is challenged from the marginal conditions of the cool north to the lush wines of the warm south. No longer can France automatically assume the role of leadership.

France produces far more red wine than white. Most of the white comes from the north; progressively more red wine is produced going from Alsace to the Loire to Burgundy, but white wine remains in the majority. Moving south, the tipping point is between Burgundy, where white wine production is still dominant, to Beaujolais, which is largely red wine. South of Lyon, production is almost 90% red. Provence is the largest region for production of rosé. The Languedoc is by far the largest area of production overall, but most is at levels below Appellation Contrôlée. Bordeaux is the largest producer of AOC wines.

The northern regions of the Loire and Alsace focus on white grape varieties that will ripen in their cool climates; the leading wines are Chenin Blanc and Sauvignon Blanc in the Loire, and Riesling in Alsace (adjacent, of course, to Germany where Riesling is even more dominant). If the Loire retains world leadership for Chenin Blanc in both dry and sweet styles, it has largely lost to New Zealand for Sauvignon Blanc. Champagne, an even more marginal climate, relies upon converting the initial, rather acid, base wine into sparkling wine.

The Rhône is really two separate regions, both focusing on red wine. Starting not far south of Lyon, the northern Rhône is almost exclusively Syrah country,

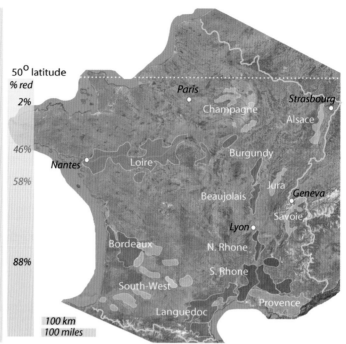

Region	AOC	Other
Alsace	15	0
Bordeaux	120	1
Burgundy	29	0
Beaujolais	22	0
Champagne	30	1
Languedoc	60	152
Loire	50	14
Provence	29	13
Rhône	78	69
Southwest	20	3
Pyrénées	13	25
Others	9	14
TOTAL	475	292

More than half of France's vineyards are AOC. Plantings (thousands of hectares) are:[1]

with the best known appellations being Hermitage and Côte Rôtie. But is it still the trendsetter given Australia's success in renaming the grape variety as Shiraz and producing its characteristically exuberant wines? The southern Rhône consists largely of blended wines, but with a wide quality range from the peak of Châteauneuf-du-Pape, where Grenache is often dominant, to the broad range of Côtes du Rhône, offering simpler wines for every day drinking.

The Languedoc in the far south is so large and disparate that it's hard to group under a single heading. Formerly known as the Midi, a source of cheap red wines from characterless, over-cropped grapes, it has made great strides towards quality in the past couple of decades. Production of table wine has been decimated, and although inferior grapes still dominate plantings, there are increasing amounts of Grenache, Syrah, and Mourvèdre, especially in rising AOC areas.

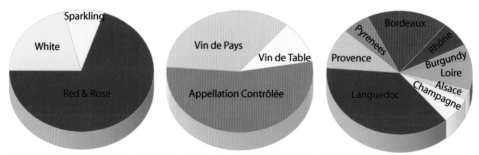

Most wine in France is red, most is Appellation Contrôlée, and the Languedoc is the largest wine-producing region.[2]

Everything is Under Control

"At its inception, the system of Appellation Contrôlée was elaborated with admirable rigor. Here was a noble idea. But when they set their minds to it the French can outwhore anybody… The current bunch in control of the INAO would have us accept the notion that a slope is flat. This is more than preposterous, it is legalized fraud," according to Kermit Lynch, the well-known American importer of French wines.[3]

Control is the operative word in "Appellation Contrôlée." It has been taken far beyond the original intention of the Appellation Contrôlée, which was to ensure authenticity of origins, and now almost every aspect of viticulture and vinification is tightly regulated. Not only does the Appellation Contrôlée system regulate the majority of wine production in France, but it was taken as the model for quality wine production in all of Europe. The big question is whether this preserves a rich patrimony from the depredations of modern industrial development, or whether it precipitates decline by failing to adapt to the modern world.

France was the first country to set up a detailed classification system for its vineyards. The roots of the system go back to the first part of the twentieth century when wine production in France was in dire straits. Phylloxera had reduced production, quality was further reduced by a series of poor vintages, and demand for wine was suppressed by a world recession. Fraud was rife, with wine from inferior sources, including substantial imports from Algeria, routinely relabeled with the names of more famous regions.

Spurred in the traditional French manner by riots in wine-producing regions, regulations were finally introduced to ensure that a geographical name on the label meant the grapes really came from a defined area. The concept of appellations originated with the law of 1905 that attempted to suppress fraud in food and wine production. The first proper regulations came into effect in 1919 (they had been delayed by the war), and further legislation followed, until the national system of Appellation d'Origine Contrôlée (AOC) was introduced in 1935.

The name describes its purpose: wines in the system have controlled origins, which means they come from specific places that are named on the bottle. This is intended to protect the producer (and more incidentally the consumer) by ensuring authenticity. An organization was created in 1935 to administer the appellation laws, and this developed into INAO, the Institut National des Appellations d'Origine, in 1947.[4]

Only the top wine-producing regions were included in the AOC.[5] Other classification systems were introduced later to cover the remaining wines. The next level down is the Vin de Pays, introduced at the end of the 1970s; it usually comes from a broad area (declared on the bottle) and may state a vintage. Vin de Pays is controlled by a different body, called VINIFLHOR. At the bottom, wine is simply described as Vin de Table. It is not allowed to have any geographical description or statement of vintage; just about the only limitation for it to be described as vin de table Français is that all the grapes should come from France.

Specific information is stated on the label at each stage of the quality scale. Vin de Table (left) states only color and national origin, Vin de Pays (center) can state cépage and vintage as well as broad geographical origin, Appellation Contrôlée (right) must state exact origin and vintage, but could not state grape varieties until recently. Some large producers have wines in all categories.

Initially the AOC system affected only French negociants and producers. Negociants in Bordeaux and Burgundy who were blending in wine from the south had to stop buying it. And the producers had to stop selling it to them. Right into the 1920s, growers in Châteauneuf-du-Pape were encouraged to produce Grenache because they got twice the price for selling it to "improve" Burgundy than they could get for Syrah or Mourvèdre.[6]

When Britain joined the common market, the need to honor the AOC descriptions put British merchants into a panic. They had to stop using Nuits St. Georges as a generic name, Sherry had to come from Spain, and Champagne could not be any old sparkling wine. They thought the end of the world was coming.[7]

The system has had an influence far beyond France. Details vary, but all countries of the European Union now have regulations based on the same principle: that wine is divided into three broad classes, where increasing restrictions on geographical origins are associated with higher quality. At the top level of equivalence to the AOC,[8] the name on the label should mean that the wine comes from a certain place and has a character reflecting the history of that place.

Every AOC wine in France has a place name on its label describing where it comes from. This is its *appellation*. Each region has a hierarchy of appellations of ascending quality, organized like Russian dolls. The details vary with the region, but each Appellation Contrôlée is generally like a pyramid, with a broad base of wines that can come from anywhere in the particular region, narrowing to a peak of top wines that can come only from more restricted sites. In ascending order, the hierarchy goes from region, to district, to commune, and finally (sometimes) to individual vineyards.[9] (But not all levels are used in all regions.) Individual AOCs vary in size from the tiny Château Grillet, a single estate in the northern Rhône of only 3.5 ha, to the broad region of the Côtes du Rhône, which sprawls over 40,000 hectares across most of the southern Rhône. Outside of the broad generic AOCs, the average individual AOC is about 1000 hectares.

Vin de Pays also reflect the French love of hierarchy. Five Vin de Pays Regionale include wine from very broad areas; within them are 50 departmental Vin de Pays, each including wine coming from a specific Département (an administrative and political unit); and within these are the much smaller Vin de Pays de Zone. But in fact the hierarchy has little significance for even an informed consumer. By far the best known Vin de Pays are those of two regions: the Vin de Pays du Val de Loire covers the whole region of the Loire (it was called Vin de Pays du Jardin de la France until 2007), and the Vin de Pays d'Oc covers a large stretch of Languedoc-Roussillon. Vin de Pays can be varietally labeled, and production of varietal Vins de Pays wines is constantly increasing, now accounting for nearly 40% of the total production.[10]

Most French wine-growing regions are covered by both AOC and Vin de Pays (the most notable exceptions until recently being Bordeaux, Burgundy, and Alsace, which had only AOCs). Most producers concentrate on either AOC or Vin de Pays wines, but some produce wines in both categories.[11] For the most part, Vin de Pays represent lower quality, using lesser grape varieties grown on inferior terroir. However, there are exceptions where a producer wants to make a high quality wine from grape varieties that are not permitted in the AOC, and as a result is forced (or for other reasons decides) to label the wine as a Vin de Pays. In fact, the constrictions of the AOC system are leading an increasing number of producers to label their wines as Vin de Pays, or even in extreme cases as Vin de Table, rather than obey the bureaucratic dictates.[12]

When the AOC was introduced, the 70 individual AOCs included about 12% of the vineyards in France, basically a small elite. Of course, these were the areas that most needed protection from cheap imitations. But the system has expanded steadily. Up to a point, this was simply recognition of improving standards. But in the 1980s the expansion gathered such pace that today there are 467 AOCs covering about 60% of the vineyards. If the authorities felt that expanding the

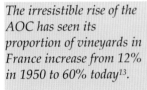

The irresistible rise of the AOC has seen its proportion of vineyards in France increase from 12% in 1950 to 60% today[13].

The proportion of vineyards making quality wine was estimated to be less than 10% before 1939.[14]

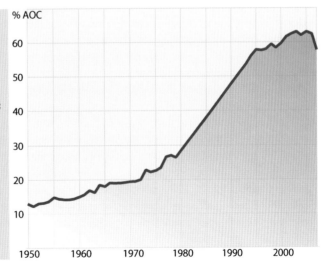

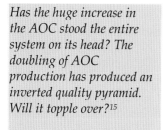

Has the huge increase in the AOC stood the entire system on its head? The doubling of AOC production has produced an inverted quality pyramid. Will it topple over?[15]

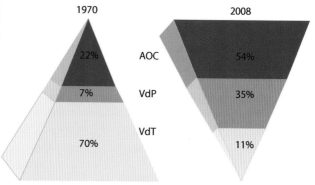

AOC was the way to compete more effectively with the New World, they may have miscalculated, because AOC has become increasingly less reliable as an indication of quality.

In fact, the pyramid of quality from AOC to Vin de Table has been completely inverted in the past half century. Since 1970, Vin de Table has shrunk from 70% of production to 11%, Vin de Pays has increased from a negligible proportion to more than a third, and AOC has doubled to become the largest single category of wine produced in France!

The vastly increased proportion of AOC partly represents growth of the vineyard areas classified as AOC, which have increased from 180,000 ha in 1950 to 475,000 ha today, and partly the decline in the overall vineyard area, from 1.4 million hectares in 1950 to 800,000 ha today. Most of the vineyards that have been pulled out were producing low quality wines that are no longer competitive—not to say that there aren't plenty left! Of course, the new vineyards in the AOC did not come from nowhere; they were reclassified from their former, lower status. This is an interesting calculation for the producer. The lower yield limits of the AOC mean that less wine can be produced. And of course this helps to alleviate the wine glut. But the higher reputation of the AOC should mean a better price for the wine. This seems fine, unless the wine really doesn't get much better and ends up selling at much the same price, in which case everyone loses, not just the producer, but also the reputation of the AOC, which is damaged by distress sales of unmarketable wine.

Indeed, the situation in the AOC became so dire that for the first time in 2004, funds were requested to distill Appellation Contrôlée wine; by 2006, more than 6% of the crop was being distilled.[16] What this really says is that a significant part of the AOC vineyards simply should not be classified at this level. Take Bordeaux as an example; all over the Gironde are petit châteaux (small producers) whose wines were viable only in an older era when there was no competition. Yet the proportion of Bordeaux described as AOC has increased from 53% in 1950 to 99.8% in 2006;[17] if anything, classification should have gone in the other direction, with poorer vineyards demoted out of the AOC.

Appellation Contrôlée has become a caricature, according to Michel Bettane (one of France's most respected tasters). "When the AOC represented 10% of the volume of wine produced in France, there was an equivalent 10% of the population interested in the cultural and historic elements of wine. But the immense farce which consisted of transforming the entire wine-producing territory of France into AOC areas lead to the creation of false AOCs. Because a certain amount of professional discipline is required for a wine to genuinely deserve this label. Paying the producer less than €2 per bottle is not sufficient to maintain this discipline. So 90% of French wines carry an AOC label, but the products do not meet the label's criteria."[18]

Part of the decline in the popularity of French wine is no doubt due to the complexity of the AOC regulations. The consumer is confused by far too many AOCs—Bordeaux alone now has 57 AOCs, almost as many today as the whole system at its inception—and the producer is bound by far too many rules that stifle rather than encourage quality. Yet INAO's most recent attempt to modernize the system took the form of a proposal from its late President, René Renou, for the introduction of yet further complexity, by introducing a new classification of elite wine regions to be called the AOCE (Appellation d'Origine Contrôlée d'Excellence). Will the real AOC stand up, please! It would be more to the point to ensure that existing regulations are relevant and to enforce them.

In 2007 INAO changed its name to Institut National de l'Origine et de la Qualité, to emphasize its supposed role in determining quality. Until now, quality has been more implied than enforced: while INAO determines the potential quality of each wine-producing region, it does little to prevent wine below standard from being sold under the label of the appellation. It is more concerned with setting a basic minimum standard (although even that can be risible in some cases) than with encouraging quality.

Part of the procedure involved in describing a wine as AOC is the need to obtain an *agrément* (an official form stating that the wine conforms to AOC standards). The French consumer organization, QueChosir, pointed out sarcastically that it is hard to believe this confers the supposed guarantee of authenticity and quality, given that 98% of submissions were approved in 2004 and 99% in 2005.[19] Wines have sometimes been turned down for being too good, however, such as Pinot Noirs from Alsace which achieved real weight in a hot vintage, thereby failing to achieve the "typicity" of the usual rosé imitations.[20] Could it be that wines showing up the others are more of a threat to the system than those of low quality?

Even the original regulations went beyond guaranteeing authenticity into attempting to ensure a certain basic level of quality and conformance to traditional local character. Slowly the rules became extended to control every aspect of viticulture and vinification, sometimes with beneficial effects on quality, sometimes inhibiting necessary innovations. INAO is responsible for defining specific regulations for each appellation, including what types of grapes are grown, how the grapevines are tended, what treatments are permitted for the wine, and how it may be described. It is INAO, for example, that determines whether French AOC wines are allowed to state the names of the grape varieties on the label.

Perhaps one of the best effects of the AOC system, aside from the guarantee of authenticity, is the reduction in yields. Reflecting the view that reducing yield enhances quality, all AOC regions have limitations on yield. Where there is a

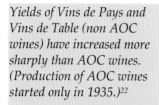

Yields of Vins de Pays and Vins de Table (non AOC wines) have increased more sharply than AOC wines. (Production of AOC wines started only in 1935.)[22]

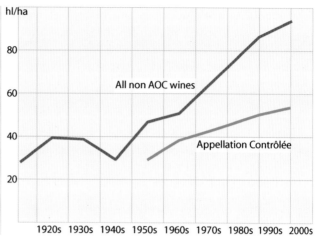

hierarchy within an AOC, higher-level appellations have lower yield limits than lower-level appellations. Certainly in many cases the limits are too high, certainly the annual farce of increasing the limits undercuts the whole scheme, but even so, yields are lower than they would otherwise have been. The average yield in France has doubled over a century, but the increase in yields of AOC wines has been much less than the increase outside of the AOC system. Within the AOC system, the increase from about 30 hl/ha to 50 hl/ha largely represents improvements in quality of viticulture. Outside the AOC system, the increase from 50 hl/ha to 100 hl/ha represents the same over cropping found everywhere in production of bulk wines that don't have much character.

The AOC remains too concerned with ripeness. Half of the AOC vineyards are in the northern part of the country where historically it has been difficult to achieve ripeness reliably, so it's understandable this should be reflected in the classification. But the system goes over the edge when it sets minimum alcohol limits as part of the hierarchy, but then permits chaptalization. Bordeaux AOC wine must have 10% minimum alcohol, while Bordeaux Supérieur must have 10.5%; but the minimum sugar requirement in the must is the same for both.[21] But when did you last see Bordeaux of any AOC at alcohol levels below 12.5%?

Because the concept of typicité is bound up with place, INAO did not allow grape varieties to be mentioned on the label (with the notable exception of Alsace). It's been considered to be an important part of the concept that the name of the AOC alone should convey the crucial indication of the character of the wine; the authorities felt that the importance of the AOC would be undercut by naming the varieties. You might wonder whether there's an element of trade protection here, since cépages are universal but place names are unique. But if this is the intention, it has backfired, because the absence of identification for grape varieties has become a big problem in competing with the wines of the New World, which boldly list grape varieties on the label as a major selling point. In 2005, INAO reversed itself and finally conceded that grape varieties could be named on AOC labels.

But now everything is changing in Europe anyway. The AOC and Vin de Pays (and their equivalents in the other countries of the European Union) are being abolished. Two new categories will be called the AOP (Appellation d'Origine Protegée) and IGP (Indication Géographique Protegée).[23] What's being protected? More likely the E.U. bureaucrats in Brussels than anything else. Certainly the system of AOC and Vin de Pays has its flaws, but, at least so far, it's difficult to see any advantage in this major disruption. The difference between the AOP and IGP is written in gobbledygook, but will presumably come down in practice more or less to a difference in quality level.[24] The new system nominally came into effect on August 1, 2009, but in fact all current AOC and Vin de Pay regions have until the end of 2011 to submit applications to become either AOP or IGP. During the interregnum, both new and old types of labels will be around, not exactly a situation to lend confidence to the consumer.

Probably the effect will be greatest at the level of Vin de Pays, where many of the smaller regions will be subsumed under broader regions. This may actually be a good thing in reducing confusion for the consumer. A handful of Vin de Pays regions may apply to be promoted to AOP. It would make sense for some struggling AOC regions to be demoted to IGP, but that is unlikely to happen. And at the bottom level, Vin de Table is being replaced by a new category called Vin de France, the major difference being that varietals and vintages can be stated on the label. So the differences in terms of what information is provided to the consumer are narrowing between the categories. Will the categories in fact be significant as markers of quality? With responsibility for both AOP and IGP being transferred to INAO (which in the meantime will be handling AOC and Vin de Pays), if the same concern for quality that has been shown for AOC is now applied to the new category, it's hard to see what will make any difference. It's not obvious what flaws in the old system will be redressed by the new: are they throwing out the baby with the bath water?

Cool Climate Variations in the Loire

The Loire river extends for about a thousand kilometers, and the wine region stretches for about 400 km (250 miles), from Nantes close to the Atlantic coast to Orleans at the east. In the nineteenth century, before the phylloxera epidemic, there were about 160,000 ha of vines. Now there are about 50,000 ha devoted to AOC wine and another 20,000 in Vin de Pays. Vineyards are found in a band along the river, but are concentrated more on the southern side. Although the region is protected from climatic extremes, its northern location means that it is generally cool for grape growing, and the whites have good acidity. Ripening can be a problem for the reds.

The Loire falls into four general regions: Nantais, Anjou, Touraine, and Central Vineyards. Each of the regions is subdivided into individual appellations, with the best known for dry wines being Muscadet in the Nantais, Savennières in Anjou, Vouvray and Chinon (red) in Touraine, and Sancerre and Pouilly Fumé in

Extending for several hundred kilometers, the Loire contains four distinct wine-producing regions.[25]

the Central Vineyards. The regional description of Vin de Pays du Val de Loire covers the whole area and accounts for almost all the Vin de Pays wine.

Although best known for its white wines, the Loire produces a wide variety of styles, not merely dry and sweet white wine, and sparkling wine, but also a good amount of rosé (largely in Anjou) and red wines from distinguished varieties in both Touraine and the Central Vineyards. In fact, white wines (including sparkling) are only just in the majority.

The white wines are dry in both the Nantais and Central Vineyards, but there are both dry and sweet whites based on Chenin Blanc in Anjou and Touraine. The best known sweet wines are Quarts de Chaumes and Coteaux du Layon in Anjou. In Touraine, where the best known appellation is Vouvray, the white wines vary from dry to sweet.

The white wines are mostly varietal-based, with the varietal changing from west to east: Muscadet in the Nantais, Chenin Blanc in the appellations of Anjou and Touraine, and Sauvignon Blanc in Sancerre/Pouilly Fumé. The red wines are based on Cabernet Franc in Anjou and Touraine (often blended with other varietals), and on Pinot Noir in Sancerre. With such diversity of varieties, you might not expect to see much universality of style, but the cool climate is reflected in the common features of good acidity and light fruits for both reds and whites. The Loire is considered to be the northern limit for viticulture; in fact, it is only due to the ameliorating influence of the river that wine can be made at all in the region.

Muscadet originated as Melon de Bourgogne in the seventeenth century, when growers were looking for a grape variety to replace the black varieties that had been killed by frost. By the eighteenth century, the Nantais had switched to white wine production, and Melon become a major variety.[26] During this period, much of the wine was exported from the port of Nantes by Dutch traders for distillation into eau de vie; the thin, acid wines of the region were ideal for this purpose. Another grape giving good results in this context was Folle Blanche, one of the principal varieties for brandy production in Cognac and Armagnac, and known in the Loire as Gros Plant because of the large size of its grapes. This became the most widely planted variety. With the balance shifting to production of white wine for drinking, Muscadet (Melon) has now become predominant, but still about a third of plantings are Gros Plant.

Muscadet describes the basic appellation, but the most important AOC is Muscadet de Sèvre et Maine, whose 10,000 hectares occupy about 80% of the total AOC area.[27] But the most important determinant of quality is a feature of production called *sur lie*. This describes the tradition of keeping the wine on the lees through the winter, and then bottling directly in the spring. The wine gains additional flavor and texture from its contact with the lees, and typically just a faint touch of spritzen from carbon dioxide remaining at the time of bottling. Unfortunately, the tradition has been honored as much in the breach as the observance. One of the major problems of Muscadet is that growers who bottle their own wine are outnumbered by negociants who buy and bottle wine, the bottling often occurring out of the immediate vicinity in Anjou. By the time the wine has been trucked to the negociant in a steel tank, it's no longer off the lees; and often enough a touch of carbon dioxide is injected to mimic the impression of authentic lees-bottling.

Muscadet bottled by a grower committed to quality can be fresh and attractive—perhaps not a competitor to Burgundy, but nonetheless a refreshing accompaniment to sea food. Many of the negociants' wines are simply characterless. Some growers are fighting the uphill battle to improve quality, and of course there are some negociants who produce good wines, but the general standard remains variable. Muscadet is a rare appellation that has an upper limit on alcohol levels, so the wine is never too heavy. Experiments using oak to produce more ageworthy Muscadet have not been a success, in my opinion.

Chenin Blanc appears to have been widely grown in the Loire for several centuries. It is sometimes called Pineau de la Loire locally, and may have originated in Anjou, in the ninth century, subsequently migrating to Touraine in the fifteenth.[29] The big issue with Chenin Blanc is always the yield. At low yields, the

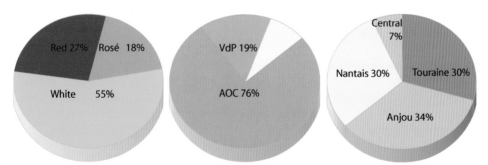

Most production in the Loire is white (including sweet wine and a variable amount of sparkling wine), and most is AOC. Overall production is divided roughly equally between the Nantais, Anjou, and Touraine, with the Central Vineyards only a minor proportion.[28]

wine can have character, but at high yields it is completely bland. It's often described as showing "wet wool" when young, together with notes of green apples from its high acidity.

The best dry wines from Chenin Blanc come from Savennières, in Anjou, where the Coulée de Serrant, a monopole owned by Nicolas Joly, has attracted much attention because of his pioneering role in biodynamic viticulture. The wines of Savennières are typically fresh when young, then close up for some years, and finally mature gracefully as the longest lived dry wines of the Loire. Due to a protected microclimate, Savennières has less rain than Touraine, so the grapes ripen more reliably, and alcohol levels are a little higher.

Vouvray is much less consistent in style. Although the wines vary from dry to sweet, the level of sweetness is indicated on the label only for the fully sweet categories of demi-sec and moelleux. Other wines may range unpredictably from dry to off-dry. This is a problem for the consumer; the only safe attitude is to assume a Vouvray is likely to be off-dry unless there is specific information to the contrary. (The off-dry is known locally as sec-tendre, but this is not officially recognized as a category.) Late harvest wines in the moelleux style can be very good and may last for decades. There's also huge variation as to whether the wine is vinified into a still style (in the better vintages) or converted into a spar- kling wine (in the less successful years), so supply is erratic.

Typically the choice of style is not made until September: when September is not sunny, production is directed toward sparkling. The average is half of each, but proportions can vary widely. With the recent warming trend, sparkling wine production has decreased over the past 5 years, and the proportion of sweet and semi-sweet among the still wines has increased. A generation ago a minority of harvests gave sweet wines; now it is a majority. Harvesting has become two weeks earlier since 2000, and botrytis occurs most years. Now the problem is lack of acidity whereas previously it was lack of alcohol.

In the early nineteenth century, Sancerre produced mostly red wines.[30] But Sauvignon Blanc has been planted at the eastern end of the wine-growing region since the sixteenth and seventeenth centuries, and was used for producing white wine together with Pinot Gris and Chasselas. Sauvignon Blanc fell out of favor and was replaced by Chasselas (an over-productive, characterless variety), and then came back again after the phylloxera epidemic.[31] But the reputation of the region for quality white wine is recent. Before Appellation Contrôlée regulations put a stop to such shenanigans in 1936, much of the white wine was sent to Champagne to augment the local product; when this stopped, the vineyards declined, until by 1960 there were only 600 ha.[32] Today plantings are up to about 2500 ha, with 80% of the production being dry white wine from Sauvignon Blanc. Just across the river is Pouilly Fumé, with about half the vineyard area, and where the wines tend to be just a fraction richer.

Sancerre and Pouilly Fumé dominated the world supply of Sauvignon Blanc until New Zealand's rise to fame. The styles are of course quite different: San- cerre and Pouilly Fumé are relatively restrained, most often having been matured in (old) oak, compared to the bright, aggressive fruits of New Zealand Sauvignon Blanc produced exclusively in stainless steel, sometimes under a coat of nitrogen to prevent even the faintest touch of oxidative influence. Certainly they share the general grassy nature of the grape, but New Zealand Sauvignon often shows tropical fruits, whereas you should not find passion fruit in Sauvignon Blanc from the Loire. That said, New Zealand has not been without influence on the Loire, and some producers now follow the modern stainless steel route; indeed, this is also emulated farther south, in Bordeaux (although there the Sauvignon Blanc is usually softened by blending with some Sémillon). At the other extreme from New Zealand, the name of Pouilly Fumé was the inspiration for the Fumé Blanc style of Napa valley, where new oak is used to mature Sauvignon Blanc. Whether the Fumé of Pouilly Fumé actually originated as a reference to a smoky, gunflint taste is somewhat debatable.

The usual international suspects have not made much impression on the Loire: it's simply too cool a climate for Chardonnay or Cabernet Sauvignon to make a great impact. The soil around Sancerre is a continuation of the same Kimmeridgian limestone found in Chablis, but Chardonnay is usually found farther to the west in the Loire, in Touraine. AOC Touraine allows Chardonnay to be used but not to be stated on the label, whereas monovarietal Sauvignon Blanc can be named on the label. An unnamed Touraine AOC Blanc may therefore be Chardonnay rather than Sauvignon, although strictly speaking the proportion of Chardonnay is supposed to be limited to 20%. There is in fact some monovarietal Chardonnay, but when it is presented for approval, the producer describes it as a blend, another example of the tricks producers are forced to play to survive in the system.[33]

The red wines of the Loire are dominated by Cabernet Franc in Anjou, most notably in Chinon and Bourgueil, and by Pinot Noir in Sancerre. There's also quite a bit of Gamay around, but the results are rarely distinguished. Chinon and Sancerre usually give wines with higher acidity and lighter style than their counterparts in Bordeaux and Burgundy, respectively. However, the recent run of warm vintages associated with climate change has brought both closer in style to the classic regions of production.

Conflicts of Style in Alsace

Alsace's reputation for quality wines is a phenomenon of the past half century. Having changed hands several times between France and Germany, production in Alsace has traditions inherited from both countries. The wines used to be regarded as low quality, mass production—what the French call vins de comptoir. One story dates this reputation from the period when Alsace came under German control following the war of 1870, and the wines were used to improve German wines. But in fact, Alsace had 65,000 hectares of vineyards (five times today's plantings!) mostly given over to high production from low quality grape varieties when the war started.[34] Nor did production habits change when Alsace became French again after the First World War.[35] Quality varietals began a slow takeover after the AOC finally came into full effect in 1962, but it was not until 1980 that the last low-grade varieties were legally excluded.

The vineyards in AOC Alsace form a band parallel with the Vosges mountains running from Strasbourg to south of Colmar. To the east of the vineyards, the Plaine d'Alsace extends for about 20 km to the Rhine.

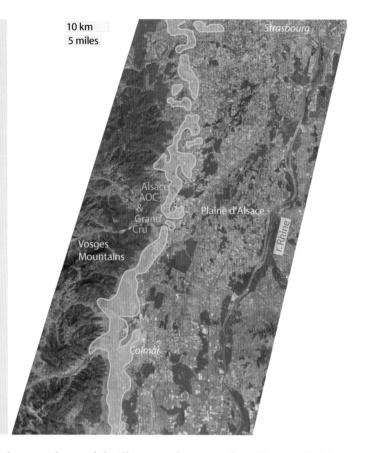

Alsace may have the most beautiful villages and vineyards in France. Driving along the Route des Vins from Strasbourg to Colmar, you pass through an endless series of beautifully preserved medieval villages, with vineyards all around. The Vosges mountains are the dominant climatic influence, interrupting the weather coming from the west. Most of the rainfall stops across the Vosges, so precipitation changes from 1,200-1,500 mm at the far, western edge, to around 2,000 mm at the peak of the mountain range, to 650 mm in the vineyards (the lowest in all of France). The vineyards extend to the east from the lower slopes of the mountains, with most of the best vineyards being on the middle slopes between 200 and 350 m, which are a degree or so warmer than the land above or below.[36] From the relatively narrow band of vineyards, the land opens out to the east into a plain extending to the Rhine (which however is too far away to have any direct influence on the climate).

Reflecting the northerly location, predominantly white varietals are grown, resembling those of Germany, including Riesling, Gewürztraminer, Pinot Blanc, Pinot Gris, and Muscat. Riesling has been grown since the fifteenth century, and Gewürztraminer and Muscat since the sixteenth.[37] Pinot Gris used to be called Tokay d'Alsace, reflecting the (improbable) legend that it was brought from Hungary in the sixteenth century; European Community rules now prevent this name from being used because of supposed confusion with Tokaji.[38] Pinot Gris was probably first grown in Alsace in the seventeenth century, and in any case came to be called Tokay only a century later.

The appellation system in Alsace is unique in France. There are only three AOCs. There are two levels of appellation for still wines in Alsace: AOC Alsace (or AOC Vin d'Alsace), and AOC Alsace Grand Cru (the grand cru is named on the label). Crémant d'Alsace is used for sparking wine. Unusually for France, the AOC Alsace is organized in terms of varietals rather than regions, and the varietal name appears on the label (96% of wines are 100% varietal, although Pinot Blanc is often a mixture with Auxerrois [39]).

Alsace today is in a full blown identity crisis. There is no agreement on whether the grand cru system is worth anything, with some growers producing wines labeled as grand crus but others refusing to acknowledge them and preferring instead to use their own place or brand names. There is no agreement on style, and wines that are not specifically identified as sweet late harvest may in fact range from absolutely bone dry to off-dry or even relatively sweet. The *agrément* that is required for a wine to be labeled as a grand cru, and which is based on tasting by a local committee, has been refused to top quality wines because they are not "typical" (perhaps based on the fear they will show up the others), while rock-bottom quality wines from some cooperatives sail easily through the system. About the only thing that can be relied upon from the label of an Alsace wine is the indication of the grape variety (unless it is Pinot Blanc!).

Yields have been reduced only slowly from the bad old days, from a maximum of 120 hl/ha in 1974, to 96 hl/ha in 1982, to 80 hl/ha today. The limitation of yields to individual varietals (as opposed to total production) was introduced only in 1999 (until then, the average for any vineyard/grower had to conform to the limit, but one varietal could be above it and another below it.) Maximum yields are much higher than allowed elsewhere in France; only Champagne is higher.[40] Yield limits do not vary with the grape variety. There is a school of thought that at least Riesling can support relatively high yields without loss of quality, but that seems to me to be rather a suspect defense.

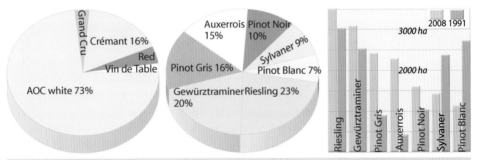

Alsace is almost entirely AOC; the vast majority is white. Plantings of Riesling, Gewürztraminer, Pinot Gris, and Pinot Noir have increased, while Sylvaner has declined, in the past two decades. The transition between Pinot Blanc and Auxerrois recognizes the reality of plantings[41].

Virtually all approved vineyards in Alsace are Appellation Contrôlée.[42] Most wine is white; there is a little Pinot Noir (traditionally almost like a rosé but in recent years of improved quality), and a fairly substantial amount of Crémant. Total plantings have increased recently, from 12,000 ha in 1982 to just over 15,000 ha today, and the increase has largely been in the quality varietals of Riesling, Gewürztraminer, and Pinot Gris. Sylvaner thankfully has decreased.

A major apparent change is a large decrease in Pinot Blanc and increase in Auxerrois, but this is presumably no more than a belated recognition of preexisting reality. Wine labeled as Pinot Blanc traditionally has included Auxerrois (a much inferior variety), and it would seem from the revision of the figures that about two thirds of what was described as Pinot Blanc in the vineyard was really Auxerrois.[43] Of course, none of this will make any difference to the consumer unless the authorities stop the newly uncovered Auxerrois from being labeled as Pinot Blanc in the bottle.

One of the biggest problems for the consumer is a completely erratic approach to sugar levels. Except for the avowedly sweet late harvest wines, there is no classification with regards to sweetness. Alsatian wines used to be vinified dry, but a trend to warmer vintages has resulted in a tendency for many to be off-dry. Perhaps in these northern climates it's regarded as such a triumph to get to full ripeness that a little residual sugar is taken as a sign of success, but for the consumer who wants to match a wine with food, it's a major disincentive to ordering an unknown bottle of wine from Alsace. Some producers' wines are always vinified to dryness, but others vary, so without detailed knowledge, you take a risk.

Hubert Trimbach of Maison Trimbach, which is known for fermenting its wines to dryness, says that the drive to include a little residual sugar came from critics who praised wines with a little sweetness about 10 years ago. Growers started picking grapes later to get enough sugar to leave some residual sweetness after fermentation. "They would not dare to say that they stop fermentation," Trimbach says with a knowing look. "This has changed the style of Alsace and has been a huge mistake."[44] Etienne Hugel of Hugel & Fils says, "Our image as a dry-wine region is at risk."[45]

A series of proposals to allow some sort of classification of sweetness on the back label have gone nowhere. Hugel is against the idea because "it means we have lost the battle." A practical difficulty is the same issue as in Germany, that the perception of sweetness depends on the acidity, but even allowing that perception of sweetness is subjective, personally, I would simply like to see the level of residual sugar stated on every bottle together with the alcohol level. It's ironic that at the time when Germany is moving to introducing more trocken (dry) wines as a better accompaniment to food, Alsace should be going in the opposite direction by increasing sweetness.

Late harvest wines have been classified separately in Alsace since 1984. Vendange Tardive describes a late harvest, (possibly with some botrytis). Selection de Grains Nobles (SGN) is produced exclusively from botrytized grapes. Even here the classification refers to the sugar level at time of harvest rather than to residual sugar after fermentation; however, given the sugar harvest levels, VT and SGN wines are always sweet. As with other Alsace wines, late harvest wines are made exclusively from single varietals, restricted to Riesling, Pinot Gris, Gewürztraminer, and Muscat. Chaptalization cannot be used for VT or SGN wines; in fact, the regulations for their production are among the strictest in France for dessert wines. Their reputation is as high as for any sweet wine anywhere, but they represent only an average 1-2% of production, with amounts fluctuating widely from year to year according to vintage conditions.[46]

The Brouhaha about Grand Crus

The grand cru system in Alsace was controversial at its introduction and has become a running saga. The lack of any hierarchy in the original classification system—all AOC wines were described simply as Vins d'Alsace—led to the establishment of a committee to consider the promotion of the best vineyards to a separate status. But the results were so controversial that several of the most important producers refuse to use the system. Grand Cru wines labeled as such account for about 4% of total AOC production in Alsace.

The Comité de Délimitation des Grands Crus assembled by INAO convened under the presidency of Johnny Hugel between 1975 and 1978. The committee started by examining the potential Grand Cru Schlossberg (between the great château of Kaysersberg and the town of Kintzheim, avowedly including some of the best terroir in Alsace). They recommended it should include a total area of about 20 hectares. But the vice president of INAO at the time was a significant proprietor of vineyards in Schlossberg. Coincidentally or not, when it turned out that few of his vineyards were to be included, the project stalled. Finally, the committee made a report to INAO saying that no more work could be done because the situation was unresolved.

At the same time, Johnny Hugel was chairing another committee that was attempting to establish classifications for the Vendange Tardive and SGN wines. This was held up in conjunction with the fracas about the grand crus. Regarding VTs as the more important objective, he resigned from the Grand Cru Committee, which was then reconstituted, and managed to find 80 hectares of suitable vineyards to include in the Schlossberg Grand Cru. This was widely regarded as a joke at the time, but mirabile dictu! the proposals for classifying VT and SGN were approved together with the enlarged grand cru. Even though the final report of the new committee in 1983 recommended only 25 of the 94 sites that had been proposed for grand cru status by growers, the scene was set for expanding grand crus beyond the best sites. More grand crus were added in a second round, with the number finally coming in 1991 to a total of 51.

It is no coincidence that most of the villages on the Route des Vins, the picturesque road running through the vineyards, have a single grand cru associated with them. Basically each village proposed its best vineyards for grand cru status, and some sort of liberté, egalité, fraternité resulted, with most villages getting one, and only one, grand cru. It's fair to say that the grand crus do include most of the best sites in Alsace, but the political nature of the process

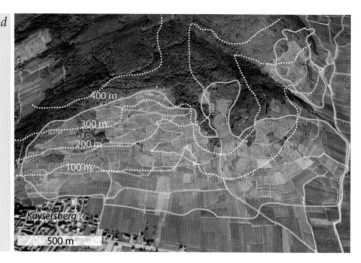

Where is the real grand cru terroir? Schlossberg runs around the mountain slopes between Kaysersberg (at the left) and Kintzheim (just off to the right) Only 25 ha were originally recommended for Schlossberg, but the final grand cru contains 80 ha.

makes the label unreliable as an indication of the very best quality. Some major producers remain resolutely opposed to the system, to the point that they do not use grand cru descriptions even for wines that come from top grand cru sites. A notable example is Trimbach's Clos St. Hune, widely acknowledged to be one of the best, in fact probably the best, Riesling from Alsace, which comes from a 1.2 ha vineyard in the Rosacker Grand Cru. Of course the firm of Hugel remains out of the system, as does Léon Beyer who says firmly, "The grand cru system is simply a marketing ploy by small estates. The problems are lack of real integrity of terroir, variation in size, and the fact that the names are all Germanic, which makes it difficult to build the reputation of Alsace as a French wine region."[47] Some estates have a different view. "Negociants were opposed to the introduction of the grand cru system because their interests lay in marketing brands, says Séverine Schlumberger.[48] "This is why they are still opposed to the system. There are 2,000 growers in Alsace but only 250 estates, who are the people interested in the grand cru system."

The grand cru appellation restricts wines to 100% varietals from Riesling, Gewürztraminer, Pinot Gris, and Muscat. In fact, most grand cru wine is either Riesling or Gewürztraminer, and there is almost no Muscat.[49] Growers have a free hand to plant any of these varieties; indeed, some plant other varieties, such as Pinot Noir, but then the wine cannot be labeled as grand cru (a recent exception allows Sylvaner specifically in the Zolzenberg Grand Cru).

Varietal labeling seems the only reliable reference point in Alsace. Indeed, until 2005 it was mandatory to include the varietal name on the label for grand cru wine. Then it was made optional, a concession to those (rare) growers who blend varieties. But now a recent proposal has called for varietal labels to be removed from grand cru wines. The rationale presumably is that attention should be focused on the grand cru's representation of terroir rather than a specific varietal.

There is in fact little doubt this would be anything other than a disaster—the grand crus are so arcane to most consumers that without the guidance of a varietal, sales would disappear. Perhaps this is no more than a provocation to draw attention to the issue, since the proposal comes from the grand cru section of the AVA (Alsace Viticultural Association) chaired by Jean-Michael Deiss, of producer Marcel Deiss who has long been committed to blending varietals.

Jean-Michael Deiss has the air of a fanatic. He expresses strong views on viticulture and terroir, on the relationship between cépages and the land. But he is a fanatic for making wine true to what he sees as the ancient tradition of Alsace: from more than one variety rather than from a single cépage. When I asked him if he uses all seven varieties of Alsace he said, "Yes, all thirteen varieties!"[50] There are the principal varieties such as Riesling (more than 50% of his plantings), then some secondary varieties (about 30%), and finally some accessory varieties, less than 10%—here his concern is to preserve the old varieties that are ceasing to be planted. Deiss is quick to point out that he does not produce his wines by assemblage, the mixing of wines made from different varieties, but as a single wine produced from grapes of different varieties that are intermingled (complanté) in the vineyard. "I don't make wines to express the cépage but to express the terroir," he told me. He believes that to express terroir, you need to grow varieties together. He points out that complanted vineyards refute the traditional view of differences between cépages, because when the vines are complanted, the different varieties mature together. This latest proposal has made him an even more controversial figure. One signatory to an open letter of protest signed by two hundred winemakers, Laurence Faller of Domaine Weinbach, said, "It is fine that Deiss makes his wines the way he wants to, but such methods should not be imposed on the rest of us."[51]

The brouhaha reflects the old argument as how best to emphasize the unique nature of French wines. If the wines carry varietal labels, other areas can produce the same varietals; why should a consumer buy a Riesling from Alsace if one from eastern Europe is half the price? But if the label carries an incomprehensible vineyard name, how does the consumer know what to expect? The Alsatians are conscious of the fact that the top wines of Burgundy, just to their south, maintain world-beating prices, but the top wines of Alsace very rarely scale the same heights. But this is likely to owe more to fashion than to labeling.

Focus on AOC in the Northern Rhône

Wine is produced all along the Rhône from just south of Lyon to south of Avignon. Production divides naturally into two regions, the northern Rhône and southern Rhône, which are about as distant and distinct from one another as they are from Beaujolais to their north. It is a mistake to consider them in the same category. The grape varieties are different, and the climates are different.

The vineyards of the northern Rhône occupy a relatively narrow band running along the river Rhône from Vienne at the north to Valence in the south. The valley has steep hillsides, and the soil is granitic in the best regions. The climate is just a little hotter than southern Burgundy. Most of the wine-growing regions are classified as Appellation Contrôlée; six of the eight appellations lie on the western side of the river, with only Hermitage and Crozes-Hermitage on the

The northern Rhône is a skinny band of vineyards running along the river for fifty miles from Vienne to Valence.[52]

AOC	Wine	1000s cases
Côte-Rôtie	red	106
Condrieu	white	52
Ch. Grillet	white	1
St. Joseph	red + white	415
Hermitage	red + white	53
Crozes-Hermitage	red + white	678
Cornas	red	42
St. Péray	white + sparkling	28

eastern side. The only permitted red grape is Syrah. With just 5% of the total production of the Rhône, the output of the north is dwarfed by the south.

The best appellations for red wines are Côte Rôtie, near Vienne, and Hermitage, at a turn in the river a bit north of Valence. Indeed, these are the most prestigious appellations in the entire Rhône. The reds of Crozes-Hermitage, Cornas, and St. Joseph are not as fine. St. Joseph is particularly variable, since the appellation was enormously expanded to include much land that used to be only Côtes du Rhône. St. Joseph grew from 97 ha in 1971 to 540 ha in 1989; today it is 1100 ha and still growing.[53] White wine is made from the varieties Marsanne and Roussanne in Hermitage (the best appellation for whites as it is for reds), Crozes-Hermitage, and St. Joseph. The appellations of Condrieu and Château Grillet make white wine from Viognier.

Hermitage is a hill in the center of the Crozes-Hermitage area. The hill rises directly up above the town of Tain l'Hermitage (originally called Tain until it was renamed to reflect the glory of the wine), with houses extending right to its base. The geography restricts the size of the Hermitage appellation to about 135 ha. There are the typical hillside problems of awkward access, and retaining walls are used to hold in the topsoil. Southern exposure is an important feature, protecting the vineyards from the north wind and giving good sunlight. "Like the Pinot Noir in Burgundy, we're at the northern extreme of the Syrah's ripening here at Hermitage," according to Jean-Louis Chave, one of the top producers.[54] Running round the hill are a series of lieu-dits, each with their own characteristics. Many of the best wines, including Chave's Hermitage, are made by blending lots from different lieu-dits, although some growers are following the international trend towards vineyard-specific bottlings. The southern exposure, hillside slopes, and granitic soil explain Hermitage's advantage over Crozes-Hermitage, which is somewhat larger, at about 1150 ha, extending to gentle slopes and flat land farther away from the river; its wines are rarely interesting.

Hermitage has always been the great name in the Rhône, although its role has changed. Ever since the eighteenth century, Hermitage was regularly sold to negociants in Bordeaux or Burgundy to strengthen their wines.[55] During the nineteenth century, as much as 80% of the production of Hermitage was bought by the Bordeaux wine trade.[56] And it was by no means the lesser wines of Hermitage that were sent up to Bordeaux. "The first growths are sent to Bordeaux to be mixed with the clarets which are made up for the English market, and only the second growths are sold in the trade as Hermitage," according to a popular report in 1874.[57] The practice was so common that it gave rise to a verb; to Hermitager meant strengthening the wines of Bordeaux (or Burgundy) with stronger wines from the Rhône.

This had to stop after new regulations came into effect at the start of the twentieth century, but the wine continued to be sold in bulk to negociants rather than bottled by growers. At this time, the white wine was more famous than the red; in fact, negociants were compelled to buy the red in order to obtain the white.[58] Things more or less collapsed after the first world war, with a large part of the wine going from small growers to a cooperative, and only four negociants han-

Côte-Rôtie runs along a series of slopes rising up along a 3 km stretch on the west side of the Rhône.

dling the wines. Bottling in the region became common only after the second world war. Today about three quarters of production is red. Hermitage can be stern when young and very long lived; its rival Côte-Rôtie is usually softer and more rounded.

Although today Côte-Rôtie has a reputation to match Hermitage, it was much less well known until recently. During the nineteenth century it used to sell at around half the price of Hermitage, but after the second world war it was being sold off for pennies.[59] Now much revived, quality is more variable than Hermitage because the appellation is not restricted to the very best terroirs; vineyard plantings have gone up and down, from 420 ha in 1907, to 72 ha in 1973, and back up to 242 ha today. Much of the revival is owed to the halo effect of Marcel Guigal's series of splendid single vineyard bottlings started in the 1970s.[60]

Côte-Rôtie means "roasted slope," but the appellation is really more a series of slopes, rising up from the river. The best plots are the hillside vineyards adjacent to the town of Ampuis—in fact, from Marcel Guigal's winery just across the railway line in Ampuis, you can see the famous slope of La Landonne—but the appellation extends into the neighboring communes of Tupin-et-Semon and St. Cyr-sur-le-Rhône. There is more variation in terroir here than in the more compact hill of Hermitage, with the plateau at the top of the slope being the least distinguished terroir.

Both Hermitage and Côte-Rôtie used to have plantings of black and white grapevines intermingled. The regulations still say that up to 15% white grapes can be included in the fermentation vat with Syrah. In the case of Hermitage, the permitted white varietals are Marsanne and Roussanne; in Côte-Rôtie, Viognier is allowed. At Côte-Rôtie, Marcel Guigal still includes some Viognier in his top Crus, about 7% in La Turque and as much as 11% in La Mouline, but the practice has largely been abandoned at most vineyards out of fear that the wine will be weakened. But in Crozes-Hermitage, it's a way to get rid of unwanted white grapes *faute de mieux*. "More growers are doing this because the red is easier to sell," according to producer Jean-Louis Pradelle.[61] The rules say that the white grapes must be included in the same fermentation vat with the red grapes;

blending red and white wines is not allowed. It now turns out that there is in fact an interesting and useful aspect to this rule, which is that copigmentation results from the mix, and increases color in the wine.[62] (Always willing to experiment, some Australian producers also make Shiraz-Viognier wines.)

The white varietals of the Rhône are unique. Viognier is grown in the northern tip of Condrieu and Château Grillet (and is the only white grape that can be included in Côte-Rôtie), whereas Marsanne and Roussanne are grown farther south in Hermitage, Crozes-Hermitage, and St. Joseph. Viognier is today the leading quality white varietal in the northern Rhône, although it nearly became extinct a few years ago. From the minimum of 13.7 ha in France in 1971, plantings have now increased to 700 ha in the Rhône, with another 1500 ha in Languedoc, as well as 1200 ha in Australia and 750 ha in California.

Viognier is an aromatic grape, and the wine can be perfumed and floral, even musky. With relatively low acidity and high alcohol, it is best drunk young. There are enormous quality differences between a top Condrieu with intense aromas and palate, and lesser versions, where the perfume may outrun the fruits; in short Viognier is a variety that needs concentrated fruits to give good balance against its perfumed background. Viognier made from inferior clones that give high yields of less aromatic fruit, of which a good number were planted when its popularity revived, can be clumsy. It can be vinified in a variety of styles from fresh and clean to heavily oaked; this makes it difficult to get a bead on any consistent style for Condrieu.

Marsanne and Roussanne, often blended together, make a dry wine with savory and herbal aromas and a nutty (sometimes almost bitter) taste. The overall impression is aromatic and a little perfumed, with a dry finish that emphasizes the perfume. Roussanne is usually reckoned to be the finer grape, giving finesse to a blend that gains body and weight from the Marsanne. Marsanne is the more widely grown, and it does not do especially well on the granite soils preferred by Syrah, but does better on the other soil types, such as clay and chalk. Roussanne is difficult to grow, and can have difficulties in the northern Rhône, but can produce superlative results farther south, as exemplified by the Vieille Vignes Roussanne produced at Château Beaucastel in Châteauneuf-du-Pape.

The Warm Sun of the Southern Rhône

The southern Rhône is where the real transition occurs to lush, fruit-driven wines. There is a long break in the wine-producing regions to the south of Valence, and the bulk of the vineyards of the southern Rhône lie between Montelimar and Avignon, spreading far on both sides of the river. The south has a more Mediterranean climate than the northern Rhône, with more sunshine and less rainfall. The valley widens out and there is a variety of terrains, including alluvial deposits, sandy areas, and limestone.

The major quality grape is Grenache, bringing a richer, sweeter, more alcoholic style; and the wines are not usually noted for being long-lived. The region is far larger than the north, and the vast bulk of production comes from generic

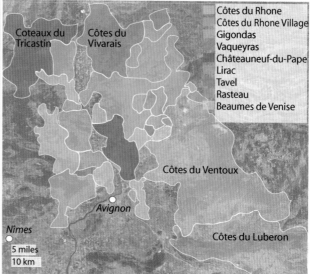

The Côtes and Coteaux occupy most of the southern Rhône.

Côtes du Rhone
Côtes du Rhone Village
Gigondas
Vaqueyras
Châteauneuf-du-Pape
Lirac
Tavel
Rasteau
Beaumes de Venise

AOCs. The Côtes du Rhône and the higher appellations of Côtes du Rhône Villages account for the major part of the region. The satellite regions of Côtes du Ventoux, Coteaux du Tricastin, and the Côtes de Luberon (the other Côtes) account for most of the rest, leaving only a small part for the top appellations, headed by Châteauneuf-du-Pape. Red wines are 86% of production, rosés are 9%,[63] and whites are only 5%. Associated with the more generic nature of the appellations comes a change in commercialization; whereas most wine is bottled by producers in the north, in the south two thirds is handled by cooperatives.[64]

Most wines in the south are blended from several varietals. Grenache is the most common grape in red wines, with Syrah and Mourvèdre adding quality, and Cinsault and Carignan reducing it. The best white wines are based on Roussanne and Marsanne. The Southern Rhône also has appellations that produce sweet fortified wines, including whites in Beaumes de Venise and reds in Rasteau.

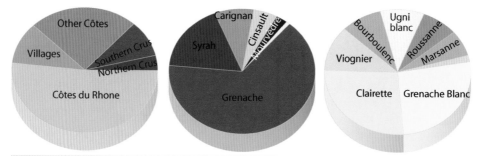

Côtes du Rhône accounts for more than half the production of the Rhône, and the Villages for another 10%. The "Crus" in the south—Châteauneuf-du-Pape, Gigondas, Lirac, Tavel, Vacqueyras, Vinsobres, Beaumes de Venise—are 9%; the entire north is only 4%. Grenache is by far the predominant black grape. The quality white grapes (Viognier [only in the north], Roussanne, Marsanne) together are just over a quarter.[65]

The best red wines come from Châteauneuf-du-Pape; other well-known appellations are Gigondas and Vacqueyras, where the wines are similar in style, but more rustic. Châteauneuf-du-Pape is a relatively large appellation of 3,164 ha. The terroir is famous for the galets, round stones that lie on the surface, which absorb and reflect heat, keeping temperatures mild at night. Actually, they are found mostly in the eastern part of the appellation, the rest being fairly sandy. Both red and white wine are made. The red wines are full bodied, with forward fruits coming from the predominant Grenache component; they tend to be alcoholic.

Châteauneuf-du-Pape has many more grape varieties than the other Rhône appellations. Thirteen black varietals and five white varietals are permitted by the appellation rules.[67] Most Châteauneuf-du-Pape is blended, although it is now rare for all of the permitted varietals to be used; Château Beaucastel is a holdout that insists on including at least a small amount of every varietal. At one time, red Châteauneuf-du-Pape used to be 80-90% Grenache, but the proportion has now dropped. Grenache usually comprises more than half of the blend, and a typical red Châteauneuf-du-Pape today might comprise 50-70% Grenache, 10-30% Syrah, and up to 20% from Mourvèdre, Cinsault, Counoise, Vaccarèse, and Muscardin, with the last three in steadily declining proportions. However, there are some famous (and often very expensive) exceptions of red Châteauneuf-du-Papes that are 100% varietal Grenache. These are usually special cuvées. In fact there is a marked tendency towards producing special cuvées, usually by selection rather than from specific plots; there are now close to 200, with a tendency to be richer in Grenache than the regular bottling and highly extracted.[68]

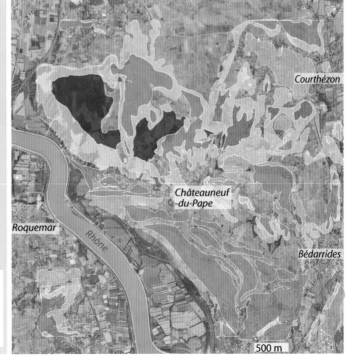

Châteauneuf-du-Pape has a variety of terroirs, with gravel and pebbles (including the famous galets) to the west and south, and sandier soils in the east and north.[66]

Sandy and rocky
Sandy & conglomerates
Calcareous
Gravel and pebbles
Hills

The galets of Châteauneuf-du-Pape absorb and reflect heat.

Photograph kindly provided by Vignobles Mayard.

Châteauneuf-du-Pape is the motor of the southern Rhône. With an international reputation, about 60% of Châteauneuf-du-Pape is exported, compared with the average of about a quarter for all Rhône wines. No doubt the special cuvées, often selling for much higher prices, lead the way on the international stage. Of course, the weakness here is that putting all your best selections into the special cuvée is not exactly going to improve the regular Châteauneuf-du-Pape. With the special cuvées now amounting to almost 10% of production, it remains to be seen whether the remaining 90% of Châteauneuf-du-Pape can withstand the loss.

Languedoc: Transformation of the Midi

Welcome to the wine lake! Overproduction of wine in Europe has been concentrated in three places: the Midi of France, southern Italy, and central Spain. Long subsidized by the European Union, winemaking in these regions has focused on bulk production of characterless wine from high-yielding varieties. Only €1.3 billion of the taxpayers' money makes it a tenable economic activity. (But what's a billion or so between friends: wine subsidies are only a small part of the €44 billion spent on the Common Agricultural Policy.)

The Midi (the middle) is a vast area of southern France, loosely defined as the region south of the Gironde, including Languedoc-Roussillon, Provence, and parts of the Rhône. Its principal contribution to the wine lake comes from the region of Languedoc-Roussillon, stretching around the Mediterranean from the Spanish border to Montpellier. Problems with wine production go back at least a century, from the riots in Montpellier in 1907 to the militant actions of CRAV (Comité Régional d'Action Viticole) in setting off explosions at bottling plants in 2009. At the start of the twentieth century, the problem was imports of cheap wine from Algeria; at the start of the twenty-first century, the enemy is the New World. "Every bottle of American and Australian wine that lands in Europe is a bomb targeted at the heart of our rich European culture," says Aimé Guibert of Mas de Daumas Gassac.[69]

The warm climate makes this a productive place to make wine, but until very recently, quantity ruled over quality. At the start of the nineteenth century, the focus was on producing wine for distillation; the Languedoc made about 40% of all spirits in France.[70] After the railway connected Montpellier to Paris in 1845, producers of table wine switched to varieties suited for bulk production to make cheap wine that could be sent to the industrial cities in the north.[71] Phylloxera wiped out the vineyards here as elsewhere. Imports of wine from Algeria and elsewhere led to the riots in Montpellier, but by the second decade of the twentieth century, recovery was under way. Production still focused on price; wine was produced as cheaply as possible, often blended with foreign imports, and sold in bulk.[72] Almost all the wine was Vin de Table, and as the demand for plonk declined, this surplus became the largest single contributor to Europe's wine lake. At its peak around 1970, the Languedoc had 450,000 hectares of vineyards.

The combination of economic difficulties with incentives to abandon production led to a substantial decline in vineyard areas. Over the past thirty years, production has declined by about half. In fact, subsidies for pulling up vineyards were a significant part of the income of the Languedoc. Today there are about 240,000 hectares of vineyards. As the number of growers has been much reduced, declining from 275,000 to 150,000, wine production has come into better balance. It remains true that much production is still in the hands of cooperatives that take grapes from smaller growers, and this can be difficult to reconcile with quality production.

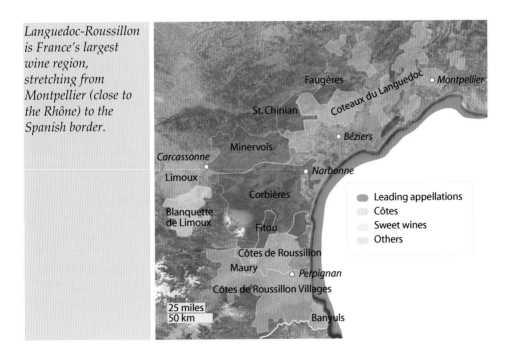

Languedoc-Roussillon is France's largest wine region, stretching from Montpellier (close to the Rhône) to the Spanish border.

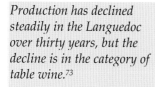

Production has declined steadily in the Languedoc over thirty years, but the decline is in the category of table wine.[73]

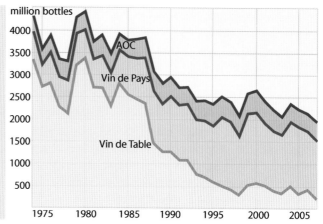

Today Languedoc-Roussillon produces 40% of all France's wine. Most is Vin de Pays. The Vin de Pays d'Oc covers the whole region (there are also several smaller Vin de Pays within it). The major change has come in the collapse of Vin de Table production, now only about 10% of what it was, and alone responsible for most of the production decline in France. Even so, almost half of France's remaining Vin de Table still comes from the Languedoc. Of course, the change is partly cosmetic: the vast increase in Vin de Pays has come from vineyards that used to be Vin de Table. AOC production has been reasonably constant for some period now, representing roughly a quarter of all production.

A major drive to improve quality focuses on "cépage amelioration," the replacement of poor qualities with better ones. Its success is indicated by the fact that today Syrah is the most planted variety in the Languedoc, whereas only a decade ago it was Carignan. In fact, there is now more Syrah in Languedoc-Roussillon than in the Rhône. For several decades the Languedoc was plagued by the characterless wines produced by the infamous trio of Carignan, Cinsault, and Aramon; today these are only a quarter of the black varieties. Grenache, a traditional variety of the region, is almost as common as Syrah, and plantings of Cabernet Sauvignon and Merlot, brought down from the north, are now substantial. Mourvèdre grows best by the coast; "it likes to get its feet wet." White varieties are less than a quarter of all plantings, with Chardonnay and Sauvignon Blanc now the leading varieties. Carbonic maceration is still widely used to produce forward, fruity wines (for example, it is used to counteract the astringency and lack of aroma in Carignan).

All of the varieties are permitted in Vin de Pays. One attempt to improve quality has been the introduction of the new Grand d'Oc category in the Vin de Pays d'Oc, which requires lower yields and ageing in barrel, but it's controversial whether these types of regulations are really compatible with the concept of Vin de Pays. The hot climate makes it natural for the region to produce dessert wines, and since 1999 the Vin de Pays has allowed late harvest wines to be labeled as Vins de Pays Doux. (They could not be called Vendange Tardive because of objections from Alsace. Evidently the winegrowers of France, whether in crisis or

Cépage amelioration is a continuing process, with Carignan, Cinsault, and Aramon declining, and Syrah, Grenache, Merlot, and Cabernet Sauvignon increasing. Carignan has more than halved and Syrah has doubled in a decade. The black varieties total 200,000 hectares; there are another 40,000 of white varieties.[74]

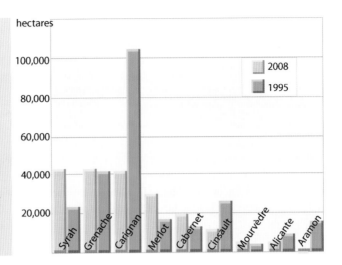

not, have never heard Benjamin Franklin's expression, "We must hang together or assuredly we shall hang separately.")

AOC regions make up only a quarter of the area. In an attempt to gain wider recognition, the region was more clearly divided into different appellations in the mid 1980s, including Minervois, Corbières, and Coteaux du Languedoc. The areas of the Coteaux du Languedoc are being classified to give more of a hierarchy. AOCs are generally restricted to growing varieties that are traditional to the region, but with the same concept of cépage amelioration promoting Syrah, Mourvèdre, and Grenache, and discouraging Carignan and Cinsault. (Some part of the problem was actually created by the authorities, however, when INAO recommended in the 1960s that producers should "cool the ardor" of Grenache by planting Cinsault. INAO would do better to cool the flowery language. Growers who accepted the advice have since been occupied pulling out the Cinsault.) Some brave producers try to make quality wine from Vieille Vignes Carignan, but personally I have yet to be persuaded that even low yields from old vines can rescue quality. There is criticism of INAO for its insistence on maintaining the original Southern varietals as the exclusive basis for AOC wines, and if you want to grow Cabernet Sauvignon or other such varieties, you can only do so as Vin de Pays.

The numbers suggest progress, with excess production coming down, and plantings of better varieties coming up, but no clear regional leader has emerged. With its (relatively) reliable hot climate, Languedoc-Roussillon better resembles the wine-producing regions of the New World than any other part of France. Why then are its wines still struggling to get out from under the image of the wine lake? There is continuing debate as to whether concentrating on making wines from the traditional varieties in the AOCs, or producing international varieties in the Vin de Pays, is the best way forward. There is no doubt that AOC wine has improved significantly, but it's fair to say that for the most part it still seems on the rustic side compared with other regions. And it's not especially easy to compete on the international stage with the same varieties that are now widely available from the New World. This is especially true for the whites, where the climate is really just a bit too hot to make interesting Chardonnay or Sauvignon Blanc. And as for the reds, the combination of small-scale production with limitations on the use of modern technology makes it difficult to compete on price.

In spite of the movement towards modernization, the Languedoc is not terribly receptive to change, and is probably the wine-producing region in France with the least foreign investment. This is unlikely to improve in the foreseeable future after the outcome of *l'affaire Mondavi*. The large Californian producer, Mondavi, proposed in 2000 to establish vineyards and build a large, modern winery at Aniane in the Hérault. Aniane is home to two of the Languedoc's top producers, Mas de Daumas Gassac and Domaine de la Grange des Pères. At the other extreme from these producers, many local growers send their grapes to the cooperative.

Daumas Gassac was established by Aimé Guibert in 1972, following advice that the terroir was suitable for producing Bordeaux blends; at the time, this was close to heresy. As Guibert recounts, "I consulted all the great oracles in Languedoc, asking them, 'How do you make great wine?' And these great professionals invariably answered, 'If it were possible to make great wine in Languedoc, we would already know about it.' They made fun of me."[75] But by 1978, the great enologist Emile Peynaud was advising the domain, and the first vintage (80% Cabernet Sauvignon) was produced. Because Cabernet Sauvignon is not permitted under local AOC rules, the wine was labeled as Vin de Table. The wines are now labeled as Vin de Pays de l'Hérault, as are those of Grange des Pères which was established in 1992, and makes its red wine from a blend of Syrah, Mourvèdre, and Cabernet Sauvignon, the last again excluding it from the AOC. Aniane is a special place, not only for its red glacial soils, but also for the protected micro climate in the Gassac Valley, where cool night winds give greater diurnal variation than elsewhere in the region.

Mondavi proposed to plant 50 hectares of vineyards, in small blocks of 5 hectares each interspersed with the garrigue (the local term for the forest, but really more of a scrub), so as to reduce disturbance to the environment. The location was on the Arboussas massif, basically scrub hillside normally closed to all development, overlooking the town of Aniane. There would also be a state of the art winery nearby. The wines were to be produced under the name of Vichon Mediterranean, a subsidiary that Mondavi had purchased previously for producing a French branded wine. The project was approved by the town authorities, who owned the land and agreed to lease it to Mondavi, but strong local opposition developed rapidly.

Part of the reaction was a genuine belief that the Massif should left untouched. Part was the anti-Americanism so common in French politics. But the heart of it was perhaps that the introduction of modern methods to make a top flight wine was seen as more of a threat to the existing order than as a promise to upgrade the whole region.[76] The leading politician against the development, Manuel Diaz, subsequently elected as Mayor of Aniane on the basis of his opposition, argued that, "To make this kind of investment profitable, he [Mondavi] would have had to buy grapes which, in the mid- or long term would have meant the closure of the local cooperative."[77] One has to wonder why it is better to preserve the local cooperative, making wines of no distinction, rather than for growers to produce better grapes and sell them to go into a wine of international reputation? Aimé Guibert was another prominent leader of the opposition, opposed to any desecration of the Massif, although the vehemence of his opposition included criticism of Mondavi's wines—"for me, Mondavi's wine is nothing better than yogurt"—which aroused some suspicion that he might be more concerned about being displaced as the most important local producer.[78] At all events, the death of the project makes it unlikely there will be other attempts on a similar scale, at least from foreign investors; it remains to be seen whether French investors might do better.

Everything is Forbidden Unless it is Permitted

Some things are sacred in France: names of grape varieties can't appear on the labels of AOC wines; oak barrels are the only means by which oak can be used in wine; rosé wine is made from red grapes by allowing a little skin contact and cannot be made by mixing red and white wines. O tempora! O mores! Knocked off its pinnacle in wine production, France is abandoning such restrictions (to be fair, abandoning the last of these was considered but rejected after protests from producers). What will be next?

Ever since Napoleon, France has been tilted towards centralized management. The statism of the French system plays out in many ways in the wine industry, from breaking up successful estates on the death of the owner, which has led to the morcelization of Burgundy, to the belief that the centralized bureaucrats of INAO can best determine which grape varieties should be allowed to be planted in each AOC vineyard in the French countryside.

So what has gone wrong in France? Its variety of terroirs from the cool north to the baking south should allow sufficient variety of wine styles to suit any palate, it has a century's history dominating the world's production of wine, and in case of trouble there is often a handout to support the producers.

It's certainly an issue that the areas that should be producing the best wines—the Appellation Contrôlée vineyards—are under stultifying regulation. Granted that a system forbidding anything that is not specifically permitted provides some protection against unscrupulous producers lowering standards, at the same time it prevents producers from responding to changing circumstances. If the present rules had been effect at, say, the time of the 1855 classification in Bordeaux, it is likely that the right bank would have been unable to make the transition from Malbec (dominant in the nineteenth century) to Merlot (dominant today). Producers of Vin de Pays are free to experiment, but (with a few notable exceptions) the inferior position of Vin de Pays in the hierarchy makes it difficult for them to provide leadership.

And, of course, while AOC may include the best vineyards, not all AOC is of the same high standard. The issue in microcosm is revealed by Bordeaux and

Burgundy, where the wines have little competition at the top, but are hard to sell at the bottom. It's even harder for the other regions where there is no halo effect from the top, except of course for Champagne where superb marketing has kept market dominance for more than a century (recent problems are just one of the usual periodic downward blips: this too will pass).

Could the answer lie in the terroir? Bordeaux has some superb terroir for producing Cabernet Sauvignon in the Médoc and for producing Merlot in Pomerol and St. Emilion; Burgundy's Côte d'Or is nonpareil for Pinot Noir. But elsewhere in either region, results are not so good, and the wines can be relatively thin and acidic in poor vintages. In fact, they show considerable vintage variation even in the best terroirs.

Contrast this with the New World, especially Australia where terroir has traditionally been ignored or even despised, because vineyards are laid out over large areas, irrigation is used to provide an even water supply, and the climate is generally reliable. Lower labor costs, better work habits, lower land costs, and freedom to use modern technology, all combine to produce reliable fruit-forward wines that appeal to the consumer and with which France cannot compete for varietals sold basically on price.

But here is a key dilemma. Sticking with traditional production on the traditional terroirs produces wines that may be unique, but which require consumers who have developed (or who are prepared to accept) a certain taste and style. Indeed, prompted by the decline in the traditional market for these wines, many French wines, including those of the most distinguished appellations, are now made in a more "international" style. But once you make the transition to a common style, you are effectively competing with others in the international market.

What a producer should be asking himself in making a wine, and what the consumer should be asking in buying it, is how it reflects the place it comes from, what's distinctive about it? If it's wine with soft fruits and tannins, with generally pleasant but indistinctive flavors not suggestive of any particular variety, what I call an interdenominational wine, aren't we in a realm in which price is the basic, perhaps the sole determinant? France just can't compete in this arena. Given that many industries have moved out of Europe to lower cost locations in other countries, why should wine be different?

Should France concentrate on what it has always proclaimed to be its strength: the unique character of its terroirs? But doesn't this require focus on the best terroirs? If they really believe in terroir in France, should they simply pull out the vines that aren't in really good terroirs? Or at the least, take them out of the AOC system and plant varieties better suited to compete in the marketplace?

"For too long, France has lived off its illustrious past reputation. It is now necessary for the wine industry to forget its haughty elitism and take the threat from New World wines seriously." This was the conclusion of the Berthomeau Report in 2001, named after Jacques Berthomeau who was commissioned by the French government to consider how to revive the wine industry.[79] The problem has been recognized, but have they slept through the wake-up call?

16

Italy: Cool North and Hot South

DOES THE REGULATION OF WINE PRODUCTION reveal national characteristics? France has a complex system of appellations based on an intellectual construction that works better in theory than in practice. Germany's system conveys a precise description of the origin and quality level of every single wine, intended to benefit producers but which certainly confuses consumers. And Italy—Italy is in permanent disorder. Having copied the French system, with wine divided into Vino da Tavola (table wine), IGT,[*] and the quality wine levels of DOC[†] and DOCG (a super-DOC category),[1] Italy finds itself in the topsy-turvy situation that the very best wines of its top regions do not qualify for the DOCG but instead are sold as IGT.[2] In Tuscany, reality is so far distant from the DOC system that many of the very best wines are known by the completely undefined category of "super-Tuscan"—basically a wine that may or may not actually meet the criteria for DOC, but that is sold at a high price under the IGT Toscana label.

Italy plays tag with France for the title of the world's largest wine producer and exporter. There's the same general trend of declining production pushed by declining consumption. Per capita domestic consumption is now half of what it was thirty years ago. About a quarter of the current annual production of 550 million cases is exported. Imports are relatively unimportant: Italians mostly drink Italian wine. The proportion of quality wine has been increasing, up from 13% in 1988 to 30% today, but that still leaves table wine as the major part of wine production. The relative increase in quality wine is mostly due to the fact that table wine production is declining more rapidly than other categories. About two thirds of the DOC(G) regions, and the majority of quality wine production, are in the northern half of the country.

---

[*] Indicazione Geografica Tipica, equivalent to the French Vin de Pays.
[†] Demoninazione di Origine Controllata.

Most of the top varieties in Italy are indigenous.[3]

	Black varieties	White varieties
1	Merlot	Trebbiano
2	Barbera	Catarratto
3	Montepulciano	Malvasia
4	Sangiovese	Muscat
5	Refosco	Chardonnay
6	Negroamaro	Garganega
7	Primitivo (Zinfandel)	Verduzzo
8	Aglianico	Ansonica
9	Cabernet Sauvignon	Prosecco
10	Dolcetto	Pinot Grigio (Pinot Gris)

The most common varieties in individual regions of Italy are more often red than white. Dominant varieties are shown under the name of each region.

DOC and DOCGs are concentrated in the northern half of the country, but production is concentrated in the south. On the right, % of DOC shows what proportion of all DOC wine comes from each region, compared to % of all wine.

DOC(G) is 29% of all production, IGT is 27%, and Vino da Tavola is 44%.[4]

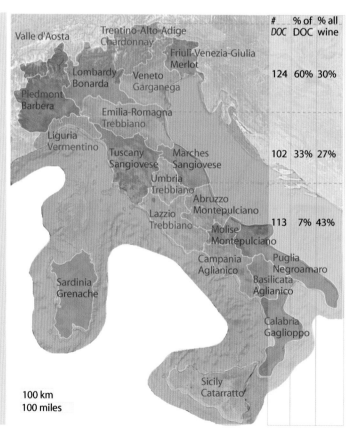

	# DOC	% of DOC	% all wine
	124	60%	30%
	102	33%	27%
	113	7%	43%

Long and skinny, extending over 10 degrees of latitude from north to south, Italy offers more diversity of climates than any other European wine producer, from cool climate Trentino-Alto-Adige in the far north, to beating hot Sicily in the far south. Italy also has an unusually high number of indigenous grape varieties. Plantings of black varieties are slightly ahead of white overall. The top red wines come from the Nebbiolo grape in Piedmont and the Sangiovese grape in Tuscany, neither of which is grown successfully anywhere else. Out of the top ten black varieties, only Merlot and Cabernet Sauvignon are shared with France; and Primitivo gave rise to California's Zinfandel. Merlot has just displaced Barbera as the most widely planted black grape. It's fair to say that, while Italy has many distinguished red wines, it's relatively hard to find an interesting white wine, perhaps explained by the fact that the predominant plantings are Trebbiano (found everywhere) and Catarratto (found in the south), although Muscat and Chardonnay now make it into the top ten. So does Pinot Gris under its Italian sobriquet of Pinot Grigio, but it's rare for it to achieve any level above the ordinary.

All regions of Italy produce both red and white wine. The most common variety in each region is usually indigenous, although international varieties are making some headway here as everywhere else. In the far north, Chardonnay has become the most common variety in Trentino-Alto-Adige, and Merlot has become the most common grape in Venezia-Friuli-Giulia (followed by Pinot Grigio and Friulano). In the Veneto, Garganega, the white grape of Soave, is planted in about equal amounts with Merlot, the leading red grape. But much of the Merlot here consists of highly productive clones giving wine that is indifferent at best.[5] Elsewhere, the indigenous varieties have a comfortable lead, Trebbiano by far the most widely distributed white, and Sangiovese the most common red. A bunch of warm-climate black grapes dominate the south, Aglianico, Negroamaro, Gaglioppo on the mainland, and Grenache, known under its local name of Cannonau, in Sardinia.

The most famous areas by far for quality wine are in Piedmont and Tuscany. Piedmont's Barolo and Tuscany's Brunello di Montalcino, made exclusively from the indigenous varieties Nebbiolo and Sangiovese, are classics. Super-Tuscans, made from any of several international varieties, can now match them for price. By comparison, many of the wines of the south continue to be somewhat rustic.

Tar and Roses

The classic description of Barolo as "tar and roses" is wonderfully evocative of the crucial contrast between the delicacy of the fruits and the stern backbone of the Nebbiolo grape. (Actually, "tar" is not found so much these days and may more reflect faults of old-fashioned wine making in the past.) Nebbiolo is successful only in Piedmont, in the northwest corner of Italy, where it prospers in a climate protected by nearby mountains (Piedmont literally means foot of the mountain) and sharpened by the morning fogs (nebbia is Italian for fog). It is at its peak in Barolo and the smaller neighboring area of Barbaresco.

On a clear day, the Alps can be seen in the far distance beyond the steep vineyards of Barolo. This view looks north over vineyards in Serralunga d'Alba.

The surrounding areas of Piedmont grow Dolcetto and Barbera, making somewhat more rustic wines, and also a great deal of Moscato (Muscat), much of it used for the sparkling wine, Asti Spumante, centered on the town of Asti a little to the north of Barolo. Gavi is a significant DOC for white wine.

Barolo and Barbaresco lie in the Langhe hills in the province of Cuneo. Langhe is the base DOC of the local hierarchy, imposing fewer restrictions on wine production than the Barolo and Barbaresco DOCGs that lie within it. Together Barolo and Barbaresco occupy only about 1750 hectares (little larger than the Margaux appellation in Bordeaux). Nebbiolo is the only grape that can be grown for either DOCG. (Other grapes are grown in the area, but carry lesser labels, such as Barbera d'Alba.) Nebbiolo is also grown in Gattinara, farther north, where it can be mixed with a little Bonarda, but here it has nothing like the same reputation.

The Barolo DOCG rules require aging for a minimum of 3 years, two of which must be in wood. Riserva wines must have 5 years of aging, but do not require any extra time in wood, so it's purely a matter of whether the producer wants to hang on to the wine longer in bottle before releasing it. Some producers certainly use "Riserva" to mark their best wines, but there is no legal requirement to do so. Until the 1980s, producers tended to use Riserva as a description for wines they had been unable to sell previously, making the label more a marketing than production decision. Since the move towards quality in the 1990s, more producers have kept Riserva to describe their best wines, but Riserva would carry more weight if there were some agreement among DOCGs as to what it should mean.

Barolo is a hair's breadth to the south of Bordeaux in terms of latitude, but the proximity of the Alps keeps the average growing season temperature a little cooler.[6] Vineyards are planted on south-facing slopes, and it's a local belief that the best sites are indicated by the places where the snow melts first in the spring.[7]

The Langhe includes Barolo
(communes indicated in
red) and Barbaresco
(communes indicated in
purple).[8]

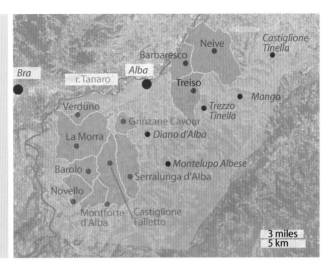

The summers can be dry, but the big climatic problem has been whether the grapes can be harvested before the autumn rains in October. Historically, there have usually been only one or two great vintages every decade, but since 1995 there has been a succession of exceptional vintages, broken only by the disastrously wet season in 2002. Of recent years, 1997 and 2001 are probably the best of a very good run. Due to global warming, harvest tends to be a few days earlier than it used to be, reducing problems with autumn rainfall.

An unusually long growing season means that Nebbiolo is not the easiest grape to grow. It tends to be productive, calling for stern pruning to keep to low yields. Like Pinot Noir, it is highly subject to mutation, and throws off clonal variations frequently. Officially three recognized subvarieties are permitted in Barolo: Lampia, Michet, and Rosé. Lampia is more productive than Michet; Rosé has pretty much disappeared because it is considered unreliable. But in reality there is much wider variation than the three names would suggest.[9] Although certainly there are differences between known clones, clonal variety is not a big issue with Nebbiolo, and most producers buy clones from local nurseries when they need to replant.

Barolo was one of the very first DOC regions in 1966, and became a DOCG in 1980 as soon as the new level was introduced. The vineyards are fragmented, with the average producer having less than 2 hectares;[10] the 1800 hectares of Barolo are divided among 1300 growers. You would think all quality vineyards must be long established, given the history of the area, but in fact the planted area increased 40% between 1999 and 2008.[11] Some growers mutter that the new vineyards are on land that will lower the overall quality of Barolo. Total production is tiny, about 11 million bottles per year, roughly one percent of the production of Bordeaux.[12]

Barolo is organized into several communes. Monforte d'Alba is a hilltop town in the center of vineyards located on steep hillsides, and gives the longest-lived Barolos. Castiglione Falletto and Serralunga d'Alba give powerful wines, the former more full bodied, the latter with more finesse. La Morra is usually de-

Morning fog descends on the vineyards of Barolo.

scribed as producing the most supple Barolos, and the readiest to drink young. It's a fine palate that can reliably discern a difference between Barolo and Barbaresco. Barbaresco is lighter, more elegant, more feminine, while Barolo tends to be more powerful and masculine. But a Barolo made solely from the lightest area, La Morra, may be hard to distinguish from a Barbaresco. Some of the difference between Barolo and Barbaresco has been due to slower ripening in Barbaresco, but the warming trend of recent years has brought convergence; some producers think that over the next decade, Barbaresco's reputation may rise to eclipse that of Barolo.

Wine has been sold under the name of Barolo since the early nineteenth century.[13] Barbaresco originated at the end of the century.[14] Barolo has gone through several transitions of wine style. In the nineteenth century, it was made in both a sweet version with residual sugar and a fully dry version. By the twentieth century, dry wine became the typical form, with high acid and tannins. Barolo used to be famous for its dense tannins, and was undrinkable when young. (It used to be the custom to warm the wine a little so as to minimize the effects of the tannins.) In the past twenty years, modernization of vinification has led to more approachable wines.

Traditionally Barolo was fermented in large oak vats. It macerated for long periods and then was matured in large casks of Slovenian oak (called botti) for several years.[15] A traditional top Barolo would take years to soften, but when mature evolves vegetal, gamey characteristics, with predominantly mineral and animal aromas. (It has to be admitted that many "traditional" Barolos were oxidized with high volatile acidity and very harsh tannins. As recently as 1983, one authoritative opinion was that "Barolo appears most often to be bitter-astringent when young and also when old... We do not know whether [Nebbiolo] is grown elsewhere, but apparently not (and justifiably so.)"[16] Indeed, it was this sort of opinion that led to the modernist movement.

Modernists versus Traditionalists

The clash between traditionalists and modernists has played out more forcefully in Barolo than most places. The methods of the modernists were introduced by a group of (then young) producers who were known as the "Barolo boys;" today they are the elder statesmen. The most obvious dividing line was the use of barriques of new oak to replace the large, old botti of Slovenian oak. Modernists believed that the barriques make more elegant wine, traditionalists that the barriques introduce flavors of vanillin obscuring Nebbiolo's delicate flavor. Leaders of the modernists included Domenico Clerico and Elio Altare; leaders of the traditionalists included Giacoma Conterno and Bruno Giacosa. However, Ceretto, who was among the first to introduce barriques (and was regarded as a dangerous radical at the time) is now considered to be mainstream. And generally acknowledged to be standing in a unique commanding position is Angelo Gaja.

The modernist movement is often represented as part of the general movement towards globalization of wine style. But this is to misunderstand the situation in Barolo in the 1960s and 1970s. Wine production was scarcely economic, and often was being abandoned; Elio Altare recollects that making wine in Barolo became regarded as something you did only if you were not capable of doing anything better.[17] Asking himself, "Why don't consumers like my wine?" and why wine production was economically successful in Burgundy but not in Barolo, he decided to adopt Burgundian methods. "The foudres used in Barolo were filthy, everyone recognized Barolo because of its barnyard smell; the typicity of Barolo was of flawed wine," he says. So he introduced modern hygiene into handling wood, and switched to barriques. "Give me an example of a

Wine maturing in the traditional botti at Giacomo Conterno.

great red wine that is made without barriques," he says, "and even if you can find one, I will find you a thousand examples of great wines made with barriques." In response to the criticism that using barriques would make all wines taste the same, he points out that Burgundy tastes of Pinot Noir and Bordeaux tastes of Cabernet Sauvignon. "The barrique is just part of modern technology," he says.

Elio credits Angelo Gaja with being the first to realize that better wine is made by using modern techniques. Gaja says that respect for tradition can be a hindrance: "It is simply ridiculous to believe that introducing barriques instead of using large casks is a problem." He too views the barrique as simply another example of equipment used in the winery. "After all, no one is using iron anymore, everyone is using stainless steel, this is not controversial, it is a benefit."[18] Altare and Gaja, and most other producers, now regard the whole question of modernist versus traditionalist as an irrelevant distraction from the real issue: making good wine. Indeed, there is now general agreement that the issue between modernists and traditionalists is largely resolved. Some merging of the two has occurred since the modernists have reduced the extent of oak flavors in their wines, and it's now a fairly common regime in the region to use one year aging in barriques (including some but not all new oak) followed by a second year in the large botti. A modern Barolo is now considered to favor sweet, ripe, finely grained tannins over harsh and astringent ones, and purity of aroma and flavor over "animal" extraction.

There's no doubt that the quality of Barolo has never been higher than it is today. Aging wine for five years or more in large casks required a great level of expertise to avoid oxidation and volatile acidity, and required very high levels of sulfur dioxide. Today the few producers who still do this are highly skilled, such as Giacomo Conterno, who makes wonderful wine; but the life of the modernist is somewhat easier. Change is inevitable, and as Angelo Gaja told me, "The profile of wine has completely changed, it is stupid for a producer to say that he makes the same wine as his great grandfather. Forget it." There is common ground with all good producers believing that the best wines are made from lower yields, good equipment (whether or not this includes barriques), and of course Nebbiolo. As Davide Voerzio of Roberto Voerzio points out, much of what is described as modernism is simply catching up with what has been done in France for a long time in both the vineyard and cellar.[19]

The basic issue with Nebbiolo is really how to handle the tannins and get them into balance with the fruit. Modern techniques of viticulture have led here, as elsewhere, to harvesting with riper tannins. Using barriques rather than botti softens the grape tannins, partly as the result of more oxidative exposure, and in many modern wineries in Barolo you see stainless steel fermentation tanks that are horizontal instead of vertical. They contain a single large paddle that rotates round slowly. This leads to gentler extraction of tannins than the conventional punch down. It's just as "modernist" as replacing botti with barriques, but is regarded as just another piece of equipment that has attracted no particular controversy.

Nebbiolo is not a grape with obviously fruity qualities. Fruit aromas can be transitory, sometimes in the same spectrum as Pinot Noir, but tending more towards cherries. Roses and violets are often mentioned in describing a Barolo's aromas. Nebbiolo can be a deceptively light garnet color, and rapidly develops an orange appearance. The light color can lead to a mistaken impression that the wine has aged prematurely. And high acidity increases the aggressiveness of the tannins. So before the DOCG regulations came into effect, it was customary to soften the wine and darken the color by including small amounts of other varietals, typically Barbera. Proposals to change the DOCG requirements in order to allow blending of small percentages of other varietals have been defeated. But today, in the modern style, fruits are more obvious, color is deeper, and the tannins are less aggressive anyway. Alcohol levels are usually high, typically about 14%, but the alcohol is naturally integrated into the palate and is rarely at all obtrusive.[20]

Until the 1960s, the production of Barolo was dominated by a handful of negociant firms who purchased grapes from many growers and blended to produce a Barolo (quality being determined by the negociant). Now grower bottling is the norm, but production is still on a fairly small scale. For the major players, Barolo and Barbaresco are only a small part of their total production; a typical producer might also have some Nebbiolo in the more general Langhe classification, vineyards of Barbera and Dolcetto, and perhaps some Arneis across the border in Roero. Barolo and Barbaresco are only 25-30% of the total production for an average producer.[21]

Behind an unobtrusive entrance in the main street of Barbaresco (on the right), Angelo Gaja makes some of the top wines of the region.

Most producers have stuck with the system, with the names of Barolo and Barbaresco bringing a substantial premium in the marketplace. But one of the major players has partly moved out of the DOCG. Gaja has been a leader in Barolo and Barbaresco, producing wines in a generally modern style (fermentation in stainless steel followed by one year in barriques and one year in large oak casks). Gaja was founded by Giovanni Gaja in 1859; under the leadership of Angelo Gaja, the dynamic fourth generation, who came into the firm in 1961, there has been enormous expansion. Gaja's headquarters are still located at the original premises in Barbaresco, but they have now bought the castle across the street, which is connected by a tunnel to their original building. In addition to 250 hectares of vineyards in Barolo and Barbaresco, Gaja now owns the Ca'Marcanda property in Bolgheri and Pieve Santa Restituta in Montalcino, and several others.

It's no exaggeration to say that Gaja's innovations reshaped Barolo and Barbaresco. He led the drive to single vineyard bottlings from Barbaresco, with Sorì San Lorenzo in 1967, followed by Sorì Tildìn (1970) and Costa Russi (1978). Sperss is a single vineyard bottling from Barolo. Not only are these now some of the most famous wines of the region, but when Gaja created the wines, he did not do so by buying existing vineyards of any reputation; he planted vineyards on land that had been used for sharecropping. His eye for land that can be converted to vineyards has not deserted him; the Ca'Marcanda property was a farm until Gaja decided it was perfect terroir for vineyards. He visited the owners every other weekend until they were persuaded it was easier to sell it to him than to spend the rest of their lives entertaining him.

Modernizing vinification and introducing single vineyard bottlings are not Gaja's only innovations in Piedmont. He reintroduced Cabernet Sauvignon to Piedmont—it had been grown there a century earlier[22]—by replanting the Darmagi vineyard. (The story goes that Darmagi, which means "what a pity," refers to the comment his father made whenever he passed the vineyard after the Nebbiolo had been uprooted.)

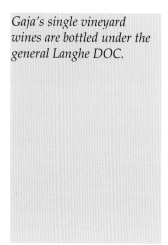

Gaja's single vineyard wines are bottled under the general Langhe DOC.

GAJA

SORÌ SAN LORENZO®

LANGHE
DENOMINAZIONE DI ORIGINE CONTROLLATA
NEBBIOLO
IMBOTTIGLIATO DA BOTTLED BY GAJA, BARBARESCO, ITALIA
RED WINE, PRODUCT OF ITALY
℮ 750 ML 14% VOL   ALC 14% BY VOL

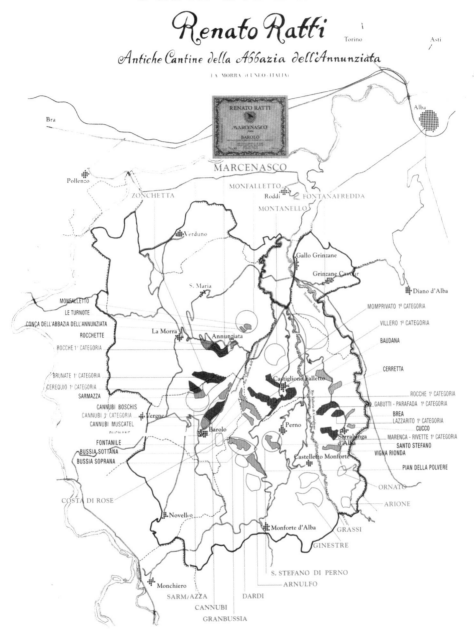

Renato Ratti's map identified two levels of Crus (red is the top level, orange the second level).

Kindly provided by Renato Ratti Winery.

Gaja's dramatic black and white labels are seen everywhere. His top wines from the single vineyards are now labeled under the general Langhe DOC to allow more flexibility in production. All have about 5% Barbera added to the predominant Nebbiolo. Given the superb quality of the wines, you have to wonder about the reasoning for the restrictions that drove them out of the DOCG. Certainly there's a case to be made that addition of a small amount of Barbera more faithfully reflects historical tradition than producing a monovarietal Nebbiolo. However, most producers are adamant that 100% Nebbiolo is the way to go for the DOCG.

The concept of Crus from named vineyards dates from the suggestion of Veronelli (an influential Italian wine critic) in the 1960s, and since 1992, the regulations have allowed Barolos to be identified as originating from individual vineyards.[23] Aficionados know the nuances between them, but there is no official classification of what would be recognized as premier or grand crus in Burgundy, although a system ascending from generic Barolo, to the commune, to individual vineyards has been advocated since the 1990s.[24] Indeed, the first classification was drawn up (unofficially) by the producer Renato Ratti in 1979.[25] Barbarescos also are identified by crus. There are still a handful of holdout producers who believe that greater complexity is obtained by blending from different areas to make a single Barolo in the old style.

Although the most famous names are well established, local politics make it impossible for there to be any official classification to promote the best vineyards to premier or grand crus. The Consorzio has finally made a geographical classification of regions within Barolo and Barbaresco, and the compromise has been to make sure that every single piece of land is entitled to a single vineyard name, thus to a large extent undermining the whole purpose of the exercise. However, this should at least stop the creation of fantasy names, although presumably those in existence will be grandfathered. It would be much better, of course, if any name on the label could be guaranteed to represent a single vineyard, but that is no more likely to happen here than in Burgundy.

The Ranks of Tuscany

The hilly terrain of Tuscany is covered in vineyards, olive groves, and forests. Many wine producers also make olive oil, although I have found scarcely any who will admit to making a profit on the olive oil; it's claimed to be more a traditional accompaniment to wine production than a profit center. It used to be said that vineyards were planted on land that could not be used to grow anything else; and olive trees were planted where you could not even grow grapevines. "Chianti was a survival economy until the 1950s or 60s," says Guiseppe Mazzocolin of Felsina. Most farms practiced polyculture, and the focus on viticulture is really a matter of the past two or three decades.

The Tuscan landscape often has olive trees planted next to vineyards.

Talk of the "rolling hills of Tuscany" is romantic twaddle; except for the coastal regions of Maremma and Bolgheri, most of the best vineyards are on relatively steep and abrupt hillsides. Driving around to visit wineries, you find many located well off the beaten track, often on unpaved roads winding up steep hillsides. Often built into hillsides or underground, cellars may be much larger than they appear, so the full scale of the investment is not evident from the exterior. Olive groves are often juxtaposed with the vineyards.[26] Tuscany has about 86,000 ha of vineyards, of which 30,000 are classified as DOC or DOCG.

The traditional red wines of Tuscany all are based on the Sangiovese grape: the DOC regions are Chianti, Vino Nobile de Montepulciano, and Brunello di Montalcino. Chianti and Montepulciano allow other varieties to be blended with the Sangiovese, but Brunello di Montalcino insists on 100% Sangiovese (of which more later). Chianti looms over everything else; altogether it accounts for about half of the DOC(G) vineyards and produces 8 million cases of wine each year. Chianti's best area, Chianti Classico DOCG, should not be confused with the lesser Chianti DOCGs.[27] Vino Nobile de Montepulciano (there is no connection with the Montepulciano grape) is roughly comparable in quality to the outlying Chianti DOCs.

In Montalcino just to the south, no one was paying much attention to red wine, until led by producer Biondi-Santi, Brunello di Montalcino emerged as one of the best red wines of Italy in the 1970s. More recently, the explosive success of Cabernet Sauvignon-based Sassicaia, at Bolgheri, close to the coast over to the west, sparked the phenomenon of the super-Tuscan, a wine that did not fit any of the traditional descriptions and was initially sold only under a generic Vino da Tavola label. However, there is no real challenge to Brunello di Montalcino as home of the greatest Sangiovese wines, except perhaps for one or two super-Tuscans, but most of the super-Tuscans use blends of international varieties.

Looking out from the Fontodi winery over their vineyards in the valley of Panzone in Chianti, there are vineyards in the foreground, forest to the left, and an olive grove in the center.

Savage Sangiovese

Sangiovese is the grape that typifies Tuscany, but Brunello di Montalcino stands alone in its history of making wine from 100% Sangiovese. Before the 1880s, Montalcino was known for sweet wines made from the Muscadello grape (a little Moscadello di Montalcino is still made). When the vineyards were attacked by oïdium, they were replanted with Sangiovese (more resistant to oïdium and already used in neighboring Chianti and Montepulciano). Brunello di Montalcino dates from 1890, but through the 1920s there were only four producers bottling wine under its name;[28] even through the 1950s there were fewer than fifteen producers because most producers were bottling their wines as Chianti Colli Senesi. Brunello di Montalcino was defined as a DOC in 1966, but really revived only in the 1970s. In 1980, it was the first region in Italy to become a DOCG. Montalcino presently has four DOC wines, of which Brunello is the most important. Brunello di Montalcino has now far outstripped Chianti on the international market, being the only traditional wine of Tuscany to vie with the price level of the super-Tuscans.

The history of Brunello di Montalcino is bound up with producer Biondi-Santi. When Sangiovese was introduced into Montalcino, Biondi-Santi identified a clone of Sangiovese in his vineyards, which he named Brunello (the little brown one).[29] The other general strain is called Sangiovese Piccolo, and this was more common in Chianti. Sangiovese Grosso is used to describe a family of clones that evolved from the original clone of Biondi-Santi. Descendants of this strain still are prominent in the production of Brunello di Montalcino, although there is very extensive clonal variation in Sangiovese, and now as many as 650 different clones have been identified in the Montalcino appellation.[30]

The production area coincides with the communal territory of Montalcino, 40 km to the south of Siena, more or less a circle with a diameter of 16 km centered on the old town of Montalcino, at an elevation of about 700 m. The terroir is varied. The area is divided into two parts: to the north is the original region; plantings in the south are more recent. Regions to the north and east are high in clay and volcanic soils, but to the south there is a high proportion of calcareous soils resembling those of Chianti. The climate of the northern half resembles Chianti, milder and wetter than the southern part, which is warmer and drier. The grapes ripen more slowly in the northern and higher altitude vineyards close to the town of Montalcino, and produce aromatic wines of greater finesse than those from the southern slopes, which tend to be fuller and richer. Producers often have vineyards in both the south and north and regard blending between them as the route to getting the greatest complexity. Roughly one third of the vineyards are in the northern half, with the majority in the south.[31]

The original regulations required long aging in oak (five years for the Riserva), which would admittedly tame the tannins, but often introduced oxidation. Regulations have changed to encourage a more modern style, by bringing the required maturation period in oak down to two years.[32] Riservas spend a year longer before they are released, but the legal difference is only how long the bottle is held before it is released to the market (although many producers do use Riserva to describe their best wines).[33]

In addition to Brunello di Montalcino itself, there is a second DOC called Rosso di Montalcino. This can be used as a second label, so producers can declassify wines that don't meet their standard for Brunello itself. Like Brunello, Rosso di Montalcino must be made from 100% Sangiovese, but the aging regime is much shorter, six months in oak and one year in total before release. However, Rosso is not just a second wine, because vineyards in Montalcino are classified as

The Montalcino DOCG describes a circle (boundary in white) around the town of Montalcino. Wineries (red circles) extend to the north and south of the town.[34]

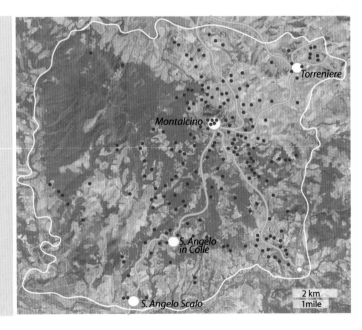

Brunello (2,100 ha), Rosso (510 ha) or IGT Tuscany (400 ha).[35] Those vineyards classified as Rosso can be used only to produce Rosso, not for Brunello, but vineyards classified for Brunello can be used for either. This being Italy, it would be too simple to suppose that the classification reflects terroir. A producer can move the classification from one vineyard to another, just as long as his total area of each type stays the same. One common use of the Rosso classification is for young vineyards that have been replanted; when they become older, they are likely to be reclassified for Brunello production. Since total production of Rosso is about three quarters of that of Brunello, a significant amount of wine from vineyards allowed to make Brunello must in fact be declassified to Rosso.[36] The terrible vintage of 2002 was an extreme case in which some producers declassified their whole crop to Rosso.

Brunello di Montalcino is traditionally described as having savory aromas and flavors, with notes of tobacco and leather, but (as elsewhere) changes in winemaking have resulted in more forward, fruitier wines that can be drunk much younger than previously, irrespective of the exact location of the vineyards. Style is perhaps now more determined by whether the producer is a traditionalist (maturing the wine in large old casks of Slovenian oak) or a modernist (using small barriques of new French oak). Guido Orzalesi of Altesino says that while the type of wood treatment used to be the difference between modernists and traditionalists, now it's more a matter of extraction, with modernists going for greater extraction in the international style, while traditionalists go for a more restrained elegance. (Claudio Basla, Altesino's winemaker, is a bit rueful about his reputation for having introduced barriques into Montalcino; it's true Altesino was the first to use them in the area, but this was not in fact for the Brunello.) Is it an exaggeration to say that the traditional wines are about red fruits, but that the modernist style is all about black fruits?

Maturation in barrique certainly smoothes the wine, adding an overlay of vanillin or other oaky notes that calm down that animal pungency. Blending in other varieties can have a similar effect. In good years, Brunello has no need of this, with the grapes achieving a ripeness that shows as tobacco, leather, even a note of chocolate on the finish. Personally, I find the traditional style wonderfully distinctive from international-style wines, giving wines of real character; while admitting that the best modernists make wines which retain enough of that character to be modern in style yet identifiable as Brunello, I like to see those intensely savory notes of traditional Sangiovese. (There has been little investigation into Sangiovese's aromatic profile; it would be a good subject for an oenology school to tackle, but producers aren't always willing to cooperate; one producer told me that a university had asked to study their clone of Sangiovese from one of the best vineyards, but they refused because they did not want the clone to become available to other producers.)

One factor in modernizing the region was the arrival of Villa Banfi in 1978. The owners are the American Mariani brothers, whose fortune came from selling Lambrusco (sweet, red, and fizzy) in the American market in the 1970s. They purchased large tracts of land, terraformed the landscape, including the construction of six lakes to provide water for irrigation, established a huge modern facility, and started to produce a wide range of wines of all types, from dry to sweet, white to red, and still to sparkling to fortified. With 155 hectares of Brunello, they are the largest producer in Montalcino, but this is dwarfed by their production of more commercial wines from a wide variety of grapes and locations.

In a world dominated by international varieties, the restriction to 100% Sangiovese in Montalcino has become controversial. You can grow other varieties in Montalcino, and the region has its own DOC to allow flexibility; Sant'Animo allows a wide variety of grapes to be used to produce either red or white wine, but it's too much of a catch-all to have acquired any significant reputation.

Does 100% Sangiovese necessarily make the best wine? It's sometimes felt to be a little hard, and there've always been rumors of blending with other grapes to soften it. These came to a head in the Brunellopoli[37] scandal of 2008 when the Italian news magazine, L'espresso, reported that 20 producers were being investigated for fraud under suspicion that they had blended Brunello with other varieties (typically Cabernet Sauvignon to bump up the color and structure).[38] The investigation was supposedly sparked by a well known producer who was indignant at others' continued flouting of the rules. Million of bottles were seized by the investigating magistrate to be tested to see whether they included other varieties. After two years, the investigation somewhat fizzled out, with an inconclusive report, and the declassification of some of the seized wines to IGT. The Consorzio (producers' association) considered the matter, and decided by an overwhelming vote that Brunello should remain 100% Sangiovese. Many producers say that allowing other varieties would diffuse Brunello's identity in the way they believe happened in Chianti when international varieties were admitted.

Superficially the argument has been resolved, but a troubling issue underlies it. Production of Brunello di Montalcino has more or less doubled in a decade.[39] This means that it has almost certainly been extended beyond the sites that are

Located close to the southern boundary of Montalcino, Castello Banfi has one of the largest wine factories in Europe, where wines from surrounding regions as well as Montalcino are made.

optimum for growing Sangiovese, creating pressure to include other varieties to "help" the Sangiovese. As Antonio Galloni remarks in The Wine Advocate, "Brunello is a wine whose fame is based on the supposedly special qualities of the Sangiovese Grosso clone... Allowing for the use of other grapes is a (not so) tacit admission that perhaps Sangiovese from Montalcino was never all that special in the first place and/or that the grape has been planted in an exorbitant number of places to which it is fundamentally ill-suited."[40] The only way out of the box is to pull back Brunello to the best sites, and to use some other label for wine from other sites (with or without other varieties in the blend).

The Hills of Chianti

A map makes it evident that in terms of total production, Chianti by far dominates wine production in Tuscany, although there is a significant difference between the Chianti Classico DOCG (the heart of the old region) and the other seven Chianti DOCGs.[41] The Classico area extends around a line between Florence and Siena; this was where Chianti gained its original reputation, and obtained the right to the description Chianti Classico in 1932. But a variety of surrounding areas gained the right to use Chianti, with individual zonal descriptions, at the same time, beginning the general degeneration of its meaning. Even worse, Chianti, with no qualification, can be used by a variety of areas elsewhere in Tuscany that have no real connection with Chianti per se. The only one of the satellite areas to have any pretension to the same quality as Chianti Classico is Chianti Rufina, just to the north. Part of the reason is that where the satellites extend into quality regions, most notably where Chianti Colli Senesi to the south includes Montalcino and Montepulciano, all wines with pretension to quality have the right to the more restricted local DOCG name.

A pile of straw-covered bottles reflects history, but has little to do with Chianti of today.

It took a long time for Chianti to recover from the post-second world war image of wine in a straw covered bottle. The bottle was certainly more interesting than the wine.[42] But slowly Chianti became a serious wine. Chianti today is a mix of artisanal and large-scale production. Half of the several hundred members of the Chianti Classico Consorzio bottle their own wine; vineyard holdings vary from as little as 1 ha to as much as 200 ha.

Chianti was (and largely still is) a blended wine. The problem was that the nature of the original blend created an issue with quality. Chianti as we know it today had its origins in 1872, when Baron Ricasoli (a future Prime Minister of Italy) recommended a blend of 70% Sangiovese, 15% Canaiolo and 15% Malvasia.[43] This formula was followed when the first DOC regulations came into effect in 1967. The rationale was that Canaiolo (an undistinguished black variety) bulked out the wine and improved the color, while inclusion of the white Malvasia softened the harsh tannins. Colorino (a grape with colored pulp but little taste) was also used to bump up the color.

Over the years, Chianti has changed. Slowly the requirements for including low quality indigenous varieties, including white grapes, were reduced. International varieties were allowed in small quantities, which were later increased. Finally white grapes were banned, and it became possible to produce monovarietal Sangiovese. These contortions all speak to the issues in winemaking with

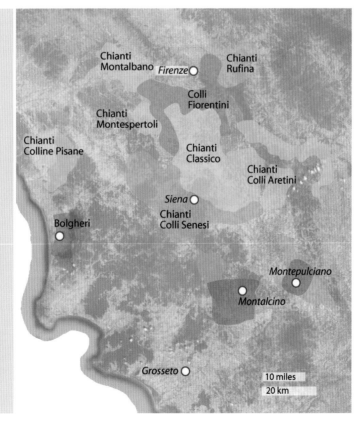

Major DOCs of Tuscany include the various Chiantis (shown in shades of orange). The most important region for Sangiovese is Montalcino (purple). Montepulciano (purple) also grows Sangiovese. Bolgheri is home to several super-Tuscans.[44]

Half a century of regulatory gyration has brought Chianti to a quality wine.

	Sangiovese	*Colorino Canaiolo*	*Malvasia Trebbiano*	*Other varieties*
1967	less than 70%	maximum 20%	minimum 10%	15% grapes permitted from other regions!
1984	minimum 75%	maximum 10%	minimum 2%	10% of international varieties allowed
1996	minimum 80% maximum 100%		maximum 6%	limit increased to 15%
2000				limit increased to 20%
2006			banned	

Sangiovese. The driving factor has always been the need to tame the tannins, typically accentuated by high acidity, whether this has led to blending with other varieties or the use of barriques instead of botti.

Perhaps the main difference in Chianti over the past twenty years has been the improvement in the quality of the Sangiovese. From the 1950s to 1970s, most plantings used a clone of Sangiovese (R10) that was too productive, giving wines with simple structure and limited aging potential.[45] In the past decade, extensive research has led to the development of better clones, with smaller, better spaced berries on smaller bunches, leading to much higher quality wine with good structure, better color, and more interesting aromatics. Several wineries in Montalcino and Chianti have actively been developing clones suited to their particular terroirs,[46] and the Chianti Classico 2000 project, supported by the Consorzio, spent 16 years testing clones in experimental vineyards.

One interesting result of all this is that the supposed advantage of Montalcino in having higher quality Sangiovese has become no more than a myth; in fact, the best clones in Montalcino, including Biondi-Santi's fabled BBS11, do not necessarily do so well in Chianti. Sangiovese somewhat resembles Riesling in the way its performance greatly reflects terroir. As Guido Orzalesi of the Altesino winery in Montalcino ruefully notes, when they tried propagating vines from their famous Montosoli vineyard in other locations, the results did not give the very special qualities of Montosoli.[47] It took 25 years to eliminate the terrible R10 clone from Chianti, but now much of the Classico region is planted with high quality clones; certainly there is no excuse for poor results.

As the quality of Sangiovese improved, lower yields and warmer conditions led to more reliable ripening of smaller berries with better color, so the inclusion of Colorino, with its dilution of taste, became undesirable. Better methods of vinification, including use of barriques instead of casks, gave riper tannins, making it unnecessary to include white grapes. Producers decided that they could best improve their Sangiovese by including more structured varieties, such as Cabernet Sauvignon. Finally the Sangiovese reached a quality level at which some producers feel they can make a one hundred percent Sangiovese that has sufficient quality in its aroma and flavor spectrum so as not to need any other grapes.

Increased fruit concentration in modern wines takes off some of the pressure to ameliorate the nature of the grape, although Sangiovese is not a variety that benefits from excessive extraction. "Applying the concept of phenolic ripeness to Sangiovese is like the tail wagging the dog," says Francesco Cinzano of Col d'Orcia in Montalcino.[48] The motto for Sangiovese should be "never too much," says Guiseppe Mazzocolin of Fattoria di Felsina in Chianti.

Sangiovese is a reductive variety, which is to say that its aroma and flavor spectrum are more affected than most by exposure to oxygen. It's not only the tannins that are changed by the aging regime, but also the aromatic profile. The characteristic organoleptic spectrum of Sangiovese, especially as aged in botti, has faintly savage, animal overtones, definitely savory, sometimes a mineral hint of gunflint. Aging in barriques suppresses those savory notes and brings out more direct fruits. Could this be because the key aromatic compounds are more oxidized when the wine is kept in barriques? So what's the true typicity (or tipicità as they would have it in Italy) of Sangiovese?

There's still some difference between those who believe that the true typicity of Chianti is best brought out by monovarietal Sangiovese and those who believe in keeping Chianti's long tradition of being a blended wine, but by using better quality varieties for the minor part of the blend. As Paolo de Marchi of Isole e Olena says, the real issue is to make the best wine. "Blending should not be used to improve poor results with Sangiovese, but to bring in a variety with complementary qualities that increases complexity... The pressure to make Chianti just from Sangiovese is taking things to excess."[49]

The success of the super-Tuscans has partially allowed Chianti to bypass the arguments about typicity that have occurred in other regions as modern techniques of viticulture and vinification have changed wine styles. It's easier to make a super-Tuscan than to fight for the soul of Chianti. But what should Chianti taste like? The admission of international varieties has certainly diluted the focus on Sangiovese, and many producers believe that the latest increase to 20% of nontraditional varieties is one step too far. On the other hand, Chianti has always been a blended wine, albeit dominated by Sangiovese, and it's not surprising that the blend should change over time. Whether or not the wine is blended, the slightly acidic, bright red cherry fruits of the past have generally given way to slightly deeper and darker flavors, following the trend of many other wine regions.

The requirements to include low quality black or white grapes, and the limit on the amount of Sangiovese, forced some quality producers out of the DOC.[50] Recent revisions of the rules have retroactively validated their response. This has all led to a definite improvement in quality, but the genie is out of the bottle, and the best wines (even those which would qualify under the new rules) are usually labeled as IGT Toscana. When you ask Chianti producers whether they would consider relabeling those super-Tuscans that would now qualify as Chianti, they usually shrug and say that they would like to help improve the DOCG, but their wine is now universally recognized as a super-Tuscan.

Bordeaux by the Sea

The land used to be marshy but has been drained. The soil is stony. The climate is maritime. Dominant varieties are Cabernet Sauvignon, Cabernet Franc, and Merlot. The major producers have large estates; often enough it is fairly difficult to arrange visits. Sounds like Bordeaux? No, it's the new area of Bolgheri on the Tuscan coast, where thirty years ago there were virtually no vineyards, but which today produces some of Italy's most famous wines from Bordeaux blends. It is perhaps an exaggeration to say that the explosive growth of Bolgheri was due to familial rivalry between the original owners of the Sassicaia and Ornellaia estates, but certainly these two great houses had a great deal to do with the success of the region. (All those wines with "aia" at the end of the name, by the way, identify Tuscan origins, because "aia" is Tuscan dialect meaning "the place of.")

The story of Sassicaia, the original super-Tuscan, perfectly illustrates the contortions of the Italian DOC system. The Marquis Incisa della Rocchetta, from an old Tuscan family, acquired the Tenuta San Guido estate in the 1930s by marriage. Inspired by a love of Bordeaux, in 1944 he planted a hectare each of Cabernet Sauvignon and Cabernet Franc at the estate; and in 1965 extended the plantings to new vineyards of Cabernet Sauvignon and Cabernet Franc. Initially the wine was consumed only in the family; the first vintage of Sassicaia to be offered on the open market was the 1968. There was no precedent in the modern Italian system for producing Cabernet Sauvignon in Tuscany, so the wine was sold only as Vino da Tavola. (However, there is nothing new under the Tuscan sun; a century earlier, a survey of foreign grapes growing in Italy said, "Even the best Tuscan wines improve notably if Cabernet is added in small quantities. Especially worthy of note are the results obtained by blending Cabernet with Sangiovese."[51])

Although the Marquis was somewhat uncertain about its potential longevity when the wine was launched, Sassicaia rapidly achieved legendary status as a rival to the top wines of Bordeaux. The 1985 is generally reckoned to have been one of the best wines produced in Italy. Eventually it became untenable for one of Italy's top wines to be merely a Vino da Tavola and a special DOC was created in 1994, Bolgheri Sassicaia, just for the one wine. The Bolgheri Sassicaia DOC specifies a blend of Cabernet Sauvignon and Cabernet Franc. A general Bolgheri DOC has been created for other wines in the zone, allowing a smorgasbord of varieties rather than attempting to impose any uniform style. The original rules required red wines to have at least 10%, and up to a maximum of 80% Cabernet Sauvignon, 70% Merlot, or 70% Sangiovese.[52] Now a change in rules allows 100% of Cabernet Sauvignon, Cabernet Franc, or Merlot. Bolgheri wines include Ornellaia's classic Bordeaux blend and Guado al Tasso, which includes 10% Syrah in the blend. These are among Italy's top wines, yet Bolgheri is only a humble DOC; perhaps in due course it will be deemed worthy to join Chianti and others in the DOCG category.

From the sublime to the ridiculous. Sassicaia now has its own DOC (left) but used to be a Vino da Tavola (right).

The 1985 vintage remains one of Italy's most famous wines, but was only a Vino da Tavola (as indicated at the bottom of the label)!

Not to be outdone in the family, Marquis Lodovico Antinori, a cousin of Sassicaia's Nicolò Incisa, created Tenuta Dell'Ornellaia in 1981 with vineyards adjacent to those of Sassicaia. Perhaps partly driven by a wish to be distinct from Sassicaia, the vineyards were planted with Cabernet Sauvignon and Merlot. The first vintage was harvested in 1985, and the winery was constructed in 1987. Among the vineyards are the 7 ha Masseto hill, where the clay is several meters deep, and the Merlot gave such extraordinary results that it was diverted to a separate wine. As a result, Ornellaia itself actually did not contain much Merlot until the subsequent purchase and planting of the Bellaria vineyard a little to the north of Bolgheri.[53] More recently, the Merlot has been decreasing to make room for a little Cabernet Franc. But the ownership has undergone a complete change. The Mondavi winery of California took a minority interest in the estate in 1999, then went into partnership with the Frescobaldi family; and then Frescobaldi purchased the estate outright after Constellation Brands took over Mondavi.

Sassicaia sparked the whole super-Tuscan phenomenon of exceptional wines that did not fit any DOC, either because they came from outside DOC areas or because they used a blend of grape varieties not permitted in the DOCs. To respond to this chaotic situation without altering the traditional DOCs, the IGT classification was created in 1992. Ironically, Sassicaia was never an IGT. Following the lead of Sassicaia and Ornellaia, Bolgheri remains devoted to Bordeaux varieties, with blends resembling the Médoc;[54] in addition there is a small amount of Syrah and an even smaller amount of Sangiovese. "Bolgheri is not a suitable area for Sangiovese, it does not do well here," says Sebastiano Rosso, the winemaker at Sassicaia.[55] Perhaps that is why Bolgheri's fame had to wait until the Bordeaux varieties were tried.

Some of the original super-Tuscans are now found under the umbrella of the Bolgheri DOC. Some remain in the IGT Toscana classification, such as Masseto, originally excluded because it is 100% Merlot. And the whole super-Tuscan phenomenon has now widened to take in other areas. Most super-Tuscans come from vineyards in the Chianti region, following the lead of Tignanello, a Sangiovese-dominated blend with Cabernet Sauvignon. Tignanello is produced on an estate in the Chianti region, but was labeled as a table wine in 1971, and later

Ornellaia nestles into the hillside in an estate including 50 ha of vineyards.

became part of the new IGT classification.[56] It contained too much Sangiovese, as well as a small proportion of the Cabernets, to be a Chianti originally, but ironically under the new regulations it could now be a Chianti Classico. Other wines that would have brought prestige to Chianti are Montevertine's Le Pergole Torte,[57] Fontodi's Flaccianello, or Isole e Olena's Cepparello, all 100% Sangiovese, made from vineyards in the heart of Chianti Classico—but labeled as IGTs first because monovarietal Sangiovese was not allowed in Chianti at the time, and now perhaps because there's more prestige in being IGT Toscana than Chianti Classico! A handful of super-Tuscans come from Montalcino, but are not made from Sangiovese, which fetches such high prices under the Brunello di Montalcino label that there is no need to declassify to IGT!

Close to half of super-Tuscans are based on Bordeaux varieties, ranging from wines based on Cabernet Sauvignon to 100% Merlots.[58] About a third have Sangiovese as the predominant variety. But there's also quite a bit of Syrah; sometimes it is included in a blend (usually with Bordeaux varieties, but there are also some 100% Syrah wines. Syrah in Tuscany gives interesting results, brighter and fresher than the wines of southern France, for example, and can be appealing. Merlot, on the other hand, does not do so well in hot climates, and although it's popular to soften the Sangiovese, tends generally to give somewhat monotonic flavors that don't reflect the terroir; "Merlot is an unfit grape for Tuscany," flatly says enologist Lorenzo Landi.[59]

The super-Tuscans first came to prominence in the 1980s. Some naysayers think the movement has run its course, and that people are now tired of powerful international-style wines, but if so, the news has yet to reach Tuscany. In fact, the number of super-Tuscans continues to increase and shows no signs of leveling off. Including wines produced in the regions of Bolgheri, Chianti, and Montalcino, there are now well over a hundred super-Tuscans. More than half come from the Chianti region, and of those about half actually could now be classified as Chianti according to current regulations.[60] The most rapidly growing new area is Maremma, just south of Bolgheri. Of course, it's a fine line as to what is a super-Tuscan and what is merely a wine using the IGT Toscana label in the way that was originally intended.

It's a moot point whether the wines of Bolgheri should all be included under the rubric of super-Tuscan. Wines that started as IGT Tuscany and later converted to Bolgheri DOC are still usually regarded as super-Tuscans. Some recently established wines are being marketed with the Bolgheri name, generally with Bolgheri Superiore used for those at the top end that might be regarded as super-Tuscans, and Bolgheri Rosso used for second labels or lesser wines. But some producers still say that super-Tuscan is the description that has recognition in the marketplace. It remains to be seen whether Bolgheri will establish its own, independent identity; if the predominant focus on Bordeaux blends based on Cabernet Sauvignon is not diluted by the admission of other varieties, it may come to be regarded as a ripe expression of Cabernet, somewhere between left and right bank in style, but definitely Old World.

Super-Tuscans aren't easy to define. Axel Heinz, winemaker at Ornellaia, points out that Tuscany is a large area, and is amused by the occasional requests for a vintage chart for super-Tuscans.[62] But let's suppose for a moment that there was actually an equivalent for a DOC for the super-Tuscan. What would its regulations be? It would have to allow any proportion of any of the grapes of Cabernet Sauvignon, Cabernet Franc, Merlot, Syrah, or Sangiovese. Perhaps the rule would state that a super-Tuscan could be any red variety or combination of varieties so long as it was aged in barrique for any period of time. It could come from any wine-producing region in Tuscany, so what would the vintage chart say—would it reflect conditions in the mountains of Chianti or at the seaside of Maremma? Perhaps the most sensible unifying regulation in order to stop the riff-raff from making wines labeled IGT Toscana would be to specify that there must be a high minimum price!

The diffusely defined nature of super-Tuscans makes it difficult to know how much super-Tuscan wine is really produced. Some super-Tuscans are produced

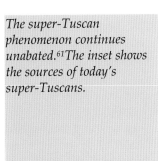

The super-Tuscan phenomenon continues unabated.[61] The inset shows the sources of today's super-Tuscans.

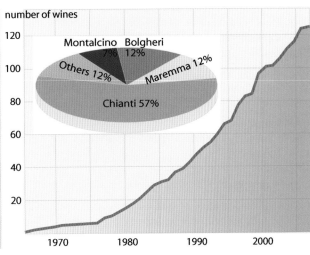

in tiny amounts, others at more than 100,000 bottles per year. Of Tuscany's annual total production of 40 million cases, about one third is DOC (of which Chianti represents almost two thirds). Probably the entire production of super-Tuscans is below 250,000 cases annually, about half of the production of Brunello di Montalcino. There's some skepticism about the point of imitating Bordeaux: "What is innovative or exciting today about experimenting with the same wines made from the same Bordeaux grapes? It's far from original," says Marco Pallanti of Castello di Ama, who is president of the Chianti Classico Consorzio.[63] But somewhat like garage wines in Bordeaux, the effect of the super-Tuscans has been disproportionate. They have raised the bar for the quality of all production in the region, although it must be admitted that success has made it all but impossible for Chianti to reach the same heights. Super-Tuscans really start where Chianti stops: the top price for any current release of Chianti from a good vintage is around $40, while super-Tuscans run from about $40 to $400 per bottle. It's striking how many Chianti producers now have an IGT Toscana as their most expensive wine.[64] But some of those wines are pure Sangiovese, a demonstration of the interest of the variety that might never have occurred without the spur of the super-Tuscans. Beyond this, the super-Tuscans gave a great boost to the confidence of producers in Tuscany that they could produce world-class wines.

The success of super-Tuscans has led to occasional imitations elsewhere, but for the most part remains confined to Tuscany. The other region of great repute, Piedmont, has not taken up international varieties to any great degree. As Angelo Gaja says, "The super-Tuscan concept does not apply in Piedmont—there is a super Piedmont and it is called Nebbiolo."[65]

Two Valpolicella in Verona

It's extraordinary how all over Italy almost every wine of quality has seen its reputation tainted by expanding the production area. Often the original area retains some shreds of dignity by adding "Classico" to the name, but that's rarely enough to distinguish it from the surrounding imitations. Valpolicella, the classic red wine of Verona, not only appears as plain Valpolicella and Valpolicella Classico, but also as *normale*, a wine made in the same way as any other red wine, and as Amarone, a very different kettle of fish.

Located just to the north of Verona, the climate is protected by the Alps and Dolomites and by Lake Garda (Italy's largest lake located just to the west), which creates warm airflow. This makes the climate as mild as Tuscany, and the vegetation is similar. The majority of production is by large concerns (50% cooperatives and 20% large industrial houses), which emphasize bulk production at low prices.

Valpolicella is made from the indigenous grapes Corvina (the predominant varietal), Rondinella, and Molinara. Corvina has aromatic fruitiness, high acidity, and low phenolic content. Rondinella is more robust but less elegant. Molinara is used for bulk, rather pale, and now is generally excluded from the blend. Since the early nineties, up to 5% Cabernet and Merlot has been allowed, but there are suspicions that some producers are using considerably more. In a now familiar story, Corvina is limited to 70% although it is notably of higher quality than Rondinella or Molinara. Some 100% Corvina wines are labeled as Vino da Tavola.

Valpolicella normale is a light, fruity wine: you might loosely compare it to Beaujolais. But Amarone is something quite different. Traditionally the grapes are dried on mats of straw in well-ventilated lofts for four months after the harvest (this is where the mild climate is important). The process is called Appassimento. By the time they are fermented, the grapes have lost up to a third of their water, so sugar levels are much higher, and the wine is much more concentrated. Originally this was used only to make a sweet wine, Recioto, where fermentation stopped before completion. Amarone results when fermentation goes to completion; ironically, this was originally regarded as a failure. The slow drying process makes the style generally oxidative, with notes of raisins showing on the palate. There's yet another variant of Valpolicella, called Ripasso, in which the Valpolicella normale wine is combined with the lees from the Recioto in the spring; this causes a minor refermentation, increasing alcohol slightly.

Amarone is an intense, concentrated wine, required to have at least 14% alcohol. The labor-intensive process of production makes it expensive. The highest profile producer in the area is Masi, who unusually produces single vineyard Amarone. Masi invented a system called NAPPAS (naturally aided Appassimento) that artificially creates the conditions for drying the grapes by controlling temperature and humidity. It's less romantic than drying grapes on straw, but more reliable.

Interdenominational Whites

The stereotypical Italian white has as much character as a dilute solution of alcohol and tartaric acid in water, to misquote Jancis Robinson slightly. (She was actually referring specifically to Trebbiano.[66]) The description remains valid for most Trebbiano and much Pinot Grigio, and indeed a fair amount of all white wine, but poking up above the parapet are some interesting wines: fresh whites in a modern style from Venezia-Friuli-Giulia, crisp Gavi di Gavi made from the Cortese grape, even the occasional Soave Classico made from the Veneto's Garganega. But the general drift is that too much flavor is too demanding.

Most white wine is made in the northern half of the country. There's not much of interest to be said about white wines from the southern half of Italy. There's lots of Trebbiano in Central Italy—well, there's lots of Trebbiano all over Italy—and almost none of it is of interest. Wines based on, or including a major part of, Trebbiano, include Est! Est!! Est!!!, Frascati, and Orvieto. Eduardo Valentini makes a Trebbiano d'Abruzzi of real quality and interest, but the grapes may actually be Bombino. Moving north, production is dominated by the three "V"s. Verdicchio, most notably Verdicchio dei Castelli di Jesi, is the best known wine of the Marches; it's described as being fuller-bodied and aging well. Vernaccia is

A map of sparkling and white wine production shows sparkling wine (yellow labels) concentrated in the north, with white wine (green labels) extending through central Italy and becoming sparse in the south.

found around the picturesque town of San Gimignano. Vermentino is found in Liguria and also in Sardinia. But it's a fine taster who can consistently get typicité in each of these varieties.

Friuli-Venezia-Giulia (together with Trentino Alto Adige) is a major source of white wine in Italy. The emphasis in Friuli is on making white wines from single varietals. The best DOC regions, Collio and Collio Orientali, have 17 different varietals; most producers make many different varietal wines. The major variety in terms of quantity is Pinot Grigio. Led by Mario Schiopetto, temperature-controlled fermentation and reductive techniques (limiting contact with oxygen) were introduced in the 1960s. The resulting style of clean, fresh, fruity wines has spread elsewhere. However, this tends to create blandness in the wines. The local variety is Friulano,[67] which tends to be slightly aromatic, but varies from dull wines to be drunk young to fresh wines that develop a nutty taste with age.

Two of the more characteristic white wines of northern Italy, Soave from the Veneto and Gavi from Piedmont, have lost much of their character as the result of expanding the production area. Soave is the most common dry white wine of the Veneto and accounts for half of its DOC production. Soave historically was made from Garganega blended with a little Trebbiano, but today Chardonnay is allowed in place of Trebbiano. Garganega is supposed to show flavors of yellow plums and citrus, but it's not often you find typicity these days. The original area for production was the hillsides near the towns of Soave and Monteforte. This is now known as Soave Classico. The DOC Soave can come from anywhere in the surrounding plain, and plain is indeed a good description for the wine. With a limit of 105 hl/ha allowed, this all too often is thin, watery, and insipid.

A major feature of the Cortese grape, the variety of Gavi, is its high acidity: good for maintaining freshness in hot years, but a problem in cooler years. Wines from the commune of Gavi itself are indicated as "Gavi di Gavi" and should be of higher quality than a simple Gavi. In an attempt to gain additional complexity, there's a move towards barrel fermentation, but it's not clear the variety really has the stuffing to stand up to this. Gavi is Piedmont's best white wine, but still it's difficult to find one with really distinctive character.

There's a small move in northern Italy to produce white wines in an international style, usually from Chardonnay, barrel-fermented with lashings of new oak. Chianti producer Querciabella produces an ambitious wine called Batàr (a play on Bâtard Montrachet) from a 50:50 blend of Chardonnay and Pinot Blanc. It's been widely praised, but it's definitely a powerful wine tending towards the New World style. Gaja makes a Chardonnay (Gaia and Rey) from a small (3.6 ha) vineyard in the Treiso zone of Barbaresco; the vineyard is named for his eldest daughter (Gaia) and his grandmother (Clothilde Rey). It's fermented in stainless steel and matured in barriques of oak from various sources. The style is forward and lush.

The most interesting winemaker in Friuli today is Josko Gravner, who moved from temperature-controlled fermentation in stainless steel in the 1970s, to fermentation and aging in barriques in the 1980s, and then in 2000 to maturation in amphorae. A visit to California convinced him of the sterility of modern methods of winemaking. Fermenting wine in amphorae is an old style of winemaking in Georgia (in the Caucasus), but Gravner has adapted it to new limits. The must is put into terracotta amphorae (glazed with honey), which are buried underground, and allowed to ferment for several months. The amphorae are large—you can climb inside to clean them out—varying from 20 to 30 hl. The must is stirred each day; the only other intervention is addition of minimal sulfur to

Josko Gravner with his amphorae (left) and during fermentation (right). Photographs kindly provided by Vias Wine and Josko Gravner.

prevent bacterial contamination. (Gravner tried making wine entirely without sulfur one year, but it was impossible.)

After a year in amphorae, the wine is transferred to large casks of Slovenian oak for 42 months of maturation before it is bottled. There are two bottlings, one of the indigenous grape Ribolla, and a blend (Breg) of several varieties.[68] The wines are deeply colored, sometimes slightly cloudy, in a generally oxidative style, with a tendency to slightly madeirized notes and a very dry, long finish. A faint touch of botrytis, made possible because Gravner harvests almost a month after everyone else, adds complexity. The very antithesis of the clean, modern Friuli style, they are not to all tastes, but the annual production of 25,000 bottles sells out quickly to aficionados. The amphorae attract attention, but are only one aspect of making wine in this style following ancient traditions of minimal intervention. Amphorae are used only to make white wine—a trial with red wine was unsuccessful because the wine lost its color—and red wine made from the indigenous variety Pignolo is matured for ten years in large wooden botti. The wines are labeled as Venezia-Giulia IGTs. Gravner is disdainful of the whole bureaucracy of winemaking: "You ask me what I think about natural Wines, if it is right for them to be certified… I don't know the answer… that is because I make Wine, my own wine, which is not dictated by any discipline or trend," he says.

The Rustic South

It gets hot in the south. Average growing season temperatures over 19 °C are pretty much at the upper limit for most of the quality black varietals.[69] So it's not surprising that viticulture in southern Italy is based on indigenous varieties adapted to the local heat. The best known are Aglianico in Campania and Basilicata, Negroamaro in Puglia, and Gaglioppo in Calabria. In Sardinia, the top black variety is in fact Grenache, known by its local name of Cannonau. In Sicily, some relief from the heat is gained by planting vineyards at higher elevations, for example on the slopes of Mount Etna. White grapes are grown in the cooler locations, but plantings concentrate on the indifferent variety Catarratto.

The best of the bunch is probably Aglianico as seen in the Aglianico del Vulture DOC of Basilicata. Vineyards are planted on the slopes of Mount Vulture, where temperatures can drop drastically at night to give much needed diurnal cooling. Of course, in typical Italian style, the DOC extends well beyond the slopes of the mountain into the surrounding plain. Aglianico is also the major black grape of Campania, where the best vineyards are at elevations of over 300 m in the Taurasi DOCG. There are some quality producers here, the best known being Mastroberardino. Prices for his Taurasi place it at the top of wines from the south and well into the sphere of quality wines.

As its name suggests, Negroamaro is both deeply colored and slightly bitter. Representing about a quarter of the plantings in Puglia, it is popular because it is easy to grow, resists local diseases, and manages well during drought. It tends to be rather rich and alcoholic. Also found in Puglia is Primitivo, the same grape as

California's Zinfandel. Reflecting the fashion for Zinfandel, and driven by increasing prices, plantings have increased. Unlike California, where Zinfandel is always produced as a single varietal, Puglia makes blends in which Zinfandel is the majority component.

Gaglioppo appears to been planted in Calabria only in the last century, in contrast with the myth that it is an ancient indigenous variety.[70] It's an unusual black variety in having red pulp; nonetheless, the wines are not deeply colored, and have a tendency to oxidize to orange and brown hues. It's also rather tannic.

The international scene has made less impression in the south than farther north, but some producers have brought modern methods to the old varieties, and there's a small amount of plantings of international varieties. In Sicily of all places, which produces 13% of Italy's wine, but is known more for quantity than quality, Planeta is the leader in the move to international style and quality. Founded by the Planeta family in the 1980s, there are now separate wineries for white and red wines. The whites include Chardonnay and the local indigenous variety Fiano; the reds include Merlot, Syrah, a Bordeaux blend, and some blends using indigenous varieties including Nero d'Avola. The wines are high in alcohol, typically 14-15%, and very powerful in the New World style; personally I find them somewhat overwhelming, but it's definitely a vast improvement over the typical rustic southern style.

Arrivederci DOC?

Will they ever learn? The focus of the DOC system away from quality has driven top producers to market their best wines as Vino da Tavola or IGT, expansion of the better DOCs into surrounding areas of lower quality has reduced their reputation, the plethora of DOCs makes the label anything but a guarantee of quality, and the cumbersome bureaucracy continues to issue rules that are years, or even decades, out of touch with reality. Giuseppe Martelli, president of the Assenologi,* says, "Although France and Spain have just as many individual appellations, Italy has a number of what I call UFOs or 'paper' appellations— which only exist on paper for political reasons."[71] Assenlogi considers that at least 20-30% of the DOCs should be abolished.

Not content merely with misregulating wine production as such, Italian regulations forbid the use of screwcaps in DOCG wines. This conforms with the widespread prejudice in Italy that screwcaps are associated with lower quality— indeed, it might be difficult to sell more expensive wines on the domestic market with screwcaps. But for those lighter wines intended to be drunk in short or medium term, especially the whites, but also at least the lighter reds, is this another stubborn example of mindless adherence to tradition at the expense of quality? In any case, it is now abundantly clear that screwcaps may be an issue of style, but they are not an issue of quality.

---

* Associazione Enologi Enotecnici Italiani

Paolo di Marchi, one of the most thoughtful and widely respected producers in Chianti, has begun experimenting with screwcaps—but because of the regulations can do so only for his top wine, Cepparello (bottled as IGT Toscana for which there is no regulation about closures). Already, he says, the screwcap and cork bottlings taste different, but the experiment has not continued long enough yet for him to decide which should represent the true taste of Cepparello. The question of corks versus screwcaps is not a major controversy yet, although one of the best known producers, Allegrini, has declassified its wines from the Valpolicella Classico DOCG to the Valpolicella DOC in order to use screwcaps. "The closure is more important to us than the denomination," says winemaker Franco Allegrini.[72] This may not become so generally pressing as debates about grape varieties, but if you compare it with the stubborn insistence on keeping white grapes in Chianti, isn't there an impression of dèja vu all over again?

Is there any way to reverse Italy's long record of spoiling the reputation of quality regions by expanding them to include the surrounding areas (of course, Italy is scarcely alone in this)? The remnants of quality in Soave are to be found only in Soave Classico, and in Valpolicella only in Valpolicella Classico (which is why it's a big deal for Allegrini to be forced to declassify its wines). Recently the two top regions, Barolo and Montalcino have increased production significantly; the vineyard area of Barolo has increased 40% in a decade, and production of Brunello di Montalcino has doubled in a decade. How can this be done without diminishing quality, and ultimately killing the golden goose?

There's a chance to sort it all out when new European regulations come into effect in 2011, requiring tighter control of classification. But already it seems that the prospective rules are so complicated that no one really understands them; some smaller DOCs could simply disappear as the result of inability to cope. There's considerable concern about the potential effects of the changes, especially that it will be much harder to change the rules after they come into effect. This is leading to somewhat of a rush to set the rules now, while there is still some flexibility, but the risk, of course, is that the law of unintended consequences will set restrictions in stone that backfire later. This would be a splendid opportunity to rationalize the system, to have a proper hierarchy based on quality. But don't hold your breath!

17

The Iberian Peninsula

WINE HAS BEEN PRODUCED IN IBERIA since ancient times. In fact, Spain may have been one of the original sites where the grapevine was domesticated. When the Romans conquered Iberia in the second century B.C., winemaking had already been established by the Phoenicians and Carthaginians. Under the Romans, Iberia became an important producer and exporter, especially from Andalucia in the south of Spain, and the Altentejo in the southern part of Portugal.[1] Even during the Middle Ages, when Iberia was under the control of the Moors, who as Muslims did not consume alcohol, wine production was allowed to continue.[2] By the middle ages, Spanish wine was exported throughout Europe. Wine from Portugal became an important export in the seventeenth century, when the war between England and France prevented the distribution of French wine.

The wine styles and regions that we know best today have relatively recent origins. Sherry and Port, the fortified wines for which Spain and Portugal are famous, depended on the rediscovery of distillation in the sixteenth century, and both regions were probably using fortification by the end of the seventeenth century. Aside from fortified wines, production is predominantly red in both Spain and Portugal today; there is no really well known white wine from either. Spain's best known region for red wine production, Rioja, established its international reputation only from the late nineteenth century, but the situation in Spain has been changing dramatically as new wine-producing regions pop up into fashion like mushrooms. Portugal still lacks much dry red wine of international reputation, although some interesting wines are beginning to emerge from the Douro, the same region where Port is produced.

Both Spain and Portugal continue to produce the majority of their wines from indigenous varieties. Tempranillo is now planted all over Spain except the extreme south; Grenache (called Garnacha in Spain) is the second most important quality variety. The situation is less clear in Portugal, because varietal character

is less obvious in fortified wine, but the best grape of the Douro, Touriga Nacional, may be one to watch in the future for its potential for dry red wine.

Spain: from Airén to Tempranillo

Spain has the largest area under vines of any country and is the world's third
largest producer (after Italy and France). Vines are grown in all of Spain's 17
provinces, although half of the total area is located in Castilla La Mancha (the
plain south of Madrid).[3] The climate is mostly hot, but as Victor de la Serna, one
of the most respected wine experts in Spain says, "Altitude compensates for
latitude to some degree."[4]

The vast area of vineyards has little relationship to either quantity or quality
of production. In fact, since 1980 the area of vineyards has been dramatically
reduced; but the level of production is about the same today as it was then. A
major part of the vineyard area used to be in such poor condition that its production was low; but the combination of subsidies for uprooting vineyards or for
replanting them has both reduced the total area and increased its productivity.[5]

Spain has the same problem as the other traditional wine consuming countries of Europe: consumption is falling steadily, and competition makes it
impossible to replace the lost sales with exports. The general quality of wine in
Spain for the first half of the twentieth century was pretty dire; it was often
mixed with lemonade to make it palatable.[7] When living standards rose after the
Franco era, many people switched to beer. As elsewhere in Europe, wine has
steadily improved, and producers are switching from producing table wine to
quality wine, but none of this compensates for the fall in consumption encouraged by the government bias against all alcohol. Except for a few years when

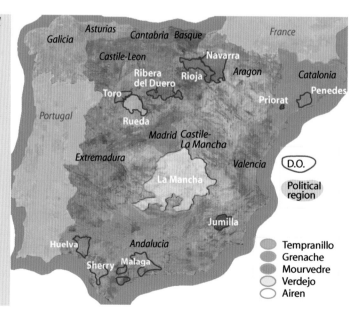

Wine is produced all over Spain. Some of the most important DO regions (Denominación de Origen) are marked together with the predominant grape varieties.[6]

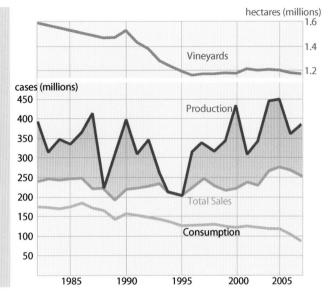

Vineyard areas have fallen steadily over 25 years, but average production has not changed much.

Consumption in Spain has been falling steady. The shaded area shows the gap between production and total sales (including exports).[11]

production was reduced by drought (before irrigation was allowed, in 1996), there has been a consistent gap between production and sales.

Over the past decade there has been a move towards black grapes, which now represent just over half of plantings.[8] Improvements in quality have seen vineyards of international varieties or other quality grapes roughly double in area, from 15% to 30%, since the turn of the millennium. Plantings of the old low grade varieties have been decreasing, although there are still large quantities of the white Airén and black Bobal.[9]

More than half of the plantings of white grapes are still Airén; at one time, there was so much of this drought-resistant, but low quality, grape that it was the most widely planted grape in the world. But the amount has been almost halved in the past decade.[10] Of the other indigenous white grapes, only Viura (also known as Macabeo) has much pretension to quality, although Verdejo and Albariño can make good wines. Of course, Palomino, although not intrinsically a quality grape, gives some wonderful results in Sherry.

Airén remains the most widely planted grape in Spain, but Tempranillo is now second.[12]

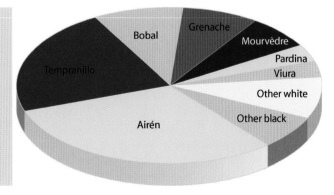

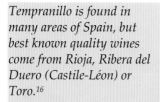

Tempranillo is found in many areas of Spain, but best known quality wines come from Rioja, Ribera del Duero (Castile-Léon) or Toro.[16]

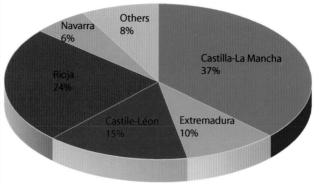

Spain's reputation for quality rests on its red and fortified wines. By far and away the star of the indigenous varieties is Tempranillo; indeed, a recent craze for planting Tempranillo has more than doubled its area in the past decade to see it become the most widely planted black grape in Spain.[13] Whether its reputation for quality can withstand this jump remains to be seen. Historically, fashion-driven trends of this sort are usually associated with planting the variety in unsuitable locations. There is also the problem that nurseries in Spain sell only three or four clones of Tempranillo, and these are not necessarily those best suited to the terroirs where they are being planted. The best producers are forced to use selection massale (planting cuttings of their own vines).

Grenache and Mourvèdre (Monastrell as it is known in Spain) are also important. Bobal, the second most widely planted black grape, is of no particular interest, but at least is in a steady decline. Spain has not been immune from the trend towards international varieties; historically there was always a little Cabernet Sauvignon, but today it is the tenth most planted variety, closely followed by Syrah, which scarcely existed in Spain 10 years ago.[14] This represents a great change in attitude. The story goes that when Carlos Falcó of Dominio de Valdepusa brought Cabernet Sauvignon into Spain in 1974, he had to hide the cuttings under a truckload of apple trees to get them over the French border.[15]

There are theories that Tempranillo was brought to Spain by monks from Burgundy, but this is mere speculation. It was clearly important by the mid eighteenth century, when it was described as the dominant variety in Rioja,[17] which historically has been by far the most important source of Tempranillo in Spain. The recent increase in other areas means that now Castilla La Mancha, that vast area to the south of Madrid, has the largest amount in Spain (much of it not in quality wine territory, however). Rioja remains the most important in terms of quality production, but wines of equivalent quality are now made in Ribera del Duero. Tempranillo in a modern style is produced also in the up and coming region of Toro.[18] Tempranillo is not usually included in the list of "noble" varieties, but in terms of the ability to produce notable, ageworthy wines, the best Tempranillo-dominated wines of Spain can certainly hold a candle to any of the international varieties.

The craze for Tempranillo has been associated with increased production of single varietal wines, but blending has always been important in Spain. "In warmer vineyards where each variety ripens fully, you do not get the same complexity you get from a single variety in a cool climate, so you need to blend," says Victor de la Serna.[19]

The system of Denominación de Origen (DO) was created in 1933, when Jerez and Malaga became the first two DOs. The law was extended in 2003, when wine was divided into quality wines (based on the DO system) and table wines. Just over half of Spain's vineyards are included in the DO system, but because yields are restricted, the DOs account for only a third of production. The majority of production in Spain as a whole is white, but the proportion of red wine production is increasing. Perhaps not surprisingly, since Spain's reputation for quality is based on red wines, more than half of DO wines are red. Exports account for a third of total production.[20]

A wine with a DO label must come from a specified area, and must be produced in conformance with local rules for viticulture and vinification. An exception is made for Cava, Spain's sparkling wine: the DO applies to the production of sparkling wine, but the wine can come geographically from many locations (although most Cava is in fact produced in Penedès, near Barcelona). Each DO is policed by a Consejo Regulador, a regulatory council that includes growers.

DOCa is a higher category of Quality Wine, but so far has been awarded only to Rioja (1991) and Priorat (2001). Nominally it requires lower yields and more rigorous selection of grapes. DO de Pago can be used for single estates of outstanding quality within DOC or DOCa areas. To date, there are only nine DO de Pagos.[21]

The DO system is extremely varied in effectiveness, to the point at which it is fair to say that "DO" by itself has little significance; the name of the particular DO is far more important. The 64 DO regions vary enormously in size, from almost 200,000 ha in La Mancha to the 42 ha of Dominio de Valdepusa (a DO with only one producer). Tenerife, scarcely one of the most important wine-producing regions, has 7 separate DOs.

Below the level of DO, there are two levels of table wine. The 46 regions of Vinos de la Tierra are the equivalent of the zonal Vin de Pays in France; they can have vintage and varietal names, but do not overlap with the DO regions. Some have achieved a good reputation, such as Sardon del Duero, just on the western boundary of Ribera del Duero. At the lowest level, Vino de Mesa is wine blended from anywhere in the country, does not have a vintage, and cannot name a grape or region name on the label.

Wine are classified by age as well as region. Joven are young red or rosé wines, harvested one year and sold the next; they have not been kept in wood, or have been aged in the barrel for less than 12 months. The year of harvest is listed on the label as "Cosecha." A wine described as "Tinto Cosecha 2000" is a red wine from vintage 2000, probably first appearing for sale in 2001.

The new wine law established some terms that can be used only for Quality Wines. Basically the quality level depends on how long the wine spends in oak. The system assumes that higher quality wines deserve longer in oak, and goes back to a period when wines were aged in barrel for much longer periods than today. (The long aging originated as a way to tame wines that were initially unappealing because of their high tannins and acid.) Quality Wines are classified as Crianza, Reserva, or Gran Reserva; the difference in the wines is whether they spend 6, 12, or 24 months in oak. They must also spend increasing time in bottle before release, but that's simply an issue of controlling availability, rather than intrinsic to quality.[22] (The intention is that the wine should be ready to drink on release.)

Rioja and the French Connection

No one knows where the name Rioja originated. The most popular theory is that it came from Rio (river) Oja; the Oja is a tributary of the Ebro river that defines the valley where Rioja is located. In fact, the Ebro is the longest river in Spain, running from the Cantábrica mountains in northern Spain until it empties into the Mediterranean some 900 km later. It enters the Rioja region through a gap in the mountains, and tributaries that empty into it create seven valleys as it passes through Rioja. It's possible that in fact it gave its name to the whole peninsula, Iberians describing the people who lived along the Iber river, which later became transmogrified to Ebro.

Wine has been produced in Rioja since Roman times. Logroño, the capital of the province, occupies the site of the Roman settlement of Vareia. Lagares from Roman winemaking—open air troughs used to tread the grapes—are dotted all over the region. Not much is known about the dark ages, but there are records from the ninth and tenth centuries referring to the cultivation of vineyards.[23] The passage of laws to protect quality suggests that wine was becoming important economically by the seventeenth and eighteenth centuries.[24]

Wine making was primitive until producer Manuel Quintano introduced techniques from Bordeaux in 1780. Among them was the use of fining with egg whites, which led him to describe his wines as *fino.* You still see Vinos Finos used on labels, implying higher quality. But Quintano was ahead of his time. The experiment with quality was short-lived, squashed by other producers; frightened of quality, in 1806 the Consejo set the price for fino below that of traditional wines.[25] Wine making generally remained primitive, including a large proportion of carbonic maceration (which gives light, fruity wines) because grapes were trodden in lagares.[26]

The modern bodegas were established in the second half of the nineteenth century under the influence of Bordeaux. The Marqués de Riscal, who had been in political exile in Bordeaux, started making wine at his bodega in Elciego in 1860. The influence of Bordeaux encouraged him to plant Cabernet Sauvignon. (In fact, Marqués de Riscal's wines still contain about 25% Cabernet Sauvignon. This is not really allowed by the regulations, but is regarded as acceptable because it is "experimental." It's a pretty good experiment that lasts more than a century!)

Bodegas Lopez de Heredia today (left) still looks much as did when it was pictured on the label at the start of the twentieth century (below).

In the 1860s, the regional government had hired Jean Cadiche Pineau, a Bordelais winemaker, to advise producers, but in a foretaste of controversy a century later, there was a feeling that while his wines were very good, they were not Rioja.[27] Pineau became the winemaker at Marqués de Riscal in 1868. Another quality bodega was established in 1872 by the Marqués de Murrieta, who had studied winemaking in Bordeaux. He built his bodega at Ygay (just south of Logroño). By this point, price controls were abandoned, and the wines of Riscal and Murrieta began to obtain higher prices, supporting the movement to modernization.

A boom in Rioja started when the railway came to the region in the 1860s. Then exports took off when a trade treaty with France cut taxes in 1882.[28] This did not establish Rioja's international reputation, because a fair proportion of the exported wine went to Bordeaux, where it was relabeled and dispatched as "Bordeaux."[29] This was by no means a new development, since Spanish wine had previously been recognized as having more strength than wine produced in Bordeaux, and it was customary to include a significant proportion when the wine was blended (although the most common source was Alicante, farther to the south).[30]

The importance of exports can still be seen in Haro, the capital of Rioja Alta, which a few miles to the west of Logroño, is the center for wine production; the oldest established bodegas are all clustered around the railway station.[31] Some of the bodegas have scarcely changed. The wine was mostly exported in bulk (bottling at the winery was a rarity reserved for a few special clients), although technicians often accompanied the shipment to bottle it for the purchaser.[32]

The connection with Bordeaux was first strengthened when the Bordelais negociants found their local supplies impacted by the attack of oïdium (a mildew) in the 1850s. Rioja was an alternative supplier until it in turn was hit by oïdium. When phylloxera decimated production in Bordeaux in the 1870s, the effect was not merely on negociants who came to buy wine; winemakers migrated across

Rioja Alavesa and Rioja Alta are to the north east of the warmer Rioja Baja.[33]

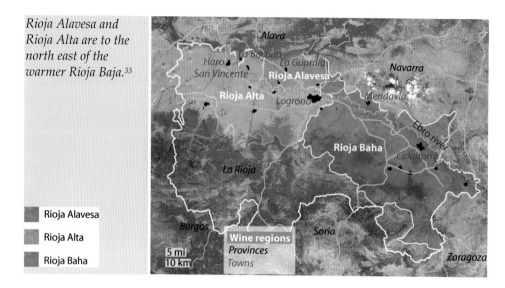

Rioja Alavesa

Rioja Alta

Rioja Baha

the Pyrenees, bringing expertise with them. By the last decade or two of the century, winemaking in Rioja generally followed the Bordeaux model.

Phylloxera decimated production in Rioja between 1901 and 1905, and the region rapidly collapsed from riches to rags. The cessation of French exports during the first world war allowed Rioja to regain some export markets, and in the succeeding period Rioja became well known in the United States and Britain, as well as more successful within Spain itself. The civil war of 1936-1939 all but destroyed the region, and revival really began only with the harvest of 1970.

Geographically, the big distinction is between the western part (Rioja Alavesa and Rioja Alta) and the eastern part (Rioja Baja). Although Rioja Alavesa is more elevated than Rioja Alta, the distinction between them is as much political as geographical (Rioja Alavesa is in the province of Alava whereas Rioja Alta is in the province of La Rioja). The usual simplification is that the wines of Rioja Alavesa have a little more body and higher acidity than those of Rioja Alta, but there's as much variation between vineyards in each region as between regions. Rioja Baja really is different: it is hotter and drier, with temperatures on average about 1 °C higher (equivalent to almost one zone on the degree day scale).

Rioja occupies a depression dominated by the Ebro river, sandwiched between mountain ranges to the north and south. The Sierra Cantábrica mountains establish a northern barrier to the Atlantic. The mountains to the south, the Sierra de la Demanda, 30-40 km away, are a barrier also, but less important. Humidity from the river has a big effect on the local climate. Vineyards in Rioja Alavesa have elevations from 400 m to 600 m, with high diurnal temperature variation, whereas those in Rioja Baja are lower, more alluvial, and have a more Mediterranean climate.

The planted area in Rioja has increased sharply in the past two decades, from 38,000 ha in 1983 to more than 63,000 ha in 2007. Rioja Alavesa and Rioja Alta account for a little under two thirds of the vineyards (with Rioja Alavesa roughly half the area of Rioja Alta).[34] The expansion has been accompanied by significant changes in the organization of the industry and in the nature of the wines of Rioja.

There has always been a division in Rioja between growers and producers. The large bodegas established in the nineteenth centuries mostly purchased grapes. (Murrieta and Riscal were unusual in planting their own vineyards.) There were the usual problems with quality in these circumstances, and the top Riojas initially were therefore premium cuvées rather than the products of single vineyards. Two decades ago, production was split more or less equally between smaller growers and producers, cooperatives, and large producers. Production has almost tripled since then, but the small operators have been disappearing, and the large producers now account for the majority of production.

The average vineyard size remains small,[35] and one of the reasons why mechanization has only reached a low proportion of vineyards is that many are below the size at which it is economic to buy the equipment. Many wines are made from a combination of grapes from the producer's vineyards and those purchased from smaller growers. There is the usual movement towards larger producers purchasing vineyards, when they have the opportunity, to own more of their sources for grapes. In some cases, the arrangement with the grower goes back several generations, and the producer would buy the land if only the grower would sell. Vineyard ownership goes along with the trend to produce wines from single Pagos (vineyards).

Production is regulated by the Consejo Regulador, which includes representatives of both growers and producers. The Consejo has gone through several incarnations since the DO was created in 1926 (and the region was given DOCa status in 1991, the first in Spain), but its present format dates from 1972. The problem is that it is dominated by large producers; inevitably, quality and typicity are not the first concerns. The quality producers express considerable reservations about its utility. "The DO prevents fraud and that's all the effect it has," one producer told me. The 300 votes are divided according to size of production, and the old established quality producers have fewer than 10 votes. No more need be said.

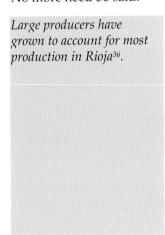

Large producers have grown to account for most production in Rioja[36].

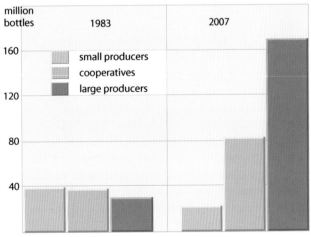

The Cantábrica mountains loom over the vineyards of Rioja Alavesa.

The New Rioja

Except for the world of wine, Rioja has been well off the beaten track. It has been generally ignored as a tourist destination for at least the past couple of centuries. "This district, devoid of pleasure and interest, may fairly be blotted out of every traveler's map," said a travel writer in 1845.[37] Even today there are guide books to many regions of Spain, including Madrid, Catalonia, and Andalucia—but still scarcely any attention is paid to Rioja. A sign that this is now beginning to change comes from the construction of the striking new hotel at the Marqués de Riscal. Oenotourism is the new phenomenon of the past five years or so, with a wine route established between friendly bodegas, and cellar door sales becoming significant. All this indicates a new success for Rioja internationally, with the various advantages and disadvantages that this entails.

Climate is responsible for a major difference between the western and eastern parts of Rioja. Conventional wisdom is that in Rioja Alavesa and Rioja Alta, the principal grape has traditionally been Tempranillo, whereas Rioja Baja is mostly devoted to Grenache. But this is now rather out of date: Tempranillo is taking over everywhere.

As with other wine-producing regions, focus has sharpened on an increasingly restricted number of grape varieties. In 1912, there were 44 varieties in Rioja, by 1942 there were only 11,[38] and today the Consejo recommends only four black (Tempranillo, Grenache, Graciano, and Mazuela [the local name for Carignan]), and three white (Viura, Malvasia, and white Grenache). And there has been a massive transition from the traditional blending of varieties towards wines dominated by Tempranillo. Like wine everywhere, Rioja is now made in a softer style, with more emphasis on upfront, fresh fruits.

In the first half of the twentieth century, Grenache in fact occupied about two thirds of plantings.[39] New plantings of Tempranillo overtook those of Grenache in 1970, and since then the growth of Tempranillo has been explosive. The total area of Tempranillo passed that of Grenache in the early 1980s, and today Tempranillo is 85% of all black grapes. There's a significant amount of Grenache left only in Rioja Baja, about 20% today,[40] a far cry from its former dominance (76% in 1981)[41]. Mazuela and Graciano are minimal; in fact, Graciano came close to extinction with less than 100 ha remaining until a recent revival brought it up to about 900 ha.

Rioja is mostly synonymous with red wine, but about 6% of production is white, mostly from Viura with a little Malvasia and white Grenache thrown in. The traditional style was heavily oxidized, but the emphasis today is on bright, fresh fruits. The decision in 2007 to allow Chardonnay and Sauvignon Blanc to be grown (although they must comprise less than half of the blend) is controversial: some producers believe it will allow Rioja to compete better, others that it will simply lead to loss of identity. The craze for international varieties is scorned by the traditional producers. Jorge Muga of Bodegas Muga thinks it would make more sense for producers to make efforts to improve their present plantings. "So Cabernet Sauvignon will improve the quality of your Tempranillo? Why don't you think instead about the quality of your Tempranillo?" he asks, concluding, "Rioja's identity rests in its own grapes."

Traditional Rioja was made by blending wines from the different regions and cépages. Fruitiness came from the Tempranillo-dominated cuvées of Rioja Alta; some austerity and acidity came from the more elevated vineyards of Rioja Alavesa, while more color, body, and alcohol came from the Grenache-dominated cuvées of Rioja Baja. Freshness came from the higher acidity of Graciano (the most acidic grape grown in Spain), offset against the softer flavors of the Grenache. Some white grapes used to be included to soften the tannins, but today this is rare.

This apparent heap of scrap metal is the hotel at the Marqués de Riscal, designed by architect Frank Geary, and opened in 2006.

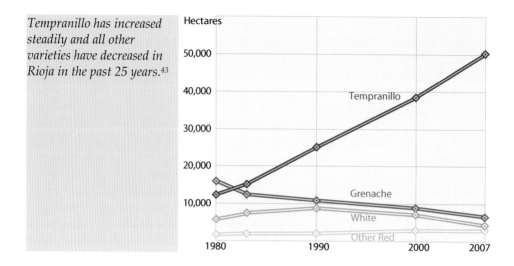

Tempranillo has increased steadily and all other varieties have decreased in Rioja in the past 25 years.[43]

None of this conventional wisdom holds any longer. Some producers feel that the rush to Tempranillo is particularly misguided in Rioja Baja, given the hot, arid conditions in the east. Jorge Muga says, "Tempranillo may be too stressed in Rioja Baja to make good wine." He thinks it would be better to make efforts to improve the Grenache. Many wines do not have even token amounts of other varietals, but now are made exclusively from Tempranillo. And a tendency towards producing wines from single vineyards, largely in Rioja Alavesa and Rioja Alta, means there is less blending from different sources. Historically, blending was regarded as crucial; when there was a shortage of white grapes in the 1960s, the Consejo even allowed white wine to be imported from other regions in Spain for blending purposes.[42] Of course, these days it's illegal to put anything except grapes from Rioja into the wine.

Rioja is now going through the same discussion about blending that dominated Barolo twenty years ago. Do you make a better wine by blending the products of vineyards with different characteristics or is it more interesting to make a variety of wines each closely reflecting the properties of a different vineyard? There's a double-edged issue here, because single vineyard wines are mostly interesting only in Rioja Alavesa and Rioja Alta; if much of these regions goes into single vineyard bottlings, what is to be done with the wine of Rioja Baja that used to be blended with them? And in Barolo, where only one grape variety is grown, the argument was confined to blending between vineyards; in Rioja it also concerns whether other varieties should be blended with Tempranillo. At Bodegas La Rioja Alta, winemaker Julio Saenz believes it's the Grenache that really determines the quality of the Crianza, and at Contino, Jesus Madrazo forcefully makes his case with tastings that the freshness of Graciano gives a huge lift to the Reservas and Gran Reservas.

What is the typicity of Rioja? Initially there was one classic style of Rioja, but now there is much variety. There is the same split here between traditionalists and modernists as in other wine regions. Some producers remain firmly traditional, with Lopez de Heredia perhaps the most committed to the old values.

Some new producers are firmly in the modern camp, such as Roda, devoted to the cult of phenolic ripeness to the extent that they assess ripeness vine by vine when selecting the harvest for their top cuvée, Cirsion. But often enough, the twist in Rioja is that the same producers make both styles, rather than committing to one side or other of the argument. Usually the modern style is presented as a new brand, not necessarily labeled with one of the traditional classifications, while the older styles retain their classic descriptions. CVNE has its traditional Imperial, but also its new style Real de Asua; Bodega La Rioja Alta has its traditional 904 Gran Reserva, but also its modern Baron de Oña. With a general move towards more international styles of vinification, bringing out riper fruit and softer tannins, there is an increasing transition from classic blended wines to monovarietal Tempranillo in the international idiom.

Oak remains a unifying theme in Rioja. Most wines at the level of Crianza and above are matured in American oak, which brings characteristic notes of sweet vanillin to the palate and finish. Indeed, when the well known Spanish wine critic José Peñin tried to define the typicity of Rioja, he concluded that the oaky nose and flavor were its most consistent features.[44] Some wines use a proportion of French oak, and these days there are experiments with oak from Hungary or Russia, but with the exception of a handful of wines matured exclusively in French oak, the flavor of American oak is a common denominator. Oak is regarded as sufficiently important for many of the larger bodegas to maintain their own cooperage, so that they can produce or repair barrels; usually they import planks of American oak so they can season the wood themselves. Because old barrels are used, repair is important, and barrels are kept in use by replacing individual staves when necessary.

The big change over the past quarter century or so is the use of more new oak and a reduction in the age of the old oak; and wines spend less time in oak than previously. Not everyone approves of the trend: "From 1971, the bodegas have vastly increased their ageing capacity using new wood... What is not acceptable

The old barrel is stained red from exposure to wine, but new wood can be seen as three staves that have been replaced.

is the presence of an oaky nose and flavor overpowering those which emanate from the grape and ageing process," said a report in 1978.[45]

Which brings us to the utility of Crianza, Reserva, and Gran Reserva, and indeed of the whole Denominación de Origen. The distinction between categories is based on the assumption that better wines should be aged for longer in oak. The regulations for Spain, dating from 1979 (calling for 6 months in oak for Crianza, 1 year for Reserva, and 2 years for Gran Reserva, followed by further time in bottle), were initially regarded as not really rigorous enough for Rioja, which demanded two years in oak for Reserva and three for Gran Reserva. But by 1981 Rioja came into line with the national regulations. Relative to the tradition of long aging in cask, these are relatively brief periods.

But is it true that all wines can be neatly divided into categories where 6 months, 1 year, or two years is an appropriate minimum in oak? Could producers make better wine if they were freed of such restraints? Of course, if 9 months in oak is deemed ideal, the wine can be given just that: but then it can sold only as a Crianza and not a Reserva. The problem here is that each category is associated with a certain price point in the market: as one producer said to me, you just cannot sell a wine labeled as Crianza at $40: it has to be Reserva. So that wine might need to be given another three months in oak (and extra time in bottle). In fact, the reputation of these categories is as much linked to market position as style: one producer has been known to label the same wine (which met Reserva standards) as Crianza or Reserva, depending on the needs of the distributors for wine at certain price points. Another, faced with an urgent need for cash flow, took wines that met the standard for Reserva and sold them as Crianza. The unclassified and Crianza wines are mostly sold within Spain, but half of the Reservas and Gran Reservas are exported.[46]

Crianza and Reservas are usually made every year, but Gran Reservas are made only in the best years; at most bodegas, Gran Reservas are made four or five times each decade. And for Gran Reserva there is a distinct view of style as well as price. In fact, this is a problem, because of the perception that Gran Re-

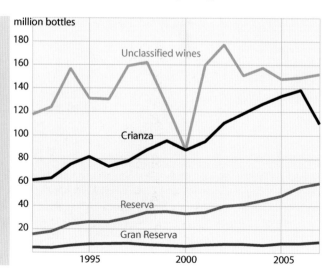

Reserva and Gran Reserva wines are only a small proportion of production.

In the most recent vintage, unclassified wines (mostly young wines) were 46%, Crianza 33%, Reserva 18%, and Gran Reserva less than 3%.[47]

servas are aged for a very long time and acquire an oxidized style. While true in the past, this is not necessarily the case today; but reducing the distinction between Gran Reserva and Reserva means that the price differential becomes more of a problem. Certainly Gran Reserva production is very small, and remains static, by contrast with a healthy increase in Reserva wines. One reason for the high cost of Gran Reservas is the expense of holding the stock longer in bottle before release, and as one producer told me, "People in Rioja are no longer making wines to age. It was the producers here who destroyed the Gran Reserva system by not wanting to keep stocks long term and preferring to go for quicker cash flow."[48] Some people believe that Rioja Gran Reserva will become extinct as a class in the next decade. (It's even less important in other areas, well under 1% of production in Ribera del Duero, for example.)[49] But there will always be some holdouts. Maria Lopez de Heredia says, "As far as Gran Reservas are concerned, we will die with our boots on."

Beyond the categories, does the DO itself make sense? The DO does not represent any homogeneity of terroir, indeed Rioja Alavesa and Rioja Alta are distinct from Rioja Baja. While not everyone would wish to go to the extreme of defining many detailed terroirs, as in Burgundy, it would certainly make sense at least to mark those areas where the best Tempranillo is grown (Rioja Alavesa and Rioja Alta) with their own geographical distinction.

And Rioja no longer stands for a single style. Leaving aside the question of oxidation, a traditional Rioja develops savory, almost animal notes of mature red fruits, with fresh acidity. The best are still good after decades. Certainly I have recently enjoyed Gran Reservas from the 1960s. But the new approach offers soft, supple, forward black fruits, more lush than acid in an interdenominational style that can be hard to distinguish from Cabernet Sauvignon, Syrah, or any other international variety. Some of these wines are good, even very good, but, as they asked more than a century ago when French techniques were first introduced, are they Rioja?

Ribera del Duero: Beyond Vega Sicilia

Ribera del Duero has been a paradox. It is home to Spain's most famous wine, Vega Sicilia, which has had a fabled reputation for more than a century. Yet whereas everyone has heard of Rioja, Ribera del Duero remained in obscurity as a wine-producing region. It began to emerge into the modern limelight after 1972, when Alejandro Fernandez founded Bodegas Pesquera. Now there are more than 250 bodegas, and, like Rioja, Ribera del Duero has become an attractive proposition for the large players, with major companies such as Codorníu making acquisitions. There are some ultra-modern international wines, such as Pingus. Certainly Ribera del Duero does not have the same international reputation as Rioja, but it can give it a close run in the Tempranillo stakes.

The 20,000 hectares of Ribera del Duero (about one third the area of Rioja) are located at elevations of 750-850 m on a wide plateau extending up from the river at the bottom of the valley. Soils tend to be sandy near the river, but become

The DO Ribera del Duero (outlined in green) extends along the river valley.[50]

progressively more calcareous going up the slope, to a point at which it becomes difficult to grow vines. The combination of higher elevations for the vineyards, a slightly cooler climate (cooler than Rioja by an average of 1-2 °C), and higher diurnal variation, gives the wines of Ribera more color, body, and structure. No subzones are officially designated, but the best wines come from a narrow strip (sometimes known as the golden mile) running between Tudela de Duero (just west of Vega Sicilia), Peñafiel, and Pesquera. Most vineyards are planted in the valley, but near Pesquera there are now also vineyards on the high ground to the north.

Irrigation is common in Ribera, but most of the producers hasten to tell you that it's used for improving quality rather than increasing quantity. Many say that the hot 2003 vintage would have been lost entirely without irrigation. The need for irrigation is more a function of distribution of rainfall than total rainfall, because there's a very sharp drop in July and August. By contrast, in Rioja Alavesa and Rioja Alta, total rainfall is not very different, but is more evenly distributed, because summer storms are trapped between the mountain ranges to the north and south, bringing significant precipitation. Irrigation is therefore less common in Rioja.

Climate is specific to the region and does not necessarily follow the pattern for Spain as a whole; the great vintages may not coincide with those of Rioja, for example. Top vintages in Ribera have been 2004, 2001, 1999, 1996, 1995, and 1989 compared with 2005, 2004, 2001, 1995, and 1994 in Rioja.

Wine has been made in the region at least since Roman times. The Romans' headquarters were at Pintia, now known as Padilla de Duero. The region became depopulated after the fall of the Roman Empire, and was not resettled until the tenth century. The area that is now the estate of Vega Sicilia was used as communal ground by the monastery at Valbuena and the town at Peñafiel. Cultivation included vineyards, which were already a significant part of the local economy, and it is likely that the monks brought their vines from Rioja.[51]

By 1536, the estate, known as the vega of Santa Cecilia (a "vega" is a fertile plain) was defined as belonging to the town of Quintanilla de Abajo. Ownership is not entirely clear until a local landowner, Toribio Lecanda, acquired the estate following the dissolution of the monasteries, in the period 1841-1847.[52] Bodegas

A vantage point looking south from the heights north of Pesquera shows a valley running east-west, filled with vineyards, between two mountain ridges.

Lecanda Valladolid, as it now became known, moved slowly into wine production. In 1864, varieties from Bordeaux were planted in addition to the local varieties.

The estate changed hands more than once as its various owners ran into difficulties, but the emphasis remained on agriculture rather than viticulture, until the famous winemaker Txomin Garramiola was hired in 1905, with the intention of making wines in the style of Rioja. In fact, the first wines were made in bulk and transported to a bodega in Laguardia, so that after aging they could be sold as Rioja![53] The first vintage to have been matured and sold as "Vega Sicilia" appears to have been 1915. The bodega was not profitable, and there continued to be transfers of ownership until the Álvarez family, who had no previous connection with wine, purchased the estate in 1982.

Profitable or not, Vega Sicilia rapidly established its legendary reputation as the best wine of Spain, one of the few that could hold a candle to Bordeaux. Indeed, the inclusion of a significant proportion of Bordeaux varieties remains true to the present day. Tempranillo is always the major component in the blend, usually around 80%, with Cabernet Sauvignon providing most of the rest.[54] There is also a little Merlot and Malbec; inclusion of the white grape, Albillo, stopped when the present owners purchased the estate.

The famous wine has been called "Unico" right from its inception, and is made only in the best vintages. The principles of its production have not changed in the last century, but it now spends a bit less time in oak than it used to, a mere 6-7 years before it is bottled to wait another three years for release. A second wine, Valbuena, which has Merlot rather than Cabernet Sauvignon as its second variety, is matured for a shorter period before release. When Unico is produced, there are usually about 80,000 bottles; Valbuena is usually around 180,000. Vega Sicilia also produces a nonvintage wine by blending different vintages, called Reserva Especiale. The estate has provided all its own grapes since 1996; previously production was supplemented by purchase of grapes.[55]

The Vega Sicilia estate comprises about 1000 ha, with 250 ha planted to vines; 150 ha are used for Vega Sicilia, and the additional 100 ha are used for a new venture, Bodegas Alion, started in 1992, which produces a wine exclusively from Tempranillo in a more modern style. Aged exclusively in new French oak, Alion was regarded as somewhat of a revolution in the region. The size of the estate has encouraged attempts to shape the microclimate, and there are recent plantings to form forests of cork trees and oak trees, which could in principle in the (distant) future provide cork for the bottles and oak for the barrels. The estate extends from the road down to the river, and up to the slope on the other side; typically the vineyards on the plateau are used for Alion and those on the slopes for Vega Sicilia.

This one estate encapsulates many of the recent trends in winemaking in Spain. There is a wine drawing on old traditions, with long maturation in old American oak, and a generally oxidative style of production. There is a second wine, made in a more approachable style. Another wine is made in a completely modern style, matured like a Bordeaux in new French oak. And there is further diversification; Vega Sicilia owns the Pintia winery in Toro and the Oremus winery in Tokaji, Hungary.

Vega Sicilia was famous long before the Denominación de Origin Ribera del Duero was created in 1982. It was by no means certain that Vega Sicilia would participate in the DO; indeed the DO needed Vega Sicilia more than Vega Sicilia needed the DO. But they decided to join, and DO Ribera del Duero was added to the label.

By 1982, Vega Sicilia was no longer completely alone in making quality wine in the region. Alejandro Fernández started Bodegas Pesquera in 1972 with 5 ha of vineyards of Tempranillo, and an initial production of 25,000 bottles. His success rapidly extended the reputation of Ribera del Duero beyond the single exception of Vega Sicilia. His wines also are traditional; indeed, until 1982 production was quite primitive, using an old lagar and wine press. Today the winery is modern, but attitudes remain traditional.

Bodegas Pesquera has 200 ha of vineyards around the town of Pesquera. The original 5 ha of vineyards on the plain in the valley have now been expanded to a block of 80 ha. The largest plot today is a block of 120 ha that Alejandro acquired 15 years ago on the plateau above the valley. This was planted with cereals until Alejandro purchased it and planted vineyards. It's a wide, flat area at an elevation of 950 m, looking down on the valley. "Everyone said I was crazy," Alejandro recollects happily, "but now everyone is planting up here." The vineyards are exclusively Tempranillo; "Spain is Tempranillo" seems an appropriate sentiment for the man who has become known as the "King of Tempranillo."

Bodegas Pesquera now produces a million bottles each year, 60% Crianza, the rest Reserva and Gran Reserva. But their top wine is Janus, a Gran Reserva made only in exceptional vintages, most recently 1995 and 2003, usually with about 30,000 bottles. It shows that classic savage intensity of Tempranillo. Its difference from Vega Sicilia's Unico points to the versatility of Ribera del Duero for quality wine production.

Grapes were trodden in a lagar and pressed in a sixteenth century wine press for the first ten years of vintages at Bodegas Pesquera.

A little to the west of Vega Sicilia is the extraordinary estate of Abadia Retuerta. Here a monastery and vineyard were established in 1146. After the dissolution of the monasteries, the estate passed through various hands until the Swiss pharmaceutical company, Novartis, bought it in 1988. At the center of the estate is the twelfth century monastery, which is presently being restored. Around it are vineyards, on which Novartis has spent more than 12 million euros for replanting. Of the 700 ha, 200 ha are planted with vines; and the modern winery, constructed in 1996 around the latest gravity flow systems, is already being replaced by an even more splendid building.

Abadia Retuerta calls itself "El Pago de la Milla de Oro," (the vineyard of the golden mile) but its vineyards are actually located in Sardon de Duero, just outside of the DO Ribera del Duero, so the wines are labeled as Vino de la Tierra de Castilla y Leon. They follow the model of Vega Sicilia in using Cabernet Sauvignon as well as the predominant Tempranillo, matured in a mix of American and French oak. Their top wines, however, are single vineyard offerings of individual varietals, including Cabernet Sauvignon, Syrah, and Petit Verdot, as well as Tempranillo. There isn't the same move in Spain that you find in Italy or France to take top wines out of the quality classification system, but making these varietals takes advantage of Abadia's status as Vino de la Tierra since it would not be possible within the confines of the DO.

A twelfth century monastery stands in the vineyards of Abadia Retuerta.

Photograph kindly provided by Bodegas Abadia Retuerta.

The prices of the top wines are up there with the leading wines of the adjacent DO, making the point that nowhere in Europe is membership of the appellation system any longer necessary for success. With a range of wines selling successfully at various price points, Abadia Retuerta is scarcely a vanity vineyard, but you have to wonder why Novartis is pouring money into wine production while at the same cutting back other operations more directly connected with drug research and development.

The Bulls of Toro and Priorat

Bulls is the right word, for these are powerful, thrusting, wines. To understand their nature, you need go no further than to compare Vega Sicilia, that most refined and elegant wine of Ribera del Duero, with Pintia, a wine produced in Toro by the same winemaking team. It is bold, big, and brassy.

Strong, very dark, alcoholic wines are traditional in Toro (half way from Ribera del Duero to the Portuguese border), made from Tempranillo (called Tinta de Toro here), sometimes also including Grenache. Tempranillo is the driving force as the regulations require wines to have at least 75% of Tinta de Toro. (Some local growers feel Tinta de Toro has diverged so far from its ancestral Tempranillo that it is really now a distinct variety. It looks different, and for a long time they refused to admit it was the same as Tempranillo, but DNA fingerprinting showed they are one variety). At one point Toro was known more for its production of relatively cheap wines, but a flood of foreign investment (foreign here meaning from other parts of Spain) has led to production of wines in the new, clean international style. Some of the wines now include Cabernet Sauvignon, which means they cannot be included in the DO.

The wines of Priorat are equally bold. The mountainous terroir has vineyards on steep slopes with an underlying bedrock of schist. The climate is hot and continental. This is Grenache territory, although there is still some Carignan, and the top wines can be incredibly lush representations of full-blown Grenache. The little hilltop town of Gratallops is the center of quality wine production in the new wave style. This initiative originated in the late 1980s, when a group of winemakers purchased plots at high elevation with the intention of producing intense wines from grapes harvested at low yield. The original idea was to produce the wines cooperatively, but today the remaining producers (Alvaro Palacios, Costers des Siurana, Mas Martinet, and René Barbier Fill) are independent and among the leaders of the new style.

Portugal: Rescuing a Derelict Industry

Port is by far and away the most important wine produced in Portugal, which is the world's seventh largest wine producer, with a total production around 70 million cases annually. This is about the same as the production level in 1900 (and roughly equivalent to Bordeaux today). Although Port has had an international reputation since the nineteenth century, production of other wines was in the doldrums until Portugal entered the E.U. in 1986.

Responding to a chaotic and desperate political situation, wine production was forced into cooperatives during the 1950s and 1960s.[56] There was a large number of individual growers (190,000), with the average holding size being only 2 ha. The monopolistic situation (combined with a heavy-handed government bureaucracy) resulted in low standards and outdated winemaking. The industry remains fragmented by small holdings, but is being modernized.

Its present organization dates from reforms required to bring it into line with E.U. regulations. Wine is divided into three classes: Vinho de Mesa is table wine, Vinho Regional comes from one of nine broad regions, and DOC (quality wines)

Quality wine is just under half of total production in Portugal.[57]

Port is 95% of the fortified quality wine.

Red wine is two thirds of all production.

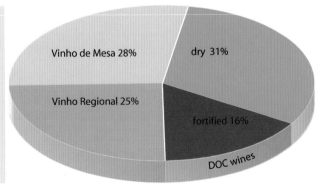

are divided into VQPRD (dry wine) and VLQPRD (sweet fortified wines). Production is split almost equally between quality wines and the rest; Port is about 16% of total production, but economically by far the most important category, accounting for more than half of all exports by value.

Portugal is interesting for a large number of indigenous grape varieties, which continue to dominate production; international varieties have made little headway here. Until recently the situation was completely chaotic, with extensive intermingling of varieties in the vineyard and multiple names for the same

Wine is made all over Portugal.[58] Regions are named in black; DOCs are named in red. DOC represents about 40% of all vineyards. Hectares in each region are:[59]

Region	DOC	Total
Minho	30,541	31,622
Trás-os-Montes	41,072	69,127
Beiras	10,598	57,306
Ribatejo	1,515	19,304
Estre-madura	152	25,107
Terras do Sado	1,965	9,313
Alentejo	8,326	23,089
Total	95,669	236,928

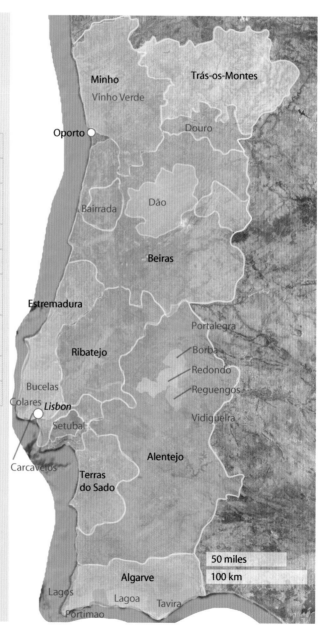

variety complicating any cataloging. The latest count identifies 341 different varieties,[60] of which perhaps about 50 can be readily equated with varieties grown elsewhere.

The best known of the white varieties is Alvarinho, the same as Spain's Albariño of Galicia, which is grown only in Monção, the northernmost area, where it is vinified as a varietal Vinho Verde. Outside of the Monção subregion, Vinho Verde is blended from several varieties, with Loureiro as the predominant variety. The white wine is light, with high acidity, some faint aromatics, and often a faint spritzen. (This used to be caused by bottling before all the carbon dioxide had dissipated from fermentation; now it is achieved by directly injecting CO_2.)

Fernao Pires (also known as Maria Gomes) is the most planted white grape in Portugal. Common in the south and in Barraida, it is versatile and used to make a range of wines including sparkling and dessert wines, but does not have much claim to character as a dry white wine.

Black varieties can be idiosyncratic. Baga is a small, dark, thick skinned grape grown in the Barraida region. Vinified as a monovarietal or dominant in a blend, it can be rather astringent. At the other extreme is Periquita (also known as Castelão Frances), which makes soft, light, appealing wines somewhat in the style of a simple Beaujolais.

Port is synonymous with the Douro, and for a long time there was nothing much else of interest coming out of the region. Now it is the source of some of the best dry red wines from Portugal. Port typically remains more than half of the annual production, and certainly is more valuable, but slowly the dry red wines have changed from heavy and tannic to more approachable. Among the top grape varieties used to make Port, Touriga Nacional and Tinto Roriz (the same as Spain's Tempranillo), can both make quality red wines (often blended also with other traditional Port varieties). Very much the same varieties are also used for producing dry red wine in the Dão, together with some other indigenous varieties, although the standard remains more rustic than in the Douro.

Portugal's only dry red wine with an iconic reputation, Barca Velha, comes from Port producer A. A. Ferreira. When it was first produced in 1952, the use of methods from Bordeaux, such as fermenting in vats (instead of open lagares), pumping over the must, and applying temperature control (initially by a primitive system using blocks of ice brought up the river from Oporto), were major innovations for the Port region (resulting from a visit to Bordeaux by Ferreira's winemaker, Fernando Nicolau de Almedia).[61] Made from a Tempranillo-based blend consisting of Tinta Roriz, Touriga Nacional, Touriga Francesca, and Tinta Barroca, the wine is produced only in the best years, only fourteen times to date. It is sold under the aegis of Casa Ferreirinha, the name used for the dry table wines from Ferreira, which is now part of Portugal's largest producer, Sogrape. Originally the wine was made at Ferreira's Quinta do Val do Meão, but Sogrape have now shifted production to Quinta da Leda, an estate in the same part of the Douro that they purchased in 1978.

Absolutely at the other extreme from the intensity of Port is the rosé phenomenon. Although very little rosé is consumed in Portugal, its production was a fantastic export success in the 1950s and 1960s, when it amounted to more than a quarter of all exported wine.[62] Both of the most important producers had their blend. José Maria da Fonseca (no connection with the Fonseca Port house) produced Lancers, a great success in the United States, while Sogrape produced Mateus, which took Britain by storm. Both vary the formula by market: they are still wines when exported to the United States, but have a slight spritzen for Europe. They are usually slightly sweet. With the style now having fallen out of fashion, production has declined sharply, although the brand names have been preserved by expanding into other types of wine.

Portugal still has some way to go to escape the impression that there isn't much of interest between the high end of vintage Port and the mass production rosé. The practical difficulty is that the region that should be producing the best red wines is, of course, the Douro, where the focus is inevitably on the better known and more lucrative fortified wine. By following the tradition of Port for declaring only exceptional vintages, even Barca Velha fails to provide a consistent halo effect that might lead the way for other red wines every year. And the south hasn't really found its way yet into producing wines that are truly competitive on the international market.

18

The Hapsburg Empire: Driving on Sugar

WHEN YOU MAKE WINE IN A COOL, MARGINAL CLIMATE, and every vintage that ripens is a triumph, naturally your thoughts often turn to sugar levels. As you anxiously measure the accumulation of sugar in the berries, the means become the end, and, directly or indirectly, sugar becomes the primary determinant of quality. Burgundy classified its vineyards into a hierarchy based on long experience of which ripen best. In Germany and Austria, classification took a different turn, and wines are classified each vintage depending on the sugar level at harvest in individual lots of grapes. Vineyard sources may be stated on the label but are not part of the quality classification.

Like the rest of Europe, Germany classifies its wines into a series of quality levels. The lowest level of Tafelwein (table wine) must be made from authorized grape varieties in one of five table wine regions (Weinbaugebiete).[1] One step up, Landwein, the equivalent of the French Vin de Pays, can come from any one of nineteen Landweingebiete, and must be vinified as trocken (dry) or halbtrocken (half dry). However, little wine is classified at either Tafelwein or Landwein levels; the vast majority of German production is at the level of quality wine.

The lowest level of quality wine is QbA.[*] Chaptalization is allowed. The bulk of wine produced at this level comes from a wide geographical area and may or may not have a varietal identity. The infamous Liebfraumilch, of which more later, is a QbA.

The higher level of quality wine is QmP (Qualitätswein mit Prädikat).[2] Chaptalization is forbidden, but the addition of süssreserve is permitted. Since süssreserve is a concentrate of unfermented juice whose main purpose is to add

---

[*] Qualitätswein eines bestimmen Anbaugebietes.

sugar, this makes a complete mockery of the concept that the wine directly reflects quality based on sugar levels achieved by the grapes.[3] In theory, up to 15% of the wine's final volume can come from süssreserve, but in practice, good producers do not use süssreserve for their quality wines, especially at the higher levels.[4]

The quality of QmP wine is classified according to the sugar level in the harvested grapes. The first three grades, Kabinett, Spätlese, and Auslese, are increasingly rich in the same style. Kabinett takes its name from the idea that the wines were special enough to be stored in a wine cabinet.[5] Spätlese literally means late-picked, and originated in a regulation that berries must be picked at least one week after the start of the harvest (today it is necessary only for the grapes to reach a specified higher sugar level). Auslese literally means selectively picked, and the bunches may have a small amount of botrytis.

The description of QmP level nominally refers to sugar level at harvest and not to sweetness in the wine, but typically vinification is performed to leave more residual sugar as the grade increases. However, a wine in any one of these categories can be vinified completely dry (trocken) or half dry (halbtrocken) and you may therefore see examples such as Kabinett trocken or Spätlese trocken on a label to indicate that the wine is dry but that it came from grapes at these QmP levels. And as if this were not enough, some producers have traditionally made distinctions within a grade by using different colored capsules—blue for Kabinett, for example, but blue with a gold band to indicate a higher grade within Kabinett. Emphasizing the fixation on sugar levels, the system has sometimes been retained even for trocken wines.

Beerenauslese and Trockenbeerenauslese (TBA) are the highest two categories of QmP wines. These wines are always sweet. The grapes are picked individually; for TBA they must be botrytized (comparable to a Sauternes from Bordeaux or Selection Grain Noble from Alsace). (Trocken in TBA refers to the berries—dried out by the botrytis—not to the style of vinification.) A Beerenauslese must have natural sugar in the grapes equivalent to more than 17.5% potential alcohol, and a TBA must have more than 21.5%. Eiswein is a specialty where the grapes are picked so late that they have frozen, becoming concentrated because

The subtle intricacies of German wine labeling reach their peak in J. J. Prüm's two Auslese bottlings, with increasing quality indicated by the gold capsule (left) and long gold capsule (right), often known as the GK and LGK bottlings.

of the loss of water due to formation of ice crystals. An Eiswein is as rich as a TBA, but is not botrytized. As with all QmP wines in the sweet style, alcohol levels are usually low, and for TBA are often as low as 8%.

The basis of the system is that in principle any vineyard can produce quality wine—all that is required is for sugar to reach a certain level in the grapes. This is a great contrast with the system in most other European countries, where only specified vineyards can produce quality wine (about 50% of the vineyards in France, for example).

German Gothic: Confusing Labels and Styles

Whether intentionally or unintentionally, German wine labels are confusing. They mention the quality level, sometimes the sweetness level, the grape variety, and have a complicated system for identifying origin that obscures the reputation of the vineyard site. But there is a clue: as Dirk Richter of Weingut Max Ferdinand Richter in the Mosel says ironically, "German labeling seems more complicated but really it is simple. The longer the term on the label, the more important it is."[6] The system reflects that search for precision in the national character, and producers can be a little defensive about it. Rowald Hepp of the famous estate Schloss Vollrads in the Rheingau says, "People who find it confusing are used to the simple description of wine."[7]

Quality wines, both QbA and QmP, carry a description of origin. The wine must come from one of the thirteen specified districts (Anbaugebiete), the best of which are the Rheingau and Mosel, followed by the Nahe and Pfalz.

Each Anbaugebiete is divided into Bereich (districts), and Bereich are divided into Grosslagen (a collection of vineyards). Within Grosslagen there can be Einzellagen (single vineyards). Grosslagen range from 60 ha to 1400 ha; Einzellagen vary from a minimum of 5 ha to 60 ha.[8] The system goes back to the rationalization of the German wine law in 1971. There was an excessive number of vineyard names, about 30,000 in all, but the reclassification threw out the baby with the bath water. The 30,000 vineyards were crunched into 2,600 Einzellagen, often enough by incorporating lesser vineyards into the great names. Grosslagen (there are about 160) were introduced to describe groups of neighboring Einzellagen, but the hierarchy deceives rather than informs.

The big problem with the German wine label is that no distinction is made between Grosslagen and Einzellagen, but in terms of quality, it's only really when a wine comes from an Einzellage that the origin means much. The name of the Bereich is incorporated into the Grosslage or Einzellage name. So in the Bereich of Bernkastel, Bernkasteler Doctor is a wine from the famous Doctor vineyard, probably the best Einzellage in the Mosel. "Bernkasteler" means "coming from Bernkastel," and then "Doctor" identifies the vineyard. Unfortunately, a wine labeled Bernkasteler Kurfürstlay comes only from the Grosslage of Kurfürstlay, which covers a wide swatch of the Bereich Bernkastel, extending through the neighboring towns of Wintrich and Minnheim (and does not include the top Einzellagen such as Doctor or Lay). Other examples of infamous classifi-

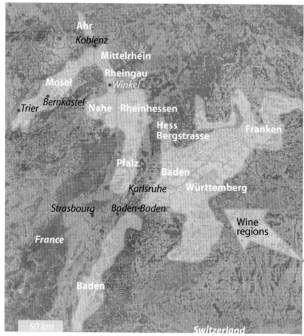

Germany's vineyards are in the southwest corner of the country.[9]

cations that mislead the consumer are Niersteiner Gutes Domtal and Piesporter Michelsberg, both huge Grosslagen that can be confused with much higher quality Einzellagen.

Bernkastel illustrates in microcosm what happened to the naming of German vineyards. Before 1971, Bernkasteler Doctor was a small vineyard, only 1.32 ha, on a steep, south-facing slope on the Mosel.[10] Then in 1971 it was expanded to cover a wider area, meeting the minimum of 5 ha. The growers protested, and this was scaled back to 3.2 ha. But this is still almost three times the size of the original vineyard. This was one of the rare cases where the growers of the top vineyard were able to protect their interests; more often, neighboring vineyards with lower reputation acquired rights to the famous name nearby.

Emphasizing that the QmP descriptions of Kabinett, Spätlese, and Auslese really do refer to sugar levels rather than to vineyard quality, they can be used for Grosslagen as well for Einzellagen. It's a myth that the description of origin on a German wine label has any significance whatsoever unless you are a real aficionado who knows the names of the Grosslagen and Einzellagen; and since this system of misleading descriptions was perpetuated when the wine law was revised in 1994, one can only conclude that the German wine authorities like it that way.

The description of sweet wines is fairly straightforward, but dry wines are another matter. If a label simply says Kabinett, Spätlese, or Auslese, the wine will be sweet—unless the label also says Trocken in which case it will be dry! If the label says Trocken or Halbtrocken, the wine won't be overtly sweet, but it might not be quite dry. Most people can taste sweetness at sugar levels over 4 g/l, but the perception of sweetness depends on the acidity level: high acidity levels can

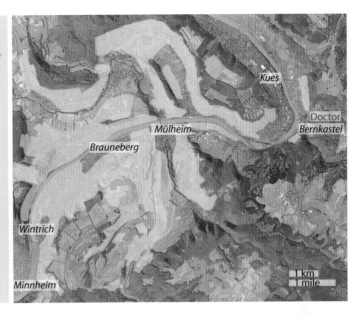

Bernkasteler Doctor comes only from a tiny vineyard of 3.2 ha (red on map), but Bernkasteler Kurfürstlay can come from anywhere in the highlighted (yellow) region of 1,354 ha.[13]

mask sweetness and make a wine appear dry even when it has more than 4 g/l of residual sugar. For this reason, German wines can be called trocken even when they have up to 9 g/l of residual sugar.[11] And a halbtrocken or half-dry wine, is allowed to have up to 18 g/l if the acidity is high enough.[12] As if this weren't bad enough, halbtrocken now is felt to be too restrictive by some producers, who instead used the term "Feinherb," which nominally describes wines between 9 g/l and 45 g/l residual sugar, pretty much covering the whole range from off-dry to medium sweet.

The problem with this argument is the inconsistency of taste it produces: some trocken wines taste bone dry although they have more than 4 g/l residual sugar, but others have a palpably sweet touch to them, all depending on the interplay of sweetness and acidity and individual perception. The rules simply permit far too much variation, and the only way to really ensure that a wine tastes dry would be to limit its residual sugar to 4 g/l. It's a pity the authorities in Germany cannot come to grips with this issue in a more decisive manner.

If you allow for all the possible combinations of the QmP hierarchy and indications of dryness, there are 12 possible stylistic descriptions on a QmP wine. You would think this was difficult enough for the consumer, but the authorities have perpetuated the problem by introducing two new styles, Selection and Classic. Selection wines must come from a Bereich; Classic wines are of higher quality and must come from an Einzellage. Both are limited to yields of 60 hl/ha and must have more than 12% alcohol (lowered to 11.5% for the Mosel). Both must be vinified dry, but this is defined as less than 15 g/l residual sugar! Will they never learn?[14] In any case, the names do not seem to have great impact on the market. Classic wines have reached only just over 1% of all production.[15] Selection appears to have been abandoned.[16]

How can the poor consumer tell that the wine on the left comes from the Goldtröpfchen vineyard (65.4 ha of a south-facing slope on the Mosel), while the wine on the right can come from anywhere in the huge Michelsberg Grosslage (1,500 ha mostly on the other side of the river)?

Perhaps somewhat in despair at the failure of regulations to ensure that the consumer gets a wine that is consistent in either quality or style, a private organization of producers, the VDP,* has introduced a voluntary classification system based on geography. The top wines are intended to be an exclusive category, generally below 5% of an estate's overall production. They can come only from sites that the regional VDP accepts as meriting classification; in the Rheingau this is 700 ha out of the total of 2,500 ha. A justification for the classification comes from old tax records showing that the sites in the VDP system tend to be those that were classified at higher tax rates more than a century ago.

VDP members agree not to use collective vineyard names, to restrict yields (with a limit of 50 hl/ha for Riesling), only to include wines reaching a must weight equivalent to Spätlese, and to eschew artificial methods for concentration. Riesling is included in the system everywhere, but individual regions can decide which other varietals they also want to include. Riesling remains the only variety allowed in the Mosel, Nahe, and Mittelrhein. In the Rheingau, Pinot Noir is allowed as well as Riesling: fair enough. But decisions elsewhere to admit varieties such as Sylvaner undermine the impression that the system is confined to top varietals.[17]

The principle is that the VDP national association provides a uniform framework, but this being Germany, the regional associations can stipulate individual conditions. The main problem already is lack of consistent nomenclature. In the Rheingau, where the scheme was first introduced in 1998, the classified sites are called Erstes Gewächs (meaning "first growths," and intended to imply a parallel with Burgundy's classification system of premier and grand crus). But the Rheingau trademarked the term and objected to its use elsewhere, so outside of the Rheingau they are called Grosses Gewächs. The collective term for both types of site is Erste Lage (but whereas Erste Gewächs and Grosses Gewächs are used

---

* Verband Deutscher Prädikatsweinguter, the Association of German Prädikat Wine Estates.

only to describe dry wines, Erste Lage describes only the site and can be used for dry or sweet wine). So in the best German tradition, the system begins with unnecessary complication. And it's not universal, but applies only to VDP members. Some producers won't use it because they think it is just too confusing.

A second problem is the old definition, "must taste dry," which becomes somewhat subjective the moment you allow more than 4 g/l residual sugar. Since Grosses Gewächs are limited to 9 g/l residual sugar, but the Rheingau allows Erstes Gewächs to reach 13 g/l for Riesling and 6 g/l for Pinot Noir, there is plenty of room for further confusing the consumer about style. Armin Diehl, of Schlossgut Diehl, former editor of the Gault-Millau guide to German wines, says, "This is a nonsense: internationally dry is less than 4 g/l."[18] When is a dry wine not dry? When it's German.

In Pursuit of Dryness

Whether Germany is still a marginal climate in the era of global warming might be debated given the extraordinary run of good vintages in the past decade. Since 2001, every vintage in the Mosel has rated excellent—there is no other decade like this in living memory. Average temperatures have been climbing steadily, and there has been a general increase in the proportion of grapes ripening to QmP levels. One side effect has been that producers have sometimes found themselves with more wine than they can easily sell at the higher grades, so they have declassified the wines by a level, with wine that could have been an Auslese selling as a Spätlese, for example. On the one hand, this can be a bargain for the consumer; on the other, if you're looking for a wine in a certain style, you may be surprised to find it somewhat sweeter than you expected.

A sea change in German wines has occurred in the past decade as production has shifted from the sweet styles of the traditional QmP wines (Kabinett, Spätlese, Auslese) to the dry (trocken) style. At the same time, restaurants in Germany have made enormous strides from a traditional rustic cuisine to a new

The proportion of QmP wine in Germany shows a general upward trend in line with an increase in growing season temperatures.[19]

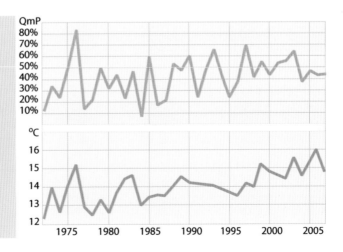

international style emphasizing purity of flavors. Is there any cause and effect here?

Until the late 1980s, most wine produced in Germany was sweet, but since then the feeling that sweet wine does not go well with food has led to increased focus on dry wine. An increase in quality came when trocken wines started to be produced from Prädikat grapes. The proportion of trocken wine has doubled in two decades, and together with halbtrocken wine, now accounts for two thirds of all production. Within the sweet wine categories, Kabinett and Spätlese have each halved, from roughly 10% to 5% of all production in the past decade, while the top grades of Auslese, Beerenauslese, and TBA amount to only about 1%. Basically the vast majority of German wine is now dry or something approximating to it.

It used to be said that Germany was an example of the great divide between domestic and export markets (with dry wines consumed at home and sweet wines exported).[20] Today producers tell you that both dry and sweet styles are exported. There's a bias in the numbers because of the huge amount of export of Liebfraumilch, a low grade semi-sweet style. In fact, exports show somewhat of a hole in the middle of the market, with a strong presence at both bottom and top levels, whereas the domestic market is more consistent because there's much less kept at home at the bottom level.

Another factor is the trend to red wine. Pushed by increasing consumption of red wine, and aided by generally warmer vintages, the proportion of vineyards devoted to red grape varieties has been increasing steadily since 1980, with a dramatic increase in the past decade. Until the mid 1990s, total plantings were increasing, but since then the planted area has been steady at around 100,000 hectares (about the same size as all Bordeaux), and producers have been replacing white grapevines with black vines. The red wines are mostly kept for the domestic market; only about 10% of exports are red. This may be partly because of high price—high quality German Pinot Noir sells into the same price range as premier crus from Burgundy, and is unlikely to be competitive on an international market.

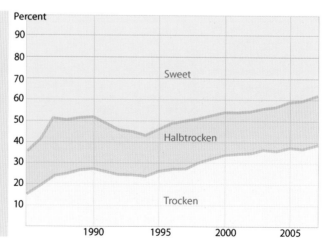

Production of dry wine has been increasing steadily in Germany.[21]

Trocken has increased from less than 20% in the 1980s to almost 40% today; halbtrocken has stayed about 20-25%.

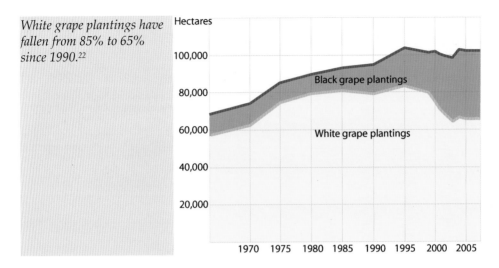

White grape plantings have fallen from 85% to 65% since 1990.[22]

Curiously, it is the most northern region of all, the tiny Anbaugebiete of the highly protected Ahr valley that has the greatest concentration of black grapes—less than 10% of its production is white wine. Aside from this, there's always been a little red wine in the north; indeed, the great monastery of Kloster Eberbach in the Rheingau started out in the twelfth century by producing red wine from vines brought by the Cistercian monks from Burgundy. But generally the more northern regions of the Rheingau, Mosel, and Mittelrhein produce mostly white wine. There is a drift to red wine production going south, with most of it focused on Württemberg, the Pfalz, and Baden. Not only has there been an increase in overall production of red wine, but there is more focus on quality with Pinot Noir.

Almost all German wine is Qualitätswein—table wine typically makes up less than 5% of total production.[24] So you might leap to the conclusion that the vine-

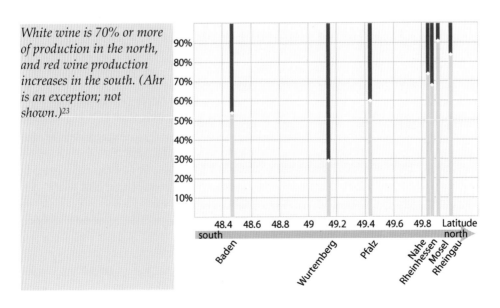

White wine is 70% or more of production in the north, and red wine production increases in the south. (Ahr is an exception; not shown.)[23]

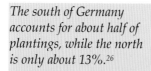
The south of Germany accounts for about half of plantings, while the north is only about 13%.[26]

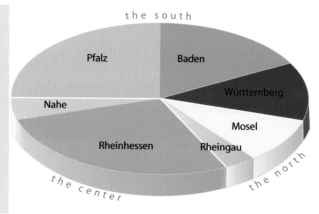

yards are redolent with plantings of quality varietals. This is not exactly true, however. Riesling, the undoubted quality leader has been about 20% of all plantings since 1980. The other white varieties, led by Müller-Thurgau and Sylvaner, with scarcely any wines from either of any interest, have declined from 68% to 42% (no great loss). The missing 26% has been made up by increased plantings of Pinot Noir (known locally as Spätburgunder, of which Germany has become a sizeable, and sometimes serious, producer) and Dornfelder (of less interest), and a variety of other black grapes, none of any great interest.[25]

Germany's reputation for quality rests largely upon Rieslings from the north, with the Rheingau and Mosel at the head of the list, but together they account for not much more than 10% of all production. Some good Rieslings are also made in the Nahe. Rheinhessen is the largest wine-producing region in Germany, concentrating on bulk wine production. In the Pfalz, most vineyards are on flat land. Baden, the most elongated region of the south, makes some good red wines, although these days excellent Pinot Noirs also come from the north.

Riesling Purity: the Rheingau and Mosel

The transition at the Prädikat level from sweet to dry styles has undoubtedly changed perception of the Rheingau and Mosel, but, dry or sweet, they remain at the forefront of quality. Wines from the Rheingau tend to be a little richer; in the sweet styles they have an unmatchable delicious sweet/sour balance. Mosel wines are slightly lighter: the best word to describe them is delicate. The Mosel typically has slightly higher acidity (which is why its "dry" wines are allowed to have a little more residual sugar) with a crystalline delineation of fruit flavors.

The Rheingau is located on the north banks of the rivers Rhine and Main. Because the river takes a large turn at this point, the vineyards face south. The land rises up from the river bank, with gentle inclines close to the river and steeper slopes farther up. Vineyards extend a mile or two back from the river along a ten mile stretch. At the points farthest from the river, the elevation is 200-300 m. At Winkel, vineyards are separated from the Rhine only by the railroad. At Rude-

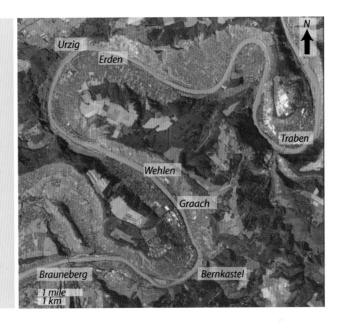

Vineyards hug the steep slopes coming straight off the twists and turns of the Mosel river.[27]

sheim, vineyards rise up sharply above the rooftops of the town, and a cable car system to the local high point swings above them. The best Rieslings come from the higher slopes. 80% of plantings are Riesling (the highest proportion in any wine region of Germany). Pinot Noir has always been well represented in the Rheingau, in fact it probably was the original variety planted by the monks who first cultivated vines at Kloster Eberbach, and it still represents about 10% of plantings.

The Mosel represents one of those rare cases where nomenclature has been simplified in Germany. Originally known as the Mosel-Saar-Ruwer after the three rivers (the Saar and Ruwer are minor tributaries of the Mosel), now it has been renamed simply as the Mosel. (Saar-Ruwer has been split into two districts, Saar and Ruwertal.) Although the Mosel river runs generally south to north, it has many wide turns and loops. Most of the vineyards run steeply up from one side of the river or the other to an elevation of 300 m or so, but because of the twists and turns of the river, their sun exposure can be full south or east or west. There are also pronounced folds in the land, so even adjacent plots may have different exposures. Most of the small flat plateaus extending from the river to the slopes are populated, the largest of them forming the small towns along the river banks. From place to place, however, plateaus with only a slight slope into the river are planted in vineyards, adding further diversity to the terroir. The soil is mostly slate—gray, blue, green, or red—and from time to time you can see outbreaks of colored rocks in the vineyards. All in all, between the soil, slope, and exposure, there is wide diversity, explaining the very different qualities of even adjacent plots of land. The finest region within Mosel-Saar-Ruwer is the Mittel Mosel, which includes the famous town of Bernkastel, directly on the river. Virtually all production is white, and Riesling predominates.

The famous Wehlener Sonnenuhr vineyard rises straight up from the Mosel (left). Sonnenuhr means sundial, and the white dot in the hillside at the left is a sundial (right). The vineyard faces south west.

Liebfraumilch Isn't What it Used to Be

When three cases of Liebfraumilch 1874 were sold in an auction at Christie's in London on February 24, 1891, they fetched the respectable price of £7, exactly the same price paid for an earlier lot at the same auction of three cases of Château Lafite Rothschild of the 1865 vintage. In the late nineteenth century, Liebfraumilch was regarded as a quality wine, equivalent to good Bordeaux. How the mighty are fallen!

Liebfraumilch came originally from vineyards around the Liebfrauenkirche (Church of Our Lady) north of the city of Worms on the banks of the Rhine in the Rheinhessen. Vineyards have surrounded the church since at least the fourteenth century, and the name literally means "milk of our lady." The merchant firm of Valckenberg exported the wine under the name Liebfraumilch in the nineteenth century, and by the time the lot came up at Christie's in 1891, Valckenberg's Original Liebfraumilch was well established as one of Germany's top priced wines.

Other growers were also using the term to describe a generic Rhine wine, however, and when the German wine law was written in 1908 to protect designated vineyards, Liebfraumilch became a regional name. (Valckenberg were also a shipper and general distributor, and had broader interests to protect than any one vineyard name.) Wine from the original vineyards then became described as Liebfrauenstift-Kirchenstueck.

The standard for Liebfraumilch declined steadily during the first half of the twentieth century. When Alsace was part of Germany (1871-1918 and 1940-1945), its wine was often included in Liebfraumilch.[28] And before 1930, Liebfraumilch often contained some French or Spanish sweet wine![29] Today it is at least exclusively German, and may be made using grapes from any one of the Rheinhessen, Pfalz, Nahe, or Rheingau. It must contain more than 18 g/l residual sugar, placing it above halbtrocken at a semi-sweet level. The grape varieties must include more than 70% of Riesling, Müller-Thurgau, Sylvaner, and Kerner, although it's usually made from Müller-Thurgau. These meaningless restrictions form an ironic counterpoint to the detailed precision with which the German system attempts to describe its quality wines.[30] Even worse, almost all Liebfraumilch is exported; in 1989, for example, this amounted to eleven million cases,[31] providing about 40% of all exports of German wine. So Liebfraumilch was the dominant impression made by German wine in the outside world.[32]

Liebfraumilch sales exploded when the firm of H. Sichel Söhne in the Rhein-hessen introduced Blue Nun in the 1921 vintage. The original Blue Nun was labeled as a Liebfraumilch Spätlese! But the quality of Liebfraumilch, if the term is at all appropriate, was driven down relentlessly by competition. After the second world war, Blue Nun was enormously successful, becoming one of the largest wine brands in the world, selling for prices comparable to good Bor-deaux. (Sales peaked in the 1970s, and after a collapse in the 1980s, it was repackaged in a drier style as a Qualitätswein.)

Coming from any one of four defined Anbaugebieten, Liebfraumilch qualifies as a category of QbA. The inclusion of Liebfraumilch as a quality wine helps to explain how 95% of German wine production qualifies as Qualitätswein. But not only does the low standard of this vaguely aromatic, semi-sweet wine of no character lower Germany's image worldwide, but the fact that it is included as a QbA damages the concept that the category of Qualitätswein counts for any-thing. In fact, Germany's reputation is somewhat besmirched by the low quality of much QbA, made from Müller-Thurgau or Sylvaner. Keeping your best prod-uct at home and exporting your worst may not be the best way to build an export market. Demoting QbA from the quality wine level would be a good place to start in restoring credibility.

The Austrian Niche

On the world scale, Austria is a tiny wine producer, with just under 50,000 ha of vineyards (half the area of Bordeaux). Located on the eastern edge of the country, bordering Slovenia and Hungary, vineyards extend between lines of latitude roughly equivalent to a range from the Loire to Burgundy in France, but the climate is more continental, with very cold winters, and more marginal for wine production. Accordingly two thirds of production is white wine. Not much of the red wine is of interest.

Although wine growing in Austria is old, the present industry dates from its reconstruction after the scandal of 1985 when wine was adulterated with anti-freeze.[33] Exports collapsed almost completely, and the only market available to producers was domestic. There was one silver lining to this great cloud: small producers benefited, because the domestic market turned against large suppliers, such as supermarkets, and consumers started buying their wines directly at the cellar door. In fact, sales were so good, rising to 50% of all production, that some producers started bottling their own wine during this period. Since then, there has been some fall off, but cellar door sales are still unusually high, at 30% of all domestic production, with specialist shops holding on to 10%, and supermarkets now scooping up the rest. Exports have now settled down at around 25% of production, so the market is still focused on domestic sales.

Wine growing areas are divided into four general regions (Weinbauregion) corresponding to individual states. Niederösterreich (lower Austria) in the north, and Burgenland (a little to the south and at the eastern edge) are the two important regions. Niederösterreich includes the premium districts for dry wines; Burgenland has the top spots for sweet wines. Steiermark, to the south, and Wien (the area around Vienna) are of relatively little importance in terms of total

The wine regions in Austria hug the eastern border of the country.[34]

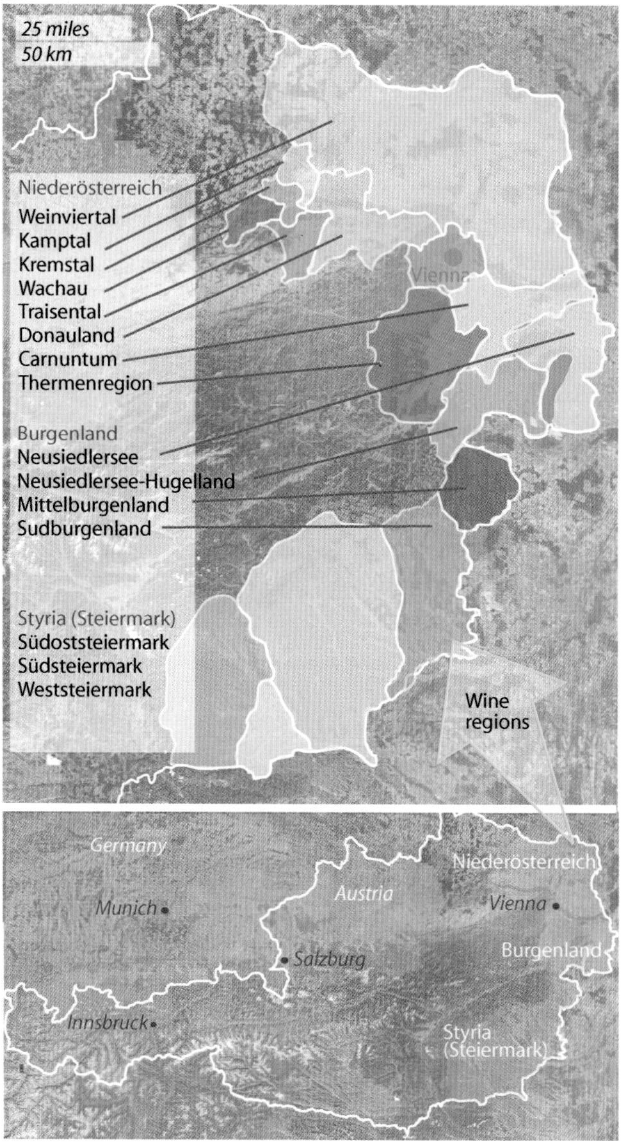

25 miles
50 km

Niederösterreich
Weinviertal
Kamptal
Kremstal
Wachau
Traisental
Donauland
Carnuntum
Thermenregion

Burgenland
Neusiedlersee
Neusiedlersee-Hugelland
Mittelburgenland
Sudburgenland

Styria (Steiermark)
Südoststeiermark
Südsteiermark
Weststeiermark

Vienna

Wine regions

Germany
Munich

Austria

Niederösterreich

Vienna

Salzburg

Burgenland

Innsbruck

Styria (Steiermark)

Niederösterreich accounts for almost two thirds of Austria's vineyards, and the two Neusiedlersee regions account for a quarter[35].

production. Each of the regions is further divided into districts (Weinbaugebiete). The Weinbaugebiete is the main geographical description on a quality wine.

Niederösterreich is the heart of dry white wine production. The major part of Niederösterreich, the Weinviertel in the north, isn't of much interest, but a cluster of high quality districts at the western edge of Niederösterreich produce both Grüner Veltliner and Rieslings. On the north side of the Danube are three regions, all within a span of about 20 miles. The best established district is Wachau, a tiny area of 1,400 ha, with the best vineyards on steep terraces overlooking the Danube. The adjoining regions of Kamptal (3,900 ha) and Kremstal (2,200 ha) to the north and east also make interesting wines. Just to the south of the Danube, Traisental (700 ha of vineyards) is coming up in importance. Terroirs are delineated within each district, and individual vineyard names are often used for the top wines.

The best known districts of Burgenland are the areas surrounding the Neusiedlersee, a shallow inland lake, whose high humidity creates perfect conditions for producing late-harvest botrytized wines. Neusiedlersee-Hugeland lies to the west of the lake, and Neusiedlersee lies to the west and north. Both regions produce red wine as well as sweet and dry whites (the proportion of sweet wines varies widely with yearly conditions). The picturesque tourist town of Rust is at the center of the wine industry in Neusiedlersee. Many of the wineries have quite deceptive exteriors, appearing to be ordinary houses in the street, but you go inside to find long courtyards surrounded by buildings containing all the usual appurtenances of wineries. These are mostly small family wineries, but some larger commercial operations are found outside of the town.

Ripeness Über Alles

Most histories of Austrian wine start with a brief mention of ancient times and then pass straight from the first modern wine law, in 1784, to the glorious revolution of 1985, as the antifreeze scandal is sometimes euphemistically glossed over.[36] This rather skips past the origins of the present system for classification, which in fact dates from the Anschluss; when Hitler took over Austria in 1938, the German wine law of 1930 became the basis for regulating wine production in Austria.

Certainly wine production in Austria is ancient. It is often claimed that winemaking in the Traisental goes back 4000 years, although evidence seems to be lacking, but grape seeds were discovered in a tomb in Zagersdorf, in Burgenland, dating from 700 B.C.[37] By Roman times, wine growing extended up to the boundaries of the empire on the Danube, and vineyards were extended under Charlemagne (742-814 C.E.). The Magyar invasion was a setback, but during the Middle Ages, the monasteries played their customary role in spreading viticulture. The banks of the Danube are littered with both Benedictine and Cistercian monasteries that were centers for wine production. The oldest wine estate still in existence is the Freigut Thallern, which was founded near Gumpoldskirchen by the Cistercians in 1141.

Wine production expanded in the sixteenth century, was heavily taxed in the seventeenth century, but then in the eighteenth century acquired a major feature that persists to this day. In 1784, Emperor Joseph II issued a decree allowing anyone to sell wine they had produced themselves. This led to the creation of the Heurigen, basically wine bars that sell wine of the current vintage together with simple food. Wine of the vintage is officially released on St. Martin's Day (11th November). A significant part of Austria's wine production is devoted to wine for these establishments.

Wines are classified by the level of sugar in the must.[38] Tafelwein and Landwein define the same categories as in Germany. The first stage of quality wines (equivalent to the German QbA) is divided into two levels: Qualitätswein (which may be chaptalized) and Kabinettwein (which may not be chaptalized, but may use süssreserve). Then the Prädikatswein (equivalent to the German QmP) is divided into ascending levels: Spätlese, Auslese, Beerenauslese, Ausbruch, and TBA. These are based on the natural sugar level. The basic differences from the German system are that Kabinettwein is included with the lower level of quality wine instead of with the QmP; and Ausbruch is an additional category, between Beerenauslese and TBA. There are also categories for Strohwein (made from overripe grapes stored on straw for 3 months) and Eiswein (made from frozen grapes).

Ausbruch is made in two styles. It can be similar to the German style, with low alcohol and high residual sugar. Alternatively, the traditional style allows must or wine from healthy grapes to be added to the must of botrytized grapes; this produces a wine with high alcohol, 60-120 g/l residual sugar, and high acidity. In the latter sense, Ausbruch is more than a classification, since it also describes the style.

This is all very well, but unlike traditional wine production in Germany, and in spite of the detailed classification system for sweet styles, most Austrian wine has always been dry. The great bulk of production is Qualitätswein, but once Prädikatswein is reached, there has not been any way to distinguish dry wines at different quality levels. Trocken and halbtrocken are used as descriptions, but not usually in association with any term other than Qualitätswein.

There is one exception. Wachau, regarded as the primary quality area for producing white wine, introduced its own classification system in 1983. Depending on the must weight, wines are classified as Steinfeder (less than 11.5%

alcohol), Federspiel (11.5-12.5% alcohol, more or less equivalent to the requirement for Kabinettwein), or Smaragd (over 12.5% alcohol, more or less equivalent to Prädikatwein). Still this reflects the idea that the climate is marginal: the best wines will be those coming from sites where the grapes achieved higher levels of ripeness. And often enough Federspiel and Smaragd come from successive harvests in the same vineyard. One weakness in the system is that the wines are supposed to be dry, but with up to 9 g/l residual sugar allowed at the Smaragd level, Smaragd may vary from dry to showing perceptible sweetness.

The impetus for introducing the classification in Wachau was competition from cheap imports from the east. Grapes could be brought into Wachau and used to make wine that was sold under the Wachau name. The classification levels were combined with a requirement that the grapes must be grown within the Wachau district. It's still an issue in Austria that consumers identify wine first by the grape variety and second by the origin, making local producers susceptible to cheap competition from foreign producers of the same varieties.

Conscious of the weaknesses of a system that does not identify quality for the majority of dry wines and that gives scant information about origins or style, Austria has now introduced a new classification system. The authorities see the situation in terms of the distinction between German and Roman wine law. "While German wine law (Austria, Germany) concentrates on the grape variety, the Roman wine law (Italy, France, and Spain) distinguishes and characterizes the wine according to its origin," they say.[39] To change to an emphasis on origin, in 2003 they introduced the DAC (Districtus Austriae Controllatus), which they describe as a system of controlled appellation of origin. But it is not quite that. And taking a cue from Germany, the DAC adds to, rather than replaces, the previous system.

The producers in each region can choose collectively whether or not to enter the DAC system, so already we have the prospect for confusion among different systems in the same country.

The first district to adopt the DAC system was Weinviertal from the 2002 vintage, followed by Mittelburgenland in 2005, Traisental in 2007, Kremstal in 2007, and Kamptal in 2008. To adopt the DAC, the producers must agree that it applies only to specific grape varieties that typify the region, and must define a required style. In Traisental, Kremstal, and Kamptal, for example, this limits it to Grüner Veltliner and Riesling; in Weinviertal to Grüner Veltliner alone, and in Mittelburgenland to the red grape Blaufränkisch.

The objective is to establish regional identity: if you buy a wine labeled Kamptal, it must be Grüner Veltliner or Riesling, reach a minimum alcohol level, be made in a dry style, with no botrytis, and no trace of oak. The downside for the producer is that other varieties cannot be labeled with the district name; they can only carry the much broader description of the general region. So a Sauvignon Blanc from Kamptal, no matter how high in quality, could only be labeled Niederösterreich, leaving it open to confusion with wines from much lower quality districts in the region. In each region, about a quarter of total production is of varieties excluded from the DAC. Is there a risk of imposing the rigidity of the French appellation system in insisting that only one or two varieties can express the typicity of the region?

But the system also harks back to the old search for ripeness. The DAC can define different levels, such as DAC and DAC Reserve; and the distinguishing feature is the alcohol level. Typically DAC requires 12% and DAC Reserve requires 13%. This is the only difference between them. When asked whether it would make sense for the higher level to have a restriction to a lower yield, producers argue that with white grapes, too much reduction in yield leads to over-ripeness and the loss of varietal character. It is, however, striking that the only restriction on yield in Austria is at national level for quality wine in general.

Wachau, which regards the DAC as simply an adaptation of its own system, is resolute about its lack of interest. "It would be a very bad idea for Wachau to become a DAC," says Lucas Pichler of F. X. Pichler, "because the idea of the DAC is that each region has a single taste, but what Wachau wants to emphasize is the winemaker."[40] Nikolaus Saahs of Nikolaihof agrees. "It's crazy for the DAC not to allow other varieties," he says, "it's bad for the region."[41] Toni Bodenstein of Weingut Prager, whose family was involved in classifying the vineyards in Wachau in the nineteenth century, is the mayor of Weissenkirchen and says that it's important for Wachau to maintain its own quality system. Increasingly concerned about the application of modern technology, the 200 producers of the Vinea Asssociation of Wachau introduced the Codex Wachau in 2006, which excludes all forms of adjustment and insists that wine is natural.

The DAC system has both strengths and weaknesses compared to a true appellation system that classifies the vineyards. In a poor year, when the berries find difficulty in ripening and do not reach the minimum sugar level, the wine will be excluded from the DAC system. Recognizing differences between vintages is not a bad idea: in fact there have been vintages when application of such a system would have saved some of the great names of Burgundy from embarrassment. But the counter side is that in a hot year, wines from the poorer vineyards, which usually do not make the DAC grade, may reach the requisite alcohol. But will they really have the extra complexity that DAC implies? Wouldn't it be better to classify the vineyards, but to insist that wines reflect grapes reaching a minimum level of ripeness in the specific vintage?

Terraces and Plantations

The focus on varieties and ripeness might suggest that terroir is of little importance in Austria. But while there may not be great variety in most regions for dry wine production, and the exposure to botrytis is the important feature in the Neusiedlersee, the top regions of Wachau, and to a lesser degree Kamptal and Kremstal, can hold a candle to Burgundy when it comes to investigating the intricate effects of terroir.

Wachau has the best terroir in Austria, consisting of terraces rising up steeply from the Danube. Slopes can be so steep as to require walls every few rows. The stone terraces increase heat during the day; and the cold nights of the Continental climate create a strong diurnal variation prolonging the growing season. The best vineyards face south. Almost half of Wachau's vineyards lie on this terrain, consisting of eroded rock, usually with a topsoil of only 20-30 cm. The remaining vineyards are on flat lands, where the soil consists of a deep layer of loess, a thick sediment formed by wind-blown silt. Kremstal occupies the valley of the river Krems and surrounding areas, mostly flat but with a high plateau of terraces looking out over the valley below. Kamptal is also a mix of flat lands and terraces. The Danube is at an elevation of about 200 m above sea level as it runs through Wachau, and the highest vineyards are at about 450 m elevation.

A theme running through all three regions is that Riesling tends to be planted on the rocky terraces and Grüner Veltliner tends to be planted on the loess-based soils. Riesling, the more demanding grape, reacts better to the more water-stressed conditions of the terraces, but Grüner Veltliner will grow anywhere. "It grows like a weed," says Toni Bodenstein of Weingut Prager in Wachau.[42] The terraces often need drip irrigation; it's less common in the vineyards on the flat lands in the valley.

One reason for the high productivity is the training system. Until after the second world war, vines were densely planted. Then winegrower Lenz Moser invented the training system named after him. He summarized his philosophy: "The grower has the task of supplying good and cheap wine."[43] The Lenz Moser system consists of trellised rows, widely separated at 3 to 3.5 meters to allow easy access by tractors, with vines at 1.25 m along each row, and a high canopy at

South-facing terraced vineyards rising up from the Danube catch the sun all day in Wachau. Photograph kindly provided by Weingut Nikolaihof.

*The Lenz-Moser
system has widely
separated rows with a
high, bushy canopy.*

*Photograph kindly
provided by Weingut
Sepp Moser.*

100 cm. This typically gives about 2,500 vines per hectare. The Lenz Moser system was widely adopted in the 1960s; now it is hard to find anything else. Many quality producers feel the Lenz Moser system is too productive, and are lowering the canopy to 80 cm and reducing its density. It's not easy to change substantially without replanting the whole vineyard, because the rows are not far apart enough simply to insert an extra row between them. But some producers are switching to Guyot systems with about 5,000 vines per hectare when they replant.

On the rare occasion that you get a chance to compare the effects of training systems, you see immediately that it's night and day. Toni Bodenstein believes that the old system gives higher quality, and has proved his point by planting over some of Weingut Prager's Grüner Veltliner in the Achleiten vineyard. Vines stand freely as bushes at a separation of 70 cm, giving an overall density of 14,500 vines per hectare. He calls the wine Stockkulture, after the name of the old culture system. This gives great diversity in the vineyard—every vine is different from the next. When I tasted the wines side by side at Weingut Prager, the increase in intensity of the Stockkulture compared with the normal bottling matched the increase in density of the vines!

After Lenz Moser introduced his training system, the tradition of replanting by selection massale was abandoned, and vineyards were planted with clones selected for bigger berries, with thin skins, forming close bunches—good for yield but not for quality. Clones have been less important with Grüner than with some varieties; their major effect appears to be on productivity. An ongoing experiment to find better clones started with 45 clones that were planted on two rootstocks in different terroirs. The experiment is now focusing on ten clones that look the most interesting.

It's evidently going to be a while before clonal selection by the authorities will have any effect on quality, but in fact there's already a history of selection seriously improving the wine. Franz Xaver Pichler started to select Grüner for small berries in 1928. He noted characteristics vine by vine, and selected the best vines for replanting. He went through 21 terraces one by one, and then repeated the process starting in 1952. Is this one of the reasons why Pichler's Grüners—today made by his grandson Lucas Pichler—have unusual density and concentration? Some people think so: Lucas sometimes finds that cuttings have been taken from his vineyards. Perhaps the selection of vines is one of the reasons why Pichler is one of the few producers whose Grüners offer the same range of complexity as Rieslings.

Concentration on full time viticulture is often a relatively recent phenomenon; many producers will tell you that it was their grandfather or father who abandoned polyculture to become a full-time wine grower. Indeed, Domain Wachau, the dominant quality cooperative in the region, still gets a fair proportion of its grapes from weekend farmers, who have very small holdings of vines.[44] The focus on viticulture has strengthened since the move away from polyculture in the 1960s; the last cow left Kamptal in 1978.

F. X. Pichler's meticulous note book records vine quality by plus and minus symbols for superior and inferior, and was the basis for selecting better quality Grüner.

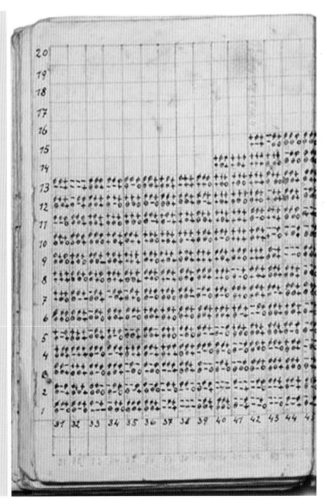

Photograph kindly provided by Weingut F. X. Pichler.

One notable feature of Austrian viticulture is the tiny size of the average holding. In spite of a halving in the total number of wineries in the past two decades, the average producer still has only 2 ha. Furthermore, individual parcels can be vanishingly small, sometimes only a few rows of vines, so even a large producer, in the Austrian context with more than, say, 20 ha, may have his vineyards broken up into individual parcels of less than a hectare each. One result is that many producers who have parcels in the top vineyards that are too small to vinify individually amalgamate them into bottlings called "Terrassen," essentially at the same level of quality as their single vineyard wines, but of course without their characteristic variations in terroir. Usually a Terrassen bottling sells just below the price of the named single vineyards.

The morcelization makes for general economic difficulties, especially in the consequences of working and harvesting the vineyards. It also impedes the move to organic viticulture, because it's very hard to work a few rows organically if your neighbor is busy spraying. Nonetheless, there are several organic producers in the region; Nikolaihof in Wachau was one of the first and has been biodynamic since 1971. They obtain supplies from a nearby biodynamic farm, and are at pains to demonstrate the difference that biodynamic viticulture makes. When you visit Nikolaihof, Nickolaus Saahs takes you to see the vineyards, but the high point is the visit to the compost heap. Running it through his hands, Nikolaus enthuses, "Doesn't it have a wonderful perfume? Look at the life in the soil!" Biodynamic farming gives physiological ripeness sooner, he says, enabling Nikolaihof to produce wines with more moderate alcohol.[45]

Although there is no classification system, individual vineyards have been recognized since the middle ages. In Wachau, the oldest classification of crus dates from 1521. At that time, there were more than 40 different monasteries under the control of 5 different bishops, with a tradition of identifying local vineyards going back to Charlemagne. The bishops were compelled to pay taxes on the vineyards but insisted on paying in relation to the quality of the wine areas, which were then classified in detail in seven quality levels.

The single vineyard wines are the pride of Wachau. The differences in the rocky foundations give a variation from site to site matching anything found in Burgundy. Some of the top vineyards are well known, such as the dramatic Heiligenstein in Kamptal, but generally the nuances between them are unappreciated by all except the most knowledgeable consumers. The terroir plays out to maximum effect in that most reflective grape, Riesling, but at the top level is also reflected in the Grüners.

Grüner Veltliner: A Grape that's Much Misunderstood

It is both fortunate and unfortunate that Grüner Veltliner has become Austria's niche grape. Fortunate in that it gives a distinct identity to Austrian wine, since nowhere else produces Grüner Veltliner. Unfortunate in that most production is of entry level wine with rather simple, forward primary fruits intended for immediate consumption. As a producer in Kremstal said to me, "Most wines are drunk young in Austria and consumers are looking for primary fruits. There is not very much difference among varieties." Certainly the lack of distinctiveness at this level might lead to the conclusion that Grüner Veltliner is a grape variety of no particular interest. Yet explore Austria's top wine-growing regions in more depth, and you can find some Grüner Veltliner's of extraordinary interest, in a range of styles matching Chardonnay's versatility.

Wine growing in Niederösterreich stopped in 1580-1590 as the result of a run of terrible vintages, cold and wet, when it was not possible to make wine. After 1590, a change in the tax laws led to imports of grapes from Hungary becoming the main source of supply. The grapes were a variety called Heunisch Weiss. It was also known as Gouais Blanc, since identified as one of the parents of several important modern varieties, including Chardonnay. According to an early nineteenth century book on wine growing in the Hapsburg Empire,[46] this variety (known by the name Grobe) was then by far the dominant grape; there was also a little Riesling and Grüner Muskateller (an early name for Grüner Veltliner).[47] Heunisch, by whatever name, is now all but extinct. Grüner started to take over when wine growing revived after Napoleon. By the start of the 1970s there were about 10,000 ha in all Austria, and then Grüner increased steadily until plantings had doubled by the 1990s.[48] In the past decade, there has been a slight decrease in Grüner Veltliner, compensated by an increase in Chardonnay and Sauvignon Blanc, and a larger increase in black varieties.[49]

Grüner is grown all over Austria. It's about half of the total plantings in the vineyards in the northern part of the country, and falls to a minority only in the more southern regions of Burgenland and Steiermark. It accounts for just over a third of plantings in the country as a whole. The general problem with Grüner is its high productivity: far too many wines show little typicity as a result. Yields on quality wine in Austria are limited to 9,000 kg/ha, equivalent to 67.50 hl/ha, and at those levels you really can't expect much character. At the levels of around 5-6,000 kg/hl, obtained by the best producers, you see a great difference.

Riesling, the other white grape of note, is concentrated in Niederösterreich, with about half the total in Wachau, Kamptal, and Kremstal, and the rest in the Weinviertel. (There's much more Welschriesling than real Riesling, but there is no need to accept the Austrian view that it's a quality grape variety.) Riesling is usually harvested at lower yields than Grüner, more towards 4,000 kg/ha. Growers who have Riesling usually plant it on their best sites, and it usually represents

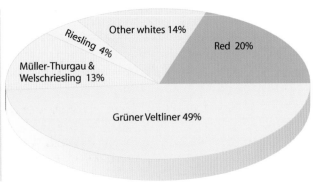

Grüner Veltliner dominates wine production in Niederösterreich.[50]

their best wine, so its importance is out of all proportion to the miniscule extent of overall production.

Reds are grown more in Burgenland than anywhere else, although all regions have a little. They are not very distinguished, consisting of Zweigelt, Blaufränkisch, and Blauer Portugieser, all the old cool-climate, high-production varieties. There's a very tiny amount of Pinot Noir (too small even to figure in the official statistics), which can be quite respectable.

Austria had a brief flirtation with international varieties in the 1980s, now sometimes referred to pejoratively as "chardonitis." In fact, Sauvignon Blanc was probably more widely planted than Chardonnay, but there isn't very much left of either now. Austrian Sauvignon Blanc can be interesting, producing a sort of halfway house between Old and New Worlds, with the aroma and flavor spectrum of the New World showing in asparagus and passion fruit, but the delicacy of the Old World showing in gentle fruits, perfumed rather than aggressive. Nonetheless, producers generally have concluded that they cannot compete with these varieties on the world stage, and it's better to focus on something unique to the country: Grüner Veltliner.

With the exception of the small proportion of Riesling occupying some of the top sites, Grüner is the name of the game. Once you get above the basic quaffing wine, which is the major proportion of production, it's usually described as showing white pepper, sometimes lentils and celery. Personally, I have a suspicion that these savory notes are associated with grapes below maximum ripeness, because I usually find them only on leaner examples of the wine. But in the hands of a top producer, Grüner can be an extremely versatile variety, offering a range from dense minerality,[51] to wine resembling old white Burgundy,[52] to wines with aromatics resembling Sauvignon Blanc.[53] If more Grüner was like this, it would take its place with the great wines of the world.

The Sweetness of Terroir

It's a real shame that Germany and Austria, where the highest quality wines are made from a grape variety that is one of the most expressive of terroir, should still be focused on classification systems reflecting the striving for ripeness. With warmer vintages likely to continue ameliorating the marginal nature of their wine production for the foreseeable future, now is the time to emphasize terroir. Some modest steps have been taken in this direction, but are they enough?

At the same time, they need to recognize that "tastes dry" is a subjective criterion not subject to a consistent classification. If there is one thing the consumer needs, it is certainty as to the sweetness of a wine. So trocken (and Smaragd in Wachau) should be restricted to wines with residual sugar below the level of detection (4 g/l). A complicated compound German term for "might be dry" would be appropriate for all those other wines presently described as trocken but with actual sugar levels above the detection threshold.

19

From Aperitif to Dessert

NOT ALL GREAT WINE HAS A VINTAGE. Capturing the heights of the vintage is certainly the ultimate expression of virtually every great table wine. But wines where—how shall we put this?—where there is more manipulation, may depend on blending or other aspects of production for their complexity. The bubbles are produced in sparkling wine by a second fermentation that greatly changes the aromas and flavors of the original base wine. Most sparkling wine owes its character to the skill of blending across several years. Fortified wines change greatly from the base wine as the result of the brutal addition of alcohol, whether this occurs after fermentation to leave a dry wine (as in the case of Sherry) or during fermentation to create a sweet wine (as in the case of Port). Age is certainly important in the complexity of Sherry, but the key factor is the length of time the wine has spent in the company of other vintages rather than its year of origin. The same is true of tawny Port, although vintage Port comes from a single year. Botrytized dessert wines owe much of their complexity to infection by the botrytis fungus, but here vintage variation can be extreme depending on whether conditions favored fungal infection. But these are all special cases where ultimate quality depends on factors beyond those involved in producing dry table wines.

All of these special situations originated as accidents. Dom Pérignon was struggling manfully to eliminate those pesky bubbles caused by refermentation in the wine at the Abbey of Hautvillers when methods were found to stabilize the wine and it became fashionable to drink sparkling wine. The process of maturing Sherry by blending vintages in the unique solera system probably originated with the need to even out vintages of varying quality. Port was probably fortified more to preserve the wine against microbial contamination, so it could be transported, than for reasons of taste. And botrytis, the noble rot, looks so disgusting on a grape that the initial reaction must certainly have been to throw out the damaged grapes; no one knows when it was discovered that the infection so concentrates the juice inside the grape that fermentation produces a delicious sweet wine. Happy accidents indeed!

The Margins of Winemaking

"We are artisans and it's not interesting to me to talk about the market or prices," says Pierre-Emmanuel Taittinger, president of Champagne Taittinger. "We are not selling perfume or soap or cars. My job is to find a million friends across the globe that drink five bottles of champagne a year."[1] But make no mistake about it, Champagne owes its dominance in sparkling wine as much to its relentless marketing campaign as to the quality of the product. "Most of the marketing is inside the bottle," says Charles Philipponnat of the Champagne house of the same name;[2] but, in fact, marketing and distribution costs are more responsible than production for the high price of Champagne. Certainly the later stages of production are unusually expensive, most especially the need to hold stock for many years, which increases the capital cost of production. But the price of Champagne is related more to what the market will bear than to its intrinsic costs of production.

That said, Champagne is indeed a unique product, although the beginnings of Champagne as a wine-producing region were not propitious. The word "Champagne" was used in the fourteenth century to describe the poor area around Reims that lacked vineyards.[3] In the sixteenth century, the wines of the region were lumped together as "wines of France," together with those produced round Paris, and the wine does not seem to have had any high repute. By 1600, the wines of the region were known by the sobriquet "Champagne." The areas considered to produce the best wines were the same as today, those of the Montagne de Reims and Ay.[4]

But the wines were not at all similar to Champagne of today. Sparkling wine had not yet been invented, and the wines of Champagne were considered competitive with those of Burgundy.[5] Pinot Noir was the most important grape variety. Sparkling wine became important at the end of the seventeenth century. And of course the image of Dom Pérignon struggling to capture those elusive bubbles is an amusing piece of marketing propaganda: in fact, his original remit was to find out how to stop the second fermentation that was creating the bubbles and spoiling production by causing the bottles to explode.

Several developments occurred during this period that set the pattern for production of Champagne.[6] It became common to blend the wine from vineyards in different parts of the region. And methods of gentle pressing allowed white juice to be obtained from black grapes. Wine producers were in fact not particularly impressed by sparkling wine, but around 1720 it became fashionable; the trend was set.[7] It was only some time later, in the second half of the eighteenth century, that juice from white grapes began to be included; this practice first became common in the region around Avize, which became known as the Côte de Blancs.[8] (Initially the additional varieties were Fromonteau, a local name for Pinot Gris, which is now scarcely used, and Chardonnay, still grown today.

The city of Reims is the center of the Champagne industry and is completely surrounded by vineyards.[9]

5 km

Actually, no one knows exactly what grapes were used in Dom Pérignon's time, as the names used then cannot be equated with modern varieties.)

Yet it was a long time before dry sparkling wine became the major product of the region. At the start of the nineteenth century, cheap red wine was 90% of production, and by 1850 it was still two thirds.[10] Champagne remained sweet until the last part of the nineteenth century, and very sweet at that, with anything from twice to five times the sugar level of a sweet champagne of the present; virtually none would have qualified as a Brut (dry) champagne today. The impetus for reducing the sugar came from British wine merchants, who found that Champagne was not competitive with other sweet wines, but that in relatively dry form, it could be sold to accompany food or (later) as an aperitif.[11] As Charles Perrier (son of the founder of Perrier-Jouët) said in 1846, "Today the English do not like Champagne too sweet. Most know that the use of high sugar levels is almost always to mask a lack of quality." Over the next thirty years there was an increasing trend towards dry styles for the English market.

By any measure, the successful production of wine, let alone wine of such prestige, is a great triumph for the Champagne area. Before the mini ice age of the Middle Ages, Champagne was the preferred supplier of red wine to Paris, but was overtaken by Burgundy when the cooling trend made it impossible to ripen Pinot Noir successfully enough to make red wine. Slowly the region was replanted to reach its present mix of grape varieties, Pinot Noir, Pinot Meunier, and Chardonnay, but conditions for ripening remain marginal in this northern climate. It was indeed remarkable to find a way of handling these grapes that allowed them to be cultivated to make such a successful product. The key is that the grapes are used only to make a base wine that needs to be a little on the acid side with low alcohol. The alcohol is then increased by the artifice of using additional sugar to cause a second fermentation in the bottle; and then the remaining acidity is counteracted by the addition of a little sweetening before bottling. At the end of the day, a marginally drinkable wine has been turned into a luxury cuvée.

The Champagne production area extends out from the city of Reims, a little less than a hundred miles to the east and north of Paris. The best regions are to the south and west of Reims, and account for three quarters of the vineyards. The Montagne de Reims produces the biggest wines and has a high concentration of Pinot Noir. The Côte des Blancs lies just to the south of Epernay, the other principal town in the region, and takes its name as the place where white grapes were first introduced; it concentrates on Chardonnay and is known for its finesse. The Vallée de la Marne produces its highest quality in the eastern part, but generally has a high concentration of Pinot Meunier, since it is considered to lack the conditions for top quality production of Pinot Noir and Chardonnay.[12] Pinot Meunier is definitely the poor man out: in fact, many houses will scarcely admit to including it in their blend. It's considered to limit longevity (although Krug, one of the few houses to state openly that they use it widely, makes one of the longest lived Champagnes).

In Dom Pérignon's day, blending from all three areas was considered to give the best quality and complexity. Because Champagne is usually a blended product, you rarely see indications of single vineyards on the label, but in fact Champagne classifies 59 of its present 319 villages into premier crus and grand

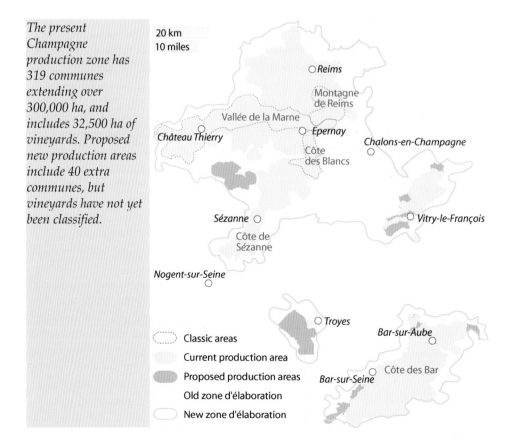

The present Champagne production zone has 319 communes extending over 300,000 ha, and includes 32,500 ha of vineyards. Proposed new production areas include 40 extra communes, but vineyards have not yet been classified.

20 km
10 miles

○ Reims

Montagne de Reims

Vallée de la Marne

Château Thierry ○   ○ Epernay

Côte des Blancs

Chalons-en-Champagne ○

Sézanne ○   ○ Vitry-le-François

Côte de Sézanne

Nogent-sur-Seine ○

○ Troyes

Bar-sur-Aube ○

Côte des Bar

Bar-sur-Seine ○

Classic areas
Current production area
Proposed production areas
Old zone d'élaboration
New zone d'élaboration

crus, situated in the Montagne de Reims or Côte des Blancs, with a handful on the eastern edge of the Vallée de la Marne. The best vineyards have thin topsoil that is rich in lignite with a subsoil of chalk beds.[13]

Going farther south, the wines become somewhat heavier. There's clearly a disjoint when you go all the way down to the Aube, which is closer to Chablis than it is to Reims, but the vineyards here have been regarded historically as part of the Champagne region. The subsoil here is mostly a Kimmeridgian clay. Today the Aube vineyards represent almost a quarter of the total vineyard area.[14] Individual vineyard holdings tend to be very small, with the present 33,000 ha broken up into 276,000 individual parcels.[15]

Champagne has contracted and expanded according to the rhythm of the day. At the end of the nineteenth century, there were 60,000 hectares of vineyards. When the area was defined as an appellation by the law of 1927, 40,000 hectares of vineyards were included in 407 villages. Responding to a decline in the market, this was reduced to 34,000 ha in 302 villages in 1951. Only 11,000 ha were used for Champagne production in the 1950s, but since then the vineyards have expanded steadily to fill the entire allotted area of the AOC. Under pressure to increase production, in 2003 the growers requested INAO to reclassify the area, this of course being a euphemism for increasing the approved area, which has reopened the controversy about where Champagne should really be made.

The region is classified in a hierarchy, with the zone d'élaboration describing the region within which it is legal to produce Champagne, the more limited zone de production covering the regions where it is legal to grow the grapes, and then within that, individual vineyards are classified. Over a three year period, INAO reviewed the zones d'élaboration and production. A leak to the press in 2007 revealed that the proposal was to include 40 new villages and to remove two existing villages. Over the next five years, INAO plans to examine vineyards in these villages in detail to decide exactly which plots can be included in the Champagne AOC, and it won't be until 2017 or thereabouts that the first new vineyards are actually planted.

The inevitable public reaction was that this is no more than a cynical ploy to increase production at the expense of quality. Certainly one is entitled to cynicism: is there any known case where expansion of the vineyards of a classic wine region has not been associated with decline in quality? But, of course, it's also true that there was much less knowledge about conditions for viticulture in 1927 when the original limits were defined, and that historical accidents influenced the outcome—such as the mayor of a village seeing no point in being included in the AOC. (When the vineyards were classified in 1927, grain, dairy, and cattle farming was more profitable than Champagne, and many landowners were aristocrats who were not interested in wine production.) The map shows that most of the new areas lie close to or within the existing areas, the two outstanding exceptions being a large expansion around Troyes and also just below Château Thierry. Public outcry might be justified, but needs to wait to see the details of the new vineyard classification.

The financial stakes are huge. Vineyards classified for Champagne production can sell for €1 million per hectare. Adjacent land that is used for other crops, such

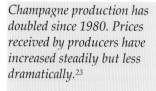

Champagne production has doubled since 1980. Prices received by producers have increased steadily but less dramatically.[23]

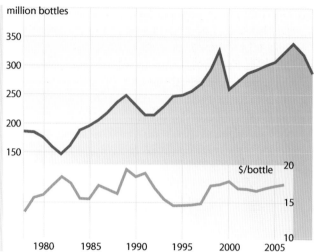

as beets or wheat, has a value around €6,000 per hectare.[16] If an additional 4,000 ha were added to the Champagne AOC, this would be making a present of €4 billion in land values to the lucky farmers. Who will be the main beneficiaries in the world of Champagne? One well known producer says meaningfully, "We have to ask who profits?" and then answers his own question by saying, "The driving force is LVMH, which needs extra production because its shareholders demand growth"—and there's no way to grow within the confines of the present land limits. While acknowledging that LVMH is a motor pulling along others in its train, and that INAO so far has done a good job in assessment, he is watching cautiously to see what effect the new classification has on quality.[17]

Virtually every classified piece of land in the Champagne AOC is planted with vines today. The area of vineyards has increased about 40% since 1980, but production has doubled.[18] So obviously yields have increased sharply. This is a sensitive issue. Yields change every year, but the current nominal limit translates to about 89 hl/ha, one of the most generous yields in the AOC system.[19] Of course, the purpose of vinification is to produce a relatively bland, neutral base wine, so high yields are not the problem they would be in another region.[20] But INAO periodically relaxes the limits by anything up to another 20%, so the nominal limit ends up being honored more in the breach than the observance.[21]

A recent fall in demand led to much publicity about a reduction in authorized yields, but this is definitely a chimera; yield limits actually remain the same, but a part of production is to be set aside as reserves for future years.[22] And with a huge number of small parcels, it's close to impossible to ensure that the rules are being followed on a lot by lot basis. (Of course, some quality producers restrict yields below the limit; so it follows there must be others who are pushing their yields well above the limit.) Would Champagne quality be better if limits were reduced rather than increased? Well let's just say that the yield limits owe more to market forces than to any investigation of the effects on quality.

Yield limitations are tied up with the division of interests between the growers and the producers. The leading Champagne houses produce two thirds of all

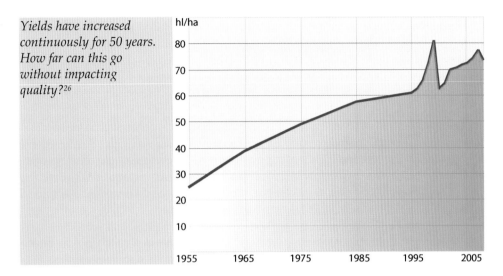

Yields have increased continuously for 50 years. How far can this go without impacting quality?[26]

Champagne, accounting for three quarters of its value, and 80% of all exports. But some 15,000 growers own 90% of the vineyards. Because the major Champagne houses own relatively few vineyards, they must buy most of their grapes.[24] Roederer, in the exceptional situation of owning enough vineyards to supply two thirds of its grapes, is much envied by the other producers. Power in the inevitable clash between growers and producers oscillates according to the state of the economy. When times are good, the growers have the whip hand, and it's dangerous for producers to turn away grapes, even if the quality is not up to their standard. When times are bad, the growers may be squeezed on price.

One of the problems of Champagne is that price does not depend on quality of the individual grapes or even of the individual vineyard, but simply on the rating of the village from which the grapes come. This perhaps is an inevitable consequence of the scattered nature of the individual holdings; with 276,000 separate parcels of vines, it's scarcely practical to distinguish each one. Every village has a rating on what is called the *échelle des crus*. At the top are grand crus at 100% and premier crus at 90-99%; other villages are rated from 90-80%.[25] Whatever price is established for the vintage as a whole is pro-rated for each village according to its position on the scale. (This is no longer entirely true, but it remains a reasonable guide.) It's a significant weakness, and to the detriment of quality, that each village is classified as a whole, so there is no recognition of the often wide variations in terroir between vineyards within the same village (or the efforts of individual growers).

The Joy of Bubbles

Fermentation produces huge volumes of carbon dioxide. The key to making sparkling wine is to trap some of that gas in the bottle. The techniques for doing this originated in the seventeenth century, although there is still controversy about who actually did it first. (It was not Dom Pérignon.) Sparkling wine may first have been made in France at Limoux, in the Languedoc, possibly because wine was bottled before fermentation had finished, and the process continued in the bottle where the bubbles were trapped. This is known as the *méthode rurale* or *méthode ancestrale*, and is still used to produce Blanquette de Limoux. In spite of claims by local producers to date the process from the sixteenth century, it is more likely to have originated around 1680.[27]

Relying on the first fermentation does not produce a great degree of sparkle. The *méthode Champenoise* developed to perfection in Champagne uses a second fermentation. The original fermentation is allowed to go to completion, generating a still base wine with low alcohol (10.5-11%). Then a solution called the *liqueur de tirage* containing wine, sugar, and yeast is added, and the bottle is sealed. A second fermentation takes place, bringing the alcohol up another per cent or so, and releasing enough carbon dioxide to create a pressure of 5-6 atmospheres in the bottle.[28] The discovery of sparkling wine was almost certainly an accident resulting from adulteration of the wine with sugar, molasses, and spices, which led to an adventitious second fermentation.

The process was invented in England well before it was tried in Champagne.[29] Two advances in technology were needed to stop bottles from exploding under the pressure of carbon dioxide: stronger glass; and corks. English glass was much stronger than French as the result of industrial improvements early in the seventeenth century;[30] and corks were (re)discovered in England a century before France. Wine was shipped in barrels to England where there was a healthy bottling trade, and some of it evidently was converted to sparkling wine, although it is not obvious why this should have been Champagne rather than any

Remuage (riddling) involves rotating the bottles gently in the pupitre until they reach an upright position. This view is from the cellars of Moët & Chandon around 1907.

other wine (perhaps initially because it was just too acid to drink as a still wine). In fact, some of the base wine actually came from the Loire, but was sold as Champagne because that was the name that gained the reputation for sparkling wine.[31]

Anyway, by 1662 the Royal Society in London had published a paper on the technique for producing sparkling wine; but the first sparkling wine was not made in the Champagne region until 1695. Dom Pérignon, who was cellar master at the Abbey of Hautvillers (near Epernay) from 1668 to 1715, was a great innovator and made many improvements in wine production; but it is entirely unclear whether he ever made sparkling wine (except inevitably by adventitious fermentation, creating bubbles that he tried to eliminate).[32]

Of course, there is more to making a successful sparkling wine than creating the bubbles. The technique of adding liqueur de tirage originated with the addition of sugar alone; at that time, no one knew the basis for fermentation. In fact, the cause was controversial; suggestions included the phase of the moon at the time of bottling.[33] It was probably well into the nineteenth century before yeast was included, as well as measuring a precise amount of sugar. Until then, the process would have been pretty much hit and miss.

The second fermentation creates a sediment of dead yeast cells. The method of dealing with this goes back to Madame Clicquot Ponsardin's disgust with the mess at the bottom of the bottle. The eponymous Veuve Clicquot had taken control of the Champagne house in 1805, and the story goes that she was infuriated by the sediment. Simply turning the bottles upside down did not work because particles continued to stick to the sides of the bottle. Experimenting with her kitchen table, she cut holes in it to hold the bottles, and discovered that all the sediment would collect in the neck if they were kept inverted and periodically rotated. By 1810 this *remuage* (riddling in English) was an established process. It was improved a few years later by the discovery that it started best by cutting holes to hold the bottles at an angle of 45°; the bottles were then rotated very gradually so that after a period of some weeks they came to a full vertical position. In due course the *pupitre* was introduced for the process, consisting of

A gyropalette holds 500 bottles and accomplishes remuage in a few days instead of a few weeks.

two boards hinged to form an inverted V, each board containing 60 holes cut at 45°.

The romantic view of Champagne production is that a skilled remueur (or riddler) can turn several hundred bottles a day, adjusting the angle minimally each day as each individual bottle requires. But today the process is largely mechanized. There's some controversy about whether the machine was invented in France or Spain, but it was first used commercially in the 1970s by Codorníu, the large Cava producer. Now it's used for virtually all sparkling wine production in Champagne and elsewhere. Called a girasol in Spain and a gyropalette in France, it holds bottles in a crate and follows a program for twisting and turning them en masse until they are vertical. It takes about three days. Less romantic, but more practical—and much more economical.

Once the sediment has collected in the neck it has to be disgorged. This is the most amazing part of the process. The necks of the inverted bottles are dipped into a refrigerated bath. The sediment in the neck becomes frozen. The bottle is turned upright, the cork is taken off, and voila!—the internal pressure ejects the sediment. Because the neck is still frozen, the wine stays in the bottle, and there is time to top it up and put on a new cork. *Dégorgement à la glace*, to give the process its full name, was invented in the late nineteenth century. The original concept is the basis for more automated machinery today.

The style of Champagne is determined by the topping-up process that follows disgorgement. The natural high acidity of Champagne needs to be counteracted

The machine for dégorgement à la glace was invented in 1884.

by some sweetness. This is done with a solution called the *liqueur d'expédition*, also called the *dosage*, which consists of sugar dissolved in wine. The nature of the Champagne is determined by the amount of sugar.

The most common style of Champagne today is *brut*, which means that the final sugar level is less than 15 g/l.[34] There is a wide range of sweetness in brut Champagnes, from those where the sugar is scarcely evident (if it is less than 6 g/l the Champagne may be called extra-brut) to those at the upper limit where it's obvious. The level of dosage is part of the style of each Champagne house, but you are entitled to be suspicious if it's too evident in a brut Champagne. Sweet Champagne is a relatively rare style today, but there's a hierarchy of descriptions for Champagnes with sugar above the brut level.

A key feature in the taste of Champagne is the date of disgorgement. Contact with the lees (the sediment containing the detritus of the dead yeast) protects the wine against oxidation and aging, giving what is considered to be a fresh flavor. As soon as it is disgorged, it begins to mature in the bottle. This is when it starts to develop the famous "biscuity" or "toasty" qualities of older Champagne.[35] Most nonvintage Champagnes do not really have the structure to withstand this development, but vintage Champagnes can become really interesting with a little age. But not everyone likes the results of development in the bottle: tastes vary enormously as to whether people prefer Champagne with fresher, recently disgorged flavors, or toasty brioche flavors from maturation after disgorgement.

This is a big issue with older vintage Champagne. A vintage Champagne will usually become available between three and four years after the vintage, but it will not all be disgorged at that point: some will be kept back to be disgorged later. It will gain increased complexity from longer time in the bottle before disgorgement, but the aromas and flavors are different from those developing after disgorgement. There may be a huge difference in flavor between a Dom Pérignon 1990 disgorged in 1996 and one disgorged in 2006. Unfortunately you can't always tell when the bottle was disgorged. There may be a hidden code on the label, but that's for the producer's convenience, not yours. However, recently the producers have become more aware of the damage done to their reputation by the unpredictable variation in older vintage Champagne, and in some cases have begun to put the date of disgorgement on the bottle. Bollinger initiated the idea of long aging before disgorgement with their RD (recently disgorged) vintage Champagne. Dom Pérignon followed suite with their Oenothèque series, which consists of recent disgorgements of older vintages.

Almost all Champagne is blended. Aside from a small proportion consisting only of Chardonnay (Blanc de Blancs) or of Pinot Noir (Blanc de Noirs),[36] most is a blend of all three grape varieties. As many as 30-40 different cuvées, coming from different parts of the region, will be included in the blend; possibly only perfume blending has the same complexity. And 85% of Champagne is nonvintage; wines from recent years are blended before the second fermentation. Each Champagne house prides itself in maintaining consistency of style by blending, and it is in fact the nonvintage Champagne that best displays the skill of each house. In vintage Champagne, which is made only three or four times a decade as and when there are vintages better than average, the style can be obscured by natural vintage variation.

One of the additional costs of producing Champagne is the need to hold large stocks, since wines from several preceding years are required for the nonvintage blend. Typically the blend will consist largely of base wine from the previous year, augmented by wines that have been kept in reserve from earlier years. Coupled with the fact that Champagne is matured in the bottle (18 months for nonvintage, three years for vintage), this means the return on investment is much slower than for dry table wine.

Blending across vintage not only allows producers to even out variations (or perhaps more to the point, to absorb the results of poorer vintages), but also enables them to react to market conditions. The significant production statistic for Champagne is not so much the size of the annual harvest as the number of bottles shipped each year. When there is high demand, Champagne is matured for the minimum period before releasing to market. When demand is low, base wines may be kept longer before blending, and Champagne may be kept longer in the bottle before disgorging, to avoid flooding the market. This actually means that in periods of low demand, the product is better.

The quality of terroir has been defined for each of Champagne's 319 villages. This isn't so different from Burgundy, around the same size with roughly 29,000 hectares, divided into 27 communes that include 375 premier crus and 32 grand crus. But in Burgundy the wines of each cru and village are vinified separately, giving a hierarchy of wines with infinite nuances of expression of Pinot Noir. In Burgundy, as in Champagne, the producer is the most important determinant of style, but imagine you were offered a Burgundy blended from 20% of Volnay for elegance, 20% of Corton for roundness, 20% Nuits St. Georges for strength, 20% Clos Vougeot for richness, and 20% Gevrey Chambertin for structure: an abomination that has destroyed the subtlety of Burgundy, you might say! Yet in Champagne, blending remains king: single vineyard Champagnes are few and far between. The important feature here is consistency between the years; acknowledging differences in terroir would only get in the way of using blending to overcome the limitations of vintage.

There are periodic cries for Champagne to produce more single vineyard wines, but I think this is misguided. To some extent the terroir would show through all the manipulations, producing interesting variety in the Champagnes for aficionados. But it wouldn't have a lot of meaning unless the Champagne was also restricted by vintage. Do we really want to see the same sort of ups and downs in Champagne as in Burgundy, with wine from the same producer and vineyard varying widely in quality from year to year?

Gentle pressing is a key feature in producing Champagne. Most of the grapes (Pinot Noir and Pinot Meunier) are black, and it's crucial that the skin color does not get into the must. So the grapes are pressed very gently in a vertical press to run the juice straight off with minimal skin contact. All Champagne, even a Blanc de Noir should be a pale golden color. Except, of course, for rosé. This can be a bit of a trick: most rosé Champagne is made simply by adding a little red wine to the base wine. This is illegal as a means of producing rosé for all wines in the

E.U. except for Champagne; and, indeed, proposals to legalize it for still wine production led to a great outcry about loss of quality. A small number of rosé Champagnes are in fact made by allowing some skin contact; is it a myth that these are more delicate? No one has ever set to testing this systematically, so far as I know. Irrespective of the means of production, most Champagne producers regard rosé with some disdain: they produce it for the market, but do not regard it as interesting in its own right.

And Champagne is not always what it seems to be. To produce Champagne, a house can buy the source material at any stage from grapes to finished product. Given that the final Champagne is blended from many base wines, it's probably reasonable enough for a house to supplement its needs by buying some wine, perhaps from one of the cooperatives in the region. But there used also to be the pernicious routine of purchasing *sur latte*. This takes its name from the period when the bottles lie flat (en latte) while maturing. In periods of high demand, a Champagne house might buy some finished sparkling wine and stick its own label on the bottles. Nominally there should be a code on the bottle to indicate that the wine was bought in.[37] Purchase sur latte is no longer legal, but don't bet money that every bottle with the name of a famous house was produced right from the start by that house.[38]

Marketing Triumph

"The success of a champagne house is very fragile and is based on a price for its raw materials that represents three quarters of its production costs," says Yves Dumont, chairman of Laurent-Perrier.[39] This is true, but deceptive. The cost of grapes is high, and this is a sensitive issue (and source of conflict) because the houses are compelled to buy most of their grapes from outside sources. But even if the cost of grapes is the major part of production expense, is this the driving force in pricing Champagne? Luxury goods are famous for the lack of relationship between cost of production and selling price; indeed, LVMH, who own several major Champagne houses, as a group spends more on marketing than on producing goods.[40]

Most Champagne is well into the class of luxury goods. The best grapes presently cost around $10 per bottle.[41] Other production costs bring total expense to about $13 per bottle. This is a lot less than the average retail price of $50 for a bottle of Veuve Clicquot, a fairly typical price for a Grand Marque Champagne. Where does the rest of the price go? Champagne producers spend a great deal on promotion, and in fact the cost of promotion is likely to be more than the cost of production, so you are really paying for the label. To add insult to injury, retail markups are high also, although they vary quite a bit in different markets. At the end of the day, the poor producer may actually be getting only a 15-20% profit, some of which is chewed up by financial and other carrying costs. Of course, since production costs are relatively fixed and promotion is such a high part of the budget, it follows that a small grower's Champagne is much better value, and the prestige cuvées at over $100 per bottle are really rather poor value.

Where your money goes on a bottle of Champagne. Producers spend more on promotion than production.

Retail margin $15-25

Producer's profit $5

Promotion $16

Production $3

Grapes $10

It's typical of the tight connection with marketing that the whole concept of the Grand Marque is tied up with brand recognition. To be considered a Grand Marque, a Champagne must be famous. In effect, this means it must be produced on a scale that gives it international recognition. The name goes back to 1912, when a breakaway group of the less successful producers left the producers' organization. Those remaining in the Syndicat du Commerce des Vins de Champagne decided that they were the grand marques, and in 1964 officially changed their name to the Syndicat de Grandes Marques de Champagne.[42] But in the early 1990s there was a brouhaha when the members of the Syndicat were asked whether their membership implied production of superior quality. The answers were equivocal: in fact, only Bollinger considered that standards of quality should be imposed on the members. After much discussion the members failed to agree on any quality standard, and as a result the Syndicat dissolved itself in 1997. At this point, the 24 Grand Marques accounted for 60% of all Champagne production. Officially recognized or not, the term persists in the concept that a relatively small number of internationally famous major houses account for the majority of production.[43]

Champagne production has become steadily more concentrated in the hands of a small number of owners. Almost two thirds of all sales come from the top five groups, the largest of which is LVMH, owning Moët & Chandon, Mercier, Ruinart, Veuve Clicquot, and Krug.[44] Another twenty groups account for another third. A remaining 5% is accounted for by thirty smaller houses.[45] The bigger fish are continuing to gobble up the smaller ones at a fairly steady pace.

The Champagne producers are a pretty ruthless lot, at least judging by the way they relentlessly enforce their name. Actually you can't blame them for insisting that "Champagne" should appear only on wine from the region, not on other sparkling wine. And at a pinch it's not unreasonable to prevent the name being used for other products that might trivialize the reputation of Champagne, but it seems to be extreme that you can't use the word "Champagne" in Europe in any context except on the label of a bottle of sparkling wine from the region.[46] More objectionable, and in my opinion somewhat extreme, is the prohibition against using "Méthode Champenoise" on sparkling wine produced elsewhere. All this means is that the fizz was introduced by a second fermentation in the bottle (as opposed to cheaper alternatives). Anywhere except Europe, such a restriction would be ruled out of court as restraint of trade. So a Crémant from elsewhere in France, a Franciacorta from Italy, a Cava from Spain, have to say "Méthode Traditionelle" if they want to indicate they use the same production method as Champagne.

Why doesn't Champagne have any successful rivals? Even though it has come under pressure with the recent financial squeeze and consumers have been switching to cheaper alternatives, this is more a choice to trade down than finding an equivalent alternative. Part of the reason is the unique balance of the climate at the marginal edge for wine production. Alternatives made in most other places are richer and heavier, reflecting warmer climates. The long history of Anglo-French rivalry comes to the fore in suggesting southern England as a future possibility; and if the climate does warm up enough for this to be really successful, certainly Champagne will be in trouble because its own climate will then be too warm. But Champagne's primacy is not under immediate threat.

Blending through the Solera

Sherry has a terrible image outside of Spain. The usual jibe is that it's drunk by your elderly aunt early in the afternoon. Fifty years ago there were 120 shippers; only about half remain today.[47] A spurt of popularity led to a large expansion in the 1980s, then there was a massive contraction. Yet Sherry is one of the most original wine products in the world, with a range from fully dry to lusciously sweet, and from sharp and salty to creamy and rich. You would think there was something here for everyone, so what went wrong?

Sherry is the antithesis of the modern emphasis on increasingly fruity wines. Its flavors reflect development during production rather than the original fruit qualities of the wine. Everything about Sherry from its alcohol level, to oxidative type of style, to sweetness, is determined by decisions made during the production process. Fashion has a great deal to do with the relative decline of Sherry. At the peak of its popularity, when the town was full of English exporters sending Sherry to England, Jerez was one of the most prosperous cities in Spain,[48] but now the province of Cádiz is one of the poorest in all Spain.

Jerez was probably founded by the Phoenicians when they moved inland from Cádiz sometime after 1100 B.C. By the time the Romans conquered Spain, wine production had probably been established in Jerez for some centuries. The Romans called the town Ceritium, and were fond of a wine they called Ceretenes. In spite of much speculation, there's no evidence it was anything like today's Sherry. When the Moors swept across Spain, the town became called Šeriš, which the Spanish changed to Jerez, and the English to Sherry. Fortunately the Moors did not suppress production of wine. The full name of Jerez de la Frontera reflects the period after Spain recaptured the town, when Jerez remained right on the frontier between Christian Spain and the Moorish empire.

English trade with Jerez goes back at least to the fourteenth century. It became substantial;[49] by 1548, two thirds of the annual production of 60,000 butts was being exported to England and Flanders.[50] This places total production at an equivalent of 3.3 million cases, comparable to the level in the 1950s, and just about half of today's average level.[51] During this period, the wine became known as Sherris or Sherry Sack (there were also Malaga sack and Canary sack);[52] it was probably sweet and drunk while young. Over the next centuries the fortunes of Jerez followed the state of war or peace between England and Spain with a series of boom and bust cycles. English shippers remained a dominant influence. A great boom at the end of the nineteenth century[53] saw the British market swamped with imitations from other countries, and it was not until Britain joined the common market that Sherry was reserved as a term for wines from Jerez.

When did Sherry become Sherry, that is, the distinctive wine we know today? This is relatively recent. In the fifteenth century there were references to both red and white wine,[54] and it appears that in the middle of the seventeenth century, wines were sometimes shipped in casks while fermentation was still proceeding.[55] This would imply the wine was from the most recent vintage and had not been fortified. The famous solera system that is now used to mature all Sherry had not yet been invented. Its origins are obscure, but probably date from the late eighteenth or early nineteenth century, possibly as a result of partial withdrawal of wine to fill orders as they arrived.[56]

A Solera consists of rows of barrels stacked three or four high. The barrels are made of old American oak but painted black (in order to detect leakages). The bodega is a large, airy warehouse open to the exterior to allow plenty of air circulation.

A traditional solera has the actual solera itself on the bottom, with successively younger criadera above.

And so to the solera system. Think of a solera as rows of barrels. Wine is siphoned out from the bottom row for bottling. The barrels are topped up from the barrels in the row above. They in turn are refilled from the next higher row. There are usually between 3 and 8 of these stages, called criadera, stacked vertically up to 3 or 4 rows deep. Soleras vary in size; when there are more than three criadera, of course the barrels can't continue to be stacked vertically, but have to form other rows. The top row (metaphorically if not literally) is topped up with wine of the current vintage (the añada).

Each stage of development is called a scale; the total number of scales in a particular solera equals the total number of criaderas plus the solera itself. (Solera has two meanings: it describes the whole system, but also refers specifically to the final row, which is usually on the bottom.[57]) The system of refreshing older barrels with wine from younger barrels is known in Jerez as "running the scales." Traditionally it was carried out with implements called the "canoe" and the "sprinkler" so that the wine falls gently into the butt. Now it is electronically controlled by modern equipment: typically the wine removed from the upper level is mixed in a tank, and then added to the barrels in the lower level to bring each up to a level of 500 l (the barrel can hold 600 l).[58]

When Sherry is bottled from a solera, it is characterized by the average age of the wine. This depends on the number of scales in the solera, the percentage of the saca (the wine that is withdrawn when a bottling is made), and the frequency of the saca. The legal limits are that a saca cannot be more than one third of the Solera on any one occasion; and no more than 30% of production can be sold in any one year (which conforms with the requirement that the minimum age to sell a wine is 3 years). Soleras vary greatly in size, from as few as 20 or so barrels to several hundred.

The story goes that every solera has its own character. By starting at the top of the system and moving slowly through to the bottom, wine is imprinted with the character of the solera by the time it emerges. Melding vintages eliminates annual variation, producing wines with more consistent quality and uniform flavor. How long a wine spends in a solera depends on how many criadera there are, and how quickly the wine is moved through them. You sometimes see references to the date when a solera was started, the implication being that if you get Sherry from a solera of 1950, there may even be a small amount of the original wine from the first year in your glass. Maybe: but not very much. After 30 years there would still be 4% of the original wine, but today there would be less than a thimbleful in a bottle of Sherry. In a one hundred year old solera, there would be less than one drop of the original wine in a bottle produced today.

The Flor on Top

A random event determines what type of Sherry develops in each butt. Actually, this is a bit of a myth: what was originally a random event, today is usually directed by the producer. The critical issue is whether *flor* forms on the surface of the wine in the barrel.

Sherry starts off as a rather neutral base wine. After fermentation, usually in stainless steel, the wine is transferred to barrels. Flor begins, or fails to begin, to form almost immediately after fermentation. It consists of a layer of the yeast Saccharomyces ellipsoideus, and can become several centimeters thick. Formation of flor protects the wine underneath from oxidation, and it matures to become a fino Sherry, very fine and delicate. If flor does not form, the wine ages in the barrel under oxidative conditions and gives an oloroso Sherry, richer and heavier. Soleras contain one type or the other; in a fino solera, all the barrels have flor, in an oloroso solera none of the barrels have flor. Sometimes the flor dies out, and when this happens in a cask where the wine is more than 3 years old, it is allowed to continue maturation in the absence of flor, to become an amontillado. [60]

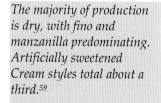

The majority of production is dry, with fino and manzanilla predominating. Artificially sweetened Cream styles total about a third.[59]

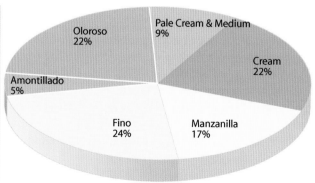

This barrel has a glass end to allow the flor to be visualized. It forms a white layer about 1-2 cm thick on top of the wine.

It used to be the case that wines were classified immediately after fermentation, depending on the level of flor, and the butts were marked with an intricate series of signs indicating what type of solera they would join. Those destined for fino would be fortified to bring the alcohol level to 15.5%, the ideal level for the growth of flor. Those destined for oloroso would be fortified up to 18%, which prevents growth of flor. After a few months the classification would be confirmed or changed. One year after the vintage, the wine would be ready to add to the youngest criadera. But this was when wine was produced at each vineyard, fermented in barrels, and there was substantial variation between the lots. In modern Jerez, the winemaker makes the wine knowing whether he wants it to become fino or oloroso; indeed, sometimes the wine for fino is seeded with the flor yeast during fermentation to ensure more rapid development. The tendency is to use free-run juice for fino and to make oloroso from the first pressing. The basic principle is that the lower the pressure of pressing (free-run being the ultimate of zero pressure, as it were) the more likely a wine is to be used for fino.

Fermentation goes to completion before the wine is fortified, so all Sherry is naturally dry. Fino has a pale color, an aromatic nose of yeast and almonds, and tangy, even pungent, salty flavors. Because the flor consumes nutrients in the wine, including glycerol, the finish is very dry. Fino has barely any residual sugar, less than 1 g/l. An amontillado, spending three years under flor, and then often as long again under oxygen, is darker in color than a fino, typically amber, with a pungent nose showing hazelnuts. An oloroso is darker as the result of its long exposure to air, and it develops rich, intense, nutty and raisiny flavors. That nutty taste you get in Sherry is due to acetaldehyde, formed by oxidation of the alcohol.

Dry styles of Sherry account for about two thirds of production, with fino about twice as common as oloroso. Fino includes the subclass of manzanilla, which is identical in its production, but distinguished by the fact that it is matured in the seaside town of Sanlúcar de Barrameda. The coastal influence makes the climate slightly milder, so that flor grows all the year round, whereas in Jerez it usually stops in the winter. The result is that manzanilla is an exceptionally fine and dry fino. Some imaginative tasters believe that it has a salty taste reflecting the sea, but really it's more of a tang resulting from the increased exposure to flor. In a sort of counterpart to terroir, it's not the location of the vineyards that is important in the distinction between fino and manzanilla, but the location of the solera; fino and manzanilla could come from the same vineyards, but the Sherry is manzanilla if the solera is located in Sanlúcar.

A very small amount of authentically sweet Sherry is produced from the Pedro Ximénez grape; grapes are dried in the sun before they are fermented, and sugar content is so high that the residual sugar after fermentation makes the wine sweet. The wine is matured in a solera system. But these PX wines are only about 1% of all production. The so-called cream sherries are made by adding rectified must (basically a sugar solution) to a dry Sherry: pale cream is made by sweetening fino, medium amontillado by sweetening amontillado, and cream by sweetening oloroso. They are about a third of production, but are hardly ever seen in Spain; almost all is exported, much of it to Britain.

Made from the Palomino grape, the base wine for Sherry is pretty neutral.[61] Given declining demand for Sherry, some producers are making a conventional white wine from Palomino, but it tends to be rather characterless.

The substantial difference between Sherry consumed in Spain and the Sherry that is exported is one of the major problems for the region. The good stuff that is kept at home is the perfect aperitif to match with tapas, a dry and savory counterpart to the food. The exported cream Sherries are all too often sickly sweet, filling neither the role of aperitif nor providing a suitable accompaniment to

The DOC is centered on Jerez de la Frontera and is known as the Sherry triangle of the three principal towns.[62]

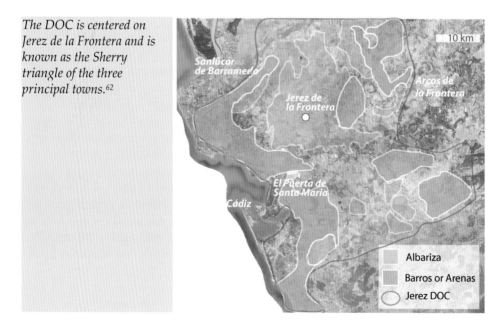

food. In a world turning more and more to fruit-driven wines, Sherry is likely to have problems anyway, but they are greatly reinforced by the mistaken perception that cream Sherry is the typical product of the region. How many people never discover the true interest of Sherry because of an off-putting experience with a cream Sherry?

Boom and Bust

The Jerez DOC is known as the Sherry triangle, after the three principal towns, Jerez, El Puerto de Santa Maria to the south, and Sanlúcar de Barrameda to the west. Vineyards are located in an area of roughly 40 km diameter extending out from the coast. Bodegas—one might almost say the remaining bodegas—are located in the three towns, although now there are few outside of Jerez itself. Sherry as such can be produced in any of the towns. Sanlúcar alone has the distinction of producing manzanilla, although the few remaining producers in El Puerta de Santa Maria will tell you that they have very similar conditions. "Here in El Puerto we *really* get flor all the year round, whereas in Sanlúcar it's not so consistent," says Carmen Pau of Bodegas Gutiérrez Colosía.[63]

You would think that terroir would be of relatively little importance in a wine matured for such long periods, and subjected to so many outside influences. A big problem in producing wine in the region is the near-drought condition of the summer. With irrigation not allowed, it's crucial to retain the water that falls earlier in the year. For this reason, the best soils are the albariza, soils that are so rich in chalk as to appear white, which retain the water. Special ditches, called deserpias, are dug along the rows to help retain water. Not much besides grapevines can grow in this soil. Barro soil is darker and gives coarser wine. Arena soil is sandy, and most of the vineyards that were planted on it have been pulled out. Some vineyards are prized because they give base wines that make especially fine fino or oloroso, but in seeking uniformity rather than individual variation, the solera is the antithesis of terroir; there are no single vineyard sherries.

The Albariza soils are white because of the high chalk content.

Photograph kindly provided by Consejo Regulador in Jerez.

Vineyard plantings have gone through the boom and bust cycles familiar to almost every viticultural region. In the 1950s, the region had settled down to about 7,000 ha. Then in the 1980s, a boom was driven by sales of cream sherries in British supermarkets; plantings increased to an unsustainable 22,000 ha. When the bust came in the 1990s, plantings contracted to around 10,000 ha, at which they've been steady for the past decade.[64] Currently vineyards are being taken out, and some producers feel that another 10-20% must go to bring supply and demand back into balance. With the ups and downs of vintages, production has fluctuated more than plantings, but has roughly halved from its peak of 16 million cases annually to around 8 million today.

Production is split between independent growers, cooperatives, and bodegas. About 38% of production is by bodegas that undertake all of the stages of production from growing grapes to selling wine. About 43% of production goes through cooperatives, and another 20% comes from independent growers.[65] Independent growers may sell either grapes or young wine to the bodegas; the cooperatives usually process grapes and produce young wine that is sold to bodegas who put it in their soleras. Only the bodegas undertake the final stages of bottling and distribution.

The recent contraction has forced out many small producers, or at least compelled them to sell to larger producers, causing increased concentration. Only a tiny number of bodegas remain in family hands. New bodegas are relatively rare; you can count on the fingers of one hand the number formed in the past decade. Jerez is now dominated by large companies, with the five largest accounting for two thirds of production.[66] The shakeout is still continuing. Most of the producers, incidentally, make both brandy and vinegar as sidelines.

Production has been modernized, with stainless steel tanks for fermentation, and controlled methods for transferring wine between butts. But the bodegas still look traditional. They were built as large, airy warehouses, open to the exterior, and designed to allow air circulation during the hot summer. Temperatures in Jerez routinely go to 40 °C in the summer, but a typical temperature in a bodega around the wine would probably be about 28 °C. One of the reasons why the

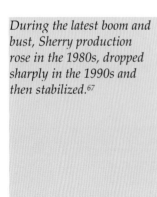

During the latest boom and bust, Sherry production rose in the 1980s, dropped sharply in the 1990s and then stabilized.[67]

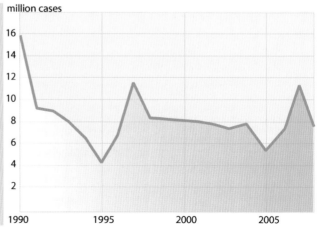

solera, which contains the oldest wine, is kept on the floor is that there is usually a 1-2 °C difference between the bottom and top rows of barrels. The bodegas mostly have not changed much, often still using sandy or gravel floors to retain humidity, and watering every week in dry conditions, as opposed to any more sophisticated control.

Almacenistas and the Move to Quality

Bodegas own about 30% of the vineyards. The gap between vineyards and producers created one of the unique features of the Sherry region, the almacenista. Literally a store-keeper or wholesaler, an almacenista would buy grapes or young wine and mature it through a solera, but would not bottle or sell it. He would in effect be an intermediary between the growers and the shippers. Sometimes an almacenista would sell a whole solera to a shipper, sometimes just some of the wine needed to make up a specific blend at bottling. A significant part of the Sherry stocks used to be held by almacenistas. Today they are of much less importance. The bodegas hold most of the 900,000 butts held in inventory; almacenistas probably account for about 60,000. Sometimes an almacenista matures into a bodega; in one case, for example, the sales arrangement failed with the bodega that had been taking the stock, so the almacenista started commercializing the wine directly.

The almacenista used to be purely part of the internal function of the market, but you may have seen "almacenista" on bottles of Sherry from the producer Lustau. Lustau was a small family firm from 1896 to 1990 when it joined the Ruiz Cabellero (brandy and Sherry) group. Lustau is now their Sherry division. About 5% of their production is by bottling finished wines from almacenistas' soleras. They have about seven almacenistas under contract at any time; these are far from the most important part of the operation economically, but bring prestige. The name of the almacenista is put on the bottle; in fact Lustau have trademarked the term almacenista, so no one else can use it now.

The system allows for considerable adjustment of style. Alcohol level is somewhat arbitrary in a fortified wine, but in response to market pressure, fino is now around 15% where it used to be 17.5%, although the exact level can vary between countries depending on local tax rates. Oloroso is usually around 18-19% after bottling. In another response to market pressure, Sherry sometimes seems to be on a convergence path with the bland white wines made from Palomino. "The market demands water, whereas the style used to be more mature," comments Xavier Hidalgo of Hidalgo La Gitana.[68]

But the Consejo Regulador (the regulatory body) is making valiant efforts to modernize Sherry. As wine that is matured in a solera, Sherry does not have a vintage. However, since year 2000 it has been possible to classify older Sherry by the average age of wines in the solera. Sherry based on wines with an average age over twenty years can be described as VOS (officially Vinum Optimum Signatum, more practically Very Old Sherry), and wines with an average age over thirty years can be described as VORS (Vinum Optimum Rare Signatum or

Very Old Rare Sherry.)[69] They are a tiny proportion of the region's production, but the Consejo hopes that they will provide a halo effect to attract attention and lift up the region. Those I have tasted certainly have great intensity of flavor. There is even now an occasional vintage Sherry; but interesting though they are, my own reaction is that they make the point about the extra complexity that comes from the solera system.

There is little else like Sherry. There are a few other cases in which a flor forms on the surface after fermentation. Vin Jaune of the Jura, Vermentino di Sardegna (which comes in both conventional and Sherry-style), and Szamorodni in Tokaji all can resemble a fino Sherry in their aroma and flavor spectrum, although they are not fortified. These wines can be very fine, but nowhere else is there such a range of styles, from fino, to amontillado, to oloroso (and actually one or two other intermediate styles that I have not mentioned),[70] now complemented by a variety of small production bottlings from almacenistas and the rarified VOS and VORS. And Sherry is ludicrously cheap compared with other wines of similar quality. Think about a Sherry that takes four or five years to pass through its solera before it is bottled; and then it sells for less than $10 a bottle. Certainly it's the antithesis of the drive for more and more fruit that has stretched from the New World to all over Europe, but I'll take a savory fino any day as the perfect aperitif or even an accompaniment to a fish meal.

Up the Douro

Less hospitable terrain for producing wine would be hard to imagine. Port is produced only in the Douro valley, which lies along the Douro river inland from the town of Oporto that gave its name to the wine. The terrain is mountainous, rising up sharply from the Douro river and its tributaries. Most grapes are grown at the lower elevations, although there are vineyards as high as 600 m. The best grapes are considered to come from close to the river (the local saying is that the best Port comes from grapes that can hear the river flowing).

Difficult to navigate, the Douro river was for long the sole source of transport through the region. Viticulture at first was possible only in the more western half, because the Cachão de Valeira canyon, a huge granite outcrop, prevented navigation farther up the river. When this was removed in the mid eighteenth century, viticulture spread along the river to the Douro Superior in the east, extending to the Spanish border. The western half is now divided into the lower (Baixo) and upper (Cima) Corgo.

Terraced vineyards run along the Douro river; the land is so steep and uninviting that often the area had to be dynamited to create the vineyards.[71] Soils are stony, typically schist with very little subsoil. The terroir has often been altered greatly from its original state, partly by the dynamiting, partly by the extensive construction of terraces. Ninety percent of the vineyards have slopes over 30 per cent, with some up to 70%.

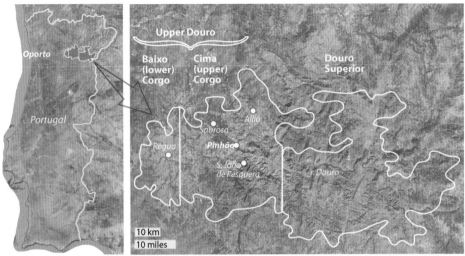

The Douro is divided into three regions:[72]		
	Baixo corgo	14,500 ha
	Cima corgo	21,000 ha
	Douro Superior	10,200 ha

Climate is different in each of the three regions. The mountains form a protective barrier against weather coming from the Atlantic. Summers are hot and dry, and winters are cold everywhere, but rainfall decreases steadily proceeding east towards the Spanish border, from about 1,200 mm per year in the Baixo Corgo, to 850 mm in the Cima Corgo, and only 400 mm in the Douro Superior (marginal for grape growing).

The closest region to the Atlantic, the Baixo Corgo is the most fertile and abundant. It tends to produce the lightest wines (ruby and tawny Port), and accounts for about half of Port production. Cima Corgo is more than double in size, and is where most of the high quality tawny and vintage Port is made. Most of the famous producers are around the town of Pinhão. This region accounts for just over a third of all Port production. The Douro Superior is the largest of the three sub-zones, the most arid and the least developed. Only a small amount of Port is produced here.

Vineyards are broken up, with around 33,000 farmers each on average working only about a hectare. The vineyards are classified into six different categories labeled "A" through "F". 20% of the vineyards are graded A or B, and 5% are graded E or F. Classification factors include productivity (the lower the yield, the higher the mark), gradient (higher points for lower altitude), aspect, soil, exposure, and vine varieties. Each factor is given a numerical value, which is then tallied up. A score of more than 1200 points out of a maximum 1680 points is given an "A". Vineyards scoring less than 200 points are given an "F". The amount of wine that can be used to make Port is limited in any given year, and the amount that can be made from any vineyard depends on its rating. Grade A vineyards are allowed to make up to 600 liters of Port per 1000 vines. F grade vineyards usually cannot be used for Port production.

Vineyards rise up in very steep terraces from the Douro river.

History still has a strong influence in the region. Obtaining grapes at optimum ripeness is complicated by extensive complantation; 70% of vineyards still have different grape varieties intermixed. Growers used to have every third vine as a different varietal as a protection against crop failures. In 1983 the E.U. started a scheme to improve plantings in the Port region by using better sites and better matching varietals to sites, so that individual varieties are now being identified and new plantings are organized in blocks.

The grape varieties used for Port were distinguished systematically only in the 1980s. About 20 grape varieties are recommended for Port out of (probably)

Five major grape varieties are used for Port	
Touriga Nacional	Low yields give deeply colored and tannic wines. This is the top varietal, considered to give the wines "grip."
Touriga Francesca	Good heat-resistance, does well in dry years, gives lighter wines than Nacional.
Tinta Roriz	Variant of Tempranillo, gives firmness and length, does best in years that are not too hot.
Tinta Barroca	Gives good color, structure, and body, with high sugar content.
Tinta Cão	Low-yielding, intense flavor, is used for wines designed for long aging.

Barco rebelo sailing boats along the Douro were the only way of transporting wine from the vineyards to Oporto until relatively recently.

about 50 varieties growing in the region. Five varietals are considered to give the best wine for Port production. All are indigenous to Portugal, except for Tinta Roriz (a variant of Tempranillo), and very little is grown elsewhere.[73]

The Colors of Port: Ruby, Tawny, and Vintage

Port owes its origins to the English merchants who settled in Oporto after Portugal freed itself from Spanish rule and then in 1654 signed a trade treaty with England. Their headquarters were established at the Factory House in Oporto.[74] By the 1680s they were exporting fortified wine from the region around Régua to Britain. Fortification appears to have been introduced to preserve the wine and perhaps to give it more body.[75] The wine was mostly fermented to dryness before the addition of brandy. Its style was somewhat harsh, but during the start of the eighteenth century, it was realized that adding brandy before the end of fermentation led to retention of sugar, making the wine sweeter and stronger. It also became obvious that some time was required for the harshness to soften, and merchants began to age the wine in cask before exporting it.[76]

In the last quarter of the eighteenth century, the development of bottles that could be stacked horizontally made it possible for aging in cask to be succeeded by bottle aging, and this was the point at which vintage Port originated.[77] The first year of vintage Port was probably 1775.[78] Even so, the wine was a far cry from that of today: adulteration was a problem, and it was so common to use elderberries to increase color that the government ordered all elderberries in the Douro to be uprooted.[79] Nonetheless, the use of *baga* (as elderberry is called in

Portugal) continued into the nineteenth century.[80] Indeed, as judged by the demand for elderberries, it may even be used today by a few minor producers.[81] By the mid nineteenth century, Port was commonly sweet, with a level of alcohol similar to today, although from time to time there was criticism that the wine was being spoiled by the addition of brandy.

Vintage Port is the pinnacle of Port matured in the bottle. Today it is bottled after two or three years of aging in cask, and then is expected to take 15-20 years before it is ready to drink. It's one of the few remaining holdouts of the old style where the consumer is expected to mature the wine. Each Port shipper must decide within two years of the harvest whether that particular year will be high enough quality to be released as a vintage Port. This is called "declaring the vintage." In a really great vintage, virtually every shipper will declare; in lesser vintages, those shippers who have done especially well, or who need a vintage perhaps because of past lack of success, will declare.

Until recently, Port was exclusively a blended wine, blended both from different grape varieties and from different vineyard sources. Since the 1980s, some single vineyard bottlings have appeared under the name of individual quintas (vineyards). Quinta is a slightly ambiguous term: nominally it means a vineyard, and can be used to identify the origin of a wine, but it is also used as the name for some famous producers, such as Quinta da Noval.

Unlike single vineyard wines in other regions, where the top vineyard in the top vintage is the best there is to offer, single quinta wines in Port are made in lesser vintages. In a great vintage, all of the wine is likely to go into the house's vintage Port. But in years just below the very top, when the vintage is not declared, the very best single vineyards may be worthy of bottling in vintage style. The most famous is from Quinta da Noval; its top vineyard is called Nacional, and has been bottled separately for much longer than most single quinta Ports. Nacional is a small vineyard still containing ungrafted vines. Many people consider the 1931 Quinta da Noval Nacional to be the greatest Port of the twentieth century, although the 1931 vintage was not commonly declared. Among single quinta Ports, Taylor's Quinta de Vargellas is also well known. A single quinta Port is made in exactly the same way as a vintage Port, and usually has the compensating qualities of coming from the best vineyard but not the best year.

The rarity of vintage Port, usually with only two or three vintages declared each decade, has spurred imitations at lower price.[82] Actually, the so-called LBV (late bottled vintage) can sometimes be good, although abuse of the name has made it unreliable. A vintage not deemed good enough for a vintage Port will go into the making of a "traditional" LBV. It is left in wood for four to six years and then bottled. The extra time in cask makes the wine ready to drink, but it can still have a heavy sediment that needs decanting. LBVs originated during the 1950s, when the market was poor, and vintage Port would remain in cask beyond the usual limits while waiting for a buyer. The style was officially sanctioned in the 1960s. At their best, LBVs can give a good impression of vintage style. The use of driven corks distinguishes the best LBVs from a lesser style of LBV, indicated by a stopper cork, where filtration and stabilization have removed all sediment to make the wine ready for immediate consumption. LBV is officially described as Ruby Port from a single vintage, the requirement for Ruby being that it is aged in bulk for three years, and bottled young. Ruby Ports tend to be fiery; certainly no one could call them subtle. LBVs under stopper corks often enough are not much different from the better ruby Ports. At one time it was possible to label ruby Port as "vintage character," but this deceptive practice has finally been stopped.

And now for something completely different. Tawny Port shows the same variety of quality and character as the range from Ruby to Vintage, but a different nature. This is a more recent style than vintage Port and its imitators. In fact, the vintage of 1797 was condemned as "very bad, tawny;"[83] a light, tawny color was the kiss of death. By contrast, tawny Port gains its light color because it is matured in wood for several years, with the color lightening, and the flavor becoming drier and nuttier from oxidation. Evaporation during its maturation in wood increases the concentration of the wine. The origins of tawny Port are not so well established as vintage Port, but by the 1840s it was reckoned that a tawny Port was ideal with 5 or 6 years in cask followed by three years in bottle.[84]

Tawny Port with no indication of age is a staple of the industry, but not of much interest. Aged tawny Ports are another matter. Tawny Ports can carry indications of 10, 20, 30, or 40 years, meaning that the wine has been aged in cask for at least that long. There is a big jump in quality from non-aged tawnies to 10-year tawnies, and again to 20-year tawnies. Gain in complexity as you go up to 30- and 40-year can be offset by an overblown quality resulting from oxidation. The aged tawnies generally originate as blends of high quality wines from undeclared vintages. Rather rare, but interesting when you can find it, is Colheita Port, which is a tawny from a single vintage. But remember that the significance of the vintage is the quality of the starting wine, with quality also influenced by the length of time in cask before bottling; little improvement occurs after bottling.

Ernest Cockburn, of the well known Port house, once famously said that the first duty of a Port is to be red (the second is to be drunk), and in this context, the less said about white Port, which comes in varying levels of sweetness, the better.[85]

Color is important in Port (so long as it is not white), one of the issues being that all the color has to be extracted from the grapes before spirits are added to stop fermentation.[86] So whereas a conventional red wine may macerate with the skins for two or three weeks, all the color for Port must be obtained in the first 36-48 hours. The traditional means of extraction was to tread grapes by foot in a trough (a lagares). The romantic myth is that this method was developed as the perfect way for gentle extraction (the pips do not get crushed, for example), but of course it owes its development to the fact that there was no electricity to run equipment, while labor was cheap.

Declining sources of labor, and increasing costs, have made this unattractive, but it's true that most alternative methods for maceration are too harsh. One of the best new systems is the robotic foot developed by Symington, which imitates the ability of the human foot to crush the grapes without squeezing the pips. This is only really practical for the high-end; cheaper Ports are made from grapes

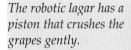

The robotic lagar has a piston that crushes the grapes gently.

Photograph kindly provided by Symington Family Estates.

fermented in autovinification tanks, where the release of carbon dioxide is used to provide the energy source for maceration. (Autovinification was necessary originally because electricity was neither widespread nor reliable.)

Port can be matured either in Port houses in the Douro or in their headquarters in Vila Nova de Gaia, the sister city of Oporto on the other side of the Douro river. Until the recent advent of air conditioning, the location made a significant difference. It is much drier in the Douro, and there are seasonal changes of up to 20 °C. A cooler climate made Vila Nova a more suitable locale for maturing the Port, and most higher quality wines were matured there. Under modern conditions the choice of location makes less difference.

Having originated with the addition of brandy to stabilize wine in casks for shipping, Port continued to be exported in cask until relatively recently. Bottling in London was more common than bottling in Portugal after the second world war.[87] In 1968, only 8% of Port was bottled before export.[88] In 1970, it became mandatory to bottle vintage Port at source, and since 1997 all Port has been bottled locally. Another change was that before 1986 Port could be exported only from Vila Nova de Gaia. But this meant that only shippers with Port lodges in Vila Nova were able to export. Allowing individual producers to export directly from the Douro opened the way for bottlings from single quintas.[89]

To Fortify or Not To Fortify

The Port industry owed much of its organization to the measures taken by Pombal, the Prime Minister of Portugal from 1755, when he introduced the first definition and regulations for Port. Production of Port was limited to the Douro valley, and a monopoly called the Real Companhia das Vinhas do Alto Douro was established to protect authenticity and set prices. In spite of howls of protest, the British shippers of the Factory House were excluded from the organization.

The situation continued until Pombal fell from power in 1777, when a free market was reestablished.

Pombal's monopoly was replaced by a privately owned successor, the Real Companhia Velha, which opened up the Douro, leading to expansion of vineyards into the Cima Corgo and the Douro Superior. During the mid nineteenth century the custom of declaring the vintage developed, and slowly the distinction began to emerge between Port that was drunk young and Port that was kept for aging.

By the mid nineteenth century, production had reached about 100,000 pipes, with roughly a quarter exported to Britain. (A pipe remains the traditional unit for Port, a large cask of old oak of about 534-550 liters.) In modern terms, this corresponds to about 6 million cases, a bit over half of today's level. Production went up and down during the first half of the twentieth century, but the main legacy from that period is the *beneficio* system, established in the 1930s to control the production of Port in response to problems caused by over production. The IVP (Instituto do Vinho do Porto: now the IVDP) sets a limit for the amount of wine that can be fortified to make Port. Wine in excess of the limit can be sold as dry table wine, but cannot be fortified. The total depends on the previous year's sales and the level of stocks held by the Port houses. It is apportioned among the growers on the basis of the classification of their vineyards.[91] The problem with this system is that, although it pays attention to potential quality (as seen in the classification of the vineyard) it does not reflect actual quality on the ground. "It is urgent that we eliminate the distortion and asymmetry caused by this antiquated system," says Adrian Bridges, managing director of Taylor Fladgate, a major group of Port houses.[92]

The beneficio system evens out the level of Port production against the background of vintage fluctuation. Over the past twenty years, Port has averaged around 9 million cases per year. The proportion of wine allowed to be fortified is usually between a half and two thirds of production. There is a big financial consequence, because grapes with a beneficio sell for about five times the price of

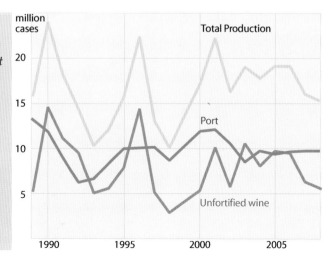

Port is more than half the production of the Douro.[90]

The volume of Port is about 79% wine and 21% added brandy.

grapes without one, reflecting the price difference between Port and Douro red wine. The grapes approved for Port are generally the highest quality, but evidently the system has not driven out the production of low quality grapes. A free market would no doubt result in more fluctuation, but growers with lower quality vineyards would probably no longer see their prices artificially inflated by the beneficio. These days the beneficio is more about protecting the small growers than ensuring quality.

Port is by far and away the most valuable wine produced in Portugal,[93] but this disguises a multitude of sins. People usually talk about two types of Port. Bottled-aged wines are bottled after only a short period in cask, and must therefore be aged in the bottle. Wood-aged wines have a longer period in cask, so the wine is ready to drink once it is bottled. But this distinction is not terribly useful because in effect, only vintage-style Ports come into the first category; everything else is ready to drink when bottled. The Port Institute, the regulatory body, draws a distinction between standard Ports and premium Ports, with production running about 80% standard and 20% premium. However, the premium category includes "tawny reserve" and "ruby reserve," neither of which improves significantly with further age.

A more meaningful distinction is really between Ports where age is important and those where age is not significant. In the first category are vintage-style Ports and aged tawny Ports; everything else is consumed in the relatively short term. By this criterion, the quality stuff is really confined to vintage, LBV, and aged tawny (with one or two other quality classes produced in amounts too small to count).[95] So basically the high end consists of about 1% vintage Port, 4% LBV, and 5% aged tawnies.[96] This is the tail that wags the dog: only about 10% of sales, but producing roughly a third of the total annual revenue of €275 million. The old British connection shows in the Anglo-Saxon dominance of the high-end market. Britain and the United States are by far the most important purchasers of quality Ports.

Although there has been increased concentration of the Port houses, they have mostly retained their individual reputations and styles. In the 1950s there

Most Port is produced ready to drink.[94]

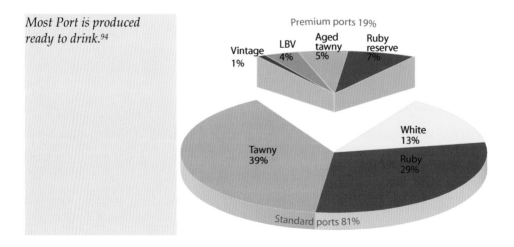

were about 80 independent producers; today there are around 30. There was a spate of purchases by international conglomerates in the 1970s and 1980s, but after 2000 most of them sold off the Port houses. This allowed some of the older houses to pick up the pieces, and now Port production is mostly concentrated into three large groups, Symington, Taylor Fladgate, and Sogrape.[97] Symington is the largest quality producer, followed by Taylor Fladgate; both are descendants of old British shippers, and the British influence remains strong. Each claims roughly 30% of the premium Port market.[98] Sogrape is a large producer of wine in Portugal, with interests extending all over the country. Aside from a few houses owned by foreign owners, the remaining houses are independent, and mostly under Portuguese ownership.

Perhaps because sweet wines are less of an acquired taste than savory wines, Port has retained its market where Sherry has lost its. Port has a long association with high living and over indulgence, going back to the days when English clubs had their "three bottle men," so named because they would drink three bottles of Port a day. The high incidence of gout among this class of elderly and indulgent gentleman led to the idea that consumption of Port causes gout. This is largely a myth, although not without a nugget of truth. Gout is an arthritic disease of the joints, caused by accumulation of uric acid. While it is conceivable in principle that high alcohol could contribute to this, it is not at all obvious why Port should be any worse than any other form of alcohol. In fact, recent studies suggest that

About half the Port houses, representing the majority of Port production, are in the hands of Symington or Taylor Fladgate, although the individual houses continue to function independently to produce Port under their original names.

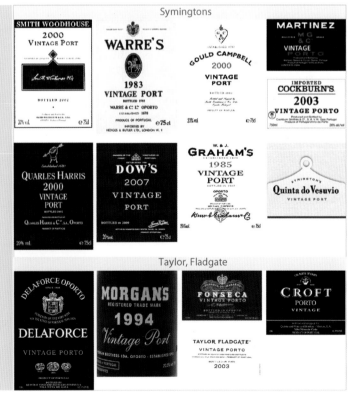

insofar as there is any connection, beer and spirits are more damaging.[99] The nugget of truth may be that Port could have been contaminated with lead, which has toxic effects producing a form of gout called saturnine gout.

Rotten to the Core

Well actually not to the core. Noble Rot, which gives sweet wines such as Sauternes their delicious piquant, honeyed quality, happens when the fungus Botrytis cinerea forms a mold on the surface of the grape. If it actually gets inside the grape, noble rot turns to gray rot, and the wine is ruined by unpleasant, mushroomy, moldy aromas and flavors. But botrytized grapes, although they look quite disgusting, give enormous concentration and sweetness to the wine.

The requirement for making botrytized wines is a long, warm, humid autumn, which creates the conditions for the fungus to infect and thrive on the grapes. These conditions are fulfilled wonderfully well in the area of Sauternes and Barsac, to the south and west of Bordeaux, essentially at the tail end of the Graves appellation, where the cool Ciron tributary empties into the warmer Garonne river. Autumnal mists created by the humidity sweep across from the junction of the rivers to the vineyards, persisting until burned off by the morning sun.[100] The alternation of damp mornings and dry afternoons (which let the surface of the grape dry out) is perfect for generating botrytis.[101]

Barsac lies on the left bank of the river, north of the Ciron, and Sauternes lies adjacent, just to its south. Barsac and Sauternes are far and away the best appellations for producing dessert wines. It would be a fine taster who can systematically tell the difference, but there is more clay in the soil in Barsac, and a substratum of limestone. This gives Barsac higher acidity in the wine, whereas Sauternes tend to be more powerful. Immediately to the north of Barsac is the lesser area of Cérons, and across the river are the appellations of Cadillac, Loupiac, and St. Croix de Mont. Wines are also made from the same grape varie-

Botrytis starts as small speckles on the grape, and finally the entire berry shrivels up. It develops unevenly in the bunch.

Botrytized sweet
wines are produced in
the region where the
Ciron meets the
Garonne. The top
regions are Barsac and
Sauternes on the left
bank. The Sauternes
AOC includes the
villages of Sauternes,
Fargues, Bommes, and
Preignac.[102]

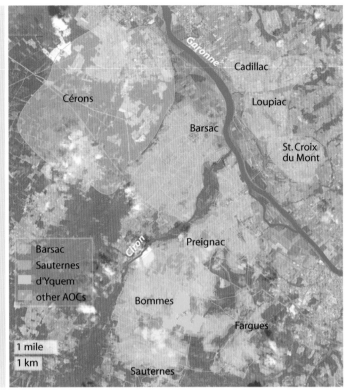

ties in the region of Bergerac to the southeast, including the appellation of Monbazillac, but do not achieve the same concentration. (Emphasizing the difference
between the requirements for producing sweet versus dry wine, the vineyards in
Monbazillac tend to face north, where fogs develop best, as opposed to facing
south to catch the sun.)

Botrytis is extremely capricious, usually attacking the grapes only three or so
times per decade. Of course, the moist, humid conditions that are ideal for botrytis are anathema to producing quality red wine, so the great vintages for dessert
wines do not usually coincide with those for red wines. In the first decade of this
century, for example, some vintages stand out for one or the other. 2000 was a
great red wine vintage but mediocre for Sauternes. 2001 was decent for reds but
superb for Sauternes. 2007 was average for reds but very good for Sauternes.
2005 was the one vintage that was top notch for both red and sweet white wines.

Any vendange tardive (late harvest) has a desiccating effect, because the
grapes dry out with the prolonged hang time. The grapes are said to be passerillé. Botrytis infection enhances this effect. The fungus breaks down the wax on
the surface of the grape, making the skin more permeable so that moisture can
escape. As the grape shrivels, the juice inside becomes more and more concentrated. By the time the grapes are harvested, the grape may be less than half of its
original weight, with sugar concentration increased by a third. In a great vintage,
many grapes will be botrytized, but in other vintages they may merely be passerillé by the late harvest.

The Ciron river is a cool, lazy stream that creates mist when it empties into the warmer Garonne.

This turn in the river is close to the village of Barsac.

The fungus does much more than concentrate the grapes. It consumes a major part of the tartaric and malic acids, but generates some acetic acid, giving that delicious piquancy to the wine. Botrytis also increases the level of glycerol. The other characteristic of botrytized wine is a honeyed taste, due to fungal production of a compound called Sotolon. On the other hand, botrytis destroys esters and terpenes, so that grape varietal character is usually lost, and it becomes more difficult to tell whether a botrytized wine originated from Muscat or Riesling. But the wine gains more complexity from the fungal additions than it loses.[103] Sotolon is produced by a series of chemical conversions from an amino acid, and it's not unique to botrytis, but is also produced by the so-called flor yeasts that grow on top of barrels of Sherry or vin jaune. At higher concentrations, its taste can change from honey to curry. The combination of high sugar concentration, increased acetic acid, glycerol, and Sotolon give botrytized wines a common sweet, piquant, viscous, honeyed impression.

Botrytis is generally associated with sweet dessert wines, but of course it can occur whenever there is a late harvest with humid conditions. It is relatively rare for it to be found in dry wines, but there are some interesting exceptions, most notably at Savennières in the Loire. At the Coulée de Serrant monopole, Nicolas Joly makes a dry white wine from grapes harvested over a period of several weeks, usually with a proportion of botrytized grapes coming from the later harvests. The botrytis adds a honeyed complexity to the savory, mineral notes usually associated with Chenin Blanc in Savennières.

Sweet wines in Bordeaux typically reverse the proportions of grape varieties used in dry white wine, with 80% coming from Sémillon and 20% from Sauvignon Blanc. Sémillon is particularly susceptible to botrytis, and its thin skin allows the fungus to penetrate more easily. Other great botrytized dessert wines are made from Riesling (in Germany, Austria, and Alsace), from Chenin Blanc (in the Loire), and from Furmint in Tokaji (Hungary). The common feature is the presence of a body of water (rivers or lakes) and warm conditions in the autumn.

This dependence was brought home forcefully at the Neusiedlersee See in Austria, a shallow lake that loses a good proportion of its water by evaporation each year; after the lake dried out completely in 1865, there was no botrytis for several years until it filled up again.

What do you do if botrytis does not develop? You can make a sweet wine simply from late harvest grapes, more passerillé than botrytized; indeed, this is not uncommon. Barring that, you can try to make a dry white wine, but there are two practical impediments. By the time you know whether or not there will be good passerillage or botrytis, it's too late to harvest the grapes for conventional vinification; and the vineyards in the Sauternes area are generally planted in the 80:20 Sémillon:Sauvignon ratio that's suitable for dessert wines rather than 20:80 ratio that would be used for a dry white Graves. However, some châteaux now regularly make at least some dry white wine as a hedge against harvest conditions. The first, and most famous, is Y (pronounced Ygrec) of Château d'Yquem, produced since 1959. Several other châteaux have followed suit, and slowly the white wines have become a limited objective in their own right as opposed to an emergency measure.

Botrytis is almost always a natural process. You might wonder why Nature couldn't be helped along a bit by spraying with botrytis spores. In fact, this was tried in California in the 1950s, when winemaker Myron Nightingale of Cresta Blanca vineyard successfully sprayed botrytis on to Sémillon and Sauvignon Blanc grapes. The climate is too dry for Botrytis to take hold naturally in the vineyard, but if both spores and moisture are provided, healthy grapes can be infected after harvesting. It takes about two weeks for the grapes to shrivel up in the winery, effectively doubling their sugar concentration.[104] The technique was used to make Beringer's Late Harvest Riesling in the 1980s; it's also been used in Australia.[105] Of course, even though metabolism is pretty much stopped for grapes sitting on the vine in late autumn, there's a difference between gradual botrytis in the vineyard and sudden botrytis in the winery. If there have been attempts to induce botrytis in the vineyard, they must generally have failed, although one winemaker in Portugal uses this approach on an experimental basis, with spores sprayed to start the infection, moisture provided by daily sprinkling with water, and humidity kept high with netting over the grapevines. It's probably only tenable on a very small scale.

At least three countries claim to have originated the production of wine from rotten grapes in spite of their appearance. In Hungary, the story goes that the 1650 vintage was delayed because Abbott Maté Szepsi, in charge of production at the Zsuzsanna Lorántfly estate in Tokaji, fled because of the impending Ottoman invasion; by the time he returned, some grapes were rotten, were pressed separately, and to everyone's surprise gave a magnificent wine.[106] At Schloss Johannisberg in Germany's Rheingau, permission to begin the harvest in 1775 failed to reach the estate from the Prince Abbott in a timely manner because the messenger was delayed by bandits. Stories placing the origins with Sauternes in the nineteenth century, and particularly with a delay in the harvest at Château d'Yquem in 1847 because the Marquis de Lur-Saluces was delayed in returning from a trip to Russia, can easily be dismissed. The Rules of Cultivation of Châ-

teau Filhot (a property owned at the time by Yquem) stated in 1740 that the fact
that the wine was made from rotten grapes should never be mentioned to customers![107] A memoir of 1716 mentions the selection of shriveled grapes, and even
earlier, in 1666 it was stated that the harvest did not usually start before mid
October. It's unclear when sweet wine actually began to be produced in Sauternes, but it seems characteristic of Bordeaux that its origins should have been
hidden.

Picking the grapes is a tricky business. Botrytis develops unevenly, so it's rare
for more than a few grapes in a bunch to be fully botrytized at any given moment. If you have the resources, grapes can be picked, berry by berry, over
several successive tries. Château d'Yquem can afford to have pickers armed with
tweezers go through the vineyards five or six times over a six week period,
selecting only the fully botrytized grapes at each pass. The overall yield is so
small that each vine gives only about one glass of wine. Lacking such resources,
lesser châteaux may resort to picking whole bunches and then sorting out the
botrytized grapes back at the ranch.[108]

All this makes it seem reasonable that Sauternes should be very sweet yet
have high alcohol. But the regulations require only a must weight of 221 g/l
(which corresponds to potential alcohol about 14% if the vine is vinified to dryness). So how does Sauternes typically come to have about 14% alcohol but
considerable residual sugar? To make a typical Sauternes naturally, the grapes
need to reach Brix of 24-25 (14% potential alcohol) by the time botrytis infection
begins; then fungal infection will increase sugar levels to around 310 g/l (20%
potential alcohol). Fermentation until the yeast die off is likely to proceed to
around 14% alcohol (a bit lower than the nominal limit of 15% completion because the effects of botrytis include inhibiting fermentation). This will leave a
wine that is naturally sweet, with around 75-100 g/l residual sugar.

Roughly the same sugar level is found in a Beerenauslese from Germany or
an SGN (selection de grain noble) from Alsace, both representing highly botrytized wines. But the difference is that with the Beerenauslese or SGN, you are
guaranteed that all the sugar will be natural, because chaptalization is forbidden.
In Sauternes, strangely it is permitted, making a mockery of the requirement for
a minimum must weight. In a great year, when botrytis concentrates the grapes,
this is not much of an issue: no one would need or want to add sugar. But in a
year with little botrytis, the only way to get to the appropriate level of sweetness
may be to chaptalize. Now nominally, sugar added before fermentation will be
converted to alcohol, but of course any sugar over the limit of 14-15% alcohol
will remain unfermented. It doesn't much matter which actual sugar molecules
get fermented; the fact is that some of the sweetness in the wine came from the
bag not the grape. I believe chaptalization should be banned for Sauternes, and
indeed, for all wines containing any residual sugar.

The common feature in all authentically sweet wines is that fermentation
stops before completion; the wine is sweet because it contains unfermented
sugar. "Authentic" means that the sugar in the wine comes from the grapes, as
opposed to wines that are sweet because sugar in one form or another was added
either before or after. In my view, wines in this latter category tend to be syn-

thetic. Sweetening wine is illegal in Europe, but it is perfectly legal, and actually quite common, in the New World.

Concentration, Desiccation, and Crystallization

Concentration is the name of the game for producing sweet wines. By one means or another, sugar concentration has to be high enough to leave residual sugar when fermentation completes. Every method of achieving concentration stamps its mark on the wine. Botrytis, of course, adds its typical spectrum of aromas and flavors as the result of the hard work put in by the fungus. Other methods of concentrating the sugar include exposure to both heat and cold. In warm climates, grapes may be put out after harvesting to dry during the autumn, so the sugar becomes concentrated by desiccation. In cool climates, grapes may be left on the vine to freeze during the start of winter, so water crystallizes out. And, of course, in this day and age there are machines to mimic these natural processes.

Grapes hanging to dry for producing Vin Santo at Altesino in Chianti.

In the south of France and the Jura, they lay out the grapes on straw mats for two months after harvesting to make a Vin de Paille (wine of straw). In Tuscany, they hang the grapes from the rafters in well-ventilated attics to dry out during the autumn to make a Vin Santo. Farther north in Valpolicella they produce Recioto by drying the grapes on mats for up to four months.[109] In Jerez they dry Pedro Ximénez grapes on the sand for a few days to make the delicious sweet style PX wine. The common feature in all these methods of desiccation is that, together with the loss of water, a slightly oxidized character creeps into the berries, giving the wine a raisiny quality, and a deep color, depending on the length of exposure.

You can also get oxidative qualities because of the way wine is matured, most notably in the *vin doux naturel* of southern France. In spite of the literal translation (naturally sweet wine), the sweetness here comes from fortifying the wine before fermentation has been completed. The principle is the same as in Port production. The level of sweetness depends on how far fermentation is allowed to proceed. The best known of these wines are made from Muscat, especially Muscat de Beaumes de Venise (in the Rhône) and Muscat de St. Jean de Minervois (in the Languedoc), or from Grenache, especially the Banyuls and Maury appellations of Roussillon.

These days most vin doux naturels are made using squeaky clean modern techniques, but traditionally oxidation was part of the production, and this is still followed by some producers. The most traditional wines develop an oxidized flavor spectrum called *rancio*, resulting from long maturation in wood and/or in glass demi-johns kept outside in the sun. The wine does not necessarily carry a vintage, but may come from a blend of several years. They are very sweet and sticky.

It's hard to believe you can make wine from frozen grapes in the middle of winter. Not surprisingly, there are various stories as to how this first happened. The one certainty seems to be that it was in Germany, around the end of the

Sweet wines maturing in glass demi-johns in the sun at Mas Amiel in Roussillon.

Frozen grapes hang on the vine until well into the winter in order to make Eiswein in the Rheinhessen.

eighteenth century or start of the nineteenth. Either in Würzburg in 1794, or in Dromersheim in 1829, unusually cold spells are supposed to have frozen the grapes before they could be harvested; and the winemakers discovered accidentally that crushing the frozen grapes gave an unusually sweet wine. Once the temperature stays below freezing for any protracted period, water crystallizes into ice within the grape, effectively concentrating everything else. If you harvest the grapes and crush them while they are still frozen, the ice is left behind, and the must becomes extremely concentrated. Because acidity is concentrated as well as sugar, the sweetness is balanced.

Eiswein was made rarely, with only ten vintages taking advantage of freak frosts between 1875 and 1962,[110] until more reliable techniques were developed by Hans Georg Ambrosi in the Rheingau in the 1960s. They include using special plastic sheets (which are porous to humidity) to protect the grapevines. It's a risky business, and Eiswein is made in tiny quantities only in occasional years. Many producers say that the costs make it unprofitable, and they do it only for the prestige, but Ambrosi famously calculated that Eiswein was in fact more profitable than making ordinary wine from the same grapes (although the calculation remains controversial).[111]

Since then, Eiswein has been produced when conditions permit, which means that the grapes must survive in good condition until there is a period of cold weather remaining below –8 °C. Sometimes the grapes are not harvested until January (but they are labeled with the vintage of the previous year).[112] Grapes are picked at dead of night in order to be pressed while still at their coldest temperatures. One side effect of global warming has been a decline in Eiswein production, because winters have not been cold enough.

Eiswein is usually made from Riesling, with a sugar level comparable to Beerenauslese (the penultimate level in the classification of botrytized wines). It shows marvelously concentrated purity, but does not (in my opinion) achieve the complexity of a botrytized wine. (Botrytis would be lethal to Eiswein production, since the grapes would simply rot.) Eiswein is also occasionally produced in Austria, and ice wine, to give it its English name, has been produced in Canada since 1974, on the Niagara peninsula, sometimes from Riesling and also from the Vidal hybrid (which is more reliable but gives much less refined wine). Canada's regulations for producing ice wine are even more restrictive than Germany's, with a Brix of 35 (equivalent to 325 g/l of sugar or potential alcohol 19%) required in the grapes, and a minimum residual sugar of at least 125 g/l required in the wine. Conditions in Canada are reliable, and ice wine can be produced every year, making Iniskillin of Niagara the world's largest producer of ice wines. Global warming does not seem to threaten the icy conditions in Niagara.

If freezing is all there is to making ice wine, why can't it be done by putting the grapes in a freezer? Well indeed it can be done, and this sort of mechanical approach is called cryoextraction. It's not legal in Europe or in Canada (where indeed they are uptight about conditions for ice wine, having taken it amiss when a producer in British Columbia trucked his grapes up a mountain to get to lower temperatures).[113] Basically the grapes are harvested as ripe as you can get them and then put in a freezer. They are pressed while still frozen, like an authentic ice wine. What's the difference? It usually seems that the imitation, sometimes pejoratively called ice box wine, has simpler flavors; even though conditions for natural Eiswein are so cold that metabolism must have stopped in the berry, the protracted period on the vine seems to produce something more complex than can be achieved in the freezer. "By hanging in the fresh air, with rain and with storms, the grapes get a totally different taste. There is much more mineral enrichment and the flavor is different," says Dirk Richter of Max Ferdinand Richter.[114] Or perhaps it's just that the grapes used for ice box wine are of lower quality, and the process can do no more than concentrate whatever is in the grape at the time of harvest. But do Eisweins improve with age in the bottle? Probably not: they are more likely to lose that initial piercing freshness.

Tokaji from the Ashes

Tokaji's claims to be the first to have discovered the delights of rotten grapes may be apocryphal, but it is certainly a very old wine-producing region, and it has a unique method for making sweet wine. First a base wine is made like any ordinary dry white table wine from ordinary, healthy grapes. Botrytized grapes are collected separately and stored until December. They are pressed to form a paste, called the aszú paste (aszú means desiccated in Hungarian), which is added to the base wine.[115] This restarts fermentation, but the paste has so much sugar that the wine remains sweet when this second fermentation finally finishes, often several months later.

No one knows when the use of botrytized grapes was introduced, but there are references to Aszú from the sixteenth century.[116, 117] The legend for the origins of the paste is that attempts to make wine from the grapes that had dried on the vine when the villagers returned after the war with the Turks gave a must that was too dense, so Abbé Szepsi refreshed it with table wine from the previous vintage.[118] One small problem with this account is that the Ottoman invasion occurred in 1650, but Abbé Szepsi had died in 1633.[119]

However, the propensity to form botrytis was a factor when the vineyards were classified into first, second, and third class between 1730 and 1772,[120] which was perhaps the earliest classification of vineyards in the world. Evidently by then the production of sweet botrytized wines must have been the norm. Of course, in Tokaji as everywhere else, botrytis is capricious: part of the quality of the aszú grapes is due to botrytis, part is due to drying out with the late harvest (passerillage), and the relative proportion of the two effects varies from vintage to vintage, just as it does in Sauternes.

The Tokaji region lies at the northeastern corner of Hungary.[121] The town itself is at the southern tip of the appellation, at the confluence of two rivers, the Bodrog and the Tisza, that create the necessary humid conditions for growth of botrytis. There are about 5,000 hectares of classified vineyards, running parallel with the Bodrog along the southerly, volcanic slopes of the Zemplén hills. The

The black mold of Cladosporium cellare covers everything in the humid cellars in Tokaji but keeps the air fresh.

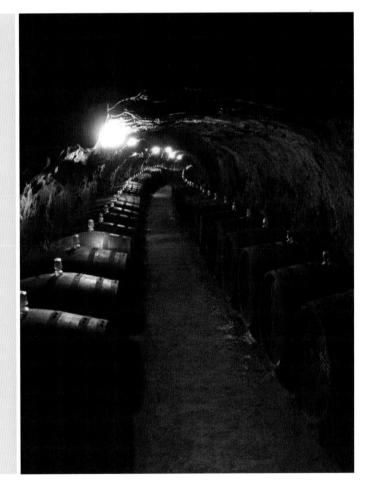

climate is continental with dry, hot summers and cold winters, but the long autumn produces misty mornings and sunny afternoons. Grapes are traditionally picked only after October 28 and before the first snow.

The sweet wine of Tokaji is called Tokaji Aszú and labeled as 3-6 puttonyos, depending on the amount of paste employed. The unit of paste is based on the puttonyo, a tub holding 20-25 kg of grapes that was traditionally used to collect the botrytized berries; a three puttonyos wine would be made by adding three puttonyos to one cask of wine (the casks being a traditional size of 136 liters called Gönci[122]). There is also a wine called Eszencia Aszú, which goes beyond even the 6 puttonyos level; the sugar level is so high that a special yeast is needed for fermentation. (This should not be confused with Tokaji Eszencia, which is made from free run juice released from botrytized grapes before the Aszú paste is prepared. It's fantastically viscous and sweet, but not in my opinion really as interesting as the Aszú wines.) As production in Tokaji has been modernized, casks have been replaced by stainless steel fermentation, and sweetness is now measured directly in terms of residual sugar.[123]

The classic description of adding paste to the base wine is bit misleading. In fact, various procedures are used. The aszú preparation may take the form of the traditional paste but also may be used in the form of whole berries. In the 1800s, it was more common to add the aszú preparation to a partially fermenting must, then in the 1900s it became usual to add the paste to the base wine, and now opinion has switched to the view that the most complex results are obtained by adding the botrytized berries to the must. The fermentation lasts 1-2 months; typically new oak is used for the highest grades (5-6 puttonyos), with 1-year or 2-year oak used for lower grades. The consistent high humidity in the region extends to the cellars, with the consequence that evaporation during maturation causes loss of alcohol, typically 0.5 to 1.0% per year, so the initial level produced by fermentation, often at 13% or more, is reduced before bottling.

Long fermentation and maturation in old oak traditionally produced wines in an oxidized style. As production collapsed in Tokaji during the communist years, winemaking skills were lost, and excessive oxidation may have become more a demonstration of poor winemaking than due to traditional style. The region revived when foreign investors took positions in the 1990s, spurred by the British wine writer Hugh Johnson with the formation of the Royal Tokaji Wine Company in 1989, followed rapidly by many others.[124] What convinced Johnson of the potential quality was wines that had been made in secret in a garage by producer István Szepsy using grapes he had held back from the Communist rulers.[125]

Some of the new producers are now making wines in a modern (non oxidized) style. Nobody really knows to what extent oxidation was deliberate in the pre-Communist years, and this remains a controversial debate between "traditionalists" and modernists. At one point, in 1999, wines in the modern style were rejected by the Wine Authorization Board. Today there is more acceptance of the fact that there are two styles of producers, some avoiding oxidation and some showing it.[126]

The grapes grown in Tokaji today are Furmint, Hárslevelü, and Muscat. None of these are mentioned in an account of the region written in 1576, when the main grape was apparently called Porcins;[127] we have no idea what this might have been. At some unknown point over the next three centuries, the modern varieties were introduced, and these became the only varieties when the vineyards were replanted following the arrival of phylloxera at the end of the nineteenth century.[128]

Furmint is by far the majority grape, accounting for some 70% of plantings. Hárslevelü is most of the rest, with a small amount of Muscat, known locally as yellow Muscat, which is the same as Muscat Blanc à Petit Grains. Furmint gives the wines high acidity, while Hárslevelü is very susceptible to botrytis. A more recent introduction is a new grape called Zéta or Oremus (a cross between Furmint and Bouvier).[129]

Not all Tokaji is sweet. Inclusion of "Aszú" on the label means the wine will be sweet, but there simply aren't enough botrytized grapes for the entire crop to make aszú wine. The remaining wine is a standard dry white table wine, with Furmint sometimes sold under a varietal label. The dry white is not especially distinguished, and it definitely has a problem competing in the international marketplace.

There's another style called Szamorodni, which is made from bunches that may include some botrytized grapes (Szamorodni means "as it comes"). It is fermented dry and aged in oak casks, where it develops a flor similar to fino Sherry. In fact, it tastes very like Sherry, although it tends to be a little less concentrated. The producers don't really quite know what to do with it.

And just to make things more complicated yet, there is an unregulated category simply called late harvest, made directly from berries that are harvested late in the same way as late harvested wines in other regions. This has the advantage for the producers that it does not involve the high cost and long process of making an aszú wine, and can provide a very necessary supplement to the cash flow. Some producers feel that the production of late harvest wines undercuts the basis for Tokaji.

So what is the real Tokaji? Its unique feature is the Aszú wine made with the paste, but (in my opinion) you have to try the 5 puttonyos to get its full complexity; the 3 puttonyos is sweet and pleasant but not complex, while the 6 puttonyos can be a little heavy, as can the Eszencia Aszú. The 5 puttonyos is the perfect balance, and whether in the modern or traditional style is unmistakably different.

20

Truth in Labeling

I HAVE A FRIEND WHO IS A SMALL WINEMAKER in the United States (well, he may not be my friend any longer after this book appears), whose winery is stuffed with chemicals that would get him fined or perhaps even jailed in France. Larger New World wineries have "chemical rooms" where the stuff is kept under lock and key. As well as the usual agents used for fining and so on, there may be acids, tannins, coloring agents, and all sorts of additives. None of this is illegal or indeed even controversial: it is unremarkable, especially in large operations, for wine to be "corrected" for sugar, acid, tannin, color by whatever means is regarded as cost effective. Yet the same treatments in Europe create controversy: is this a double standard?

Because winemaking is so highly regulated in Europe, we are highly sensitized to which techniques are banned or allowed. So it remains a running controversy as to whether and how much sugar can be added for chaptalization, whether techniques such as reverse osmosis should be permitted, or what forms of oak may or may not be used to flavor the wine. Any change in the rules is highly visible, and infractions are a matter for publicity. So while we may not necessarily know whether any particular wine is treated in a certain manner, it's public knowledge as to whether a particular approach is permitted in a given appellation.

The contrasting freedom in the New World makes it completely unremarkable whether a wine is matured in oak barrels or tainted with oak flavors by adding some oak dust or extract. Only really extreme cases, such as adding flavors, attract any comment. No one knows or cares whether a wine is made a little sweeter by tipping in some sugar or made a little sharper by adding some acidity, although in Europe such actions would be a matter for shocked publicity and possibly even criminal action. Does the double standard mean that wine is a more natural product in Europe?

A consumer charter for wine requiring truth in labeling would reveal some interesting things on the back label. "This wine shows delicate nuances of French oak" might have to be replaced by "Oak flavors were added by dunking oak chips in the wine for 48 hours." "This wine shows a perfect balance of acidity and sweetness" might need to be changed to "Tartaric acid was used to boost the acidity and some sugar was added to cut the dry finish." As for chaptalization, who wants to say, "This was not a very ripe vintage, so alcohol was boosted 20% by adding some beet sugar to the wine before it was fermented?" And for those deeply colored wines, perhaps honesty would require a note saying, "That deep color and *je ne sais quoi* aroma of a classic hybrid come from the judicious addition of a tiny amount of Mega Purple."

Would such changes serve a useful purpose? Well yes, if they stopped the deception that expensive options had been used. After all, if a consumer can be fooled by superficial oak flavors coming from chips that cost a few cents a bag instead of from barrels costing several hundred dollars each, what's the incentive for producers to stay with quality? Just as bad money drives out good, so cheap imitations will undercut the real thing. And there's the rub: are the cheap imitations inferior? We might like to believe that doing it the authentic way, using oak barrels, minimizing additives, and so on, will produce a better wine: but does it?

The situation for a consumer who wants to buy a natural product is both better and worse for wine compared with food. Organic produce is widely available and clearly labeled as such, whereas certified organic wines are rare. Unfortunately, however, organic food is a farce, and there's no guarantee an "organic" chicken will have been treated any better than a battery chicken or that it will taste any better (in fact it may well be the result of similar industrial mass production).[1] An organic label on wine really refers mostly to viticultural practices; there will not have been any pesticides or other such treatments, and the grapes will have a natural origin. There's less emphasis on winemaking, although, ironically, the first organic wines acquired a bad reputation because of a winemaking issue; sulfur dioxide was so low that many were spoiled. But organic or biodynamic certification somewhat bypasses the issue of whether the wine is natural, whether it was made without undue manipulation, no matter how the grapes were grown. What we really need is a label to indicate that a wine was produced naturally, without artificially adjusting its alcohol, acidity, or sweetness, beefing up the color, adding oak flavors or tannins, and so on.

We have to decide what sort of wine we want and how much we care about how it is made. The agri-industrial complex can make technically better wines, better adjusted to the taste of the average consumer, than any individual small producer. But do we want wine to suffer the same sort of industrialization that has made so much food tasteless, or are we prepared to pay the price, in the form of imperfections as well as higher cost, for a natural product? Is it possible for both to survive in the same market?

Bibliography

Beeston, John, *The Wine Regions of Australia* (Unwin and Allen, Australia, 1999).

Belfrage, Nicholas, *Barolo to Valpolicella: the Wines of Northern Italy* (Faber & Faber, London, 1999).

Belfrage, Nicholas, *Brunello to Zibibbo: the Wines of Tuscany, Central and Southern Italy* (Faber & Faber, London, 2001).

Bert, Pierre, *In Vino Veritas. L'Affaire des Vins de Bordeaux* (Albin Michel, Paris, 1975).

Bird, Owen, *Rheingold: the German Wine Renaissance* (Arima Publishing, London, 2005).

Blom, Philippe, *The Wines of Austria* (Faber & Faber, London, 2000).

Brook, Stephen, *The Complete Bordeaux* (Mitchell Beazley, London, 2007).

Coates, Clive, *The Wines of Burgundy* (University of California Press, Berkeley, 2008).

Cooper, Michael, *Wine Atlas of New Zealand* (Hodder Moa Beckett, 2002).

Dion, Roger, *Histoire de la Vigne et du Vin en France des Origines au XIX Siècle* (Paris, 1959).

Faith, Nicholas, *Australia's Liquid Gold* (Mitchell Beazley, London, 2002).

Fielden, Christopher, *Is This the Wine You Ordered, Sir?: The Dark Side of the Wine Trade* (Christopher Helm, London, 1989).

Garner, Michael & Paul Merritt, *Barolo. Tar and Roses* (Wine Appreciation Guild, San Francisco, 1991).

Goode, Jamie, *The Science of Wine. From Vine to Glass* (Mitchell Beazley, London, 2005).

Hallgarten, Fritz, *Wine Scandal* (Sphere Books, 1987).

Halliday, James, *Wine Atlas of Australia and New Zealand* (HarperCollins, Australia, 1999).

Jackson, Ron. S., *Wine Science: Principles, Practice, Perception* (Academic Press, New York, 2000).

Jeffs, Julian, *Sherry, 4th edition* (Little Brown, New York, 1992).

Kramer, Matt, *New California Wine* (Running Press, Philadelphia, 2004).

Lapsley, James T, *Bottled Poetry: Napa Winemaking from Prohibition to the Modern Era* (University of California Press, Berkeley, 1997).

Lewin, Benjamin, *What Price Bordeaux?* (Vendange Press, Dover, 2009).

Livingstone-Learmonth, John, *The Wines of the Northern Rhône* (University of California Press, Berkeley, 2005).

Livingstone-Learmonth, John, *The Wines of the Rhône*, 3rd edition (Faber & Faber, London, 1992).

Mayson, Richard, *Port and the Douro* (Faber and Faber, London, 1999).

Mayson, Richard, *The Wines and Vineyards of Portugal* (Mitchell Beazley, London, 2003).

McGovern, Patrick E, *Ancient Wine: The Search for the Origins of Viniculture* (Princeton University Press, Princeton, 2003).

Penning-Rowsell, Edmund, *The Wines of Bordeaux, 6th edition* (Penguin Books, London, 1989).

Petrini, Carlo & Victtorio Mangnelli, *A Wine Atlas of the Langhe: The Greatest Barolo and Barbaresco Vineyards* (Slow Food Editors, 2003).

Pinney, Thomas, *A History of Wine in America : From Prohibition to the Present* (University of California Press, Berkeley, 2005).

Radford, John, *The Wines of Rioja* (Mitchell Beazley, London, 2004).

Richards, Peter, *The Wines of Chile* (Mitchell Beazley, London, 2006).

Rosso, Maurizio and Chris Meier, *The Mystique of Barolo* (Omega Edizione, 2002).

Stevenson, Tom, *The Wines of Alsace* (Faber & Faber, London, 1993).

Stevenson, Tom, *The World Encyclopedia of Champagne and Sparkling Wine* (Wine Appreciation Guild, San Francisco, 1999).

Sullivan, Charles L, *Napa Wine: A History from Mission Days to Present* (Wine Appreciation Guild, San Francisco, 1995).

Sullivan, Charles L, *Zinfandel: A History of a Grape and Its Wine* (University of California Press, Berkeley, 2003).

Taber, George, *To Cork or Not to Cork* (Scribner, New York, 2007).

Unwin, Tim, *Wine and the Vine: An Historical Geography of Viticulture and the Wine Trade* (Routledge, London, 1996).

Waldin, Monty, *Wines of South America* (Mitchell Beazley, London, 2003).

Wilson, James, *Terroir* (Wine Appreciation Guild, San Francisco, 1998).

Notes

References cited in the Bibliography are given in the notes by author and short title. Other references are given in full the first time cited in each chapter, and by author and short title with the indication *op. cit.* for subsequent citations in that chapter.

Organizations abbreviated by acronyms are:

AWBC: Australian Wine and Brandy Corporation.

AWRI: Australian Wine Research Institute.

BIVB: Bureau Interprofessionnel des Vins de Bourgogne.

CIVB: Conseil Interprofessionnel du Vin de Bordeaux.

CIVC: Comité interprofessionnel du Vin de Champagne

INAO: Institut National des Appellations d'Origine.

OIV: International Organization of Vine and Wine.

ONIVINS: Office National Interprofessionnel Des Vins (now known as VINIFLHOR).

USDA NASS: United States Department of Agriculture, National Agricultural Statistics Service.

TTB: United States Department of the Treasury; Alcohol and Tobacco Tax and Trade Bureau.

Chapter 1: The Grapevine

[1] A species is often defined as a group of organisms capable of interbreeding and producing fertile offspring. By this definition, all Vitis members would be one species. Because of the ability to interbreed, the exact number of Vitis subspecies is hard to define. However, I shall follow conventional terminology and describe the different varieties as "species" in the text.

[2] One of the best known of the other species is Vitis labrusca, which accounts for 80% of grape juice production in the United States. The Concord variety has been used to make wine, but the wine is marred by a characteristic "foxy" flavor.

[3] Most Vitis species are described as Euvitis (true Vitis). All Euvitis species are interfertile. In addition, there is a group of three species called Muscadinia. These split off from the Euvitis about 2 million years ago, and are found only in North America. They cannot breed with Euvitis species.

[4] Mutations suppressed development of male stamens in female plants and suppressed development of ovaries in male plants.

[5] Wild grapevines technically are known as Vitis vinifera ssp. silvestris and cultured grapevines are called Vitis vinifera ssp. sativa (or vinifera).

[6] McGovern, *Ancient Wine*, p. 7.

[7] Ibid., p. 72.

[8] Ibid., p. 16.

[9] Patrice This et al., *Historical Origins And Genetic Diversity Of Wine Grapes* (Trends in Genetics, 22, No. 9, 2006).

[10] R. Arroyo-Garcia. et al., *Multiple Origins Of Cultivated Grapevine (Vitis Vinifera L. Ssp. Sativa) Based On Chloroplast DNA Polymorphisms* (Molecular Ecology, 15, 3707-3714, 2006).

[11] Unwin, *Wine and the Vine*, p. 64.

[12] McGovern, *Ancient Wine*, p. 85.

[13] Theophrastus, *Enquiry into Plants*, trans. A. F. Horton, Heinemann, London, 1916.

[14] Unwin, *Wine and the Vine*, p. 118.

[15] Richard C. Selley, *The Winelands Of Britain: Past, Present & Prospective, 2nd Edition* (Petravin, London, 2008), pp. 13-19.

[16] Dion, *Histoire de la Vigne et du Vin*. p. 128.

[17] N. G. Davies and A. H. Gardiner, *Ancient Egyptian Paintings* (University of Chicago Press, Chicago, 1936), plate XXVIII.

[18] Dion, *Histoire de la Vigne et du Vin*, p. 3.

[19] The first Cistercian monastery, and the headquarters of the Cistercian Order, was established at Citeaux, close to Nuits St. Georges in Burgundy, in 1098. Kloster Eberbach, in the Rheingau of Germany, was established in 1136. These were the two most prominent monasteries in wine-producing regions. Both were important wine producers and innovators. The rules of the order (the "Carta Caritatis") required all monasteries to follow uniformity of custom. They were supposed to be self sufficient agriculturally. It is therefore possible that even the northern monasteries beyond the normal limits for wine production attempted to grow vines and produce wine. See also note 26.

[20] Unwin, *Wine and the Vine*, p. 146.

[21] Locations for monasteries producing wine were identified by Desmond Seward, *Monks and Wine* (Mitchell Beazley, London, 1979). The map shows only the major monasteries of the major orders. Identification of monasteries not making wine is less certain, but in all cases shown there are at least references to the purchase of wine by the monastery, and there is no record for wine having been produced in situ. For example, wine is known to have been produced at Altzel (south of Leipzig) and transported along the Elbe to Cistercian abbeys in northern Germany.

[22] Unwin, *Wine and the Vine*, p. 157.

[23] There were roughly 55 ha of vineyards, making the average vineyard around 1 ha in size (Tim Unwin, *Saxon and Early Normal Viticulture in England*, J. Wine Research, 1, 61-76, 1990). For a list of vineyards, see Selley, *The Winelands of Britain*, op. cit., p. 24.

[24] Hugh Barty-King, *A Tradition of English Wine: the Story of Two Thousand Years of English Wine Made from English Grapes* (Oxford Illustrated Press, Oxford, 1977), p. 40.

[25] By 1609 there were 139 vineyards in England and Wales, but later in the century the dissolution of the monasteries and the cooling climate led to their decline (ibid, p. 57).

[26] The Abbot of the Cistercian monastery near Bergen (the first to be established in Scandinavia, by monks who came from the Fountains Abbey in England in 1146), complained in 1338 that wine no longer came from England, suggesting that in Scandinavia even the Cistercians met their limit and were forced to bring in wine from other monasteries (Henry Goddard Leach, *The Relations Of The Norwegian With The English Church, 1066-1399, And Their Importance To Comparative Literature*, Daedalus, Proceedings of the American Academy of Arts and Sciences, XLIV, No. 20., May, 1909, p. 558.)

[27] Norman John Greville Pounds, *An Historical Geography of Europe, 1500-1840* (Cambridge University Press Archive, Cambridge, 1949), pp. 41-42.

[28] Unwin, *Wine and the Vine*, p. 162.

[29] Gary L. Peters, *American Winescapes: The Cultural Landscapes of America's Wine Country* (Boulder, CO, Westview Press, Swinchatt, Jonathan and Howell, 1997), p. 17.

[30] Its official name is now *Daktulosphaira vitifoliae*.

[31] Jeffrey Granett et al., *Biology and Management of Grape Phylloxera* (Annual Reviews Entomology, 46, 387-412, San Francisco, 2001), p. 403.

[32] Ibid., p. 396.

[33] Christy Campbell, *Phylloxera. How Wine Was Saved For The World* (Harper Perennial, London, 2007).

[34] Gilbert Garrier, *Le Phylloxéra. Une Guerre De Trente Ans 1970-1900* (Editions Albin Michel, Paris, 1989).

[35] Ibid., p. 38.

[36] The Concord grape takes its name from its origins in Concord, Massachusetts, where it was developed by Ephraim Bull. It was selected from 20,000 seedlings developed from Vitis labrusca. Because it is a hermaphrodite, it has been suggested that it has some Vitis vinifera in its parentage. One possibility is that the male parent (pollen donor) may have been Catawba, which is probably derived from Vitis labrusca and Vitis vinifera.

[37] Campbell, *Le Phylloxera*, p. 147.

[38] Le Journal Illustré, September 28, 1878. The legend says "The official commission visiting vineyards suspected of having phylloxera." The personages are not named, but are recognizable.

[39] In fact, it was recommended well before phylloxera became a problem as a means for improving quality in grapevines (Armand d'Armailhacq, *De La Culture Des Vignes, De La Vinification Et Des Vins Dans Le Médoc,* Chaumas, Bordeaux, 1867, p. 287).

[40] Although it proved impossible to graft Vitis vinifera directly on to Vitis berlandieri, a cross between the Chasselas variety of Vitis vinifera and Vitis berlandieri generated the "41B" rootstock that did well enough on chalk and had sufficient resistance to phylloxera.

[41] According to this analysis, in 1862 there were 2.32 million ha and in 1929 there were 1.6 million ha of vineyards. Distribution by département according to Genevieve Gavignaud, *Aspects de l'Evolution du Vignoble Français d'Après les Enquêtes Statistiques Agricoles (1806-1929).* In A. Huetz de Lemps et al. (Eds.), *Géographie Historique des Vignobles, Tome I Vignobles* Francais (CNRS, Paris, 1978), pp. 93-110.

[42] Author's discussion with Francesco Cinzano at Col d'Orcia, October 2009.

[43] A report issued by the University of California commented that AxR1 had "only moderate phylloxera resistance," but nonetheless recommended it as "the nearest approach to an all-purpose stock." (Lloyd A. Lider, *Phylloxera-resistant grape rootstocks for the Coastal Valleys of California,* Hillgardia, 27, 287-318, 1958). AxR1 then became the rootstock of choice. The University should have known better.

[44] Data source: Garrier, *Le Phylloxéra,* op. cit., p. 175.

[45] Granett, *Biology and Management of Grape Phylloxera,* op. cit., p. 401.

[46] A "biotype" is no more than a new variant of the species. Biotypes of phylloxera were first proposed in the 19th century, but could not be substantiated (Michael C. Smith, *Plant Resistance to Arthropods: Molecular and Conventional Approaches,* Springer Science & Business, 2005, pp. 347-352). Renewed claims in the late 1980s identified A and B biotypes, which supposedly differed in their ability to feed on AxR1. B multiplies twice as rapidly as A on AxR1 (Jeffrey Granett et al., *Evaluation Of Grape Rootstocks For Resistance To Type A And Type B Grape Phylloxera,* Am. J. Enol. Vitic. 38, 293-300, 1987). However, it is not clear whether this is relevant to the final outcome: death of the plant irrespective of biotype. In fact, there appears to be a general lack of correlation between genetic variants of phylloxera and susceptibility of rootstock hosts (A. Fornceck, *Ecological And Genetic Aspects Of Grape Phylloxera Daktulosphaira Vitifoliae (Hemiptera: Phylloxeridae) Performance On Rootstock Hosts,* Bull. Entomol. Res. 91, 445-451, 201).

[47] Frank Prial, *Wine Talk* (New York Times, August 12, 1992).

[48] Discussion with author, August 2008.

[49] Penning-Rowsell, *The Wines of Bordeaux,* p. 192.

[50] This would not be an easy project, because resistance to phylloxera probably involves many genes. The properties of hybrids show that sensitivity is more or less correlated with the proportion of Vitis vinifera parentage.

[51] Vitis International Variety Catalog (2007). See www.vivc.bafz.de.

[52] This includes Thompson seedless, which accounts for the majority of the world's white table grapes.

[53] Most new cultivars are results of crosses between existing domesticated grapevines, but it is still possible for crosses to occur between domesticated grapevines and wild grapevines. One relatively recent example of the introduction of genes from the wild may have been Riesling, which was probably generated by a cross between a variety called Heunisch Weiss (which was at one time widely distributed in Eastern Europe) and either a wild grapevine or a grapevine that was itself a cross between the domestic Traminer and a wild grapevine (Ferdinand Regner et al., *Heunisch x Fränkisch, ein wichtiger Genpool Europäischer Rebsorten (Vitis vinifera L sativa),* Viticultural and Enological Sciences, V. 53, p. 114-118, 1998).

[54] Charles Sullivan, *Zinfandel. A History Of The Grape And Its Wine* (University of California Press, Berkeley, 2003).

[55] Quoted in Jordan Ross, *Balancing Quality & Yield: Impact Of Vine Age, Clone, And Vine Density,* Practical Winery and Vineyard, November, 1999.

[56] The growing season is April-October in the northern hemisphere. In the southern hemisphere, it is October-April.

Chapter 2: The Vineyard

[1] This is not so odd as it sounds, since one aspect of the Lenz-Moser training system, which is widely used in Austria, is a high canopy, one reason for which was to make it easier to harvest the grapes.

[2] Figures calculated from the declared vineyard area and total production for 2005.

[3] Quoted in Jordan Ross, *Balancing Quality & Yield: Impact Of Vine Age, Clone, And Vine Density*, Practical Winery and Vineyard, November, 1999.

[4] Ibid.

[5] Richard Smart, *Higher Yields Cause Lower Wine Quality*, Wine Business Monthly, November 2005.

[6] Jordan Ross, *Balancing Quality*, op. cit.

[7] A. J. Winkler et al. (General Viticulture. University of California Press, Berkeley, 1974), pp. 140-153; Linda Bisson, *In Search Of Optimal Grape Maturity* (Practical Vineyard and Winery, July 2001).

[8] This can be formalized as the maturation index, which divides the must sugar concentration in g/l by the titratable acidity expressed as tartaric acid equivalents per liter. It provides a valid comparison only within a variety, since different varieties have different typical indices.

[9] Brix × 0.9 gives the grams of sugar per 100 gms of juice. Fermentation generates 1% alcohol from 16.83 g/l of sugar. So Brix × 0.9 / 16.83 = Brix × 0.55 gives the per cent potential alcohol.

[10] Its level goes down by about half in the two weeks after veraison, largely due to dilution as the berry expands with the synthesis of other compounds.

[11] Uli Fischer and Ann C. Noble, *The Effect of Ethanol, Catechin Concentration, and pH on Sourness and Bitterness of Wine* (Am. Soc. Enol. Viticult., 45, 6-10, 1994).

[12] Abbé Tainturier, *Remarques sur la culture des vignes de Beaune et lieux circonvoisins* (Editions de l'Armançon (2000), Précy-sous-Thil, 1763).

[13] Unwin, *Wine and the Vine*, p. 107.

[14] IPT is measured by the optical absorbance at 280 nm (multiplied by 100). A rough equivalent in mgm equivalents of gallic acid /liter is given by multiplying the IPT by 0.08.

[15] IPT was typically about 62 in Bordeaux in 1982, 70 in year 2000, and 78 in year 2005.

[16] Pascal Ribéreau-Gayon et al., *The Handbook of Enology, Volume 1, The Microbiology of Wine and Vinifications* (John Wiley & Sons, New York, 2000), p. 357.

[17] One issue is that the physiological processes governing sugar and malic acid accumulation are much more dependent on temperature than those governing the color, aroma, and tannin levels that result from phenolic development. In cooler climates, phenolic ripeness is achieved at lower sugar levels than in warmer climates, which is part of the reason why higher alcohol (resulting from higher sugar) is associated with phenolic ripeness in warm climates.

[18] Helga Willer, *Organic Viticulture In Europe: Development And Current Statistics* (16th IFOAM Organic World Congress, Modena, Italy, June 16-20, 2008); Tom Stevenson, *Wine Report 2009* (Dorling Kindersley Publishing, London, p. 341).

[19] Official figures underestimate the extent of organic viticulture, because the expenses of certification are an impediment for small growers.

[20] Some growers in Germany's Rheingau, for example, who would like to be organic, feel that it's just too risky because their entire vineyards are devoted exclusively to Riesling, and an infection could spread too rapidly to be treated by organic methods.

[21] Copper accumulates in the top layer of soil and does not dissipate.

[22] Personal communication, Jean-Michel Comme, March 2009.

[23] This is now published annually (Maria Thun & Matthias Thun, *The Biodynamic Sowing and Planting Calendar*, Floris Books, Edinburgh, 2009).

[24] The movement is most highly developed in France, where biodynamic wine producers include Domaine d'Auvenay and Domaine Leflaive in Burgundy, Nicolas Joly and Didier Dagueneau in the Loire, Marcel Deiss and Marc Kreydenweiss in Alsace, Chapoutier in the Rhône, Domaine Gauby in Languedoc.

[25] Monty Waldin, *Biodynamic Wines* (Mitchell Beazley, London, 2004), p4.

[26] Guy Renvoisé, *Le Monde du Vin. Art ou Bluff* (Editions du Rouergue, Parc St Joseph, 1994), p. 156.

[27] On the occasion of a tasting of Château Musar in New York, October 2009.

[28] The certifying organization is Demeter, except in Australia where there is a government standard. See www.demeter.net.

[29] According to Demeter International, as of 2008 there were only 107,200 ha of certified biodynamic farms (including all types of agriculture) worldwide.

[30] The cost of certification is significant. The fee is 2% of net sales plus a charge for an annual inspection. See www.demeter.net.

[31] Claude Bourguignon, *Le Sol, La Terre Et Les Champs* (Sang de la terre, Auxerre, 1996).

[32] But note that this was an extremely brief report made at a Congress and that there appears to have been no detailed follow up or subsequent supporting study (Claude Bourguignon & Lydia Gabucci, *Comparisons Of Chemical Analysis And Biological Activity Of Soils Cultivated By Organic And Biodynamic Methods*, In H. Willer & U. Meier (Eds.), Proceedings 6th Annual Congress on Organic Viticulture, Basel, 2000, pp. 92-94).

[33] With permission from Maria and Matthias Thun, *The Biodynamic Sowing and Planting Calendar 2008*, Floris Books, Edinburgh.

[34] Jennifer Reeve et al., *Soil and Wine Grape Quality in Biodynamically and Organically Managed Vineyards* (Am. J. Enol. Vitic., 56, 367-376, 2005).

[35] Maria and Matthias Thun, *When Wine Tastes Best 2010* (Floris Books, Edinburgh, 2009).

[36] The Guardian, *Why Good Wine May Taste Like Moonshine Today*, April 18, 2009.

[37] Discussion with author, February 2010.

[38] Unfortunately, biodynamics has such an aura of mysticism that serious scientists are frightened to investigate the issues because they are concerned they will lose face with their peers (and, more practically, have difficulty getting grants).

[39] Interview with a winemaker in Napa Valley, February 2010.

Chapter 3: Terroir

[1] John Locke, The Works of John Locke, vol. 9 (Letters and Misc. Works, 1685) paragraph 1073.

[2] Dictionnaire de l'Académie Françoise, Nouvelle Edition, tome II, Paris, 1777, p. 542.

[3] It is mentioned by William Douglass, *A Summary, Historical And Political, Of The First Planting, Progressive Improvements And Present State Of The British Settlements In North America* (R. & J. Dodsley, London, 1760).

[4] Denis Morélot, *Statistique De La Vigne Dans Le Département De La Côte-D'Or* (Huzard, Paris, 1831), p. 4.

[5] Jake Hancock, *Terroir: The Role of Geology, Climate, and Culture in the Making of French Wines* (J. Wine Research, 10, 43-49, 1999).

[6] James Wilson, *Terroir* (Wine Appreciation Guild, San Francisco, 1998).

[7] Quoted in Michael Veseth, *Globaloney: Unraveling the Myths of Globalization* (Rowman & Littlefield, New York, 2005), p. 146.

[8] Matt Kramer, *The Notion Of Terroir*, in *Wine and Philosophy: A Symposium on Thinking and Drinking*, ed. Fritz Allhof, Wiley-Blackwell, Oxford, 2007, p. 228.

[9] The average size of vineyard holdings in Europe is around 2 ha, whereas in California or Australia it is 75-100 ha.

[10] "The answer lies in the soil" was the famous catch phrase in a British comedy radio program in the 1960s; the deep profundity of this expression, however, was far beyond their ken.

[11] Cornelius Van Leeuwen & Gerard Seguin, *The Concept of Terroir in Viticulture* (J. Wine Research, 17, 1-10, 2006).

[12] Marcus Vitruvius Pollio (27 B.C.), book VIII. In Vitruvius: The Ten Books on Architecture, by Morris H. Morgan, Harvard University Press, Cambridge, 1914. p. 236.

[13] Gerard Seguin, *Terroirs And Pedology Of Wine Growing* (Experientia, 42, 861-873, 1986).

[14] Author's discussion with Stefano Carpeneto at Tignanello, October 2009.

[15] Alex Maltman, *The Role of Vineyard Geology in Wine Typicity* (J. Wine Research, 19, 1-17, 2008), p. 5.

[16] Uptake of minerals is affected by the pH (acidity) of the soil, but uptake of potassium (most directly connected with lack of acidity in the plant) shows no effect over the pH range that grapevines can grow under (Jackson, *Wine Science*, p. 162).

[17] One study purporting to establish a relationship grew grapevines hydroponically. Increasing calcium carbonate in the hydroponic medium caused a 30% decrease in potassium concentration in the leaves of the plant, with a corresponding increase in acidity (Garcia et al., *Effect of various potassium-calcium ratios on cation nutrition of grape grown hydroponically*, J. Plant Nutrition, 22, 417-425, 1999). But no one has the faintest idea how the concentration of calcium carbonate in solution relates to effective concentration in soil, although this makes it plausible that increased available calcium in the soil could increase acidity in the grapes.

[18] Jennifer M. Huggett, *Geology and Wine: a review* (Proc. Geologists' Assoc., 117, 239-247, 2006), p. 240.

[19] The only difference between black and white grapes is that the former produce anthocyanins. These colored pigments do not contain iron; perhaps people have confused them with the blood pigment, hemoglobin, which requires iron! There appears to be no relationship between grape variety and iron content (Bruce W. Zoecklin et al., *Wine Analysis And Production*, Springer, 1995, p. 202).

[20] Soil areas based on Wilson, *Terroir*, p. 248. Topographic map from Google Earth.

[21] See décret in Journal Officiel, January 8, 1967, p. 412-413.

[22] See décret 78-238 of February 27, 1978.

[23] Jennifer M. Huggett, *Geology and Wine: a review* (Proc. Geologists' Assoc., 117, 239-247, 2006).

[24] Jake M. Hancock and Jennifer Huggett, *The Geological Controls in Coonawarra* (J. Wine Res., 15, 115-122, 2004).

[25] Maltman, op. cit., p. 10.

[26] Iron, Manganese, Boron, Molybdenum, Copper, Zinc, Chlorine, Cobalt.

[27] Alex E. Martin & R. John Watling, *Determining The Geographical Origin Of Wine* (Government of Western Australia, DAF, *Wine Industry Newsletter*, 89, 6-7, 2008).

[28] Maltman, op. cit., p.8.

[29] Taste thresholds for some metals are: Copper - 3 ppm; Iron - 0.1 ppm; Manganese - 1 ppm; Zinc - 4 ppm. Some comparable legal limits for concentrations in wine are: copper in wine in the E.U. is 1 ppm; zinc in wine in Australia is 0.005 ppm.

[30] For example, copper was ~1 ppm in must but ten-fold less in wine (C. M. Almeida and M. T. Vasconcelolos, *Multielement Composition Of Wines And Their Precursors, Including Provenance Soil And Their Potentialities As Fingerprints Of Wine Origin,* J. Agricult. Food Chem., 51, 4788-4799, 2003). Another study, attempting to demonstrate a reproducible relationship between concentrations of elements in soil and wine, showed widely variable levels influenced to some degree by berry ripeness (as seen in sugar levels and titratable acidity) (D. E. Mackenzie and A. G. Christy, *The Role Of Soil Chemistry In Wine Grape Quality And Sustainable Soil Management In Vineyards*, IWA Publishing: Water Science and Technology, 51, 27–37, 2005).

[31] Ron S. Jackson, *Wine Science*, p. 50.

[32] Takatoshi Tominaga et al., *Contribution of Benzenemethanethiol to Smoky Aroma of Certain Vitis vinifera L. Wines* (J. Agric. Food Chem., 51, 1373–1376, 2003).

[33] In the first edition of his book, *Burgundy*, in 1982, Anthony Hanson offended some people by writing "Great Burgundy smells of shit." In the second edition of 1995, he acknowledged an oversimplification, and implied that the odor might be due to microbial action (Anthony Hanson, *Burgundy, 1st edition,* Faber & Faber, London, 1982, p. 147; Anthony Hanson, *Burgundy, 2nd edition,* Faber & Faber, London, 1995, p. 151).

[34] ETS Laboratories, *Technical Bulletin - Eucalyptol*, February 8, 2009.

[35] Glynn Ward et al., *Smoke Taint in Western Australia*, Wine Business Monthly, September 15, 2008.

[36] Pliny the Elder (70 C.E.). The XIIII book of the history of nature. Containing the Treatise of Trees bearing fruit. Chapter VI.

[37] Unwin, *Wine and the Vine*, p. 111.

[38] James Busby, *A Treatise On The Culture Of The Vine And The Art Of Making Wine, Compiled From The Works Of Chaptal And Other French Writers ; And From The Notes Of The Compiler During A Residence In Some Of The Wine Provinces Of France* (R. Howe, Government Printer, Australia, 1825), p. 14.

[39] Ibid., p. 11.

[40] Jennifer M. Huggett, *Geology and Wine: a review* (Proc. Geologists' Assoc., 117, 239-247, 2006), p. 243.

[41] Ibid., p. 241; Alex Maltman, *Wine, Beer and Whisky: the Role of Geology* (Geology Today, 19, 22-29, Blackwell, Oxford, 2003).

[42] Adam, Smith, *An Inquiry into the Nature and Causes of the Wealth of Nations*, 1776, Book 1, Chapter 11, p. 41.

[43] Joseph Capus, *Proposition De La Loi Sur La Protection Des Appellations Contrôlées*, Revue du vin de France, July 25, 1935, cited in Philip Whalen, *'Insofar as the Ruby Wine Seduces Them': Cultural Strategies for Selling Wine in Inter-war Burgundy* (Contemporary European History, 18, 67-98, Cambridge University Press, Cambridge, 2009), p. 71.

[44] Lewin, *What Price Bordeaux?*

[45] Philip Whalen, *'Insofar as the Ruby Wine Seduces Them', op cit.*, p. 71.

[46] "The majority of wines sold behind respectable labels are more often the product of the chemist's laboratory rather than the vintner's cellar" (Gaston Roupnel, *La Crise Du Vin*, Dépêche de Toulouse, November 2, 1922).

[47] The protagonists in favor of terroir were the producers Gaston Roupnel, Albert Noirot, Georges Gouges, and the Marquis d'Angerville, and the legal cases were fought between 1924 and 1936 (Whalen, op. cit., p. 81).

[48] J. Lavalle, *Histoire et Statistique de la Vigne et des Grands Vins de la Cote d'Or* (Picard, Dijon, 1855), appendix.

[49] Walter Moran, *The Wine Appellation as Territory in France and California* (Annals Association American Geographers, 83, 694-717, Blackwell, Cambridge, Massachusetts, 1993), pp. 702, 714.

[50] Walter Moran, *Crafting Terroir: People In Cool Climates, Soils, And Markets* (Sixth International Cool Climate Symposium for Viticulture and Oenology, Christchurch, New Zealand, 2006).

[51] Ibid.

[52] Dion, *Histoire de la Vigne et du Vin*, p. 108.

[53] According to the Gimblett Gravels Winegrowers Association history of the region. See www.gimblettgravels.com.

[54] Ibid.

[55] Topographic map from Google Earth.

[56] John Schreiner, *Icewine. The Complete Story* (Warwick Publishing, Toronto, 2001), p. 36.

[57] Publicity brochure for J. L. Wolf.

[58] Personal communication from Christoph Graf (November 2008).

[59] Lewin, *What Price Bordeaux?*, p. 71.

[60] In 1710, when a ban was imposed on new plantings because there had been a surge of over-planting, gravel-based lands were excluded because of their known superiority (René Pijassou, *Le Médoc: Un Grand Vignoble De Qualité. Tomes I & II*, Tallandier, Paris, 1978, p. 421.)

[61] A little farther inland, roughly 10 km from the river, soils are also gravel-based, but here the mix also includes more sand and clay on a limestone plateau.

[62] Gérard Seguin, *Influence Des Facteurs Naturels Sur Les Caractères Des Vins. In Traité D'ampélologie*, (Sciences et Technique de la vigne, Bordas, Paris, 1980); Wilson, *Terroir*, p. 188.

[63] www.atlaspeakappellation.com/elan.html

[64] Topographic background from Google Maps.

[65] Quoted in James Conway, *Napa. The Story of an American Eden* (Houghton Mifflin, New York, 2002), p. 363.

[66] The subsequent story was not entirely happy; most of the original partners in the deal bailed out during the 1990s, the vineyards finally came under the control of Antinori, there were unsuccessful attempts to make a Sangiovese wine, then the brand name became the property of Beam vintners (who own nearby William Hill Vineyards), and now the vineyards themselves have reverted to Antinori, although the brand name remains the property of Beam.

[67] Conway, *Napa*. op. cit., p. 130.

[68] Wine Business Monthly, *Wine Business Insider, Sierra Club Lawsuit Triggers Hillside Moratorium: CEQA Applies, Napa County Says,* January 29, 2000.

[69] Conway, *Napa,* op. cit., p. 58.

[70] www.winespectator.com/Wine/Daily/News/0,1145,1664,00.html

[71] Topographic background from Google Earth.

[72] Richard Smart, *Terroir Unmasked* (Wine Business Monthly, June 15, 2004).

[73] Randall Grahm, *The Phenomenology of Terroir: A Meditation by Randall Grahm* (University of California, Davis, Terroir Conference, March, 2006).

[74] A variation called partial root drying was introduced by two Australian scientists in the early 1990s. Two separate irrigation lines are placed on either side of the vine. Water is shut off from one side, and the root zone is permitted to dry while the other side gets irrigation. Then the situation is reversed. Each side is used 2-3 times per week. Drying out causes the root system to generate a signal that it is under stress. This causes the vine to close its stomata (pores) under the leaves where most of the water evaporates from the vine, in order to minimize water loss. The net result is to mimic the effects of a water deficit stress, but without the harmful consequences of water loss (P. R. Dry et al., *Partial Rootzone Drying - An Update.* The Australian Grapegrower and Winemaker, Annual Technical Issue, 2000, pp. 35-39). The technique is controversial because it's not entirely clear whether it really offers advantages over simply reducing the amount of water provided during deficit irrigation.

[75] See page 358.

[76] Until the 1989 vintage it was labeled Grange Hermitage, in reference to the great Syrah-based wines of Hermitage in the Rhône, but since then it has stood on its own as just Grange.

[77] Max Schubert, *The Story of Grange* (Paper delivered at the first Australian National University Wine Symposium, Canberra, 1979).

[78] Data source: Langton's auctioneers, Melbourne, Australia; see www.langtons.com.au/images/pdfs/grange_guide.pdf

[79] Topographic background from Google Earth.

[80] The range is from 100% to 86% Shiraz.

[81] Bureau National Interprofessionel du Cognac (www.cognac.fr).

[82] Jake Hancock & Richard Selley, *Coquand's joke,* Geoscientist, 13, 17, 2003.

[83] Kyle Jarrad, *Cognac. The Seductive Saga of the World's Most Coveted Spirit* (John Wiley, New York, 2005), p. 89.

[84] Richard C. Selley, *The Winelands of Britain: Past, Present & Prospective* (Petravin, London, 2008), p. 50.

[85] Location of chalk-based soils from Richard C. Selley, *The Winelands of Britain,* op cit., p. 51. Topographic background from Google Earth.

[86] Wilson, *Terroir*, pp. 211-213.

[87] One study tried to assess terroir in terms of describing features such as soil types and the presence of slopes. But the wines were all from the Médoc in Bordeaux, damning the study with a basic misunderstanding of the nature of wine production in Bordeaux, where the châteaux have large landholdings, showing diversity of terroir that is not susceptible to simple description. Critics' ratings or prices were used to assess quality, which encounters the difficulty discussed in the text. The authors concluded that wine-making features show a better correlation with critics' ratings than does terroir; but in fact the only strong correlations with putative quality were manual picking and use of new

oak, both of which could be consequences of the château's ability to make better wine rather than the cause of it (Olivier Gergaud and Victor Ginsburgh, *Natural Endowments, Production Technology, and the Quality of Wines in Bordeaux. Does Terroir Matter,* The Economic Journal, 118, F142–F157, 2008). Any study of this type may be futile, but better results might be obtained with Burgundy, where my analysis shows a correlation between price and level in the AOC hierarchy, supposedly determined by terroir (see pp. 380-384 in Chapter 14 of this book).

Chapter 4: Vintage & Global Warming

[1] Dion, *Histoire de la Vigne,* p. 120.

[2] Following a detailed discussion of different pitch and resins, Pliny commented that "the pitch most highly esteemed in Italy for preparing vessels for storing wine is that which comes from Bruttium. It is made from the resin that distils from the pitch-tree; that which is used in Spain is held in but little esteem, being the product of the wild pine." (*The Natural History Of Pliny,* Volume 3, edited John Bostock and H. T. Riley, Kessinger Publishing, p. 267).

[3] A transition to storage in barrels took place in Roman times, but increased the risk of spoilage by exposure to air. And as soon as the wine was transferred from the barrel to a smaller container, its life was measured in days if not hours.

[4] This depended on the introduction of sulfur as a preservative, allowing wine to be kept in barrels for 3-4 years before bottling, and the development of bottles that could be sealed with corks so the wine could be kept by the consumer.

[5] The proverb came to mean: there is no drawing back. It was famously used to stiffen Louis XIV's courage at a battle in 1710 (Alphonse Mariette, *French and English Idioms and Proverbs with Critical and Historical Notes,* Hachette, Paris, 1896, p. 43).

[6] A contemporary view in 1751 of the merits of wine of different ages noted, "wine begins to degenerate as it enters its second year." (L'Encyclopédie de Diderot et d'Alembert, 1751, tome 17, p. 290.)

[7] At first it was used by individuals for wine (or cider or beer) bottled at home, but by the end of the century it came into use by wine merchants (John Worlidge, *Vinetum Britannicum, Or, A Treatise Of Cider And Other Wines And Drinks From Fruits Growing In This Kingdom,* Thomas Dring, London, 1678).

[8] Tim Unwin, *Wine and the Vine,* p. 266.

[9] René Pijassou, *Le Médoc: Un Grand Vignoble De Qualité,* Tallandier, Paris, 1978, p. 597.

[10] Ibid., p 537.

[11] There were some occasional reports early in the century that wines forgotten in a cellar might taste better than the current vintage; but this was clearly contrary to expectation (Asa Briggs, *Haut-Brion,* Faber & Faber, London, 1994, p. 5).

[12] The Writings of Thomas Jefferson (1905). Issued under the auspices of the Thomas Jefferson Memorial Association of the United States.

[13] The proprietors of the first growths believed Jefferson may have been drinking his wines too young (James M. Gabler, *Passions: The Wines and Travels of Thomas Jefferson,* Bacchus Press, 1995, pp. 118-119).

[14] George Saintsbury, *Notes on a Cellar Book,* MacMillan, London, 1931, p. 51.

[15] For example, the average price of wine in the Médoc varied over a 4-fold range in the period from 1741 to 1774, according to data shown in Pijassou, *Le Médoc,* op. cit., p. 1408.

[16] For example, prices at Château Latour showed as much as 4-5-fold variation from year to year in the second half of the 19th century (Lewin, *What Price Bordeaux?,* p. 97).

[17] Range for Cabernet Sauvignon taken from Gregory Jones, *Climate and Terroir: Impacts of Climate Variability and Change on Wine,* in *Fine Wine and Terroir - The Geoscience Perspective,* Macqueen, R.W., and Meinert, L.D., (eds.), Geoscience Canada Reprint Series Number 9, Geological Association of Canada, St. John's, Newfoundland, 2006.) This was based on relationships between phenological requirements and climate for high to premium quality wine production in the world's benchmark regions for the variety over the period prior to 1999.

[18] Orley Ashenfelter, David Ashmore, and Robert LaLonde, *Bordeaux Wine Vintage Quality and the Weather* (Harris School Working Paper Series 04.13, 1995); Orley Ashenfelter, *Predicting the Quality and Prices of Bordeaux Wines* (American Association of Wine Economics, Working Paper #4., 2007).

[19] More precisely, the formula explains auction prices in terms of age of the wine and quality of the vintage. Wines become more valuable as they become older (if the vintage was good), but I have adjusted the formula to assign a rating to each vintage by omitting the age factor.

[20] The main deficiency in the formula is that it does not allow for a transition when increase in temperature becomes too much (as in 2003, which is vastly overrated on Ashenfelter's scale) or when there is too much rain earlier in the season. Another major mistake is 1997, rated very highly by Ashenfelter: "the 1997 vintage... is probably the only seriously under-priced vintage currently available." I hope he did not buy too much of it.

[21] Of the 25 leading brands in the United States, 17 have no vintage.

[22] Sales data from Adams Wine Handbook, Norwalk, CT, 2008.

[23] Data from Instituto dos Vinhos do Douro e Porto.

[24] Global warming is attributed to the excessive accumulation of greenhouse gases such as carbon dioxide, methane, nitrous oxide, sulfur hexafluoride, perfluorocarbons, and hydrofluorocarbons, which are mostly produced by human activities. Fluorocarbons are being phased out in industrialized countries, but because they persist in the atmosphere for ~200 years, they will continue to contribute to global warming for some time. It may be impossible to reverse the trend in the next 20-30 years.

[25] Carbon dioxide was probably 270 ppm pre industrial age. It began to increase with the industrial revolution, rising from 310 ppm to 370 ppm over the period 1961-1997; the trend extrapolates to 700 ppm by 2050. Increases for methane and nitrous oxide show similar proportions (J. R. Ehleringer and T. E. Cerling, *Atmospheric CO2 and the Ratio of Intercellular to Ambient CO2 Concentrations in Plants*, Tree Physiol. 15, 105-111, 1995; Wuebbles et al, *Global Change: State of the Science*, Environmental Pollution, 100, 57-86, 1999).

[26] Projections for temperature increase out to 2080 have been used to suggest that by then the north of England might grow Pinot Noir and Chardonnay, while the south might grow Merlot (Selley, *The Winelands of Britain,* op cit., p. 97).

[27] The chalk subsoil of the South Downs, for example, is not unlike the underlying structure in Champagne.

[28] Martin Hickman, *Top Champagne House May Buy English Vineyards*, The Independent, November 17, 2007.

[29] See for example extensive differences between J. Esper et al., *Low-Frequency Signals in Long Tree-Ring Chronologies for Reconstructing Past Temperature Variability*, Science, 295, 2250-2253, 2002, and A. Moberg et al., *Highly Variable Northern Hemisphere Temperatures Reconstructed From Low- And High-Resolution Proxy Data*, Nature, 443, 613-617, 2005.

[30] Jean Ribéreau-Gayon and Emile Peynaud, *Traité d'Oenologie*, Tome I, Librairie Polytechnique, Paris, 1960, p. 122.

[31] According to the Australian Bureau of Statistics, Australian Wine and Grape Industry Report 1329.0, 50% of current vineyards were planted between 1998 (total 78,709 ha) and 2008 (total 172,676 ha).

[32] According to New Zealand Winegrowers Vineyard Surveys, 50% of current vineyards have been planted in the past six years, bringing the total from 13,787 ha in 2002 to 29,310 ha in 2008.

[33] Temperatures are rolling five year averages from P. D. Jones and M. E. Mann, *Climate Over Past Millennia,* Reviews of Geophysics, 42, RG2002, 2004. They are generally in the middle of range when comparing other temperature estimates (which actually vary considerably). For details of the origins of particular varieties, see Chapter 7.

[34] Albert Julius Winkler et al., *General Viticulture* (University of California Press, 1962), p. 61.

[35] Degree days were originally defined in Fahrenheit, but you can also calculate them in Centigrade using a base of 10 °C.

[36] Winkler et al., *General Viticulture*, op. cit., pp. 64-65.

[37] Other, more sophisticated systems for assessing climate also include the effects of moisture (rainfall and relative humidity), sunlight, cloud cover, soil characteristics, difference between maximum and minimum daily temperatures, wind conditions, air pollution, and solar radiation. One heat summation method is the Huglin index, which puts more weight on maximum temperature and adds a parameter for latitude to reflect the effect of increasing hours of sunlight. The formula sums average temperature minus 10°C plus maximum temperature minus 10°C, multiplied by a coefficient for latitude that increases from 1.02 at 40° to 1.06 at 50°. It has been used to establish limits for the minimum values required to ripen each variety successfully. It includes days from April 1 to September 30 (P. Huglin, *Biologie Et Ecologie De La Vigne*, Payot, Lausanne, Switzerland, 1986).

[38] More recent analyses would place them close to a zone apart.

[39] The most accurate way to do this is to take the average of daily temperatures during the growing season. It can be done with less accuracy by using monthly averages. The difference between average temperature and degree days is only significant if the calculation is done on a daily basis (in which case days at the beginning and end of the season where average temperatures do not reach 10 °C count as zero for degree days, but do contribute to average temperature).

[40] See note 44.

[41] The average difference in temperature during the growing season (April-October) was calculated for the two periods 1945-1990 and 1991-2009 for weather stations operating during both periods. Data source: National Climatic Data Center, US Department of Commerce, GHCN (Global Historical Climatology Network)-Monthly Version 2.

[42] Gregory Jones, *Climate and Terroir: Impacts of Climate Variability and Change on Wine.* In Fine Wine and Terroir - The Geoscience Perspective. R. W. Macqueen & L. D. Meinert (eds.), Geoscience Canada Reprint Series Number 9, 2006, Geological Association of Canada, St. John's, Newfoundland.

[43] Data from the Goddard Institute database of weather stations.

[44] Optimum growing season temperature for each variety was calculated as the average of growing season temperature in its classic region for the best vintages (taken as those rated 90 points or more in the Wine Advocate). Projected optima were 14.3 °C for Riesling (the Mosel), 15.8 °C for Pinot Noir (Burgundy), 15.9 °C for Chardonnay (Burgundy) 16.2 °C for Sauvignon Blanc (the Loire), 17.3 °C for Cabernet Sauvignon (Bordeaux), 18.6 °C for Nebbiolo (Barolo), 18.9°C for Grenache (Southern Rhône), and 19.3 °C for Sangiovese (Tuscany). Similar growing season optima have also been calculated on the basis of a regression analysis by Gregory Jones et al, *Climate Change and Global Wine Quality* (Climatic Change, 73, 319–343, 2005).

[45] The temperature projected for 2025 assumes the same average annual increase after 2005 as occurred between the periods 1986-1995 and 1996-2005. This gives 15.2 °C for the Mosel, 16.5 °C for Burgundy, 16.8 °C for the Loire, 18.6 °C for Bordeaux, 19.2 °C Ribera del Duero, and 19.3 °C for Tuscany. Temperatures for wine regions in 2049 have been projected previously by Gregory Jones et al, *Climate Change and Global Wine Quality* (Climatic Change, 73, 319–343, 2005).

[46] Isotherms show average growing season (Apr-Oct) temperatures for the period 1945-1990 based on weather station data from National Climatic Data Center, US Department of Commerce, GHCN (Global Historical Climatology Network)-Monthly Version 2.

[47] Burgundy for 1996-2005 shows the same average growing season temperature as Bordeaux from 1961-1970; based on analysis of monthly data from the weather stations at Dijon and Merignac as available on the Goddard Institute database.

[48] Locations of isotherms based on data in National Climatic Data Center, US Department of Commerce, GHCN (Global Historical Climatology Network)-Monthly Version 1. Topographic background from Google Earth..

[49] B. Ganichot, *Evolution De La Date Des Vendanges Dans Les Côtes Du Rhône Méridionales* (Proceedings of the 6th Rencontres Rhodaniennes, Institut Rhodanien, pp. 38- 41, Orange, France, 2002).

[50] Harvest dates became later during the mini-ice age around 1500, and then stayed stable, with the exception of a warmer period in the 17 century, until the past half-century (I. Chuine et al., *Grape Ripening As A Past Climate Indicator,* Nature, 432, 289-290, 2004).

[51] Data from the cliflo database of New Zealand weather stations. The change is from about 15.3 °C to about 16.3 °C.

[52] Increase from 17.7 °C to 18.7 °C at the weather station at Nuriootpa in Barossa Valley between 1953 and 2008 (Australian Government Bureau of Meteorology).

[53] Weather data: Goddard Institute; Harvest dates: Fédération des Grands Vins de Bordeaux.

[54] Data from Roger Dubrion, *Trois Siècles de Vendanges Bourguignon* (Editions Féret, Bordeaux, 2006).

55 Based on data of Gregory V. Jones, *Climate Change in the Western United States Grape Growing Regions* (Acta Horticulturae (ISHS), 689, 41-60, 2005) and M. A. White et al., *Extreme Heat Reduces And Shifts United States Premium Wine Production In The 21st Century* (Proc. Nat. Acad. Sci. USA, 103, 11217-11222, 2006). Topographic background from Google Earth.

[56] AWRI 2003 Annual Report, p. 44.

[57] Hans Schultz, *Climate Change In Viticulture: A European Perspective On Climatology, Carbon Dioxide And UV Effects* (Austr. J. Grape and Wine Research, 6, 2-12, 2000).

[58] The grapes for QmP wine must have a minimum sugar level equivalent to 9.1-10.0% alcohol, depending on the German wine region.

[59] Results obtained at the University of Bordeaux from a test plot of Cabernet Sauvignon grapes harvested in the Médoc. Merlot would have a higher level of potential alcohol. Actual wine would be a blend of varieties and very likely be chaptalized to increase the alcohol level. See www.oenologie.u-bordeaux2.fr..

[60] Data for sugar levels at harvest from the Grape Crush Report, California Department of Food and Agriculture, Sacramento. Data for seasonal growing temperatures from the Goddard Institute.

[61] At the Grandes Pagos tasting in London, March 12, 2010.

[62] Data from the Goddard Institute database of weather stations.

[63] Jonathan Leake, *The Great Climate Change Science Scandal,* The Sunday Times, London, November 29, 2009.

[64] Based on this type of assumption, estimates forecast a further increase of 1.8-2.5 °C warming by the middle of the century (Intergovernmental panels on climate change (IPCC), 1992, 1994, 1998, 2001).

Chapter 5: Grape Juice into Wine

[1] The best known teinturier is Alicante Bouschet, sometimes used in blends to add extra color. It was popular during Prohibition in the United States because the grapes transported well and gave deeply colored wine.

[2] Olivier de Serres, *Le Théâtre D'agriculture Et Mesnage Des Champs,* 1600.

[3] This became common in Bordeaux only after the 1970s, but the advantages have in fact long been known. A book published in California in 1911 advocated temperature control for fermentation, and several wineries in Napa Valley introduced cooling systems in the 1930s (Lapsley, *Bottled Poetry,* pp. 53, 59). By the late 1940s it was common in Napa (Wines and Vines, February, 1949).

[4] This happened in the 1945 vintage in Bordeaux.

[5] Yeast convert vanillin extracted from the oak into the odorless vanillin alcohol, giving a more subtle balance to the wine.

[6] Pasteur's involvement started when the father of one of his students asked him to resolve some problems he was having in manufacturing alcohol from beetroot. The fermentations often went sour, producing lactic acid (Patrice Debré et al., *Louis Pasteur,* Johns Hopkins University Press, Baltimore, 2000, pp. 82-114.)

[7] Photograph under common license from flickr.com.

[8] When alcohol was produced, the fermenting mixture contained cells that appeared round under the microscope; but when lactic acid was produced, the cells were elongated like rods (Debré et al., *Louis Pasteur,* op. cit.).

[9] Although this is true, fermentation usually gets off to a better start with a kick of oxygen to provoke the yeasts. Oxygen exposure also helps to avoid the development of reduced aromas, which can happen during fermentation.

[10] Debré et al., *Louis Pasteur,* op. cit., pp. 232-233.

[11] Cultured yeasts have been used since the 1960s. Cakes of compressed yeast became commercially available in the United States in 1963 (Lapsley, *Bottled Poetry,* p. 168).

[12] Pascal Ribéreau-Gayon et al., *The Handbook of Enology, Volume 1, The Microbiology of Wine and Vinifications, 2nd edition* (John Wiley & Sons, New York, 2000), p. 46.

[13] Winemakers who practice fermentation with indigenous yeast argue that if they get into trouble, they can always overwhelm the must by inoculating with cultured yeast.

[14] Personal communication from Sebastiano Rosa (winemaker at Sassicaia), October 2007.

[15] Once Brettanomyces has infected a winery, it is impossible to remove. It can be eliminated from wine by filtration or prevented by using compounds that are toxic to yeast.

[16] Two types of compounds are responsible for Brett. Low concentrations of tetrahydropyridines may show as bread, popcorn or cracker aromas, but at high concentrations they turn to mousy aromas. Tetrahydropyridines are not volatile and so are not detected on the aroma, but only as a result of tasting, usually on the aftertaste. The major cause of barnyard aromas is the production of volatile phenols, including 4-ethyl phenol (band-aid aroma) and 4-ethyl guaiacol (wet burnt wood aroma). These compounds are only produced by Brettanomyces, and the presence of 4-ethyl phenol is used as a quantitative marker for the level of Brettanomyces infection.

[17] This usually occurs with red wine, because of the higher polyphenol levels (which form substrates for Brettanomyces to form its typical phenols) and because pH is higher (that is, acidity is lower, forming better conditions for bacterial growth).

[18] Sam Harrop MW, *Production of High Quality Syrah-based Wines,* Institute of Masters of Wine Dissertation, 2003.

[19] See note 33 in Chapter 3.

[20] The amount of alcohol generated per unit of sugar is called the conversion ratio. For unknown reasons, it seems to have increased slightly in recent decades.

[21] Jean-Antoine Chaptal, *L'Art de Faire le Vin* (Bouchard-Huzard, Paris, 1801, 1807, 1839).

[22] It is possible that the technique was used previously. The chemist Pierre Joseph Macquer proposed that cassonade (brown sugar) should be used rather than honey or molasses to increase alcoholic strength, so as not to affect flavor (Jean-François Gautier, *Le Vin Et Ses Fraudes,* Presses Universitaires De France, 1995, p. 16). Addition of sugar may have been practiced regularly at Clos Vougeot before 1790 (Hallgarten, *Wine Scandal,* p. 64).

[23] The recommended dose was 15-20 livres of sugar per muid (456 liters).

[24] Denis Morélot, *Statistique de la Vigne dans le Departément de la Cote-d'Or* (Ch. Brugnot, Dijon, 1831), p. 250.

[25] Harry W. Paul, *Science, Vine, and Wine in Modern France* (Cambridge University Press, Cambridge, 1996), p. 130.

[26] Christopher Fielden, *Is This the Wine You Ordered, Sir?: The Dark Side of the Wine Trade* (Christopher Helm, London, 1989), pp. 67-68.

[27] Paul, *Science, Vine, and Wine,* op. cit., p, 128.

[28] Fortification was sometimes practiced with the wines of Bordeaux in the mid nineteenth century (Lewin, *What Price Bordeaux?,* p. 59).

[29] It is generally agreed that more than 1-1.5% increase creates an unbalanced wine.

[30] Consider a vineyard where the costs of production are €7 per kg of grapes (a typical price in Champagne), which will give about 0.75 liters of wine, corresponding to €9/liter. You can buy a kilo of sugar for €0.85; this will increase the volume of the wine by 0.66

liters, corresponding to a cost of €1.25/liter. The legal limits allow 3.6 kg of sugar to be added to a hectoliter of red wine, or 3.4 kg to a hectoliter of white wine, basically diluting the wine by 2-3% of volume at the low production cost of the sugar.

[31] One measure of the profitability of chaptalization was contained in an official report of the Institut des Vins de Consommation Courante (the old name for Vin de Table) in 1974, stating that the cost of wine per degree-hectoliter was 2.90F, compared with an average sale price of 9F.

[32] Pierre-Marie Doutrelant, *Les Bons Vins et les Autres* (Editions du Seuil, Paris, 1976), p. 197.

[33] Decanter on line, December 13, 2007 and March 18, 2009; see www.decanter.com/news/169103.html; www.decanter.com/news/news.php?id=278929.

[34] A bit below the use of sugar for ice cream. Data from the statistics memo of CEDUS LeSucre at www.lesucre.com.

[35] The sugar producers report usage of sugar for chaptalization over the period 2002-2006 varied from a low of 11,180 tonnes in the hot year of 2003 to a high of 30,359 tonnes in 2002. Assuming that chaptalization was performed at the legal limit of 3.5 kg/hl, the amount of treated wine would be 6.7% in 2003 and 16.7% in 2002. If chaptalization was performed at the more reasonable limit of 2.5 kg/hl (this is about the limit for avoiding change in the organoleptic quality), the corresponding proportions would be higher, at 9.4% and 23.2%. Data from the statistics memo of CEDUS LeSucre at www.lesucre.com.

[36] Bacteria that perform malolactic fermentation had actually been identified long previously by H. Müller-Thurgau and A. Osterwalder in 1913 (Ian Spencer Hornsey, *The Chemistry and Biology of Winemaking*, Royal Society of Chemistry, London, 2007, p. 224.)

[37] Peynaud published a paper in 1959 reporting successful induction of MLF (CR Seances Acad. Agric. France, 45, p. 355.)

[38] Malolactic fermentation removes one of the two acidic groups from malic acid by converting it into lactic acid with the release of carbon dioxide.

[39] Champagne houses have varying views on whether to perform MLF, but there's a tendency to use it to make the wine more drinkable for nonvintage (which will be consumed young), but not for vintage (where it may detract from aging potential).

[40] Robert Parker, *Bordeaux, 4th edition* (Simon & Schuster, New York, 2003), p. XVII.

[41] Lewin, *What Price Bordeaux?*, pp. 192-193.

[42] The name, carbonic maceration, reflects the fact that carbon dioxide dissolves in water to form a (very weak) solution called carbonic acid.

[43] Jan Read, *Wines of the Rioja* (Sotheby Publications, London, 1984), p.35.

[44] John Radford, *The Wines of Rioja* (Mitchell Beazley, London, 2004), p. 41.

[45] As exemplified in several thousand hits on google for "wine is a living thing."

[46] The suspended compounds are negatively charged, and many fining agents are proteins with positive charges that bind by electrostatic interaction to the compounds in the wine. The clay bentonite is used for the opposite case when a wine has too much protein in it.

[47] "Oxygen penetration...has been measured as 2-5 ml/l per year. It depends on the thickness and type of wood...In tuns where the staves are 5 cm thick, it is virtually nil." (Emile Peynaud, *Knowing and Making Wine*, 2nd edition, Wiley-Interscience New York, 1984, p. 245).

[48] Discussion with author, June 2009.

[49] Chilling is the traditional method. More recent methods include crystallization, when potassium bitartrate is added to nucleate the formation of crystals, or electrodialysis when tartrate ions pass specifically across an ion-exchange membrane. Removal of tartrate by any method reduces acidity by the amount of tartaric acid that has been extracted.

[50] Sterile filtration uses membranes with a pore size <0.45 µm. (This is usually not possible with sweet wines, where the viscosity blocks the filter, and slightly larger sizes must be used.) Filtration at < 0.8 µm removes all yeast, and filtration at <1.2 µm removes most yeast. Alternatives to membrane filtration include depth filtration, when the wine is pushed through sheets that trap solid particles.

[51] Pascal Ribéreau-Gayon et al., *The Handbook of Enology, Volume 2, The Chemistry of Wine Stabilisation and Treatments,* 2nd edition (John Wiley & Sons, New York, 2000), p. 362.

[52] Ibid., p. 364.

[53] Robert Parker, *Parker's Wine Buyer's Guide*, 5th Edition, 1999, p. 29.

[54] Tannins take their name from their use in tanning animal hides into leather. Technically they are polyphenols formed by plants, falling into several different classes, but all sharing the feature that they have multiple phenol rings with hydroxyl and other groups that are negatively charged and can bind to proteins. Their binding to animal proteins is the basis for the tanning reaction.

[55] Because the stalks contain water, but not sugar, and absorb alcohol, destemming also increased alcoholic strength by up to 0.5%. It was advocated by Peynaud in his book of 1970 (later translated as Emile Peynaud, *Knowing and Making Wine,* Wiley-Interscience, New York, 1984, p. 146).

[56] The reason tannins in stalks and seeds are more bitter is that they are smaller than those found in the skin. Larger tannins are less astringent.

[57] Some methods measure ability to bind to proteins, some measure oxidative capacity, and so on, so the various methods for measuring total polyphenols can differ as to exactly which set of compounds is included in each assay. Total phenols are usually measured in grams/liter, with a typical level (depending on the black variety) in the range of 4-6 g/l.

[58] Variations on pump-over include délestage (rack-and-return) in which the juice is pumped through a screen to remove the seeds and then sprayed on to the cap (to ensure oxidative exposure), the auto-fermenter (which uses the pressure generated by carbon dioxide released during fermentation to drive the pumping-over), and rotary fermenters (which lie on their sides and rotate to keep the juice in contact with the skins).

[59] Enzymes used in extraction include pectinase, cellulase, hemicellulase, and protease activities. Breakdown of cell walls encourages extraction of skin tannins, giving the wine a more full-bodied nature.

[60] A high concentration of sulfur dioxide together with low temperature (10 °C) is used to prevent fermentation.

[61] Leonard Barkan, *Time, Space, And Burgundy* (The Yale Review, 92, 109-127, 2008).

[62] Free anthocyanin content can vary in young wines from 100 mg/l in Pinot Noir to 1500 mg/l in varieties such as Shiraz and Cabernet Sauvignon, to a minimum of 50 mg/l or less during aging.

[63] Stable color results from interactions between anthocyanins and tannins to form polymeric color pigments that are stable. Tannin levels can therefore influence color by stabilizing the anthocyanins.

[64] Copigmentation is due to an association of components, not a chemical reaction.

[65] Roger Boulton, *The Copigmentation of Anthocyanins and Its Role in the Color of Red Wine: A Critical Review* (Am. J. Enol. Vitic., 52, 67-87, 2001).

[66] Because the effect depends on extraction of cofactors from the skins during fermentation, it is not achieved by blending wines.

[67] Author's discussion with Roger Boulton, UC Davis, December 2009.

[68] This was common in Rioja, Chianti, and at Côte-Rôtie and Hermitage in the northern Rhône. It no longer occurs in Rioja or Chianti, but it is still legal to include up to 15% of permitted white varieties with Syrah (the only permitted black grape) in Côte-Rôtie and Hermitage.

[69] Flavonoids are found in most plants. The most important with regards to white wine are quercetin and kaempferol.

[70] Terms used to describe rosé wine in various countries are: Italy - Rosata, Chiaretto; Spain - Rosado; Portugal - Branco; Germany - Bleichert, Rotling.

[71] Acidity is reduced because potassium is extracted from the skins.

[72] Author's discussion with Jorge Muga, May 2009.

[73] Suzannah Ramsdale, *Fury At E.U. Rosé Wine Plans*, Decanter magazine on line, March 16, 2009.

[74] John Lichfield, *E.U. Abandons Plan To Allow Blended Rosé Wine*, The Independent, June 8, 2009.

[75] Edward Cody, *French Vintners Find E.U. Concoction Unpalatable*, Washington Post, May 4, 2009.

[76] The introduction of sulfur as a preservative made it possible to keep wine in barriques for 2-4 years without spoilage. The technique was invented by the Dutch, in the form of burning a sulfur candle in a barrel before it was filled with wine, and became known as the "allumettes hollandaises." It was used when barriques were initially filled and when wine was racked (moved) from one barrique to another. By the mid eighteenth century it was in common use. (René Pijassou, *Le Médoc: Un Grand Vignoble De Qualité: Tomes I & II*, Tallandier, Paris, 1978, p. 494.)

[77] Jackson, *Wine Science*, p. 312.

[78] In the United States, it is a requirement that no sulfur dioxide is used before a wine can be labeled "organic," although it can be described as "made from organic grapes" if the vineyard is certified as organic but sulfur dioxide is used at low levels (<100 ppm). In other countries, low levels of sulfur dioxide addition are allowed in production of organic wine.

[79] A study at Hallcrest Vineyards in Santa Cruz, California, during the 1991 harvest showed that wines fermented without any added sulfur dioxide had levels varying from 0 to 41 ppm after fermentation. While it is a myth that fermentation *always* produces some SO2, it certainly can produce low levels, depending on the conditions of fermentation.

[80] The major problem is for the 0.1% of people who lack the enzyme sulfite oxidase and therefore cannot metabolize sulfites.

[81] Sulfur dioxide is measured in ppm (parts per million). Legal limits in the European Union are 160 ppm for dry red wine, 210 ppm for dry white wine and rosé, and 300-400 ppm for various classes of sweet wines. In the United States it is 350 ppm for all wines. In Australia it is 250 ppm for dry wines and 350 ppm for sweet wines.

[82] Harry W. Paul, *Science, Vine, and Wine in Modern France* (Cambridge University Press, Cambridge, 1996), pp. 197-198.

[83] Ibid., pp. 189-190; Anthony Hanson, *Burgundy*, 2nd edition (Faber & Faber, London, 1995), p. 417; Frank Prial, *Wine Talk*, New York Times, November 26, 1997.

[84] Levels of allergens including sulfur dioxide and histamines are much lower in wine than many other foods, but alcohol may enhance the effects of histamine, so that its effect becomes significant for sensitive people.

[85] I tasted both wines from the 2007 vintage at Sepp Moser in August 2009. They were the Grüner Veltliner Kremstal Schnabel 2007 and Kremstal Schnabel MINIMAL 2007, both trocken with virtually no residual sugar (1.2 g/l) and 13.5% alcohol.

[86] Certainly there are different views as to what constitutes minimalist winemaking. Rowald Hepp at Schloss Vollrads in the Rheingau says that their winemaking attempts to achieve minimal intervention focus on going straight from fermentation in stainless steel into the glass bottle with minimal exposure to outside influences including oxygen (Author's discussion with Rowald Hepp, August, 2008).

Chapter 6: The Alchemist's Delight

[1] In the United States tolerance in labeling is reduced to 1% for wines above 14% alcohol.

[2] Michelle Waterman of Brochelle Vineyards, Paso Robles, discussion with author, January 2010.

[3] Troy Bunnell of Coyote Canyon Wines in the Santa Lucia Highlands, discussion with author, January 2010.

[4] 16% of winemakers use it routinely, 33% use it occasionally, 48% never use it, 2% do not know what it is (survey of winemakers in California conducted by the author in January 2010).

[5] Kathleen Inman of Inman Family Wines in Russian River Valley, discussion with author, January 2010.

[6] Douglas Braun of Presidio Winery in Santa Barbara County, discussion with author, January 2010.

[7] www.vinovation.com/alcadjustment.htm.

[8] Clark Smith, *Some Like It Hot*, Appellation America, September 2007.

[9] Felicity Lawrence, *Blanc Check For Wine Purity*, The Guardian, January 24, 2004, London.

[10] Michael Fridjhon, *Wine column*, Business Day, February 19, 2004.

[11] Charlotte Matthews, *KWW Fires Cheating Wine Makers Over Fruity Sauvignon*, Business Day, December 7, 2004.

[12] Acidity in g/l determines the taste of the wine, but another measure used by winemakers is the pH. This is a logarithmic scale indicating the concentration of hydrogen ion. pH varies from 0 to 14; pH of 7 is neutral, and lower pH means more acidity. pH is important because it determines the effectiveness of sulfur dioxide and the inhibition of bacterial growth. pH and acidity in g/l are not exactly correlated, which is why both are used.

[13] If grapes start with 9 g/l, after alcoholic fermentation the wine will have about 8 g/l (due to conversion of some malic acid to alcohol), and after malolactic fermentation acidity will be down to about 6 g/l (due to conversion of the rest of the malic acid to lactic acid).

[14] See p. 99.

[15] Double salt deacidification uses ACIDEX (calcium carbonate double seeded with small amounts of calcium tartrate-malate). This removes both tartaric acid and malic acid by forming crystals of the insoluble calcium tartrate-malate, but it is expensive.

[16] Per-Henrik Mansson, *Vive Le Vin Nature!* (Wine Spectator, February 3, 2000).

[17] The International Riesling Foundation has a scale based on the ratio of sugar to acid, where wines <1.0 are described as dry, ratios of 1.0-2.0 are called medium dry, ratios of 2.1-4.0 are medium sweet, and >4.1 is sweet.
See www.drinkriesling.com/tastescale/thescale/

[18] Quoted in Jamie Goode, *Residual Sugar*, Wine Business, April 2007.

[19] This is called back-blending, and the technique was developed in Germany after the second world war. In fact, it was more a rediscovery of an old technique, since the Romans knew that lowering the temperature would prevent fermentation, and they used this to preserve some unfermented grape juice that they could use later for sweetening wine they considered too dry.

[20] RCGM is also somewhat more expensive than using raw sugar.

[21] Grape juice contains two sugars, glucose and fructose, in roughly equal amounts. Yeasts ferment glucose first, so when sweetness is achieved by stopping fermentation, it is usually due to unfermented fructose. Fructose is usually reckoned to be almost twice as sweet as glucose. When süssreserve is added, it consists of both glucose and fructose, and the balance is different, because more sugar must be added to reach the same sweetness level, and the sweetness integrates less well.

[22] Quoted in Dan Berger, *Mega Purple* (Wines & Vines, March, 2006).

[23] There are several hybrids resulting from crosses of Aramon and Rupestris, the best known being AxR1 (infamously used as a rootstock in California), which is Aramon Rupestris Ganzin #1.

[24] Nick Dokoozlian, *Rubired*, in *Wine Grape Varieties in California* (University of California Agricultural and Natural Resources Publication 3419, Oakland, 2003). pp. 126-129.

[25] It is in seventh place in the list of leading varieties (Grape Crush Report, California Department of Food and Agriculture, 2009).

[26] Alternatively if it is added to the must rather than to the wine, the sugar will ferment to give alcohol.

[27] Berger, *Mega Purple*, op. cit.

[28] Ibid.

[29] Concentrate represents almost 20% of all crushed grapes in California, with 80% of the concentrate produced from white varieties, largely Thompson seedless, and 20% from red varieties, primarily Rubired, Royalty, and Salvador.

[30] Corie Brown, *What's Really In That Wine?*, Los Angeles Times, March 28, 2007.

[31] The latest idea is to try polyethylene which has "breathing capabilities."

[32] Some producers who punch-down the cap find that the conical shape is important because it allows better submersion of the cap.

[33] Technically the defining feature is the presence of a sulfur-hydrogen moiety.

[34] This is produced when yeast do not have enough nutrients during fermentation.

[35] It's usually reckoned this gives up to 0.5% less alcohol in the wine.

[36] Sometimes it is used with wine being matured in barrel as an alternative to racking, since it has the same effect in counteracting the reductive effect of the lees. This is called clicage and is popular on the right bank of Bordeaux, where it has been legal since 1997.

[37] He produces wines from Coonawarra, Clare Valley, and Adelaide Hills at Petaluma Wines.

[38] Although the top producers, such as the first growths in Bordeaux, have usually replaced all their oak every year given their greater resources.

[39] Light toasting might be 10 minutes duration at 120-180°C, medium is 10 minutes at 200°C, and heavy is >15 minutes at 230°C.

[40] Altogether about 100 volatile compounds have been reported to come from exposing wine to oak (Pascal Chatonnet, *Incidence Du Bois De Chêne Sur La Composition Chimique Et Les Qualités Organoleptiques Des Vins. Applications Technologiques*, Thesis, Université de Bordeaux II, 1991).

[41] Flavors derived from oak:

Compound	Effects on wine	Effect of toasting
Lactones	Coconut aromas; responsible for much of the "oaky" aromas in wine.	Levels reduced.
Vanillin	Extraction depends on the stage at which the wine is exposed. Barrel fermentation reduces concentration.	Derived from lignins, levels are greatest at medium toast.
Furfural, 5-methylfurfural	Butterscotch and caramel aromas.	Generated from sugars during toasting.
Eugene	Clove-like aromas.	A volatile phenol, increased by seasoning and toasting.
Coumarone	Cinnamon-like aromas.	Cinnamon acid derivatives extracted from oak.
Guaiacol, 4-methylguaiacol	Smoky aromas.	Formed by degradation of lignins during toasting.
Ellagitannins	More astringent than grape tannins.	Heavy toasting decreases concentration.

[42] Two types of oak trees are mixed in French forests (Quercus robur and Q. pedunculata), but it is mostly Q. robur that is used for barrel-making. The major forests in France are Limousin, Tronçais, Nevers, Allier, Jupilles, Vosges. Each has its own characteristics. Oak in Limousin grows fast and forms wide rings; it is mostly used for aging cognac. Allier oak from central France grows slowly, with tight rings. Tronçais is a small forest within Allier, forming even tighter grain. Nevers is a medium grain. Jupilles is very tight grain. In the past, the forest of origin was emphasized, but the trend at coopers now is more to select by the grain of the wood (finer is better).

[43] Quercus alba.

[44] Based on an analysis reported by ETS Laboratories, Technical Bulletin, February 8, 2009.

[45] StaVin Inc, Sausalito. see www.stavin.com/tanksystems/oakbeans.htm.

[46] Aurélia Rivier, *The Alchemy of Oak Add Ins* (Nadalie, USA, 2004); see www.nadalie-usa.com /pdf/nadalie_add-ins_alchemy.pdf.

[47] The Vines & Wines listing of oak alternatives suppliers has 4 providers for oak extract, 10 for oak dust or granules, 14 for chips, 5 for cubes, 12 for segments, 13 for tank inserts, 15 for staves to give a rough idea of relative popularity (Vines & Wines, April, 2008).

[48] Oak chips have been allowed in Vin de Pays but not at higher quality levels. The ex-

tension was recommended in a report commissioned to improve the competitiveness of French wines and will apply to all wines in France except for individual AOCs that ban the procedure (Bernard Pommel, *Réussir l'Avenir De La Viticulture Française. Plan National De Restructuration De La Filière Viti-Vinicole Française,* Ministry of Agriculture, Paris, 2006).

[49] As reported by Panos Kakaviatos, Decanter, March 30, 2006.

[50] TCA is estimated to be responsible for about 85% of corked wines, but the taint can also be produced by other, related compounds. Of course, sometimes there is a tendency to ascribe any problem with mustiness to the cork, and it can also be produced in other ways. See Mark A. Sefton & Robert F. Simpson, *Compounds Causing Cork Taint And The Factors Affecting Their Transfer From Natural Cork Closures To Wine - A Review* (Australian J. Grapes Wine Research, 11, 226-240, 2005).

[51] The value of cork exports was €850 million in 2007 according to the Portuguese National Institute of Statistics), representing 0.7% of Portugal's GDP. The total value of all wine exports was €575 million according to the IVV (*Vinha e do Vinho*: Vine and Wine Institute).

[52] The cork starts out with an average diameter of 24 mm (just under 1"), is compressed to 16 mm to fit it into the bottleneck, and expands to 18 mm after insertion.

[53] Those also implicated in wine include TeCA (2,3,4,6-tetrachloroanisole) and TBA (2,4,6-tribromoanisole).

[54] George Taber, *To Cork or Not to Cork,* pp. 71-79.

[55] Pascal Chatonnet, *Nature et Origin des Odeurs de "Moisi" dans les Caves, Incidences sur la Contamination des Vins* (J. Int. Sci. Vigne Vin, 28, 131-151, 1994).

[56] George Taber, *To Cork or Not to Cork,* pp. 31-35.

[57] According to John Kolasa of Château Canon, one of the few producers to be open about the problem, as reported in Conan, *L'Inavouable Maladie du Vin,* see note 58.

[58] Eric Conan & Jean-Paul Géné, *L'Inavouable Maladie du Vin* (L'Express, December 24, Paris, 1998).

[59] Ibid.

[60] Taber, *To Cork or Not to Cork,* pp. 181-191.

[61] H. R. Buser et al., *Identification of 2,4,6-Trichloroanisole as a Potent Compound Causing Cork Taint in Wine,* J. Agricultural and Food Chemistry 30, 359–38, 1982.

[62] Taber, *To Cork or Not to Cork,* p. 35.

[63] The Diamond process developed by Sabaté (now known as Oeneo) consists of treating corks with CO_2 in a "supercritical state," in which it is at the interface between gaseous and liquid conditions. As gas, it extracts TCA from the cork; as liquid it solubilizes it. It is much more efficient than previous techniques for washing corks, although more costly. The ROSA (Rate of Optimal Steam Extraction) process developed by Amorim uses steam treatment to extract volatile compounds; this reduces the level of TCA by 70-80%. However, it deforms the cork, but is useful with technical corks (corks made from agglomerated particles.

[64] This analogy was suggested to me by Paolo di Marchi.

[65] Jeffrey Grosset, famous for his Polish Hill Riesling, took the lead, and recruited 13 of the 25 winemakers in Clare Valley who produced Riesling.

[66] Taber, *To Cork or Not to Cork,* p. 49.

[67] The figures in the original study superficially suggest a difference of 1000-fold between the tightest and loosest corks. This may be misleading, and the real variation in corks is probably a few fold (Alan Limmer, *The Chemistry of Post–bottling Sulfides in Wine* (Chemistry in New Zealand, 69, 2-5, 2005).

[68] A. Hart and A. Kleinig, *The Role of Oxygen in the Aging of Bottled Wine* (Aust. N.Z. Wine Ind. J. 20, 46-50, 2005).

[69] Richard Alleyne, *Screwcaps Blamed for Tainting Wine*, Daily Telegraph, London, September 20, 2006.

[70] 1,1,6-trimethyl-1,2-dihydronaphthalene.

[71] Peter Godden et al, *Towards Offering Wine To The Consumer In Optimal Condition - The Wine, The Closures And Other Packaging Variables, Part II* (Infowine, Internet J. Viticul. Enol.,

Enoforum, Piacenza, March 2005).

[72] Pascal Ribéreau-Gayon et al., *The Handbook of Enology, Volume 2, The Chemistry of Wine Stabilisation and Treatments,* 2nd edition (John Wiley & Sons, New York, 2000), p. 405.

[73] Emile Peynaud, *Knowing and Making Wine* (Interscience, 1984), p. 254.

[74] packagingnews.co.uk, May 6, 2009.

[75] Victor Hugo, *Les Contemplations, La Fête Chez Thérèse,* I, 22.

Chapter 7: Thousand Cultivars

[1] This figure is biased by the fact the Airén is planted at an unusually low density, typically about 1500 vines per hectare. If the numbers were calculated in terms of number of vines planted rather than area planted, Airén would come out somewhat lower in the list.

[2] It's enormously difficult to get accurate figures on a worldwide basis. Data sources: for 1990 - Patrick Fegan, The Vineyard Handbook: Appellations, Maps and Statistics, 2nd edition, Chicago Wine School, Chicago, 2003; for 2004 - Jancis Robinson, Oxford Companion to Wine, 3rd edition, 2006, p. 746. The main difficulty is to keep up with the pace of change, which can outrun the official statistics. The trends shown in the figure are undoubtedly correct, but the exact numbers should be regarded as an approximation.

[3] Data based on the latest census for grape variety plantings in each country. There are some inconsistencies because data are more timely for the New World than for Europe.

[4] Data sources for plantings of varietals in individual countries are: Argentine Instituto Nacional de Vitivinicultura (Registro de Vinedos y Superficie), Australian Bureau of Statistics (Annual Reports 1329.0), California Department of Food and Agriculture, Sacramento (California Grape Acreage Reports), Catastro Viticola Nacional, Chile; SAWIS (South Africa Wine Industry Information and Systems; Statistics of Wine Grapes); ONIVINS (Les Principaux Cépages De Cuve / Departements Principaux : Blancs, Noirs); New Zealand winegrowers statistical annual, 2008; Moldova WineGuild MoldovaWein Dossier.

[5] The mutations are not in the genes actually coding for the enzymes that produce anthocyanins, but in regulatory genes that control expression of the anthocyanin genes. There are two (very similar) regulator genes, either of which can turn on anthocyanin synthesis. Both of them are inactivated in white grapevines. The two mutations (a different one in each regulator gene) are identical in 55 different cultivars that were examined (Amanda R. Walker, *White Grapes Arose Through The Mutation Of Two Similar And Adjacent Regulatory Genes,* The Plant Journal, 49, 772-785, 2007).

[6] Relationships were determined by DNA mapping of 222 cultivars and 22 wild grapevines (Mallikarjuna K. Aradhya et al., *Genetic structure and differentiation in cultivated grape, Vitis vinifera L,* (Genet. Res., 81, 179-92, 2003).

[7] This does not necessarily mean they were the first to be cultivated, but does indicate that they have been better preserved since their cultivation; many original cultivars from Greece and Italy, for example, may have been lost.

[8] Rosso, *Mystique of Barolo,* p. 18.

[9] According to the Unione Produttori Vini Albesi (Alba).

[10] Giovanni Battista Croce, *Della Eccellenza E Diversità Dei Vini Che Nella Montagna Di Torino Si Fanno E Del Modo Di Farli.*

[11] Dion, *Histoire de la Vigne,* p. 297.

[12] The origins of one such clone were analyzed by H. Yakushiji et al., *A Skin Color Mutation Of Grapevine, From Black-Skinned Pinot Noir To White-Skinned Pinot Blanc, Is Caused By Deletion Of The Functional Vvmyba1 Allele* (Biosci. Biotech. Biochem., 70, 1506-1508, 2006). Another is referred to by Amanda R. Walker et al., *Two New Grape Cultivars, Bud Sports Of Cabernet Sauvignon Bearing Pale-Coloured Berries, Are The Result Of Deletion Of Two Regulatory Genes Of The Berry Colour Locus* (Plant Mol. Biol., 62, 623-635, 2006).

[13] Pierre Gouges says that a white mutant was discovered in 1936 in the Clos des Porrets vineyard in Nuits St. Georges by his grandfather. Some cuttings were propagated in

1938, but it was not until 1947 that the major planting, 400 vines in the Perrières vineyard, was made. In 1997 a larger area was planted just outside Nuits St. Georges and is used to produce a Bourgogne Pinot Blanc. The cultivar was called Pinot Gouges at the oenological school at Montpellier (personal communication, Pierre Gouges, October 2009).

[14] Freddie Price, *Riesling Renaissance* (Mitchell Beazley, London, 2004).

[15] Jean-Alexandre Cavoleau, *Oenologie Française, Ou Statistique De Tous Les Vignobles Et De Toutes Les Boissons Vineuses Et Spiriteuses De La France, Suivie De Considérations Générales Sur La Culture De La Vigne* (Huzard, Paris, 1827).

[16] John Bowers et al., *A Single Pair Of Parents Proposed For A Group Of Grapevine Varieties In Northeastern France* (Acta Hort., 528, 129–132, 2000).

[17] Widespread genetic variety is consistent with the idea that it originated in the region. As a working rule, the greatest genetic variation in grape variety is found closest to its point of origin.

[18] Giovan Vettorio Soderini, *Trattato Della Coltivazione Delle Viti,* Firenze, 1590.

[19] Di Cosimo Trinci Pistojese, *Agricoltore Sperimentato*, Venezia, 1738; Gallesio, Pomona Italiana, Niccolò Capurro, Pisa, 1830.

[20] José F. Vouillamoz et al., *The Parentage Of 'Sangiovese', The Most Important Italian Wine Grape* (Vitis 46, 19-22, 2007).

[21] George M. Taber, *Judgment of Paris: California vs. France and the Historic 1976 Paris Tasting That Revolutionized Wine* (Scribner, New York, 2006).

[22] Is it a sign of progress that the estimate for aroma complexity does not come from direct measurement of ability to smell, but from genetic analysis of the human genome, which shows several hundred genes coding for odorant receptors? By contrast, there are only five types of taste receptor genes, and the largest family (for bitter taste) has only 25 members.

[23] A. F. Blakeslee, *Unlike Reaction Of Different Individuals To Fragrance In Verbena Flowers,* Science, 48, 298-299, 1918.

[24] Andreas Keller and Leslie B. Vosshall, *Better Smelling Through Genetics: Mammalian Odor Perception,* Curr. Opin. Neurobiol., 18, 364-369, 2008.

[25] The range is from 10 to 10,000 depending on the odor (Yehudit Hasin-Brumshtein et al., *Human Olfaction: From Genomic Variation To Phenotypic Diversity,* Trends Genetics, 25, 178-184).

[26] Different combinations of the proteins coded by these genes are used to detect sweet and unami.

[27] Dennis Drayna, *Human Taste Genetics* (Ann. Rev. Genomics Human Genetics, 6, 217-235, 2005).

[28] Beverly J. Tepper, *Nutritional Implications of Genetic Taste Variation: The Role of PROP Sensitivity and Other Taste Phenotypes* (Annu. Rev. Nutr. 2008., 28, 14.1–14.22, 2008).

[29] Stephen Wooding, *Phenylthiocarbamide: A 75-Year Adventure in Genetics and Natural Selection* (Genetics, 172, 2015-2023, 2006).

[30] The gene is called TAS2R38. Inactive variants are recessive. There is one major inactive variant in the human population, and several minor variants, one of which causes intermediate sensitivity to bitterness. Although the inactive variants do not react with PTC, it is possible they are active with some other (unidentified) bitter compound (U. K. Kim and Denis Drayna, *Genetics Of Individual Differences In Bitter Taste Perception: Lessons From The PTC Gene,* Clin. Genet., 67, 276-280, 2004).

[31] 6-n-propylthiouracil.

[32] Linda M. Bartoshuk et al., *PTC/PROP Tasting: Anatomy, Psychophysics, And Sex Effects* (Physiol. Behav., 56, 1165-1171, 1994).

[33] I have been unable to find any published scientific support for the connection with morning sickness (obviously more difficult to prove than the others since it rests on anecdotal evidence). One study that tested for a connection in pregnant women themselves found no increase in morning sickness for super-tasters (Sipiora et al., *Bitter Taste Perception And Severe Vomiting In Pregnancy,* Physiol Behav., 69, 259-267, 2000). Another showed a preference for high salt intake in infants whose mothers had morning sickness (Susan R. Crystal and Ilene L. Bernstein, *Infant Salt Preference and Mother's Morning Sick-*

ness, Appetite, 30, 297–307, 1998). However, unpublished results obtained by consumer research of the Napa Seasoning Company are reported to show directly a correlation between morning sickness and bitter sensitivity in offspring (personal communication, Tim Hanni MW, February 2010).

[34] PTC and PROP are thiols (sulfur-containing) substances, and it has been thought that the receptor recognizes compounds containing the thiocyanate (N-C=S) structure. This is not found in tannins or caffeine. The range of compounds to which PTC/PROP tasters have increased sensitivity also includes saccharin, salt, potassium benzoate.

[35] Super-tasters have greater sensitivity to a wide range of features in red wine, including acidity, saltiness, textural factors, and astringency (Gary J. Pickering and Gordon Robert, *Perception Of Mouthfeel Sensations Elicited By Red Wine Are Associated With Sensitivity To 6-N-Propylthiouracil,* J. Sensory Studies, 21, 249–265, 2006).

[36] Based on data of Dennis Drayna et al., *A Model System for Identifying Genes Underlying Complex Traits* (Cold Spring Harbor Symp. Quant. Biol., 68, 365-371, 2003).

[37] Super-tasters are not reliably predicted by threshold tests. Instead, methods called suprathreshold testing are used. These basically rely on the tasters' reported reactions to a given dose (see note 32). If super-tasters detected a lower absolute threshold, they would occupy the far right part of the curve, but in fact they appear to be distributed among the entire taster population. Their reported response is strong whatever their threshold levels. This is shown by the fact that people can be divided into the same groups of nontasters, tasters, super-tasters when tested with PROP over a 100-fold concentration scale (Gary J. Pickering, Katerina Simunkova, and David DiBattista, *Intensity of taste and astringency sensations elicited by red wines is associated with sensitivity to PROP (6-n-propylthiouracil),* Food Qual. Pref. 15, 147–54, 2004, table 1).

[38] Gregory K. Essick, et al., *Lingual tactile acuity, taste perception, and the density and diameter of fungiform papillae in female subjects* (Physiol. Behav., 80, 289-302, 2003).

[39] Juyun Lim, Lenka Urban, and Barry G. Green, *Measures of Individual Differences in Taste and Creaminess Perception* (Chemical Senses, 33, 493- 501, 2008).

[40] The association of super-tasters with bitter perception may simply be due to a historical accident: that diagnosis has been performed with PTC/PROP. This has the consequence that nontasters for PTC/PROP cannot be assessed. It might be that with a different test, super-tasters would also be present in the PTC-nontaster population, which would give a broader perspective on the phenomenon. A real understanding of the super-taster phenomenon requires a more objective measurement for supertasting than is presently available.

[41] Alexey A. Fushan et al., *Allelic Polymorphism within the TAS1R3 Promoter Is Associated with Human Taste Sensitivity to Sucrose* (Current Biol., 19, 1-6, 2009).

[42] Martha R. Bajec and Gary J. Pickering, *Astringency: Mechanisms and Perception* (Crit. Rev. Food Science Nutrition, 48, 858–875, 2008).

[43] Incidentally, it is not only the senses of taste and smell that differ among individuals, but also vision. There are two different red eye pigments in the human population, with the result that different individuals do in fact see slightly different red color spectrums, so presumably will have slightly different views of red wines (Benjamin Lewin, *On Neuronal Specificity and the Molecular Basis of Perception,* Cell, 79, 935-943, 1994).

[44] Pavla Polásková et al., *Wine flavor: chemistry in a glass* (Chem Soc. Rev., 37, 2478-2489, 2008).

[45] Christian Lindinger, *When Machine Tastes Coffee: Instrumental Approach To Predict the Sensory Profile of Espresso Coffee* (Anal. Chem. 2008, 80, 1574-1581).

[46] John E. Bowers & Carole P. Meredith, *The parentage of a classic wine grape, Cabernet Sauvignon* (Nature Genetics, 16, 84-86, 1997).

[47] J.-M. Boursiquot et al., *Parentage of Merlot and related winegrape cultivars of southwestern France: discovery of the missing link* (Australian J. Grape and Wine Research, 15, 144-155, 2008).

[48] Ibid.

[49] France 60,800 ha (including 30,382 ha in Bordeaux and 19,299 ha in Languedoc), Chile 40,765 ha, United States 30,769 ha, Australia 27,309 ha, Spain 19,430 ha, Argentina

17,921 ha, Bulgaria 16,600 ha, South Africa 12,252 ha. Data sources; see note 4.

[50] Armailhacq comments in his book that Cabernet had been spreading rapidly in recent years (Armand d'Armailhacq, *De la culture des vignes, de la vinification et des vins dans le Médoc*, Chaumas, Bordeaux, 1867, p. 37).

[51] Lewin, *What Price Bordeaux?*, p. 60.

[52] Ibid., p. 161.

[53] John Livingstone-Learmonth, *The wines of the Northern Rhône*, p. 237.

[54] Serine d'Ampuis (from Côte-Rôtie) and Syrah de l'Hermitage were only recognized as being the same variety in the twentieth century.

[55] Not to be confused with the grape today sometimes called Petite Syrah in California, which is really Durif.

[56] John Livingstone-Learmonth, *The Wines Of The Northern Rhône*, p. 16.

[57] Ibid., p. 16.

[58] James Halliday, *The History of Shiraz in Australia* (World of Fine Wine, issue 20, 2008).

[59] France 67,800 ha; Australia 42,806 ha; Spain 16,586 ha; Argentina 12,772 ha; South Africa 9,754 ha; United States 6,896 ha; Chile 4,795 ha. Data sources: see note 4.

[60] Burgundy has 10,040 ha, including 5,800 ha on the Côte d'Or and 2,800 ha on the Côte Chalonnaise. California has almost 5,000 ha, with half in Sonoma and rest spread among Napa, Santa Barbara, and Monterey. Germany's main area is Baden, with 5,729 ha. New Zealand now has 4,650 ha. Data sources; see note 4.

[61] France 27,900 ha (11,650 ha in Champagne and 10,040 ha in Burgundy); Germany 11,371 ha; United States, 11,038 ha (3,268 ha in Oregon and 4,982 ha in California); New Zealand, 4,650 ha; Switzerland 4,659 ha; Australia, 4,208 ha; Italy, 3,287 ha; Moldova accounts for most of the other plantings in Europe, with 8,200 ha. Data sources; see note 4.

[62] Jackson, *Wine Science,* p. 50.

[63] The genetic map is shared with two other varieties, Pinot Moure and Pinot fin teinturier (which has colored juice).

[64] Paul K. Boss & Mark R. Thomas, *Association of dwarfism and floral induction with a grape 'green revolution' mutation* (Nature, 416, 847-850, 2002).

[65] S. Hocquigny, *Diversification within grapevine cultivars goes through chimeric states* (Genome 47, 579–589, 2004).

[66] France, 43,887 ha (13,500 in Burgundy; 9,000 ha in Languedoc); United States, 39,728 ha; Australia, 30,820 ha; Italy, 11,686 ha; Chile, 8,753 ha; South Africa, 8,327 ha; Argentina, 6,613 ha; Spain, 5,423 ha; New Zealand, 3, 861 ha. Data sources; see note 4.

[67] There is one prominent exception. The Chardonnay Musqué clone has strong aromatics with some grapey, Muscat-like features. This is ENTAV-INRA clone 809. The comparison with Muscat is based solely on gustatory experience; there appears to have been no direct analysis of volatile compounds. There's a little grown in Macon, and some in northeastern Italy; otherwise it's favored by some New World producers who want to make a more aromatic wine than you usually get from Chardonnay's neutral profile.

[68] One vineyard block was given over to the experiment. There were six rows of each clone, giving 5-10 barrels of wine per clone.

[69] The number of clusters per vine varied from 20 to 28, the number of berries from 68 to 125, the weight per berry from 1.0 to 1.4 g, total range of yields varied from 1.7 to 4 tons per acre, the Brix at harvest varied from 23.4 to 25, acidity varied from 8.1 to 9.7 g/l tartaric (personal communication from Mark Lingenfelder).

[70] Comments on properties of individual clones from the author's tasting notes.

[71] France, 22,062 ha (divided between the Loire, Bordeaux, and the Languedoc); New Zealand, 13,988 ha (two thirds in Marlborough); Chile, 8,862 ha; South Africa, 7,753 ha; United States, 5,697 ha; Australia, 5,327 ha. Data sources: see note 4.

[72] IBMP levels were measured in Cabernet Sauvignon grown in Tarragona by Christina Sala et al., *Contents of 3-alkyl-2-methoxypyrazines in musts and wines from Vitis vinifera variety Cabernet Sauvignon: influence of irrigation and plantation density* (J. Science Food Agric., 85,1131-1136, 2005).

[73] The intensity of each aroma on the spider chart is indicated by its distance from the center. Red shows fermentation with a yeast that has increased carbon sulfur lyase activity

compared to the yeast used for the blue fermentation (Jan H. Swiegers et al., *Enhancement of Sauvignon blanc wine aroma through yeast combinations,* Wynboer, South Africa, 2000).

[74] The detection threshold is 2 ppm; levels in wine vary from 2 ppm to 40 ppm (Jan H. Swiegers et al., *Meeting consumer expectations through management in vineyard and winery,* AWRI Report, 2005).

[75] 4-MMP is 4-mercapto-4-methylpentan-2-one. The others are 3-MH (3-mercapto-hexan-1-ol) and 3-MHA (3-mercaptohexyl-acetate).

[76] The perception threshold is only 0.8 ppb. Typical levels in wine are 4-24 ppb (Denis Dubourdieu et al., *The role of yeasts in grape flavor development during fermentation: the example of Sauvignon Blanc,* Am. J. Enol. Vitic., 57, 81-88, 2006).

[77] Threshold levels give impression of broom, tropical fruits before the 25 ppm level, first signs of cat's pee by 50 ppm. 3-MH and 3-MHA require much higher levels relative to threshold before they turn to cat's pee (personal communication from Sakkie Pretorious).

[78] The inactive form is bound to the amino acid cysteine. The enzyme that releases the volatile compound is called a carbon-sulfur lyase. Both 4-MMP and 3-MH are formed by this mechanism. 3-MHA is not present at all in the berry and is synthesized by yeast enzymes by modifying 3-mercaptohexanol (Jan H. Swiegers et al., *The Influence of Yeast on the Aroma of Sauvignon Blanc Wine* (Food Microbiology, 26, 204–211, 2009).

[79] Ibid.

[80] W. R. Sponholz and T. Hühn, *Einflussfaktoren von Klonenmaterial und verwendetem Hefestamm auf die Alterung von Riesling Weinen (Factors influencing the ageing of Riesling wines : Clonal material and used yeast strain),* Wein-Wissenschaft, 52, 103-108, 1997.

[81] Although it is fair to say we don't fully understand all the factors determining when and how much develops, it can reach levels of 200 μg/l in aged wines, some ten times greater than the threshold for detection (Uli Fischer, *Wine Aroma,* Wine Aroma – Flavours and Fragrances. Chemistry, Bioprocessing and Sustainability. Ed. R.G. Berger, Springer Verlag, 241-267., Berlin, 2007).

[82] Tom Cannavan's wine-pages.com; see www.wine-pages.com/guests/tom/riesling-petrol-2.htm.

[83] Germany, 20,627 ha; Australia, 4,270 ha; France, 3,480 ha (mostly in Alsace), United States, 1,802 ha; Austria, 1,642 ha; New Zealand, 917 ha. Data sources: see note 4.

[84] About 40 terpenes have been found in grapes. All terpenes are based on a five-carbon unit called isopentenyl pyrophosphate (IPP). They are named for the number of these 5-carbon units: hemiterpenes (one 5-carbon), monoterpenes (2), sesquiterpenes (3), etc. Terpenes can be simple hydrocarbons (endings in "ene"), aldehydes (endings in "al"), alcohols (endings in "ol"), ketones (endings in "one"), acids and esters.

[85] Albariño is an exception where the majority are free.

[86] Jan H. Swiegers et al., *Yeast and bacterial Modulation of Wine Aroma and Flavor* (Austra-lian J. Grape and Wine Research 11, 139–173, 2005), p. 157; Uli Fischer, *Wine Aroma* (Wine Aroma. Flavours and Fragrances. Chemistry, Bioprocessing and Sustainability. Ed. R.G. Berger, Springer Verlag, 241-267., Berlin, 2007).

[87] Jancis Robinson, *The Oxford Companion to Wine* (Oxford University Press, Oxford, 1994), p. 649.

[88] Manna F. Crespan and N. Milani, *The Muscats: A molecular analysis of synonyms, homonyms and genetic relationships within a large family of grapevine cultivars* (Vitis 40, 23-30, 2001); Cecilia B. Agüero, *Identity and Parentage of Torrontés Cultivars in Argentina* (Am. J. Enol. Vitic., 54, 318-321, 2003).

[89] Robinson, *The Oxford Companion,* op. cit., p. 651.

[90] Unidentified "Muscat" represents 38% of plantings, Muscat d'Alexandrie is 29%, Muscat Blanc à Petits Grains is 14%, Muscat Ottonel and Hamburg are 9% each. Data sources; see note 4.

[91] Christian Lindinger, *When Machine Tastes Coffee: Instrumental Approach To Predict the Sensory Profile of Espresso Coffee* (Anal. Chem. 2008, 80, 1574-1581.)

[92] Based on the original aroma wheel of Ann Noble of the University of California.

[93] This was the highest proportion for a genetically modified crop. Cotton was 47%, maize 23%, and rapeseed 21% (Clive James, *Global Status of Commercialized Biotech/GM*

Crops: 2008. ISAAA Brief No. 39., ISAAA, International Service for the Acquisition of Agri-Biotech Applications, Ithaca, NY; see also GMO Compass, www.gmo-compass.org).

[94] The sequence of the grapevine genome has 30,434 genes (Olivier Jaillon et al., *The grapevine genome sequence suggests ancestral hexaploidization in major angiosperm phyla*, Nature, 449, 463-467, 2007).

[95] C. L. Barker et al., *Genetic and physical mapping of the grapevine powdery mildew resistance gene, Run1, using a bacterial artificial chromosome library* (Theor. Appl. Genet., 111, 370-377, 2005).

[96] Actually, special techniques are required because Muscadinia has a different number of chromosomes from Vitis, so it would not be possible simply to breed the gene into a cultivar.

[97] Institut National des Appellations d'Origine.

[98] These vines actually are 41B rootstocks modified to resist the nematode that carries fanleaf virus. They come from an experiment started by Moët and Chandon in Champagne in 1996, but the vines were pulled up there in 1999 as a result of public protests.

[99] Two examples would be the widespread use of the Pinot Droit clone of Pinot Noir in Burgundy in the 1960s, and the more recent use of clones based on the over-productive Grosse Syrah strain in the northern Rhône.

[100] 124 samples of table grapes were purchased in supermarkets in Germany, France, Holland, Hungary, and Italy in 2008. 123 contained detectable pesticide residues, with an average content of 0.65 mg/kg. The study was reported by MDRGF (Mouvement pour le droit et le respect des générations futures) in France; see www.mdrgf.org.

[101] Melané A.Vivier and Isak S. Pretorius, *Genetically tailored grapevines for the wine industry* (Trends Biotechnology, 20, 472-478, 2002); Isak S. Pretorius & Peter B. Hoj, *Grape and Wine Biotechnology: Challenges, Opportunities and Potential Benefits* (Australian J. Grape and Wine Research, 11, 83–108, 2005).

[102] Isak S Pretorius & Florian F Bauer, *Meeting the consumer challenge through genetically customized wine-yeast strains* (Trends Biotechnology, 20, 426-432, 2002).

[103] ML01 is basically the same as the parental strain Prise de Mousse S92, one of the standard cultured yeast strains for wine fermentation, except that it can also perform malolactic fermentation. It was created by the insertion of two genes. One is the malate permease gene, obtained from another yeast strain, S. pombe; this allows the yeast to take up malic acid. The second is the malolactic gene, obtained from Oenococcus oeni (the bacterium usually responsible for malolactic fermentation), which causes the yeast to convert malic acid to lactic acid (John I. Husnik et al., *Metabolic engineering of malolactic wine yeast*, Metabolic Engineering, 8, 315-323, 2006).

[104] The authors claim that the wine has lower content of histamine (reducing risk of migraines), because biogenic amines are usually produced by bacteria during MLF. It also has lower volatile acidity (less acetic acid) (John I. Husnik et al., *Functional Analyses of the Malolactic Wine Yeast ML01*, Am. J. Enol. Vitic., 58, 42-52, 2007).

[105] It was approved by the FDA and has been available on the United States market since 2005. It was initially distributed by Springer Oenologie, but now does not have a commercial distributor, although it is available directly from its creator, Hennie van Vuuren, in the United States and Canada. It is not known how many wineries are using it, because none is presently prepared to admit publicly to its use.

[106] It was ordered to be pulled out in Lorraine in 1598 and in Besançon in 1731 (Pierre Galet, *Cépages et Vignobles de France: L'Ampelographie Française*, Paul Dehan, 1956, p. 146).

[107] Grape varieties arising from crosses between Gouais Blanc and Pinot include Aligoté, Aubin Vert, Auxerrois, Bachet noir, Beaunoir, Chardonnay, Dameron, Franc Noir de la-Haute-Saône, Gamay Blanc Gloriod, Gamay noir, Knipperlé, Melon (Muscadet), Peurion, Romorantin, Roublot, and Sacy (John Bowers et al., *Historical Genetics: The Parentage of Chardonnay, Gamay, and Other Wine Grapes of NorthEastern France*, Science, 285, 1562-1565, 1999).

[108] Müller-Thurgau was created by Dr. Hermann Müller (who was born in the Swiss canton of Thurgau) at the Geisenheim Institute in Germany. It was originally thought to

be a cross between Riesling and Sylvaner, but recently it was discovered that Sylvaner is not the other parent. After confusion arising from the fact that several cultivars in the reference grapevine collections were misclassified, which led to the misidentification of Chasselas as the other parent, DNA mapping showed that the second parent was the Madeleine Royale cultivar from the collection in Montpellier (Büscher et al., *On the origin of the grapevine variety Müller-Thurgau as investigated by the inheritance of random amplified polymorphic DNA (RAPD)*, Vitis, 33, 15-17, 1994; Erika Dettweiler et al., *Grapevine cultivar Muller-Thurgau and its true to type descent*, Vitis, 39, 63-65, 2000).

[109] Currently most new grapevine plantings in France are clones.

Chapter 8: Global Wine Trends

[1] Unwin, *Wine and the Vine*, p. 128.

[1] Quoted in *Wine War. Savvy New World marketers are devastating the French wine industry*, Business week cover story, September 3, 2001.

[1] Phil Davies and Dermot Walsh, Alcohol problems and alcohol control in Europe, Gardner, 1990. p. 74.

[2] DGDDI (Direction Générale des Douanes et Droits Indirects); INSEE (National Institute for Statistics and Economic Studies).

[3] The Wine Institute (California) figures for U.S. consumption, 1937-2007.

[4] "Plonk" may have originated as a generic term for cheap wine as a transmogrification of "vin blanc" by British soldiers in the first world war (Ian Gately, *Drink. A Cultural History of Alcohol*, Gotham Books, New York, 2008, p. 361).

[5] Lewin, *What Price Bordeaux?*, p. 67.

[6] Data from the vines.org auction database of prices for auctions at Christie's, Sotheby's and Acker Merrall in London and New York for wines of vintages after 2000 sold at auctions through 2009. Numbers refer to different types of wines reaching a price over $100 per bottle.

[7] In terms of total sales of wines at more than $100 per bottle at the auctions during the first decade of the 21st century, France accounts for 90% of revenue, with Bordeaux twice as important as Burgundy. See note 6.

[8] The numbers of wines in individual regions are: Burgundy, 144; Bordeaux, 61; Rhône, 36; Napa, 47; Sonoma, 41; Piedmont, 12; Tuscany, 12; Rioja, 8; Barossa, 15; McLaren Vale, 7. See note 6.

[9] Brands from the USA: Gallo, Mondavi, Beringer, Blossom Hill, Sutter Home, Inglenook, Kendall Jackson; Australia: Hardy's, Jacob's Creek, Lindemans, Yellow Tail, Banrock Station, Wolf Blass, Penfolds; Chile: Concho y Toro; Spain: Torres; South Africa: Kumala (Intangible Business, *The Power 100. The World's most powerful spirits and wine brands*, London, 2008).

[10] Jean-Bernard Marquette, *La Vinification dans les Domaines de l'Archeveque de Bordeaux a la fin du Moyen Age* (In A. Huetz de Lemps et al. (Eds.), Géographie Historique des Vignobles, Tome I Vignobles Français, CNRS, Paris, 1978).

[11] Some sample prices from a Christies' auction in April 1820 (recalculated per dozen bottles) are: Port, £3.15; East India Madeira, £4.24; White Creaming Champagne, £3.54; Hock (Mannheim), £4.05.

[12] It has been claimed that in the early nineteenth century, Riesling from Germany's Rheingau became the most expensive wine in England, at 50s per bottle representing twice the price of any other wine (John Hurley, *A Matter of Taste: The History of Wine Drinking in Britain*, The History Press, 2005, p. 84.) I am unable to substantiate this claim from Christies' auction records, which suggest to the contrary that Riesling (usually identified only as "Hock" or "Moselle") was generally priced close to claret.

[13] Samples prices from a Christies' auction in June 1860 (recalculated per dozen) were: Claret (Cos d'Estournel, 1848), £3.30; Sherry (1820 vintage), £3.45; Madeira (old Boal), £4.20; Port (Quarles Harris, 1840), £4.30.

[14] Christies auction records for the 1890s show sales mostly of three dozen lots, with prices (recalculated per dozen) for some typical lots as follows: Pommery 1874, £10.25-

12.00; Veuve Clicquot 1874, £6.24-7.00; Perrier-Jouet 1874, £7.75-12.50; Lafite 1870, £3.30-4.75; Lafite 1864, £5.36; Margaux 1870, £2.36; "Port" 1847, £6.25; Sandeman 1863, £4.67; Yquem 868, £5.00; Yquem 1870, £4.20; Steinberg Cabinet 1862, £6.75; Liebfraumilch 1874, £2.33; Romanée-Conti 1868, £6.50; Le Montrachet (Bouchard) 1870, £4.00.

[15] In 2009, boxes of Franzia Chablis could be bought on the U.S. market for $1.60 per 750 ml; the most expensive wine of the Bordeaux 2005 vintage, Château Ausone, came on the market for $2200 per bottle.

[16] Hugh Johnson, *The Story of Wine* (Mitchell Beazley, London, 2005), p.145.

[17] Prices for 1890 taken from Christies' auction results (see note 14). Prices for 2010 taken for current releases of the most expensive wine in each category (Red Burgundy – Romanée-Conti; Bordeaux – Château Ausone; Napa – Screaming Eagle Cabernet; Sauternes – Château d'Yquem; Rhône – Côte-Rôtie La Turque; White Burgundy – Le Montrachet; Champagne – Dom Pérignon, Roederer Cristal.

[18] See Chapter 1.

[19] James Conaway, *Napa* (Mariner Books, New York, 2002), p. 9.

[20] Tim Unwin, *Wine and the Vine*, pp. 102-104.

[21] Thomas Pellechia, *Wine. The 8000 year old story of the wine trade* (Running Press, Philadelphia, 2006), p. 48.

[22] Unwin, *Wine and the Vine*, pp. 108-109.

[23] By 1959, Peynaud published a scientific paper showing that malolactic fermentation could be induced by inoculating wine with the appropriate bacteria (CR Seances Acad. Agric, France, 45, p. 355).

[24] Quoted in Frank Ward (Connoisseur magazine, New York, May issue, 1987).

[25] According to châteaux identified on the web sites of the oenologists or oenologists identified on the web sites of the châteaux.

[26] Decanter magazine (U.K.) was founded in 1975, Finigan's Private Guide to Wines (U.S.) became national in 1977, The Wine Advocate (U.S.) was founded in 1978, and The Wine Spectator (U.S.) in its present form dates from 1979. Alles über Wein in Germany dates from 1982. Only in France does consumer criticism go back substantially earlier, to the Revue du Vin de France founded in 1927.

[27] The Private Guide finally ceased publication in 1990.

[28] Author's discussion with a château proprietor in Margaux, March 2009.

[29] Lewin, *What Price Bordeaux?*, pp. 145-148.

[30] David Darlington, *The chemistry of a 90+ wine*, New York Times, August 7, 2005.

[31] Michael Steinberger, *Grape Rot. The new Wine Spectator's distinct aroma of fishiness* (Slate, December 26, www.slate.com/id/2075720/, 2002).

[32] James Suckling, *Magnificent Wines From a Flawless Vintage*, Wine Spectator, July 31, 2004.

[33] Chateau St. Jean was founded in 1973, became known for the elegance of its Cabernet Sauvignon and Chardonnay, and was bought by Beringer Wine Estates in 1996.

[34] Michael Steinberger, *Grape Rot*, op. cit.

[35] Ibid.

[36] Ibid.

[37] Amanda Hessser, *A Wine Award that Seems Easy to Come By*, New York Times, July 9, 2003.

[38] Details are on Robin Goldstein's blog at blindtaste.com.

[39] Quoted in Jerry Hirsch, *Hoax leaves bitter taste for wine magazine*, Chicago Tribune, August 24, 2008.

[40] Omer Gokcekus and Andrew Fargnoli, *Is Globalization Good for Wine Drinkers in the United States?*, J. Wine Economics, 2, 187-195, 2007.

[41] Robert Joseph and Joel Payne, *Wines Without Frontiers*, Wine Business International, January 2007.

[42] Ibid.

[43] Examples of globally-sourced brands: Blue Nun has 20 wines from Germany, France, Chile, Australia, and the United States; Bernard Magrez has wines from France,

Italy, United States, Morocco, Spain, Uruguay; Mateus includes wines from Portugal and Spain; Torres has wines from Spain and Chile; Lindemans has wines from Australia. South Africa, and Chile; Ravenswood has wines from the United States and Australia. Ibid.

[44] A total of 5.73% from Gallo, Franzia, Carlo Rossi, Tavernello, Almaden, Sutter Home, Woodbridge, Beringer, JP Chenet, and Riunite in 2002 (Liz Thach & Tim Matz, *Wine: A Global Business, 1st edition,* Miranda Press, 2004, p. 7).

[45] Gallo, Hardy's, Concho y Toro, Mondavi, Beringer, Jacob's Creek, Lindemans, Blossom Hill, Yellow Tail, and Sutter Home were the top ten in 2008 according to Intangible Business, *The Power 100. The World's most powerful spirits and wine brands,* London, 2008.

[46] Ellen Hawkes, *Blood and Wine: The Unauthorized Story of the Gallo Wine Empire* (Simon & Schuster, New York, 1993), p. 167.

[47] Accurate numbers on a worldwide basis are difficult to obtain; these are approximations, especially given the rapidly of change. Total worldwide consumption is about 32 billion 750 ml-equivalents. Glass accounts for around 19.68 million, approaching two thirds. Of the glass bottles, about 13 billion are sealed with natural corks, 2.8 billion are technical corks, and 2.5 billion are synthetic (plastic) corks (Skalli & Rein, *Global Wine Closure Report,* 2006). The hardest number to assess is the proportion under screwcap, because it has been increasing so rapidly. In the 2006 report it was stated as 1.24 billion, but more recent estimates vary from 1.7 billion from cork producer Amorim to 2.5 billion from Italian screwcap producer Guala and synthetic cork producer Nomacorc (Jamie Goode, *Screwcaps take 15% of Global Market,* Decanter, March 9, 2009). No one knows the breakdown of the other types of packaging, but bag-in-box, tetrapak, and P.E.T. bottles are probably used in declining order of importance.

[48] Energy consumption measured in a study of a winery in Italy was 28.1 MJ/bottle of wine produced, but only 13.2 MJ/750 ml of bulk wine (Fulvio Ardente et al., *POEMS: A Case Study of an Italian Wine-Producing Firm,* Environmental Management 38, 350–364, 2006).

[49] Study performed for Nomacorc (producer of synthetic corks) using the Bilan Carbone method, April 2008. Similar results were reported previously in a study performed for Oeneo, reported by Jamie Goode, *The Carbon Trail of Closures* (Wine Business, April, 2007). Another study was performed for Amorim in October 2008 by PriceWaterhouseCoopers, *Evaluation of the environmental impacts of Cork Stoppers versus Aluminium and Plastic Closures* (Amorim, 2008).

[50] Unwin, *Wine and the Vine,* p. 132.

[51] Dion, *Histoire de la Vigne,* p. 31.

[52] Total revenue was Ff380 million, which was 15% of all revenue (Charles K. Warner, *The Winegrowers of France and the Government since 1875,* Columbia University Press, New York, 1960, p. 1).

[53] Unwin, *Wine and the Vine,* p. 242.

[54] For example, The World Health Organization's European Charter on Alcohol proposes that each Member State should: "Promote health by controlling the availability, for example for young people, and influencing the price of alcoholic beverages, for instance by taxation."

[55] Peter Anderson and Ben Baumberg, *Alcohol In Europe. A Public Health Perspective. A report for the European Commission,* Institute of Alcohol Studies, London, June 2006, p. 385.

[56] The effect of price increases is least for beer, in the middle for wine, but quite effective for spirits (Anderson and Baumberg, op cit., p. 259).

[57] The pattern is slightly different among young people, but the same principle holds. The high tax countries of Britain, Sweden, Norway are at the top; the low tax countries of France and Italy are at the bottom (Anderson and Baumberg, op cit., pp. 93, 105).

[58] Ibid.

[59] Consumption in liters of pure alcohol per person per year from European health for all database (HFA-DB) (data.euro.who.int/hfadb/). Data for tax on wine from individual countries.

[60] Data for U.K. market from Wine and Spirit Trade Association, London, September

2009; data for U.S. market from Wine Institute, California, *Proposed Excise Tax Surcharge on California Wine*, Stonebridge Research report, January 2009.

[61] l'Association Nationale de Prévention en Alcoologie et Addictologie (ANPAA)

[62] The fine was imposed by the Tribunal de Grand Instance de Paris on December 20, 2008.

[63] Quoted in The Times, London, September 19, 2008.

[64] The advice was apparently based on a claim by INCA, the French national cancer institute, claiming that any consumption of alcohol increases risk of mouth and throat cancer. Other authorities regard this as flawed (Decanter, February 20, 2009).

[65] Tyler Colman, *Wine Politics: How Governments, Environmentalists, Mobsters, and Critics Influence the Wines We Drink* (University of California Press, 2008), p. 57.

[66] www.heineken.fr now gives a message "Le site www.Heineken.fr est momentanément indisponible." Unfortunately, "momentanément" is a euphemism.

[67] Recent government guidelines in Britain recommend, entirely without any evidence, that children under 15 should not be allowed to consume alcohol even at meals with their parents. See www.direct.gov.uk/en/Nl1/Newsroom/DG_174464.

[68] Most countries fit the pattern, although there are some exceptions (Griffith Edwards and Marcus Grant, *Alcoholism: New Knowledge and New Responses*, Croom Helm, London, 1977, p. 25).

[69] This should be better evidence than the correlation between different countries because there are fewer variables. However, there is almost as good a correlation between the drop in alcohol consumption and a drop in accidental poisoning! (WHO Global Status Report on Alcohol, 2004.)

[70] As one measure of the contrast, moderate drinking is considered to be a couple of glasses of wine per day. Statistics show that 14% of alcoholics who drink the equivalent of 2 bottles of wine or half a bottle of spirits every day for 8 years will develop cirrhosis (Robert E. Mann, *The epidemiology of alcoholic liver disease*, Alcohol Research & Health, Fall, 2003).

[71] Roy Porter, *The Creation of the Modern World. The Untold Story of the British Enlightenment*, W. W. Norton, 2001, p. 81.

[72] Raymond Pearl, *Alcohol and Longevity* (Alfred Knopf, New York, 1926).

[73] One weakness in the study is lack of clear definition of the groups, with the moderate group extending from those who took only an occasional drink to those who drank regularly but in small amounts.

[74] Extrapolations from effects on other organisms, such as mice, suggest that people would require 20 mgm of resveratrol per day for any anti-aging effect to become noticeable (but note that such extrapolations are extremely unreliable). There are roughly 160 µg of resveratrol per fluid ounce of red wine. This means that roughly 5 bottles of red wine would be required for the daily dose.

[75] Aside from cirrhosis of the liver, there is increased risk for cancers of the pharynx and esophagus (M. Gronbaek, *The positive and negative health effects of alcohol and the public health implications*, J. Internal Medicine, 265, 407-420, 2009).

[76] Probably a function of the lower average body weight of women.

[77] It's not completely certain, but it seems that premenopause women have increased susceptibility; postmenopause there is no increased risk except for those on estrogen therapy (Gronbaek, op. cit.)

[78] Richard Doll et al., *Mortality in relation to consumption of alcohol: 13 years' observations on male British doctors* (British Medical Journal, 309, 911-918., 1994).

[79] It was first diagnosed in 1973 as a consequence of heavy drinking, defined as more than 4-5 drinks per day.

[80] A review of an international meeting on FAS says in the introduction "Wherever heavy drinking occurs, FAS can be detected," and then moves in its conclusion to the recommendation "no alcohol drinking during pregnancy is safe," without ever explaining the transition from heavy drinking to no alcohol (Edward P. Riley et al., *Prenatal Alcohol Exposure: Advancing Knowledge Through International Collaborations*, Alcohol Clin Exp Res, 27, 118–135, 2003).

[81] A summary of the reason for the new position refers to studies on exposing rat brain to alcohol, the review of a meeting discussing the syndrome (see note 80), and a study of behavioral changes in children whose mothers drank. There were no new data on exposure levels of pregnancy and their effects (Raja A S Mukherjee, *Low level alcohol consumption and the fetus. Abstinence from alcohol is the only safe message in pregnancy*, British Medical Journal, 330, 375–376, 2005).

[82] A typical piece of scare mongering from the BBC (July 19, 2004) reads "A mother drinking while pregnant will not necessarily have a child with FAS, although there is no known safe level of alcohol consumption during pregnancy." A study of 400,000 women in 1997 who consumed less than 8.5 drinks per week did not report any cases of FAS (S. Wilkie, *Global overview of drinking recommendations and guidelines*, AIM Digest (Supplement), June, 1997, 2-4).

[83] Ernest L. Abel, *Fetal Alcohol Syndrome: A Cautionary Note* (Current Pharm. Design, 12, 1521-1528, 2006).

[84] Quoted in Iain Gately, *Drink. A cultural history of alcohol* (Gotham Books, New York, 2008), p. 468.

[85] House of Commons, Public Accounts Committee - Forty-Seventh Report, *Reducing alcohol harm: health services in England for alcohol abuse*, July 2009..

[86] Unfortunately there is a common trend to diagnose a medical problem among chronic alcohol abusers (who are relatively easy to identify) and to commit the error of assuming that a low level of alcohol will be associated with the disease at proportionately reduced frequency. This is not necessarily true. Another example of such a mistaken extrapolation is with osteoporosis (which is clearly associated with alcohol abuse). But advice to post-menopausal women to avoid alcohol could be ill-advised because in fact the response curve may be J-shaped, so that a small amount of consumption could even be beneficial (Karina M. Berg et al., *Association between alcohol consumption and both oesteoporotic fracture and bone density*, Am. J. Med., 121, 406-418, 2008).

Chapter 9: International Wine Trade

[1] Unwin, *Wine and the Vine*, pp. 99, 131.

[2] Gaston Roupnel, Histoire de la campagne française, Éditions Bernard Grasset, Paris, 1932, p. 194

[3] Ibid., p. 231.

[4] The OIV gives a total world consumption of 2.6 billion cases in 2007, of which France accounted for 360 million, Italy for 300 million, the United States for 295 million, Germany for 220 million, China for 145 million, Spain for 140 million, United Kingdom for 135 million, Argentina for 120 million, and Russia for 115 million (6th General Assembly of the OIV, Verone, 2008). Another report suggested that Italy overtook France as the largest consumer in 2007 (source: see note 5).

[5] A report commissioned by Vinexpo from International Wine and Spirit Record in January 2009 projects United States as world's largest consumer by 2012. Total spent by consumers on wine in 2007 was $22 billion, which would make the USA the largest market by value.

[6] Latest figures show beer production at 1.7 billion hl (equivalent to 226 billion 750 ml bottles), wine at 240 million hl (32 billion 750 ml containers), and spirits at 26 billion bottles. Sources: Beer Institute (Washington DC), Brewers Almanac; VinExpo-IWSR (International Wine and Spirit Record, 2009).

[7] $100 billion is a conservative estimate for receipts by producers. Total market value was estimated at $152 billion in the Vinexpo/IWSR study of 2010 (without stating which basis was used). Comparative figures for markets for different forms of alcohol usually use figures nearer $250 billion.

[8] Data sources: Datamonitor, *Drinks: Global Industry Guide*, April 2009; and industry guides for individual countries, March and April 2009. See text for explanation of discrepancies in total wine market value.

[9] Because beer, wine, and spirits have different levels of alcohol, total alcohol consumption is usually expressed in terms of the amount of pure alcohol consumed, assuming beer at 4.6%, wine at 12%, and spirits at 40%.

[10] Germany, 11.99 liters, Britain 11.75 liters, Spain 11.68 liters, France 11.43 liters, Italy 8.02 liters per adult per year (WHO, *World Health Statistics 2008*).

[11] Cases of 12 bottles of 750 ml of wine; cases of 24 bottles of 500 ml of beer.

[12] In fact, there has been a general convergence of wine-drinking patterns in the past half century; a survey of 36 countries shows that wine consumption has declined in many traditional consuming countries and has increased in many traditional beer-drinking countries (Joshua Aizenman and Eileen Brooks, *Globalization and Taste Convergence: the Cases of Wine and Beer*, Review of International Economics, 16, 217–233, 2008).

[13] OIV figures for 2008 report 500,00 ha of vineyards with production of 12 million hl, a level between Argentina and South Africa.

[14] Data sources: France - IREB (Institute de Recherches Scientifiques sur les Boissons), Paris, *Mémento Alcool Edition 2008*; Britain - Institute of Alcohol Studies, London, *Drinking in Great Britain, factsheet 2008*.

[15] OIV State of the vitiviniculture world report, 2007, claims that up to 35 million hl is absorbed in this way.

[16] Data sources: OIV statistical report, 2005; OIV State of the vitiviniculture world report, 2007.

[17] Bottling capacity in the UK has increased sharply, from 130 million bottle equivalents in year 2000, to 240 million in 2006, and to 450 million by 2009 (Wine and Spirits Trade Association, U.K.). Part of the recent increase is due to Constellation's new packaging and bottling plant, with a capacity for 120 million bottles each year (Packaging News, U.K., March 15, 2007).

[18] In 2006 and 2007, the equivalent of approximately 6 million cases of Blossom Hill was shipped from Santa Vittoria, according to Diageo's Corporate Citizenship Report, 2007.

[19] This has a collateral effect in distorting trade figures, since the same wine shows up as imported into Italy from the United States, but also is included in Italy's export figures to Britain. Italy's total reported exports to Britain were 25 million cases in 2007, according to the Global Trade Atlas. The inclusion of Blossom Hill therefore inflates the figure significantly. Italy's total imports of wine are about 20 million cases annually (OIV statistical report, 2005), having increased sharply when Blossom Hill began bottling at Santa Vittoria.

[20] Data sources: OIV statistical report, 2005; OIV State of the vitiviniculture world report, 2007.

[21] In the early nineteenth century, Hungary had 572,000 hectares of vineyards, making it Europe's third largest wine producer (David Copp, *Hungary: its fine wines and winemakers*, András Wiszkidensky, Budapest, 2006, p. 25).

[22] Data for 1880 from George Goudie Chisholm, *Handbook of Commercial Geography* (Longmans, Green & Co., London, 1913), p. 88. Data for 2007 from Euromonitor.

[23] Quoted by Kym Anderson, *Wine's New World* (Foreign Policy, 136, 46-54, 2003), p. 47.

[24] Production figures from the FAOstat database for 1950-85; for subsequent years from OIV annual statistical reports, 1999-2005.

[25] Yield in Europe is usually expressed in terms of wine volume per area as hl/ha. In the New World it is more often expressed in grapes harvested per area, as tonnes/acre. (Very) roughly, 1 hl/ha = 16 tons/acre.

[26] Production figures from OIV (latest available 2006).

[27] Sources. *France*: Gilbert Carrier, *Le Phylloxéra* (Albin Michel, Paris, 1989), p.175; Marcel Lachiver, *Vins, Vignes et Vignerons* (Fayard, Paris, 1988), pp. 616-619; ONIVINS. *California*: U.S. Dept Agriculture, National Agricultural Statistics Service. *Australia*: James Halliday, *Wine Atlas of Australia and New Zealand* (Harper Collins, New York, 1998), p. 26; Australian Bureau of Statistics, Australian Wine and Grape Industry Report #1329.0, 1994-2008. Some figures have been converted from tons/acre to hl/ha, so may be approximate.

[28] OIV World Statistics, 6th General Assembly, Verona 2008.

[29] The most extreme example is that total plantings in Argentina stayed between 200,000 and 220,000 ha from 1990 to 2007, but plantings of quality varietals increased from 20,000 to 80,000 hectares over the period (Argentine Instituto Nacional de Vitivinicultura, Registro de Vinedos y Superficie).

[30] In California, international varieties increased from 15% to 65% of production between 1982 and 2009. In Australia, quality varieties increased from 30% in 1978 to 75% in 2008 (annual statistical report 1329.0 from Australian Bureau of Statistics). In Chile, Cabernet Sauvignon overtook País (an indigenous, low quality, grape) as the principal black variety in 1997.

[31] Total hectares increased from 760,000 in 1990 to 1,200,000 in 2007; quality varietals (defined as in note 32) increased from 100,000 ha to 450,000 ha, that is from 13% to 37%.

[32] The plantings for each country include: Cabernet Sauvignon, Merlot, Pinot Noir, Syrah, Chardonnay, Riesling, Sauvignon Blanc, and Sémillon comprise the vast majority; Cabernet Franc, Mourvèdre, Nebbiolo, Petit Verdot, Sangiovese, and Tempranillo are also included. Data sources: Argentine Instituto Nacional de Vitivinicultura (Registro de Vinedos y Superficie), Australian Bureau of Statistics (Annual Reports 1329.0), California Department of Food and Agriculture, Sacramento (California Grape Acreage Reports), Catastro Viticola Nacional, Chile; SAWIS (South Africa Wine Industry Information and Systems; Statistics of Wine Grapes).

[33] Lewin, *What Price Bordeaux?*, p. 224.

[34] Data source: annual reports of OIV.

[35] Data sources: E.U. report AGRI/EVALUATION/2002/6, and AGRIVIEW, Wine History Survey, 2008.

[36] The major reduction was 216,000 ha in Spain; other reductions were 137,000 ha in Italy, 101,000 ha in France, 37,000 ha in Greece, and 14,000 ha in Portugal. Data source: E.U. commission reports.

[37] Distillation was regarded as an "exceptional" measure until 1982, when it became the main means of regulation (Unwin, *Wine & Vine*, p. 322).

[38] Philip Whalen, *'Insofar as the Ruby Wine Seduces Them': Cultural Strategies for Selling Wine in Inter-war Burgundy* (Contemporary European History, 18, 67-98, Cambridge University Press, Cambridge, 2009), p. 69.

[39] The system has continued unabated ever since the 1930s. From 1935 to the mid 1950s, the average amount of distilled wine was about 65 million cases each year, corresponding to about 10% of production (Charles K. Warner, *The Winegrowers of France and the Government since 1875*, Columbia University Press, New York, 1960, p. 191). Distillation reached a peak in 1961-1962 when one third of all table wine production was distilled (Leo A. Loubère, *The Wine Revolution in France* (Princeton University Press, Princeton, 1990, p. 132).

[40] Proposals adopted by the Council of Ministers in April 2008 (Regulation 479/2008).

[41] Data source: European Commission DG AGRI and AGRIVIEW Wine History Survey. Numbers apply only to table wine. In addition, a small amount of Quality Wine is distilled.

[42] Unwin, *Wine & Vine*, p. 115.

[43] The ostensible reason was that the land was needed to produce grain (Dion, *Histoire de la Vigne*, p. 128).

[44] Ibid., p. 133.

[45] It is disputed whether the trigger was concern about excessive wine production, possible disruption to production of corn, or simple protectionism (Société Académique d'Agen, *Recueil des Travaux*, 1908, pp. 342-344; Alan I. Forrest, *The Revolution in Provincial France: Aquitaine, 1789-1799*, Oxford University Press, Oxford, 1996, p. 125).

[46] Adam, Smith, *An Inquiry into the Nature and Causes of the Wealth of Nations*, 1776, Book 1, Chapter 11, p. 37.

[47] European Union directive EU/NR 40/08, *Adoption of wine reform to balance markets, preserve rural areas and simply rules for producers and consumers*, April 29, 2008.

[48] Details: one small plot of land in the Rutherford area of Napa was sold for $350,000/acre (personal communication) although the quoted top rate is $250,000/acre (Dan Levy, *Slump takes hold of Napa Valley*, International Herald Tribune, March 9, 2010), giving a rate around $700,000/ha; producers in Barolo say that Cannubi sells at about €1 million/ha if available; the top rate for land in Champagne is quoted as €1.1 million/ha in the Valeur Venale; a Médoc Grand Cru Classé sold for €2 million/ha; land in Pomerol is quoted as €2-3 million/hectare; the top rate for Grand Cru Burgundy is quoted as €4 million/ha in the Valeur Venale (and premier cru is quoted as €800,000), but other figures place it as up to €6 million/ha (Business Week, April 23, 2009); and it is reported that a very small parcel of Le Montrachet sold for a rate of $20,000,000/ha (Decanter, November 2009).

[49] Based on grape and land prices in the San Joaquin Valley as reported in a study by Tony Correia, *Valuing Vineyards* (Royal Institution of Chartered Surveyors, New York, 2008).

[50] Overall sales in supermarkets are USA - 25%; Japan - 40%; Italy - 50%; France - 62%; Britain - 80%; Denmark - 80%; Netherlands - 80%; Germany - 82%. The United States is bimodal because individual states regulate whether or not supermarkets can sell wine (it is permitted in 35 states), so the level is high in Florida but zero in New York.

[51] Market share of the top five retailers: more than 75%, Norway, Sweden, Finland, Denmark; 60-75%, Belgium, Poland, Switzerland; 50-60%, Germany, France, Austria, Britain, Netherlands, Spain.

[52] The proposal failed. Large distributors, such as Diageo, campaigned furiously against it, although not openly (their efforts were channeled under the guise of protecting small stores).

[53] Quoted in Long Island Business News, February 5, 2009.

[54] Women purchase more wine than men, a significant part in the context of the weekly household shopping at supermarkets (Wine Intelligence Seminar, March 2006).

[55] Data source: A. C. Nielsen.

[56] Quoted in Simon Bowers, *Wine world soured as half-price offers are labelled misleading*, The Guardian (U.K.), August 14, 2006.

[57] Bowers, *Wine world*, op. cit.

[58] Roughly 60% of wine is sold below the £3.99 price point in Britain.

[59] Tim Atkin, *Super Mark-Ups*, The Observer, October 5, 2003.

[60] According to the 2007 annual report, Constellation Wines had $3.8 billion of sales, comprising $2.7 billion of branded wine and $1.1 billion of other wine sales.

[61] Since Constellation's figures refer to retail sales, the best total for comparison is probably the $220-250 billion range for total value of all sales worldwide.

[62] Coca Cola has annual sales of $32 billion (and accounts for 50% of cola sales), beer company Annheuser-Busch has annual sales of $22 billion, and the largest spirits company, Diageo, has sales of $16 billion (which includes some wine) (Forbes Global 2000 report, March 2009).

[63] The three largest wine companies probably have wine sales of around $7 billion. For other sectors see: coffee (Jelle Bruinsma, *World agriculture: towards 2015/2030*, Food and Agriculture Organization of the United Nations, 2005, p. 277; coffee and chocolate (Jagjit Plahe, *The global commodity chain (GCC) approach and the organizational transformation of agriculture*, working paper 63/05, Monash University Department of Management, 2005); beer (Peter Swinburn, *Global beer brewing industry and the Coors Molson merger*, Global Executive Forum, University of Colorado, 2005).

[64] Data from annual reports for 2008 for public companies; private companies estimated from public information (for Gallo see Chapter 11).

[65] Joel B. Payne, *Pernod-Ricard's Wine Empire* (Wine Business International, January, 2006).

[66] Annual cash turnover in 2000 according to Kym Anderson, *The World's Wine Markets: Globalization at Work* (Edward Elgar Pub, 2005), p.67; see also Raúl Green et al., *Global market changes and business behavior in the wine sector* (LORIA (Laboratoire d'Organisation Industrielle Agro-alimentaire, INRA), cahier 2003-02, 2003). For current data see note 74.

All figures are adjusted to show cash turnover from wine only, excluding beer and spirits, when information is available.

[67] The largest acquisitions were BRL Hardy in 2003 for $1.4 billion, Robert Mondavi in 2004 for $1.03 billion, Vincor in 2006 for $1.3 billion, and Beam Estates in 2007 for $885 million.

[68] See Pinney, *A History of Wine*, p. 256.

[69] The brand name is in fact licensed from R.A.B. Foods, which markets several brands of kosher food including Manischewitz matzo. The wine is sweetened with fructose from corn syrup, except for a special Passover bottling which is sweetened with cane sugar.

[70] At an annual rate of increase of 2.6% according to *Wine: Global Industry Almanac* (Datamonitor, May 2009).

[71] Lewin, *What Price Bordeaux?*, p. 107.

[72] Actual production volumes (millions of cases per year) are:

Country	Company	Company Production	Country Total
South Africa	Distell	41.0	92
Chile	Concho y Toro	26.6	92
United States	Gallo	67.0	260
New Zealand	Montana	3.5	16
Argentina	Peñaflor	26.9	155
Australia	Constellation	17.5	136
Spain	Garcia Carrion	30.0	377
France	Castel Frères	37.5	560
Italy	Riunite	20.8	545

[73] Share is measured by volume. Sources: Wine Business Monthly, Top 30 Report, February 2009; New Zealand Wine Industry, PriceWaterhouseCoopers report, 2007; Australia Bureau of Statistics reported by winebiz.com.au; Jane Anson, *The Place de Bordeaux* (Wine Business International, February, 2007); Castel Freres company web site; Michéle Shah, *Up by the boot hell. Doing the Italian job* (Wine Business, January, 2007); Gary Greenfield, managing director, Distell Europe, Just-drinks.com, November 27, 2006; Chile, Concho y Toro company web site; Argentina, Peñaflor company web site; personal communication from Food and Wines from Spain, Spanish Embassy, London, November 2009. For actual production levels see note 72.

[74] Discrepancies between the top-3 and top-5 shares shown in this table and those for the top companies in the previous chart are probably due to differences in measuring market share by volume versus value and to whether only table wine is included. There are also difficulties in obtaining accurate data when the companies are privately held. Where possible, share is calculated by volume. For Australia, there was a large drop in market share of the leading companies in 2009; Fosters market share by value was 28.5% in 2005 but 21.2% in 2009, while Constellation (Australia) moved from 22% to 13.5% (Nigel Austin, *Wine families strike back*, Herald Sun, Melbourne, December 8, 2009). Producer number refers to the number of wineries that make wine; the number of growers is usually larger. Data sources: Rabobank Global Focus, *Australian wine – the easiest growth comes first*, winter 2007; Victor de la Serna, *Spanish eyes seeing red* (Wine Business International, March, 2007); Argentine Instituto Nacional de Vitivinicultura (Registro de Vinedos y Superficie); Australian Bureau of Statistics (Annual Reports 1329.0); California Department of Food and Agriculture, Sacramento (California Grape Acreage Reports); *The Top 30 U.S. Wine Company profiles*, Wine Business Monthly, February 2008; Catastro Viticola Nacional, Chile; SAWIS (South Africa Wine Industry Information and Systems; Statistics of Wine Grapes).

[75] According to the Wine Institute (an association of Californian producers) only 17% of its members currently had complete national distribution as of 2005.

[76] In 2008 there were 2,843 bonded wineries in California and 6,368 in the United States as a whole according to the Wine Institute.

[77] Thomas Pinney, *A History of Wine in America : From Prohibition to the Present*, p. 347.

[78] Costco is a buying club, with an annual membership fee of $50. It offers a relatively small selection of wines (fewer than 150 different wines in each store compared with 1000 or more at a typical supermarket), but the wines change frequently, are different in each store, and pricing is very keen, driven by a maximum markup of 14% above wholesale. Wine sales in 2007 were $800 million. Sources: Kevin McCallum, *Costco: The high quality, mass market retailer*, Wine Business International, October 20, 2007; The Wine Economist, November 7, 2009.

[79] John R. Emshwiller & Alix M. Freedman, *Early Relationships Help Shape Southern Wine & Spirits' Image* (Wall Street Journal, October 4, 1999).

[80] Alix M. Freedman & John R. Emshwiller, *Vintage System: Big Liquor Wholesaler Finds Change Stalking Its Very Private World --- Southern Wine & Spirits Is A Mandated Middleman Under Increasing Attack --- A Vineyard Breaks the Mold* (Wall Street Journal, October 4, 1999).

[81] Tyler Colman, *Wine Politics: How Governments, Environmentalists, Mobsters, and Critics Influence the Wines We Drink* (University of California Press, 2008), p. 97.

[82] The case was Granholm versus Heald. Technically it argued that it was unconstitutional for a state to ban shipment to consumers from wineries out of state if it allowed shipment from wineries within the state. The 5-4 decision on May 16, 2005 agreed that this was an unconstitutional protection of the in-state wineries. This left states the option of allowing all shipments or banning all shipments; as a practical matter, banning shipments within the state would often simply kill the local industry.

[83] Freedman & Emshwiller, *Vintage System*, op. cit.

[84] Freedman & Emshwiller, *Vintage System*, op. cit.

[85] Business Wire on line, January 26, 2010.

[86] It's really quite remarkable that in the context of an overall worldwide surplus of 450 million cases annually, Australia was able to double its production since 1995 to its present level of 130 million cases without running into trouble sooner. But supply has now really outrun demand, and probably close to 20% of the vineyards are uneconomic.

[87] This was seen at its most dramatic in the high end of the New York wine auctions, where prices collapsed by more than 50% in matter of a few weeks during November 2008.

Chapter 10: Fraud

[1] Thomas Pellechia, *Wine. The 8000 year old story of the wine trade* (Running Press, Philadelphia, 2006), p. 30.

[2] Ibid., p. 35.

[3] Pliny XXIII.1.

[4] Andrew Dalby, *Empire of pleasures: luxury and indulgence in the Roman world* (Routledge, London, 2000), p. 49.

[5] Hugh Johnson, *The Story of Wine* (Mitchell Beazley, London, 2005), p. 36.

[6] Lynn Thorndike, *A history of magic and experimental science*, Columbia University Press, New York, 1923, p. 132.

[7] Bee Wilson, *Swindled: the dark history of food fraud, from poisoned candy to counterfeit coffee*, Princeton University Press, 2008, p. 57.

[8] Fielden, *Is This the Wine You Ordered, Sir*, p. 169.

[9] Lewin, *What Price Bordeaux?*, p. 211.

[10] Jean-Alexandre Cavoleau, *Oenologie Française, ou statistique de tous les vignobles et de toutes les boissons vineuses et spiritueuses de la France, suivie de considérations générales sur la culture de la vigne* (Huzard, Paris, 1827).

[11] Cyrus Redding, *A History and Description of Modern Wines* (Henry Bohn, London, 1833).

[12] James M. Gabler, *Passions: The Wines and Travels of Thomas Jefferson* (Bacchus Press, Lutherville, Maryland, 1995), p. 133.

[13] René Pijassou, *Le Médoc: Un Grand Vignoble De Qualité. Tomes I & II*, Tallandier, Paris, 1978, p. 845.

[14] Josef Eisinger, *Lead and Wine. Eberhard Gockel and the Colica Pictonum* (Medical History, 26, 279-302, 1982).

[15] Ibid., p. 288.

[16] S. C. Gilfillan, *Lead poisoning and the fall of Rome*, J. Occup. Med., 7, 53-60, 1965.

[17] Christian Warren, *Brush with death: a social history of lead poisoning*, Johns Hopkins University Press, Baltimore, 2001, p. 23.

[18] Ibid.

[19] Eisinger, *Lead and Wine,* op. cit., p. 295.

[20] Ibid., p. 298

[21] Warren, *Brush with death, op. cit.,* p.24.

[22] David Hunter, *Handel's Ill Health: Documents and Diagnoses*, RMA Research Chronicle, 41, 69, 2008.

[23] Maynard Amerine, Composition of Wines II Inorganic Constituents, In Advances in Food Research, Emil Mark, Mrak (Ed.), John Wiley, New York, 1958, p. 191.

[24] Study by the U.S. Bureau of Alcohol, Tobacco, and Firearms.

[25] J. H. Graziano & C. Blum, *Lead exposure from lead crystal* (Lancet, 337, 141-2, 1991); E. Guadagnino et al., *Estimation of lead intake from crystalware under conditions of consumer use,* (Food Addit. Contam., 17, 205-218, 2000).

[26] Fielden, *Is This the Wine You Ordered, Sir*, p. 67.

[27] Arm. Gautier, *On the Fraudulent Coloration of Wines*, J. Chem. Soc., 30, 426-446, 1876.

[28] Quoted in Fielden, *Is This the Wine You Ordered, Sir?*, p. 101.

[29] Ibid., p. 97.

[30] Iver Peterson, *Plea of Not Guilty in Tainted-Drink Death*, New York Times, July 13, 2004.

[31] Fielden, *Is This the Wine You Ordered, Sir?*, p. 86.

[32] Fritz Hallgarten, *Wine Scandal*, p. 29.

[33] Fielden, *Is This the Wine You Ordered, Sir?*, p. 87.

[34] Total production in Austria in 1984 was a bit over 2 million hectoliters, or 250 million bottles. 15 million liters (20 million bottles) were stated to have been confiscated by August 10. Ibid., p. 89.

[35] Data source: Austrian Wine Marketing Board, *Austrian Wine*, December 2008 edition.

[36] Fielden, *Is This the Wine You Ordered, Sir?*, p. 84.

[37] Roberto Suro, *Italy acting to end sale of methanol-tainted wine*, New York Times, April 9, 1986.

[38] In the *Encyclopédie, ou dictionnaire raisonné des sciences, des arts et des métiers,* published in France between 1751 and 1772, article by Chevalier Louis de Jaucourt. See Jean-François Gautier, *Le Vin Et Ses Fraudes* (Presses Universitaires De France, 1995), p. 14.

[39] Based on calculations of the gap between wine consumption minus production plus imports, first made by Armand Gautier, *La sophistication des vins: méthodes analytiques et procédés pour reconnaitre les fraudes* (Baillière, 1898), p. 3.

[40] Alessandro Stanziani, *La Falsification Du Vin En France, 1880-1905: Un Cas De Fraude Agro-Aliminetaire* (Revue d'Histoire Moderne et Contemporaine, v. 50, 2003), p. 154.

[41] See note 35 in Chapter 5.

[42] Fritz Hallgarten, *Wine Scandal*, p. 68.

[43] According to the chief prosecutor, 6,270 tons of liquid sugar were used in the Pfalz, 4,070 tons in the Mosel, 1,150 in Rheinhessen, and 550 in the Nahe over a three year period (Ibid). Annual production in these regions totaled about 5 million hl, making the usage of sugar close to 1 ton/thousand hl/year. One ton of sugar will convert 300 hl of table wine to the high grade of Auslese, so this "improvement" of quality may have affected a major part of production.

[44] Fielden, *Is This the Wine You Ordered, Sir?*, p. 78.

[45] P. E. Schneider, *France's wine casks are in the red* (New York Times magazine, December 8, 1957).

[46] Decanter on line, December 13, 2007 and March 18, 2009; see www.decanter.com/news/169103.html; www.decanter.com/news/news.php?id=278929.

[47] Fielden, *Is This the Wine You Ordered, Sir?*, p. 72.

[48] Ibid., p. 47.

[49] Hallgarten, *Wine Scandal*, pp. 176-177.

[50] Fielden, *Is This the Wine You Ordered, Sir?*, p. 46.

[51] Ibid., pp. 49-51.

[52] Oliver Styles, Vin de Pays d'Oc in massive US fraud scandal. Decanter online, February 9, 2009.

[53] The case came to court in January 2010 (*Carcassonne. Faux pinot : prison et amendes*, La Depeche, January 26, 2010).

[54] Decanter online, February 18, 2010.

[55] The wine merchant Ducasse, who sold the wine to Sieur d'Arques was purchasing wine for €58 /hl compared with the price of Pinot Noir at €97/hl. The difference on 110,000 hl (1.3 million cases) would be several million euros per year. It was stated in court that overall the illicit profits amounted to €7 million, with Ducasse taking €3.7 million and Sieur d'Arques making €1.3 million (Rory Mulholland and Suzanne Mustacich, French plonk scam spreads to world's top wine group, AFP News, February 18, 2010).

[56] Institut National des Appellations d'Origine.

[57] Le Figaro, May 23, 1973, p. 4.

[58] Bert, *In Vino Veritas*, p. 128.

[59] Faith, *The Winemasters*, p. 266.

[60] Hallgarten, *Wine Scandal*, p. 141.

[61] Ibid., p. 134.

[62] Benjamin Wallace, *The Billionaire's Vinegar* (Crown Publishing, New York, 2008).

[63] Patrick Keefe, *The Jefferson Bottles*. New Yorker, September 3, 2007.

Chapter 11: North America

[1] Frank Schoonmaker and Tom Marvel, *The Complete Wine Book,* Duell, Sloan and Pearce, New York, 1934.

[2] Lapsley, *Bottled Poetry*, p. 92.

[3] Ibid., p. 93.

[4] Restrictions on use of place names from other countries were agreed at the Convention of Madrid in 1891 by many European nations, and later reinforced by the regulations of the European Union. The United States did not sign the convention, and its use of place names today is subject only to regulations introduced as the result of bilateral agreements.

[5] Sullivan, *Napa Wine*, p. 135.

[6] Wine Review (1941). *Defense Program for U.S. Wines: an Editorial.* July issue, p. 7. (The Wine Review was an industry publication from 1933 until 1950, when it merged with Wines & Vines.)

*[7] Lapsley, *Bottled Poetry*, pp. 94-95.

[8] Maynard A. Amerine, *Wine Bibliographies And Taste Perception Studies* (Regional Oral History Office University of California, The Bancroft Library Berkeley, California, 1985).

[9] Maynard A. Amerine and Paul Scholten, *Varietal labeling in California* (Wines and Vines 58, # 11, 1977), pp. 40-41.

[10] Lapsley, *Bottled Poetry*, p. 22.

[11] Varieties included Alicante, Barbera, Cabernet, Charbono, Folle Blanche, Gamay, Mondeuse, Petite Syrah, and Zinfandel.

[12] Curiously Sauternes was used for dry white wines (Pinney, *A History of Wine,* p. 91).

[13] Sullivan, *Napa Wine*, p. 40.

[14] Ellen Hawkes, *Blood and Wine: The Unauthorized Story of the Gallo Wine Empire* (Simon & Schuster, New York, 1993), p. 243.

[15] Frank Schoonmaker and Tom Marvel, *The Complete Wine Book,* op. cit.

[16] Varietals account for some 80% of wines originating in the New World and sold in the United States.

[17] Generic descriptions are most often based on French place names such as Burgundy or Chablis.

[18] Based on a survey conducted by the author of still table wines produced on the West Coast (California, Oregon, and Washington). The analysis refers to the numbers of different wines available, and does not reflect sales volumes; it excludes sparkling and fortified wines. White Zinfandel has been excluded, since it is ambiguous as to whether it should be a brand or a varietal. It was about 25% of the wines in this sample under $5 per bottle.

[19] Impact Databank (2007).

[20] Pinney, *A History of Wine*, p. 167.

[21] Production in 2008 was:

American varieties	37,958
Hybrid varieties	9,386
Vitis vinifera	7,144 (tons)

Concord was 90% of the American varieties, but much of it is used to make grape juice (USDA NASS New York Field Office, Fruit Report, January 2009).

[22] Vitis rotundifolia is now considered not to be a member of the Vitis family, but to belong to the Muscadinia, which are considered to have evolved parallel with Vitis rather than to have descended from it.

[23] Pinney, *A History of Wine*, p. 168.

[24] Ibid., p. 165.

[25] Fortunately this is unique to the United States. In Europe, wine can be produced only from Vitis vinifera by law. And the habit of making wine from other Vitis species never became established elsewhere in the New World.

[26] The TTB (the regulatory agency in the U.S.A.) defines amelioration as: "The addition to juice or natural wine before, during, or after fermentation, of either water or pure dry sugar, or a combination of water and sugar to adjust the acid level." The limit of 35% for grape wine is increased when fixed acidity is greater than 7.69 g/l. Current rules were updated in January 2005. Source: www.ttb.gov/rpd/td403.htm

[27] DNA fingerprinting shows the Mission variety to be identical with an obscure Spanish variety called Listán Prieto (Alejandra Tapia et al., *Determining the Spanish Origin of Representative Ancient American Grapevine Varieties*, Am. J. Enol. Vitic. 58, 242-251, 2007.)

[28] Thomas Pinney, *A History of Wine in America. From the Beginnings to Prohibition* (University of California Press, Berkeley, 1989), p. 280.

[29] Ibid., p. 282.

[30] The common view is that originally phylloxera was indigenous only to the east of the Rockies; it penetrated to the west of the Rockies when carried there with imported grapevines. Some viticulturalists believe it may have been in California all along—it was discovered in Sonoma in 1873—but its effects became manifest only when Vitis vinifera was more widely planted.

[31] California State reports show a total number of gallons equivalent to 19 million cases. Most of it was probably shipped in bulk. A report on grape production gives the tons crushed, which would translate to about 22 million cases (USA NASS, California Wine Grapes, 1920-2007).

[32] Sullivan, *Zinfandel*, p. 77.

[33] California had 55% of production devoted to dry table wine (California State Board of Agriculture, Statistical report, 1914). This made it the quality leader, since in the country as a whole, consumption of table wine was probably only around a third (Pinney, *A History of Wine*, p. 57).

[34] Sullivan, *Zinfandel*, p. 80.

[35] Pinney, *History of Wine*, p. 9.

[36] Grape shippers included names that are familiar today, including Gallo, Mondavi, Italian Swiss Colony.

[37] Soon after the start of Prohibition, in 1920, the price of Alicante grapes was $180/ton compared with $130/ton for Zinfandel (New York Times, *Home Wine Making Saves Grape Growers*, October 30, 1921, p. 38.)

[38] Edward Behr, *Prohibition: Thirteen Years that Changed America* (Arcade Publishing,

New York, 1996), p. 86.

[39] Deborah Blum, *The Chemist's War*, Slate, February 19, 2010.

[40] Lapsley, *Bottled Poetry*, p. 3.

[41] An ancillary effect of Prohibition was a transition from bulk sales to sales in bottle. After Repeal, most states restricted the sale of wine in bulk (largely to improve tax collection rather than to serve any useful purpose). This meant that almost all imported and most domestic wines were sold in bottle (Pinney, *A History of Wine*, p. 50).

[42] Louis Roos Gomberg, *Analytical perspectives on the California wine industry, 1935-1990*, Oral history transcript, Bancroft Library. Regional Oral History Office, University of California, Berkeley, 1990, p. 8.

[43] Ibid., p. 9.

[44] Consumption of beer declined ~70%, consumption of wine increased ~65%, and consumption of spirits increased ~10% (C. Warburton, *The Economic Results of Prohibition*, Columbia University Press, New York, 1932, p. 260).

[45] Of course, the usual data are not available since most of the consumption was illegal. It is sometimes stated that overall alcohol consumption declined during Prohibition, but there was a shift towards wine. Most analyses are based on assuming that a decline in cirrhosis of the liver must have been due to a decline in alcohol consumption. There have also been attempts to rely on crime statistics. It's plausible there was a modest decrease in overall alcohol consumption.

[46] Pinney, *A History of Wine*, p. 20.

[47] Ibid., p. 42.

[48] Prior to Prohibition, in 1919, California had 4 times more Zinfandel than Alicante. New plantings and replanting reversed their proportions so that Alicante outsold Zinfandel by 2.5 to 4 times over the period from 1925 to the end of Prohibition after 1932 (Sullivan, *Zinfandel*).

[49] Probably 80% of production was shipped out of state in bulk for bottling elsewhere (Lapsley, *Bottled Poetry*, p. 99).

[50] Gomberg, *Analytical perspectives*, p. 14; Lapsley, *Bottled Poetry*, p. 104, 115.

[51] The figures for growth of table wine for the 1960s are a bit deceptive, because flavored wines of various sorts were included in the same statistic (Pinney, *A History of Wine*, p. 229).

[52] Data from The Wine Institute of California (www.wineinstitute.org). Assignment of wines to categories is not exact. Total wine includes sparkling wine, dessert wine, vermouth, various "natural" wines as well as table wine. Table wine may be underestimated slightly, especially in recent years, because wine over 14% alcohol is not included in this category. Fortified wine quantities are calculated from the difference between total wine and other categories.

[53] Both the BATF and TTB are departments of the Treasury.

[54] The shortsightedness of the industry is indicated by the violent opposition in this period to proposals to introduce a more stringently regulated category with 85% of the named variety and 95% from the named area (Lapsley, *Bottled Poetry*, p. 205).

[55] Lapsley, *Bottled Poetry*, p. 90.

[56] Pinney, *A History of Wine*, pp. 355-356.

[57] The TTB list of authorized AVAs had 191 entries when updated in November 2008.

[58] AppellationAmerica.com.

[59] Napa Valley Vintners (St. Helena).

[60] Lapsley, *Bottled Poetry*, pp. 206-209.

[61] Ray Johnson and Johan Bruwer, *The Balancing Act between Regionality and American Viticultural Areas (AVAs)* (J. Wine Research, 18, 163-172, 2007).

[62] Sullivan, *Napa Wine*, p. 174.

[63] James Conaway, *Napa* (Mariner Books, New York, 2002), p. 412.

[64] Paul Franson, *Napa Ridge Winery Gains a Home to Match its Presence* (Wine Business Monthly, August issue, 2002).

[65] Production was 400,000 cases in 1989 (Sullivan, *Napa Wine*, p. 348).

[66] The basis for the lawsuit was a claim that Federal regulations should be followed. The case was Bronco Wine Co. *v.* Jolly, 04-945.

[67] Jerry Hirsch, *Vintner Agrees to Drop 'Napa' from Wine Label* (Los Angeles Times, April 29, 2006).

[68] Of course, in the first half of the twentieth century it was common for Burgundy to be adulterated with wine from the south of France, but this was stopped by the introduction of Appellation Contrôlée regulations.

[69] TTB data for 2007.

[70] The scale shows average daily temperature (°C) between April 1 and October 31. Data for United States from Western Region Climate Center, Nevada; data for France from Goddard Institute for Space Studies, New York.

[71] Figures from the individual States are usually restricted to wine made from grapes. However, Federal numbers also include "other natural wines."

[72] Only ~10% of New York's production is from Vitis vinifera. See note 21.

[73] For all practical purposes, this means California.

[74] Zinfandel was 30%, Alicante 22%, and Carignan 15% (Pinney, *A History of Wine*, p. 63).

[75] In 1940, 28% of the crop was wine grapes, but 54% was crushed to make wine (Lapsley, *Bottled Poetry*, p. 99).

[76] In 1944, only 55% of new plantings were wine grapes, and more than half were low-quality, high-yield varieties (Burger, Carignan, Palomino, Mission) (Lapsley, *Bottled Poetry*, p. 106).

[77] E. L. Markell, *Grapes in the Land of Sunshine* (Wines and Vines, August, p. 11, 1941).

[78] Even as late as the 1960s, wineries were used as a salvage operation to turn excess grapes into wine or to rescue damaged table grapes (they were usually distilled) (Pinney, *A History of Wine*, p. 206).

[79] Ibid., p. 232.

[80] In 2007, Cabernet Sauvignon from Napa average $4,300 per ton, compared to $334 per ton in San Joaquin. USDA NASS, California Crush Report.

[81] USDA NASS, California Crush Report, 1974-2008.

[82] Ibid.

[83] Wines produced from grapes grown in Washington were taxed at a much lower rate than wines from other states and only local wineries could sell directly to wholesalers and retailers.

[84] Pinney, *A History of Wine*, p. 310.

[85] Ibid., p. 312.

[86] Stimson Lane is a subsidiary of U.S. Tobacco. It owns Chateau St. Michelle, Columbia Crest, Canoe Ridge Estates, Col Solare, Snoqualmie Winery, Erath, Northstar, Red Diamond, Saddle Mountain, Stimson Estate Cellars, Spring Valley Vineyard, and Whidbeys in Washington, as well as Villa Mt. Eden and Conn Creek in Napa Valley. They are secretive about production levels, but it appears that Chateau St. Michelle and Columbia Crest alone account for some 3.5 million cases out of the 8 million produced annually in Washington.

[87] Data sources: California: TTB, USDA NASS, Wine Institute; Washington: Washington Wine Commission, USDA NASS Washington Field Office; Oregon: Oregon Wine Board, USDA NASS Oregon Vineyard and Winery Report.

[88] Pinney, *A History of Wine*, p. 322.

[89] The actual number of producers is significantly greater, because not all have bonded wineries.

[90] The Wine Institute, California; 70.9% of dry table wine as of December 2008.

[91] California still had 85% of the domestic market at the start of the 1990s, but the proportion has been dropping steadily. California sales are increasing in absolute volume and value because the market is still growing.

[92] Pinney, *A History of Wine*, p. 216.

[93] The original 9 members of the association grew to 28 by 1958, but by 1960 the association was effectively defunct in all but name (Ibid., p. 215).

[94] Date source: Gomberg-Fredrikson report. See Goodhue et al., *California wine industry evolving to compete in 21st century* (California Agriculture, vol 62, pp. 12-18, 2008).

[95] Revenues for each category can be estimated by assuming average prices:

Category	1995 Revenues	2006 Revenues
Jug (<$3)	35%	13%
Popular ($3-7)	35%	22%
Premium ($7-14)	23%	37%
Super-premium (>$14)	8%	29%

[96] For both San Joaquin and Napa, more than 80% of plantings consist of three varieties. Top planted varieties in 2007 for white and black (data source: USDA, NASS.):

	San Joaquin	Napa
Chardonnay	65%	71%
Sauvignon Blanc	11%	19%
Pinot Gris	9%	-

	San Joaquin	Napa
Cabernet Sauvignon	25%	52%
Zinfandel	43%	6%
Pinot Noir		6%
Merlot	18%	22%

[97] Data sources: USDA NASS, California Crush Report and Grape Acreage Report for 2007. Crush as tons/acre was:

	San Joaquin	Napa
Black	8.99	3.25
White	9.58	3.51

[98] Data source: USDA NASS. The data are expressed as hl/ha for convenience of comparison with other information, but absolute values are only approximate as the original data were measured as tons of grapes harvested per acre.

[99] Calculating yields by comparing production levels with planted areas is complicated by the fact that there is some overlap between wine production and use as table grapes. The mix varies from year to year, and not all the grapes reported as crushed are necessarily used to produce wine.

[100] An approximate conversion from the crush in tons/acre given in note 97.

[101] Sullivan, *Napa Wine*, p. 145.

[102] Topographic background from Google Earth.

[103] Discussion with the author, January 2010.

[104] USDA NASS, California Acreage Report 2007 and California Crush Report 2008.

[105] Topographical background from Google Maps.

[106] When the AVAs were proposed, there was a proposal for further sub-appellations to be called Rutherford Bench and Oakville Bench. Growers within them generally supported the proposal, while those outside were against. "There is no geological evidence of bench land in the Napa Valley," according to Joe Heitz of the eponymous winery (Sullivan, *Napa Wine*, p. 361.) The existence of an alluvial fan creating the Rutherford Bench is generally accepted, but the existence of the Oakville Bench is certainly doubtful.

[107] While the Rutherford area is certainly among the best terroirs on the valley floor, the notion of the distinctive taste of Rutherford dust may be more marketing than reality.

[108] Sullivan, *Napa Wine*, p. 362.

[109] Ibid., p. 9.

[110] Ibid., p. 19.

[111] Ibid., p. 27.

[112] Lapsley, *Bottled Poetry*, p. 41.

[113] Ibid., p. 42.

[114] Petite Syrah was 40%, Alicante another 25%, with Zinfandel at 15% (Ibid., p. 43).

[115] In (descending) order of production: Beringer, Beaulieu, Christian Brothers, Martini, Larkmead, Inglenook (Lapsley, *Bottled Poetry*, p 23.)

[116] Lapsley, *Bottled Poetry*, p 23.

[117] Ibid., p. 112.

[118] Ibid., p. 131.

[119] Ibid., p. 170.

[120] According to the USDA NASS California Crush Report for 2007, 107,580 tons of black grapes crushed from Napa included 104,289 tons from Cabernet Franc, Cabernet Sauvignon, Malbec, Merlot, Petit Verdot, Pinot Noir, Sangiovese, Syrah, Tempranillo, and Zinfandel.

[121] The total for black quality varieties excepting those shown individually includes Cabernet Franc, Carmenère, Mourvèdre, Nebbiolo, Pinot Meunier, Petit Verdot, Sangiovese, Syrah, Tempranillo, and Touriga Nacional.

[122] Data from the USDA NASS California Acreage reports for 1969-2007.

[123] Known in the trade during the 1980s as the "white wine craze" (Sullivan, *Zinfandel*, p. 308).

[124] Ibid., p. 268.

[125] Stony Hill, built in 1951, might be considered the first.

[126] Conaway, James, *Napa* (Mariner Books, New York, 2002); Conaway, James, *The Far Side of Eden* (Houghton Miflin, New York, 2003)

[127] Sullivan, Charles L, *Like Modern Edens: Winegrowing in Santa Clara Valley and Santa Cruz Mountains 1798-1981* (California History Center, 1982).

[128] Mick Winter, *Who Owns Napa Valley's Vineyards?* (Wine Business Monthly, May 23, 2001).

[129] Roughly 50% of the harvest in 2007 was available for purchase, compared with the one third that would be available according to the wineries' claim (USDA NASS California Crush Report.) Larger discrepancies have been noted for earlier years (Sullivan, *Zinfandel*, p. 365).

[130] Discussion with the author, January 2010.

[131] Discussion with the author, February 2010.

[132] Pinney, *A History of Wine*, p. 126.

[133] Ibid., pp. 241-243; Sullivan, *Napa Wine*, p. 295.

[134] Cabernet Sauvignon had been planted previously, but Niebaum introduced the small-berried clone 29 (which subsequently was lost from Bordeaux) personal communication, Larry Stone MS).

[135] The profitable year was actually the last one before it was sold (personal communication, Larry Stone MS).

[136] United Vintners paid $1.2 million for the original purchase in 1964; Heublein received $10 million for the winery and vineyards in 1995.

[137] In the 1950s-1960s, the major wineries owned or controlled between a quarter and third of all vineyard areas, so since then the proportion has increased as well the sizes of the individual companies (Lapsley, *Bottled Poetry*, p. 171).

[138] Lewin, *What Price Bordeaux?*, p. 65.

[139] Data updated from public records for sales and purchases, but based on the original analysis of Mick Winter, *Who Owns Napa Valley's Vineyards?* (Wine Business Monthly, May 23, 2001).

[140] Discussion with the author, February 2010.

[141] Discussion with the author, February 2010.

[142] Discussion with the author, February 2010.

[143] Discussion with author, February 2010.

[144] USDA NASS California Crush Report 2008.

[145] USDA NASS, California Acreage report 2007.

[146] USDA NASS California Crush Report 2008.

[147] Topographic map from Google Earth.

[148] Discussion with the author, February 2010.

[149] Approximate yields are 60 hl/ha for Chardonnay in Napa Valley and 160 hl/ha in San Joaquin Valley. Basically this is no different from the average for white grapes for each region (see note 97). You have to wonder what varietal typicity could possibly be produced at yields over 100 hl/ha. Figures converted from the crush and acreage reports from USDA NASS California (2007).

[150] USDA NASS California Crush Report 2008.

[151] Ellen Hawkes, *Blood and Wine: The Unauthorized Story of the Gallo Wine Empire* (Simon & Schuster, New York, 1993), p. 56.

[152] Hawkes, *Blood and Wine.*, op. cit., p. 82.

[153] Topographic map from Google Earth.

[154] Hawkes, *Blood and Wine*.op. cit., p. 119.

[155] News report in The Modesto Bee, October 28, 1938.

[156] Hawkes, *Blood and Wine,* op. cit., p. 136.

[157] Ibid., pp. 156, 158.

[158] Ibid., p. 166.

[159] Ibid., p. 177.

[160] They moved into first place by volume of sales in 1960, with total production of 12.6 million cases (Jerome Tuccille, *Gallo Be Thy Name,* Phoenix Books, Beverley Hills, 2009, p. 120). This was equivalent to almost 20% of total consumption in the United States that year.

[161] In 1989 Gallo stopped selling Thunderbird and the similar Night Train brand to retailers located in low-income areas (New York Times, September 23, 1989).

[162] Its alcohol level has been reduced slightly to 18%.

[163] According to Time magazine, November 27, 1972.

[164] The brand was introduced in 1981. It has a wide range of fruit flavors. Gallo also owns the Boone's farm line of fruit wines.

[165] Fruit wines include coolers, spirits include vermouth, popular & premium include wines from $3-16/bottle, prestige is over $25 from Napa or Sonoma. Based upon sales data from Adams Wine Handbook (Adams Media Inc., New York, 2008); price data from Gallo Winery and from www.wine-searcher.com. The analysis represents revenues of $3.4 billion from sales of 64 million cases from wines produced and sold within the United States.

[166] The Livingston plant is about half the size of Modesto; Healdsburg is much smaller.

[167] Production from U.S. sources is about 65 million cases, roughly 10 million cases are imported from Italy, France, and Australia, and roughly 10 million cases are exported (Wine Business Monthly, February 15, 2008).

[168] Gallo's market share has been steady. It was estimated at 26% by Fortune magazine (issue of September 1, 1986).

[169] Frank Prial (New York Times, March 7, 2007).

[170] It was overtaken in first place when Constellation expanded as the result of acquisitions in 2003.

[171] But estimates vary wildly. Annual revenues in 2007 were estimated at $3.7 billion by Wine Business Monthly, February 15, 2008. The Hoover's company profile gives a figure of $3.15 billion. An older estimate of $1 billion annual revenues with a $50 million profit margin was made by Fortune magazine, September 1986.

[172] Quoted in *American Wine Comes of Age* (Time Magazine, Nov. 27, 1972). Perhaps to be taken with a pinch of salt as this was the cover story of the issue, devoted to Gallo.

[173] Lapsley, *Bottled Poetry*, pp. 175-176.

[174] Hawkes, *Blood and Wine*, p. 246.

[175] Louis Martini was purchased in 2002; William Hill was purchased in 2007.

[176] Probably around 90% of the wines in the popular and premium class come from grapes of San Joaquin Valley.

[177] Wine prices taken from RRPs stated on the Gallo web site, February 2009. Actual store prices could be a little lower.

[178] This analysis refers to table wines only; sources as in note 165.

[179] Pinney, *A History of Wine*, p. 317.

[180] Topographic map from Google Earth.

[181] Topographic map from Google Earth.

[182] USDA, NASS, Washington Field Office, Grape release, January 2009.

[183] USDA, NASS, Oregon Field Office, Vineyard and Winery Report, February 2008.

[184] 68% of the vineyard area and 62% of the wineries.

[185] Under the GATT rules (the General Agreement on Tariffs and Trade).

[186] Penny Hope-Rose, *From the Vine to the Glass: Canada's Grape and Wine Industry* (Statistics Canada, 2006).

[187] Owen Roberts, *Obsolete law works against our grape growers*, Guelph Mercury, July 10, 2009.

[188] *Blended deceit from the nanny state*, The Economist, September 10, 2009.

[189] Gordon Hamilton, *Wine consumers 'dumbfounded'' over faux B.C. wines*, The Vancouver Sun, September 23, 2009.

[190] Canada's production breaks down to: Ontario 65%, British Columbia, 31%, Quebec 2%, Nova Scotia, 1%. Ibid.

[191] Grape Growers of Ontario, Vine Census 2006.

[192] Vidal is a cross between the Seibel variant of Vitis labrusca and the undistinguished Ugni Blanc cultivar of Vitis vinifera.

[193] Cabernet Sauvignon, Cabernet Franc, and Merlot were 12% of the volume of single varietal wines in 2009 (Vintners Quality Alliance Ontario, 2009 Annual Report).

[194] Production in these far north vineyards is very small; together they have only around 300 ha of vineyards (Hope-Rose, *From the Vine to the Glass, op. cit.*).

[195] See page 150.

Chapter 12: Australia and New Zealand

[1] Wine Export Approval Report, AWBC, June 2006.

[2] Data from Australian Bureau of Statistics, Australian Wine and Grape Industry Report #1329.0, 1978-2008.

[3] Exports grew at a rate of 20% or better from 2000 through 2003, but only at 14% in 2004 and 2005, which was insufficient to accommodate the 40% growth in production.

[4] Data from CIVB, Bordeaux and Australian Bureau of Statistics.

[5] A Rabobank report in 2007 pictured Australian wine exports as passing from their mature phase to a declining phase (Rabobank Global Focus, *Australian wine – the easiest growth comes first,* winter 2007).

[6] Robinson, Jancis, *Tasting Pleasure: Confessions of a Wine Lover* (Viking Press, 1997), p. 200.

[7] There are still a few surviving bottles of the 1951 vintage. One was sold at auction for $50,000 in 2004 (ABC news, June 17, 2004).

[8] For the full story, see page 62.

[9] A book on Barossa Valley wineries in 1970 discussed Penfolds under the heading "Penfolds and Port," with only a passing mention of dry red wines (Bryce Rankine, *Wines and Wineries of the Barossa Valley,* The Jacaranda Press, Melbourne, 1971, p. 24).

[10] Faith, *Australia's Liquid Gold*, p. 47.

[11] St. Hubert was produced at the de Castella estate in Victoria, which set the local standard for innovation and quality (Faith, *Australia's Liquid Gold*, p. 76). Hubert de Castella published a book in 1886 called *John Bull's Vineyard*, reflecting the importance for Victoria of exports to Britain.

[12] Faith, *Australia's Liquid Gold*, op. cit., p. 72.

[13] The transition is striking. In 1983 Australia exported 3% of its wine production. Today production is 5 times larger and 60% is exported (Data from Australian Bureau of Statistics, Australian Wine and Grape Industry Report #1329.0, 1978-2008).

[14] James Halliday, *A history of the Australian wine industry, 1949-1994* (Australian Wine and Brandy Corp, Australia, 1994), p. 57.

[15] Data from Australian Bureau of Statistics, Australian Wine and Grape Industry Re-

port #1329.0, 1978-2008.

[16] Out of 70,000 ha, Cabernet Sauvignon, Mourvèdre, Riesling, Sémillon, and Syrah accounted for 20,000 ha (Data from Australian Bureau of Statistics, Australian Wine and Grape Industry Report #1329.0, 1978-2008).

[17] Totaling 31,228 ha out of a total of 146,177 ha (Data from Australian Bureau of Statistics, Australian Wine and Grape Industry Report #1329.0, 1978-2008).

[18] Data from Australian Bureau of Statistics, Australian Wine and Grape Industry Report #1329.0, 1978-2008.

[19] Australian Bureau of Statistics, Australian Wine and Grape Industry Report #1329.0, 2008.

[20] Second annual lecture, Wine Press Club of NSW, Sydney, November 2004.

[21] The national average is 88%. Greatest dependency is in South Australia where 93% of vineyards are irrigated (Australian Bureau of Statistics, Australian Wine and Grape Industry Report #1329.0, 2008).

[22] In Barossa Valley, for example, the historical average is about 550 mm per year, well below the 700 mm minimum required by the vine (Australian Bureau of Meteorology).

[23] Data from Australian Bureau of Statistics, Australian Wine and Grape Industry Report #1329.0, 2008.

[24] Some vintages, such as 1995, have identified the source as South Australia..

[25] Each wine region on the map is an official Geographical Indication. Production figures from Australian Bureau of Statistics, Australian Wine and Grape Industry Report #1329.0, 2008.

[26] The top six brands account for a quarter of production (see page 313).

[27] *Directions to 2025*, AWBC, Adelaide, 2027.

[28] Australian Bureau of Statistics, Australian Wine and Grape Industry Report #1329.0, 2008.

[29] James Halliday, *Wine Atlas of Australia*, p. 67.

[30] Topographic map from Google Earth.

[31] Shiraz was 2658 of the total 6750 ha planted in 1969-1970 (Bryce Rankine, *Wines and Wineries of the Barossa Valley,* The Jacaranda Press, Melbourne, 1971, p. 87).

[32] See page 47.

[33] Comparison of production (tonnes crushed) in Barossa Valley and Coonawarra:

	Barossa	*Coonawarra*
Shiraz	22,409	7,025
Cabernet Sauvignon	6,788	17,830
Merlot	3,052	3,379
Grenache	3,694	0
Other Black	2,022	1,019
Chardonnay	3,737	3,364
Riesling	3,385	1,085
Sémillon	4,135	0
Other White	2,379	950
Total	51,601	29,253

Data source: 2009 South Australian Winegrape Utilisation and Pricing Survey, Phylloxera and Grape Industry Board of South Australia, September 2009.

[34] The style of the Riesling used to be oxidized as the result of wood aging. This changed when Orlando introduced its first Barossa Riesling in 1953, using the techniques developed in Germany after the second world war (Bryce Rankine, *Wines and Wineries of the Barossa Valley,* The Jacaranda Press, Melbourne, 1971, p. 14). Much later there was a subsequent revolution to the modern, dry, steely, fruit-driven style.

[35] Data sources: 2009 South Australian Winegrape Utilisation and Pricing Survey, Phylloxera and Grape Industry Board of South Australia, September 2009; Australian Bureau of Statistics, Australian Wine and Grape Industry Report #1329.0, 2008.

[36] Exports have increased steadily from 265,000 cases in year 2000, to 520,000 in 2003, and over 1.1 million in 2006. Winefacts database, AWBC, November 2009.

[37] See page 137.

[38] James Halliday, *Wine Atlas of Australia*, p. 269.

[39] John Gladstones, *Viticulture and Environment* (Winetitles, Adelaide, 1992), p. 77.

[40] John Gladstones, *The climate and Soils of South Western Australia in Relation to Vine-growing* (J. Australian Inst. Agric. Sci. 31, 275-288, 1966).

[41] George M. Taber, *In search of Bacchus. Wanderings in the wonderful world of wine tourism* (Scribner, New York, 2009), p. 108.

[42] Langton's auction house classifies Australian wines by auction prices; see page 315.

[43] Taber, *In search of Bacchus*, op. cit., p. 112.

[44] Quoted in Katherine Lindh, *John Casella: the brains behind the brand*, Winebiz feature of the week, www.winebiz.com.au/features/default.asp?VIEW=88.

[45] Quoted in Peter Steane and Yvon Dufour, *Casella wines and the success of [Yellow Tail]* (Macquarie Graduate School Of Management Case Studies In Management, 2006).

[46] Data sources: Rabobank Global Focus, *Australian wine – the easiest growth comes first*, winter 2007; Adams Wine Handbook (Adams Media Inc., New York, 2008); Australian Bureau of Statistics, Australian Wine and Grape Industry Report #1329.0.

[47] Ibid.

[48] Jacques Berthomeau, *How can we improve French wines' positioning in export markets?*, report to the French Ministry for Agriculture, July 2001.

[49] Brian Croser, *Brand or Authenticity* (WSET Annual Lecture, February, 2004).

[50] Interview with Phil Laffer reported by about.com (wine.about.com/od/winearoundtheworld/a/JCheritagerange.htm).

[51] Quoted in Nicholas Faith, *Australia's Liquid Gold*, p. 187.

[52] The leading brands underestimate the concentration of the large companies; Fosters alone produced 30 million cases of wine in 2008 and Constellation (Australia) produced another 20 million. Data sources: personal communication from Casella Wines, November 2009; Chris Snow, *Major production of lightweight wine bottles in Australia*, Decanter online May 11, 2009; Fosters, *Wine Review Outcomes*, February, 2009; Robert Fenner and Frank Longid, *Foster's Targets Increased Domestic Sales of Australian Wine*, Blomberg News Report, March 2009.

[53] Brian Croser, *Brand or Authenticity* (WSET Annual Lecture, February, 2004).

[54] Quoted in Tony Love, *Brian Croser blames big business for wine industry problems*, The Advertiser, Adelaide, February 10, 2010.

[55] A statement to the wine industry by the Winemakers' Federation of Australia, Wine Grape Growers' Australia, the Australian Wine and Brandy Corporation and the Grape and Wine Research and Development Corporation, November 2009.

[56] The Wine Advocate, October 31, 2005, p. 3.

[57] The 2005 classification has 11 exceptional wines, 22 outstanding wines, 34 excellent wines, and 34 distinguished wines. The 101 wines include 67 of the 89 wines that were in the previous classification of 2000 (Langton's, Melbourne and Sydney, Australia).

[58] The average price of exported New Zealand wine is the highest of any exporting country.

[59] Michael Cooper, *Wine Atlas of New Zealand*, p. 19.

[60] Rosemary George, *The Wines of New Zealand* (Faber and Faber, London, 1996), p. 27.

[61] Michael Cooper, *Wine Atlas of New Zealand*, p. 23.

[62] Data source: New Zealand winegrowers statistical annuals.

[63] Prices in Hawke's Bay were NZ$4800/ha, but prices in Marlborough were in the range of NZ$600-1200. Montana purchased 14 farms totaling 1600 ha, and planted 390 ha of vines (Oz Clarke, *Oz Clarke's New Wine Atlas: Wines and Wine Regions of the World*, Harcourt, 2002, p. 316).

[64] Montana have substantial vineyard holdings, but now also supplement their grape supply by purchases from growers in the region (whom they persuaded to plant vines instead of using the land for grazing sheep).

[65] Rosemary George, *The Wines of New Zealand* (Faber and Faber, London, 1996), p. 241.

[66] Map from Google Earth. Production data from New Zealand winegrowers statistical annual 2009.

[67] Average for the past decade of 15.75 °C in Marlborough compares with 16.1 °C in Burgundy. Based on weather station data from NIWA (National Institute of Water & Atmospheric Research, New Zealand) and Goddard Weather Center.

[68] Together with the predominance of mechanical harvesting, this increases the level of skin contact with juice before vinification starts, which can give a more phenolic impression to the wine.

[69] George M. Taber, *In search of Bacchus. Wanderings in the wonderful world of wine tourism* (Scribner, New York, 2009), p. 132.

[70] The winery takes its name from the bay at the eastern end of Wairau Valley, named by Captain Cook in 1770.

[71] New Zealand winegrowers statistical annual 2008.

[72] Ross Spence at the Te Kauwhata Research Station propagated UCD1 from a single healthy vine in the Corbans vineyard and put it into production at Matua Valley in 1974. Cuttings were sold to Montana for their first vineyard in Marlborough. Spence also propagated clone UCD2 of Sémillon, which was the sole supply of Sémillon for New Zealand (Rosemary George, *The Wines of New Zealand*, Faber and Faber, London, 1996, pp. 55, 57).

[73] Quoted in Hannah Summers, *New Zealand wine country rattles the French*, Metro World News, Calgary, March 3, 2010.

[74] Data source: New Zealand winegrowers statistical annual 2008.

[75] The first efforts with Pinot Noir were partially confounded by a poor choice of available clones. The Bachtobel clone was predominant in the first New Zealand plantings, but its lack of intensity makes it really suitable only for sparkling wine. Quality improved when the Dijon clones became available in the past decade (Rosemary George, *The Wines of New Zealand*, Faber and Faber, London, 1996, pp. 83-84).

[76] Gavin Evans, *New Zealand Cuts Sauvignon Blanc Output to Avoid Glut*, Bloomberg News, February 19, 2009.

[77] Sales increased 42% in 2009 compared with the previous year.

[78] Sauvignon Blanc accounted for 30% of white wine sales in 2009.

[79] Guy Woodward, *Australian producers rally to stem flood of New Zealand Sauvignon*, Decanter online, November 9, 2009.

[80] Quoted in James Lane, *It's a Kiwi savalanche… and the Aussies love it*, New Zealand Herald, March 5, 2010.

Chapter 13: South America and Africa

[1] Data source: Registro de Viñedos, Instituto Nacional de Vitivinicultura, Argentina.

[2] Success with white wine was retarded by a period during which it was difficult to obtain foreign currency to buy temperature controlled equipment (Christopher Fielden, *The Wines of Argentina, Chile, and Latin America*, Faber & Faber, London, 2001, p. 33).

[3] Cecilia B. Agüero, *Identity and Parentage of Torrontés Cultivars in Argentina* (Am. J. Enol. Vitic. 54, 318-321, 2003)

[4] Data source: Registro de Viñedos, Instituto Nacional de Vitivinicultura, Argentina.

[5] Topographical maps from Google Earth.

[6] Terrazas de los Andes say that at 800 meters the thermal amplitude (difference between day and night temperatures) is 13 °C, but at 1200 meters it is 16 °C.

[7] Madeleine Stenwreth, *The effect of altitude on Malbec in Mendoza, Argentina*, Institute of Masters of Wine, Dissertation, 2008.

[8] Christopher Fielden, *The Wines of Argentina, Chile, and Latin America* (Faber & Faber, London, 2001), p. 35.

[9] Ibid., p. 105.

[10] Ibid., p. 107.

[11] Quoted in Peter Richards, *The Wines of Chile*, p. 30.

[12] ODEPA (Ministry of Agriculture).

[13] Data sources: Servicio Agricola y Ganadero, Minustry of Agriculture, Chile; CORFO, Chilean Economic Development Agency.

[14] Vineyards increased from 53,093 ha in 1994 to 117,559 in 2007. País is now 15,042 ha; other unnamed varieties are 15,395 ha.

[15] Peter Richards, *The Wines of Chile*, p. 21.

[16] Cabernet Sauvignon, 40,675 ha; Merlot, 13,283 ha; Carmenère, 7,283 ha; Chardonnay, 8,733 ha; Sauvignon Blanc, 8,862 ha; other quality varieties include principally Syrah, Pinot Noir, Cabernet Franc, Malbec. País is still 15,042 ha. Data source: Catastro Viticola Nacional, Chile, 2007.

[17] Richards, *The Wines of Chile*, op. cit., p. 24.

[18] Vinos Viníferos y Vinos de Variedad sin indicación geográfica.

[19] Servicio Agricola y Ganadero, Ministry of Agriculture, Chile; CORFO, Chilean Economic Development Agency.

[20] Topographic map from Google Earth.

[21] Cooperative Winemakers' Society of South Africa Ltd.

[22] Quality varieties are largely Cabernet Sauvignon, Syrah, Merlot, Pinotage, Chardonnay, and Sauvignon Blanc. The dashed line in the middle is obtained if Chenin Blanc is also included. Data from Wines of South Africa.

[23] For a detailed account of the history and status of the variety see Peter F. May, *Pinotage* (Inform and Enlighten, St Albans, England, 2009).

[24] There are tiny amounts in other New World countries, but it is more of a curiosity than anything else. There is none in Europe.

[25] Percentages refer to proportion of all vineyards. Data from Wines of South Africa.

[26] Quoted in Peter F. May, *Pinotage,* op cit., pp. 140.

[27] Peter F. May, *Pinotage,* op cit., pp. 142-150.

[28] Jane MacQuitty, *Burly South Africans*, The Times (London), October 17, 2007.

[29] Barry Bearak, *A Whiff of Controversy and South African Wines*, New York Times, June 28, 2009.

[30] Topographical map from Google Earth. Production data from SAWIS (South Africa Wine Industry Statistics), annual report, 2008. The areas used to describe production do not coincide exactly with the geographically named areas.

[31] Wine production (millions of cases)

	Domestic	*Exported*
Dry table wine	34.7	34.4
Fortified	3.8	0.04
Sparkling	1.1	0.3

Data from SAWIS annual report, 2008.

[32] Ibid.

Chapter 14: Bordeaux and Burgundy

[1] Dewey Markham, *A History of the Bordeaux Classification* (John Wiley & Sons, New York, 1997).

[2] J. Lavalle, *Histoire et Statistique de la Vigne et des Grand Vins de la Cote d'Or* (Phenix Editions, reprint, 2000).

[3] The first recorded use of "château" in the context of wine production was in the diary of Lord Hervey of Bristol, a connoisseur of his time, who mentioned "Château Margou Claret" in 1724 (René Pijassou, *Le Médoc: Un Grand Vignoble De Qualité. Tomes I & II*, Tallandier, Paris, 1978, p. 321). The term came into wider use in the first half of the nineteenth century, but when the leading producers were classified in 1855, its significance was still more architectural than viticultural; only 4 of the 80 properties that were classified were described as "châteaux" (Lewin, *What Price Bordeaux?*, p. 31).

[4] "Châteaux" multiplied quite quickly after the classification; by the 1868 edition of Cocks & Féret there were just over 300, including all the first growths of the Médoc and a quarter of the Grand Cru Classés overall (Charles Cocks & Edouard Féret, *Bordeaux et ses*

vins classés par ordre de mérite, 8th edition, Editions Féret, Bordeaux, 1908). During the century, "château" became a successful marketing term implying a significant producer with a good reputation; by 1908 there were 1600 "châteaux (Lewin, *What Price Bordeaux?,* p. 31).

[5] 68% for Bordeaux, 55% for Burgundy (see following note).

[6]

Percent sales by volume to different countries

	Bordeaux	Burgundy
France	68%	55%
E.U. except U.K.	16%	18%
U.K.	5%	10%
China	2.7%	0.2%
U.S.A.	2.3%	6.2%
Japan	2.3%	4.5%

Total sales and revenues

	Bordeaux	Burgundy
Bottles (millions)	661	177
Revenue (€ million)	337	1.1

Sources: CIVB Memento 2007; Daily Telegraph, London, March 11, 2010; BIVB press dossier, 2009.

[7] According to the BIVB, negociants account for 58% of the sales of Burgundy, including 7% of wines produced from vineyards that they own. The 3,800 domaines viticoles (grower-producers) account for 26%, which represents an increase of one third over 7 years. The remaining 16% is handled by 23 cooperatives.

According to the CIVB Mémento économique du Vin de Bordeaux for 2006, 47% of the châteaux sent their wine to 47 cooperatives, and this amounted to 26% of the crop. 42% of wine was bottled by the proprietor at the château. Negociants account for the rest, although this includes 12% that they bottled at the château.

[8] Topographic map from Google Earth.

[9] Until recently there were several appellations called Côtes or Coteaux, but now they have been combined into a single Côtes de Bordeaux.

[10] Data from the FGVB and CIVB. Production figures are based on 2007 vintage, when Bordeaux AOC was 49%, Côtes was 15%, Médoc & Graves was 16%, Libournais was 11%, dry white was 8% and sweet white was 2%. Proportions of revenues are calculated from average prices for each region as reported for CIVB and give approximately 34% for Bordeaux AOC, 14% for Côtes, 31% for Médoc & Graves, 16% for Libournais, and 5% for dry white.

[11] INAO lists Cabernet Sauvignon, Cabernet Franc, Merlot, Malbec, Carmenère, and Petit Verdot as the only permitted black varieties. Sémillon, Sauvignon Blanc, Sauvignon Gris, and Muscadelle are listed as "principal" white varieties, with the lower quality varieties Colombard, Merlot Blanc, and Ugni Blanc listed as "accessory" varieties (CDC Bordeaux Homologation, June 11, 2008).

[12] CIVB census (2000).

[13] CIVB census (2000).

[14] Lewin, *What Price Bordeaux?*, p. 183.

[15] The emphasis on red wine may partly reflect the fact that in effect white wines can only be made from Sauvignon Blanc and Sémillon. What would be happen if Chardonnay was allowed?

[16] Ministry of agriculture viticultural census (1968, 1988, 2000); Charles Cocks & Edouard Féret, *Bordeaux et ses vins classés par ordre de mérite, 12th edition* (Editions Féret, Bordeaux, 1969); CIVB Census (1988, 2000).

[17] Provided by Pichon Lalande.

[18] An increase in total plantings contributes to the increase in proportion of Merlot. The very best areas, identified long ago, are planted with Cabernet Sauvignon. New areas naturally are not such good terroir, and therefore tend to be planted with Merlot.

[19] Dion, *Histoire de la Vigne,* p. 367.

[20] A. D. Francis, *The Wine Trade* (Adams & Charles Black, London, 1972), p. 9.

[21] At the start of the 14th century, Bordeaux wines accounted for only 120,000 hl out of a total exported of 850,000 hl. See Pijassou, *Le Médoc,* op. cit., p. 307.

[22] Pijassou, *Le Médoc,* op. cit., p. 304; Thiney, *Fascinant Médoc,* pp. 166-168.

[23] Because of problems with spoilage, wines were exported as soon as possible. Most exports took place in an intensive period of 6-8 weeks relatively soon after the harvest, and the wines would arrive in England in time for Christmas (Dion, *Histoire de la Vigne,* p. 386).

[24] A contemporary view in 1751 of the merits of wine of different ages noted, "wine begins to degenerate as it enters its second year." (L'Encyclopédie de Diderot et d'Alembert, 1751, tome 17, p. 290.)

[25] This happened in the twentieth century; barrels were still more than 90% of exports at the start of the century (Cocks & Féret, *Bordeaux,* op. cit., 1908, p. 87).

[26] "Purchasers must leave the wines in the chais of the château, at their expense, risks, and perils, including that of fire, until the moment of bottling, which will be obligatory at the château for the entire harvest,", quoted by Pijassou, *Le Médoc,* op. cit., p. 840.

[27] Lewin, *What Price Bordeaux?,* p. 124.

[28] One indication of the transition occurring during the 1970s may be that prices were quoted on the Place de Bordeaux in tonneaux (barrels of 900 liters) until 1978, when most quotations changed to a price per bottle.

[29] When the en primeurs are first released, their relative prices in all consumer markets closely reflect the initial release price, partly due to an unwritten understanding on margins. As the initial supply is sold, and once the initial period of honoring the margins passes, readjustment occurs, especially with increased markup of wines that have been perceived as too cheap.

[30] Jane Anson, Wine and Spirits Magazine, 2006.

[31] Union des Maisons de Bordeaux (2008). *L'economie du vin.* www.vins-bordeaux-negoce.com/economie.asp

[32] Today there are fewer than 20 negociants in the vicinity of the Quai des Chartrons. In 1950, there were close to 200 (Réjalot, *Les Logiques du Château,* p. 143).

[33] Réjalot, *Les Logiques du Château,* pp. 241, 249.

[34] Prices in livres/tonneau were: Médoc, 386; Graves, 298; palus, 257 (Pijassou, *Le Médoc.* op. cit., p. 511).

[35] By 1740, a document from the chamber of commerce in Bordeaux described 19 separate subdivisions within the Médoc, and remarked how the qualities of certain Crus depended on the efforts of their proprietors (Markham, *A History of the Bordeaux Classification,* p. 47; Thiney, *Fascinant Médoc,* p. 182.)

[36] Pontac (Haut Brion), Latour, Lafite, and Margaux were selling at 4-5 times the price of other wine from the Médoc (Pijassou, *Le Médoc,* op. cit., p. 371.)

[37] Pijassou, *Le Médoc,* op. cit., p. 1408.

[38] Markham, *A History of the Bordeaux Classification,* op. cit., presents an extensive history of the classification on which I have drawn in this chapter.

[39] The term Grand Cru Classé is now restricted by law to châteaux in Bordeaux.

[40] Lewin, *What Price Bordeaux?,* p. 42.

[41] Actually a total of 57 châteaux were classified in 1855, but since then some have been divided, increasing the total number of classified growths to 61. In Sauternes, 21 châteaux were classified.

[42] The Cru Bourgeois classification was drawn up in 1932 by the Bordeaux wine brokers, under the authority of the Chamber of Commerce and the Chamber of Agriculture. 444 châteaux were ranked into three levels of Cru Bourgeois. The list was never made official but was used for more than 50 years. The Syndicat des Crus Bourgeois du Médoc was established in 1962, and was authorized by a ministerial decree in 2000 to reclassify the Cru Bourgeois. This led to a classification that was published in 2003, with the intention of being revised every 12 years.

[43] The appellations take the names of individual villages, except for Margaux, which

includes five communes, so wines in any of Arsac, Cantenac, Labarde, Margaux and Soussans can state "Appellation Margaux Contrôlée."

[44] The only one of these classifications to take terroir into account at all is in St. Emilion, where INAO has the right to refuse the classification if a château buys extra land with terroir considered to be inferior.

[45] The classification included 13 châteaux, all located in Pessac-Léognan (which subsequently separated from the Graves, in 1974). The classification was modified in 1959 to give Cru Classé status to some châteaux for their white wine, but otherwise has never been changed. The 9 châteaux classified for white wine included 7 of the original 13 classified châteaux plus an additional two that are classified only for white wine.

[46] It was revised twice at roughly 15-year intervals (in 1969 and 1986), but since then has been revised more systematically every decade (in 1996 and 2006).

[47] The heart of the criticism is that the judges did not taste the wines in a completely blind manner.

[48] Quoted in Roger Voss, *St. Emilion's classification suspended*, Wine Enthusiast online, March 30, 2007.

[49] Wilson, *Terroir*, pp. 187-191.

[50] The only one not to conform completely is Château Margaux, where some of the vineyards are on bedrock rather than gravel (and some people consider that in fact this makes it the best terroir in the Médoc) (Wilson, *Terroir*, pp. 194-198).

[51] Wilson, *Terroir*, pp. 198-199.

[52] The total vineyard area of the Grand Cru Classés in 1855 occupied about 2,650 hectares (Thomas George Shaw, *Wine, the Vine, and the Cellar, 2nd edition*, Longman, London, 1864, p. 263). It probably dropped to about 1,800 ha in the mid twentieth century; today it is 3,380 ha (Lewin, *What Price Bordeaux?*, p. 62).

[53] Lewin, *What Price Bordeaux?*, p. 87.

[54] Based on a survey by the author of châteaux in Bordeaux in 2007.

[55] 25% of second wines are made exclusively from young vines (Lewin, *What Price Bordeaux?*, p. 201).

[56] Ibid.

[57] In 1997, the worst vintage of the past decade, many châteaux used less than half of their production for the grand vin. In the more normal 2006 vintage, grand vin provided an average 69% of production compared to 31% for second wine. (Based on a survey conducted by the author in 2007.)

[58] The length of time spent in oak varies from 10-24 months for grand vins, and from 6-18 months for second wines. Most second wines are matured in old oak, but a minority of 10% see no oak at all (Lewin, *What Price Bordeaux?*, p. 205).

[59] The grand vins of the left bank on average have 52% Cabernet Sauvignon, but second wines have 44%. There is less difference on the right bank (Lewin, *What Price Bordeaux?*, p. 205).

[60] The history of Carruades de Lafite, the second wine of Château Lafite Rothschild, casts an interesting light on this question. This was produced until 1966, when it was discontinued because of confusion among consumers. It was reintroduced in 1974, and represented about a third of the crop made from young vines, but did not use the name of Lafite on the label. However, there was little demand, so in 1985 the wine was again labeled Carruades de Lafite—and demand revived (Edmund Penning-Rowsell, *The Wines of Bordeaux, 6th edition*, Penguin Books, London, 1989, p. 192). Today it sells especially strongly in Japan, where the name of Lafite is magical.

[61] Since 1990 the law has restricted "château" to AOC or VDQS (a classification for regions awaiting promotion to AOC) wines on condition that the grapes are harvested solely from the château's own vineyards and are vinified on the premises (Code du Vin, Article 6 of Règlement 3201/90, October 16, 1990).

[62] A rough count suggests that more than 10% of labels purporting to be châteaux may really be no more than subsidiary marques or alternative bottlings. Out of 7000 "châteaux" listed by the FGVB, more than 1000 have addresses and phone numbers that belong to another château. In some cases, as many as 10 or 20 "châteaux" all have the

same address and phone number! (Lewin, *What Price Bordeaux?*, p. 203).

[63] Ibid., p. 204.

[64] Frank Prial, *Wine Talk: $1,000 Wines You Never Heard Of* (The New York Times, October 25, 2000).

[65] Lewin, *What Price Bordeaux?*, p. 166.

[66] Interview with the author, April 9, 2008.

[67] Dion, *Histoire de la Vigne,* p. 119.

[68] Ibid., p 137.

[69] According to Dion, *Histoire de la Vigne,* p. 147; another view is that it may have been earlier because of the disappearance of imported amphorae in archeological evidence from 50-150 C.E. (Loïc Abric, *Le Vin de Bourgogne aux XIX Siècle,* Editions de l'Armançon, Précy-sous-Thil, 1993, p. 21).

[70] Dion, *Histoire de la Vigne,* p. 142.

[71] Ibid., p 286.

[72] Loïc Abric, *Le Vin de Bourgogne,* op. cit., p. 22.

[73] Dion, *Histoire de la Vigne,* p. 297.

[74] Unwin, *The Wine & the Vine,* p. 17.

[75] Gilles Laferté, *La Bourgogne et ses vins: image d'origine contrôlée* (Belin, Paris, 2006), p. 19.

[76] Production is 114 million bottles of white wine (60%), 85 million bottles red (34%), and 13 million bottles crémant (7%). Data sources: BIVB, *Chiffres-clés de la Bourgogne Viticole,* 2006; BIVB, *Eléments clés de la Bourgogne viticole.*

[77] Topographic background from Google Earth. Data source: BIVB, *Chiffres-clés de la Bourgogne Viticole,* 2006.

[78] Quoted by Jancis Robinson, *Bust-up in Burgundy,* jancisrobinson.com, July 8, 2009.

[79] Chablis produces 35 million bottles (19%), the Cote d'Or 40 million (22%: 14 million on the Côte de Nuits, 26 million on the Côte de Beaune), Côte Chalonnaise is 10 million (5%), Mâconnais is 45 million (24%). Generic Bourgogne is 57 million (31%), including 26 million from the Côte de Beaune and 31 million from the Mâconnais. These figures do not include production in the Beaujolais. Data source: BIVB, *Chiffres-clés de la Bourgogne Viticole,* 2006.

[80] The Hospice owns 61 hectares, mostly premier and grand crus.

[81] Philip Whalen, *'Insofar as the Ruby Wine Seduces Them': Cultural Strategies for Selling Wine in Inter-war Burgundy* (Contemporary European History, 18, 67-98, Cambridge University Press, Cambridge, 2009).

[82] Gilles Laferté, *La Bourgogne et ses vins: image d'origine contrôlée* (Belin, Paris, 2006), p. 22.

[83] Ibid., p. 29.

[84] This was by no means a unique situation. For example, in the late nineteenth and early twentieth centuries, wines produced in Napa were largely sold to merchants in San Francisco, who sold it under their own names rather than those of the growers (Charles L. Sullivan, *Napa Wine,* p. 107).

[85] Laferté, *La Bourgogne,* op. cit., p. 51.

[86] The negociants stated their position by saying that they "corrected wines that were healthy, but imperfect, by controlling the course of their development. They could not accept the law of 1919 which relied on the origin of a wine instead of its basic quality." (Olivier Jacquet, *Un Siècle de construction du vignoble bourguignon,* Editions Universitaires de Dijon, Dijon, 2009, p. 169.)

[87] Gaston Roupnel, *La crise du Vin,* Dépêche de Toulouse, November 2, 1922.

[88] Anthony Hanson, *Burgundy, 1st edition* (Faber & Faber, London, 1982), p. 132.

[89] Ibid., p 130.

[90] Hectares owned by the leading producers in the Côte d'Or:

Producer	Village	Premier	Grand
Bouchard	128	74	12
Faiveley	37	16.5	10.5

Louis Latour	48	15	27
Joseph Drouhin	75	31	
Louis Jadot	75	75	
Patriarche	100?	?	

Information provided by the producers.

[91] Land in the major communes of the Côte d'Or is classified into village, premier cru, and grand cru, as follows (in hectares):

Commune	Village	Premier	Grand
Gevrey Chambertin	369	86	87
Morey St Denis	64	42	40
Chambolle Musigny	94	60	26
Vougeot	5	12	51
Vosne Romanée	105	58	75
Nuits St Georges	175	143	-
Aloxe Corton	90	38	160
Beaune	128	322	-
Pommard	212	125	-
Volnay	98	136	-
Meursault	305	132	-
Puligny Montrachet	114	100	33
Chassagne Montrachet	180	159	-
Total	1939	1412	471

[92] Topographic background from Google Earth.

[93] Clive Coates, *Cote d'Or: A Celebration of the Great Wines of Burgundy* (University of California Press, Berkeley, 1997), p. 114.

[94] Mouton Cadet started in 1934 with the declassification of the crop of Mouton Rothschild. It was so successful that it became first a brand incorporating other wine from Pauillac, and then a generic Bordeaux. The objection to its name is simply that it implies a connection with Mouton Rothschild that no longer exists.

[95] According to the BIVB, 55% of all Burgundy is sold by maisons de negoce.

[96] Lewin, *What Price Bordeaux?*, p. 51.

[97] Data from CIVB, Bordeaux and Australian Bureau of Statistics.

[98] A record amount of Bordeaux wine is now being distilled; by 2006 this had reached the equivalent of 4 million cases annually (CIVB, 2008). See www.bordeaux.com/Data/media/DP08_FR_VinsDeBdxChiffres.pdf.

[99] Although it should be said that much of the decline was due to forcing out poor, old-fashioned producers; the standard of what is left is much improved.

[100] The basic problem remains that its low reputation makes it impossible to get an economic price. In 1991, much of the market was lost when prices were forced up to uncompetitive levels by low yields. The same could happen with the 2008 vintage, where yields are down about 40% on the previous year.

[101] Grants of €15,000 per hectare were offered (L'Express, May 15, 2007). This was the limit set by the Ministère de l'Économie, as stated in the Journal Officiel of September 9, 2006, p. 2490.

[102] Between 2005 and 2007, less than 3000 ha were uprooted; see CIVB report (2008).

[103] Rebecca Gibb, *Bordeaux is in Crisis: Chadronnier*, Decanter online, November 12, 2009.

[104] There would be no reduction in yields or any other difference that would translate into higher quality.

[105] Quoted in Jane Anson and Rebecca Gibb, *New Bordeaux appellation attacked*, Decanter

online, August 26, 2009.

[106] Alain Vironneau, Annual general assembly of the Syndicat des Vins de Bordeaux, 2005.

[107] Syndicat des Vignerons Coteaux du Languedoc, report on 2005, as stated on web site.

[108] Discussion with the author in Bordeaux, March 2009.

[109] The legal limit is the average Rendement de Base for all Burgundy (excluding the Beaujolais). Limits for Bourgogne AOC are 50 hl/ha, for communes and premier crus usually around 40 hl/ha, and for Grand Crus usually around 37 hl/ha, with the overall average of 46.5 hl/ha. Actual yields in each year are taken from INAO statistics.

[110] Vintages rated on a 100 point scale, taking the average for each year of the ratings for Burgundy in *The Wine Advocate.*

[111] Coates, *The Wines of Burgundy*, pp. 18-19.

[112] Data source: INAO.

[113] Le Nouvel Observateur, Paris, September 15, 2005.

[114] INAO Communiqué de Presse, September 9, 2005.

[115] Data sources: for 1850, William Franck, *Traité sur les vins du Médoc et les autres vins rouges et blancs du Departément de la Gironde,* Chaumas, Bordeaux, 1864); for 1900, New International Encyclopedia, Dodd Mead, vol 23, 1907, p. 697.

[116] Prices obtained by the author from negociants' archives for the period 1996-2005. To avoid bias between years, prices were set for each year relative to 100% as the average for the first growths of the Médoc. Some châteaux are not included because their production is too small to allow reliable prices to be obtained every year.

[117] There have been some amateur attempts at revising the classification. The trading firm of Liv-ex produced a classification based on its records for prices for wines in bond in London for vintages 2003-2007 as of December 2008 (Liv-ex, *Bordeaux Classification,* London, 2009). They divided the wines of the Graves and Médoc into price bands, 1st Growths: £2,000 a case and above, 2nd Growths: £500 to £2,000, 3rd Growths: £300 to £500, 4th Growths: £250 to £300, 5th Growths: £200 to £250. There are several problems with this approach. When the brokers created the original classification in 1855, prices were relatively stable, and they were able to look at a period of many years. The Liv-ex classification has the twin problems that the period of assessment is too short (allowing for over-influence due to fads of the moment) and prices vary significantly between vintages; with 2005 showing much higher prices than any other vintage, a simple comparison based on average price over the years gives much greater emphasis to the result in 2005 than any other year. Classification needs to reflect the results of a château in poor years as well as the best. It's also a problem that the results are based on trading prices in London, since it's not necessarily true that this represents the world wide market.

[118] Lewin, *What Price Bordeaux?*, p. 242.

[119] Le Petit Mouton, the second wine of Mouton Rothschild, would probably also be in this group, but it is produced in such small quantities that there is not enough price data to place it.

[120] Based on prices on the Place de Bordeaux for the period 1996-2005 obtained by the author from negociants' archives, augmented by retail prices for a small number of châteaux that are not included on the *Place*. To avoid bias between years, prices were set for each year relative to a first growth average of 100%. The difference from the classification presented previously (Lewin, *What Price Bordeaux?*, p. 246) is the expansion of the list to include châteaux from Graves.

[121] Interview by the author at Château Sociando-Mallet, April 7, 2008.

[122] Lewin, *What Price Bordeaux?*, pp. 236-241.

[123] Quoted in *Wine War. Savvy New World marketers are devastating the French wine industry*, Business week cover story, September 3, 2001.

[124] Lewin, *What Price Bordeaux?*, p. 249.

[125] Prices for 1820-1829 are averages for the decade calculated from the original data reported by Loïc Abric, *Le Vin de Bourgogne aux XIX Sièele,* (Editions de l'Armançon, Précy-sous-Thil, 1993), pp. 30-49. The range was from around 160 francs per pièce (228 liters) for

Santenay to 400 francs per pièce for Romanée or Chambertin. Prices for 1910-1919 are averages for the decade as seen on the negociant market, ranging from Ff 1894 for Chambertin to Ff 536 for Monthélie (presumably per tonneau or equivalent unit) calculated from the data reported by Gilles Laferté, *La Bourgogne et ses vins: image d'origine contrôlée* (Belin, Paris, 2006), p. 263. Current prices are based on retail prices for the period 2002-2007 as determined by the author's survey of leading merchants in the U.S., U.K, and France. They range from $23 per bottle for Santenay to over $300 average per bottle for Chambertin, and as much as $10,000 for Romanée-Conti (2005 vintage).

[126] Gilles Laferté, *La Bourgogne et ses vins: image d'origine contrôlée* (Belin, Paris, 2006), p. 23.

[127] The average for 1810-1875 showed Chambertin just ahead of Romanée: Chambertin 528 Ff, Romanée 523 Ff, Richebourg 481 Ff, Corton 416 Ff, Vosne 387 Ff, Nuits 383 Ff (Abric, *Le Vin de Bourgogne)*, p. 49).

[128] The cadastral plan of 1860 was followed with some modifications reflecting changes in regulations that had been passed between 1920 and 1936 (Gilles Laferté, *op. cit*, p. 63).

[129] Richard Olney, *Romanée Conti* (Rizzoli, New York, 1995), pp. 96-97.

[130] Typical prices from the Valeur Venale (a French government record of land prices) state regional Bourgogne in the Côte d'Or as €30,000, village as €340,000, premier cru as €800,000, and grand cru as €2,760,000 (Journal Officiel De La République Française, February 5, 2009).

[131] Quoted by Nick Passmore, *First-class white Burgundy at a second-class price*, Business Week, April 23, 2009.

[132] The vineyard was only a small fraction of a hectare, but the rate was reported to be over $20 million per hectare (Decanter, November 2009).

[133] Based on a survey of prices in the U.S., U.K. and France for current vintages (vintages 2002-2007 were analyzed over the period 2007-2010). Prices for appellations were compared for individual producers in each vintage, and then the data sets were merged on the basis of relative appellation prices. Some very small crus (especially if they are monopoles) are not included because of lack of data.

[134] Ranking of the top producers on the basis of price relative to DRC = 100 is::

Domaine Leroy	137
Domaine de la Romanée-Conti	100
Domaine Bernard Dugat-Py	64
Claude Dugat	64
Comte de Vogüé	35
Denis Mortet	33
Domaine Ponsot	31
Domaine Trapet Père et Fils	31
Domaine Jacques Frédéric Mugnier	30
Domaine Henri Perrot-Minot	30

[135] Based on analyzing relative prices for vintages 2002-2007. The hierarchy is on the basis of *relative* prices, not who produces the most expensive wines in absolute terms. That is, if a specific appellation wine for one producer consistently sells at a higher price than the same appellation wine from another producer, the second producer has a lower rank.

[136] It is made by putting whole clusters of grapes into the press and using carbonic maceration, when fermentation occurs inside the berry without extracting tannins from the skin. It's rapidly stabilized, so there is no malolactic fermentation to reduce acidity, and bottled (see page 100).

[137] Dion, *Histoire de la Vigne*, pp. 576, 585.

[138] Ibid., 587.

[139] Sometimes exceptions are made to allow more economical shipping. Moving the

Beaujolais by air is usually necessary outside of Europe (in fact special arrangements have to be made to move such a large volume in such a short time) and this is expensive. In 2008, the authorities agreed to allow two-thirds of the Beaujolais going to the United States to leave earlier in order to be shipped by sea (Emily S. Ruer, *Rolling out the Beaujolais Nouveau*, New York Times, November 20, 2008).

[140] Beaujolais Nouveau was around 13 million bottles out of a total production of 80 million bottles of all Beaujolais until 1970 (Gilbert Garrier, *L'Etonnante Histoire de Beaujolais Nouveau*, Larousse, Paris, 2002, p. 23).

[141] Data source: UIVB (Union Interprofessionnelle des Vins du Beaujolais).

[142] The phrase is supposed to have originated when Louis Orizet, the Inspecteur Général of INAO responsible for dealing with frauds, spotted it written on a bar window (Garrier, op. cit., p. 29).

[143] Michel Deprost, *Beaujolais. Vendanges amères* (Golias, Villeurbanne, 2004), pp. 103, 104.

[144] UIVB.

[145] Quoted in Eric Asimov, *Discovering a 'new' and finer Beaujolais*, New York Times, October 4, 2007.

[146] Michel Deprost, *Beaujolais. Vendanges amères* (Golias, Villeurbanne, 2004), p. 80.

[147] Average production is 5 million cases of Beaujolais Nouveau, 3.5 million of Beaujolais, 2.7 million of Beaujolais Villages, and 4 million of the various Crus. Average price per bottle in France for the 2005 vintage was €3.38 for Beaujolais Nouveau, €3.14 for Beaujolais, €4.04 for Beaujolais Villages, and €5.61 for the Crus. The average price for the various Crus ranges from the same range as Beaujolais or Beaujolais Villages to €7 for Moulin à Vent and €8 for Fleurie at the top. Data from the Union Interprofessionnelle des Vins du Beaujolais.

[148] Brouilly, Chénas, Chiroubles, Côte de Brouilly, Fleurie, Juliénas, Morgon, Moulin à Vent, Régnié, Saint Amour.

[149] Quite a bit of Beaujolais is distilled already. And in 2002 the UIVB took a bank loan to reduce the surplus by buying up a million cases, to be variously distilled, turned to vinegar, or declassified to table wine (Michel Deprost, *Beaujolais. Vendanges amères*, Golias, Villeurbanne, 2004, p. 12).

Chapter 15: Northern France, Rhône, and Languedoc

[1] Topographic background from Google Earth. Data from INAO: *Superficie et récolte revendiquées pour la campagne 2005-2006.*

[2] France produces about 450 million cases of wine each year (with another 70 million produced for distillation into brandy). 315 million cases (70%) are red or rosé (the official figures do not distinguish between them), 90 million (21%) are white, and 40 million (9%) are sparkling (of which 75% is Champagne). Some 250 million cases (54%) are AOC, 164 million cases (35%) are Vin de Pays, and 53 million cases (11%) are Vin de Table. With 170 million cases the Languedoc produces more than 37%, followed by Aquitaine (mostly Bordeaux) at 80 million cases (18%). Other average production levels are Provence (46 million), Pyrenees and Southwest (28 million), Rhône (31 million), Burgundy (18 million), Loire (35 million), Alsace (12 million), and Champagne (31 million). Data from ONIVINS for vintages up to 2008.

[3] Kermit Lynch, *Adventures on the Wine Route* (New York: Noonday Press, 1988), p. 179.

[4] Wine is only a part of the AOC system, which applies to a wide variety of agricultural products—there are AOCs for spirits, olive oils, cheeses, and chickens (such as the famous Poulets de Bresse).

[5] INAO also administers a level just below AOC called VDQS which consists of regions being considered for promotion to AOC.

[6] John Livingstone-Learmonth, *The Wines of the Rhône*, p. 328.

[7] Fritz Hallgarten, *Wine Scandal* (Sphere Books, 1987), p. 85.

[8] Formally defined by the European Union as QWPSR (Quality Wine Produced in a

Specific Region).

[9] It's a basic principle of the AOC system that wine from higher-level appellations can always be declassified to the lower level appellations that contain them. So if a producer decides that wine produced from a district vineyard isn't really good enough (or if in the past the authorities decided he had produced too much wine), the wine can be sold instead under the regional appellation. So any wine produced in Graves could be sold as AOC Bordeaux.

[10] Varietal-labeled Vin de Pays can be made from one or two varieties; when a single variety is named, it must comprise 100% of the content (although general E.U. law requires only 85%).

[11] According to the agricultural census of 2000, 25% of the producers of AOC wines also produced a Vin de Pays wine (Jean Strohl et al., January 2005, Agreste #157: La Statistique Agricole, Service Central des Enquêtes et Études Statistiques, Paris).

[12] The trend is growing nationally. In the 2000 vintage, 10% of wines that could have been labeled AOC were in fact labeled as Vin de Pays, largely in the various appellations of the south. Ibid.

[13] Data from Charles Cocks & Edouard Féret, *Bordeaux et ses vins classés par ordre de mérite, 13th edition* (Editions Féret, Bordeaux, 1982) and from ONIVINS. (The proportion of AOC wine is less than the hectarage because yield limits are lower in the AOC.)

[14] Gilles Laferté, *La Bourgogne et ses vins: image d'origine contrôlée* (Belin, Paris, 2006), p. 18.

[15] Data from INAO.

[16] €300 million were requested in 2004. By 2006, the equivalent of 4 million cases was being distilled. CIVB (2008). See www.bordeaux.com/Data/media/DP08_FR_VinsDeBdxChiffres.pdf

[17] Cocks & Féret, *Bordeaux*, 1908, 1982; Lafforgue *Le Vignoble Girondin* (Louis Larmat, Paris, 1947); Philippe Roudié, *Vignobles et vignerons du Bordelais*, p. 349; CIVB.

[18] Michel Bettane, 2005, Forum Vinexpo.www.academie-amorim.com/us/rencontres/actes_vinexpo_gb.pdf.

[19] see www.quechoisir.org.

[20] There are reports from all over France of wines being refused the AOC agrément because they are not "typical." Sometimes, of course, they are indeed flawed, but there is a trend to exclude wines with originality, especially those made by completely natural means. "It is becoming increasingly difficult for the small minority of natural winemakers to continue to work in the context of the AOC because the AOCs want to enforce a uniform and mediocre style with no tolerance for originality and authenticity... [The] bureaucrats ... have flattened out, if not lowered quality and made many of France's best winemakers the targets of an intolerant offensive." (Louis/Dressner Selections, 2007); see louisdressner.com/basicsearch/?s=brun].

[21] 178 g/l, which would usually give about 10.5% alcohol anyway at a normal conversion rate. So the difference between Bordeaux AOC and Bordeaux Supérieur AOC is a distinction without meaning (INAO regulations: AOC Bordeaux, Bordeaux clairet, Bordeaux rosé, Bordeaux sec, Bordeaux Côtes de Francs, Bordeaux Haut-Benauge, 1988; AOC Bordeaux Supérieur, 2006.)

[22] Data sources: AOC yields calculated from Charles Cocks & Edouard Féret, *Bordeaux et ses vins classés par ordre de mérite, 13th edition* (Editions Féret, Bordeaux, 1982).Total yields calculated from Vicente Pinilla, *'Old' And 'New' Producing Countries In The International Wine Market, 1850-1938*, IEHC 2006 Helsinki Session 117, 2006), and ONIVINS.

[23] The change is not specific to wine but applies to all food and drink products using the old system, for example, cheese.

[24] E.U. regulation 510/2006 states that "the two levels of geographical description are different. AOP designates a product whose production, transformation, and elaboration must be connected with a specific place having a recognized and noted savoir-faire. IGP indicates a link with the territory for at least one of the stages of production, transformation, or elaboration."

[25] Topographic background from Google Earth.

[26] Roger Voss, *Wines of the Loire* (Faber & Faber, London, 1995), p. 7.

[27] Two other appellations signifying higher than average quality are Muscadet Coteaux de la Loire and Muscadet Côtes de Grandlieu, more recently introduced to try to bring some distinction, but with only a couple of hundred of hectares each, production is scarcely significant set against Muscadet de Sèvre et Maine.

[28] Data from Viniflhor based on DGDDI and from Vals de Loire.

[29] Pierre Galet, *Cépages et Vignobles de France, Tome III Les Cépages de Cuve* (Paysan du Midi, Montpellier, 1962), p. 1929.

[30] André Jullien, *Topographie de tous les vignobles connus* (Paris, 1816).

[31] Voss, op. cit., p. 7.

[32] Voss, op. cit., p. 32.

[33] It's an ironic comment on the effectiveness of the assessment for the AOC agrément that one producer had their monovarietal Chardonnay accepted without demure, but their Sauvignon Blanc was rejected as atypical (Author's interview with château proprietor, April 2006).

[34] In the eighteenth century the predominant variety was Burger, by the nineteenth century it was Knipperlé, but the mark of both is very high yields of flavorless wine (Stevenson, *The Wines of Alsace*, p. 9).

[35] For example, chaptalization was performed by adding sugar in solution, with the result that the total volume of must was increased, resulting in significant dilution. This ceased only in 1962.

[36] Stevenson, *The Wines of Alsace*, p. 49.

[37] Ibid., p. 6.

[38] There is no known connection between Pinot Gris and the varieties grown in Tokaji today nor any reason to suppose that Pinot Gris was previously grown in Tokaji.

[39] Auxerrois here is a white variety; no connection with its use as a synonym for Malbec in Cahors!

[40] Typical recent yields for Alsace average 75 hl/ha, whereas Champagne has reached 82 hl/ha. (Data from Viniflhor based on DGDDI.)

[41] Data from Viniflhor based on DGDDI.

[42] The only alternative to AOC is Vin de Table (about 4% of all production), since there is no Vin de Pays.

[43] The ONIVINS website of the French government distinguishes between Pinot Blanc (1,111 ha) and Auxerrois (2,289 ha), but the CIVA (Conseil Interprofessionnel des Vins d'Alsace) remains in denial, with no mention of Auxerrois in its statistics and a figure of 3,303 ha for Pinot Blanc, curiously almost exactly the sum of the Pinot Blanc and Auxerrois according to ONIVINS!

[44] Author's discussion with Hubert Trimbach in June 2008.

[45] Quoted in Sue Style, *Alsace sweetness levels*, Decanter, November 6, 2009.

[46] CIVA.

[47] Author's discussion with M. Beyer in June 2008.

[48] Author's discussion with Sévérine Schlumberger in June 2008.

[49] Riesling 41%, Gewürztraminer 38%, Pinot Gris 19%, Muscat 1% (Data from CIVA for 2008).

[50] Author's discussion with M. Deiss in June 2008.

[51] Quoted in Panos Kakaviatos, *Alsace vintners attack reforms*, Wine Business International, July 14, 2009.

[52] Topographic background from Google Earth.

[53] The local Syndicat has finally taken the situation in hand and proposes to remove unsuitable vineyards from the appellation, but it still acknowledges 3,500 ha of potential vineyards!

[54] Quoted by Livingstone-Learmonth, *Wines of the Northern Rhône*, p. 245.

[55] Ibid., p. 237.

[56] Lewin, *What Price Bordeaux?*, p. 213.

[57] George Ripley & Charles Anderson Dana, *The American Cyclopaedia: A Popular Dictionary of General Knowledge: France (Wines of)*, (Appleton, 1874), p. 412

[58] Livingstone-Learmonth, *Wines of the Northern Rhône*, p. 244.

[59] Ibid., p. 37.

[60] La Turque, La Landonne, and La Mouline.

[61] President of the Crozes-Hermitage growers' union. Quoted by Livingstone-Learmonth, *Wines of the Northern Rhône*, p. 341.

[62] This would not happen if wines were made separately and then blended; see page 108.

[63] Mostly from the Tavel AOC.

[64] Interprofession des Vins AOC Côtes du Rhône & Vallée du Rhône.

[65] Total production figures are Côtes du Rhône Régional, 230 million bottles; Côtes du Rhône Villages, 50 million bottles; other Côtes, 105 million bottles; southern Rhône Crus 40 million bottles; northern Rhône Crus, 17 million bottles. Out of a total of 79,045 ha, 39,648 are in Côtes du Rhône and another 9,495 in the Villages, 17,693 ha in the other Côtes, and only 12,209 in the Crus altogether. Data source: Ibid., *Chiffres Clés*, 2007.

[66] Topographic background from Google Earth.

[67] The 13 varietals that are permitted in red Châteauneuf-du-Pape are: Bourboulenc, Cinsault, Clairette, Counoise, Grenache, Mourvèdre, Muscardin, Picardan, Picpoul, Roussanne, Syrah, Terret Noir and Vaccarèse. The 5 varietals that are permitted in white Châteauneuf-du-Pape are Bourboulenc, Clairette, Picardin, Roussanne, and Grenache Blanc. Although white varietals can legally be included in red Châteauneuf-du-Pape, this practice has all but disappeared.

[68] Harry Karis, *The Châteauneuf-du-Pâpe Wine Book* (Kavino, Roermond, Netherlands, 2009), p. 105.

[69] Quoted in *Wine War. Savvy New World marketers are devastating the French wine industry*, Business week cover story, September 3, 2001.

[70] Paul Strang, *Languedoc-Roussillon: the Wines and Winemakers* (Mitchell Beazley, London, 2002), p. 12.

[71] Olivier Torrès, *The Wine Wars. The Mondavi Affair, Globalization and 'Terroir'* (Palgrave Macmillan, London, 2006), p. 48.

[72] Paul Strang, *Languedoc-Roussillon: the Wines and Winemakers* (Mitchell Beazley, London, 2002), p. 12.

[73] Data source: La Direction Régionale de l'Alimentation, de l'Agriculture et de la Forêt (DRAAF) of Languedoc Roussillon.

[74] FranceAgriMer statistics.

[75] Quoted in C. Gourtorbe, *Aimé Guibert de la Vaissière:" je suis un cul-terreux"*, Terre de Vins, December 1999.

[76] Olivier Torrès, *The Wine Wars. The Mondavi Affair, Globalization and 'Terroir'* (Palgrave Macmillan, London, 2006).

[77] Quoted, ibid., p. 104.

[78] Ibid., p. 92.

[79] Jacques Berthomeau, *Comment mieux positioner les vins français sur les marchés d'exportation* (Ministère d'Agriculture, Paris, 2001).

Chapter 16: Italy

[1] The "G" stands for "Garantita," which signifies that wines are guaranteed for authenticity (not quality). DOCG also carries more restrictive conditions on viticulture and vinification.

[2] There are 120 IGT regions, 316 DOC regions, and 41 DOCG as of 2008 (Istituto nazionale di statistica).

[3] Based on data of grape census in 2000.

[4] Sources: Michéle Shah, *Up by the boot hell. Doing the Italian job* (Wine Business, January, 2007); ISTAT production figures 2007.

[5] Franco Ziliani, *New Wave Merlot In Italy*, Wine Business Monthly, January 2001.

[6] Garner, *Barolo. Tar and Roses*, p. 10.

[7] This belief is not unique to Piedmont. Charlemagne is supposed to have had the Cis-

tercian monks plant Pinot Noir on the Rhine opposite his palace at Ingelheim, where he could see that the hill, which later became Schloss Johannisberg, showed the snow melting earlier than on his side of the Rhine.

[8] Topographic background from Google Earth.

[9] Belfrage, *Barolo to Valpolicella*, p. 53, suggests there are about 40 distinct clones of Nebbiolo.

[10] Rosso, *Mystique of Barolo*, p. 37.

[11] Planted area in Barolo was 1,283 ha in 1999 and increased to 1,796 ha by 2008 (personal communication from Dr. Giancarlo Montaldo).

[12] The average production between 2004 and 2008 was 10,920,138 bottles per year; production in 2008 was 11,548,485 bottles (personal communication from Dr. Giancarlo Montaldo).

[13] Rosso, *Mystique of Barolo*, p. 24.

[14] Ibid., p. 34.

[15] This was necessary to tame the harsh tannins, but often produced oxidized wines; modern methods, including reduction of the time in oak, have solved this problem.

[16] Maynard A. Amerine & Edward B. Roessler, *Wines: Their Sensory Evaluation, 2nd edition* (W. H. Freeman & Co., New York, 1983), p. 121.

[17] Author's discussion with Elio Altare, October 2009.

[18] Author's discussion with Angelo Gaja, October 2009.

[19] Author's discussion with Davide Voerzio, October 2009.

[20] The minimum permitted alcohol in Barolo DOCG is 13%.

[21] I am greatly indebted to Dr. Giancarlo Montaldo for this calculation.

[22] The school of viticulture and oenology in Alba reported in the late nineteenth century that blends of Cabernet Sauvignon with Dolcetto were "very encouraging" (Edward Steinberg, *The Vines of San Lorenzo*, Ecco Press, New Jersey, 1992, p. 97).

[23] The names that have been used in the past do not always coincide with the official sottozona (subzones).

[24] Garner, *Barolo. Tar and Roses*, p. 240.

[25] Rosso, *Mystique of Barolo*, p. 43.

[26] In the central provinces (including Tuscany) production of olives is about 20% of that of wine grapes. In Italy as a whole, olive groves occupy 1,161,000 ha whereas vineyards amount to only 782,000 ha. (ISTAT, *Survey on agricultural holdings*, 2007).

[27] Until 2009, Chianti Classico DOCG was part of the general Chianti DOCG, but then they were separated, and now there are separate Consorzios to represent them.

[28] Biondi-Santi, Colombini, Franceschi and Angelini.

[29] A government commission to define the boundaries for Chianti production in 1932 noted that "Brunello... is a recent creation of Dr Ferruccio Biondi-Santi of Montalcino. It is a wine produced exclusively from a subvariety of Sangiovese that is called Brunello." (Ministero dell'Agricoltura e delle Foreste, *Per la tutela del Vino Chianti*, Bologna, 1932).

[30] Roberto Anzani et al., *The pursuit of excellence* (Castello Banfi, Montalcino, 2008), pp. 149-152.

[31] Information from the Consorzio del Vino Brunello di Montalcino, October 2009.

[32] It was originally 42 months, then was lowered to 3 years, and in 1998 was lowered further to 2 years. The reduced aging requirement helps the wines of weaker vintages, which do not stand up so well to the oxidation that occurs during long aging in wood. The producers asked in 2001 for the period to be shortened further to only one year in wood. They claim this will produce a fruitier wine without affecting its ability to age.

[33] This is the same issue discussed on p. 422 for Barolo.

[34] Topographic background from Google Earth. Locations of wineries from the Brunello Consorzio.

[35] Information from the Consorzio del Vino Brunello di Montalcino, October 2009.

[36] Production under the DOCs is 550,000 cases/year of Brunello, 400,000 cases of Rosso, 60,000 cases of Ant'Antimo, and 7,000 cases of Moscatello (Consorzio del Vino Brunello di Montalcino, September 2009).

[37] The scandal takes its name from the Tangentopoli (Italian for Bribesville) scandal of

the 1990s and was first reported by the Italian journalist Franco Zilani.

[38] Emiliano Fittipaldi, *Nel Brunello c'è il tranello*, L'espresso, April 3, 2008.

[39] The Consorzio del Vino Brunello di Montalcino reports average production in the 1990s at 3.1 million bottles, and production in 2008 at about 6.8 million bottles.

[40] The Wine Advocate, issue 183, June 2009, p. 102.

[41] Technically there are two DOCGs: Chianti Classico; and Chianti. The latter is divided into seven subzones: Chianti Colli Aretini, Chianti Colli Fiorentini, Chianti Colli Senesi, Chianti Colline Pisane, Chianti Montalbano, Chianti Montespertoli, and Chianti Rufina.

[42] It was phased out as much because it was uneconomic to continue the manual process of adding the straw as because it was damaging the reputation of Chianti. The bottle is amusingly called a fiasco.

[43] This popular impression may not be quite correct. It now seems that Baron Ricasoli may have actually developed two formulae: one for quality wines consisting only of black grape varieties, and one for common wines that made use of the white grapes that were prevalent in Chianti at the time (personal communication from Vincenzo Zampi, March 2010).

[44] Topographic background from Google Earth.

[45] Belfrage, *Brunello to Zibibbo*, p. 9.

[46] Castello Banfi in Montalcino worked with the University of Milan to identify the best clones for their vineyards in southern Montalcino; Castello di Fonterutoli tested 37 different clones in their Belvedere vineyard and then selected the best for general propagation; these are only a couple of examples of the intense research in both regions.

[47] Author's discussion with Guido Orzalesi, October 2009.

[48] Author's discussion with Francesco Cinzano, October 2009.

[49] Author's discussion with Paolo de Marchi, October 2009.

[50] It's only possible legally to produce 100% Sangiovese in Chianti Classico; the other Chianti DOCs still have a limit of 90%.

[51] Salvatore Mondini, *I vitigni stranieri da vino caltivati in Italia (Foreign wine grapes grown in Italy)*, published in Florence in 1903.

[52] There are actually several Bolgheri DOCs: Bolgheri White, Bolgheri Vermentino, Bolgheri Sauvignon (must have 85% Cabernet Sauvignon), Bolgheri Rosé, Bolgheri red (described in the text), Bolgheri Superiore (must have more than 12.5% alcohol and be aged at least one year in barrique and six months in bottle), and, of course, Bolgheri Sassicaia (according to the Consortium of the Bolgheri DOC).

[53] Ornellaia now comes about 50% from the original block and about 50% from the Bellaria vineyard.

[54] Overall more than 80% of plantings are the major Bordeaux varieties (45% Cabernet Sauvignon, 24% Merlot, 7% Cabernet Franc, 7% Petit Verdot). There is also 7% Syrah and 1% Sangiovese (data from Bolgheri DOC, October 2009).

[55] Author's discussion with Sebastiano Rosso, October 2009.

[56] Tignanello actually originated as Chianti Classico Riserva vigneto Tignanello in 1970, as a traditional blend of 75% Sangiovese, 20% Canaiolo, and 5% of the white grapes Trebbiano and Malvasia. White grapes were no longer included from 1975. It has included Cabernet Sauvignon since 1978. Since 1982 it has been a constant blend of 85% Sangiovese, 10% Cabernet Sauvignon, and 5% Cabernet Franc according to its producer, Antinori, who describes it as "the original super-Tuscan," and claims it was the first Sangiovese to be aged in barriques and blended with a nontraditional variety.

[57] This was actually the first 100% Sangiovese wine to be made in the Chianti area, in 1972. It had a great influence on other producers.

[58] The blend of varieties is more constant from year to year than in Bordeaux, because ripening is more reliable for all varieties.

[59] Quoted in Kerin O'Keefe, *Rebels without a cause? The demise of super-Tuscans* (World of Fine Wine, issue 23, 2009).

[60] Based on the author's survey of 160 wines identified as super-Tuscans by criteria of origin and price.

[61] Data based on a survey of 100 producers of super-Tuscan wines conducted by the author, November 2009.

[62] Author's discussion with Axel Heinz, October 2009.

[63] Quoted in Kerin O'Keefe, *Rebels without a cause? The demise of super-Tuscans* (World of Fine Wine, issue 23, 2009).

[64] A survey of releases from the 2006 vintage shows that 72% of producers who sell Chianti on the international market have an IGT Toscana that prices significantly higher than their Chianti.

[65] Author's discussion with Angelo Gaja, October 2009.

[66] Jancis Robinson, *Vines, Grapes and Wines: The Wine Drinker's Guide to Grape Varieties* (Mitchell Beazley, London, 1997), p. 197.

[67] Friulano used to be known as Tocai Friulano, but the E.U. in its infinite wisdom decided that producers could no longer use Tocai because it might be confused with Tokaji wine from Hungary. For the same reason, Tokay Pinot Gris in Alsace had to be called simply Pinot Gris.

[68] 45% Sauvignon Blanc, 15% Chardonnay. 30% Pinot Grigio, 10% Welschriesling.

[69] For Caraffa de Catanzaro in Calabria, according to records on Goddard Weather Center.

[70] Nicholas Belfrage, *Brunello to Zibibbo*, p. 308.

[71] Michéle Shah, *Up by the boot hell. Doing the Italian job* (Wine Business, January, 2007).

[72] Decanter online, April 10, 2008.

Chapter 17: Iberia

[1] Luis Hidalgo & Miguel Urrestarazu Gavilán, *Tratado de viticultura general*, Mundi-Prensa Libros, 2002, p. 66.

[2] The Muslim presence lasted eight centuries in the south, but the Christian reconquest moved steadily down from the north, so that Toledo was reconquered in 1085, Seville in 1248, and all of Portugal by 1249. By 1300 only the southeastern corner was still under Muslim control.

[3] The total of 1,130,000 hectares in 2008 was divided among provinces as:

Castilla-La Mancha	580,080
Extremadura	88,178
Valencia	75,903
Castilla Y León	68,313
Cataluña	61,117
La Rioja	49,672
Aragón	46,880
Murcia	37,812
Andalucia	31,476
Navarra	27,445
Galicia	26,102

Data from Observatorio ESPAÑOL del Mercado del VINO.

[4] At the Grandes Pagos tasting in London, March 12, 2010.

[5] E.U. data show that 216,000 ha were grubbed up between 1988 and 1996; and 140,000 ha have been replanted to a better standard using a E.U. subsidies since year 2000 (Victor de la Serna, *Spanish eyes seeing red* (Wine Business International, March, 2007).

[6] Data from the various DOs show that Tempranillo is more than 95% of Ribera del Duero, more than 85% of Rioja, and 90% in Toro; Tempranillo is 40% of Navarra and Grenache is 28%, Grenache is 40% of Priorat, and Monastrell (Mourvèdre) is more than 80% of Jumilla. All proportions are relative to total plantings of black grapes. In Rueda, Verdejo is more than 76% of all plantings. (Data from the DO for each region provided in 2009).

[7] Victor de la Serna, op. cit.

[8] Black grapes were 43% of plantings in 2000 but reached 53% of plantings by 2007. Data source: Observatorio Español Del Mercado Del Vino, *Superficie de Viñedo en Espana*, 2007.

[9] The increase is from 188,000 ha in 2000 to 325,000 ha in 2007. Ibid.

[10] Airén was more than 400,000 ha in the 1990s; today it is 284,000 ha. Ibid.

[11] Data sources: Kym Anderson & David Norman, *Global Wine Production, Consumption and Trade, 1961-2001* (University of Adelaide, CIES, 2003), DGA/ICEX (Instituto Español de Comercio Exterior), Victor de la Serna, *Spanish eyes seeing red* (Wine Business International, March, 2007).

[12] The top varietals by area are: Airén, 284,623 ha (26.0%); Tempranillo, 206,988 ha (18.9%); Bobal, 85,124 ha (7.7%); Grenache, 75,399 ha (6.9%); Monastrell (Mourvèdre), 63,244 ha (5.8%), Viura (Macabeo), 34,401 ha (3.1%), Pardina, 31,440 ha (2.8%). Data source: Observatorio ESPAÑOL del Mercado del VINO, Superficie de Viñedo en Espana, 2007.

[13] Tempranillo was 74,000 ha in the 1990s, reached 112,000 ha in 2000, and was 207,000 ha by 2007. Data source: Observatorio Español Del Mercado Del Vino, *Superficie de Viñedo en Espana*, 2007.

[14] Cabernet Sauvignon has increased from 5500 ha in 2000 to 19,430 in 2007; Syrah has increased from zero to 16,500 ha (Ibid).

[15] Dominio de Valdepusa in Toledo was a pioneer in planting these varieties. Cabernet Sauvignon and Merlot were first planted in 1974. The first vintage of Syrah was 1993. There is also a varietal Petit Verdot. The wine is called Marqués de Griñon.

[16] Rioja, 50,083 ha; Castille-La Mancha 76,874 ha (including 23,353 ha from DO La Mancha); Castile-Léon 30,538 ha (including 20,173 ha from DO Ribera del Duero); Navarra, 17,500 ha (data source: see note 13, and figures for 2007 from the DO for each region).

[17] The description dates from 1762 (F. Martinez de Toda & J. C. Sancha, *Variedades de Vid Cultivadas en Rioja a lo Largo de la Historia*, Zubia Monografico, 7, 9-13, Logroño, 1995).

[18] see note 6

[19] At the Grandes Pagos tasting in London, March 12, 2010.

[20] Exports are 87% still wines, 7% sparkling, 5% fortified.

[21] Six DO Pagos are in Castille-La-Mancha, three are in Navarra. The first five were Dominio de Valdepusa, Finca Elez, Guijoso and Dehesa del Carrizal (all in Castilla La Mancha) and the Señorío de Arinzano vineyard in Navarra (part of Bodegas Julián Chivite).

[22] Crianza red wines must spend 6 months in cask and two calendar years undergoing maturation (e.g. the harvest of year 2000 can first be sold on January 1, 2003). Whites must mature for 12 months with at least 6 in cask.

Reserva red wines must spend at least 3 calendar years before sale, including at least one in oak, and the rest in bottle. Whites must mature for two years including 6 months in wood.

Gran Reserva must spend at least 5 years before sale, including at least 2 in cask and the rest in bottle. Whites mature for 4 years with at least six months in cask.

There is some controversy because standards are not uniform; each DO can set its own. When the regulations were introduced, Rioja required longer periods in cask. Presently La Mancha requires only 18 months in cask for its Gran Reservas (DO regulations as of 2009). Most DOs are as described above.

[23] Radford, *The Wines of Rioja*, p. 10.

[24] Ibid., p. 13.

[25] Jan Read, *Wines of the Rioja* (Sotheby Publications, London, 1984), p. 31.

[26] Ibid., p. 35.

[27] Radford, *The Wines of Rioja*, p. 17.

[28] Ibid., p. 18.

[29] Lewin, *What Price Bordeaux?*, p. 214.

[30] Ibid, pp. 59, 213.

[31] Lopez de Heredia in 1877, CVNE in 1879, Gómez Cruzado in 1886, La Rioja Alta in 1890; some even had their own railway lines directly into the station.

[32] Read, op. cit, p. 39.

[33] Topographic background from Google Earth.

[34] Official statistics may give planted areas in terms of the political units, that is, La Rioja, Alava, and Navarra, but the DO gives current areas (in 2009) as 12,934 ha for Rioja Alavesa, 26,786 ha for Rioja Alta, and 23,873 ha for Rioja Baja.

[35] Half of the vineyards are less than one hectare in size; 10% are larger than 50 ha (Emilio Barco Royo, *Análisis de un sector: el Rioja entre dos siglos,* Gobierno de La Rioja, Logroño, 2008), pp. 43, 53. The average was 4.5 ha in 1984 and is about 7.5 ha today (Read, op. cit., p. 72).

[36] Data sources: Royo, op. cit., p. 89, and the Consejo Regulador, Rioja. (Large producers are defined as more than 2,500,000 bottles annual production.)

[37] Richard Ford, *Handbook for Spain*, 1845, quoted in Read, op. cit., p. 21.

[38] Radford, *The Wines of Rioja*, p. 35.

[39] There were 6,500 ha of Grenache and only 3,000 ha of Tempranillo in 1935 (Read, op. cit., p. 67).

[40] *Tres Siglos de La Rioja Alta,* 2009 (ISBN 978-84-613-0615-2), p. 87.

[41] Data source: Angel Jaime Baro et al., *Atlas de los Vinos de Rioja* (Diputacion de la Rioja Unidad de Cultura, Logrono, 1982)

[42] Read, op. cit., p. 53.

[43] Data sources: Barco Royo, op. cit., p. 49; Angel Jaime Baro, op. cit.

[44] José Peñin, Manual de los vinos de Rioja (Penthalon, Madrid), 1982.

[45] Manuel Ruiz Hernández, *Estudios sobre el vino de Rioja,* Gráf. Sagredo, Logroño, 1978.

[46] The average over the past decade was 27% export for unclassified, 23% for Crianza, 42% for Reserva, and 55% for Gran Reserva (data source: Royo, op. cit., 137, 152).

[47] Ibid., pp. 137, 152.

[48] A producer in Rioja Alta, June 2009.

[49] Between 0.3% and 0.9% during the period 2003-2009, according to data from the DO.

[50] Topographic background from Google Earth.

[51] José Peñin, *Vega Sicilia. Journey to the Heart of a Legend* (Bodegas Vega Sicilia, Valbuena, 2002), p. 28.

[52] Ibid., pp. 35-45.

[53] Ibid., p. 59.

[54] The lowest proportion of Tempranillo was 60% in 1979; the highest was 85% in 1991.

[55] Peñin, op. cit., p. 121.

[56] Richard Mayson, *Portugal's Wines and Winemakers, 2nd edition* (Wine Appreciation Guild, San Francisco, 1998), p. 10.

[57] Data from Vinhos e Aguardentes de Portugal, Anuário 09, Instituto da Vinha e Do Vinho.

[58] Topographic background from Google Earth.

[59] Data from Vinhos e Aguardentes de Portugal, Anuário 09, Instituto da Vinha e Do Vinho.

[60] Ibid.

[61] Richard Mayson, *Portugal's Wines and Winemakers,* op. cit., p. 115.

[62] Ibid., p. 10.

Chapter 18: Hapsburg Empire

[1] Table wines can be blended between the regions. Quality wines all are restricted to the individual region that is named on the label.

[2] Officially shortened to Prädikatwein from 2007.

[3] Süssreserve must come from the same region as the wine. Better producers use süssreserve from the same source as the wine itself. But what difference does this make?

[4] The sugar balance is different, with more glucose when süssreserve is added (see note 21 in Chapter 6).

[5] The term Kabinett was used at Kloster Eberbach in 1730, but according to Rowald Hepp, Schloss Vollrads had used it previously in 1728 to declare the 1718 vintage as something special. (Author's discussion with Rowald Hepp, August 2008.)

[6] Ibid.

[7] Ibid.

[8] The law of 1971 set the minimum size for an Einzellage as 5 ha, but there are a couple of Einzellage where protests from growers resulted in dispensations to allow a size below the minimum.

[9] The Anbaugebiete are: Ahr, Baden, Franconia, Hessische Bergstrasse, Mittelrhein, Mosel (used to be called Mosel-Saar-Ruwer, but the name was simplified), Nahe, Palatinate, Rheingau, Rheinhessen, Württemberg, plus Saale-Unstrut and Saxony (which were part of the former East Germany and lie farther to the north; not shown on the map). Topographic background from Google Earth.

[10] It was so small that demand greatly exceeded supply, and wine was sold as blends with adjacent vineyards such as Doctor und Graben, Doctor und Badstube, but this became illegal after 1971 (S. F. Hallgarten, *German Wines,* Publivin, London, 1981, p. 58).

[11] Higher sugar levels require that the wine has higher acidity to offset the sweetness.

[12] At lower acidity levels, wines above 12 g/l are considered to be medium dry (a misnomer for a wine that is actually palpably sweet), while sweet wines *per se* start at 45 g/l.

[13] Topographic background from Google Earth.

[14] For an account of the first attempts to define an "Internationally Dry" style that tastes dry because of high acidity, although technically within the halbtrocken range, see the description of the Charta movement, the forerunner of the VDP in the early 1980s (Bird, *Rheingold,* pp. 136-138).

[15] Relative to average annual production around 10 million, the average amount of Classic wines produced in the three years 2006-2008 was 117,000 hl. (German Wine Institute, *Deutscher Wein Statistik,* 2008-2009, table 11, and personal communication from Ernst Buescher at the DWE.)

[16] Average production of Selection wine in the period 2006-2008 was only 1000 hl each year (personal communication from Ernst Buescher at the DWE).

[17] The rationale is that Sylvaner really does produce excellent results in Franken. But it's an exception that proves the rule.

[18] Author's discussion with Armin Diehl, August 2008.

[19] QmP percents do not correlate exactly with vintage, because reported statistics refer to wine available rather than produced each year. Proportion of QmP calculated from data of German Wine Institute, *Deutscher Wein Statistik,* annual reports. Annual growing season temperature from the weather station at Trier in the Mosel as reported at the Goddard Institute for Space Studies.

[20] More sweet wine may have been consumed in Germany than is usually admitted, however.

[21] See note 19.

[22] Data source: German Wine Institute, *Deutscher Wein Statistik,* annual reports.

[23] Ibid., table 12.

[24] German Wine Institute, *Deutscher Wein Statistik,* 2008-2009, table 8.

[25] Ibid, table 4.

[26] Latest figures from the German Wine Institute (for 2008) show: Rheinhessen, 26,333 ha; Pfalz, 23,389 ha; Baden, 15,892 ha; Württemberg, 11,526 ha; Mosel, 8,981 ha; Franken, 6,081 ha; Nahe, 4,135 ha; Rheingau, 3,097 ha; Saale-Unstrut, 665 ha; Ahr, 552 ha; Mittelrhein, 457 ha; Saachsen, 441 ha; Hessische Bergstrasse, 436 ha.

[27] Topographic background from Google Earth.

[28] Hallgarten, *Wine Scandal,* p. 76.

[29] Ibid., p. 72.

[30] An excellent account of the debacle is given by Bird, *Rheingold,* pp. 29-34.

[31] Jancis Robinson, *The Oxford Companion to Wine* (Oxford University Press, Oxford, 1994), p. 566.

[32] Total exports were around 28 million cases (German Wine Institute, *Deutscher Wein Statistik*, 2008-2009, table 11).

[33] See pp. 244-245.

[34] Topographic background from Google Earth.

[35] The 30,003 ha of Niederösterreich include 1,390 ha in Wachau, 3,868 ha in Kamptal, 2,175 ha in Kremstal, and 682 ha in Traisental; Weinviertel is half of the total at 15,892 ha. Neusiedlersee has 8,326 ha and Hugeland-Hugeland has 3,291 of the total 14,563 in Burgenland. Steiermark has 3,290 ha and Wien has 678. Data source: Austrian Wine Marketing Board, *Austrian Wine*, December 2008 edition.

[36] Philippe Blom, *The Wines of Austria*, p. 18.

[37] Lebensministerium Öffentlichkeitsarbeit, Austria, November 17, 2008.

[38] The system of measurement used in Austria is the KMW (Klosterneuburger Mostwaage).

[39] Austrian Wine Marketing Board, *Austrian Wine*, December 2008 edition, p. 85.

[40] Discussion with author, August 2009.

[41] Discussion with author, August 2009.

[42] Quoted in Freddie Price, *Riesling Renaissance* (Mitchell Beazley, London, 2004), p. 122.

[43] Quoted by Philippe Blom, *The Wines of Austria*, p. 19.

[44] Author's discussion with Roman Horvath at Domain Wachau, August 2009.

[45] Discussion with author, August 2009.

[46] Franz Schams, *Ungarns Weinbau in seinem ganzen Umfange, oder vollständige Beschreibung sämmtlicher berühmten Weingebirge des ungarischen Reichs in statistisch-topographisch-naturhistorischer und ökonomischer Hinsicht*, 3 volumes, Wigand, Pest, 1832-1835.

[47] The origins of Grüner Veltliner aren't entirely clear. One parent has been reported as "Traminer", a somewhat generic name for a set of varieties including Gewürztraminer and Savagnin (Ferdinand Regner and H. Kaserer, *Investigations into the genetic variability of Traminer clones*, Mitteilungen Klosterneuburg, 52, 177-186, 2002). More recently it has been reported that the other parent is St. Georgen, an almost extinct variety found in Burgenland, somewhat distant from the main concentration of Grüner Veltliner (Susanne Eiweck, *Grüner Veltliner: passed paternity test*, Kurier, Vienna, August 7, 2009).

[48] Austrian Wine Marketing Board, *Austrian Wine*, December 2008 edition, p. 57.

[49] Total hectares of 48,514 in 1999 increased to 52,319 in 2007. White plantings decreased slightly from 36,162 ha to 35,619 ha; blacks increased from 12,351 ha to 16,700 ha. According the Austrian Wine Marketing board, the most significant changes were:

Variety	1999 ha	2007 ha	Change	Current
Grüner Veltliner	17,479	17,033	-2%	32.56%
Welschriesling	4,323	4,323	-	8.26%
Müller Thurgau	3,289	3,009	-8%	5.75%
Chardonnay	2,953	3,460	17%	6.61%
Riesling	1,642	1,874	14%	3.58%
Sauvignon Blanc	314	753	139%	1.44%
Zweigelt	4,349	6,511	49%	12.45%
Blaufränkisch	2,640	3,340	26%	6.38%
Blauer Portugieser	2,358	2,222	-6%	4.25%
Blauburger	883	1,001	13%	1.91%
Cabernet Sauvignon	311	518	66%	0.99%
Merlot	111	551	393%	1.05%

[50] Ibid.

[51] F. X. Pichler's single vineyard bottlings at the Smaragd level offer intense citrus and

stone fruits with a mineral backbone. They are more forward than his Rieslings, which are like coiled springs waiting to be released, and require more time.

[52] Sepp Moser's Kremstal Schnabel MINIMAL 2007; see p. 114.

[53] In the top-rated year of 2006, Prager's Achleiten Stockkulture achieved an aromatic density resembling a top Sauvignon Blanc; in other years it has been less aromatic.

Chapter 19 From Aperitif to Dessert

[1] Doreen Carvajal, *Bubbles at a Discount for Consumers Trading Down*, New York Times, November 14, 2009.

[2] Ibid.

[3] Dion, *Histoire de la Vigne*, p. 615.

[4] Ibid., p. 632.

[5] Ibid., p. 636.

[6] Ibid., p. 639.

[7] Ibid., p. 643.

[8] Ibid., p. 644.

[9] Topographic background from Google Earth.

[10] Hugh Johnson, *The Story of Wine* (Mitchell Beazley, London, 2005), p. 176.

[11] Ibid., p. 180.

[12] Regional focus is strong: Vallée de la Marne is 62% Pinot Meunier, Côte des Blancs is 82% Chardonnay, Montagne de Reims is 40% Pinot Noir, Côte des Bars is 87% Pinot Noir (CIVC).

[13] Maggie McNie, *Champagne* (Faber & Faber, London, 1999), p. 9.

[14] The total of 32,902 ha breaks down as 78% in the Département de la Marne (Montagne de Reims [7,960 ha = 24%], Vallée de la Marne [11,232 ha = 35%], Côte des Blancs [6,129 ha = 15%]), 6,817 ha = 21% in the Aube (Côte des Bar), and the rest in the outlying areas (CIVC).

[15] CIVC.

[16] Average prices from Valeur Venale, Journal Officiel De La République Française, February 5, 2009.

[17] Author's discussion with the CEO of a Champagne house, December 2009.

[18] Average area in 1980-1989 was 25,159 ha compared to 32,902 ha in 2008 (CIVC).

[19] The limit is that 14,000 kg of grapes can be harvested from each hectare, and 2,550 liters of must can be pressed from every 4000 kg of grapes. This is equivalent to 89 hl/ha.

[20] Yields in most years are fairly close to the limit, often over 80 hl/ha; in 2004 they exceeded the limit (INAO statistics).

[21] And the nominal limits have gone up steadily from 12,000 kg/ha in the 1980s to 15,500 kg/ha in 2007.

[22] Because of the turn down in the market in 2009, the CIVC limited current production to 9,700 kg/hectare. This was a compromise between the growers (who wanted a higher limit) and the houses (who wanted a lower one). However, the remaining 4300 kg/ha can be harvested and used for reserve stocks for future years.

[23] Production figures from CIVC show the number of bottles shipped each year. Average price per bottle (adjusted for inflation) from Francis Declerck and L. Martin Cloutier, *The Financial Value of Champagne Houses in a Cobweb Economy* (110th EAAE Seminar, Innsbruck-Igls, Austria, 2008).

[24] The growers own 29,295 ha and the houses own 3,427 ha (CIVC).

[25] Grand crus account for 4,500 ha, and premier crus for 5,700 ha.

[26] The curve is slightly smoothed out because production is in terms of bottles shipped, as opposed to actual harvests. In terms of harvests the peak yield would be 89 hl/ha. Data from CIVC records.

[27] Tom Stevenson, *The World Encyclopedia of Champagne*, p. 136.

[28] Typically the sugar content will be 22-24 g/l in the liqueur de tirage, and its fermentation adds an alcohol level of 1.3-1.5%.

[29] Tom Stevenson, *The World Encyclopedia of Champagne,* p. 9; Christopher Fielden, *Is This the Wine You Ordered, Sir?,* p. 54.

[30] This was an accident resulting from a ban imposed on the use of oak in glass furnaces by James I in 1615; intended to preserve the supplies of oak for naval use, it had the unintended effect of increasing furnace temperature when coal was substituted for the oak. This led to stronger glass.

[31] Christopher Fielden, *Is This the Wine You Ordered, Sir?,* p. 57.

[32] Dom Pérignon is credited with developing techniques for producing white wine from black grapes, harvesting under cool conditions to preserve freshness, and (crucial for Champagne) introducing the idea of blending wines from different vineyards to make a more complex wine.

[33] Chanoine Godinot, *Manière de Cultiver la Vigne et de Faire le Vin en Champagne* (Chez Bethélémy Multeau, Reims, 1718), p. 32.

[34] Approximately 90% of Champagnes are labeled brut.

[35] Resulting from the Maillard reaction between nitrogenous compounds and sugars.

[36] Technically a Blanc de Noirs is a Champagne made from black grapes, which means Pinot Noir and Pinot Meunier. But most high quality Blanc de Noir is made from Pinot Noir.

[37] The nature of the producer of Champagne must be indicated on the label by a code:

RM - récoltant-manipulant describes a vigneron who harvests the grapes and vinifies the wine

NM - négociant manipulant describes a producer who buys the grapes and then vinifies the wine. This is true of most of the large houses.

CM - cave coopérative produces wine from grapes harvested by its members. Nicolas Feuillatte is a prominent example.

RC - récoltant manipulant describes a grower who affixes his own label to wine produced by a cooperative to which he belongs.

MA - marque d'acheteur applies to a wine that was produced by someone else and has then been sold under the label of the final owner.

[38] Trading sur latte became illegal among negociants in 2004. Champagne can still be purchased sur latte from a grower or cooperative, but should be shown on the label as "distribué par" rather than "elaboré par" the negociant, but it is unlikely this distinction will have any significance for the consumer.

[39] Caroline Brothers, *Bright Holidays for 'Fragile' Champagne Makers,* Reuters, December 23, 2005.

[40] LVMH Annual Report.

[41] The most recent price for top grapes according to the Syndicat Professionel des Courtiers en Vins de Champagne is €5.33 per kilo. With production limited to 2,550 liters per 4000 kilos, this translates to €6.4 for a bottle, almost $10.

[42] The group of Grand Marques defined in 1964 was Ayala, Billecart-Salmon, Bollinger, Veuve Clicquot, Canard-Duchène, Delbeck, Deutz, Gosset, Heidsieck Monopole, Charles Heidsieck, Henriot, Irroy, Krug, Lanson, Massé, Mercier, Moët & Chandon, Montebello, Mumm, Perrir-Jouët, Joseph Perrier, Laurent Perrier, Piper-Heidsieck, Pol Roger, Pommery, Prieur, Roederer, Ruinart, Salon, Taittinger.

[43] The CIVC lists 76 leading Maisons de Champagne and states 10 criteria for being considered a Grande Marque, from which quality of production is significantly absent.

[44] The top five groups are:

LVMH: Moët & Chandon, Mercier, Ruinart, Montaudon, Veuve Clicquot, Krug.

Boizel Chanoine: Lanson, Burtin Besserat de Bellefon, Boizel, Chanoine, Philipponnat, De Venoge, Alexandre Bonnet

Vranken-Pommery: Vranken-Pommery, Charles Lafitte, Heidsieck & C° Monopole, Demoiselle

Laurent-Perrier: Laurent-Perrier, De Castellane, Salon-Delamotte, Lemoine

Pernod-Ricard: Mumm, Perrier-Jouët.

[45] CIVC.

[46] Products, including bread, cookies, and still wine—all absolutely nothing to do with sparkling wine— that have been labeled for more than 1000 years with the name of the town of Champagne in the Vaud region of Switzerland had to stop using the name after a court case brought by the champagne producers in 2008 (John Tagliabue, *Champagne, Switzerland, can't use its own name,* International Herald Tribune, April 27, 2008).

[47] Personal communication from César Saldaña, Jerez Consejo Regulador.

[48] Possibly the richest city in Spain in the early nineteenth century (Hugh Johnson, *The Story of Wine,* Mitchell Beazley, London, 2005, p. 172).

[49] Manuel Gonzalez-Gordon, *Sherry: the Noble Wine* (Quiller Press, London, 1990), p.32.

[50] Julian Jeffs, *Sherry,* p. 22.

[51] Personal communication from César Saldaña, Jerez Consejo Regulador.

[52] One possible origin for "sack" is *saca,* meaning withdrawal of wine, but there have been many more fanciful explanations (Gonzalez-Gordon, *Sherry,* op. cit., p. 40).

[53] At the peak in 1864 Sherry accounted for 43% of wine imports into Britain (Hugh Johnson, *The Story of Wine,* op. cit., p. 172).

[54] Ibid., p. 36.

[55] Ibid., p. 40.

[56] Julian Jeffs, *Sherry,* p. 212.

[57] Solera probably takes its name from *suela,* Spanish for floor.

[58] The traditional unit of measure in Sherry is the butt, a barrel filled with 500 liters of wine.

[59] Data from the Memoria de Actividades of the Consejo Regulador of Jerez.

[60] Amontillado originally meant that the wine had the style of one made in Montilla (another region near Jerez that also produces wines in a solera system).

[61] One problem was that acidity tended to be too low. The traditional way of handling this was to add gypsum, either by sprinkling on grapes or later, to increase acidity. This practice goes back to Roman times, when it was recommended by Columella. Gypsum is basically calcium sulfate, which reacts with potassium hydrogen tartrate in the must to generate (soluble) potassium sulfate, precipitating calcium tartrate and releasing tartaric acid. Today if acidity is needed it is added directly.

[62] Topographic background from Google Earth.

[63] Discussion with author, September 2008.

[64] See note 59.

[65] Ibid.

[66] Personal communication from César Saldaña, Jerez Consejo Regulador.

[67] Data from the Memoria de Actividades of the Consejo Regulador of Jerez.

[68] Discussion with author, September 2008.

[69] This does not apply to fino because fino soleras are limited to 8-9 stages; otherwise the flor dies off.

[70] The most significant is Palo Cortado, a special style resulting from an early transition from flor to oxidative development. This used to occur when the flor failed to develop at an early stage; now it is more a matter of selection on the basis of the organoleptic qualities of the wine. After a few months development under flor, it is fortified to 18-20% cent alcohol, and develops into a halfway house between Amontillado and Oloroso, with an aroma similar to Amontillado, but the body associated with Oloroso. One theory is that these wines occur when an unusually high content of malic acid leads to a malolactic fermentation.

[71] "The Portuguese in these parts regard dynamite with familiarity amounting to affection. No festival is complete without fusillades of rockets carrying aloft one or two sticks of dynamite." (H. Warner Allen in André L. Simon, *Wines of the World,* McGraw-Hill, New York, 1967, p. 449).

[72] Topographic background from Google Earth.

[73] Touriga Francesca is now known officially as Touriga Franca, to avoid confusion with the quite different grape Tinta Francisca. There is a story that Tinta Francisca is a descendant of Pinot Noir, brought to Portugal by Count Henry of Burgundy around 1095.

Further cuttings are supposed to have been brought in the 17th century by Robert Archibald, the owner of Quinta de Roriz (Ben Howkins, *Rich, Rare & Red, 3rd edition,* Wine Appreciation Guild, San Francisco, 2003, p. 34). There appears however to be no evidence to support this idea. It's not even known whether Pinot Noir was grown in Burgundy in the eleventh century (see page 360); it's quite unlikely anyone should know whether cuttings were of the same variety six centuries later. It's an amusing story but a myth. So far there are no DNA fingerprinting studies to address the origins of the Portuguese grape varieties.

[74] The Factory House was not a factory for production but the headquarters of a business association (John Delaforce, *The Factory House at Oporto,* Christies, London, 1979).

[75] Richard Mayson, *Port and the Douro,* p. 11.

[76] Tim Unwin, *Wine and the Vine,* p. 264.

[77] Ibid., p. 265.

[78] H. Warner Allen, *The Wines of Portugal* (Rainbird, London, 1962).

[79] The edict was issued in 1756 but was not effective (Richard Mayson, *Port and the Douro,* p. 11).

[80] It was reported in 1851 that Port was commonly adulterated with a mixture called geropiga, consisting of 57 pounds of elderberries, 60 pounds of brown sugar, 78 gallons of unfermented grape juice, and 39 gallons of coarse brandy (Cyrus Redding, *History and Description of Modern Wine,* Third edition Henry G. Bohn, London, p. 242).

[81] At the time of the 1998 vintage, the price for elderberries was 500 escudos/kilo, twice that for Touriga Nacional (Richard Mayson, *Port and the Douro,* p. 137).

[82] Most Port in the vintage style carries a vintage, but Crusted Port, named because of the heavy deposit or crust that forms in the bottle, is a blend of wines from two or three vintages, aged in wood for two years like vintage Port, and then bottled.

[83] H. Warner Allen in André L. Simon, *Wines of the World* (McGraw-Hill, New York, 1967), p. 433.

[84] Ibid., p 447.

[85] Wyndham Fletcher, *Port: an introduction to its history and delights* (Sothebys, London, 1978), p. 52.

[86] The spirits used to stop fermentation are a 77% alcoholic solution called aguardente (not brandy); originally this was made by distilling wine in the Douro, then producers were required to purchase it from other sources in Portugal, but since 1992 producers have been able to use any spirits of the appropriate strength.

[87] Richard Mayson, *Port and the Douro,* p. 46.

[88] Ben Howkins, *Rich, Rare & Red, 3rd edition* (Wine Appreciation Guild, San Francisco, 2003), p. 58.

[89] These days most Port is actually shipped from the new Port of Leixòes (10 km north of Oporto). But by law the shippers have to have their offices in Vila Nova de Gaia.

[90] Data source: annual reports of IVDP (Port and Douro Wine Institute).

[91] The organization for assigning beneficios was the Casa do Douro. This got into trouble when it purchased a Port house in difficulties, the Royal Oporto (the descendent of the Real Companhia Velha), and a new body, the CIRDD, was created in 1995 to handle the beneficios. Now all these bodies have been merged into the IVDP.

[92] Quoted in the Wine Report, 2009, Dorling Kindersley, London., p. 153.

[93] Port accounts for 26% of exports by volume but more than 70% by value.

[94] Statistics for 2008 from the IVDP (Port and Douro Wine Institute).

[95] Colheitas are 0.4%, crusted Ports are 0.04% (for the 2008 vintage as reported by the IVDP).

[96] Naturally the proportion of vintage Port varies according to the quality of recent vintages.

[97] Symingtons hold Dow, Graham, Warre, Quarles Harris, Gould Campbell, Smith Woodhouse, Martinez, and Cockburn; Fladgate own Taylor, Fonseca, Croft, Delaforce, Osborn, and Romariz; Sogrape include Sandeman, Ferreira, Morgan, and Offley. In addition, Sogevinus now owns Cálem, Burmeister, Barros, Kopke, and Gilberts. Individual international owners are AXA, who own Quinta do Noval, Roederer, who own

Ramos-Pinto, and Vranken Pommery who own Rozès. The remaining independent houses are Churchill, Messias, Montez Champalimaud, Quinta do Crasto, Poças, and Niepoort. Royal Oporto has the distinction of being owned by the authorities.

[98] Ben Howkins, op. cit., p. xv.

[99] There was no connection with consumption of table wine, but a correlation with alcohol levels consumed in the form of beer or spirits. Oddly enough in view of the history, Port was not specifically tested (H. K. Choi et al., Alcohol intake and risk of incident gout in men: a prospective study, Lancet, 363, 1277-1281, 2004).

[100] It is not particularly wet here, in fact there is slightly less rainfall in Sauternes and Barsac than farther north in Graves (Jeffrey Benson & Alastair MacKenzie, *Sauternes, 2nd edition,* Sotheby's Publications, London, 1990, p. 18).

[101] If botrytis penetrates into the berry (called gray rot), it makes the grapes susceptible to other, pernicious infections (called sour rot). If either gray rot or sour rot sets in, there is nothing to do but throw away the grapes. Dry spells are the best protection against this happening.

[102] Sauternes has 1670 ha of vineyards, Barsac is much smaller at 600 ha. There are not many vineyards in the area of Cérons; the appellations on the right bank have a combined acreage of about 1000 ha. Topographic background from Google Earth.

[103] Jackson, *Wine Science,* p. 522.

[104] Stephen Brook, *Liquid Gold. Dessert Wines of the World* (Constable, London, 1987), p. 311.

[105] Ibid., p. 322.

[106] But see pp. 540-541.

[107] Jeffrey Benson & Alastair MacKenzie, *Sauternes, 2nd edition,* Sotheby's Publications, London, 1990, p. 11)

[108] Stephen Brook, *Sauternes and other sweet wines of Bordeau,* op. cit. p. 28.

[109] The name Recioto refers to the ear of the grapes, from the old habit of selecting the top of the bunch which is ripest, because it gets the most sunlight.

[110] Stephen Brook, *Liquid Gold. Dessert Wines of the World* (Constable, London, 1987), p. 165.

[111] John Schreiner, *Icewine. The Complete Story* (Warwick Publishing, Toronto, 2001), p. 27.

[112] Between 1961 and 2000, harvest dates at Max Ferdinand Richter in the Mosel varied from November 2 to January 28 the following year (Schreiner, op. cit., p. 44).

[113] Schreiner, op cit., p 168.

[114] Ibid., p. 31.

[115] It used to be possible to use base wine from the previous vintage, but the law now requires the base wine to be from the current vintage.

[116] "Aszú grape wine" was mentioned in a textbook glossary in 1570, and the Nomenclatura of Fabricius Balázs Sziksai which was published posthumously in 1576, discussed the grapes used in Aszú wine (Ben Howkins, *Tokaji. A Classic - Lost and Found,* International Wine and Food Society, London, 1999). A will of 1571 is supposed to mention Tokaji Aszú (Tim Atkins, *Tradition And Innovation In The Tokaji Region,* Dissertation, Institute of Masters of Wine, London, 2001).

[117] The Fukier cellar in Warsaw was reported to have many cases of the 1606 vintage before the second world war (ibid.) And Crown Estates of Hungary (formerly Tokaji Kereskedőház) have a bottle of Tokaji Aszú from the 1680s in their museum, and a bottle reported to date from 1641 was sold at Christies.

[118] Ibid.

[119] Ibid.

[120] 76 vineyards were classified as first class, and two (Mezes Maly and Szarvas) were classed as Great first growth. Ibid.

[121] Two of the villages that used to make Tokaji ended up across the border in Slovakia. They stopped labeling their wine as Tokaji only in 2004 as the result of an international agreement.

[122] The casks were made in the village of Gönc.

[123] Tokaji Aszú of 3 puttonyos has 60-90 g/l residual sugar, 4 puttonyos has 90-120 g/l, 5 puttonyos has 120-150 g/l, 6 puttonyos has 150-180 g/l, and Tokaji Aszú Eszencia has more than 180 g/l.

[124] Including most notably Hetszölö in 1991 (a joint venture between the state and GMF of France and Suntory of Japan), Disznokö in 1992 (a joint venture between the state and French insurance company AXA), and Oremus in 1993 (an investment from Vega Sicilia in Spain). For an account of the start of foreign investment see Mathilde Hulot, *Tokaj, Hungary: An Impressive Diversity*, Wine Business Monthly, November 5, 2001.

[125] Tim Atkins, op. cit.

[126] The modernists include Hétszölö, Oremus, Disznókö, Château Pajzos and Megyer, a roll-call of the leading foreign investors; the traditionalists include Crown Estates and Hungarovin.

[127] Ben Howkins, op. cit.

[128] Tim Atkins, op. cit.

[129] There is about 5% Muscat and 1% Oremus.

Chapter 20: Truth in Labeling

[1] Michael Pollan, *The Omnivore's Dilemma* (Penguin, New York, 2006).

Index